*The publisher gratefully acknowledges the generous
contribution to this book provided by the
Ahmanson Foundation Humanities Endowment Fund
of the University of California Press Foundation.*

THE TOUR DE FRANCE

UNITED KINGDOM

FRANCE

Low   Hills   Mountains

BELGIUM

GERMANY

English Channel

Channel
Islands

•Caen

Seine

LUXEMBOURG

Metz •

Strasbourg•

★

Paris

*VOSGES
MOUNTAINS*

Rhine

•Brest

•Rennes

Seine

Saône

SWITZERLAND

Nantes
•

Loire

Loire

*Atlantic
Ocean*

Vichy •

Lyon •

ALPS

ITALY

N

Bordeaux
•

*MASSIF
CENTRAL*

Garonne

Rhône

Bay of Biscay

Toulouse
•

Marseille
•

SPAIN

PYRENEES

*Mediterranean
Sea*

ANDORRA

0   50   100 Miles

0   50   100 Kilometers

The TOUR de FRANCE

A CULTURAL HISTORY

Updated with a New Preface

Christopher S. Thompson

UNIVERSITY OF CALIFORNIA PRESS

BERKELEY   LOS ANGELES   LONDON

University of California Press, one of the most distinguished university presses in the United States, enriches lives around the world by advancing scholarship in the humanities, social sciences, and natural sciences. Its activities are supported by the UC Press Foundation and by philanthropic contributions from individuals and institutions. For more information, visit www.ucpress.edu.

Parts of this book were previously published in different form and appear here by permission of their original publishers: part of chapter 1, Christopher Thompson, "Regeneration, *Dégénérescence,* and Medical Debates about the Bicycle in Fin-de-Siècle France," in *Sport and Health History,* ed. Thierry Terret (Sankt Augustin, Germany: Academia Verlag, 1999), 339–45; parts of chapters 1 and 4, Christopher Thompson, "Bicycling, Class, and the Politics of Leisure in Belle Epoque France," in *Histories of Leisure,* ed. Rudy Koshar (Oxford: Berg Publishers, 2002), 131–46; parts of chapters 1 and 4, Christopher Thompson, "Controlling the Working-Class Hero in Order to Control the Masses?: The Social Philosophy of Sport of Henri Desgrange," *Stadion* (Fall 2001): 139–51; part of chapter 5, Christopher Thompson, "The Tour in the Inter-War Years: Political Ideology, Athletic Excess and Industrial Modernity," *International Journal of the History of Sport* (www.tandf.co.uk) 20:2, special issue on the Tour de France 1903–2000 (June 2003): 79–102.

University of California Press
Berkeley and Los Angeles, California

University of California Press, Ltd.
London, England

ISBN: 978-0-520-25630-9 (pbk. : alk. paper)

The Library of Congress has catalogued an earlier edition of this book as follows:

Library of Congress Cataloging-in-Publication Data
Thompson, Christopher S., 1959–
    The Tour de France : a cultural history / Christopher S. Thompson.
       p.   cm.
    Includes bibliographical references and index.
    ISBN-10 0-520-24760-4 (cloth : alk. paper),
    ISBN-13 978-0-520-24760-4 (cloth : alk. paper)
    1. Tour de France (Bicycle race)—History.   2. Bicycle racing—Social aspects—France.   I. Title.
GV1049.2.T68T56   2006
796.6'2'0944—dc22   2005023760

Manufactured in the United States of America
17   16   15   14   13   12   11   10   09   08
10   9   8   7   6   5   4   3   2   1

The paper used in this publication meets the minimum requirements of ANSI/ASTM D5634-01 *(Permanence of Paper).* ∞

CONTENTS

PREFACE TO THE 2008 EDITION

In late July 2006, just days after the conclusion of the Tour de France and shortly after this book was published, I was cycling back to my apartment in Paris from a training ride around the Hippodrome de Longchamps in the Bois de Boulogne. As I rode up Boulevard Pereire, a teenage boy on the sidewalk stared at me and then shouted: "Sale dopé [Dirty doper]!" A few days later, I was in southwestern France, engaged in a 113-mile solo ride over three of the major Pyrenean peaks of the Tour. As I struggled up the steep slopes of the Col du Soulor I had ample time to note two words that had been painted in large letters on the stone wall that borders the narrow road leading to the summit: "Vilains dopés [Evil dopers]!" Less than a year earlier, in the fall of 2005, I had concluded the epilogue of this book by reflecting on the implications of the doping scandals that have plagued the recent history of the Tour de France. I suggested that, far from being limited to the intimate world of professional cycling, the repeated revelations about illicit doping by Tour racers—including many of the sport's stars—raised important questions about the place of high-performance spectator sports and top-flight athletes in contemporary societies. The anecdotal evidence provided above from my own recent experience suggests that these questions continue to be relevant: cycling remains in crisis.

The questions raised by the apparently never-ending succession of doping affairs in professional cycling defy easy answers, in part because of the sheer number of the sport's stakeholders and their at times conflicting interests. They include the racers, represented by national and international professional associations; the sport's commercial sponsors, who provide the financial backing for teams and competitions; the race organizers; the communities that invest considerable sums to host competitions for the economic benefits and favorable exposure they expect will ensue; the national and international cycling federations, which govern the sport; the scientific and medical communities, which are continually developing new therapies and drugs that improve human physiological capacities; the media, who cover the sport and seek to profit from that coverage (a dual objective fraught with conflicts of interest); the national and international antidoping agencies, which are leading an increasingly global campaign against illicit performance-enhancement by athletes; the antidoping laboratories, which process the racers' samples and at times fail to follow the rigorous guidelines established to guarantee athletes due process; and national governments, which have passed a variety of antidoping laws and exhibited differing levels of commitment in enforcing them. To date these parties have failed to formulate a common vision for cycling's future, in large measure because they cannot agree about how to address the challenge that doping poses to the racers' health and the sport's image.

In the less than two years since I completed this book, the sport's doping crisis has deepened as legal investigations into, and revelations about, the extent of the practice among professional racers have multiplied. On the eve of the 2006 Tour, the so-called Puerto Operation broke in Spain, implicating dozens of professional racers in an apparent blood-doping enterprise of unprecedented scale.[1] Determined to put behind them Lance Armstrong's seven-year reign over the event, which was dogged by repeated suggestions that he had doped, the organizers decided to exclude from the 2006 Tour any contestants implicated in the Spanish affair, before any of the latter had been formally charged or had the chance to present a legal defense.[2] Among the banned racers were several of the prerace favorites and top finishers of the 2005 Tour. Such a draconian housecleaning—one that did not spare the sport's stars—allowed some to hope, not for the first time, that a new, "cleaner" era in cycling was dawning.

These hopes were soon dashed. In the days that followed his dramatic come-from-behind victory in the 2006 Tour, it was reported that the American Floyd Landis had tested positive for synthetic testosterone, a banned substance. The positive result had come from a sample taken the day of his remarkable solo breakaway in the mountains, which had allowed him to recover most of the time he had lost the previous stage when he had collapsed on the final climb. Headlines extolling Landis's exploit, which was among the most riveting in the event's recent history, were soon replaced by ones accusing him of cheating and disgracing the Tour. For the first time in history a Tour champion faced the very real prospect of being stripped of his victory after the fact for a doping violation.

A year later, both the Puerto and Landis affairs were ongoing as the parties in each continued to work through the complicated legal and scientific issues involved.[3] Meanwhile, just a few weeks before the 2007 Tour a third major doping scandal made headlines; it involved a German team prominent since the 1990s, known first as Deutsche Telekom and more recently as T-Mobile. Jef d'Hont, a former employee with a half century of experience in the sport, revealed in interviews promoting his professional memoir that doping had been widespread among the team's racers, including the Dane Bjarne Riis, who won the 1996 Tour, and the German Jan Ullrich, who won the 1997 Tour, finished second several times, and is now implicated in the Puerto affair in Spain.[4] Although Ullrich asserted categorically that he had never doped, many of his former teammates, some of them now retired from racing, broke with the long-standing code of silence that has prevailed among racers on the subject and acknowledged that they had in fact engaged in more or less systematic doping during their careers.[5]

Realizing that the credibility of the 2007 Tour would be damaged by the participation of racers implicated in highly publicized doping affairs, in the days preceding the start of the race the organizers took an unprecedented step to reassure the public about the integrity of the competition: all racers wishing to compete in the Tour were required to sign an antidoping pledge as a precondition for their participation. In doing so they declared that they were not involved in any doping affair, promised never to infringe the antidoping rules of the UCI (Union Cycliste Internationale, the international cycling federation) in the future, and agreed to substantial penalties in the event that they violated the pledge. Although their professional associations were not entirely behind this initiative, which put the entire onus on the racers and was not required of their support staff, the *directeurs sportifs* (team managers), the federation officials, or the race organizers, more than 200 racers had signed the pledge by the end of June. The 2007 Tour thus began with the expected number of teams and competitors and, perhaps more important, with the hope that the race would represent a decisive turning point in the battle against doping.[6]

As had been the case a year earlier, such optimism proved to be unjustified. This time, however, the scandal extended well beyond the racer in the yellow jersey. The first sign of trouble came when the positive result of an antidoping test done in early June on Patrik Sinkewitz, a German member of the T-Mobile team in the Tour, was made public during the race. At the time of the test Sinkewitz had been training with his team in the Pyrenees. In a disturbing echo of the Landis case, his test had revealed excessive levels of testosterone. Sinkewitz, who had already withdrawn from the Tour after a collision with a spectator, asked that a second test be done to confirm or invalidate the positive result: an athlete's A and B samples must both test positive for him to be convicted of doping. In the meantime, he was suspended by his team even as a German court initiated legal action against him for defrauding his partners (the team's sponsors). A few days later, Sinkewitz withdrew his request to have his B sample tested, an implicit admission of doping, and was immediately fired by T-Mobile. He then publicly acknowledged having used a testosterone cream on the eve of the test to "improve [his] recovery after difficult training sessions," a mistake for which he apologized.

By the time the Sinkewitz case was resolved, the Tour had been hit by more damaging doping affairs involving prominent racers. The Danish racer Michael Rasmussen, who was leading the Tour at the time, was forced by his Rabobank team to withdraw from the race in the wake of revelations that he had missed antidoping tests in the weeks preceding the Tour and had apparently lied about his whereabouts during that period; casting further doubt on the integrity of Rasmussen's performances were allegations by a former racer who implicated Rasmussen in a blood-doping scheme in 2002.[7] Rabobank had initially left Rasmussen, who was emerging as the odds-on favorite to win the Tour, in the race, hoping perhaps to weather the storm of bad publicity and bring him to Paris clad in the yellow jersey. The team removed him only in the wake of public statements by the president of the UCI, the Tour organizers, and other racers (some of whom openly expressed skepticism about Rasmussen's missed tests and his remarkable performances in the mountains), all of which made it clear that the Dane's continued participation was unwelcome, even if it was permitted by the sport's regulations. Perhaps the most important factor in Rabobank's decision to pull their racer out of the Tour was the fact that he was being booed vociferously by crowds along the itinerary—hardly the public relations boon a sponsor hoped to gain from having a racer leading the Tour. The team suspended Rasmussen and then fired him for violating its "internal rules," specifically for breach of trust (lying). Rabobank did, however, keep its other racers in the Tour.[8]

The Astana and Cofidis teams were arguably even less fortunate. As the Sinkewitz and Rasmussen affairs were playing themselves out, Alexander Vinokourov, a prerace favorite, tested positive for homologous blood-doping (using the blood of a compatible donor) on the very day he won a Tour time trial; acceding to a request from the organizers, his entire team, Astana, withdrew from the race. A few days later, Vinokourov's B sample confirmed the positive result, but the racer continued to deny having doped and hired the lawyers who had represented Landis in his doping case. He was nevertheless fired by his team, which, shaken by this and other doping affairs, decided to suspend its season for a month while it decided how to proceed.[9] Meanwhile, Cristian Moreni, an Italian member of the Cofidis team, which itself had temporarily suspended its season a few years earlier in the wake of a major doping scandal, tested positive for exogenous testosterone. He acknowledged having doped and apologized; without waiting to hear from the organizers, Cofidis withdrew its racers from the Tour, fired Moreni, and decided to take a brief break from competition.[10]

Until recently, the parties most directly affected by cycling's doping crisis have typically refused to acknowledge that the persistence of widespread doping reflects a systemic dynamic driven by the logic of competition—racers are continually seeking an edge over their adversaries—and important economic interests. The athletes, sponsors, race organizers, federations, and media all profit from cycling's popularity and have therefore generally sought to present as pristine an image of the sport as possible. This has led them, when forced to confront the issue, to dismiss doping as the result of reprehensible or misguided individual decisions taken by a few untalented racers who thereby sully the reputation of the sport and of the vast majority of their peers, who are "clean." Things appear to be changing, however.

A tipping point may have been reached with the latest doping affairs. For the first time, large numbers of racers are ignoring the code of silence with respect to doping. Not only are they openly voicing suspicions about their peers, but in the wake of Vinokourov's positive test and with the much-contested Rasmussen still wearing the yellow jersey, six French and two German teams staged a public antidoping protest at the start of the sixteenth stage: as the other racers set off, these teams stood their ground, delaying their start for thirteen minutes to the applause of the same crowd that had just booed Rasmussen. The eight teams went further, creating the Mouvement pour un cyclisme crédible.[11]

The mounting frustration expressed by these teams, by other stakeholders in the sport, and by numerous commentators about the continued wide-spread (and effective) doping by professional cyclists raises the important issue of the sport's authenticity. The legitimacy of recent Tour champions has been called into question as never before. According to the three-time Tour winner Greg LeMond, who retired from the sport just as the era of new, more sophisticated, and more effective doping was getting underway, "over the past fifteen years it is impossible to know who the best cyclist of this generation was. Today, doping makes it possible to improve a racer's capacities by 30 percent. It has thus completely altered the hierarchy."[12]

At least one recent Tour champion agrees with this assessment. In contrast to his former teammate Jan Ullrich, in the wake of d'Hont's revelations Bjarne Riis confirmed that he had doped during the latter years of his career when he suddenly emerged from mediocrity to claim the 1996 Tour and the fame and fortune that accompany the sport's greatest prize. A national hero, Riis came under heavy criticism at home, at least from government officials, and was expelled from Denmark's Sports Hall of Fame. He apologized for having doped his way to a Tour victory, acknowledged that he had not deserved to win the race, and expressed his willingness to return his yellow jerseys and forfeit his victory.[13]

The Tour organizers were only too happy to oblige Riis, wiping his 1996 victory from the race's official records. Beyond its obvious symbolic and public-relations value, what this decision actually meant was unclear, as the sport's statute of limitations for revising the results of a competition had expired. The organizers did not, as one might have anticipated, transfer Riis's victory—even symbolically—to the racer who finished second that year, for that racer was none other than Jan Ullrich. Nor could they look to the Frenchman who finished third: Richard Virenque, an admitted doper, was a member of the Festina team at the center of the doping scandal that rocked the 1998 Tour, itself won by another confirmed doper, Marco Pantani. The fourth-placed racer in 1996, Laurent Dufaux, was also not a viable option, for he too had been part of the disgraced Festina team. The 1996 Tour is not the only one whose victor remains a mystery: the Tour organizer Christian Prudhomme ruefully predicted before the 2007 Tour that we would probably know the identity of the 2007 winner before that of the 2006 winner, as the Landis case was likely to drag on in appeals. He was right.

What Prudhomme did not predict was that the victory of the young Spaniard Alberto Contador in the 2007 Tour would itself be greeted with considerable skepticism and suspicion. Even before the race reached Paris, at least one contestant pointed out that like the now disgraced Rasmussen, Contador had not seemed to be suffering in the mountains (which he had ascended in most instances as quickly as the Dane). *Libération* published an article by a professor of physical education and sport who had been a trainer for the Festina team; he argued that the power (measured in watts) deployed by many Tour racers in 2007, including Contador and Rasmussen, like that of top performers in recent Tours, could be explained only by their having had recourse to "incredibly effective medical substances."[14] After reviewing legal documents relating to the Puerto Operation, *Le Monde* revealed that Contador's name and initials appeared in those documents several times, along with those of some of his teammates. Unlike the latter, however, his name did not appear next to doping substances; as a result, the Spanish federation had not taken action against him. When interviewed by the investigating judge in Spain, Contador claimed that he did not know the doctor at the center of the Puerto affair. He refused, however, to provide a DNA sample, which would have allowed the authorities to determine whether or not his blood was among that found at the doctor's office.[15] Characterizing Contador's Tour victory as "the greatest fraud in the history of sport," the German antidoping expert Werner Franke claimed to have seen documents from the investigation that showed that Contador had taken insulin and a testosterone booster.[16] In the wake of these revelations, the organizers of a major one-day race in Hamburg in August publicly announced that Contador was not welcome to participate in their event. However Contador's case plays itself out, the voicing of such doubts in so many quarters is a sign of how badly the Tour's—and the sport's—credibility has been damaged.

The fallout of these affairs extends well beyond the reputations and careers of implicated racers and their support staff. Commercial sponsors of teams who stayed the course through previous doping affairs are beginning to withdraw from professional cycling. Some have publicly concluded that associating their brand with a sport so tainted by doping and as yet unable to organize an effective campaign against the practice is a counterproductive marketing strategy.[17] On the other hand, the sponsors of the three main Tour classifications (the yellow jersey of the overall leader, the green jersey of the points leader, and the polka-dot jersey of the best climber) all wish to maintain their relationship with the race. LCL (formerly Le Crédit Lyonnais), which sponsors the yellow jersey, explained that although it deplored that cheaters were wearing the yellow jersey, its research showed that its clients were able to distinguish between the discredited racers and the company.[18]

Communities are also rethinking their involvement with the sport. Stuttgart, which had been selected to host the 2007 world cycling championships (held in September), threatened to back out in light of recent doping scandals but reconsidered after being promised that the number of antidoping tests at the championships would be increased.[19] Local authorities in Germany suspended their financial partnership with the organizers of the Tour of Rhineland-Palatinate, putting the event in jeopardy. Other races, including the century-old Championship of Zurich, have already been canceled for lack of financial backing, and television coverage of the sport is being reduced.[20]

Even television coverage of the Tour may no longer be the financial sure bet it once was. In Germany, for example, the two networks televising the 2006 Tour registered a 43-percent drop in their audience, no doubt in large measure due to Ullrich's last-minute exclusion from the race as a result of his implication in the Puerto affair.[21] Without a guarantee from the organizers to allow the sport's stars to participate as long as they have not actually been convicted of doping, will some networks no longer be willing to risk immense sums on transmission rights? On the other hand, given how long the investigation and prosecution of an alleged doping violation can take, the organizers feel the need to take preemptive action, even if this violates the presumption of innocence. It would hardly serve their interests to admit racers who would be competing under a cloud of suspicion and might in the end actually be found guilty of having doped.[22]

On this front, too, events are moving rapidly and in unprecedented directions. On the eve of the 2007 Tour and in the wake of the T-Mobile and other recent doping scandals, the ARD and ZDF German television networks threatened to stop televising the Tour in the event of another case of doping involving a German racer or team: "We are prepared to support cycling," they announced, "but only if it is clean, that is to say free of doping and banned substances." They were as good as their word: upon the news of Sinkewitz's positive A sample the two networks immediately suspended their Tour broadcasts, much to the consternation of the organizers and racers. On the other hand, the French public networks that cover the race, while deploring the cheaters and dopers, stood by the event; they were comforted in part no doubt by stable ratings for the 2007 Tour, except for the final week, when the succession of doping affairs contributed to a significant decrease in the number of viewers. For the private German station Sat.1, which obtained the transmission rights to the 2007 Tour after ARD and ZDF canceled their coverage, the news was bleak: disappointed by the ratings in Germany, which it attributed to the Tour's lack of credibility, Sat.1 was leaning toward no longer televising the sport at all.[23]

The doping scandals of the 2007 Tour sparked calls in the French press for the race's cancellation. *France-Soir* announced sarcastically that the Tour had succumbed "at age 104, after a long illness."[24] Across the rest of Europe—in England, Belgium, Germany, Spain, and the Czech Republic—the press hypothesized about the death of the Tour, speculated about the event's and the sport's credibility, and wondered whether and how the sport could be reformed.[25] For its part, the major Swiss newspaper *Tages-Anzeiger* decided to limit its Tour coverage to doping stories and the results.[26]

Perhaps most alarming for the sport's stakeholders, the public's tolerance of repeated doping scandals, which has long seemed limitless, is showing signs of fraying. Not only are commercial sponsors, television stations, newspapers, and host communities reconsidering their involvement in the sport (presumably at least partly in response to the public's mounting disgust with the doping scandals), but there is evidence that live television audiences, even for a major "classic" one-day race like the Tour of Flanders, are on the decline.[27] The Tour itself is not immune: observers noted that the crowds that came out for the race in 2006 were smaller than in previous years. The live television audience for the 2006 Tour also declined significantly, not just in Germany, but also in the United States (where Lance Armstrong's retirement no doubt was a factor) and even in France. These trends suggest that the Puerto affair—coming after so many other recent doping scandals—alienated at least part of the event's fan base that year.[28] A year later, some reports suggested that Tour crowds in the Pyrenees had declined in the wake of the 2007 doping affairs.[29]

Public opinion polls in France near or at the conclusion of the 2007 Tour indicated both the public's disenchantment with the succession of doping affairs and the continuing, if somewhat reduced, popularity of the race among the French. A poll published on 22 July in *Le Journal du Dimanche* revealed that 78 percent of the respondents had doubts about the "integrity" of the racers' performances, but that 52 percent still liked or loved [*aimer* can mean either] the Tour de France.[30] In another poll a few days later, 46 percent of the respondents declared that they had no interest in the Tour, compared with 29 percent who expressed at least some interest in the race (down from 38 percent in 2005).[31] For his part, the newly elected president of France, Nicolas Sarkozy, assured the Tour organizers of his support, declaring to his ministers: "The Tour de France is one of the symbols of French identity, and a month of July without the Tour de France is not a month of July."[32]

Are we witnessing the chaotic, collective suicide of an immensely popular and profitable sport with a history rich in legendary exploits and great champions? Is time running out on professional cycling's stakeholders, who seem unable to put aside their differences for the sake of their common interest in an economically (and ethically) viable sport, notwithstanding their repeated claims to be aggressively confronting the doping crisis? Is it conceivable that, President Sarkozy's sentiments notwithstanding, in the not-too-distant future French summers will not include the joyful, century-old ritual that draws millions of spectators to the side of the road every July as hundreds of millions more watch the Tour live on television? It is still too early to tell: in the last four decades the Tour has survived the drug-related death of the English racer Tom Simpson in 1967, as well as major doping scandals in 1978 and 1998. But the fact that the question of the Tour's survival can now seriously be posed suggests that, whatever its ultimate fate may be, the race continues to raise the important questions that inspired me to write this book in the first place—questions about the roles and meanings assigned to sport and athletes in modern societies.

Those questions, as readers will discover in the chapters that follow, relate to definitions of heroism, conceptions of human rights and dignity, ideas about work and about workers' rights and duties, and public health. Over the past century, these issues have been addressed, ignored, and finessed in various ways by the sport's stakeholders. But what of the public's role in, and responsibility for, the crisis that currently confronts the Tour de France and, more generally, professional sport? This dimension of the story rarely generates much discussion, despite the obvious fact that without public interest in and support for the race it would rapidly cease to be.

Tour de France racers have been celebrities since the first Tour was held in 1903, when many—although by no means all—French newspapers and illustrated magazines sought to increase sales by featuring articles and images of France's new "giants of the road." Major advances in communications technology over the past century have dramatically expanded this media-fueled celebrity culture. But Tour racers have always been more than mere celebrities: the media has helped to create and disseminate an image of them as heroic survivors confronting horrific suffering as they struggle to complete the world's most grueling sporting event. In France especially, such courage and perseverance have endowed Tour racers with a moral standing as public exemplars of qualities to which their (male) fans should aspire. A society composed of such individuals can look to the future with confidence, a prospect that has been especially meaningful to the French, given the often mortal challenges their nation has faced during the last century.

Thus, as elsewhere in the modern world, in France athletes—especially Tour racers—have been burdened with an important symbolic role: they are widely associated with virtues essential to the health, prosperity, and even survival of the national community. First idealized a century ago, the racers have been idolized ever since. Yet what is generally glossed over in the transformation of Tour racers into moral exemplars is that the event that conditions their public elevation to heroic status is a professional competition, and their motivation is first and foremost economic: Tour racers have typically hailed from humble backgrounds, enjoyed limited career options, and faced a lifetime of modestly paid and often unpleasant labor should they fail at cycling. That economic incentive, combined with the competitive essence of sport, which motivates athletes to seek an advantage over their opponents, and the particularly grueling nature of cycling, have led—and continue to lead—Tour racers to seek ways to ease their suffering and maximize their prospects for success. Hence their recourse to doping.

Is it not time for the public to confront its contradictory expectations of these men? On the one hand, it wishes to celebrate Tour racers as heroes and moral exemplars. On the other, the public expects the racers to live up to their lofty status by performing feats that lead large numbers of them to dope. In the process, racers put their health and lives at risk in a manner that is difficult to view as either virtuous or heroic. Although they are adult men and thus at least partly responsible for their actions, professional cyclists have long been, and continue to be, trapped in a sinister dynamic not solely of their making—a dynamic shaped and driven by the profit motives of race organizers, sponsors, and much of the media. History offers us many examples of public campaigns that have taken on major economic interests and effectively addressed social evils, such as slavery, child labor, environmental threats, and various forms of discrimination. Why not doping?

Several factors help explain the public's passivity to date. For one thing, it has been encouraged to live in denial about doping by the repeated refusal of racers, team staffs, race organizers, commercial sponsors, federation officials, and members of the media who knew what was going on to acknowledge a reality that would jeopardize what they perceived to be their self-interest. Spasms of media coverage of the latest "affair" have been typically followed by sober requests to avoid simplistic generalizations and a return to the inspirational rhetoric of exploits and heroes. Sustained attention to, and investigation of, the issue remained the province of a few mavericks who could be plausibly marginalized as publicity-seeking sensationalists. Raised in a celebrity culture that promotes the uncritical admiration of elite athletes, the public has been far more likely to believe the categorical denials of the "giants of the road" than the accusations of anonymous journalists, especially when many prominent reporters either remained silent or sided with the athletes.

A second reason for the public's passivity is that, unlike the other interested parties, it is not, nor can it easily be, effectively organized. Racers have their professional associations, teams and race organizers their respective umbrella organizations, and the sport its national and international federations. The public, however, remains scattered—admittedly in the hundreds of millions—across neighborhoods, cities, countries, and continents, divided by geography, language, and culture. Moreover, the public divests itself of any direct responsibility by assuming that governments will address illegal conduct such as doping, which in fact most governments have been loathe to do until quite recently. Finally, the scientific and legal issues are often so complex that the public defers to experts acting on behalf of democratically elected governments, who, presumably, are implementing the will of the people. In fact, however, the public has often sided with the racers under investigation rather than with the investigating authorities, and resents the latter for singling out athletes who seem overmatched by the awesome power and resources of the state.

Perhaps the most important reason behind the public's failure to mobilize against doping is that most people do not identify the practice as a serious social problem, in spite of compelling evidence that the illegal use of banned performance-enhancing drugs is both widespread among professional cyclists (and other high-performance athletes) and a threat to their health.[33] Unlike racism or an environmental menace, doping in professional cycling, it can be argued, directly affects at most a few thousand individuals worldwide—the professional racers.[34] The public also rebels against the criminalization of doping by athletes, because it is founded on distinctions that are difficult to grasp. Where does the boundary lie between an athlete's presumably legitimate right to recover quickly and completely from an extreme effort and his presumably illegitimate attempt to extend through pharmacological and other means his physiological limits? Why are a few thousand racers denied drugs and therapies that are prescribed to millions of ill or elderly people as a matter of course?[35]

Seeking answers to these difficult questions demands an honest attempt to grapple with complex issues and subtle distinctions. In the final analysis, effectively addressing doping by athletes will require nothing less than a cultural shift by the public: other social problems, once they were defined as such, were not solved solely by legislation and regulation; major changes in public attitudes were also required. Such a sea change with respect to doping, which may now be in its initial stage, would significantly bolster official attempts to eradicate the practice. Should that shift occur, it may again be possible to train in the Bois de Boulogne without provoking the opprobrium of a teenager indulging in guilt by association, and to ride in the Pyrenees without encountering signs impugning the character of the "giants of the road." In the meantime, we can seek to understand how cycling and its premier event reached this difficult juncture in the first place. One of my motivations for writing this book was to contribute to that effort.

Muncie, Indiana
October 2007

1. The Puerto affair involves an investigation into a blood-doping operation in Spain allegedly run by a Dr. Eufemiano Fuentes, whose offices were found to contain about 100 bags of frozen blood when they were raided by the Spanish authorities. DNA testing has to date implicated two of the sport's biggest stars, Ivan Basso and Jan Ullrich. Basso acknowledged that, tempted by the prospect of blood-doping, he had turned to Dr. Fuentes, but he claimed that he had not actually followed through with his plan to dope. He received a two-year suspension. Ullrich maintained his innocence and soon announced his retirement from the sport.

2. On the doping crisis in American cycling, see David Walsh, *From Lance to Landis: Inside the American Doping Controversy at the Tour de France* (New York: Ballantine Books, 2007), which is a follow-up to the book he coauthored with Pierre Ballester (see the bibliography).

3. In September, the arbitration panel in the Landis case ruled against him 2–1, stripping him of his Tour victory. Landis then appealed the ruling to the Court of Arbitration for Sport. In October, Oscar Pereiro, who had finished second in the 2006 Tour, was formally recognized as the race's winner in a ceremony by the organizers.

4. Jef d'Hont, *Memoires van een wielerverzorger* (Leuven: Uitgeverij van Halewijk, 2007).

5. The racers who admitted to doping when with the team acknowledged that they had done so systematically and over a significant period of time—with one exception: Erik Zabel claimed that he doped only briefly in 1996 and has otherwise been "clean." His assertion needs to be balanced against his impressive record of victories over the last decade, when he has been one of the most successful racers in professional cycling (and when so many of the racers he was defeating were apparently doping), and against the fact that as he is still racing, he has a stake in presenting himself as "clean." His current team has kept him on. In the wake of Zabel's admission, the Tour organizers took the symbolic measure of erasing him from the official records of the 1996 Tour, in which he had won the green jersey of points leader for the first time (he would win the points competition in five subsequent Tours). They did so despite the inconvenient fact that the sport's statute of limitations for changing the results of a competition had expired.

In addition to racers and support staff, the Deutsche Telekom/T-Mobile affair implicated two prominent German doctors at a leading sports clinic, who were soon fired. The affair rose to the highest levels of the German state as Chancellor Angela Merkel implored racers who had doped to "come clean and break 'a cartel of silence.'" Associated Press, 25 May 2007 (accessed at ESPN.com, 27 May 2007). Soon thereafter, "the German Minister of Sport announced . . . the formation of a special working group to combat doping in sport." Agence France-Presse, 30 May 2007.

6. The full text of the pledge is as follows:

> I do solemnly declare, to my team, my colleagues, the UCI [the international cycling federation], the cycling movement and the public that I am not involved in the Puerto affair nor in any other doping case and that I will not commit any infringement to the UCI antidoping rules. As proof of my commitment, I accept, if it should happen that I violate the rules and am granted a standard sanction of a two-year suspension or more, in the Puerto affair or in any other antidoping proceedings, to pay the UCI, in addition to the standard sanctions, an amount equal to my annual salary for 2007 as a contribution to the fight against doping.
>
> At the same time, I declare to the Spanish Law that my DNA is at its disposal, so that it can be compared with the blood samples seized in the Puerto affair. I appeal to the Spanish Law to organize this test as soon as possible or allow the UCI to organize it. Finally, I accept the UCI's wish to make my statement public.

No doubt responding to complaints that such a commitment to a doping-free sport (and the serious penalties involved in the event of violations) should not be limited to the racers, the UCI asked the racers' managers, doctors, and all other support staff, as well as the *directeurs sportifs* of the teams, to sign a similar pledge.

7. Rasmussen had been among the last to sign the antidoping pledge required to participate in the Tour, claiming that being forced to do so represented an "intrusion" into his "private life." For its part, the UCI noted that, consistent with its rules and procedures, Rasmussen had been given a formal warning in the wake of his missed tests, but that as he was not subject to further disciplinary action, he was within his rights to continue competing in the Tour.

8. At the end of the Tour, the organizers froze Rabobank's prize money as they awaited the UCI's ruling in the Rasmussen case.

9. The Astana team had already made doping-related news just before the start of the race, when Vinokourov acknowledged that he was consulting with the Italian doctor Michele Ferrari, whose name has repeatedly come up in doping affairs. Moreover, Astana had suspended two of its racers for doping just before the Tour began (later firing one of them), while a third, the German Jörg Jaksche, who was implicated in the Puerto Operation, had agreed to come clean and collaborate with the police, the German courts, and sports officials.

10. Bad news on the doping front extended beyond the Tour's finale on the Champs-Élysées. Twenty-four hours after the race ended it was revealed that Iban Mayo of the Saunier Duval team, a Spaniard who had finished sixteenth, had tested positive for the oxygen-boosting hormone EPO during a rest day before the last major mountain stage. The UCI suspended him immediately, and his team pledged to fire him should his B sample confirm the positive result.

11. Ironically, one of the French teams involved in the strike was none other than Cofidis, which would soon withdraw in the wake of Moreni's positive test result.

12. *Le Monde,* 27 July 2007. "The credibility of [the] sport is ruined," the *directeur sportif* of one of the French teams concluded. "The gangrene follows us; it won't leave us alone." Ibid.

13. Riis stayed on, however, as the manager of the CSC team (one of the most successful in professional cycling), a fact many observers found disturbing, but he did not accompany his team to the 2007 Tour.

14. *Libération,* 27 July 2007.

15. *Le Monde,* 29 July 2007.

16. *Libération,* 30 July 2007; *USA Today,* 1 August 2007.

17. Landis's team's sponsor, Phonak, discontinued its sponsorship soon after his positive result was announced. Lance Armstrong's last team, Discovery Channel, announced before the 2007 Tour that it would not renew its sponsorship of the team as a result of the sport's ongoing doping crisis. *New York Times,* 28 June 2007. In July 2007 a spokesman for the Gerolsteiner team said that the sponsor's continued involvement was a 50–50 proposition. Adidas indicated that it might terminate its partnerships with the T-Mobile team as well as with the French and German

national teams. Audi, too, was considering discontinuing its involvement in the sport. Meanwhile, in the wake of the Sinkewitz affair, T-Mobile was reconsidering its sponsorship of a team and was planning to make a decision soon after the Tour's conclusion. Other teams' sponsors have decided to stay in the sport and committed, at least in their public statements, to a renewed battle against doping. For the Caisse d'Épargne bank, which sponsors a team, the sport remains a viable and remarkably inexpensive promotional strategy for reaching a broad audience. The bank, however, retains the right to cancel its sponsorship at any moment in the event that one of its racers is convicted of doping. *Libération,* 26 July 2007; *Le Monde,* 31 July 2007.

18. *Libération,* 26 July 2007; *Le Monde,* 31 July 2007.

19. *USA Today,* 3 August 2007. In an embarrassing twist, the winner of the professional road race in Stuttgart was none other than the defending world champion, Paolo Bettini, whom the organizers had unsuccessfully sought to exclude because he refused to sign the antidoping pledge.

20. *New York Times,* 13 May 2007.

21. *Le Monde,* 23 July 2006.

22. The succession of doping scandals in the 2007 Tour led to mutual recriminations between the organizers and the UCI president. Accusing the UCI of not having waged a sufficiently rigorous campaign against doping, the organizers broke with the international federation and asked for the resignation of its leaders. The UCI president characterized this reaction as "irrational" and noted that the UCI was but one of a number of institutions involved in the antidoping campaign and thus was not responsible for the way every doping case was handled.

23. *Libération,* 26 July 2007; *Le Monde,* 31 July 2007.

24. *USA Today,* 27 July 2007.

25. *Libération,* 26 July 2007.

26. *USA Today,* 26 July 2007.

27. *New York Times,* 13 May 2007.

28. *Le Monde,* 23 July 2006.

29. Ibid., 27 July 2007.

30. Ibid., 28 July 2007.

31. *L'Équipe,* 29 July 2007.

32. *Le Monde,* 27 July 2007.

33. Fans who understand the dangers of doping may be in denial, preferring not to acknowledge their role as more or less unwitting enablers of the doping racers.

34. This case has been countered by the argument that juniors and amateurs who hope one day to break into the professional ranks will be drawn to doping, and that the practice will thus never be limited to adult professionals. See chapter 6.

35. On this question, see especially the work of John Hoberman (see the bibliography).

ACKNOWLEDGMENTS

It is humbling, at the conclusion of a project so often solitary, to reflect on how much its successful completion owes to individuals and institutions without whose encouragement, advice, financial support, and cooperation this book could not have been written.

Research for this book and for the dissertation on which it is partially based was supported by a number of generous grants. These included a Châteaubriand Scholarship from the French government, a Dean's Dissertation Fellowship from the Department of History at New York University, a Summer Research Grant from NYU's Remarque Institute (made possible by the generosity of the Mellon Foundation), a Summer Research Stipend from the National Endowment for the Humanities, and three grants from Ball State University: a new Faculty Summer Research Grant, a Supplemental Equipment and Travel Grant, and a Faculty Summer Research Grant. I also thank Ball State University for generously covering the cost of the book's illustrations.

The staffs of the following institutions deployed equal parts patience and perseverance in helping me to track down the primary sources on which this book is based: the Bibliothèque Nationale (Salle des Imprimés and Salle des Périodiques); the Bibliothèque de France; the INAthèque; the Paris police archives; the municipal archives of Longwy-Bas, Sens, Rennes, Strasbourg, and Caen; and the departmental archives of Meurthe-et-Moselle, Meuse, Ille-et-Vilaine, and Calvados. Many thanks also to the interlibrary loan staff at Ball State University for their tireless efforts on my behalf.

I am indebted to Serge Laget for his willingness to share his unrivaled knowledge about the Tour, for providing me with access to a copy of the unpublished report *L'Auto* produced about its wartime activities, and for setting up interviews with the late Jacques Goddet, the former editor in chief of *L'Équipe,* and Victor Cosson, a former Tour racer. John Hoberman, one of the most thought-provoking historians of sport, also has been a great resource. I thank him for reading chapter 6 and for sharing his insights on the history of doping in sports.

Three people were kind enough to grant me interviews that enhanced my understanding of important aspects of the Tour's history. M. Goddet graciously answered all my questions about the race's history going back to the 1930s. M. Cosson, who finished third in 1938, arrived at the offices of *L'Équipe* on his bicycle and regaled me with stories about racing in the 1930s and 1940s. Finally, Helen Hoban could not have been more forthcoming in discussing her experience as a Tour racer's wife, including the tragic death during the 1967 Tour of her first husband, the English racer Tom Simpson. I can never repay her willingness to speak openly about such private matters.

I have benefited from the advice, suggestions, criticisms, and guidance of scholars on both sides of the Atlantic. In Paris, Jacques Revel enthusiastically supported this project from the beginning. Georges Vigarello guided my preliminary research on the Tour's history, and Patrick Fridenson lent me a rare primary source and suggested I look at a master's thesis, both of which proved most helpful. Pascal Ory and Steven Kaplan invited me to present my research at the Université de Versailles Saint-Quentin-en-Yvelines and Cornell University, respectively. I am also grateful to the American Historical Association, the Society for French Historical Studies, the Western Society for French History, and the International Society for the History of Physical Education and Sport for giving me the chance to present papers at their annual conferences. These were all invaluable opportunities to test my arguments and benefit from the insights of the scholars in attendance.

I could not have hoped for a more stimulating environment in which to pursue a doctorate in modern French history than the one I found at New York University. Three professors, in particular, played pivotal roles. The late Nicholas Wahl, the first director of the Institute of French Studies, supported me unstintingly from my arrival at the institute. My two principal dissertation advisers could not have been more helpful. I am grateful for Professor Tony Judt's attention to detail, his unfailing accessibility (on whichever side of the Atlantic he happened to find himself), and his rapid reactions to drafts of my dissertation chapters. Professor Molly Nolan's doctoral seminar on modern Germany introduced me to the kinds of historical problems I continue to find most stimulating, and her insights into the organizational and conceptual challenges of my dissertation made me a more thoughtful and more careful historian. Meanwhile, my classmates were always ready to listen to my musings about the Tour and offer their suggestions. I am especially grateful to John Savage, who encouraged me to explore the extent to which my dissertation topic intersected with several important themes in the history of the Third Republic. I also greatly benefited from the insights of two friends who preceded me at the Institute of French Studies: Janet Horne patiently helped me work through one of the key arguments of this study, and Shanny Peer assisted me in thinking more rigorously about social class.

My colleagues in the History Department at Ball State University also made important contributions. René Marion and Carolyn Malone commented on early drafts of two chapters, and Rob Hall put his encyclopedic understanding of the historiography of European class identities at my disposal. I am grateful for his patience in helping me work through certain thorny—at least to me—conceptual issues. I owe a special debt of gratitude to Jim Connolly, whose eye for argument, impatience with unnecessary evidence, and gift for organization were of great benefit as I confronted large amounts of data and looked for the best way to tell an often complicated story. He read the entire manuscript and made suggestions that improved the flow and the argument of two chapters in particular. I am fortunate indeed to count such intelligent and congenial historians among my friends.

The University of California Press was from the beginning enthusiastically supportive. I thank the two historians who read the manuscript for the press for their encouraging assessments and helpful suggestions. At the press, Sheila Levine offered timely advice and exhibited much-appreciated patience throughout what must at times have seemed an interminable process. I thank her for understanding that this book would take time to write. More recently, Niels Hooper, Rachel Lockman, Laura Harger, and Erika Büky have shepherded the manuscript through the production process. Lindsie Bear provided welcome guidance and helpful suggestions for the first paperback edition. I am grateful for their determination to make the finished product as good as possible, and for their skill and professionalism in doing so.

I thank my family for their support throughout the researching and writing of both my dissertation and this book, especially my father, who read the entire dissertation and suggested stylistic changes that improved my prose. Perhaps even more important than their encouragement, generosity, and hospitality, three generations of Thompsons continually offered me timely reminders that there may in fact be more to life than cycling. I look forward to testing that hypothesis with them in the years to come.

Finally, I wish to recognize the special contributions of my friend Myra van Hus. In addition to putting me in touch with Helen Hoban, over the past thirty years Myra has always been there for me, through the good times—of which there have been so many—and the difficult moments, which she inevitably finds a way to ease. I will never be able to thank her enough for her humor, her enthusiasm for the good things in life, and her courage and selflessness in confronting its challenges.

Introduction

≡

In early August 1971, a few days before my twelfth birthday, my family moved to Brussels. I already knew how to ride a bicycle. I soon realized, however, that I knew nothing about cycling. Alternating between the Flemish- and French-language television stations or glued to my radio, I discovered a sport I could never have imagined. Bloodied, mud-splattered racers careened over the treacherous cobblestones of northern France, the strongest inexorably pulling away, meter by painful meter, from the rest. Less selective races concluded dramatically with scores of contestants gathering themselves for a perilous sprint, swerving acrobatically as they fought their way to the front of the pack. Stretched out over kilometers, participants in the Tour de France inched up the great climbs of the Alps and Pyrenees and rocketed down the descents, leaving the motorcycles of the television camera crews in their wake.

This new world had its own mysterious language. There were *pelotons* (packs of racers) and *sprints massifs* (group sprints); *démarrages* (attacks), *attaques,* and *échappées* (breakaways); *cols* (climbs), *défaillances* (collapses), and *abandons* (withdrawals). A new calendar restructured my sense of time from February to November, as one-day races, week-long stage races, national and world championships, and the three-week Tours of Spain, Italy, and France succeeded each other at a dizzying pace. I learned of new places, from the legendary Tourmalet and Galibier climbs in the Tour de France to cities like Milan and San Remo, Paris and Roubaix, that have been linked for more than a century by the race itineraries they evoke. Above all, I was introduced to new characters with exotic names, whose posters, carefully unstapled from *Le Miroir du Cyclisme,* covered my bedroom walls. There

1

were tanned champions from the Mediterranean, like the star-crossed Spaniard Luis Ocaña, the gracious Italian Felice Gimondi, and the stocky Joaquin Agostinho of Portugal. There was the good-natured Frenchman Raymond Poulidor—"Pou-Pou" to his legions of fans—with his lovable knack for finishing second in the most important races, and the enigmatic Dutchman Joop Zoetemelk, in whom the same knack was somehow less lovable. And of course there were rugged Flemings like Roger de Vlaeminck and Freddy Maertens, who excelled at the prestigious one-day *classiques,* never more so than when the weather was cold and wet and the terrain the slick country roads of their native Flanders. Reigning above them all was another Belgian, Eddy Merckx: the "Cannibal" dominated European professional cycling during this period with an unquenchable thirst for victory I found utterly captivating.

Cycling had its own history. I pored over the sports pages of the Brussels daily *Le Soir* and each issue of my cycling magazine, gradually piecing together the careers of earlier champions with magical names like Fausto Coppi, Louison Bobet, and Jacques Anquetil. Their exploits had created a heroic mythology that stretched back in time, full of tense rivalries, hard-won victories, and bitter defeats. That *légende,* I came to understand, was founded on a set of core values: courage, perseverance, the tolerance of pain, and, in the case of the greatest champions, *panache.* No sport was more grueling and, thus, to the awestruck adolescent sports fan, no group of men more worthy of admiration. With its virtuous heroes, epic moments, and legendary places, cycling was a world of its own.

Or so I believed when we left Belgium in July 1975. Some fifteen years later, enrolled in graduate school, I was fishing around for a dissertation topic when one of my professors made a passing comment about the popularity of the Tour in the 1930s. On reflection, it struck me that far from being a world of its own, the race was inextricably and meaningfully connected to the world around it. For one thing, it epitomized the rise of mass spectator sport, a phenomenon with far-reaching social, cultural, political, and economic consequences (which, curiously, has received relatively little attention from historians of modern France).[1] For another, it offered a new lens through which to view twentieth-century French history, one that was likely to yield original insights into developments both in sport and in other aspects of French life. The race I had watched as a boy was more than trivial entertainment; it was a legitimate subject of historical study.

My dissertation explored the social, cultural, and political history of bicycling under the Third Republic, including aspects of the Tour. When it came time to develop the dissertation into a book, I focused on the topic that had first inspired me: the race itself. I was especially fascinated by the diverse meanings with which the French have invested the Tour since its creation in 1903. They are important for two reasons. First, they deepen our understanding of the impact of sport on modern France. Second, they reveal much about the hopes and fears of the French as they confronted the challenges of an often traumatic twentieth century. Together, these meanings constitute the Tour's cultural history.

My approach to that history has been informed by two historiographic trends. Recent scholarship on the construction of identities has argued that, rather than being the self-evident expression of certain supposedly natural, timeless, and universal roles, social identities are historically contingent, shaped by tensions and conflicts within a given society at a particular time. Although often promoted as objective and neutral, representations of class or gender identities, for example, reflect specific interests, values, and social visions. This explains why they are so often challenged by alternative representations designed to advance competing interests, values, and social visions. Some of the most interesting scholarship on identity has been influenced by the new cultural history, itself inspired by disciplines such as cultural anthropology and literary criticism.[2]

In seeking to understand the socially constructed nature of identities, practitioners of the new cultural history have shown particular interest in events, activities, places, and individuals previously ignored or dismissed as insignificant. Resurrecting such subjects and inserting them into historical narratives has required exploiting a broad range of primary sources in popular culture and the history of everyday life, many of which had heretofore received scant attention from historians. My own research led me to examine advertising posters, postcards, and press photographs; poems, songs, and novels; films and television coverage; the Parisian and provincial press; and the words of politicians, military officers, physicians, cycling club members, sports officials, the Tour's organizers, its public, and, of course, the racers and their families.

These sources have helped me to reconstitute what I believe are the most important public narratives inspired by the Tour. They address a range of subjects, including war, the nature of heroism, women's emancipation, industrialization, class relations, and the often ambiguous relationship between local and national identity. Various groups—the race's organizers, the racers, the press, and different constituencies within its vast public—have sought to control the Tour's image, infusing the event with meanings that furthered their specific interests or reflected their particular worldview. The result has been a variety of depictions of France, ranging from idealized portrayals of a traditional, stable, and united community to disturbing visions of a modern, chaotic nation riven by social conflict and political polarization. To understand the complex, often contradictory ways the French have experienced their Tour is to understand the stories they have told to themselves and to each other about who they are, whence they came, and where they are heading. It is to shed light on their attempts to embrace, control, or reverse the dramatic changes of the past century. And it is to affirm the importance of sport in that process.

The French have found the Tour a particularly productive site for competing narratives about France and Frenchness. The race quickly established itself as the nation's most popular sporting event, attracting ever more extensive media coverage. Unlike the soccer World Cup or the Olympic Games, which are held only once every four years and shift from continent to continent, the Tour de France is held annually in the same general area. Each summer *la grande boucle* (the great loop), as the race has been known from its earliest days, provides the French with a familiar and very public screen on which to project their understandings of the past, assessments of the present, and aspirations for the future. From year to year, and from generation to generation, they have used these projections to evaluate the changes and challenges, but also the continuities, that have shaped their lives.

Most of these Tour-inspired narratives reflect their often conflicted relationship with modernity. This is hardly surprising. The race itself was made possible by a number of trends associated with modern life, including technological innovation, the development of a mass press (and subsequently other media), and the emergence of a society characterized by increased leisure and the mass consumption of nonessential goods. As a result, the relationship between the French and their Tour has been double-edged. On the one hand, their ambivalence toward the modern has shaped French thinking about and experience of the race. On the other hand, they have often turned to the Tour to make sense of the twentieth century, notably with respect to such important issues as class relations, gender roles, social cohesion, national unity, the nature of work, and public health. They have done so by using the race to tell stories about both what it means to be French and what it means to be modern.

These stories have been as varied as the motivations and perspectives that inspired them. Some have sought to resolve perceived tensions between the two terms *French* and *modern* by celebrating the Tour as a manifestation of the irresistible and resolutely positive march of progress. Others have embraced the Tour as embodying a traditional France that must be defended against the nefarious forces of modernity. Still others have attacked the race as emblematic of the destructive pathologies of modern life, from the numbingly repetitive work of the assembly line to widespread drug abuse.

This book is organized both chronologically and thematically. Chapter 1 addresses the convergence of inventions, institutions, interest groups, and motivations that led to the birth of cycling in the late nineteenth century, setting the stage for the Tour's creation in the early twentieth. It then examines the race's evolution as an athletic competition, a commercial enterprise, and a media event. The chapter is structured around two often contested concepts, modernity and progress, that play a central role in the narratives analyzed in subsequent chapters. Chapter 2 illustrates how the ever-changing itinerary of *la grande boucle* has been exploited to generate diverse and often opposing views of French society, history, and identity. Chapter 3 focuses on representations of Tour participants as heroic, hypermasculine *géants de la route* (giants of the road), explains the motivations behind and the enduring appeal of this image, and examines how and why women have been limited to carefully prescribed, traditionally female roles in this male universe and in the stories told about it.

The final three chapters address images of the Tour and its racers in relation to notions of work. The physical and psychological conditions of the race and the racers' status as national heroes placed them at the center of French debates about work and class. As individuals who improved their socioeconomic condition by their physical strength and endurance rather than through their social networks or educational qualifications, professional bicycle racers challenged the assumptions of bourgeois society, threatened the status quo, and provided a potentially disruptive model for the masses. Chapter 4 examines attempts by the sports daily that organized the race through 1939 to defuse this potential threat by celebrating Tour participants as exemplary *ouvriers de la pédale* (pedal workers) and publicly punishing those who deviated from rigorously enforced rules of appropriate conduct. Racers often resisted this campaign to transform them into "respectable" members of the (lower) middle class and remained true to their working-class identity. Chapter 5 explores how opponents of the Tour during this period undermined representations of racers as model workers, describing them instead as slave laborers. These commentators exploited the Tour's much-celebrated extreme nature to formulate a broad critique of the exploitation of labor which, they argued, characterized the increasingly rationalized factories of early-twentieth-century France. Finally, chapter 6 examines postwar debates about the Tour as work, relates them to the racers' longstanding practice of doping, and explores the implications of that practice for their heroic image as France's *géants de la route*.

ONE

La Grande Boucle
Cycling, Progress, and Modernity

≡

The late nineteenth century was a time of dramatic change for the French. The Second Empire had collapsed abruptly in military defeat at the hands of a Prussian-led coalition of German states in the fall of 1870. A republic, France's third, was immediately proclaimed, but, as had been the case since the revolution of 1789, *republic* meant different things to different people. To the workers of Paris, unable or unwilling to flee the German troops who now laid siege to the capital, the new regime represented an opportunity to implement direct, local, and social democracy under the Commune. For more conservative citizens attempting to make the best of military debacle, foreign invasion, and the political vacuum resulting from Napoleon III's abdication, the republic's value lay elsewhere. In the words of its first president, Adolphe Thiers, it was the regime that "divides us the least." After weeks of stalemate and under pressure from Bismarck, Thiers sent French troops into Paris, where they massacred thousands of *communards,* bringing the latter's experiment in self-government to a violent conclusion and sending many of the survivors into exile. The dual trauma of military defeat and civil war was compounded by the foundation, at Versailles no less, of a united German Empire led by the Prussian king. The existence of a dominant, ambitious, and populous neighbor to the east was made all the more threatening to the French by their own stagnant demography and the cession of Alsace and part of Lorraine to the new German Reich.

Confronted with so much apparent evidence of national decline, the

French were particularly sensitive to the radical changes occurring as the nineteenth century drew to a close. Although much of that change was contested by social conservatives and the Third Republic's political opponents, the new regime had a good deal of which to be proud. The reparations imposed by Germany were paid off faster than even the most optimistic French could have hoped. Universal male suffrage was once again the law of the land, and early challenges by monarchists and other political opponents of the republic were successfully parried. To shore up and expand their base, the republicans passed legislation making primary schooling obligatory and free. New public schools opened their doors in communes across the country, promoting a republican civic culture, offering educational opportunities to all children, and suggesting the coming of a secular, meritocratic age. Universal conscription also promoted patriotism and unity by bringing together young Frenchmen of all regions, social classes, and political convictions, and suggesting that each was prepared to lay down his life for *la patrie*.

While revenge against Germany remained an uncertain proposition at best, France found other ways to rebuild its international prestige, pursuing a policy of colonial expansion and, in the early 1890s, emerging from diplomatic isolation by concluding an alliance with Russia. Meanwhile, France's self-proclaimed *mission civilisatrice* was not aimed exclusively beyond its frontiers: secondary railroad lines were reaching deep into the French countryside, linking previously isolated mountainside hamlets and farming communities to the rest of the nation and in the process transforming rural France.[1] The nation's urban landscape was also changing dramatically. The great steel and glass architecture of the period spawned monumental structures, most notably the Eiffel Tower in Paris, where the Métropolitain opened at the turn of the century. Inventors and entrepreneurs promoting new locomotive technologies such as the bicycle, automobile, and airplane were challenging traditional conceptions of time and space.[2] As if to consecrate these diverse achievements, the International Exhibitions of 1878, 1889, and 1900 allowed the French to present to the world and, perhaps more important, to themselves a self-confident image of accomplishment, flair, and technological know-how.

Modernity was not confined to new technologies and feats of engineering; nor was democratization limited to the political sphere. Department stores like the Bon Marché were revolutionizing the shopping practices of the expanding French middle classes, not just in Paris but nationwide, thanks to the introduction of mail-order service made possible by the growing railroad network. Exploiting the new mass-production techniques of the Industrial Revolution, these stores contributed to the emergence of a mass consumer culture—one of plentiful and comparatively inexpensive quality goods—that reflected bourgeois values and aesthetics even as it democratized consumption.[3]

If the mass consumption of goods characterized the era, so too did the mass consumption of leisure. As legislation reduced the working hours of the lower classes and their real wages increased (if at times only marginally), opportunistic businessmen launched excitingly modern forms of entertainment, such as the Musée Grévin and its wax figures, the music hall, and the first movie theaters.[4] No form of leisure or entertainment touched more people during this period than sport. Whether as members of recently founded clubs, participants in newly created competitions, spectators of a rapidly growing number of amateur and professional events, or fans perusing the sports coverage of a burgeoning mass press, the French engaged in (or with) physical recreation as never before. Of all the sports from which they had to choose—including gymnastics, boxing, soccer, rugby, tennis, and track and field—none captured their imagination, time, energy, or discretionary income more than cycling, and none sparked more debate.

Optimists and those profiting from the transformations under way equated change with progress and the promise of a great future for France. Conversely, those who saw their nation as weakened or corrupted by change called for measures to contain these new threats to France's identity, to its social stability, indeed to its very existence. Some commentators, for example, saw sport as the key to national regeneration, a solution to physical and military weakness, demographic stagnation, and political and social divisions. For others, concerned with its disruptive impact on the social order, sport was on the contrary a contributing symptom of France's multifaceted decline. Survival versus extinction, progress versus decadence and chaos, activity and expansion versus prudence and the status quo—such were the choices that seemed to lie before the French nation in the closing decades of the nineteenth century and the first years of the twentieth. Although some French adopted uncompromising positions for or against the changes associated with modern life, many remained ambivalent, facing their uncertain future with a mixture of trepidation and hope.

During this time the bicycle came to symbolize for many both the promise of modernity and its dangers. This would have been inconceivable until the final third of the nineteenth century, when the wooden hobbyhorse, invented by a German aristocrat named Drais in the early years of the century, underwent a remarkable transformation.[5] The modernization of the *draisienne* began in 1861 when Pierre Michaux, a French locksmith and builder of mechanical vehicles, connected pedals to its front wheel with cranks. This created an easier, more efficient way of propelling this *vélocipède* (the generic nineteenth-century French term for human-propelled vehicles). In the final years of the Second Empire, a hundred or so bicycle-related patent applications were registered, including the key innovation of the freewheel, made possible by the use of ball bearings.[6]

In the wake of the Franco-Prussian War, during which French cycle manufacturers had converted their establishments to wartime production, European leadership in the field crossed the Channel to England. There the unwieldy penny-farthing, named for coins of different sizes and known in France as the *grand bi* (short for *grand bicycle*), was launched.[7] The invention of individual spokes linking the hub to the rim in a crossing pattern increased the rigidity and dependability of its wheels while reducing its weight. Still, the penny-farthing remained dangerous both for its precariously perched rider and for passers-by. The 1880s saw its gradual replacement by the first modern bicycle, whose momentum, generated by turning the pedals, was transmitted to the rear wheel by a chain rotating on sprockets. Between 1888 and 1891 a more rigid frame was developed; its basic shape has remained much the same to this day. Meanwhile, primitive wheels of wood or metal were being replaced first by solid rubber wheels, then by hollow rubber tires. These innovations improved shock absorption, an important achievement given the roughness of public roads. The final major invention was the derailleur, which allowed riders to choose from several gears as they negotiated uneven terrain. Invented in Britain in 1887, its commercialization on both sides of the Channel began in earnest during the first decade of the twentieth century.[8]

By the turn of the century, a series of refinements had transformed dangerous curiosities into relatively comfortable and reliable machines. Even more important, as manufacturers adopted mass-production techniques, the price of a bicycle plummeted. What had until the 1890s been an expensive hobby, notwithstanding the artisans and mechanics who rode machines they had built themselves, broadened its social base.[9] Manufacturers now began to offer a range of models to their increasingly diverse clientele. In 1893 the Hirondelle company offered a *démocratique* model (185 francs) targeted at artisans, workers, and employees; a *service administratif* model (280 francs) for mailmen, bailiffs, delivery men, and borough surveyors; *routier* models with air-filled tires (300 and 380 francs) for traveling salespeople, veterinarians, and doctors; and a 385-franc model designed for soldiers, tourists, and hunters. Finally, there were two top, *extra-supérieur* models intended for bicycle tourists, typically members of the upper classes.[10] By 1909 one could purchase a new Clément bicycle in the northern mining community of Longwy-Bas for 150 francs and a used one for only fifty.[11] Even humble workers and junior shop clerks, who were unlikely to make less than five francs a day, could now afford a bicycle. It was largely from their ranks that the first generations of Tour racers would emerge.

Michaux's invention of the pedal and the innovations that followed sparked the creation of a new sport, which would develop rapidly as the price of the bicycle dropped and various economic and political actors saw in cycling an opportunity to advance their interests. During the sport's infancy, cyclists experimented with a variety of events. In 1868 the Englishman James Moore won a 1,200-meter race in the Park of Saint-Cloud, defeating nine other contestants before a crowd of Parisian socialites. The same year, a race inspired by medieval exercises (an *épreuve de la bague*) was held in Bordeaux, and another was organized at Château-Gontier in Brittany. The first race in Alsace seems to have been a *course de lenteur* held in 1869 in Thann: the winner was the cyclist who took the longest to complete the eighty-meter course without putting a foot to the ground or wobbling into an opponent's lane. Such events were more acrobatic contests than races, and they quickly disappeared as it became clear that spectators were drawn to high speeds and feats of endurance.[12]

Road races linking towns and cities soon became popular. The first was Paris-Rouen on 7 November 1869, also won by James Moore. Other races followed. After 1880 they rarely covered less than thirty kilometers; many exceeded two hundred kilometers, and some linked cities five hundred kilometers apart. Contestants often spent most of the day—sometimes longer—on their machines. Competitive long-distance road-racing reached unprecedented heights in early September 1891, when one of the sport's first stars, Charles Terront, arrived at the Porte Maillot in Paris to be greeted by some ten thousand admirers on winning the inaugural Paris-Brest-Paris race. He had completed the 1,200-kilometer race in 71 hours and 35 minutes, averaging 400 kilometers a day over three days without rest. This prodigious feat enhanced his own popularity and that of the sport. In the final decade of the century, dozens more road races were created, including *classiques* such as Paris-Roubaix that remain important events on the international cycling calendar today. A vast spider's web of competitions now linked communities across the nation. Although particularly popular in France, the road-racing phenomenon also spread across the continent. Races that crossed national borders were created, among them Milan-Munich and Paris-Milan, the latter run in separate stages over several days.[13]

By the late nineteenth century, the aristocratic ladies and gentlemen who had witnessed James Moore's victory in 1868 had given way to much larger, more socially diverse crowds who lined roads and filled town squares to greet racers at the start and cheer them along the route. Contemporary photographs and press coverage suggest that these crowds were largely composed of middle- and working-class men. Women were a distinct minority; those in attendance appear to have been primarily from the middle classes and probably accompanied male friends and relatives. As a new century dawned, the bicycle racer—dusty, mud-splattered, and bloodied, hunched over his machine and battling his rivals and the elements—was increasingly celebrated as the heroic personification of courage and perseverance. This image and the celebrity of the top racers would provide the foundation on which the creators of the Tour de France built the race's appeal.

Meanwhile, another form of competitive cycling became arguably the most popular sport in the Western Hemisphere at the turn of the century: velodrome racing. Competitions held in arenas enjoyed a number of advantages over road races. Events could be run on a precise schedule, spectators could follow races in their entirety, and organizers could charge entry fees and sell refreshments. Whether in sprints or endurance events, such as the twenty-four-hour Bol d'Or and Six-Day races, racers risked their lives as they achieved high speeds, attempted daring passing maneuvers, and cycled to the point of exhaustion. Falls were frequent, spectacular, and sometimes fatal.[14]

The first French velodrome was built in Paris in 1879. Velodrome construction took off in the 1890s, as municipal governments came under pressure to provide venues for this new entertainment and entrepreneurs recognized the profits to be made from the sport's soaring popularity. By 1899 there were almost three hundred velodromes in France. In the Paris area alone, six were built between 1892 and 1897.[15] Tickets went for different prices, resulting in socially diverse, spatially segregated crowds. Dressed in their evening finest, the upper classes often came for a late dinner, enjoying the opportunity to display their social standing through the conspicuous, refined consumption of new entertainment. Meanwhile, the lower classes in the cheap (often standing-room) sections reveled in the excitement of a night out in modern arenas where there was always someone to watch, on the track or in the stands. Although they may not actually have rubbed elbows, racegoers from different social classes were no doubt acutely aware of each other's presence in this new public space, which may have been one of its most titillating attractions.[16]

For all its novelty, the development of competitive cycling was often facilitated by its inclusion in traditional or official celebrations. Bicycle races accompanied municipal festivities and the national holiday on July 14. The latter, first officially celebrated in 1880, was marked by locally organized concerts, dances, firework displays, torchlight retreats, bonfires, and parades. Various contests were held: *boules* and *quilles,* races on stilts or skates, wheelbarrow and sack races, swimming and foot races. New sporting activities such as gymnastics and cycling also found a niche in these festive commemorations. Bicycle races became popular toward the end of the nineteenth century, especially in cities.[17]

In some instances, cycling owed as much, if not more, to Catholic rituals. In Brittany, for example, each village celebrated its *Pardon:* dressed in their Sunday best, people came from miles around to ask the patron saint of the local parish for forgiveness for their sins and to earn indulgences. They then celebrated the purification of their souls with parades, food and drink, games, dances, fairs, singing contests, and sporting events. The last included wrestling competitions, foot races, sack races, and horse races, as well as *soule,* a traditional and violent French ball game, and its modern cousin, soccer. In the late nineteenth century, bicycle races frequently replaced horse races and became an integral part of the scheduled festivities. Soon these races became the focus of the *Pardon,* eclipsing the religious aspect as well as other entertainment.[18] The popularization of cycling in Brittany and elsewhere was thus in part a parasitic process: the new sport fed off festivities that provided a pretext and a venue for races. Once established, cycling often grew so popular as to dominate the civic or religious celebration of which it had initially been but one facet.

Cycling clubs or *associations vélocipédiques* also played a significant role in the sport's development in France.[19] The first such clubs were founded in the final years of the Second Empire, but their creation stalled until around 1880, no doubt because the high cost of bicycles limited the number of members. During the next three decades, however, their increase was spectacular: by 1910, there were eight hundred cycling clubs in France with a total of some 150,000 members. Areas with a high concentration of clubs included the Paris region, Normandy, the North, and a string of departments surrounding the Massif Central, from the lower Loire to the Rhône. The bicycle remained comparatively rare in the less prosperous, more isolated, or more mountainous regions, as illustrated by the absence of clubs in a large part of Brittany and in the *départements* of Lozère, Aveyron, Creuse, Nièvre, Hautes-Alpes, and Corsica. French cycling in the fin de siècle was essentially an urban phenomenon, except in west-central France, where the establishment of a cycle industry countered the general pattern.[20]

Although the representation of specific trades and occupations depended on local employment patterns, the members of cycling clubs were generally petty bourgeois and skilled artisans intent on providing activities and an opportunity for male sociability for their town, neighborhood, or profession. Clubs held their meetings in local cafés and participated actively in the life of their communities by organizing local *fêtes de bienfaisance* (charitable festivals).[21] Their goals, as defined in their official statutes, invariably included the desire to "establish and maintain friendly relations among the cyclists of the region" and "develop appreciation for and the use of the bicycle by organizing rides, trips, [and] races."[22] The last, in particular, provided local opportunities for young racers to develop and exposed communities to the new sport, thereby laying the foundation for the popularity of cycling's greatest event. Reflecting the growing interest in competitive cycling and the need to provide it with an organizational structure, the Union Vélocipédique de France (UVF, the French Cycling Federation) was founded in 1881. Its membership grew rapidly: from ten thousand in 1889, it had reached eighty thousand by 1909.[23]

Cycling's particular vitality at this time owed much to the financial support it received from one of France's most dynamic industries. In 1874, despite the disruption caused by the Franco-Prussian War and the Commune, there were more than sixty cycle manufacturers in Paris alone and some fifteen more in the provinces. The largest company at the time, the Compagnie Parisienne of the Olivier brothers, produced two hundred bicycles a day—a dramatic increase over the four hundred machines Pierre Michaux had built in his workshop in all of 1865. As demand for bicycles grew, manufacturers adopted modern mass-production and advertising techniques, and workshops increasingly gave way to factories.[24] Innovative entrepreneurs like Gustave Adolphe Clément rapidly forged a name and a fortune for themselves in the new industry. Born in the Oise *département* in 1855, in 1878 Clément came to Paris, where he opened a cycle workshop and published catalogues advertising his wares to such good effect that he soon had four hundred workers in his employ. Clément's fortune was made when, having grasped the potential of Dunlop's invention of the air-filled rubber tire, he acquired an exclusive sales permit for the *pneumatique*. In 1894 he founded the Société des Vélocipèdes Clément, which he merged the following year with two other great cycle brands of the period, Humber and Gladiator. For the next decade he comanaged the new company. In 1904 he broke away to become the sole owner of the Bayard-Clément brand, with its immense factories in Mézières and Levallois and two thousand workers.[25]

Around 1890 some thirty bicycle stores as well as the headquarters of the French cycling federation graced the Avenue de la Grande Armée in Paris, which was accordingly nicknamed "L'Avenue du Cycle." In January 1894, when the first Salon du Cycle was held at the Salle Wagram in Paris, almost three hundred cycle manufacturers displayed their wares with such success that a second Salon du Cycle was held that December, and the event was repeated annually thereafter.[26] Bicycle shops opened in many French towns. At the turn of the century, the town of Rennes in Brittany had at least nine, as well as a store that sold cycling attire for men and women. A decade later, Longwy boasted six or seven bicycle merchants, at least one of whom offered lessons and rented bicycles to customers.[27] The number of bicycles in France grew rapidly after 1890, when there were some fifty thousand bicycles in the country. In 1900 there were 975,878 registered (and taxed) bicycles in France; a decade later there were 2,724,467. Thousands more went unregistered and thus unrecorded in official statistics. On the eve of World War I, there were some three and a half million registered bicycles in France, almost one for every ten Frenchmen.[28] This increase directly reflected the drop in prices, itself the result of the rapid modernization of the production process.

The cycle industry's growth created other commercial opportunities. The Delaux-Chatel et Fils hosiery specialized in clothing for the new sport. The great department stores Belle Jardinière and Bon Marché introduced sports departments and devoted pages of their catalogues to items of interest to the growing market of cyclists. Tire companies profited. Wolber produced inner tubes and tires for bicycles and motorcycles sold under the Liberty-Wolber brand name. These companies organized races to publicize their products: Michelin ran Paris–Clermont-Ferrand, a race open, not surprisingly, only to riders of bicycles equipped with air-filled rubber tires. Quick to grasp the advertising potential of popular champions winning races with their products, cycle and tire manufacturers signed the sport's stars to exclusive contracts and sponsored teams to compete in the most prestigious events. Along with companies in related sectors, cycle manufacturers controlled or financially supported numerous Parisian and provincial papers, either directly as investors or through advertising. These papers in turn created and organized races, ranging from local and regional events to the Tour de France itself.[29]

The creation of specialized sports and cycling papers in the later nineteenth century was part of a broader transformation of the French press. By this time a mass press had emerged in France, feeding off a potent combination: almost universal literacy, which created a potential readership of unprecedented proportions, and improved printing technology, which made it possible to mass-produce newspapers cheaply. The specific raison d'être of the cycling press was to report on the exploits of racers in the recently created track and road competitions.[30] Although a significant number of these newspapers were Parisian, the development of a specialized cycling press, like that of the sport it covered, was a national phenomenon. Provincial papers appeared weekly or monthly, whereas some of the Parisian papers were dailies.[31] As cycling papers struggled in an increasingly competitive environment to secure and expand their readership, they sought to create their own market demand by founding and organizing many—indeed, perhaps most—of the road races held during this period. The first intercity road race, Paris-Rouen, was organized by *Le Vélocipède Illustré* in 1869; *Véloce-Sport* created Bordeaux-Paris in 1891; and two years later the Parisian *La Bicyclette* organized the first Paris-Brussels race.[32]

Sponsoring races was both a form of publicity for a paper and a means of increasing its sales.[33] Fans seeking in-depth information about a race would purchase the sponsoring newspaper, which offered the most complete coverage. This was especially true in the case of road races, for even fans who watched from the side of the road witnessed only a few seconds of the competition as the contestants shot by. They wanted additional coverage, such as postrace reactions, in-depth interviews, gossip and controversies, injury reports, and biographical features on contestants.[34] Sport was an important factor in the development of the French press in general at this time. Determined to capitalize on the increasing public appetite for *faits divers,* sporting contests, and spectacles, the four major mass-circulation Parisian dailies created a variety of events. *Le Petit Journal* organized the Paris-Brest-Paris bicycle race in 1891 and the Paris-Rouen automobile race in 1894. *Le Matin* organized the Tour de France automobile race in 1899, the Marche de l'Armée in 1903, the Paris-London dirigible race in 1906, the Circuit de l'Est airplane race in 1910, and a long-distance horse-trekking event in 1911. That year, not wishing to be outdone, *Le Journal* organized the Circuit Européen airplane race, while *Le Petit Journal* organized the Paris-Rouen airplane race and *Le Petit Parisien* sponsored a Paris-Madrid event.[35]

THE BIRTH OF *L'AUTO-VÉLO* AND THE TRIUMPH OF *L'AUTO*

In such a competitive environment, a new sports paper's survival was anything but assured. It was with this grim thought in mind that, on a December day in 1902, Henri Desgrange, the editor in chief of the sports daily *L'Auto-Vélo,* invited Géo Lefèvre, his young assistant and the head of the paper's cycling division, to join him for lunch at the Zimmer Madrid on Boulevard Montmartre in Paris. The paper had celebrated its second anniversary in October, but whether it would survive to witness its third was increasingly in question. Financed by leading cycle and automobile industrialists, *L'Auto-Vélo* was pitted against Pierre Giffard's dominant sports daily *Le Vélo,* founded in 1892. Itself backed by a leading French automobile manufacturer, *Le Vélo* had organized immensely popular long-distance bicycle races such as Paris-Brest-Paris, Bordeaux-Paris, and Paris-Roubaix. Besting such a rival would require a spectacular initiative.

Lefèvre, who had started at Giffard's paper before joining Desgrange's staff, suggested beating his former employer at his own game by organizing an even bigger, more popular race, whose coverage by *L'Auto-Vélo* would draw readers from its rival. "Why not a Tour de France?" he suggested. "We would organize it in stages with rest days in between." The autocratic Desgrange, never one to suffer fools easily, inquired sarcastically whether his assistant had taken leave of his senses and wished to kill off the great cyclists of the day. Refusing to be intimidated, Lefèvre evoked the Six-Day track competitions, in which racers covered hundreds of kilometers daily for almost a week. Large provincial cities, he noted, were continually asking for events featuring the best racers and would support a Tour de France. When Victor Goddet, *L'Auto-Vélo*'s treasurer, supported the idea, Desgrange was won over, and the paper began to make plans to launch the first Tour de France the following summer.[36] In the meantime, Giffard sued to have *L'Auto-Vélo* drop the second term from its name, arguing that it constituted an infringement of his paper's name. On 15 January 1903 he prevailed, and Desgrange renamed his paper *L'Auto*.[37] This would prove a pyrrhic victory, for the Tour de France was fatal to *Le Vélo*, which closed shop in 1904.[38] Building on the success of its prize event, *L'Auto* and its post–World War II heir, *L'Équipe*, thereafter dominated the French sports press.

L'Auto-Vélo's desire to bring down Pierre Giffard's *Le Vélo* was fueled by economic and political considerations. Giffard's paper had been financed from the start by Darracq, a powerful automobile manufacturer. Some of Darracq's competitors, among them Count Albert de Dion (of Dion-Bouton Cycles and Automobiles) and Gustave Adolphe Clément, now a successful cycle and automobile manufacturer, resented the virtual monopoly enjoyed at the turn of the century by *Le Vélo*, not to mention its advertising rates.[39] The commercial stakes were considerable, given the rapidly expanding market for cycles and the lively competition between French automobile manufacturers in the early twentieth century: in 1901, of an estimated 7,600 automobiles produced in France, Darracq accounted for 1,200; among his competitors who launched *L'Auto-Vélo*, Dion-Bouton produced 1,800, Panhard-Levassor 723, and Renault 347.[40]

Giffard and his paper also constituted a political irritant. In the Dreyfus affair, which polarized France in the late 1890s, Giffard had sided with the falsely accused Jewish officer Alfred Dreyfus in a number of articles in *Le Petit Journal* and *Le Vélo*. This did not sit well with some of the future backers of *L'Auto-Vélo*, including the violently anti-Dreyfusard Dion and Count Chasseloup-Laubat, the president of the Auto-Club de France Baron de Zuylen de Nyevelt, the tire magnate Édouard Michelin, and Clément.[41] Although they too had strong (if opposite) political views, they believed Giffard's political engagement violated the sacrosanct neutrality of sport, which they wished to preserve.[42] To exacerbate matters, when Giffard was defeated by Dion in legislative elections, he retaliated by boycotting the Dion-Bouton brand in his paper.[43] Deciding the time had come to act, Dion and his like-minded associates persuaded some of their prominent peers and friends to join them and founded *L'Auto-Vélo*.[44]

The original stock issue was four hundred shares worth five hundred francs each, for a total initial outlay of two hundred thousand francs. Cycle, automobile, and tire manufacturers accounted for three-quarters of the total (302 shares), with Dion-Bouton Cycles and Automobiles alone purchasing 192 shares.[45] The statutes of *L'Auto-Vélo*, registered on 15 September 1900 with a Parisian notary, specified that the paper was "especially and exclusively interested in all issues involving sports and transportation, races, [and] sporting events of all kinds, railroad transportation, automobile transportation, and other [forms of transportation] and all events or incidents linked directly or indirectly with sports and transportation." On 4 October the General Constitutive Assembly of the new company selected its first board of directors.[46] They in turn hired Henri Desgrange as the paper's editor in chief. In its first issue he pledged that *L'Auto-Vélo* would be devoted to popularizing the bicycle and the automobile by "toast[ing] the glory of the athletes and the victories of the Industry."[47] Desgrange was to lead the paper for almost four decades, during which time his authority and vision shaped the Tour de France. His legacy influences the race to this day.

Although only thirty-five at the time, the man chosen in 1900 to run *L'Auto-Vélo* was already an important figure in French cycling.[48] Born in Paris in 1865, Desgrange earned a law degree in 1889, registered with the Paris Bar, and was hired in 1891 as the principal clerk in the offices of a Parisian solicitor.[49] His legal career was brief, for Desgrange had already become smitten with the bicycle around 1890. He obtained an amateur racer's license from the Amicale Vélo Amateur, began to train, and rapidly expanded the range of his cycling activities. By 1895 Desgrange was the head of advertising for the bicycle manufacturing firm of Clément et Cie., the president of the Chambre Syndicale des Coureurs Vélocipédiques founded that year, and the proud owner of the first hour record set without a trainer.[50] The late 1890s was the professional point of no return for Desgrange: in 1897 he resigned from the Paris Cour d'Appel and began to devote himself almost exclusively to his many responsibilities in Parisian cycling. The previous year he had become manager of the Vélodrome de la

Seine, which closed down not long thereafter, and later he ran the Vélodrome du Parc des Princes with his longtime associate, Victor Goddet. Throughout this period he contributed articles to magazines and newspapers, including *La Revue des Revues,* his soon-to-be archrival *Le Vélo,* and *Le Journal des Sports.*[51] He also published a training manual for young cyclists and a novel about Parisian velodrome racing.[52]

Desgrange's financial standing was at first modest.[53] A few years into the new century, however, the Tour de France's dramatic impact on *L'Auto*'s sales (see below), the elimination of *Le Vélo,* and Desgrange's other ventures, velodrome management in particular, began to pay off handsomely. In January 1907 he purchased a *hôtel particulier;* by 1927 he owned several other properties, including one on the Côte d'Azur at Beauvallon. His professional success was reflected in social recognition. He was awarded the Palmes Académiques as an advertiser in 1898 and was subsequently named Chevalier du Mérite Agricole, Chevalier de la Légion d'Honneur, and finally Officier de la Légion d'Honneur. He was also a member of the Automobile Club and the Aéro-Club, founded by Dion. Desgrange's awards indicate that his conduct, morality, and politics—notwithstanding his association with Dion and other opponents of the republic—were officially considered beyond reproach.[54] For Desgrange the critical issue was not the regime but the nation. Committed, like so many of his compatriots, to national revival, he saw sport as the field in which he could best serve that end. Desgrange's patriotism led him to volunteer for the army in April 1917. He served for the balance of the war in the 29th Infantry Regiment based in Autun and was released with the rank of lieutenant in January 1919, four days shy of his fifty-fourth birthday.

Desgrange's social, financial, and professional ascent indicates that in the new and expanding world of French sport men of energy, initiative, and determination could rapidly overcome their modest origins and initial lack of capital to build impressive careers. As preposterous as the idea initially seemed to him, the Tour de France paid immediate dividends for *L'Auto.* At the end of the nineteenth century, the sports and cycling press competed for a limited number of readers, a figure one historian has estimated to be in the neighborhood of 150,000. Of these, 80,000 were readers of *Le Vélo,* a measure of the latter's dominance at the time *L'Auto-Vélo* was launched in October 1900.[55] As we have seen, the first three years were precarious ones for Giffard's fledgling competitor. Its initial average daily circulation stood at 20,000. These numbers improved gradually, but *L'Auto*'s survival was hardly assured, especially when sales dropped from a daily average of 30,000 in 1902 back down to 20,000 in 1903.[56]

Public interest in the first Tour de France changed everything. *L'Auto*'s daily sales rose to 30,000 during the pre-race buildup in June, and to 65,000 in July during the race itself.[57] By 1913 the paper's average daily circulation had reached 120,000 issues; in July, however, daily sales surpassed 250,000 issues, establishing a pattern of more than doubling the paper's circulation during the Tour that held until World War II.[58] If *L'Auto*'s performance compared favorably to that of the political dailies, its figures paled in comparison with the success of the four major mass-circulation Parisian dailies—*Le Petit Journal, Le Petit Parisien, Le Journal,* and *Le Matin*—which in 1914 together were printing 4.5 million copies daily *(Le Petit Journal* had reached a million copies a day by 1890).[59] Press competition was fierce and growing fiercer, but it was not until the interwar years that the nonspecialized press began to devote considerable coverage to sports.[60] Consequently, during the years leading up to World War I, *L'Auto* had the opportunity to develop a loyal audience and succeeded in doing so: its annual circulation trebled between 1903 and 1913, and its average daily circulation reached 320,000 during the final prewar Tour in July 1914.[61]

The development of cycling in late-nineteenth- and early-twentieth-century France, then, resulted from the timely intersection of mutually reinforcing trends that allowed the sport to sink deep roots into French life, particularly in towns and cities. Technological innovations transformed the primitive hobbyhorse into a reliable, cheap, mass-produced machine as demand was growing for organized sports entertainment in an era of increased leisure time for the lower classes. Entrepreneurs and municipal governments responded by building and managing velodromes and organizing meets. Lower-class men not only attended races; they created cycling clubs whose members enjoyed new athletic and social opportunities. Many became amateur racers, and some reached the professional ranks. The sports press, the cycle industry, and related sectors sought to profit from and fuel public interest in the new sport by organizing track and road races, and by publicizing the exploits of courageous young men who were willing to suffer for long stretches on their machines as they strove for victories, fame, and the economic rewards that would follow.

In England, a much smaller country, the twin forces of industrialization and urbanization had favored the growth of cities with large working-class communities. This growth in turn had sparked the popularity of soccer, played in stadiums before large crowds that, except in Paris, would have been impossible to assemble in France. The French, on the other hand, remained relatively spread out over a large territory. This no doubt explains the appeal of cycling's road races, which were unique in that they "exported" athletic contests to the doorsteps of their spectators, who often lived far away from soccer stadiums, tennis courts, and rugby fields. For many French, these races were their first (and for a while perhaps only) exposure to modern sport.[62]

By 1903 this complex dynamic had made it possible to actually conceive of a Tour de France bicycle race. That such potent trends and interest groups contributed to its creation did not mean that the race's popularity was somehow preordained; of this the organizers were fully aware. To ensure the success of their ambitious gamble, they tirelessly strove to link it in the minds of the public with a national revival that only the modern march of progress could make possible.

A MODERN RACE FOR A MODERN FRANCE?

As the start of the first Tour approached, *L'Auto* hailed the race as "the most grandiose competition there has ever been" and "the gigantic professional race that will revolutionize the world of cycling" and "constitute one of the great dates of our history."[63] It was understandable that to attract readers the paper would trumpet the historical significance and unprecedented scale of the Tour, especially as contestants were slow to register and the organizers feared they might have to cancel the race. Their self-serving hyperbole should not, however, obscure the fact that the organizers sincerely believed that by popularizing the bicycle and inspiring the nation to exercise, their new event would have a significant impact on French society. Géo Lefèvre imagined the astonishment of peasants at the arrival in isolated villages throughout France of "white demons . . . at top speed, as if in flight." He predicted that once Tour racers had demonstrated that one could "cover considerable distances on a bicycle," peasants would adopt the new technology, resulting in dramatically increased sales for cycle manufacturers. One of the great racers of the day, Hippolyte Aucouturier, confirmed that there remained regions deep in the French countryside where the bicycle "still astonishes," as well as cities and towns where the sport of cycling was unknown. He too concluded that the Tour de France "will revolutionize the lives of all those people."[64]

Once the race was under way, *L'Auto* reported that all along the itinerary "cities dead to sport are awaking," inspired by the racers, "these unconscious messengers of progress." The organizers celebrated the regenerative role of these "admirable men, truly exceptional beings, carrying in them extraordinary qualities that they will transmit . . . to the race they will create one day." As the paper prepared for the second Tour in 1904, it confirmed the "enormous impression" made by the first, "especially in regions that had until then been the most impervious to the sport of cycling." In Grisolles, "since the Tour de France everywhere you go you see the JCG (Joyeux Cyclistes Grisollais)," whose membership now exceeded one hundred riders and whose president, Jean Dargassies, was a veteran of the first Tour and a hometown hero. In Castelnaudary, a cycling club founded only six months earlier had more than 140 members; in Montauban five cycling clubs had been created since the end of the first Tour. In 1905 *L'Auto* described the Tour as a "great moral crusade" whose contestants, "our apostles," were demonstrating that "human energy is without limit" and converting "thousands of the ignorant to the beauty of sport."[65]

Other commentators agreed. An observer in Vire attributed the founding of a local cycling club to the Tour's passage and thanked the organizers for having "shaken our fellow citizens out of their apathy."[66] *Le Toulouse Cycliste* described the race as "a stimulant, an example, a lesson" for local cyclists inspired by the "performance of the [Tour's] courageous road racers."[67] Obsessed with the specter of national decline, many French clearly shared *L'Auto*'s view that cycling epitomized France's revival through competition, physical exercise, and the adoption of modern technology. *Le Vélo* had since its inception enthused that cycling was "a social good," poets and politicians associated the bicycle with progress, and a doctor asserted that the new sport could "play a significant role in the functioning of modern society, [and] be beneficial to human development to a degree that no one can foresee."[68]

Others, however, far from equating modernity with progress, believed the two terms were fundamentally incompatible. They condemned the bicycle as an instrument of chaos and degeneration. The bicycle's proponents were fully aware of the hostility it inspired. Speaking to a sports club in Tours in 1888, M. Garsonnin, of the recently founded French cycling federation, described his audience as "overly disposed . . . to make merry at the expense of cyclists."[69] Louis Baudry de Saunier, a prolific author of works on the bicycle, claimed that "cycling has encountered more enemies than any other form of exercise."[70] A few months before the first Tour, the vice-president of one of France's oldest cycling clubs praised the "moral energy" of his predecessors, "who as early as 1869 came together to spread in a hostile environment the ideas that triumph today."[71]

As *L'Auto*'s references to crusades and apostles confirm, the bicycle's partisans often invoked religious imagery. Garsonnin described his lecture as a "profession of faith" and alluded to "velophobic persecution."[72] Baudry de Saunier referred to "the *communion* of man and bicycle."[73] Cycling, he claimed, was "a religion whose dogmas you fiercely defend," its earliest practitioners "old men on tricycles who, besieged by the incessant sarcasm of their friends, resemble martyrs pierced with arrows." He urged "bicycle racers to consider the sport a vocation" and hoped there would never be "priests unworthy of that religion."[74] At a time of heightened conflict in France between church and state, such rhetoric conveyed the intensity of this peculiar *guerre de religion*. Whether celebrated for personifying national regeneration through sport and science, or vilified as a symbol of the perils implicit in the unrestrained application of modern technology, the cyclist had become a focus of debates about progress in fin-de-siècle France. Those debates are important not just because they shaped the cultural context for the first Tours, but also because the controversial association between cycling, modernity, and progress has informed representations of the race ever since.

THE CYCLIST:
CHAOS OR PROGRESS PERSONIFIED?

The bicycle's appearance in French towns and cities had hardly been harmonious. Accidents, sometimes fatal, were widely reported in the press as cyclists crashed into pedestrians, other vehicles, and each other, and came to grief over railroad and tram lines, slick cobblestones, and dogs.[75] Bicycle enthusiasts conceded that the machine's early users had often been irresponsible menaces but claimed that this was no longer the case by the late 1880s.[76] This was wishful thinking: in the early twentieth century, bicycle-related accidents continued to fill the *chronique locale* columns of French newspapers.[77] As early as 1869, some of the larger French cities had passed municipal by-laws to control this new public hazard: an 1874 ordinance banned bicycles from certain roads in Paris and other cities. During the next few decades, local governments across France passed *arrêtés municipaux* restricting bicycle traffic. One such measure in Sens required cyclists to attach warning bells to their machines, a lantern when traveling at night, and a sort of license plate with their name and address. They could not exceed 10 kilometers per hour or use certain roads required for other traffic, and they had to dismount when passing through markets, fairs, festivals, and other crowded areas. Nor could they ride on sidewalks or other spaces reserved for pedestrians.[78]

Perhaps in part to counter views of the bicycle as an urban danger, by the late 1880s cycling advocates were outlining a broad program for its use by gendarmes, rural policemen, postmen, telegraph employees, and officials responsible for maintaining the nation's roads and bridges.[79] An advertising poster for Hurtu bicycles depicted a cycling mailman handing letters to the occupants of an automobile, while in the background a peasant walked beside his ox-driven haycart: the bicycle, like the railroads, was improving rural France's ties with the rest of the nation. Such representations extolled the utilitarian modernity of the bicycle, which anecdotal evidence supported. A cycling telegraphist reported that he did his work faster on his bicycle and thus saved his customers and the government time and money.[80] On 1 April 1900, *Le Petit Parisien,* noting that the Bois de Boulogne and the Bois de Vincennes had become increasingly dangerous, announced that policemen in those areas would henceforth be mounted on bicycles, which would allow them to supervise a larger sector and intervene more quickly.[81] By World War I these *agents* were familiar figures. Cyclists were also employed as deliverymen and messengers.[82] Improved service, reduced costs, and new professional opportunities: for all its detractors, the bicycle clearly had a significant impact on a number of occupations and the people they served.

Civilians were not alone in appreciating the bicycle's potential for improving efficiency and performance. In a period of heightened tension in Europe, armies across the continent attempted to adapt bicycles to military use. From the 1880s through World War I, considerable sums were spent on the creation of corps of infantrymen on wheels. In France alone, dozens of works on the topic were published, including instruction and regulation manuals, tactical studies of both French and foreign military uses of the bicycle, and, after the war, histories of the wartime experiences of *chasseurs cyclistes.*[83] Posters advertising the merits of a given make of bicycles often showed military cyclists during maneuvers.[84] Many on both sides of the Rhine believed that cycling troops were "necessary in a modern, scientific army in which the rapidity of transportation and communication appears to be a dominant quality," and that they would play an important role in a future conflict.[85] The Germans went so far as to train dogs to attack French and English military cyclists, while the French hoped that battalions of cyclists would compensate for their stagnant demography and smaller cavalry forces.[86] French experts clearly saw the issue in the technological and industrial terms of an arms race: "We must know how to profit from the advantages which industrial progress, whatever form it takes, may, at a given moment, provide to the national army." Not to do so was to be doomed to being overtaken by France's "neighbors," Germany in particular, as they exploited the bicycle for military purposes.[87]

The French army began experimenting with cycling infantrymen in the late 1870s; by the 1890s it had formulated official regulations on military cycling that covered the organization and responsibilities of corps of infantry cyclists, who were principally to be used as liaison officers transmitting orders and other communications.[88] To maximize the bicycle's wartime utility, in 1890 Captain Gérard, the leading French advocate of military cycling and the commander of the cycling company based in Saint-Quentin, designed a folding bicycle that soldiers carried on their backs over unfavorable terrain. After rigorous testing, a military *commission d'expérience* concluded that the folding bicycle was "good for wartime use."[89] The increasing importance and potential contributions of military cycling were officially recognized in 1901, when cycling infantrymen paraded down the Champs-Élysées during the July 14 celebrations and Gérard himself was received by the president of the republic. Four years later Gérard, now a major, was in command of a battalion of four companies of cyclists. In October 1913, as the war loomed ever closer, the French army created ten groups of *chasseurs cyclistes,* each of which had four hundred men.[90]

The bicycle's greatest feature, for civilians and the military alike, was that, as one early commentator observed, it "erases time and space."[91] Quite apart from the champions who were regularly setting records, average citizens were covering unheard-of distances: one fifty-year-old man cycled 343 kilometers in twenty-four hours, a performance officially supervised and recorded by the French cycling federation. Such achievements led to suggestions that the bicycle might compete successfully with the railroads, which only a few decades earlier had themselves challenged established conceptions of time and space.[92] One contemporary advertising poster depicted a man pedaling effortlessly on an elaborate quadricycle as a train rumbled by in the background, implicitly comparing these two modern machines and perhaps implying the superiority of the former.[93] Apparently, such a comparison was not absurd to many observers: one claimed that bicycles provided far more flexibility than trains, which were limited by schedules and the location of tracks and stations. Celebrating the regenerative promise of the new sport, another cycling enthusiast asserted that two days of cycling were less tiring than one spent on a train.[94] A third argued that the railroad system should have been restricted to its primary axes, leaving the bicycle to service areas for which the new secondary lines were responsible. The latter, he claimed, had profoundly perturbed the mores and interests of rural France, bringing numerous modern ills, including "depression, slavery [!], a feverish obsession with business, disappointed speculations, mental illnesses and the abandoning of roads that unify the countryside and bring men together."[95] The bicycle was thus a technological advance whose value derived from its ability to correct the evils and excesses of other recent locomotive technology; unlike the railroads, it did not upset his admittedly idealized view of traditional French life.

Such nuanced views were rare. Most bicycle enthusiasts, like Baudry de Saunier, unabashedly celebrated "the birth of a new human type, the cyclist" as the emblematic figure of modernity: "The cyclist is a man made half of flesh and half of steel that only our century of science and iron could have spawned. An era that had invented the steam engine, the telegraph, the telephone, the phonograph, . . . etc., etc., was bound to invent this new machine, the bicycle: *The bicycle is a machine that multiplies the ambulatory power of man.*"[96]

Some even dreamed of a day in the not-too-distant future when the bicycle would conquer gravity, perceived as the next great challenge of locomotive science. For these commentators, the bicycle heralded a new age of unrestricted scientific horizons; it was "a sign of extreme civilization or of the transition to a superior civilization that we have never known."[97] Contemporary postcards celebrating French colonial expansion reinforced this view, portraying the bicycle as the advanced technology of a superior culture that was "civilizing" backward "savages."[98]

The bicycle's opponents also recognized that the new machine symbolized the profound transformations of the day, but, fearing those changes, they rejected the bicycle as a symptom of the terrible ills afflicting France. Of those, none was of greater concern than the nation's moral and physical degeneration.

Military defeat in 1870, civil war, the amputation of Alsace-Lorraine, and the formation of the German Empire in 1871, along with France's stagnating demography, provided powerful evidence of a potentially fatal national decline.[99] The military authorities blamed the psychological and physical weakness of their troops for the defeat, described by the prominent Italian fatigue researcher Angelo Mosso as "the triumph of German legs." French physicians, public hygienists, moral crusaders, and physiologists concurred.[100] Some commentators placed the crisis in a longer historical perspective. The journalist Émile Weber, writing in 1905 in *Sports Athlétiques*, attributed it to "several centuries of laxity" and "the muscular laziness of our ancestors." He warned that "it will take our people several generations, not to recognize the need for physical exercise, but to acquire the physical courage to tolerate its hardships."[101] Dr. Philippe Tissié, a prominent advocate of physical education and a major figure in the burgeoning sports movement, explained that the mental and psychic state of the present generation in France was the result of psychological traumas experienced by their mothers during the wars of the French Revolution and the First Empire: "The generations from around 1870 to 1875 were born tired, which explains their particular psychological state, their appetite for stimulants *[les excito-moteurs]* and for erotic or decadent literature."[102]

The commentaries of both men are characteristic of the period. Their emphasis on the hereditary nature of such disorders was consistent with the influential new doctrine of social Darwinism; Tissié's reference to drug abuse echoed widespread concern among physicians, social commentators, bourgeois moralists, and politicians about working-class alcoholism. Their obsession with fatigue as the key to understanding the physical, mental, and moral shortcomings of their compatriots reflected a contemporary preoccupation throughout the Western, industrialized world. Finally, their linking of physical symptoms with moral decadence—particularly a deficit in willpower and courage—was typical of French explanations for the defeat of 1870. Tissié even placed French physical weakness in the context of a more general French inferiority, evident "in the areas of trade and industry": France's "neighbors" were at an advantage because they knew "how best to employ their productive energies, having learned at school how to work, and especially how to relax." His solution to France's general crisis was seductively simple: "Physical education is the great key to our physical, intellectual, and moral regeneration."[103]

Many of Tissié's contemporaries agreed that physical education and sports could reverse numerous symptoms of France's crisis, including depopulation, neurasthenia, fatigue, alcoholism, prostitution, and organic diseases of the urban masses.[104] According to Garsonnin of the French cycling federation, young French cyclists "have learned, thanks to the various sports they have played, to fear nothing. Fatigue and the outdoors are, to a certain extent, schools of courage and dedication." His words, like those of so many of his contemporaries, substantiate Robert Nye's description of the sportive nationalism that emerged during this period as "a profoundly compensatory movement" that not only replaced "an unrealizable military revenge on Germany" but also helped convince the French that they had not succumbed to irreversible physical and moral decadence.[105] Indeed, sport and physical education were seen as ways to ensure that *la revanche* was merely postponed: when the opportunity arose to reverse the humiliating 1871 settlement, French youth would be physically and psychologically prepared to do so.[106]

Cycling clubs were determined to do their part. As their statutes and newsletters indicated, *associations vélocipédiques* were committed to supporting military cycling. The rides they organized would help produce a generation of healthy, strong, and determined patriots, ready to make the ultimate sacrifice in a future war with Germany. Although some clubs actually participated in mobilization drills, their most immediate and tangible contribution to military cycling was the organization (along with local and regional newspapers, the French cycling federation, and bicycle and tire manufacturers) of special races called *brevets militaires.* These generally covered set distances of 50, 100, or 150 kilometers, which had to be completed within a time limit, usually based on a minimum pace of twenty kilometers an hour.[107] Cycling clubs also organized military cycling championships for various army corps.[108] In addition, cycling had a place in the programs of thousands of clubs that received government subsidies in the early years of the twentieth century as officially recognized *sociétés de préparation militaire.*[109] By the summer of 1914, as tensions mounted across the continent, the new sport was intimately associated with national defense and military preparedness.[110]

The fact that the bicycle's popularization coincided with the search for a cure to French *dégénérescence* at a time of widely perceived national vulnerability explains the wide-ranging debate among French doctors as to the physiological and psychological effects of cycling. The bicycle's opponents within the French medical establishment were convinced that it was "the source of all sorts of ills, that it [caused] terrible dangers."[111] The new machine, they claimed, overdeveloped leg muscles, harmed joints, neck muscles, and the head's vascular system, and deformed hands and feet. It caused curvature of the spine, varicose veins, weight loss, hunger, respiratory disorders, narrow chests, arthritis of the knee, physical laziness, a repulsion for walking, cardiac disorders, fevers, albuminuria, eye problems, sudden death (particularly as a result of overexercising), and disorders (including both erections and temporary impotence) of the genitourinary organs, so essential to the production of healthy future generations.[112] Had they prevailed, these dire medical assessments might well have stalled the development of cycling in late-nineteenth-century France.

For every doctor who railed against the bicycle, however, there was one who praised cycling for curing or helping to cure an equally impressive list of ailments. These included hernias, physical deformations and curvature of the spine, arthritis, neurasthenia, gout, rheumatism, anemia, phthisis, tuberculosis, obesity, and sterility. Doctors claimed that cycling was good for one's bones, fibrous tissues, joints, and skin. The sport stimulated the elimination of toxins from the body, increased endurance, expanded the thoracic cage and lung capacity, corrected poor posture, facilitated the digestive process, and stimulated the appetite. Alleged threats posed by cycling, such as cardiac ailments and arthritis, were rejected outright or downplayed as negligible.[113] Such dramatic disagreements underscore how little was known about the physiological effects of exercise. This lack of knowledge, however, did not discourage doctors from making a wide range of often contradictory assertions, which they were careful to couch in medical terminology. Scientific discourse concealed their ignorance and established their professional credibility with their compatriots, many of whom were seeking a medical diagnosis of France's perceived decadence. After all, what science could explain, science could no doubt cure.

Meanwhile, cycling enthusiasts within the French medical profession were themselves divided: some advocated moderation, whereas others claimed that extraordinary performances by cyclists were redefining the limits of human strength and endurance. The former, fearing the consequences of overexercising, argued that excessive cycling was bad for one's intelligence and that fatigue, such as that caused by endurance events, resulted in profound *ennui,* reduced memory, personality disorders, amnesia, and temporary cases of hypermnesia and insanity. They warned that overexertion *(le surmenage)* caused phlebitis, autointoxication resembling typhoid, and general weakness, and that it provoked the same psychological disorders and psychopathological phenomena exhibited by individuals suffering from hysteria, neurasthenia, mental instability, hypnotic sleep, hallucinations, illusions, phobias, paramnesia, obsession, automatism, and *dégénérescence.*[114] Their concerns reflected a broader contemporary obsession with fatigue and its relationship to intensive athletic training. As Europeans attempted to come to grips with the disturbing sense of their own decline, many physicians, physiologists, hygienists, and psychologists identified fatigue as the nemesis of progress and the source of social disorder and moral decay in late-nineteenth-century Europe. Between 1880 and 1930, along with engineers and social reformers, they waged a scientific campaign against fatigue, defined as a physical and moral disorder characterized by weakness, the inability to control passions and violence, and a decrease in rationality and willpower.[115]

Among the most prominent of these scientists was Tissié. He advocated a national hygiene program of moderate physical exercise, including cycling, to foster individual and collective health and counter fatigue. Athletes given to overexertion, he warned, would father "degenerate" offspring, whereas moderately and rationally trained individuals could pass on their acquired fitness to their descendants. This view was consistent with Jean-Baptiste Lamarck's influential (though incorrect) theory of the hereditary transmission of acquired characteristics.[116] Tissié argued that the advantages of moderate cycling were moral and psychological as well as physical, and thus the sport addressed all facets of France's perceived decline. His promotion of moderate physical exercise was in part a reaction against the emergence of a new culture of extreme athletic performance, encapsulated in the motto "Faster, Higher, Stronger" of the Modern Olympic Games, which the French aristocrat Pierre de Coubertin founded in 1896.[117]

Scientific interest in the psychological and physiological dimensions of athletic performance increased dramatically during the 1890s. New instruments permitting the precise measurement of the body's performance piqued public interest in quantitative records. Cycling, particularly endurance events such as the grueling Six-Day races so popular at the time, were more than athletic contests; they were scientific experiments concerned with the physiology of stress and the relationship between pain and fatigue.[118] Noting the remarkable recuperative powers of the day's most celebrated long-distance bicycle racers, one doctor enthused that as a result of methodical and regular preparation, "every year we see athletes go further and faster." A racer examined a week after a thousand-kilometer race in 1893 exhibited no traces of fatigue and was back to training with the same intensity and speed as before the event.[119]

The Tour de France was thus created at a time when the French were investing the bicycle with their deepest hopes and fears as they digested recent traumas, experienced dramatic change, and confronted an uncertain future. Despite—or perhaps because of—contemporary misgivings about cycling, *L'Auto's* editorial line never wavered. In a lengthy front-page article in 1913, Desgrange noted that the invention of the bicycle had modified society by contradicting retrograde theories that opposed physical exercise: a nation's greatness was measured not only by its literary, artistic, and scientific achievements but also by its athletes and the "solidity of its children's bodies." The great sporting events of which the Tour was "the greatest crusade" had convinced "new crowds" of the importance of physical exercise as the foundation of a good life and future healthy generations. Today's French youth were far more resolute, audacious, and willful than their predecessors of thirty years earlier (who, he did not need to remind his readers, had lost the Franco-Prussian war). This "new France," aware of the dangers facing the nation, was impatient for combat.[120] These were ambitious claims indeed, but the scale and difficulty of *L'Auto's* great bicycle race appeared to justify them.

A "GREAT LOOP" INDEED

As we have seen, road racing was already widespread and popular when the first Tour de France was launched in 1903. Until that point, however, most races, even the longest intercity events, like Paris-Brest-Paris, were organized as one continuous leg without scheduled rests. The Tour thus represented a novelty: it was run in six stages from July 1 through July 19 (the race has since then been held in July, occasionally spilling over into late June or early August).[121] There were two or three rest days between stages to allow racers to recover from their efforts, which were considerable given the distances they were required to cover: Paris-Lyon (467 kilometers), Lyon-Marseille (374 kilometers), Marseille-Toulouse (423 kilometers), Toulouse-Bordeaux (268 kilometers), Bordeaux-Nantes (394 kilometers), and Nantes–Ville-d'Avray (471 kilometers), a total of 2,397 kilometers.[122] The racers started each stage together in a *peloton,* or pack. The standings were based on each contestant's overall time, the sum of his individual stage times. Of the sixty racers in the field, only twenty-two finished (see chapter 3 for more on attrition rates). The winner, Maurice Garin, an established star and one of the prerace favorites, took ninety-four hours and thirty-three minutes to complete the race, coming in almost sixty-five hours ahead of the last-place finisher. In 1904 the stages were essentially the same, but they covered a slightly greater distance (2,542 kilometers) and took the racers back into Paris on the final day.

The following year the organizers almost doubled the number of stages, to eleven, and reduced the number of rest days between stages, a change justified by the shorter distances of the stages. These ranged from 168 to 342 kilometers, with the Tour covering a total of 2,975 kilometers. The overall winner was determined according to a formula that attributed points for place finishes in each stage. It was thus possible for a racer who had lost considerable time during one bad day to remain competitive and even win the Tour. While this arrangement encouraged participants not to drop out, it also meant that the racer with the best overall time at the end might not win. Desgrange and his successors continually tinkered with the race's *formule* to maintain suspense and oblige racers to ride hard. The points system was used through the 1912 Tour, after which it was definitively replaced by accumulated time.

From 1906 through 1926, the race ranged in length from 4,407 kilometers (1908) to 5,741 kilometers (1926) and was divided into thirteen to eighteen stages. The average Tour was fifteen stages and 5,193 kilometers; the average stage length was 347 kilometers. Racers often spent most of the day in the saddle. The winning times for the stages of the first Tour averaged fifteen hours and forty minutes. The 1914 Tour saw all but two of the fifteen stages require the winning racer over twelve hours to complete; the longest took sixteen hours, thirteen minutes, and forty-five seconds. In 1926 Lucien Buysse averaged over fourteen and a half hours for the seventeen stages of the longest Tour in history—and he won the race! The racer who finished last that year averaged over sixteen hours a stage. Adding to the race's difficulty in its early decades were poorly surfaced roads and comparatively primitive equipment, as Desgrange did not permit the use of derailleurs until 1937 (see chapter 3 for more on this restriction). In the interwar period, the organizers added individual and team time trials, which remain important features of the race. In 1927 they increased the number of stages to twenty-four and further reduced the number of rest days. Since then, stages have numbered between twenty and twenty-five, except in 1939, when there were only eighteen.

Beginning in 1934, certain stages were divided into two or three relatively short legs held a few hours apart. This change allowed the organizers to bring the Tour to more towns and cities, increasing the revenues paid to them by host communities. It also increased the drama and the number of potential stage winners, which in turn maximized fan interest and newspaper sales. From 1927 through 1970 the average Tour was twenty-two stages and 4,574 kilometers long, and the average stage length was 208 kilometers. Since 1971, the Tour's length has only occasionally exceeded 4,000 kilometers, and never by much. The tendency in recent years has been to keep the race under 3,500 kilometers over twenty days of racing, with one or two rest days. Today's Tour racers generally spend between four and eight hours in the saddle during a stage.

Impressive as these distances are, what truly set the Tour apart from other races was the inclusion of mountains in the itinerary. The first serious climbs were incorporated in 1905, when the Tour passed over the Ballon d'Alsace (1,150 meters), the Col Bayard (1,250 meters), and the Côte de Laffrey. Two years later, the three climbs of the Massif de la Chartreuse (with its Col de Porte at 1,326 meters) were added, and in 1910 four great Pyrenean summits that remain regular features of the race: the Tourmalet (2,115 meters), the Aubisque (1,710 meters), the Peyresourde (1,545 meters), and the Aspin (1,500 meters). The following year, the racers were introduced to France's other great mountain range, the Alps, with climbs of the Galibier (2,645 meters) and the Allos (2,250 meters). Subsequently, other peaks in the Alps were added, including the Vars (2,111 meters), the Izoard (2,361 meters), and the famous Alpe d'Huez climb (1,860 meters), introduced in 1952.[123] Although the mountains selected vary from year to year, the Pyrenean and Alpine stages remain the high points, literally and figuratively, of the race.

The number of contestants starting the Tour has also varied. Before World War II, it ranged from a low of 60 in 1903, 1905, and 1934 to 162 in 1928. From World War II to the early 1980s, there were at least 100 racers (and generally between 120 and 130) at the start. As television coverage expanded beyond Europe, non-European sponsors became interested in the global exposure provided by fielding a team in the race. In response, the organizers increased the number of teams from thirteen or so to as many as twenty-two or twenty-three. As a result, since 1982 the trend has been towards larger *pelotons,* sometimes exceeding two hundred racers.

L'Auto organized the Tour from 1903 through 1914, and 1919 through 1939 (the race was not held during World War I). In 1939 the press magnate Raymond Patenôtre, who owned *Le Petit Parisien, Le Lyon Républicain,* and *Le Petit Niçois,* purchased a majority stake in *L'Auto,* which he sold to the Germans in November 1940, a few months after the fall of France. The Tour was not held again until 1947. After the war, newspapers that had appeared during the German occupation of France and were therefore tainted by their association with the collaborationist Vichy regime were outlawed by the provisional French government. *L'Auto,* which had continued to cover sports during the war, closed its doors and lost its rights to the Tour. In February 1946 Jacques Goddet, Victor's son and Desgrange's chief assistant in the 1930s, founded *L'Équipe,* which rapidly emerged as the dominant sports daily in postwar France. Following the passage of a law in May 1946 establishing acquisition procedures for the rights and possessions of banned newspapers, *L'Équipe* bought *L'Auto*'s materials and equipment, as well as one-half of the rights to the Tour de France.

The other half of those rights was purchased by a major Parisian daily, *Le Parisien Libéré,* which had acquired what had previously been *Le Petit Parisien.* For almost twenty years *L'Équipe* and *Le Parisien Libéré* organized the Tour jointly as equal and independent partners. In 1964 *L'Équipe* was bought by Éditions Émilien Amaury, which owned *Le Parisien Libéré,* and the two papers continued to organize the race together under the joint leadership of Goddet and *Le Parisien Libéré*'s editor, Félix Lévitan. Lévitan was dismissed by the Groupe Amaury in 1987; the following year Goddet, at the age of eighty-three, retired as race director. In recent years, a separate entity, the Société du Tour de France, owned by Éditions Philippe Amaury, has run the Tour and a number of other prominent bicycle races. In 1989 Jean-Marie Leblanc, a sports journalist and former racer, became its technical director, responsible for the planning, preparation, and management of the Tour.[124]

Organizing the Tour has always been an immense logistical challenge. Given the length of stages and the organizers' desire to have the stages conclude in the afternoon so that the results could be covered in the following morning's issue of *L'Auto,* during the Tour's first decades, the racers set off in the middle of the night and cycled for hours in pitch darkness. This arrangement made supervising their progress—in particular to prevent cheating—an arduous affair for race officials, involving multiple check-points and frantic train and car trips. The itinerary was chosen months in advance: a staff member covered every meter of it by car to ensure its via-bility. Communities along the proposed route had to be willing and able to provide lodging for the racers, their support staff, and the organizers, as well as security and other assistance at start and finish lines and checkpoints. The last, called *contrôles,* served several purposes: food and beverages were pro-vided to the participants, who were required to sign in on a special *feuille de contrôle,* while race officials ensured that they were adhering to the Tour's many rules. The location of some *contrôles* was kept secret from the racers and served to check that they were not bypassing the race's difficulties, tak-ing shortcuts, or receiving illicit assistance.

Desgrange not only changed the race's itinerary and rules on a regular basis, but he continually experimented with different categories of racers and teams to maximize sportsmanship, fairness, and public interest in the race, as well as to maintain control over the participants and their com-mercial sponsors. From 1903 to 1908 each contestant competed, in prin-ciple, as an individual racer against all the others. This theoretical equality was immediately undermined by the cycle and tire manufacturers, who sought good publicity by sponsoring the best racers. For example, Alcyon Cycles, which sponsored successful racers during this period, saw its sales rise from 9,772 bicycles in 1906 to 31,813 in 1910.[125] With so much at stake, each company was determined to maximize its star's chances. To do so it hired less talented racers (known as *domestiques*) to shield the champion from the wind, chase down his opponents, maintain a rapid pace to dis-courage breakaways by his rivals, and pass him their bicycles, tires, food, and drink as needed. This support allowed a top racer to preserve his strength for the critical moments when the race was decided.

Confronted by the sponsors' strategies, Desgrange soon realized that to guarantee the participation of champions he would have to permit the par-ticipation of their *domestiques.* Between 1909 and 1914, contestants were separated into sponsored *coureurs groupés* and unsponsored *coureurs isolés.* In 1910, 1913, and 1914, the sponsored riders competed in teams named after their sponsors, whereas in the other years they competed, at least theoreti-cally, as sponsored "individual" racers. The first postwar Tours saw the cre-ation of similar categories: "A" and "B" racers in 1919, and "first class" and "second class" racers from 1920 through 1922. Between 1923 and 1927, the contestants were separated into three categories: a "first category" of top

Before launching the Tour de France in 1903 as the editor in chief of *L'Auto,*
Henri Desgrange was an avid racer and even, briefly, a world-record holder.
He is pictured here in the 1890s in a photograph from *Miroir des Sports.*
(Courtesy of Abaca.)

This photograph of the winner of the first Tour de France, Maurice Garin, and his son was featured on the cover of *La Vie au Grand Air*'s Tour de France special issue in July 1903. (Courtesy of Abaca.)

The French racer Hippolyte Aucouturier arrives at the finish line of the Lyon-Marseille stage in the first Tour de France. Note the lack of security, as evidenced by the spectators and even a dog spilling out into the street. (Courtesy of Abaca.)

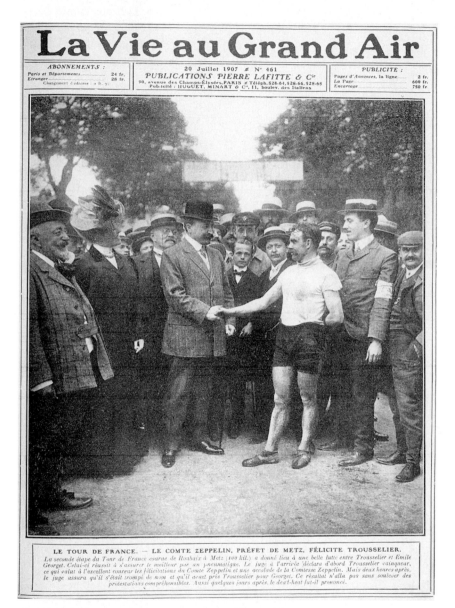

La Vie au Grand Air

ABONNEMENTS :
Paris et Départements .... 24 fr.
Étranger .... 28 fr.
Changement d'adresse : 0 fr. 75

20 Juillet 1907 ≠ N° 461
PUBLICATIONS PIERRE LAFITTE & Cⁱᵉ
90, avenue des Champs-Élysées, PARIS ≠ Téléph. 528-64, 528-66, 528-68
Publicité : HUGUET, MINART & Cⁱᵉ, 11, boulev. des Italiens

PUBLICITÉ :
Pages d'Annonces, la ligne .... 2 fr.
La Page .... 600 fr.
Encartage .... 750 fr.

LE TOUR DE FRANCE. — LE COMTE ZEPPELIN, PRÉFET DE METZ, FÉLICITE TROUSSELIER.

La seconde étape du Tour de France course de Roubaix à Metz (400 kil.) a donné lieu à une belle lutte entre Trousselier et Émile Georget. Celui-ci réussit à s'assurer le meilleur par un pneumatique. Le juge à l'arrivée déclara d'abord Trousselier vainqueur, ce qui valut à l'excellent coureur les félicitations du Comte Zeppelin et une accolade de la Comtesse Zeppelin. Mais deux heures après, le juge assura qu'il s'était trompé de nom et qu'il avait pris Trousselier pour Georget. Ce résultat n'alla pas sans soulever des protestations compréhensibles. Aussi quelques jours après, le déat-hest fut-il prononcé.

On this July 1907 cover of *La Vie au Grand Air,* Count Zeppelin, the prefect of Metz in German Alsace-Lorraine, congratulates the 1905 Tour winner, the Frenchman Louis Trousselier, after his victory in the first stage of the 1907 Tour. (Courtesy of Abaca.)

A virile "giant of the road." François Faber, known as the "giant of Colombes," adjusts his headgear. This photograph was featured on the cover of *La Vie au Grand Air* in July 1909. Faber dominated the Tour that year, winning six of the fourteen stages and the overall title. Note the goggles and inner tubes, the tools of Faber's trade, which contributed to *L'Auto*'s celebration of Tour racers as model workers (see chapter 4). Faber died a hero's death in World War I, attempting to save a fallen comrade in no-man's-land. (Courtesy of Abaca.)

The French racer Octave Lapize, photographed by *La Vie au Grand Air,* climbs the Tourmalet during the 1910 Tour. This was the first time that the Pyrenees were included in the race's itinerary. The Alps were added in 1911. (Courtesy of Abaca.)

The racer Joseph Müller, joined by his wife and daughter, is surrounded by fans at the conclusion of the Geneva-Strasbourg stage during the 1923 Tour. (Courtesy of Abaca.)

The *forçats de la route* controversy is launched. Having just dropped out of the 1924 Tour, Henri and Francis Pélissier, leaning against the window of the café in which they have paused, offer their criticisms of the Tour to the famous investigative journalist Albert Londres, who was covering the race for the mass-circulation daily *Le Petit Parisien*. (Courtesy of Abaca.)

The racer Joseph Rivella pauses to sign in at the checkpoint at the top of the Peyresourde climb in the Pyrenees during the 1927 Tour. (Courtesy of Abaca.)

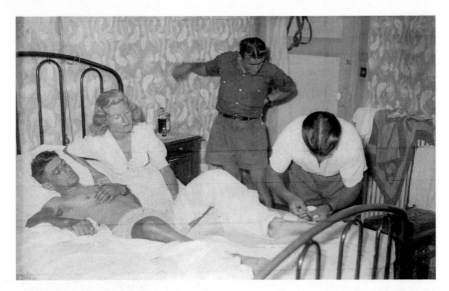

During the rest day in Nice during the 1947 Tour, the French veteran racer René Vietto, one of the prerace favorites, relaxes in his hotel room as a doctor attends to his injured toe. Mme Vietto "attentively supervises the procedure" (*Le Parisien Libéré,* 8 July 1947) and sits next to her husband "to give him moral support" (*L'Équipe,* 8 July 1947). (Courtesy of Abaca.)

Leaving behind the devastated city of Caen, the racers of the 1947 Tour set off on the final stage to Paris. Such images, the Caen municipal council hoped, would convey both the terrible toll exacted by the war on the city and the determination of Caennais to rebuild in its wake. (Courtesy of Abaca.)

The newly married Jean Robic receives a bouquet from his young bride at the Parc des Princes after winning the 1947 Tour. The couple's devotion to each other during the race was a regular feature of that year's Tour coverage. (Courtesy of Abaca.)

During the St. Malo–Sables d'Olonne stage of the 1949 Tour, the young Breton racer Louison Bobet, who later became the first racer to win three consecutive Tours (1953–55), pauses to embrace his wife and daughter in his hometown. (Courtesy of Abaca.)

sponsored racers, a "second category" of lesser but accomplished racers, and a third category of quasi-amateurs called *touristes-routiers*. After an initial period in the early 1920s, when the war-weakened cycle manufacturers banded together in a consortium called La Sportive, individually sponsored teams like Automoto-Hutchinson and Alcyon-Dunlop reemerged. In 1928 there were also nine regional teams (replacing the second-category racers) and a number of *touristes-routiers*. In 1929 Desgrange experimented with only two categories, top racers called *as* (aces) and modest *touristes-routiers*.

By 1930 Desgrange was unhappy with the increasing control exercised by the top teams, which had resulted in the late 1920s in unsuspenseful Tours won by well-supported but often unspectacular racers. He decided to do away with commercially sponsored teams, substituting in their place national teams (and, in 1930 and 1939, French regional teams), whose members were selected by the organizers. During that decade teams were fielded by France, Belgium, Italy, Germany, Spain, Switzerland, Australia, Luxembourg, the Netherlands, Yugoslavia, Romania, Great Britain, and Austria. Anywhere from three to eleven national teams competed each year. Some teams were made up of racers from more than one country, whereas countries with many great racers, like France and Belgium, might field two or even three national teams. Between 1930 and 1937, Desgrange also allowed the participation of lesser racers, dubbed *individuels, isolés,* or *touristes-routiers*. In some years the *individuels* were placed in their own national teams and were called up to their nation's "varsity" to replace members who had dropped out. This guaranteed that the top teams remained at full strength and maintained their competitiveness. Exploiting widespread athletic chauvinism, these changes revived public interest in the race.

The national and regional teams were reinstated after World War II and persisted through the 1961 Tour. During that period there were between five and nine national teams each year, representing France, Belgium, Italy, Switzerland, West Germany, Luxembourg, Australia, Austria, Spain, Great Britain, and the Netherlands. Again, some countries occasionally entered more than one team, while other teams were made up of riders from two or more nations. There were also between three and six French regional teams each year, including a North African team in the early 1950s, just a few years before Tunisia, Morocco, and Algeria gained their independence from France. In the 1950s sponsorship from the moribund cycle industry gave way to team sponsors from other sectors. The Tour's national teams did not prevent cycle manufacturers from gaining exposure for their product lines, but *extra-sportif* sponsors derived publicity from cycling primarily when their racers' corporate jerseys appeared in press photographs and on television screens during race coverage. They exerted considerable pressure on the Tour organizers, who resurrected commercially sponsored teams in 1962.[126] Since then the Tour has been contested exclusively by such teams, with the exception of a short-lived return to national teams in 1967 and 1968. In the 1980s the Tour's *peloton* expanded beyond Europe and Australia as racers from North and South America participated, reflecting the internationalization of the sport and the Tour's increasingly global commercial appeal. In the 1990s they were joined by racers from Eastern Europe and the former Soviet Union, who had been excluded from the Tour since 1947 as a result of the Cold War.

COMMERCIAL MODERNITY AND MASS-CONSUMER SOCIETY: SPONSORSHIP, NEW MEDIA, AND THE TOUR

The development of various motorized forms of locomotion and the proliferation of consumer goods during the Tour's early decades soon rendered anachronistic the bicycle's image as a symbol of technological modernity and of the burgeoning consumer culture of early twentieth-century France. Yet while the bicycle's modernity faded, the Tour itself remained modern. As its successive organizers sought to establish the race first as France's, then Europe's, and finally the world's most popular annual sporting event, they not only relied on but actually fueled innovations in two trends that have characterized modern societies in the twentieth century: the increasingly pervasive commercialization of sport and the development of new mass media capable of covering athletic competitions for ever-expanding audiences.

Both trends are of critical importance to the cultural history of the Tour, for together they ensured that representations of the race and its participants would be widely disseminated throughout French society (and ultimately around the world). As a result of its commercialization and *médiatisation,* the race itself became big business: as an advertising strategy for a variety of businesses and as a commodity in itself, to be marketed, packaged, and sold to millions of fans through increasingly effective and technologically sophisticated media. For all their editorial bravado during the Tour's early years, it is unlikely that Desgrange and his collaborators at *L'Auto* could have foreseen the day when the race would be sponsored by huge multinational corporations and broadcast—often live—all over the planet.

Little about the race's economics in those early years would have justified such an ambitious vision. Initially, *L'Auto* provided virtually all of the official prize money designed to attract racers to the world's most grueling race. In 1903, when a young male worker typically earned about 5 francs a day, that sum was 19,625 francs.[127] In addition, members of communities through which the race passed offered numerous *prix spéciaux*. Café owners, for example, often gave an award (usually between 25 and 100 francs) to the first contestant to race by their establishment. In 1908 a local Peugeot dealer promised 25 francs to the first racer on a Peugeot bicycle to pass through Béziers, and the Club Sportif Alcyon offered the same amount to the first contestant on an Alcyon bicycle to sign at the Toulouse checkpoint.[128] By such awards local entrepreneurs signaled their support for the courageous participants, attracted customers curious to see who had won the prize, and drew attention to their product lines. Offering prizes also allowed associations and individuals to support racers from their own town, region, or profession and enabled municipal governments to associate their communities with an event popular with their constituents. Prizes along the itinerary multiplied over the years, especially in communities with checkpoints, and included plaques, medals, bouquets, cash, shoes, bottles of calvados, cycling clothes, and artwork. In 1920 the organizers announced that all prizes offered by the public would henceforth have to be in cash amounts of at least ten francs; this rule was a response to the unmanageable quantity and variety of these prizes, which reflected the Tour's popularity.[129] This restriction did not deter the public. Cycling and other sports clubs, local organizations of merchants and artisans, military schools, hotels, garages, shopkeepers, café owners, and private citizens continued to donate sums to specific racers, as did transplanted foreigners supporting their compatriots.[130]

More explicit commercial sponsorship of the race was slower to develop, perhaps because businesses were initially reluctant to invest their advertising budget in an event that had yet to attract broad press coverage. In 1903 the publishing house of Plon, Nourrit et Cie. donated fifty francs toward the prize money for each stage as well as for the final classification.[131] Five years later, cycle and tire manufacturers as well as the press offered special prizes to racers as promotional devices. The Wolber tire company sponsored

Le Prix Wolber (five thousand francs to be shared by the top three finishers who completed the Tour using removable tires); Labor Cycles and the Hutchinson tire company created Le Prix Labor Hutchinson (one thousand francs to be distributed among the first three racers to reach the Tour's four major summits). *Sports Populaires* and *L'Éducation Physique* offered Le Prix du Courage (one hundred francs and a silver gilt medal) to the racer who demonstrated "the most remarkable energy." Meanwhile, Labor also promised to "adopt" the unsponsored racer who performed best in the 1908 Tour and provide him with bicycles the following season.[132] As the general press began to increase its sports coverage after World War I, commercial sponsorship reached new heights: in 1924 the Produits Gibbs soap company donated forty-five thousand francs, to be shared by the stage winners and the top two finishers in the final overall standings.[133] Although Gibbs remained the major player by far in this area for the rest of the decade, other companies followed suit at more modest levels. Their involvement foreshadowed the commercial revolution of the 1930s.

In 1929 the Tour's official prize money had reached 150,000 francs, but the race was in trouble because powerful team sponsors had engineered a series of predictable victories by unspectacular racers.[134] Seeking to revive flagging public interest, in 1930 Desgrange replaced commercially sponsored teams with national and regional teams.[135] *L'Auto* provided all participants with identical bicycles and all national team members with lodging, food, accessories, and spare parts (except for bicycle seats, racing shorts, and handlebars), as well as doctors, masseurs, and mechanics.[136] Although it effectively limited the involvement of the racers' corporate sponsors, this arrangement dramatically increased the organizers' financial burden. In response, *L'Auto* created the *caravane publicitaire,* exploiting previously untapped commercial interests for whom the race's greatest selling point was its itinerary: each sponsor paid a fee to enter one or more vehicles in a noisy, colorful procession that preceded the racers along the route. From these vehicles sponsors broadcast their advertising jingles and slogans and distributed flyers, samples, and gifts to millions of spectators patiently awaiting the racers.[137] The *caravane publicitaire* quickly became one of the Tour's main attractions, both along the itinerary and in host communities, where it provided an evening of entertainment.

The new formula immediately proved an immense success. The 1931 Tour, for example, offered 733,000 francs in prize money, of which only 152,900 was provided by *L'Auto.* Forty-six sponsors gave between 5,000 and

40,000 francs each.[138] They included nineteen beverage companies (alcoholic and nonalcoholic), eight manufacturers of bicycle-related products, five from the clothing sector, five representing food (cheese, bananas, and chocolate), two motorcycle manufacturers, two tire companies, the Belle Jardinière department store, and the Parc des Princes velodrome, which hosted the Tour finale.[139] Other sponsors were makers of polish, soaps, phonographs, and records. Although most were French, German and Belgian businesses also viewed the Tour as an effective advertising ploy in their efforts to penetrate the French market. Furthermore, the participation of their national teams guaranteed public interest in and media coverage of the race in their domestic markets. The success of the *caravane publicitaire* was such that in 1935 the prize money reached 1,059,350 francs. Two years later, the La Vie insurance company donated a record 200,000 francs to be awarded to the winner.[140] In a few short years, businesses in a variety of sectors had come to see the Tour as an invaluable advertising strategy. They were not alone.

Increasing numbers of communities, particularly those hosting stages, contributed more than prize money: in 1936, for example, in addition to almost four thousand francs in prize money awarded by the city of Évian and its famous water company, support was provided by the local *comité des fêtes,* the tourist bureau, and the association of merchants. The thermal establishment placed its "luxurious facilities" at the racers' disposal, and the city's hotel owners agreed "graciously" to receive the *touristes-routiers,* whose lodgings the organizers no longer covered.[141] As *L'Auto* was happy to point out, such hospitality reflected an understanding in communities along the Tour's route that the race represented a significant economic opportunity. Hotel and café owners, souvenir shops, ice-cream vendors, and cycle manufacturers were obvious beneficiaries. The automobiles of the *caravane publicitaire* required gas and oil. Spectators and journalists took photographs, a boon to photography shops, while the state-owned postal and communications service, the PTT, benefited from the increase in postcards, telephone calls, and telegrams sent during the race.[142] Many communities came to see the Tour as more than a one-time boost to their economies. Particularly after the advent of paid vacations for workers, legislated by the Popular Front government in 1936, favorable media coverage of a town's hospitality and attractions could translate into long-term gains from expanding tourism.[143] Not surprisingly, given *L'Auto*'s increased costs and the benefits derived by host communities, the organizers demanded much larger municipal subventions from the latter in the 1930s and insisted that they also cover the cost of crowd and traffic control.[144]

The Tour had become a big business on which hundreds of other economic actors, extending well beyond the traditional cycle and tire manufacturers of the race's first decades, depended—at least for a few days or weeks each summer. This heightened commercialization owed much to expanding media coverage of the race after World War I. Before the war, the mass-circulation Parisian press generally offered only brief, episodic coverage of sports, and regional papers usually devoted only a quarter of a page to the subject. During the 1920s, however, the press took note of *L'Auto*'s impressive sales: between 1920 and 1930 its daily circulation increased from 100,000 to 300,000, numbers that doubled during the Tour. The Frenchman Henri Pélissier's triumphant 1923 Tour saw *L'Auto*'s daily circulation reach almost half a million copies. Ten years later, it was up to 730,000 during the victory of his compatriot Georges Speicher. Responding to the evident public interest in sport, mass-circulation dailies developed their own sports sections, which by the end of the 1920s often occupied an entire page. New sports magazines, such as *Miroir des Sports* and *Match,* were launched.[145]

In the 1930s no paper was more aggressive than *Paris-Soir* at exploiting sports—the Tour in particular—to attract readers. On acquiring the paper in 1930, Jean Prouvost dramatically expanded its sports coverage and use of photography. The results were immediate: daily circulation exploded from sixty thousand in 1930 to one million in June 1933 and almost two and a half million in April 1936. To consolidate its position, in July 1935 *Paris-Soir* created the weekly sports magazine *Sprint.* By the mid-1930s *Paris-Soir* was sending as many reporters to the Tour as *L'Auto* itself: its 1935 coverage mobilized forty employees, two airplanes, eight cars, five motorcycles, a bus, and another vehicle in which photographs of the race were instantly developed, thanks to a newly devised portable system, before being flown to the paper's headquarters for publication in that evening's issue. *Paris-Soir* thus scooped *L'Auto*'s coverage, which appeared only the following morning. Other mass-circulation dailies, such as *Le Petit Parisien,* followed suit. During the 1939 Tour, one hundred cars were required to accommodate the press covering the race. For the press, too, the Tour had become big business.[146]

Meanwhile, a completely new media phenomenon, radio coverage of the Tour, began in the late 1920s. Between the wars, the French state and newspapers—including *L'Auto, L'Intransigeant, Le Petit Parisien,* and Prouvost's company—founded, bought, and invested in radio stations. By 1939 France was covered by a network of twenty state-owned and twelve private transmitters. During the 1927 Tour Radio-Toulouse offered a nightly quarter-hour summary of the day's racing. The first live broadcasts of the race took place in 1929 when Jean Antoine of Paris-PTT/*Intran*/*Match* provided fifty-five *reportages en direct.* Radio coverage radically changed the way the public experienced the race, creating a dramatic immediacy the print press was obviously unable to match. When the race leader, Victor Fontan, had to drop out because of mechanical problems, fans for the first time learned about his calamity as it happened. On hearing of their son's crash on the radio during the 1930 Tour, André Leducq's parents hurried to the Galibier climb in the Alps, where they were relieved to learn he had been able to set off again, preserving his position as race leader. In the early 1930s Antoine's broadcasting team provided a hundred or so programs during the Tour: an early-morning report giving the overall standings and approximate time the racers were expected at various points along that day's itinerary; a lunchtime update halfway through the stage; coverage of the finish; and an evening summary of the day's racing, accompanied by a presentation of the main features of the next stage. Meanwhile, responding to public interest with its more limited means, Radio-Lyon offered live coverage of Tour stages in its region.[147]

Just as press coverage of the Tour spurred technological innovation, notably in photography, so too did radio coverage. In 1932 Antoine and his team used a recently invented system that allowed them to record interviews with racers right after a stage, when they were most accessible; these were later played during the evening wrap-up show. This technology also made it possible for Antoine and his colleague Alex Virot to transmit from Luchon their coverage of the racers' passage over the great Pyrenean summit, the Aubisque, recorded earlier in the day. Soon, *L'Intran-Match*'s bus, with its studio, technical room, ten staff members, modern radio equipment, and reporters perched on the roof, became one of the Tour's attractions. In 1938 a live sports program was produced at high altitude for the first time as Tour racers passed over the Iseran peak (2,769 meters). By the late 1930s fans could tune in several times a day on a number of radio stations for updates and live reports of the race (*L'Auto* provided a daily schedule of radio coverage). During a Pyrenean stage in 1937, for example, four radio stations between them offered fourteen Tour reports between 7:40 A.M. and 7:45

P.M., including live coverage of the racers negotiating the Tourmalet and Aubisque peaks.[148]

No doubt in part because of the public's desire to follow the Tour and other sporting events as closely as possible, the number of radios in France rose dramatically throughout the 1930s, from a half million in early 1930 to about five and a half million in July 1939 (approximately one for every seven people).[149] Those who did not own a radio had one more reason to frequent their neighborhood café or cycle shop, which, in a savvy move, tuned in to the race and provided their clientele with regular updates on slate tablets.[150] During this period, the organizers shortened the stage lengths, keeping racing to a daytime schedule that maximized the benefits of radio coverage. They also introduced individual time trials, in which racers left the starting line at intervals of several minutes and rode alone against the clock. This addition heightened the drama for fans following the race, thanks to the live reports and frequent updates provided by radio. Meanwhile, host communities and commercial sponsors benefited from exposure on this new medium, despite French government restrictions on radio advertising.[151]

A third medium, newsreels shown in movie theaters, further contributed to the Tour's popularity during the interwar years. Filmed news coverage got its start in France with Pathé-Journal (initially called Pathé–Fait Divers) in 1908 and Gaumont-Actualités in 1910. It covered spectacular events such as official presidential trips, visits of foreign rulers, coronations and funerals, natural catastrophes, great exhibitions, military and naval reviews, and sporting events. After the war these *journaux d'actualité* reported on innumerable commemorative ceremonies as well as fashion shows, new dances, automobile races, boxing matches, and Tour de France stages. In 1923, still traumatized by four years of trench warfare, the French assembled in movie theaters to celebrate the victories of Suzanne Lenglen in tennis and Henri Pélissier in the Tour, as well as the French pilot Sadi Lecointe's world altitude record of 11,145 meters. The genre enjoyed its greatest success from 1929 to 1939, as it benefited from innovations in moving-picture and sound technology without having to face the competition that would come from television after World War II. In Paris in the 1930s newspapers like *Le Journal* opened *cinéacs,* theaters located near train stations and devoted to *actualités.*[152]

Makers of feature films also sought to capitalize on the public's fascination with competitive cycling and the Tour in particular. Their films included *Le roi de la pédale* (1925), set during an imaginary Tour de France and based on a recent novel; *Hardi les gars* (1931); *Rivaux de la piste* (1932); and *Prince des six jours* (1933). Both *Le facteur du Tour de France* (1934) and *Pour le maillot jaune* (1938) were shot partially on location during the Tour. Occasionally, top racers played roles in cycling films: Charles Pélissier, the youngest of three famous racing brothers, acted in a film about velodrome racing in the 1930s. Documentaries were also made, the first of which was probably *Le Tour de France* (1935).[153] Meanwhile, when the *caravane publicitaire* set up its festive camp in a host community, its entertainment often featured a filmed summary of the just-completed stage, projected on a huge screen in the town square. At the end of the Tour, hundreds of movie theaters across France showed a summary of the race. Thus, at precisely the time Desgrange was aggressively pursuing commercial sponsorship, vastly expanded and innovative press, radio, and film coverage made the Tour an increasingly attractive advertising opportunity.

After the war, Goddet and Lévitan modernized the logistical organization of the Tour. As part of these efforts, they hired advertising professionals to take charge of the Tour's publicity and, in 1957, created a mobile press room with modern communications equipment to allow journalists to cover the race in the best possible conditions. Reflecting the increasing scope of its responsibilities in postwar French society, as well as its recognition of the importance of the Tour in the nation's life, the state provided the logistical support of the PTT in communications.[154] The *caravane publicitaire* returned as a prominent feature of postwar Tours and continued to expand and innovate as commercial sponsors like Ricard, Pernod Fils, and the private radio station Europe No. 1 hired entertainers to perform for host communities. These included accordionists like Fredo Gardoni and Maurice Alexander as well as established and up-and-coming singers such as Darcelys, Tino Rossi, Charles Trénet, Johnny Halliday, Gilbert Bécaud, Petula Clark, and the Bordeau sisters.[155] The Tour exposed young entertainers like Line Renaud, the first singer to accompany an entire Tour de France, and the prizewinning accordionist Yvette Horner to millions of potential fans across France, helping to transform both young women into stars.[156]

Meanwhile, a new medium—television—was beginning to revolutionize the relationship between the Tour and its public; in the process, it dramatically increased the race's viability as a promotional vehicle. First demonstrated in France in 1931, television was still a curiosity in 1948, when there were only five thousand television viewers in the entire country. To increase its audience, French television provided live coverage of sporting events, including the Tour's conclusion at the Parc des Princes that summer. The following year, it experimented with an evening news program five times a week. Recognizing that the Tour was the most spectacular and most popular event in France, television officials scheduled the first *journal télévisé* nightly for the duration of the race. Fans without televisions flocked to cafés, where they huddled around sets to see their heroes in action. The experiment was a success: the *journal télévisé* resumed definitively that October and continued to rely on important sporting events to attract viewers. In 1950 the program followed the Tour from start to finish in the official media *caravane,* providing viewers with an unprecedented window on the race's subtleties: how racers broke away and were chased down, how and what they ate during stages, and how they collaborated with their team managers.[157] Echoing Desgrange's rhetoric of a half century earlier, *L'Équipe* heralded this achievement in a headline describing the Tour as a "source of progress." As with radio, sport—the Tour in particular—inspired a number of technical advances in television coverage.[158]

In the early 1950s the Tour remained the great attraction of French television news programming: in July television sales spiked as fans decided to invest in their own sets. Increased race coverage, which expanded to three daily news programs in 1952, contributed to the decline of the weekly filmed *actualités,* which the race had helped to make popular before the war. By 1959, although rural France still lagged behind the rest of the country, there were eight hundred thousand television sets nationwide, and 70 percent of the French population could receive programs. For those who could not afford their own set, the 1950s saw the development of *téléclubs,* which helped popularize the new medium in rural communities and exposed inhabitants of many villages, primarily workers and small farmers, to the Tour.[159] In 1960 French television broadcast nine hours and twenty minutes of race coverage (including four hours of live coverage); by 1970 coverage had increased to about twenty-eight hours, four-fifths of it live.[160]

The French government, which owned and controlled French television during this period and was determined to use the new medium for educational and cultural purposes, banned all commercial advertising until 1968. The Tour emerged as a valuable alternative for corporate interests, who could bypass this prohibition by sponsoring aspects of the race, and, after 1961, teams. For example, Peugeot became the official supplier of vehicles for the Tour in 1954 and was soon providing dozens of cars and trucks that appeared continually in television coverage of the race, generating enormous exposure for the company. The organizers initially feared that allowing sponsors to exploit fully the opportunities for televised publicity would damage the Tour's traditional character. They faced financial difficulties, however, and had few options: the RTF (Radio-Télévision Française) began to pay for the right to cover the race only in 1960, and fees for broadcasting rights remained minimal until the 1980s. Furthermore, the national-teams formula, in effect through the 1961 Tour, denied the organizers income from team sponsors. As a result, the organizers opted to exploit television's income-generating possibilities, and sponsors extended their involvement in the Tour beyond the *caravane publicitaire,* as Peugeot's initiative illustrates.[161]

Businesses sponsored specific stages and "officially" provided laundry services for racers and officials, drinks and timekeeping at the finish line, gas and oil for the *caravane,* and health care for the contestants.[162] Perrier, "the water of champions," and later Coca-Cola paid the organizers for the right to photograph each stage winner drinking their product. Corporations sponsored the race leader's yellow jersey, the points leader's green jersey, the "king of the mountains" championship for the best climbers, and other symbols of athletic excellence or good character.[163] Classifications and *challenges* increased dramatically as ambitious new sponsors came to the Tour. The 1979 Tour, for example, featured sixteen such competitions, each rewarding a daily leader and an overall winner at the end of the race.[164] The proliferation of such prizes not only increased commercial sponsorship of the Tour; it also created a host of secondary competitions that encouraged lesser racers to compete aggressively. This in turn heightened the action for the public and gave the media more exploits to cover. Since becoming technical director of the Tour in 1989, Jean-Marie Leblanc has reduced the number of classifications based on athletic performance to the six most significant, in the hope of reducing the pressure on racers to resort to performance-enhancing drugs.[165] Meanwhile, deregulation in the French audiovisual sector, begun in the early 1980s, has further increased the promotional value of television coverage of the race.[166]

As media coverage expanded, making the Tour an even more attractive advertising option than before the war, so did the *caravane publicitaire.* In 1978, for example, 155 trucks, cars, and motorcycles covered the entire itinerary, and forty-seven additional vehicles participated in parts of the race. In addition, a Tour-Expo composed primarily of vehicles from the *caravane* set up an advertising exhibition near the start and finish of each stage. One hundred sixty-two vehicles participated in this Tour-Expo for the entire race, and another 73 did so for part of the Tour only.[167] In 1992 the *caravane publicitaire* contained 200 vehicles, 180 of which completed the entire Tour. Twenty were "regional" and joined the *caravane* for two or three stages— further evidence of the organizers' flexibility in meeting the needs of diverse sponsors. In 1991 and 1992, for example, several Beaujolais wineries limited their participation to a regional publicity operation. In the 1990s as in the 1930s, the *caravane* included food and beverage firms, but these were now often vast international concerns headquartered outside Europe, such as Coca-Cola and Café de Colombie. Other important sponsors included banks, computer-related businesses, automobile manufacturers, insurance companies, and the PMU (the off-track betting concern).[168]

The Tour's commercial viability increased as television coverage expanded in duration and global scope. The race was broadcast for the first time in the United States in 1979 and in Japan in 1985; in 1995, Chinese television provided its viewers with a twenty-six-minute daily Tour summary. French public television packaged and sold race coverage in Asia, Australia, South Africa, and Latin America. In 1986 it was estimated that a billion viewers in seventy-two countries watched the race on television. That year, for the first time, a Tour stage (in the Pyrenees) was covered live virtually from start to finish by French television. In 1989 the media present on the Tour included 580 journalists, 150 photographers, and 620 chauffeurs and technicians, representing 190 newspapers, 45 radio stations, 26 television stations, 18 international news agencies, and 14 international photographic agencies. Today, viewers in the vast majority of the world's countries can follow the Tour on television, either live or in the form of regular race summaries. Television rights provide the organizers with an ever-expanding source of income, from 1.56 million francs in 1986 to 40 million francs in 1995. Most of this revenue comes from French public television, which by 1995 was providing 110 hours of live coverage. The Tour today has the largest television audience of any annual sports event in the world.[169]

CONCLUSION

The Tour's successive organizers have consistently sought to associate the race with modernity and progress. Henri Desgrange and his journalists argued that the Tour would introduce the recently invented bicycle to rural

France and inspire a listless generation of Frenchmen to exercise. The race's unprecedented scale and difficulty provided seemingly incontrovertible evidence that the alliance of modern sport and modern technology would develop the moral and physical virtues required for French regeneration. *L'Auto* also celebrated the Tour's commercialism as evidence of the economic opportunities the race offered: team sponsors, participants in the *caravane publicitaire,* and communities along the itinerary all profited from the Tour's popularity, itself made possible by expanding and innovative media coverage.

After World War II, Jacques Goddet continued to emphasize the Tour's relationship to technological modernity, reflected no longer by the bicycle but rather by the modernization of the Tour's logistical organization and advances in television coverage, even if he initially feared that the new medium might erode the Tour's traditional essence.[170] Goddet, too, celebrated the race's commercial expansion, describing the *caravane publicitaire* as a "fantastic exhibition of commercial intelligence" that proved that the Tour was modern and "foreshadowed progress."[171] He saw the *caravane*'s modernity reflected in the diverse entertainment it provided for host communities the evening of a stage; for Goddet, the Tour quite simply "engendered modern life."[172] Referring to the global media attention and international sponsorship the Tour attracts, his successor has also evoked the race's modernity. For Jean-Marie Leblanc, the Tour is "a myth perfectly adapted to the exigencies of the modern world."[173]

Although such self-serving claims must be evaluated critically, the Tour's modernity, particularly with respect to its commercialization and media coverage, is indisputable. The race has inspired technological innovations in and fueled the popularization of new media and has been at the forefront of the commercialization of modern sport—from the cycle and tire manufacturers who sponsored the first champions to the creation of the *caravane publicitaire,* from the sponsorship of the yellow jersey by a French wool company in 1948 to the more recent involvement of huge international concerns like Coca-Cola. These two features of the race's modernity are of course linked: the commercial exploitation of the Tour would have been unthinkable without media coverage that has made the race increasingly appealing to potential sponsors.

Beyond this economic function, expanding media coverage of the Tour has played an important cultural role. By presenting images—whether verbal or visual—of the race and its contestants, it helped to shape how the

French public understood and experienced the Tour as well as broader trends with which the race came to be associated. Not all commentators have followed the lead of the Tour's successive organizers in equating modernity with progress. Echoing early opponents of the bicycle, many have criticized the Tour for epitomizing the dangers and excesses of modern life, including repetitive industrial labor, exploitative capitalism, hypercommercialism, and drug abuse. We shall turn to these representations in due course, for they constitute important chapters in the race's cultural history. That history, however, begins with the symbolic power of the race's itinerary and the narratives it inspired about France and the French. For as its name indicates, the Tour de France is first and foremost an itinerary.

TWO

Itineraries, Narratives, and Identities

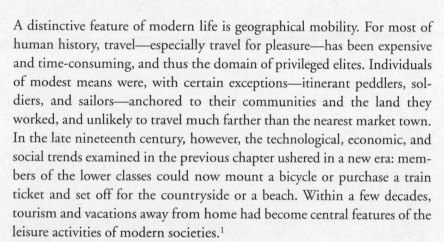

A distinctive feature of modern life is geographical mobility. For most of human history, travel—especially travel for pleasure—has been expensive and time-consuming, and thus the domain of privileged elites. Individuals of modest means were, with certain exceptions—itinerant peddlers, soldiers, and sailors—anchored to their communities and the land they worked, and unlikely to travel much farther than the nearest market town. In the late nineteenth century, however, the technological, economic, and social trends examined in the previous chapter ushered in a new era: members of the lower classes could now mount a bicycle or purchase a train ticket and set off for the countryside or a beach. Within a few decades, tourism and vacations away from home had become central features of the leisure activities of modern societies.[1]

In France, as elsewhere, such travel increased contacts between inhabitants of quite diverse regions. Unprecedented numbers of people experienced firsthand the differences to be found among others with whom they shared a nationality but—it often seemed—little else: local customs, crafts, dialects, clothing, religious practices, gastronomic specialties, histories, and natural environments varied dramatically. This was especially true of France: the centralizing impulses of absolute monarchs and democratic republics notwithstanding, the size of the national territory and the piecemeal way it had been cobbled together over the centuries had long militated against cultural homogenization or a strong sense of national identity.

This extraordinarily varied physical and cultural landscape, and the complex history with which it was imbued, provided the spatial and psychological environment for the Tour de France. Embodying the era's new-found mobility, the racers connected their public to the past as they negotiated an itinerary sprinkled with historic sites that evoked important moments or figures in the nation's life. This was, of course, true in a literal sense for the spectators who lined the race route, but it was also true for the millions who experienced the race indirectly. From the very first Tour, media coverage of the race was a way of imagining the nation, interpreting its history, and defining its people.

Such coverage was thus a profoundly political act founded on conscious choices. Which sites and events were to be celebrated, and which ignored? Which historical interpretations were to be promoted, and which discredited? Which images of the people were to be presented as authentic, and which dismissed as false? These were fundamental questions to which the French offered varied, even contradictory responses. Broad agreement that the Tour was a preeminent symbol of France simply begged a far more complicated question: which "France" did the race symbolize?

COMMEMORATING THE PAST,
LOOKING TO THE FUTURE

In early January 1919, less than two months after the armistice that ended World War I, *Le Petit Journal* announced that it was organizing a bicycle race to commemorate the battles of the Western Front. The aptly named Circuit des Champs de Bataille was to be run in seven stages between April 28 and May 11. It would cover some two thousand kilometers, beginning and concluding in the recently recovered Alsatian city of Strasbourg and pausing along the way in other cities that had experienced or been threatened with German occupation: Luxembourg, Brussels, Amiens, Paris, Bar-le-Duc, and Belfort.[2] The race was one in a series of sporting events the paper organized that year to symbolize the postwar regeneration of France, particularly that of its recently liberated northeastern sector. These included a Soccer Cup of the Liberated Regions (Belgium, northern France, and Alsace-Lorraine), a cross-country foot race, an airplane race, a swimming competition, and a boxing match involving the great French heavyweight Georges Carpentier. But it was above all the battlefield circuit of the bicycle race that *Le Petit Journal* expected would spark "global interest" as it traced the "glorious stages of Victory."[3]

Other commentators, too, celebrated the race's commemoration of four years of fighting for "law and justice" by heroic French soldiers.[4] *L'Auto* predicted that the itinerary through a countryside "devastated by the *Boche*" would inject the competition with an unprecedented emotional charge. The racers would draw energy from visiting such "magical" sites as Verdun and be acclaimed across the Alsatian plain by "those who, for a half-century, have been awaiting liberation."[5] Rejecting the assessment of a number of newspapers that the local roads would be unusable, the organizers argued that it was precisely their abominable condition that conferred prestige on the race: had not military cyclists courageously negotiated the very same roads during the war while dodging machine-gun fire and rock fragments?[6]

Doubts about the region's capacity to host such a race were well founded. One of the country's richest agricultural and industrial areas, northeastern France had been devastated by the war. Villages, towns, and cities had been razed; over five million acres of agricultural land, contaminated by chemicals and unexploded artillery shells, were at least temporarily out of commission; and some two and a half million farm animals had been expropriated by the Germans. After four years of exploiting the region's mineral resources, they had, on their retreat, laid most of its industrial infrastructure to waste, flooding mines and destroying factories. Iron production had been reduced by almost 60 percent, coal production to almost nothing. The war's impact on the region was such that in 1919 national figures for metallurgical production stood at just 29 percent of 1913 levels. Many of the area's railroads, waterways, and roads were unusable. Even more devastating was the war's human toll. France had lost proportionately more men than any of the other major combatant nations: in addition to some 1.3 million dead—about 10 percent of the male work force in 1913—another 1.1 million Frenchmen returned from the front as invalids, many of them permanently incapacitated.[7] For a nation long obsessed with its low birth rate, the demographic implications of these losses were disastrous.

A week before the Circuit des Champs de Bataille was to start, the classic Paris-Roubaix race was held in conditions so appalling that only five of the forty automobiles accompanying the racers were able to reach the finish. *L'Auto* dubbed the event "the hell of the north," a nickname that has survived to this day.[8] Evoking the material devastation suffered by northern France, Desgrange wondered what had become of the Roubaix velodrome, which "used to welcome our heroes." The race's itinerary cut across "the tragic lines, penetrating resolutely into the 'no man's land' where so many of our [lads] fell heroically for the noblest of causes," and passed through communities "systematically devastated by the barbaric and ignoble *boche*." The Germans had robbed France of some of its greatest racers (including Tour winners François Faber and Lucien Petit-Breton), who, along with countless others, had been killed in the war—a crime "we shall never forgive." Each village along the itinerary had lost young men whose mothers grieved for them. Still, the sports daily hailed Paris-Roubaix as a welcome sign of cycling's "renaissance" after five years of cancellations due to the "appalling events" caused by "the vile *boches*." Beyond its commemorative function, Desgrange argued, the race symbolized renewal and a gradual return to normal for a convalescent nation.[9]

The conditions for the Circuit des Champs de Bataille were even worse. As a result of war-induced shortages, contestants were inadequately supplied with food and other necessities and equipped with tires of poor quality. Fields were flooded, and the roads, where they still existed, were reduced to a muddy mess. Strong winds blew rain, hail, and snow over the ravaged countryside, battering increasingly demoralized racers as they struggled to reach the next *ville-étape*.[10] The race's attrition rate reflected the apocalyptic conditions: of the eighty-seven starters, seventy-one qualified for the second stage, fifty-one for the third. By the sixth stage only twenty-one racers were left. Of these, just thirteen—15 percent of the original *peloton*—made it back to Strasbourg.[11]

Far from seeing in these results a disturbing confirmation of the war-ravaged state of the French people, *Le Petit Journal, L'Auto,* and a major regional paper celebrated the "heroic survivors" as symbolizing national revival through sport. Their coverage emphasized the huge, enthusiastic crowds who turned out to applaud the courageous, persevering racers, especially in the *villes-étapes*, despite the bad weather and the delays it provoked.[12] The public's support of the race in the face of the difficulties of the day was confirmed by the fact that the racers were more often than not housed by local residents.[13] At its conclusion, the organizers described the circuit as a "victory . . . for the French race," for such competitions tested and made the French aware of their energy, inspiring in them an enthusiasm for "useful effort." *L'Auto* congratulated *Le Petit Journal* for the "lesson of energy" it had given the crowds on the very sites where French soldiers, representing Right, had gloriously fought to save the human race.[14]

As counterintuitive as it might seem given the race's severe attrition rate, such optimism was rooted in prewar hopes about the contributions sport might make to the nation. Since the Franco-Prussian war, numerous commentators had identified sport and physical education as the keys to reversing French *dégénérescence*. It is hardly surprising, then, that in the wake of a far more destructive conflict, the French sought evidence of national resurrection in the perseverance, endurance, and courage of athletes, especially those confronted with such frightful conditions. Beyond the regenerative promise attached to sports in general, road races were endowed by commentators with special meaning: their itineraries solemnly commemorated the very land on which so many French soldiers had made the ultimate sacrifice and, by symbolically reclaiming territory once occupied by the enemy, reaffirmed the existence of an eternal France defined by her physical borders. That these borders were themselves anything but eternal, having expanded and contracted over the centuries with the ebb and flow of French power, was conveniently ignored as the French celebrated the expulsion of the Germans from the eastern provinces lost in 1871.

No bicycle race—indeed, no sporting event—has been more intimately associated with French geography and the identities it has shaped than the Tour de France. Some commentators, first and foremost among them *L'Auto,* have portrayed the race's itinerary as an annual pilgrimage into the nation's glorious, if often painful, history. As such, the Tour's function was to cement the national community by stressing the common experiences and territory that bind the French together as one nation. This was particularly true following both world wars. Others, however, have used the Tour's route to offer alternative readings of French history that emphasized division and exclusion. Observers have thus exploited the itinerary to generate multiple, often contradictory visions of the nation and formulate historical narratives that served specific ideological ends. Such efforts were facilitated by the fact that the organizers selected a different itinerary every year and that their inclusion of specific regions and host communities was at times motivated by the desire to make a political statement or recognize a historic event.

That the itinerary of France's national bicycle race should be closely associated with French identity is hardly surprising. Along with a common language, shared traditions, self-government, and a sense of a unique history, a distinct territory constitutes an essential feature of modern nationhood. In France, earlier "tours" had made at least some Frenchmen aware of the land they shared: the French king had toured his kingdom, visiting its borders and symbolically tracing the physical limits of his sovereignty. Although most of his subjects rarely strayed beyond the region of their birth, among those who did travel around France under the ancien régime and well into the nineteenth century were journeymen, members of national associations for artisans in training called *compagnonnages*. These men spent several years completing their professional *tour de France des compagnons,* moving from town to town along a well-established route. At each stop they worked for artisans, perfecting the skills required to be recognized as master artisans and granted the right to open their own workshops by a local craft guild.[15] *L'Auto's* first two Tours actually followed the typical journeymen's circuit, stopping in Paris, Lyon, Marseille, Toulouse, and Nantes.[16] Thereafter, as the organizers lengthened the race, increased the number of host communities, and included the Alps and Pyrenees, the race departed from this route. For some, however, it continued to evoke the workingman's tour: on the eve of World War II, the mayor of Rennes noted that the race reminded him of the three-year *tour de France des compagnons* he had completed as a young man.[17]

By the late nineteenth century the ancien régime and its royal tours had been relegated to French history books, the fantasies of unreconciled monarchists notwithstanding. As industrialization disrupted traditional work patterns, the journeymen's tour gradually became a thing of the past. The idea of a tour of the nation was given new life, however, in the primary-school curriculum under the Third Republic, as the regime sought to defuse the nation's recent legacy of polarization and conflict. Since 1789 the French had experienced three revolutions, three republics, three monarchies, two empires, a directorate, a consulate, and the civil war of 1871. Political instability was fueled by and in turn sparked social unrest, particularly as France industrialized and workers increasingly sought to advance their interests. At the same time, conflict over the role of the Catholic Church in French public life poisoned relations between republicans and socialists on the Left and monarchists, bonapartists, conservative nationalists, and Catholics on the Right. The new republic sought to address these tensions and foster national unity through educational reform. Laws passed in the early 1880s made primary education obligatory for all children and resulted in the massive expansion of the public school system. Each commune now had its public school, whose teachers, trained in the republic's normal schools, not only taught reading, writing, and arithmetic but also introduced students to French history and geography in ways that celebrated the unified national community.

The centerpiece of this republican pedagogy of national unity was an elementary-school textbook called *Le tour de la France par deux enfants*. Adopted in 1877, this text told the story of two orphaned brothers who leave their cherished Lorraine in 1871 after its annexation by the German Reich and embark on a journey throughout France in search of an uncle. They follow the classic itinerary of the journeymen and tour France's frontiers and fortifications before visiting other regions. Along the way, the boys (and French schoolchildren reading about their adventures) learn to appreciate their country's remarkable diversity, which is conveyed by more than two hundred illustrations. They consume local gastronomic specialties and encounter stereotypical inhabitants of France's various regions. Places they do not visit are integrated into the narrative through their exposure to people and artifacts. The textbook treats regional diversity as a gift to a nation in which separatist urges have long evaporated, leaving a united citizenry.

The manual also introduced schoolchildren to French history, if selectively, often through the lives of famous men who had left a positive but politically neutral trace, such as fortifications, on the nation's landscape. The French Revolution of 1789, so divisive a memory for the young republic, was given scant coverage; the regime itself was treated as an idea rather than a historical outcome, presumably because it had hardly been the product of a peaceful, consensual process. On the other hand, the defeat of 1870 and the amputation of the eastern provinces were addressed, no doubt because they were expected to spark uncomplicated feelings of national unity. The role of the Catholic Church was carefully negotiated. If priests, masses, and confessions were conspicuously absent, the boys still visited churches, and people prayed. After the separation of church and state in 1905, even these relatively innocuous references to religion disappeared.

The textbook emphasized France's agricultural, rural, and artisanal identity, neglected its proletarians, and offered examples of solidarity, cooperation, and social cohesion that rendered moot any notion of class conflict. At the conclusion of their travels, Julien and André, an apprentice locksmith, find a home and a job on a farm.[18] The divisions resulting from France's geography and history are thus defused in a transcendent vision of a harmonious, fraternal national community. *Le tour de la France par deux enfants* depicted a country enriched by its regional diversity, strengthened by the unstinting reciprocal commitment of its citizens, and impervious to the siren call of particularism and internecine conflict.

This text was but the most prominent of a whole series of primary-school textbooks, many of them local monographs, designed by the education ministries and schoolteachers of the Third Republic to achieve three essential objectives. In the wake of the defeat of 1870 and emergence of a dominant Germany, the republic's elites sought a rationale for national pride consistent with the assumption that France had a unique, universalist vocation embodied in the republic and the principles of 1789 (liberty, equality, fraternity). The manuals argued therefore that France did more than any nation on earth to provide its inhabitants with everything required for human happiness. Evidence for this proposition was conveyed through a detailed examination of the unparalleled diversity of France's fauna, flora, soils, climates, and topography.

The second objective of these textbooks was to foster patriotism and promote national identity through the celebration of France's distinctive local cultures. Children were introduced to the resources, geography, specialties, and history of their own *petite patrie*. This effort was intended to spark a local patriotism founded on concrete experience that would in turn foster a love of the nation, the *grande patrie*. Children examined the achievements of local "great men" and learned that they had contributed not only to their region's but also to France's glory. They studied local dolmens (the stone monuments of the ancient Gauls), castles, cathedrals, churches, and statues to illustrate broader national developments. The history of the *petite patrie* was linked to national history, even presented as a concentrated version of the latter. Local textbooks evoked the actual moment when a region was attached to the French kingdom as the result of a natural process, sometimes even of an early French patriotism shared by nobles and commoners alike. Adversarial relations between social classes, so important a feature of nineteenth- and early-twentieth-century French history, were excised from this idealized France by representations of the people as a collection of harmonious local communities.

The third aim of these manuals was to emphasize the nation's timeless unity, as epitomized by its traditional peasant identity. The latter accommodated diverse regional stereotypes, each of which reflected the natural environment in their respective *petites patries*. This approach allowed textbooks to present French identity as impervious to the disruptions of recent history and modernity. Not surprisingly, the nation's expanding industrial working class, including the hundreds of thousands of immigrants who came to France during this period, were largely ignored and, in the interwar years, increasingly presented as problematic: untamed industrialization, and the urbanization and rural exodus with which it was associated, challenged the idealized France promoted by the manuals.[19] As evidence mounted of political, economic, and social developments that threatened French unity, the educational establishment of the Third Republic emphasized an increasingly anachronistic image of the nation.

The themes and style of these textbooks were consonant with those of another new genre, tourist guidebooks; one anthology of geographical texts actually included articles taken from publications of the Touring Club de France.[20] Early guidebooks, notably those published by Hachette beginning in the 1850s, were inspired by the development of French railroads, which created a captive market of voyagers along fixed itineraries for information about the communities and countryside through which they were passing. The most famous French guidebook series of the period, the *Guides-Joanne* (which became the *Guides Bleus* in 1910), were designed to "educate and seduce" travelers, who were introduced to French geography and a conservative vision of French history through a series of itineraries that reordered their mental maps of the nation: France became a vast network of intersecting lines that connected neighboring communities to each other and, ultimately, to the nation.[21]

The educators of the Third Republic and the burgeoning French tourism industry were not alone in recognizing the possibilities of a didactic narrative rooted in the nation's geography. *L'Auto*'s journalists had been educated in the very schools where the new republican pedagogy was being implemented; some no doubt had traveled through France with a *Guide-Joanne* stuffed in a pocket. They understood that their own "tour" might serve, and be served by, a similar presentation of France, which would resonate with readers accustomed to seeing France as both a collection of regions and a network of itineraries. From the earliest Tours through 1939, the paper sought to exploit the Tour's itinerary to generate narratives that reconciled diversity with unity, and to promote France to a growing market of potential tourists.

RACERS, CROWDS, AND PLACES: *L'AUTO*'S NARRATIVE OF UNITY IN DIVERSITY, 1903–1939

L'Auto sought to reconcile French unity with diversity through a three-pronged rhetorical strategy. First, the organizers continually emphasized that the race attracted athletes from every corner of France. Over the years they and others implemented a variety of initiatives to ensure that the composition of the Tour's *peloton* lived up to these claims. Second, while celebrating the distinct regional flavor and social diversity of the Tour's crowds, *L'Auto* stressed the unity of communities throughout France as they assembled along the itinerary to await their heroes. Third, the paper described and photographed innumerable sites along the race's route. Emphasizing this shared patrimony allowed *L'Auto* to celebrate an indivisible, timeless French identity and promote the emerging tourism industry.

Fielding racers from all over France was a priority for the organizers from the very first Tour. Each spring, in the weeks leading up to the race, *L'Auto* announced the registration of "provincial" contestants before concluding that "all the regions of France are represented" and assuring fans in the provinces that "their representatives will accomplish prodigies of valor and energy in our Tour de France."[22] The paper's headlines and final list of contestants typically identified the region, department, or city from which "the best children of the provinces" hailed, as the organizers welcomed "the brilliant legion of Northerners" or announced that "the Midi is on the move."[23] Especially during the early Tours, when the single largest group of contestants came from the Paris area, *L'Auto* was determined to counter the impression that the race, like so much of the country's affairs, was dominated by the capital.[24] Even a cursory glance at *L'Auto* in the weeks before the race would convince readers that the Tour de France was a Tour for the whole nation. In 1903 the organizers were so keen to involve provincial contestants, who might have been put off by the Tour's difficulty or the cost of traveling to Paris for the start, that they allowed racers to sign up just for the stage that went through their home region. This was a one-year experiment, perhaps because, as the organizers noted the following year, the race was attracting regional racers even from departments not included in its itinerary.[25]

Beyond its symbolism, a representative field served the financial interests of *L'Auto* and the sport's commercial sponsors. In addition to established national stars, including less prominent racers with a local following from as many regions as possible helped maximize interest in, and press coverage of, the race throughout the country. The organizers promoted the idea of *régionaux de l'étape*—racers from the region visited by a particular stage—and reported that they were often honored in local cafés by their supporters on the evening of their "home" stage.[26] *L'Auto*'s success in assembling a diverse *peloton* for the Tour was not lost on other commentators. Describing the *isolés* in 1911, a regional paper echoed the growing interest in folklore and local traditions that was influencing the primary-school manuals of the day: "Picturesque, humble people, from all occupations and from all corners of the country of France, each one of them brings to this event, as if to a sort of ethnic museum, both the accent and the savory particularities of his province."[27] Meanwhile, *L'Auto,* like the manuals, reinforced this impression by deploying regional stereotypes to describe the racers: Bretons prayed devoutly and crossed themselves at the foot of climbs, southern racers were "loquacious children of the Midi," Flemings were stubborn and silent, Basques intrepid, and Normans clever.[28]

L'Auto's regionalist vocation was supported in the 1920s by provincial newspapers, perhaps confirming the organizers' self-serving claim that there was an unofficial competition between regions to see which could enter the most contestants in the race.[29] Some papers covered the expenses of local racers during the Tour; others collected donations from the public to do so.[30] Such initiatives maximized a newspaper's sales as fans sought to follow the progress of their local hero. By 1926 *L'Auto* was envisaging ways to ensure the regional diversity of the Tour's *peloton.* Two years later, nine regional teams, supported by regional newspapers, were selected to participate, and *L'Auto* catered to their fans by running a regular column, "The Race of the Regional Teams."[31] Regional teams also competed in 1930 and 1939 against the national teams introduced at the beginning of the decade.[32] In 1938 *L'Auto* selected a team of up-and-coming French racers, named the Bleuets, and noted that its members hailed from "almost all the great regions of French cycling"—perhaps to divert attention from the fact that a third of the team came from the Île-de-France region around Paris. When there were no formal regional teams, a variety of qualifying competitions reasserted the importance of regional representation in the 1930s.[33]

By encouraging provincial racers to enter, implementing measures that ensured their participation, downplaying the disproportionate number of contestants from Paris and its suburbs, and relying on regional stereotypes to describe the racers, *L'Auto* did indeed transform the race into an itinerant, national "ethnic museum." Just as French schoolchildren presumably identified with the orphans of *Le tour de la France par deux enfants* as they explored their nation, so *L'Auto*'s readers identified with the participants of its Tour. As a result, French unity was reinforced on two levels. Racers from every corner of France came together to negotiate an itinerary grounded in the national territory, the concrete foundation of French identity. Their fans in turn were united by the common experience of reading *L'Auto*'s accounts of the race, which allowed them to experience vicariously the racers' journey through France.[34]

The Tour's spectators also featured prominently in *L'Auto*'s race coverage, which, as in its profiles of the racers, deployed stereotypes to celebrate regional identities. Bretons were stubborn, religious, and lived in a "Bretagne *bretonnante*," a traditional, Breton-speaking Brittany. Crowds in the Midi were enthusiastic, undisciplined, noisy, exuberant, gay, turbulent, and good-natured. Southern peasants were lazy, lived off the labor of their women, wore sandals, played *boules,* and took their Pernod liqueur twice daily. Basque men wore berets; their tanned young women had large eyes and beautiful white teeth. The villagers of the Arriège in the Pyrenees worked hard in the local mines, quarries, and chemical industry; in their free time they hunted wild boar, fished for trout, and played rugby.[35] Photographs reinforced these stereotypes, showing, for example, a shepherd of the southwestern Landes applauding the racers while perched on his traditional stilts.[36] So did the paper's cartoons: one in 1927 depicted Normans, Bretons, and Basques in traditional garb, a Landais shepherd on his stilts, sporting young *bourgeois* from the wealthy Le Vésinet suburb of Paris, and elegant young *bourgeoises* from Perpignan in the short hairdos and sleek dresses that were all the rage in the roaring twenties.[37] If the tone of such coverage was playful, its content nevertheless sought to educate readers, most of whom were unlikely to travel widely or encounter compatriots from distant regions. In keeping with the general tenor of patriotic discourse under the Third Republic, *L'Auto* treated the regional particularism of the Tour's crowds as quaint, picturesque, and interesting. In this way, too, the race's itinerary exposed the French to their cultural diversity.

L'Auto depicted the Tour's spectators as socially diverse but united by their passion for the race:[38] "We had never seen such a crowd," the organizers claimed in 1930. "Factories, schools, barracks, seminaries, to name but a few! Everyone had the day off. The customs officials and the gendarmes, the lumberjacks and the shepherdesses, the priests and the Capuchins, the workers and the pretty girls . . ."[39] In 1932, at the Tourmalet peak in the Pyrenees, *L'Auto* noted that "the crowd at the summit is as heterogeneous as could be: elegant, dressed-up young women who had arrived in sedans; athletic gentlemen in knickerbockers pretending to be great voyagers; inhabitants of the region in Basque berets and leather cardigans; motorcyclists, . . . and finally bicyclists in sweaters and golf britches."[40]

Songs about the Tour from the late 1920s through the 1930s reinforced the image of united communities celebrating the racers' passage. In the 1930s the organizers commissioned songs for the race, often organizing competitions to select the official Tour anthem. The songs were then played over loudspeakers or by accordionists in the *caravane publicitaire* as it traveled along the route.[41] Their lyrics made numerous references to giddy, diverse crowds assembling along the itinerary, admiring, applauding and cheering their heroes: "And starting at dawn the crowd runs to the roadside to hail the lads of the Tour: . . . the girl from the tobacconist's, the firemen, the [municipal] councilors, and the road menders."[42] The songs were often set in idealized small communities whose entire population took a break from its routine to watch the race go by.[43] One even described a parish priest who was late for a wedding because he had gone to bless the Tour racers as they sped through his village.[44]

Such depictions of crowds and communities implicitly erased social, political, and religious conflicts. Their quarrels magically forgotten, workers and their bourgeois employers united in admiration of the "giants of the road."[45] At Sedan in 1906, *L'Auto* noted that "civilians, military men, everyone is on the bridge." Occurring in the aftermath of the Dreyfus affair, which had tarnished the army's public image, and in the city where Napoleon III had surrendered in 1870, this scene symbolically reconciled the nation with its twice-compromised army.[46] *L'Auto*'s description of workers and soldiers pressed together to watch the Charleville-Dunkerque stage in 1927 implicitly refuted the cliché of troops violently repressing labor unrest in France's industrial north.[47] The divisive confrontation between the republic and the Catholic Church, which led to the separation of church and state in 1905, was defused by *L'Auto*'s descriptions of parish priests and public schoolteachers sharing the same stretch of road as they awaited the racers.[48] In Brest, in Catholic Brittany, *L'Auto* observed that both public and parochial schoolteachers had brought their students to see the end of a stage.[49]

The organizers' thesis was clear. The Tour attracted a representative sample of the French population who reflected both the nation's diversity and its fundamental cohesion. Desgrange himself defined the Tour as "the reunion over thousands of kilometers, in a single act of encouragement and applause" of all casts and classes—proletarians, peasants, bourgeois, and nobles. For *L'Auto,* the simple act of attending the race was an expression of unity, while the united communities it described were microcosms of, and models for, a diverse nation.[50]

Like the primary-school manuals, *L'Auto*'s Tour coverage evoked the rich geographical, historical, and cultural patrimony on which France's universalist vocation and its people's happiness were founded: "The Tour de France is a month-long parade of adorable skies, wonderful countrysides, provincial costumes; it's the music of accents, *patois*, colors. It's the ever-renewed tableau of immense horizons or of alpine or Pyrenean walls of rock, of all the riches of our ancient soil, of all our wines, of all our fruits, of all our dairy products, of all our herds, of all our peaceful villages, of our tumultuous cities, of our cathedrals kneeling in the distance in their robes of stone, of our Roman arenas, of our dolmens, of our belfries."[51]

The paper turned the race's itinerary into an annual lesson in French geography, featuring maps, topographical profiles, and detailed schedules of the racers' expected times of arrival in communities along the itinerary. Readers were exposed to a barrage of geographical information, including the altitudes of mountains, distances between major cities and towns, and the administrative division of the national territory into departments.[52] Maps and topographical profiles of specific stages closely resembled those of the *Guides-Joanne* (and later of the *Guides Bleus*), which became more lavishly illustrated with maps during this period.[53] Within a few years of the race's creation, *L'Auto* and other entrepreneurs were selling maps of the Tour's itinerary to fans.[54] Occasionally, *L'Auto*'s maps were humorous, caricaturing the regions visited by the Tour; others included drawings of typical local scenes. Such initiatives combined geography with cultural information that exposed fans to France's diverse heritage.[55]

In keeping with their didacticism, the organizers frequently provided examples of how teachers and their students put the race to educational use. The itinerary became a subject, a pedagogical methodology, and—when the students actually watched the racers shoot by—a temporary classroom.[56] This resulted in powerful images of youthful patriotism, as when some fifty six- and seven-year-olds stood outside their school waving tiny French flags in honor of the Tour.[57] In 1923 *La revue de l'enseignement primaire et primaire supérieur,* a professional journal for primary-school teachers, published an article describing the Tour de France as a lesson in hygiene, geography, and willpower, combining the moral (cleanliness, determination) with the educational (geography).[58] On a less serious note, *L'Auto*'s cartoons poked fun at the unintended consequences of such initiatives, parodying the classroom refrains of French schoolchildren—"France is divided into eighty-six departments and fifteen stages"—and noting that, when asked where Dinan was located, a student responded: "In the fourth stage, sir."[59] A humorous piece in 1934 imagined a student excelling on an oral examination about the artisan's tour de France by drawing on an understanding of national geography gained from press coverage of the race.[60]

One corporate sponsor sought to exploit the Tour's educational dimension. In 1937 and 1938 the Byrrh aperitif company sponsored a bus from which deserving high-school students followed several stages of the race and wrote essays about the Tour. These were published in *L'Auto,* which noted that the students had observed the diverse composition of the race's crowds.[61] In 1938 the Tour received further validation of its pedagogical worth when the Minister of Education Jean Zay toured an exhibit of mural paintings, including one of the Tour de France, that the government had ordered for the nation's schools.[62]

From the very first Tour, *L'Auto* combined its pedagogical vocation with the promotion of French tourism, embellishing its race coverage with lyrical descriptions of sites encountered along the itinerary. Such passages faithfully reproduced the style of contemporary primary-school manuals and the new *guides touristiques,* as in this first-person narrative from 1903: "I found La Rochelle, her old towers and her thick walls guarding the tranquil port where the fishing boats sleep with their pink and white sails tinged with gold by the sun, which was already rising over the unruffled mirror of the Atlantic."[63] Imitating publications like the monthly magazine of the Touring Club de France and *Sites et Monuments,* and complementing the expanding postcard industry, *L'Auto* illustrated its descriptions with countless photographs of forts, fountains, castles, bell towers, statues, churches, cathedrals, dams, bridges, city gates, clock towers, theaters, medical schools, squares, viaducts, bullfighting arenas, and government buildings such as city halls and court houses.[64] Such coverage encouraged affluent readers to travel and provided a vicarious journey to those of more limited means.

The organizers invited their readers to experience with the racers their admittedly "tough tourism." According to Desgrange, the less talented racers in particular had the "souls of tourists" and took great pleasure in the "charms of this enormous panorama of six thousand kilometers that unfolds before them," as they explored a "beautiful and rich and sweet-smelling" France in all its agricultural, viticultural, climatic, and topographical diversity: "The racers . . . notice . . . , like tourists, the perpetual changes of nature, the accents that change, the skies that change under different climates . . . all things that make the kilometers lighter."[65] The contestants, most of whom were from the lower classes, were the unlikeliest of tourists; still, their example was to be followed by anyone wishing to appreciate the beauty and variety of France.[66] In the interwar years, newspapers, tourist agencies, and railroad companies offered special deals and a variety of Tour de France travel packages for fans.[67] In the 1930s the race also promoted tourism through the annual *film du Tour,* which was shown in hundreds of French movie theaters at the race's conclusion and, according to *L'Auto,* included "sites of a rare beauty."[68]

Industrial modernity posed a grave threat to these sites. *L'Auto* addressed this issue, particularly after World War I. Occasionally, the paper's coverage was positive: industrial development in Mulhouse had been carefully controlled to avoid an aesthetic affront, as demonstrated by the recently constructed individual housing for workers. More often, *L'Auto* deplored the ecological and aesthetic impact of industrialization, complaining in 1928, for example, that in Évian "factories, whose soul is hydroelectric power, stain the countryside with a dirty note of brutal and realistic modernism." Four years later, provoked by a partial view of the Briey industrial basin, *L'Auto* exclaimed: "God! How sad these rich regions are. Is this monotonous [countryside] of factories, chimneys, or wheat fields the ransom [to be paid] for wealth? The shepherd, in his mountainside pastures, is less comfortable, less endowed with material goods, but he has all the luxury of nature and of scenery that the Alps compose for him alone."[69]

During the race's early years *L'Auto,* like the primary-school textbooks, emphasized a traditional France of ancient cities and bucolic countrysides. As the century advanced, the sports daily, again like the manuals, exposed a new, ugly, industrializing France that challenged the nation's conventional image as a rural society of small agricultural and artisanal producers. *L'Auto* was in an ambiguous position. Launched by automobile and cycle manufacturers who epitomized modern industry, mass production, and consumer society, the paper celebrated the bicycle's modernity as a vector of progress. Yet, as the organizer of many outdoor sporting events, none more celebrated than the Tour, *L'Auto* had an interest in defending a pristine and eternal rural France from the ravages of industrial modernity.

L'Auto's Tour coverage clearly extended beyond the racers' exploits. Influenced by the Third Republic's educational policies and the beginnings of modern tourism, the organizers recognized that an effective way of marketing the race was to use its itinerary as the basis for a selective lesson in

French *histoire-géo.* This was never more evident than when France reappropriated Alsace-Lorraine after World War I.

RESURRECTION, COMMEMORATION, AND HOPE: *L'AUTO*, THE TOUR, AND ALSACE-LORRAINE

On 10 May 1871, the newly constituted German Reich and its defeated neighbor signed the Treaty of Frankfurt, according to which France agreed to Germany's annexation of her eastern provinces: Alsace, much of whose population spoke a German dialect, and half of Lorraine.[70] Even before the treaty was finalized, elected representatives of the two provinces issued the "declaration of Bordeaux," in which they tied French regeneration to the future recovery of Alsace-Lorraine. In the decades that followed, the French ignored their own incremental, haphazard acquisition of the border provinces, as well as the cultural factors that made Alsace as German as it was French, and transformed the "lost provinces" into potent symbols of a national unity that only a successful *revanche* against Germany could restore.[71]

France's obsession with Alsace-Lorraine took many forms. While generally not endorsing a military solution, teachers used classroom maps, reading assignments, and exercises in a number of disciplines to remind their pupils of the injustice done to France. The *Guides-Joanne* devoted increasing attention to the sieges and battles of the Franco-Prussian War, and to the museums, ossuaries, and monuments commemorating them. *Images d'Épinal* (popular, mass-produced drawings of "authentic" French scenes), novels, songs, and poems of the period also kept alive the memory of the "lost provinces." The passion elicited by their amputation was fueled by the mystical nationalism of the day, according to which a nation was defined by *la terre et les morts* (its land and ancestors) and by the widespread assumption that France's political borders should conform to the self-evident boundaries Nature had provided. Because France's "natural frontier" to the east was the Rhine, the nation required the reattachment of Lorraine and Alsace.[72] The territorial loss of 1871 was thus a painful reminder not only of a military debacle and the erosion of France's position among the European great powers but also of the nation's unfulfilled geographic destiny.

Understanding the psychological impact of including the lost provinces in the Tour itinerary, from 1906 through 1910 *L'Auto* persuaded the German authorities to allow the race to pass through Alsace-Lorraine. Thereafter, with tensions mounting between the two countries, the Germans refused. Sensibly, given its dependence on German goodwill during this five-year period, *L'Auto* expounded on the political neutrality of great sporting events. Yet even while claiming to be "unmotivated by any political thought" and asserting that "sport has no fatherland," *L'Auto* observed that posters in Alsace-Lorraine announcing the Tour's arrival were the first since 1870 composed exclusively in French. One even heard the "Marseillaise" as the racers passed through the annexed provinces.[73]

The display of French symbols in Alsace-Lorraine during the Tour did not always go over well. In Metz, a policeman confiscated a Luxembourg flag from children on the indignant insistence of a doctor who had mistaken it for the French flag. Meanwhile, the Germans forbade cars carrying race officials and support staff to fly the tricolor. Still, *L'Auto* trumpeted the racers' triumphant entry into the city in 1907. By 1910, however, the organizers were conceding that the Tour's visit evoked painful historical memories: Metz was "a city, yesterday still French, but which is being Germanized little by little, thanks to the stubborn and patient efforts of her conquerors."[74] No doubt to drive home this point, high-ranking German civilian and military officials, including the governor of Alsace-Lorraine, attended stage finishes in the annexed provinces. If in 1911 *L'Auto* still remembered the "sincere enthusiasm" with which inhabitants of Metz had greeted the Tour, the following year it observed how much more enthusiastically the racers were welcomed in Longwy, where "we are in France and truly in France."[75] Confronted with a political reality it could not alter, *L'Auto*'s symbolic reappropriation of the "lost provinces" had failed.

The outbreak of war in early August 1914 reignited the Tour itinerary's symbolic charge. Just days into the conflict, a French soldier wrote *L'Auto*, suggesting that the 1915 Tour go through Metz and Strasbourg. Recalling the Tour's passage through Alsace-Lorraine as painful confirmation of illegitimate German authority over French territory, Desgrange responded that such an itinerary would depend on the soldier and his mates. It was not until the summer of 1919, when the Tour's start coincided with the popular celebration of the signing of the Treaty of Versailles, that the organizers were able to grant this wish.[76]

On the eve of the first postwar Tour, *L'Auto* commemorated "the dear ones the *Boches* have taken from our affections" and celebrated the example of moral and physical regeneration provided to the French as "a new generation of great and handsome athletes" reconnected with one of the "traditions interrupted by the dirty *Boches*." Evoking "the France of tomorrow, daring, energetic, willful, and healthy" that "the most beautiful of crusades" would help to build,[77] *L'Auto* designed the 1919 itinerary to symbolize France's territorial reunification: "Strasbourg! Metz! And it is not a dream! We are going there, *chez nous*. We shall see, from Belfort to Hagenau, the entire blue line of the Vosges. . . . We shall go along the Rhine. . . . With Strasbourg and Metz our ambitions are satisfied; the Tour de France is complete."[78]

As the Tour entered the eastern provinces, *L'Auto* combined somber commemoration with triumphalism and hope, describing the disastrous condition of the "devastated regions" and exulting in the presence of "repugnant" German prisoners along the itinerary. The Geneva-Strasbourg stage was "the day of glory," a phrase lifted from the opening line of the French national anthem.[79] Strasbourg-Metz was "the stage of memory," "the stage of victory," and "the stage of glory" that symbolized the "triumph of French muscle, of French will, of French rage over *boche* barbarism." In Metz the finish was staged in front of a model of a proposed monument in honor of the French soldiers who had liberated the city; in Strasbourg, in front of a new statue of a French infantryman.[80] Subsequent Tours made a point of going through Alsace and Lorraine, and *L'Auto* continued to evoke "the reconquered provinces," link the war of 1870 to that of 1914–18, and commemorate the French soldiers whose graves dotted the fields of northeastern France.[81]

L'Auto's use of the Tour's itinerary to honor the sacrifices of so many French soldiers reflected a broader commemorative movement. Faced with a tragedy of unprecedented scale that had touched virtually every family, the French felt the need to inscribe their collective mourning in public ritual and iconography. The aftermath of the Franco-Prussian War had seen the erection of relatively few, privately funded war memorials in cemeteries, battlefields, and the hometowns of fallen soldiers—a commemoration situated in large measure in the war zone rather than across the country. In contrast, in the years following World War I, the French erected thirty-eight thousand *monuments aux morts,* whose design and construction were supervised, partially funded, and officially recognized by the state. Most of the memorials were erected not in cemeteries but at the village entrances, in squares or parks, or in front of churches, schools, or town halls. Each monument listed the community's war dead. If the community could afford it, the monument included a statue, often of a realistically carved French infantryman, sometimes victorious but more often on guard, injured, or dying. The memorials became the destination of somber Armistice Day rituals. Consistent with the overwhelming sense of loss that the war inspired and the expressed wish of veterans' associations, the parades, speeches, and ceremonies were devoid of military triumphalism. Instead, they stressed the horrific cost of victory, honored the sacrifices of the dead and the surviving veterans, and celebrated the end of the mass slaughter. Schoolchildren participated by laying flowers at the monument, reciting a poem (often Victor Hugo's "Hymn to the Dead"), and uttering the refrain "died for the fatherland" after each name in the roll call of fallen local soldiers. Their involvement in honoring the republic's dead patriots was intended to initiate them into the national community, whose future they represented.[82]

Postwar Tours, according to the organizers, fulfilled several important functions. By reminding the French of prewar days, this free, joyous form of popular festivity allowed them to begin to put the war behind them, easing their return to "normal." Evidence of reconstruction along the itinerary reinforced *L'Auto*'s message of French regeneration, symbolized by the athletes who took on this great challenge.[83] Above all, the itinerary symbolically reattached the "lost provinces" to France and inspired the morally necessary evocation of the tragic recent past with its legacy of suffering and sacrifice.

Given the extent to which *L'Auto* and others celebrated the Tour's reappropriation of Alsace-Lorraine, it is ironic that the organizers' relationship with the Strasbourg municipal government had soured so badly by the late 1920s that, after stopping in the city nine times between 1919 and 1929, the race bypassed it for the rest of the interwar period, except in 1932 and 1938. The Strasbourgeois had enthusiastically welcomed the return of the Tour in 1919 as they celebrated their liberation from German occupation and reattachment to France, but the city's subsequent refusal to guarantee the organizers large subventions and crowd control caused growing tensions. For some Strasbourgeois, the conflict pitting the powerful Parisian sports daily against their city epitomized their postwar treatment by the French government: in its determination to assimilate a province that had been under German control since 1871 and had a long history of cultural and political autonomy, the government implemented policies that so alienated Alsatians that an autonomist movement emerged; by the late 1920s it enjoyed significant electoral success. In the 1930s Alsatians resented the Tour organizers' insensitivity to their cultural specificity, which appeared to mirror the attitude of the republic, and the German-language press criticized the race as a chauvinistic exercise organized by distant Parisians who discriminated against the province's German speakers.[84] As Bretons and communists in the 1930s would confirm, *L'Auto*'s attempt to assert a master narrative of national unity through the Tour's itinerary sometimes met with resistance and inspired counternarratives of exclusion and division.

BRETON AND COMMUNIST COUNTERNARRATIVES IN THE 1930S

Given *L'Auto*'s depiction of the Tour as symbolizing and reinforcing French unity, communities repeatedly left off the race's itinerary sometimes came to interpret this neglect as evidence of their marginal standing within or even exclusion from the nation. This was even more likely if they were located in a geographically peripheral, once-independent state with a distinct cultural identity, a national reputation for backwardness, and a recent history of regionalist, autonomist, and nationalist movements. Such was the case in Brittany in the 1930s.

Long an independent duchy, Brittany had maintained considerable sovereignty over its internal affairs after its attachment to the French kingdom in 1532. During the French Revolution, however, the National Assembly not only abolished the autonomy, rights, and privileges Brittany had enjoyed for some two and half centuries but actually erased it from the new administrative map of France, dividing the province into five departments. Tension between Brittany and the revolutionary government mounted in the early 1790s over the Civil Constitution of the Clergy (which drastically curtailed the Catholic Church's authority), the military draft, and political centralization. A decade-long peasant insurrection in Brittany and other western regions was brutally repressed by the central government. In the wake of the Revolution and the Napoleonic era, Bretons had gained a national reputation as backward, conservative, Catholic, and counterrevolutionary.[85]

Nineteenth-century developments reinforced this reputation. Susceptibility to disease and adult mortality in Brittany were well above the national average. Its population was comparatively rural: by the late nineteenth century, when only 23 percent of Bretons worked in industry (much of it traditional), peasants were increasingly perceived as "savages" who needed to be "civilized," a view confirmed by *L'Auto's* references to the Tour as a "modernizing crusade." The province remained a conservative, Catholic bastion, confirming its backwardness, at least for the resolutely anticlerical Third Republic. This tension extended to the world of sport: both the clergy, through its *patronages,* and republicans founded soccer clubs in their attempts to rally Breton youth to their respective causes. After World War I the influence of the church remained strong: almost half of Breton children attended private Catholic primary schools. Despite the Republic's prohibition against its use in schools, on the eve of World War I the Breton language was still spoken by one and a half million people, and an attempt had been made to harmonize three of its four dialects. After the war, however, the erosion of Breton accelerated. Meanwhile, Brittany's infrastructure remained among the most underdeveloped in France, and insufficient employment opportunities led some 215,000 Bretons to leave the region during the first postwar decade. Adding insult to injury, Breton railroad concessions, industries, banks, and even the local tourist industry were increasingly owned or controlled by external interests, both French and foreign. During the economic crisis of the early 1930s, Brittany's difficulties were exacerbated by the French government's emphasis on protecting the great industries in northern and eastern France and around Paris. The exodus continued, averaging twenty thousand Bretons a year between 1932 and 1939.[86]

In light of Brittany's history and culture, it is hardly surprising that various groups sought to exploit the notion of a distinct Breton identity to advance their interests and promote their vision of the province's future. Breton nobility and clergy defended Breton language and identity in their attempt to resist the cultural imperialism of the French state, liberalism, anticlericalism, and Protestantism—or, as one bishop put it in 1846, the threat of "modern civilization" to the "religious character" of the Bretons. Cultural associations promoted Breton culture and history and sought to thwart the hegemonic linguistic policies of the Third Republic, which was determined to undermine the influence of Breton-speaking clergy. Historians of the province evoked an alleged Breton nationalism to counter the assimilationist thrust of French nationalism. At the turn of the century, Bretons concerned with the leftward tilt of the Republic founded regionalist political organizations that, while not questioning Brittany's attachment to France, favored a more decentralized arrangement. Meanwhile, the National Breton Party demanded the right to self-determination for Brittany, arguing that its language and history proved that it was a distinct nation. Largely the affair of conservative religious, economic, and social elites, these movements did not engage the masses and failed to achieve any significant gains.[87]

Spurred by the war's disproportionately heavy toll on the province's population (estimated at 12 percent of total French war fatalities), Breton autonomism emerged in the early 1920s, culminating in 1927 with the foundation of the Breton Autonomist Party. Autonomists emphasized Brittany's history as a once-independent duchy whose attachment to France had never been intended to jeopardize its internal autonomy, and they demanded a Breton parliamentary government within a federal system. Unable to attract sufficient support to remain viable, in 1931 the autonomist movement collapsed, splitting into the Federalist League of Brittany and the more extreme Breton Nationalist Party. On the four-hundredth anniversary of the 1532 treaty, terrorists affiliated with the latter blew up a statue at the Rennes City Hall of a female Brittany kneeling before the King of France. This act was generally condemned by the regional press, although *Le Nouvelliste de Bretagne* noted that many Bretons had criticized the statue for depicting their province in a humiliating pose. Meanwhile, cultural initiatives galvanized Bretons in the 1930s. By 1939 the general councils of all five departments and a majority of communes in Brittany were demanding that Breton be taught in their schools. As Bretons sought to salvage their athletic heritage, some traditional sports were able, at least temporarily, to survive the erosion of rural traditions and competition from new sports and modern entertainment. Ultimately, they too declined, increasingly eclipsed by gymnastics and marksmanship clubs and new sports, notably cycling.[88]

Some of France's earliest cycling clubs were founded in Brittany, where bicycle races, often grafted onto religious celebrations, soon became popular. The first long-distance intercity road race, Paris-Brest-Paris, linked the French capital to the tip of the Breton peninsula in 1891. Other such races—Paris-Nantes (1924) and Paris-Rennes (1927)—followed, as did important competitions confined to Breton territory, including the Circuit de l'Ouest (1931), which attracted regional, national, and foreign stars. By the 1920s Brittany also had a significant number of velodromes, which drew large crowds. The province produced stars, including the record-setting Corentin Corre in the 1890s and Lucien Mazan, the Tour winner in 1907 and 1908, who, though raised in Argentina, was widely known as Petit-Breton. In the late 1920s and throughout the 1930s, Breton racers, such as the professional French road-racing champions Ferdinand Le Drogo and René Le Grévès, were among the sport's elite. Several were selected for the French national Tour teams, including Le Grévès, who won sixteen stages.[89] Breton papers covered the performances of local racers in the Tour with columns devoted to "our Bretons," reported on receptions and races organized in their honor, and invited readers to celebrate their achievements, determination, and attachment to Breton language and traditions.[90]

Two major Breton cities hosted Tour stages under the Third Republic: Brest, situated at the western point of the peninsula, and Rennes, the provincial capital, located further inland, where Brittany merges with the rest of the nation. Brest had been a regular *ville-étape* since the early Tours, hosting stages from 1906 through 1914 and 1919 through 1931, and again in 1939. When, during the race's early years, the organizers wished to follow the nation's contours and introduce the bicycle to backward, rural areas, the city's location had made it an obvious choice.[91] Rennes, however, was a different story: after hosting a stage in 1905, it was not selected as a *ville-étape* again until 1933, and then again in 1937 and 1939. By the mid-1930s the local press was expressing exasperation and resentment at this discrimination. In so doing, Breton commentators deployed *L'Auto*'s longstanding emphasis on the unifying and pedagogical functions of the Tour's itinerary against the organizers.

Invoking the symbolic role of the itinerary in tracing France's periphery, *La Province* noted that the 1933 Tour had followed France's frontiers in the Alps and Pyrenees as well as its Mediterranean coastline, but had avoided its western and northern coastlines. The race's timid incursion into Brittany for the Rennes stage hardly seemed to count. Four years later, the paper wondered why the organizers had selected Geneva, but not Brest, as a *ville-étape:* "We ask simply that the Tour de France do the tour of France."[92] On learning in 1935 of Rennes's inclusion in the 1937 itinerary, *La Bretagne Sportive* observed sarcastically that "Brittany will become French again, as far as the Tour de France is concerned, but not before 1937."[93] The Breton sports paper evoked the primary-school geography lessons that defined France as "an immense territory that stretched from the limits of Germany to the Ocean's shore" and noted that as children Bretons had read enthusiastically of racers completing "an immense circuit baptized 'Tour de France.'" Recently, however, their "poor province" had been "mercilessly" excised from *L'Auto*'s "sportive map of France," to the point that a father who planned to use the Tour to teach his children French geography could not include Brittany in his lessons.[94]

La Bretagne Sportive also gave *L'Auto* a lesson in regional geography. Contesting the organizers' claim that they bypassed Brittany because its flat terrain made for boring racing, the paper observed that the province was in fact full of steep inclines, which explained why it had produced so many good climbers. The province was "a breeding ground for cyclists," many of whom distinguished themselves in the Tour. All these factors further justified its inclusion in the itinerary.[95] *La Bretagne Sportive* even turned Bretons' reputation for separatism on its head, describing Brittany's prolonged exclusion from the Tour's itinerary as "a flagrant case of French separatism" and urging *L'Auto* to reconsider its neglect of the province, which gave ammunition to Breton autonomists.[96] Venting its own sportive separatism, the local sports paper concluded that "since M. Desgrange neglects Brittany, Brittany must neglect him," and proposed the creation of a Tour of Brittany that would pit Breton racers against the best European teams.[97] Meanwhile, Breton papers dismissed the Tour as a commercial venture and suggested that *L'Auto* had in fact been avoiding Brittany largely because it received better financial offers from velodromes, sports clubs, and cities in other regions.[98]

The timing of Bretons' criticism of the Tour organizers was curious.[99] After avoiding Rennes for almost three decades, *L'Auto* selected the city as a *ville-étape* three times between 1933 and 1939. The larger context suggests an explanation. Accusing the organizers of neglecting Brittany for crass commercial reasons allowed Breton papers to reflect widespread public anxiety about the province's problematic relationship with the rest of the nation, specifically its difficult assimilation and reputation for backwardness under the Third Republic. Unemployment and infrastructural underdevelopment, external ownership of Breton businesses, demographic exodus, and the erosion of traditional practices all pointed to a region in crisis. Although they were electorally insignificant, autonomist and nationalist movements focused public attention on Breton identity and Brittany's place in the French nation, at times through symbolic acts of terrorism. So did more popular cultural initiatives, such as demands to have Breton taught in schools. The Tour's popularity in Brittany, its status as a national institution, and the symbolism of its itinerary made the race a particularly effective device for communicating a range of grievances about Brittany's unsatisfactory and sometimes demeaning treatment by the nation. Thus, Breton commentators noted the irony that a region so rich in great racers was neglected by the national competition those athletes served so well. They proposed a regional Tour pitting Breton racers against European (rather than French) teams, not out of some reflexive autonomism but to highlight the disjunction between the Republic's and *L'Auto*'s geography lessons and the incomplete, exclusionary nation traced by recent editions of the Tour. Exploiting the symbolism of the Tour's itinerary, Breton commentators challenged the organizers, and by implication the Republic, to be true to their rhetoric of unity.

The French communists, too, used the Tour's itinerary in ways that contradicted *L'Auto*'s portrayal of a unified nation. In its coverage of the 1935 race, their official organ, *L'Humanité,* ran a regular column, "Following the Tour: Struggles of Yesterday and Today," which exposed cases of class conflict and exploitation, going back centuries, in sites along the itinerary.[100] *L'Humanité*'s coverage also addressed contemporary issues. On the Riviera these included high milk prices, the activities of Italian Fascists, the impact of the economic crisis on small businesses and hotels, the struggles of the local proletariat, and increases in the membership and electorate of the French Communist Party (PCF). In western France, *L'Humanité* evoked the region's past as a hotbed of royalist and Catholic reaction during the Revolution, only to congratulate peasants in Brittany and Vendée for participating in recent antifascist demonstrations. Countering *L'Auto*'s crowd descriptions, *L'Humanité* described the "grandiose welcome" its representatives received from the "red suburbs" around Paris.[101]

Far from uniting social classes in common admiration of the Tour's racers, the itinerary provided communists with an opportunity to expose the urban segregation, political polarization, and social inequalities generated by capitalism. For example, *L'Humanité* blamed the 1907 revolt of vineyard workers and small and medium-sized wineries in the southwest on plummeting wine prices resulting from overproduction and fraud by bigger producers. The latter had maximized profits at the expense of quality and the "appalling misery" of smaller producers. The lesson of 1907 for the current economic and political crisis was clear: "Agricultural workers, small and medium wine producers, assisted by the Communist Party, will know how to unite with urban workers against the big proprietors and the capitalists, against the bourgeois state, against the Laval government and the fascist leagues that support it and are supported by it. They shall reinforce the popular front."[102]

The communist exploitation of the Tour's itinerary in 1935 reflected recent developments, both domestic and international. Even as it stressed class conflict, *L'Humanité* reached out beyond its traditional proletarian constituency by broadening its definition of capitalism's victims to include agricultural laborers and small entrepreneurs, who had in fact been hit particularly hard by the economic crisis of the 1930s. This tactical shift was also driven by Hitler's rise to power and the brutal liquidation of the German Communist Party in early 1933, and the unsuccessful attempt by antiparliamentary *ligues* on the French far Right to overthrow the Third Republic a year later. In response to this threat to democracy, and in keeping with the will of their base and orders from Moscow, the PCF adopted the new "popular front" strategy of international Communism: French communists, socialists, and other democratic forces now coalesced in defense of the republic against the various imitators of Nazism and fascism in France, who, according to *L'Humanité*'s analysis, served the interests of big capitalists and the conservative governments under their sway.[103] As a result, in 1935 the PCF exploited the Tour to offer a reading of French history and a vision of contemporary France radically different from those of *L'Auto* and the Republic's public schools. The united, harmonious national community of a traditional, rural France was replaced by a polarized society, in which progressive political forces sought to protect capitalism's diverse victims from big business and its fascist minions.

WORLD WAR II AND THE TOUR

The outbreak of hostilities a few weeks after the end of the 1939 Tour prevented the race from being held again until 1947. In early May 1940, Germany invaded France and swept to a rapid victory. On 22 June, having been granted "full powers" by a demoralized parliament, the World War I hero Marshal Philippe Pétain signed an armistice with the victors. In its wake was born the collaborationist Vichy regime, which Pétain led during the four years that followed. The Germans granted Vichy authority over much of central and southern France while directly administering the northern half, including Paris, and the Channel and Atlantic coastlines. This arrangement lasted until November 1942, when the Allied landing in North Africa led Germany to occupy all of France in order to defend its Mediterranean coastline, which now lay exposed. Thereafter, the Vichy regime continued to collaborate with the Nazis, helping them to govern France, combating Resistance cells, rounding up Jews for deportation to death camps, and providing the German war machine with equipment, raw materials, and workers. Many French who refused to accept the German victory as final or the Vichy regime as legitimate organized resistance movements, which were ultimately united under General Charles de Gaulle.

For the French, World War II was thus a far more ambiguous experience than World War I. In the summer of 1940 a long-simmering civil war between partisans and opponents of parliamentary democracy came to a boil—a far cry from the much-celebrated, if increasingly strained, Union Sacrée of the previous war. Total defeat offered Pétain and his circle a chance to remake France according to their conservative, authoritarian, and ruralist vision. They replaced the republican regime and its democratic principles, which they held responsible for the divisions and disorders of recent French history, with a new slogan—"Work, family, fatherland"—and a "national revolution" designed to resurrect a corporatist, hierarchical, and Catholic society presumably devoid of conflict.[104]

Although the Tour was not held during the war, it continued to play a symbolic role for its organizers, Vichy, and the Germans. Less than three weeks before the armistice, with the German invasion well under way, Henri Desgrange proposed holding a week-long Tour de France around the capital, along a star-shaped itinerary that reached out to the provinces in a poignant evocation of national unity. Once established, the Vichy regime initially refused to allow L'Auto to organize the Tour: the race's internationalism, commercialism, and professional racers were incompatible with the amateur mass sport the regime was intent on promoting to improve the nation's physical and moral condition and to teach French youth respect for authority, team spirit, and the subordination of the individual to the national interest. In addition, both the Germans and Vichy were unwilling to set aside the gasoline and equipment required to hold the race, whose running would have been further complicated by the demarcation line between the occupied and Vichy zones.[105]

Jacques Goddet, who succeeded Desgrange upon his death in August 1940, initially favored holding the race. He argued that the Tour would contribute to France's economic revival by promoting the French cycle industry, which provided jobs for thousands of workers. Evoking the schoolchildren and teachers who had flocked to the itinerary in happier times, Goddet reminded his readers that the race was a lesson in heroism, constancy, and effort. At the same time, suspicious of the uses to which the Germans and Vichy wished to put French sport and determined to maintain *L'Auto*'s independence, he argued that sport and the sports press must remain politically neutral. *L'Auto*'s staff therefore avoided dealing with or sought to obstruct German propaganda and sports officials as well as Vichy's Commissariat Général à l'Éducation Générale et Sportive, with whom Goddet had numerous conflicts.[106]

In the years that followed, although he sometimes lamented the Tour's absence, Goddet limited *L'Auto* to the organization of smaller, much less expensive events that would not drain valuable resources from a nation confronting significant shortages. Sensitive to the propaganda value of France's most popular sporting event, he understood that organizing the Tour would require authorizations, favors, and material support from the Germans and Vichy and thus lead to unacceptable compromises. In 1941 the German-run *Paris-Soir* attempted to pressure *L'Auto* into coorganizing the Tour, but Goddet managed to scuttle the project. The following year, aware that its popularity was collapsing in the wake of its decision to send French workers to Germany in exchange for French prisoners of war, Vichy sought to resurrect the Tour. Hoping that the revival of this French tradition would convey the impression that life in wartime France was normal and peaceful, the Germans were now prepared to provide the organizers with the necessary equipment, food, vehicles, and fuel, as well as to facilitate the race's passage between the occupied and unoccupied zones. Again Goddet came under pressure to organize the race, this time in tandem with the collaborationist *La France Socialiste*. Again he refused.[107]

Undeterred, in the fall of 1942 *La France Socialiste* went ahead with its own race, Le Circuit de France, a six-stage, 1,650-kilometer competition held in both zones. Both the organizers and the regime they served sought to exploit the Circuit to promote a vision of France consistent with Vichy's national revolution, Franco-German collaboration, and the prospect of an Axis victory that would give birth to a new order.[108] The itinerary's symbolic unification of France was appreciated by no less a figure than Pierre Laval, then head of the Vichy government, who described the race as a "national" event—by inference, one that might fulfill the symbolic role *L'Auto* and like-minded commentators had previously attributed to the Tour. Although the Circuit's organizers agreed as to the symbolism of the itinerary, they also took pride in drawing distinctions between the Tour and their race.[109] Rather than national teams, the race would feature six multinational teams (sponsored by cycle manufacturers) who would provide the edifying image of "champions of diverse nationalities" struggling "together towards a common goal." At a time when "the world is torn by gigantic struggles," *La France Socialiste* claimed that it was up to athletes to provide "an early image of the unified world that must emerge." The Circuit would "unite the youth of several countries" as they worked together for "the greatest glory of their common profession." In a clear reference to Vichy's corporatist vision, *La France Socialiste* claimed that this collaboration would revive the "old corporate pride," presumably in contrast to the divisive class loyalties generated by uncontrolled, modern capitalism.[110]

Rather than the wasteful, excessively commercial races of the past (a clear swipe at the Tour and its *caravane publicitaire*), the organizers promised a sober "Circuit of Armistice France" that would not offend a population struggling to meet its most basic needs. Racers would use ration tickets and wear jerseys made of *fibrane* and wool (rather than lighter, more expensive material). Their lodgings would be humble, at times simple dormitories. They would not be permitted to throw away food or water bottles to lighten their bicycles as they prepared for a sprint finish. Rather than use their ultralight prewar competition inner tubes, which they threw away after a race, they would compete on the more resistant inner tubes they used for training.[111] According to *La France Socialiste,* it was the successful negotiation of these difficulties, rather than the race's length and mountains, that would redound to the credit of racers who completed the Circuit, which symbolized "the daily task successfully completed despite the obstacles [confronted] every day." Even as it reflected France's dire circumstances, the Circuit also held out the promise of national revival. It represented "the return to the virile age"—another theme dear to the Vichy regime, which accused the Third Republic of weakening and corrupting the French—and demonstrated in a sport perfectly suited to the regeneration of the French, "that our race still knows how to suffer and show courage."[112]

The organizers' descriptions of enthusiastic crowds of all ages and both sexes notwithstanding, the Circuit was a disaster, because of terrible weather, logistical and supply problems, and the organizers' inexperience. Despite Laval's favorable assessment and plans to expand the race in 1943, it was never held again.[113] The Allied invasion of North Africa a month after the Circuit, followed by Soviet gains a few months later on the eastern front, radically altered Germany's priorities. The Nazis were no doubt unwilling to waste more resources on a race for propaganda gains that were illusory in a France they now occupied completely. As for the Tour, Goddet maintained that it had no place in France's wartime circumstances, which represented too great a rupture with the prewar period when the race—identified with honor, glory, and a sense of heritage—had been an important feature of French cultural life. The Tour's rebirth, he affirmed, would only occur once the war was over.[114]

In the months following the war's conclusion, the three major parties of the Resistance were directly or indirectly involved in the battle to acquire the rights to the Tour in the new press environment created by the banning of all newspapers, including *L'Auto,* that had appeared officially under the occupation and the Vichy regime. The communists' vehicle was *Sports,* the socialists' *Élans.* Goddet, for his part, hoped to use his Gaullist contacts in French publishing to obtain the Tour for *L'Auto*'s heir, *L'Équipe,* which began appearing on 28 February 1946. *L'Équipe* purchased *Élans* in mid-June, gaining a decisive advantage over *Sports,* which went out of business soon thereafter. It still faced rivals for the right to organize the Tour, including the communist sports weekly *Miroir-Sprint,* a national press syndicate, and French bicycle manufacturers. Some commentators suggested "nationalizing" the race, in keeping with the trend in a number of important French industries. Proposals included a publicly owned Tour corporation, funding the race through the national lottery, and including the cost of organizing the race in the budget of the Ministry of Sports. Meanwhile, as the struggle for the rights to the Tour intensified, both *Sports* and *L'Équipe* (the latter in collaboration with *Le Parisien Libéré* and the Parc des Princes stadium) organized short stage races in July 1946. No doubt to strengthen their case, *L'Équipe* and its allies resurrected familiar features of the Tour in their Monaco-Paris event, which they dubbed "La Course du Tour de France": it included six national teams, five French regional teams, and a yellow jersey for the race leader. After months of debate and negotiation, in early June 1947 the government formally awarded the Tour to the Parc des Princes. This entity had obtained the financial backing required to organize the race from *Le Parisien Libéré* and *L'Équipe,* which became the organizers.[115]

In the weeks preceding the 1947 Tour, the political divisions of postwar France intensified as the nascent Cold War drove a wedge between the Communists, whose ministers were expelled from the cabinet in May, and the Socialists and Christian Democrats.[116] In this context *L'Équipe* promised to remain independent of politics.[117] Meanwhile, commentators across the political spectrum—from the conservative *Le Figaro* to Louis Aragon, the surrealist intellectual and editor of the communist *Ce Soir*—presented the Tour as a unifying, apolitical event that would provide the French with a welcome distraction from the difficult conditions and uncertain future they faced.[118] "The Tour," Jacques Goddet asserted, "reopens the era of *joie de vivre*. It spontaneously establishes an entirely free community, it convenes a good-natured society that makes no distinctions of class or political affiliation. The giants of the road are magicians who bring a happy truce."[119] The race was "a message of joy and confidence" that "intensely evoked the idea of peace . . . a heroic ride from which hatred is excluded."[120] An official of the national government concurred, describing the Tour as "a great work of peace" because the people communed together along the roads of France, inspired by the sporting ideal. He warned, however, that the race could become "a terrible instrument of division" were it to be exploited for the purposes of political propaganda.[121] Such concerns notwithstanding, and despite the severe shortages facing the nation, the Ramadier government concluded that during the Tour the French would not think about politics, and it provided the organizers with everything they required to make the race a success.[122]

The gamble paid off handsomely for both the government and the organizers: a hopeful consensus emerged that the 1947 Tour signaled France's postwar recovery. According to the socialist *Le Populaire*, the spectators along the itinerary demonstrated that neither the beauty nor strength of the French was degenerating: "A magnificent youth . . . has proven to us that the love of sport and naturism preserves physical and moral health."[123] *Ce Soir*'s Aragon saw in the racers' effort, sweat, and "voluntary pain" a "lesson of national energy"; the Tour provided evidence "that France is alive."[124] *Le Monde* described the race's "resurrection" as a "symbol" that would allow the French to move beyond the terrible period just concluded. Demonstrating a selective recollection of the 1930s, *Le Populaire* claimed that the Tour would link the "happy" prewar era to "that which in the eyes of the world must signal our desire for recovery in all domains."[125] *Le Parisien Libéré* noted that, although "still torn, still convalescent," France in 1947 would have "a Tour de France worthy of her past, worthy of her future." The "liberating start" of the race would usher in "a new life after the long and painful years of the war."[126] Commentators congratulated the organizers on a job well done, which was all the more impressive given the extraordinary material obstacles they had had to overcome.[127]

The organizers were only too happy to agree. Until very recently considered "unrealizable" given the condition and meager resources of the country, the race was experiencing a "definitive resurrection," according to *Le Parisien Libéré:* "There were so many difficulties! . . . One had to have faith not to be discouraged and to overcome one by one all the obstacles." They listed the extensive material requirements of the race, reinforcing the widespread view that the 1947 Tour was an inspiration for the French as they faced the daunting task of rebuilding their country.[128]

That challenge was great indeed. Whereas the destruction of World War I had been confined to areas near the western front, the massive bombing of civilian targets in World War II devastated communities across the nation. Almost a quarter of all French buildings had been destroyed, and one million families were homeless. Industrial production in 1944 stood at 38 percent of its 1938 level, agricultural production in 1945 at 57 percent. The nation's transportation infrastructure was in a terrible state: fewer than half of France's railroad tracks were operational, 7,500 bridges had been destroyed, and the country lacked coal, locomotives, railway cars, and trucks.[129]

The region most affected by wartime destruction was Normandy. Its major cities had been devastated: 42 percent of Rouen, 58 percent of Évreux, 77 percent of Saint-Lô, and 82 percent of Le Havre had been destroyed. Twenty thousand Normans had been buried under bombed ruins; over half a million were homeless. Many spent the final winter of the war in wooden huts, and some continued living in them for the next decade. Even before the war's conclusion and for several years thereafter, Normans came to see the destruction of 1944 as a horrific and unjust disaster that required complete restitution.[130] For one Norman city in particular, the Tour de France took on a special resonance.

THE RESURRECTION OF A "MARTYRED CITY": CAEN, 1947

On 4 January 1946, the municipal council of Caen convened under the leadership of Mayor Guillou, who was not only the vice president of the Association of French Mayors but also the president of the Permanent Commission of Mayors of Disaster-Stricken Communes. There was no question that Caen qualified as a *commune sinistrée:* as the Allies liberated northern

France in the summer of 1944, nearly three-quarters of the city, including almost all its housing, had been destroyed, and its port was badly damaged by bombing. The fighting left Caennais struggling for survival amidst the rubble and ruins.[131] It was thus with palpable anger that the mayor informed his councilors of the criticism the city's recovery efforts had recently received in Parisian newspapers such as *Front National, Forces Libres, Combat,* and *Franc-Tireur.* Under the headline "The Museum of the Catastrophe," *France-Soir* had described women cooking over open fires among the ruins, as if "nothing had been touched in the past year," and implied that someone, presumably the city government, wanted to turn Caen into "a symbol of giving up."[132] In late February the mayor noted that the provincial press was also emphasizing the inadequate efforts of the local authorities to restore water, gas, and electricity to the city's inhabitants.[133] Clearly, Caen had an image problem: in a nation of stricken communities, Caennais were being portrayed as incapable of the organization, effort, and fortitude required to clear away debris and rebuild their city.

As luck would have it, the first postwar Tour, symbolic of the nation's resurrection, provided an opportunity to correct this perception: the organizers planned to have the penultimate stage conclude in Caen, which would then host the start of the final stage into Paris. In March 1947 the municipal council met to decide whether to host the race and addressed the potential impact of the Tour's visit on Caen's image. The mayor hoped that the press would report that Caen was being reborn and argued that the substantial financial outlay required to prepare the city to be a *ville-étape* was justified in order that "the entire world know that the city of Caen has received a terrible blow and that the destruction here is immense." A councilor agreed: Caen's condition would move the international press, which would not fail to report the disaster that had befallen Normandy. When another councilor argued that hosting a music competition would be a better investment for the city, the assistant mayor responded that the Tour would generate far more coverage. Apparently swayed by the likely economic and public relations benefit to be derived from the Tour's visit, the council voted unanimously in favor of subventions totaling the required 450,000 francs.[134] Hosting a stage of the Tour offered the city a unique opportunity to achieve two objectives that were otherwise difficult to reconcile: media coverage of the race's passage through the city would provide incontrovertible evidence of the horrific damage it had sustained, and welcoming an event that symbolized French resilience and recovery would allow Caennais to demonstrate their commitment to the great challenge of reconstruction. The city would be doubly vindicated and its critics silenced.

The council's public-relations objective was largely realized. Television coverage (and, presumably, filmed footage) showed ruined houses along the route as the narrator gravely intoned that "it is from Caen, martyred city, that the last stage will start."[135] *L'Équipe* thanked the "martyred city" for the "moving" efforts it was making to ensure that the race was as well received as before the war. Its coverage hit the very notes for which the city council had hoped: "Caen. A sportive city, but also a martyred city. Caen can only show the Tour de France her skeleton. But a magnificent heart continues to beat under the ruins. There was truly something moving about the welcome provided the champions of the road."[136]

The regional press concurred. Proclaiming in a huge headline that "Caen, Martyred City, Welcomes the 54 Survivors of the 34th Tour de France," *Liberté de Normandie* congratulated the local authorities on overcoming "numerous difficulties" resulting from the war and the German occupation through their hard work, attention to detail, and organization: in less than four months, and despite early pessimism, they had rebuilt the city's sports infrastructure to receive the stage finish, prepared the necessary technical support for the organizers, race officials, and journalists, and taken the security measures required to guarantee the safety of racers and spectators alike. Fans awaiting the racers enjoyed a full program of track events at the local velodrome, where the stage finish took place. Perhaps most impressive, the local Tour committee had found the 386 hotel rooms required for the teams, race officials, and press, as well as additional lodgings for the members of the *caravane publicitaire*. According to *Ouest-France,* despite a torrential downpour, both the velodrome races and the stage finish in Caen were "an unprecedented success."[137] Meanwhile, in their Tour coverage, Caen's erstwhile critics in the Parisian press made no mention of the city's alleged failure to address the challenge of postwar recovery.[138]

A DEAFENING SILENCE?
VICHY, 1952

It was one thing to use the Tour to illustrate the national and local will to rebuild in the wake of war. Far more complicated was the challenge of exploiting the race to defuse the legacy of polarization and hatred generated by four years of civil war under foreign occupation. Yet this may well have been the organizers' intent when they decided that the final stage in 1952 would link Vichy, the capital of Pétain's État Français, to Paris, France's eternal capital; it is a choice otherwise hard to explain. After all, Vichy had never before been selected as a *ville-étape,* and, when it was slow to accept the organizers' invitation and another community in the region (Montluçon) stepped forward, the organizers waited patiently for Vichy to meet their conditions.[139] Furthermore, the 354-kilometer Vichy-Paris stage was eighty kilometers longer than the next-longest stage, a disparity difficult to justify on a purely competitive basis.[140] Above all, it is difficult to imagine that, only seven years after the end of the war, at the very moment the French were debating and passing amnesty laws for crimes relating to wartime collaboration, the organizers could select Vichy without considering the historical and political implications of such a choice.

Whatever the organizers' intent, unlike Caen, Vichy was not about to use the Tour to focus national attention on its wartime experience, which, as Vichy was the capital of the now-discredited collaborationist regime, had been largely tranquil. At the same time, like Caen, Vichy was preoccupied with its economic future, specifically with recovering its prewar prosperity as a spa catering to the leisured classes. In this regard the 1952 Tour might play a useful role.

France's postwar economic difficulties profoundly affected Vichy, which had been largely dependent on the discretionary spending of curists (and their companions) who came to its hydropathic establishments for their health. Building on the development of seaside resorts where the European aristocracy sought the alleged curative benefits of salt water while creating a vibrant social life for itself, the commercial exploitation of French inland spas began under the First Empire.[141] By the 1820s Vichy was already one of the elite spas in Europe, each year welcoming almost a thousand visitors who were attracted in part by the decidedly nontherapeutic activities provided by the local casino: in addition to gambling (prohibited during much of the July Monarchy), visitors enjoyed billiards, plays, dancing, concerts, and reading rooms. At midcentury Vichy and other hydropathic centers received a dramatic boost from Napoleon III's commitment to their development and from recent railroad construction, which brought them increasing numbers of visitors. In response, many spas invested in ambitious construction programs, resulting in grand new parks, hotels, promenades, and casinos. Vichy now boasted a theater for 1,200; by 1866 its summertime population had reached 21,000.[142]

As spa communities developed, so did their leisure offerings, which continued to be centered on the casino. These included theater, concerts, and opera; dancing, piano, and fencing lessons; balls and *fêtes;* and various card and other games. Entertainers of all kinds, from great stars of the Paris stage and opera to comics, performed during the summer season. Reflecting a broader trend, from the late nineteenth century, sport began to represent an important share of the leisure offerings of spas, which hosted automobile, yacht, sailboat, and horse races, regattas, and airplane events, and offered polo, golf, tennis, pigeon-shooting, hunting, fishing, and even donkey rides in the country.[143] At the turn of the century Vichy boasted almost six hundred hotels, evidence that huge profits were being made and reinvested in the booming spa. In 1913 the city welcomed 108,000 spa-goers.[144]

The clientele of spas like Vichy was a self-selecting, leisured elite initially made up of aristocrats but soon including bourgeois notables, retired businessmen, military officers, and Catholic clergy.[145] Members of the middle classes began to join their social betters at spas from the 1860s onward, but this did not prevent late-nineteenth-century Vichy from remaining "one of Europe's most fashionable resorts . . . where the rich and famous came to take the waters and attend the opera." In the mid-1930s Vichy attracted nearly 130,000 curists a year.[146]

By the late 1940s hotel owners in the region were concluding that although there were as many curists as before the war, their numbers were unlikely to increase in the future, and they were now coming unaccompanied. Attracting the curist's companion back to Vichy would require "providing the holiday attractions and pleasures that he increasingly pursues elsewhere." Meanwhile, foreign tourists were neglecting the center of the country in favor of Paris, Brittany, the Alps, the Basque coast, and the Riviera.[147] The city's political and economic leaders soon realized that Vichy's recovery depended on attracting a broader range of visitors by organizing spectacles, competitions, and activities, including sporting events, that went beyond the offerings of the spa's traditional summer season.[148] In 1951 the city opened an *office du tourisme,* which negotiated reciprocal arrangements with other French and foreign tourist destinations to ensure that Vichy received better exposure.[149] Despite these initiatives, the 1951 season actually saw a 25 percent decrease in hotel-room occupancy in the region. Some of this decline was attributable to bad weather, but there were also deeper, structural causes. Local critics argued that Vichy had to rethink its conventional program of activities and entertainment. In an increasingly competitive European market, more attractive, less expensive vacation packages were being offered by other countries, whose governments were implementing a variety of policies designed to modernize their hotels.[150]

In 1952, in response to the crisis of the region's tourism industry, Vichy's *syndicat d'initiatives* proposed an aggressive publicity campaign. The municipal council set aside 4.5 million francs for a variety of initiatives designed to increase Vichy's national and international profile, paid the Havas Agency five million francs to publicize Vichy's attractions, and allotted millions more to its own *comité des fêtes* and the local and national horse-racing associations.[151] The program planned by the *syndicat d'initiatives* from May through September included automobile races, an air show, international regattas, clay and live pigeon-shooting, and an international soccer match; golf, tennis, fishing, and equestrian events; ballet, opera, and film festivals; an international music competition, theater, a dog show, a "Garden Party," a ball, a nocturnal *fête* at a local castle, a "Nautical Carnival," and various commercial fairs and exhibitions.[152]

Although clearly inspired by prewar activities, the 1952 program was not limited to them, as the Tour's visit to Vichy demonstrated.[153] The time trial between Clermont and Vichy on 18 July was expected to draw huge crowds, benefit local merchants and hotel owners, and, through the race's international appeal and media coverage, bring Vichy to the attention of future tourists.[154] Arguing that the Tour was "a construction, instead of the passive instrument of geographical fate," one tourism journal described the final stage on 19 July as linking the "Hydropathic Capital" to the "Capital of France," and it celebrated the fact that the race had departed from the borders and coastlines that had traditionally determined its itinerary.[155]

On 18 July, as expected, huge throngs lined the itinerary of the time trial, while a record-setting crowd of 150,000 converged on Vichy, filling the velodrome for the stage finish and later enjoying the entertainment provided by the *caravane publicitaire* in front of the City Hall.[156] Much of the local and regional press reported positively on the crowds, security dispositions, and entertainment associated with the race, describing the Tour's visit to the city as a great and joyous fair.[157] Commentators deployed familiar images of the race as a unifying respite from difficult times, which attracted a "motley crowd where all the classes of society were rubbing shoulders [sharing] the same pleasure, the same enthusiasm" before returning to their respective hotel rooms, boarding houses, and tents.[158] Like *L'Auto* and other prewar observers, they celebrated the Tour for bringing the French together, an achievement implicitly heightened by the fact that it had occurred in a city associated with recent national divisions and civil war.

Not all local reactions to the Tour's visit were so positive, however. Months earlier, during the debate over whether to host the race, several members of the *syndicat d'initiatives* had voiced concern about the noise from the Tour's vehicles, particularly those of the *caravane publicitaire*.[159] There were also reports that Vichyssois were reluctant to lodge members of the *caravane publicitaire* for fear that they would behave "like certain Parisians when they camp in the fields." After the Tour, one regional paper criticized the "cacophony" and poor taste of the *caravane publicitaire* and the "even more lamentable" attitude of the crowds, "suddenly stricken with stupidity," who pressed forward to grab candies and samples of laundry detergent, endangering the safety of mothers and children.[160] A Vichy paper for curists ridiculed the *caravane* for transforming the race into a "Tour of noise" in which spectators fought each other over Cinzano caps tossed into the crowd.[161] The transformation of Vichy from a prewar spa catering to an elite clientele to a postwar tourist destination for a broad cross-section of French and foreign vacationers did not sit well with local traditionalists or with the curists themselves, a fact noted by some of the national press.[162] In ridiculing the Tour's commercialism and spectators, they vented their resentment at the corruption of the spa's summer season by popular entertainment and audiences.

If commentators, both local and national, addressed the economic and social implications of the Tour's visit to Vichy in 1952, they were silent about its historical and political significance. There was no discussion of Vichy's role as the capital of collaborationist France, no lyrical evocation of the Vichy-Paris stage as symbolic of national reconciliation. Even *L'Humanité*, which commemorated the Resistance "martyrs" of the Auvergne in its Tour coverage, made no mention of Vichy's role during the war.[163] Such willful amnesia confirms the findings of the historian Henry Rousso, who has studied the evolving postwar reactions of the French to the Vichy regime as they struggled to come to terms with the crimes committed in the name of France by Pétain's État Français.[164]

Along with its supporters and other pro-German French people, Vichy had been responsible for imprisoning 135,000 people, interning another 70,000, dismissing 35,000 civil servants, investigating 60,000 Freemasons (549 of whom died in the camps), contributing 650,000 French workers to the German war machine, and deporting 76,000 Jews, almost all of whom perished en route to or in the camps. The decade following the Liberation, according to Rousso, was characterized by "an emotional commitment to the idea of the French people united in resistance," whose corollary was that Vichy's crimes were the acts of an unrepresentative minority who took advantage of the nation's defeat in 1940 to advance an agenda in utter contradiction with the core values of the French people. At the same time, even as the French embraced "the reassuring image of a resisting France," they wished "to forget the exceptional circumstances of the Occupation" and "return to normality" as quickly as possible.[165]

Nowhere was this a greater challenge than in the city that had hosted the ministries and bureaucrats of Pétain's État Français and whose name had quickly become shorthand for the regime.[166] Vichy's selection as the capital of the unoccupied zone in the summer of 1940 had resulted from its many advantages for the new regime: its proximity to the occupied zone; the availability of more than three hundred hotels with some fifteen thousand rooms; a well-to-do, conservative population used to receiving politicians and other high-ranking dignitaries and unlikely to be a hive of contestation; an army garrison in nearby Clermont-Ferrand; a modern post office and telephone exchange; and good roads, as well as a direct rail connection, to Paris. Thirty thousand government employees moved to the new capital during the war, working and residing in its hotels and helping to transform a community of twenty-five thousand into a bustling city four times larger.[167]

If such rapid expansion inevitably created stresses for the local inhabitants as they sought to meet the state's demands in the face of energy and food shortages, it also created opportunities which the Vichyssois embraced.[168] There were obvious economic benefits for hotel, restaurant, and café owners, who now enjoyed a large clientele year-round. As behooved a capital, particularly that of an authoritarian regime, the city was safe and immaculately maintained; to reflect its new status, it was elevated to the administrative rank of *sous-préfecture*.[169] Another advantage for the Vichyssois was the rarity and relative discretion of Germans, who tended, with the notable exceptions of the Gestapo and German police, to avoid the capital, even after they occupied the entire country in November 1942.[170] The État Français even authorized attempts to revive the city's hydropathic economy, within limits imposed by the war and the requirements of decency in such difficult circumstances: certain activities—sports, films, theater, concerts, opera—were revived in combination with new, more serious fare, such as lectures and charity events.[171]

Complicating postwar attempts by Vichyssois to put the recent prominence of their town behind them was the fact that they had done more than simply work for the regime as secretaries, clerks, cooks, drivers, and servants. As Adam Nossiter notes, they had also been the regime's most prominent "extras": as the center of Pétain's personality cult, Vichy had hosted innumerable parades, rallies, and speeches that its inhabitants had attended, enthusiastically chanting refrains assuring the old marshal of their loyalty. Not only was the regime's escalating anti-Semitic campaign of purges, expropriations, roundups, and deportations organized from Vichy, but the city and the Allier *département* were, according to Nossiter, "uniquely inhospitable [to Jews] as a matter of government policy." In 1942 Jews were banned from the department; more than 130 Jews from the Vichy area alone "did not return from deportation or were otherwise killed." A local company provided buses for the regime's roundup of foreign Jews in the department. Given its role as the capital of the collaborationist regime and its inextricable association with the regime's crimes, at the liberation Vichy endured a purge that may have been, proportionally, the largest of any French community: seven hundred Vichyssois were detained, ranging from former ministers and prominent local residents to low-level employees and staff.[172]

By the early 1950s, French attempts to assign responsibility for acts of collaboration and punish the guilty were being complicated by national and international developments. The neo-Vichyite Right had found its voice, questioning the "myth" of a national Resistance movement, ridiculing *résistants* whose heroic commitment coincided with the war's final days, defending the memory of Pétain, and, along with many on the moderate Right, rejecting the postwar purges of *collabos* as excessive, summary, and indiscriminate. Meanwhile, the unimpeachable Resistance leader Colonel Rémy, one of the founders of the Gaullist Rally for the Republic in 1947, publicly sought a reconciliation with Pétain's supporters. Claiming to echo the assessment of de Gaulle himself, Rémy argued that "France has always had two strings in its bow. In June 1940 it needed the Pétain 'string' as much as the de Gaulle 'string.'" The beginning of the Cold War further muddied the waters: from 1947, the political party most associated with the nation's resistance against Nazi tyranny and Vichy, the French Communist Party, became identified with international communism and the Soviet Union, which many French now perceived as the greatest threat to their freedom. In this context, support for amnesty for individuals convicted of collaborationist crimes grew among those, especially on the Right, who wished to effect national reconciliation and repair the excesses of the postwar purges. The first amnesty law was passed in January 1951; the second, which affected all but the most serious criminals, in July 1953. Six months earlier a special, highly controversial amnesty had been granted to Alsatian soldiers who, conscripted forcibly—by their accounts—into the Waffen SS, had participated in the massacre of 642 inhabitants of Oradour-sur-Glane.[173]

The Tour thus paused in Vichy at a moment when many French were both reassessing and seeking to put behind them complicated questions of guilt and innocence, victimhood and responsibility, memory and reconciliation. In such a context it was hardly surprising that the city would use the 1952 Tour as part of a broad program of economic recovery but not as a symbol of its moral reintegration into the nation. After all, most French had simply sought to survive the war and German occupation; whatever their public posture in the years that followed, they likely saw themselves as neither heroic *résistants* nor abject *collabos*. Why should average Vichyssois be any different, feel any more guilty, or be required to expiate the sins of collaborators simply because the latter had chosen Vichy as their capital? If, right after the war, the local newspaper invited suggestions for a new name for the city, this response to the taint of collaboration was apparently unrepresentative of local attitudes: even the hotels most prominently identified with the ministries, agencies, and leaders of the period, including those occupied by the Gestapo and the Milice, refused to change their names.[174]

In 1952 Vichy's political and business leaders were certainly interested in recasting their city's identity by attracting tourists from a broader social stratum than before the war. Their efforts, however, had nothing to do with Vichy's wartime prominence, about which they and the local press remained silent. Meanwhile, as we have seen, the national press also avoided the issue. At a time when so many of their compatriots were seeking to put the *années noires* of 1940 to 1944 behind them, commentators across the political spectrum apparently decided that exploiting the symbolic potential of Vichy's selection as a *ville-étape* would be a risky and ultimately fruitless enterprise. Complex, fractured, and ambiguous, France's experience in World War II defied the kind of commemoration afforded by the Tour's itinerary.

CONCLUSION

Reconciling regional and political loyalties with national identity has often been a challenge in modern France. *L'Auto*'s attempt to use the Tour to do so and the reactions of Strasbourgeois, Bretons, and communists in the interwar years only confirmed the persistence of particularisms the race was expected—and to some extent designed—both to celebrate and to defuse. The contradictory representations of the Tour over its first half century illustrate the difficulties inherent in reinforcing unity while celebrating diversity, a challenge hardly unique to France, even as they affirm the symbolic role of the Tour in doing both. These representations also confirm that the race's image belonged to no single newspaper, political movement, or interest group; that its image could be controlled neither by its organizers nor by municipal or national (or even German) governments, however much each might wish to do so; and that its itinerary could be used to both emphasize and undermine national unity and social cohesion. Just as the French have disagreed about their history, they have disagreed about how their Tour helps to define them. What they have repeatedly taken for granted, however, is that the race is an important cultural and political *enjeu,* a semantic battleground worth contesting.[175] As a result, attempts to impose historical master narratives by means of the Tour have generated counternarratives, as in Brittany in the 1930s, or silence, as in Vichy in 1952—a silence as pregnant with meaning as the spoken or written word.

In the years that followed the Tour's visit to Vichy, the race's organizers looked beyond France's borders and beyond its past to the future, endorsing the general trend in Western Europe toward integration by "exporting" the Tour to neighboring countries. In the 1960s the race visited West Germany for the first time; in the 1970s it crossed the Channel to England. In 1992 the organizers celebrated the Treaty of Maastricht by organizing stages in all of France's European Union neighbors, a choice that offended traditionalists who bemoaned the fact that a distinctly French tradition had been compromised by a European (and Europeanist) itinerary, amputated of its major Pyrenean climbs. The following year, perhaps chastened, the organizers returned to a more traditional French itinerary. Some, including the late Jacques Goddet, have proposed a transatlantic Tour that would start on the East Coast of the United States and continue in France, but the logistical difficulties and cost involved have to date discouraged any attempt to implement this unprecedented expansion of the race's itinerary.[176] In 2002 the mayor of Quebec proposed that the 2008 Tour de France include his city to mark the four-hundredth anniversary of its founding by the French explorer Samuel de Champlain. After studying the idea, the Société du Tour in 2004 decided that it posed insuperable organizational challenges. Beyond their commercial motivations, such ambitious proposals reflect, a century on, the enduring power of the Tour's itinerary to carry meanings that transcend sport.

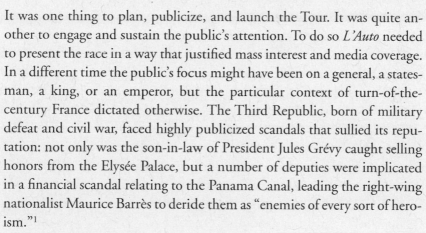

THREE

The *Géants de la Route*
Gender and Heroism

It was one thing to plan, publicize, and launch the Tour. It was quite another to engage and sustain the public's attention. To do so *L'Auto* needed to present the race in a way that justified mass interest and media coverage. In a different time the public's focus might have been on a general, a statesman, a king, or an emperor, but the particular context of turn-of-the-century France dictated otherwise. The Third Republic, born of military defeat and civil war, faced highly publicized scandals that sullied its reputation: not only was the son-in-law of President Jules Grévy caught selling honors from the Elysée Palace, but a number of deputies were implicated in a financial scandal relating to the Panama Canal, leading the right-wing nationalist Maurice Barrès to deride them as "enemies of every sort of heroism."[1]

If politics offered no heroes, neither did the military. To be sure, in the 1880s the dashing, popular General Boulanger served for a time as minister of war and blustered about a *revanche* against Germany. However, fearing arrest by the government, which hoped to defuse the appeal of his increasingly antirepublican nationalism, Boulanger fled to Belgium, where he committed suicide on the grave of his mistress. The Dreyfus affair at the turn of the century further damaged the army's image as it became clear to many that the Jewish officer convicted of spying for Germany had been framed. If the conquest of a colonial empire second only to Britain's allowed the French to applaud, in the words of a contemporary hit song, "the heroes who crossed Africa and planted the French flag on the banks of the Nile," that opportunity was short-lived.[2] In 1898—the very year the novelist Émile Zola published his famous Dreyfusard editorial, "J'accuse!"— France backed down in a confrontation with Britain in the Sudan. Lyrics extolling French imperial and military heroism rang hollow in the wake of the humiliating retreat at Fashoda.

In this context, and amid widespread anxiety about national decline, male athletes emerged as symbols of physical prowess and courage, particularly given the popular belief that France's many ills could be reversed by physical exercise. As sporting events proliferated, thousands of new fans demanded information about the young men whose performances they had witnessed in person or heard about in their neighborhood cafés. What, however, would they find appealing about the Tour? Soccer and tennis were characterized by creativity, finesse, and imaginative shot making; rugby players and boxers demonstrated their power, quickness, and courage in violent and spectacular confrontations. Cyclists, on the other hand, applied their strength to an impersonal machine in an endlessly repetitive act. Furthermore, while most sports were held in an enclosed space, allowing the crowd to witness a competition in its entirety, no spectator saw the whole Tour, let alone a complete stage.

During the race's early decades, hardy fans on bicycles accompanied the racers for a while; others followed in cars, but even they had to choose which competitors to follow once the pace, terrain, and weather broke up the *peloton*. The vast majority of spectators waited by the side of the road, catching a few seconds of the event as the contestants sped by. Before radio coverage they did not know what attacks, punctures, injuries, and withdrawals had occurred during the stage they were witnessing or how these developments affected the standings. The challenge facing the organizers in 1903 was to sell such an event to a public that enjoyed an increasing number of entertainment options within and beyond the world of sport.[3]

Using the Tour to educate the French about their history and geography while celebrating their diversity and unity was hardly sufficient to generate mass interest in the race. Instead *L'Auto* elaborated a cult of effort, suffering, and survival that informed the way the media, sponsors, public, and athletes themselves thought about the event. The grueling nature of the Tour inspired representations of a specific kind of heroism that resonated particularly well with a public seeking confirmation of France's resurgence. Echoed by other journalists and commentators, the organizers portrayed Tour racers as hypermasculine "giants of the road," implicitly countering widespread anxiety, exacerbated by the defeat of 1870 and later by the horrific death toll of World War I, that French men during this period lacked virility.

Although the pivotal actor in this new cult of athletic performance was the French press, other new media and cultural forms also played their part. Fears of a multifaceted national decline, characterized by a deficiency in masculinity, helped to spawn a new literary genre, sports fiction, whose authors celebrated the physical and moral value of sport. Recognizing the contributions of these writers to its own efforts to increase public awareness of the importance of physical exercise, the French sports press featured their texts; both *Le Vélo* and *L'Auto* offered literary prizes for sports writing.[4] New visual images also fueled the era's cult of athletic heroism. The press included dramatic photographs of the racers in its Tour coverage, postcards featuring star racers were sold to the public, and cycle and tire manufacturers placed advertisements in the press and posters along city streets, vaunting the performances of champions using their equipment.[5]

If, as we saw in chapter 1, such a positive image of Tour racers served important commercial interests, using the race to celebrate a new, hypermasculine French manhood in early-twentieth-century France was not as self-evident as it might appear at first blush. Fears about the lack of virility of French men were magnified during the belle époque by *female* cyclists and their close identification with the hotly debated topic of female emancipation: if women could so easily become proficient cyclists, how could cycling, let alone less demanding sports, provide French men with the self-confidence, courage, and strength they seemed to be lacking? For *L'Auto* and other commentators, extolling Tour racers as heroic men who overcame obstacles by virtue of their distinctly male qualities was not enough. Their race coverage also celebrated nurturing, supportive mothers and wives and admiring *spectatrices* attracted to the muscular, brave young men who took on a prodigious challenge from which fragile women were naturally excluded. This rigidly gendered presentation of the race was reinforced by continual references to its contestants as heroic soldiers and to the Tour as a war that emotional women witnessed from the side of the road or experienced on the "home front," away from the action.

Although developed in the particular context of pre–World War I France, the Tour's heroic ethos has endured to the present day, in large measure because it serves the same purpose it did a century ago. By asserting the timeless nature of conventional gender roles, heroic Tour narratives have continually offered a conservative counterpoint to fears that increasingly emancipated and empowered women were blurring fundamental sexual differences and undermining social stability as they gained new rights and opportunities. Not surprisingly, defining Tour heroism as exclusively male has had a debilitating impact on competitive female cycling in France. Long after other women's sports have attracted significant media coverage, sponsorship opportunities, and prize money, women's cycling remains marginalized, despite the creation of a Tour *féminin* in 1984 and the fact that the dominant female racer of the past quarter century, and the greatest in history, is French. To understand why this is so we must go back to the early days of cycling and to the emergence of a new French hero.

INVENTING A HERO:
THE *GÉANT DE LA ROUTE*

As it sought to shape public perceptions of the Tour, *L'Auto* emphasized the race's theatrical dimension. Géo Lefèvre heralded the event as "a great athletic drama whose magnitude will captivate [the public's] attention during almost three weeks" as "the giants of the road offer us six consecutive tragedies, [each] with its particular ups and downs, its *dénouement*."[6] Commentators have long made the connection between sport and drama: like a compelling play, an athletic competition introduces characters, ranging from great stars to their anonymous supporting cast, into a situation full of conflict and obstacles, subjects them to a plot with twists and turns ("la glorieuse incertitude du sport"), and builds to a climax in which the conflict is resolved and the characters meet their respective fates. Georges Speicher, who won the 1933 Tour, observed that "as in the theater, they [the racers] represent a complete range of humanity. There are the powerful and the weak, the fortunate and the unlucky. Their names change as the years go by; but the characters are fundamentally the same."[7]

Where sport trumps theater is in the fact that a competition, barring collusion or a fix, is by its nature open-ended. Its plot is a work in progress: a prohibitive favorite can crash or puncture and lose the race; a once-dominant star can be bested by a gifted newcomer. No sporting event contained this dramatic uncertainty as much as the Tour de France. The succession of natural obstacles to overcome—most notably the mountains—and the race's division into stages allowed tension, conflict, and suspense, carefully woven into an epic narrative by journalists covering the race, to build over several weeks. Such a narrative, *L'Auto* hoped, would appeal to a public primed by weeks of prerace reporting and accustomed to serialized novels in mass-circulation dailies.

As quickly as it came to dominate the French sports press, *L'Auto* could not have ensured the Tour's popularity on its own. The race's popularity nationwide, and thus its commercial viability, required coverage by hundreds of papers, a fact the organizers fully appreciated: "The provincial press has understood the importance of our event, and does not spare us its encouragement or publicity. We must thank it deeply, for that will contribute in no small way to the success of the Tour de France, by making it known in the smallest villages."[8] *L'Auto*'s gratitude notwithstanding, press coverage of the Tour was uneven at best in prewar France. While some papers provided brief daily, or almost daily, Tour updates, with stage results and the overall standings, others only occasionally mentioned the race, and many paid it absolutely no heed. By exaggerating the extent of Tour coverage, *L'Auto* hoped perhaps to elevate the event to the rank of a national happening and thereby encourage delinquent papers to add or expand their coverage.

In its own coverage, *L'Auto* stressed the conditions and scale of the race, which underscored the racers' heroic performances: "The most abrupt mountains, the coldest and blackest nights, the most violent and atrocious winds, the most unfair and repeated bad luck, the longest roads, the never-ending climbs and the paths lengthening forever [before them] . . . nothing has overcome the stubbornness and the willpower of these men."[9] The paper continually evoked the indefatigability, valor, and willpower of athletes "bent over their pedals, pulling desperately on their handlebars, forever finding new energy," as they confronted "high mountains and vertiginous descents, precipices always at their side, . . . incredible roads, veritable cross-country paths, . . . grandiose peaks all around." Such a "battle against nature" required "unfailing endurance, muscles of steel, and an iron temperament" as well as "unshakable willpower."[10] Borrowing a phrase coined by two journalists at *Le Vélo* four years earlier in their book on Bordeaux-Paris (one of the longest races of the day), *L'Auto* dubbed these new heroes the "giants of the road."[11]

Meanwhile, the Tour's classic nickname, "the Great Loop," was reinforced by expressions emphasizing its "monstrous," "colossal," and "gigantic" dimensions. As the contestants forged their way through the Pyrenees in 1910, *L'Auto*'s headline, "Pygmies against Giants," highlighted the unequal battle that pitted mortal racers against nature's true giants.[12] From the Tour's earliest years, other newspapers echoed the organizers' hyperbole.[13] *L'Ouest-Éclair* marveled at these "men accustomed to all forms of fatigue, wonderfully trained and toying with the thousand difficulties of the road, the sun, the hills, the punctures, thirst, etc."[14] *Le Toulouse cycliste* celebrated "the extraordinary resistance of the human machine, the things of which willpower [and] energy are capable, and the prodigious feats of endurance and strength that man can accomplish."[15]

Starting in the late nineteenth century and reaching their high point in the 1920s, novels about competitive cycling also contributed to the emerging heroic mythology of the bicycle racer, as fans turned to fictionalized accounts of athletic exploits to supplement press coverage of real competitions. These novels generally described the rise of a working-class youth from the amateur ranks to the fame and fortune of professional stardom. The sports that inspired the greatest number of novels were boxing and cycling, both of which exemplified a rugged virility, provided dramatic confrontations, and, more than other sports of the day, allowed for a tragic dimension to the plot because they involved so much effort, sacrifice, and suffering. A Tour racer struggled as much against his own limits, the elements, and the environment as against his rivals. He became the hero of an athletic epic.[16] Cycling fiction was complemented by biographies and autobiographies of racers, including one about the Tour champion François Faber subtitled "Le géant de la route" (suggesting that the phrase was already widely used).[17] Meanwhile, on the eve of the race, many newspapers and magazines came out with a *numéro spécial* that covered its history, the heroic moments and sites of its growing *légende,* and biographical sketches of the racers.

Advertisements along city streets complemented verbal accounts of racers' exploits. Bicycle posters had initially featured historical icons, such as Henri IV (one of France's most beloved monarchs), Marianne (the symbol of the French Republic), and a female version of Vercingetorix (the great leader of the Gauls).[18] This iconography made sense in the early days of the sport, when racers had not yet become household names. From the 1890s onward, however, bicycle posters shifted to portrayals of champion racers now sufficiently well known to justify a credible advertising campaign.[19] In 1908, for example, Peugeot produced a poster titled "Two Great Winners,"

Seeking relief from the ferocious heat of the 1950 Tour, racers take a spontaneous break from competing to bathe in the Mediterranean, an escapade for which they were fined by the organizers. (Courtesy of Abaca.)

The young accordionist Yvette Horner plays to a crowd from her Suze car during the 1954 Tour. Repeatedly hired during this period to entertain Tour crowds by sponsors participating in the *caravane publicitaire*, Horner took advantage of this exposure to become a huge star. (Courtesy of Abaca.)

A publicity vehicle for La Vache Qui Rit cheese ascends a hill during the 1955 Tour, providing an entertaining spectacle for the crowd awaiting the racers. (Courtesy of Abaca.)

The English racer Tom Simpson, clearly in distress, climbs the Mont Ventoux during the Marseille-Carpentras stage of the 1967 Tour. (Courtesy of Abaca.)

The Tour's doctor, Pierre Dumas, seeks in vain to revive Tom Simpson after his doping-related collapse on the Mont Ventoux during the 1967 Tour. (Courtesy of Abaca.)

The Tour organizer Jacques Goddet lays a wreath during the 1970 Tour at the monument honoring Simpson on the Mont Ventoux. In the background, the Tour leader Eddy Merckx removes his cap as he passes the monument. (Courtesy of Abaca.)

An image typical of the suffering of Tour racers. The victim of arguably the most famous fall in Tour history, the Spaniard Luis Ocaña, wearing the yellow jersey and enjoying a commanding lead over his rivals, has just crashed in a downpour in the mountains during the 1971 Tour. Officials, including the Tour organizer Jacques Goddet (in the background on the left), try to help him. Too badly injured to continue, Ocaña was forced to withdraw, allowing the Belgian Eddy Merckx to win his third straight Tour. Ocaña went on to win the 1973 Tour. (Courtesy of Abaca.)

The famous "strike" of Valence-d'Agen in the 1978 Tour. Before a stunned and hostile crowd, the racers arrive in Valence-d'Agen well behind schedule and walk their bicycles to the finish line to register their dissatisfaction with their work conditions. They are led by several of the Tour's top racers, including Michel Pollentier, in the polka-dotted jersey of the Tour's top climber (third racer from right, front row); Freddy Maertens, in the green jersey of the Tour's best sprinter (at right); and the French national road-racing champion Bernard Hinault (second from right), who is discussing the situation with the Tour organizer Félix Lévitan (front right, in jacket). (Courtesy of Abaca.)

The Frenchman Laurent Fignon and the American Marianne Martin, winners of the 1984 men's and women's Tours, celebrate their victories at the closing cere- mony in Paris. On the left, the mayor of Paris, Jacques Chirac, clasps Fignon's raised hand, while the French prime minister, Laurent Fabius, and Tour organ- izer Félix Lévitan look on from the far right. (Courtesy of Abaca.)

The 1998 doping scandal. Outraged by their treatment at the hands of the authorities who searched their hotel rooms and jailed some of their peers, the racers
remaining in the Tour refused to contest the seventeenth stage from Albertville
to Aix-les-Bains. Instead, they used the stage for a collective protest that was
covered live by French television. Here they cross the finish line together, led by
members of the TVM team, one of the teams at the center of the affair. Note the
gestures of the fans at the finish line: although denied a competitive finish and
despite a lengthy wait, they appear to support the racers' action. (Courtesy of
Abaca.)

Wearing a skin-tight cycling outfit and aerodynamic helmet, and mounted on the latest model of time-trial bicycle, Lance Armstrong takes full advantage of the most recent scientific and technological advances as he launches his successful bid for a seventh and final Tour victory during the opening individual time trial in 2005. (Courtesy of Abaca.)

depicting the great racer Petit-Breton standing next to Napoleon I. Each holds a banner: while Napoleon's lists his military victories over a ten-year span, Petit-Breton's much larger banner lists the victories gained in 1908 alone by racers on Peugeot bicycles, including French and world championships, the top four places in the Tour de France and all fourteen of its stages, the Paris Grand Prix, the Tour of Belgium, and Paris-Brussels.[20] In such posters Tour champions supplanted the great figures of French history as the preeminent national heroes of early-twentieth-century France. After all, every French schoolchild knew that Napoleon's career, for all its triumphs, had ended in debacle at Waterloo.

Meanwhile, newspapers and magazines quickly understood that providing a curious public with pictures of the race would increase their sales: advertisements for the 17 July 1903 issue of *La Vie au Grand Air* emphasized that it would include photographs taken on the roads of the first Tour de France.[21] The press favored shots of the racers against the awesome backdrop of a Pyrenean or Alpine skyline or surrounded by crowds as they raced through city streets toward the finish of a stage. Both types of image confirmed the racers' heroic standing, the former by illustrating the physical obstacles they surmounted, the latter by demonstrating the adulation they inspired throughout France.

Postcards of individual contestants and teams also disseminated heroic images of racers.[22] Some featured posed photographs on a velodrome track, often accompanied by a list of the racer's main achievements. Others depicted the heat of competition, frequently in the mountains: the roadside is sprinkled with the parked cars of the wealthier spectators, crowds are assembled near a tavern or along the road, and majestic, snow-capped peaks reinforce the immensity of the task facing the racers. Some postcards included a map of the Tour's itinerary, emphasizing its daunting dimensions. Many were advertisements for the brakes, tires, and bicycles used by top racers to overcome the Tour's obstacles. Grasping the postcard's appeal as a collectible item, entrepreneurs featured great French racers as part of a series or issued smaller cards and albums to reward customers for their purchases.[23] The athlete was thus commodified; his likeness could be replicated ad infinitum and sold to his fans.

Ultimately, of course, it was the public that decided to worship these new "giants." As coverage of the Tour by *L'Auto* and other papers emphasized, in town after town, whatever the time of day or night, crowds came out to encourage the racers on their journey through France. On the evening after a stage, receptions at clubs and city halls were held in their honor. Local notables attended, including the mayor, municipal councilors, the garrison commander, the priest, the schoolteacher, and sports-club officials. Bands played, streets and squares were decorated as if for a national holiday, and torchlight parades wound through the town. At the Tour's conclusion, the racers' hometown fans welcomed them back, greeting them at the local train station with great pomp and circumstance before honoring them at a reception in a café or the headquarters of a sports club (often one and the same). Bicycle stores displayed dusty bicycles used by Tour racers to attract curious passers-by.[24] These machines were celebrated as the instruments of the racers' heroism—hence the shopkeepers' refusal to clean them—even more than as symbols of technological modernity. Tour champions became so popular that Petit-Breton, originally from Argentina, was received at that country's Paris embassy. François Faber was asked by a minister of the Luxembourg government in 1913 to lecture on the origins of the bicycle, its practical uses, and the value of bicycle races. Top racers became the toast of Paris, embraced by its cultural elites, including leading actors and writers.[25]

By the eve of World War I several important factors had converged to transform the Tour racer into a *géant de la route*. First, his visibility was dramatically increased by the development of various media, the most important of which was a mass press made profitable by almost universal literacy. Visibility begat celebrity, which in turn was molded into a heroic image by epic narratives and dramatic pictures. Second, considerable profits could be made from such a positive image. As indicated by the advertising strategies of their first commercial sponsors and the tone and content of press coverage, the "giants of the road" sold bicycles, tires, newspapers, and magazines. Above all, the unmatched scale of the Tour set racers apart from other men at a time when the French, obsessed with the specter of their decline, were seeking models of physical and psychological vigor. Gigantism has long evoked the freakish or monstrous, and the Tour, continually described as both "gigantic" and "monstrous," appeared to perpetuate this association. However, when used to describe the energy, courage, and endurance of Tour racers, references to giants were an unequivocal refutation of French degeneration. Therein lay a curious paradox: for many commentators in the belle époque, the decadence the "giants of the road" were called on to reverse was epitomized by *female* cyclists.

FEMALE CYCLISTS AND FRANCE'S CRISIS
OF MASCULINITY

French men were not alone in enjoying the new sport of cycling in the late nineteenth and early twentieth centuries: women, particularly middle-class women, soon followed the example of their brothers, fathers, and husbands. In so doing they sparked considerable concern among observers (of both sexes) who saw these cyclists as representative of a profoundly disturbing de-velopment: women's emancipation.[26] During the early decades of the Third Republic, women obtained new rights and educational and professional op-portunities. At the same time, the plummeting French birthrate exacerbated anxiety sparked by the defeat of 1870 and the foundation of an ambitious, populous German Empire in its wake.[27] By the final decade of the nineteenth century, a variety of social commentators, especially on the Right, were blam-ing feminism for the decline in France's birthrate.[28] Any activity that appeared to hinder France's demographic expansion by distracting women from their reproductive duty to the nation became an obvious target for all those con-cerned with national security and the viability of the French "race."

Cycling appeared to be just such an activity. Seeking attire better adapted to the sport than their long skirts, petticoats, and restrictive corsets, women adopted new clothing clearly inspired by men's trousers: *culottes* (bloomers) and hybrid *jupes-culottes* (skirts with bloomers). For many commentators, both male and female (including proponents of female cycling), this sarto-rial revolution signaled a fundamental and troubling reorientation of female identity. Women who wore bloomers were rejecting the skirt and with it, the argument went, the attributes of conventional femininity: mystery, charm, elegance, grace, and beauty. The appropriation by female cyclists of masculine clothing thus appeared symbolic of a broader feminist attack on the traditional bourgeois gender order.[29] Had not Maria Pognon, the pres-ident of the 1896 Feminist Congress, celebrated the liberating impact of the egalitarian bicycle?[30]

As a result, for many French, the trend toward increased female in-dependence came to be personified by women cyclists. For their part, physi-cians debated whether pedaling resulted in female masturbation and might lead women to seek sexual pleasure on their new machines rather than in the marital bed.[31] This debate was symptomatic of a broader concern in the decades preceding World War I about the mysterious and "uncontrollable" nature of women's sexual feelings (and their emotions in general) and the perceived threat such feelings posed to the bourgeois order.[32]

Anxiety about France's stagnant population and its implications for national security thus intersected with male insecurity at the apparent assertion by women of an autonomous sexuality. The bicycle operated as a convenient lightning rod for such anxiety, for it evoked women voraciously pursuing sexual and other pleasures on their own and, in the process, abandoning their traditional duties in the home.[33] Fully aware of the widespread concern that women cyclists threatened social stability, doctors and other commentators who favored female exercise argued that cycling actually strengthened marriages and families by providing a wholesome activity for couples and their children to enjoy together.[34] Still, the fact that mothers joined fathers in leading their children on educational bicycle tours of the French countryside suggested that the new sport, even when it appeared to reinforce the family, did so in ways that increased a woman's responsibilities and visibility.

Female cycling was particularly provocative given the widespread conviction that the principal way for French men to overcome their widely assumed deficit in masculinity was through sport. According to many fin-de-siècle commentators, athletic competition reproduced the psychological and moral conditions of the battlefield and would thus provide men with the qualities required for a successful war against Germany.[35] At a time when many French felt that newly empowered women were undermining the traditional gender order, female participation in sport seemed to signal a deep-rooted masculine decadence, itself symptomatic of a general national decline.[36] Although hygienists promised an increase in the French birthrate if women exercised rationally, women's sports violated taboos inspired by conventional representations of women as emotional, gentle, maternal, and delicate domestic beings.[37] The underlying assumption appears to have been that France possessed a finite amount of virility: if women were becoming more masculine, men must therefore be undergoing a process of feminization, becoming what Maurice Barrès contemptuously dismissed as *"demi-mâles."*[38]

France's alleged crisis of masculinity explains why advocates of female cycling reaffirmed traditional sexual stereotypes even as they encouraged women to bicycle.[39] Physicians formulated numerous restrictions for female cyclists founded on widely accepted "scientific" explanations of women's "natural" inferiority; the appeal of such explanations increased throughout the nineteenth century, even as classic bourgeois conceptions of sexual roles and differences were being contested, not least by women on bicycles.[40]

Manèges, the newly created cycling schools that catered to the middle classes, often charged women an additional three francs for lessons, assuming, no doubt, that they would take longer to learn than men.[41] A cycling manual of the day claimed that it was a man's duty to ensure that his delicate female companion was comfortably equipped and to protect her from vehicles and pedestrians during a ride.[42] An article in a local sports newspaper urged that a woman's handlebars be set higher than on a man's bicycle to conceal her cleavage by keeping her torso vertical (this aerodynamically inefficient position would of course also limit her speed).[43] Founded on the conventional image of women as weak, inept, and irresponsible, such recommendations promoted a less autonomous form of female cycling by asserting male control and medical authority over the activity and reinforced distinctions between the sexes that recent advances by women had begun to erase. These distinctions were now deemed all the more important as they permitted the restoration of virility in a society many feared had become excessively effeminate.[44]

DESIRABLE MEN, DANGEROUS WOMEN, AND "RACIAL" REGENERATION

For those worried by women's emancipation in the belle époque, the "giant of the road" provided a useful counterpoint to the "new woman," first, by reasserting a male monopoly over virility, and, second, by equating virility with heroism. Masculinity of this sort, *L'Auto* repeatedly observed, went neither unnoticed nor unappreciated by French women. There were, of course, housewives among the throngs lining the race route, but the organizers were more likely to note the presence of young women in their "elegant" and "fresh" summer outfits, "pretty girls" with "healthy and honest smiles," or "beautiful girls of the Midi" who enthusiastically cheered the racers on. Checkpoints were crowded with "lots of women, and, well, pretty women! [who have] come to applaud our racers." *L'Auto* continually reported the effect Tour racers had on *spectatrices,* who "wished to contemplate" such exceptional men.[45]

The curiosity of female fans, which recalled that of their ancestors beholding the "wonderful athletes" of ancient Greece, was fueled by their incredulity at the racers' performances: "They push each other, they bump each other, they press forward; I believe that, given the chance, they would like to feel the steel muscles to make sure that a little motor is not hidden in them." One slender "little brunette with pretty black eyes," the maid of honor of a wedding party that had interrupted its celebration to watch the Tour, acknowledged with eyes modestly downcast that she would willingly follow the racers for the rest of the race. Women unable to make it to the itinerary wrote to ask racers for autographs and photographs. Others accompanied their menfolk to the local train station to welcome home a Tour participant with kisses and added an "elegant note" at the "charming" celebratory banquet honoring the hometown hero.[46]

The message of such anecdotes was clear: Tour racers embodied a rugged virility that made them irresistible to French women—particularly young, single women—whom *L'Auto* portrayed as passive, innocent, healthy, and attractive. The racers, in turn, were generally depicted as confident, decent young men, who appreciated their female fans without taking advantage of them, apart from the harmless, playful remarks, pinches, and kisses that entertained *L'Auto*'s readers.[47] To a nation obsessed with its low birthrate and "racial" degeneration, the Tour's organizers offered a comforting vision of archetypal gender identities that augured well for its future.

The staggering fatalities sustained by France in World War I, combined with the crippling psychological and physical toll inflicted by trench warfare on many survivors, only exacerbated fears about the emancipation and empowerment of women. Veterans returned from the war as outsiders to a home front that seemed populated by newly independent, assertive women who had replaced working men sent to the front. After the war female cyclists were no longer the focus of French debates about gender roles: by 1918 a generation of women had used their machines to no demonstrable ill effect, and the French medical community, although arguably now even more concerned about the nation's health and fertility, no longer saw the bicycle as a threat. Instead, as Mary Louise Roberts has shown, postwar debates about gender revolved around images of modern, single, boyish women: *la femme moderne, la femme seule,* and *la garçonne.* Like the bloomer-clad "new woman" of the belle époque, these female types redefined female identity in ways that challenged conventional views of femininity and appropriate womanly conduct. Their sleek fashions, short hairstyles, and apparently hipless and bosomless bodies masculinized them in the eyes of many of their contemporaries. Their perceived life choices—work outside the home and the rejection of marriage and motherhood (both of which were largely necessitated by the lack of potential husbands)—reinforced the sense that young women were opting for an autonomy that destabilized society and threatened France's survival.[48]

No doubt sensitive to these concerns, *L'Auto* redoubled its efforts to describe the feverish adulation virile racers inspired in their female fans. Women cheered their favorites along the itinerary, braved cold, windy conditions to watch them conquer the mountains, blew them kisses, gave them gifts (ranging from bouquets and gold medals to silk stockings and racing jerseys), and wrote them letters, asking for a signed photograph or including one of themselves that could "wake up the most serious of hermits."[49] Henri Decoin, a writer who frequently contributed to *L'Auto,* described the effect of the "athletes of the road" on "cities and villages where the young women quiver at the sight of men passing by." The sports novelist Robert Dieudonné, a columnist for the paper in the 1930s, opined that women's interest in sport was a "sign of the times" and a significant change from "not so long ago when women knew almost nothing about sport and athletes." He explained that their admiration was coupled with romantic feelings inspired by "the champions."[50]

L'Auto provided ample evidence of such feelings, describing "blushing girls who slip into the garage to touch our dust-covered monsters." A sixteen-year-old girl reported her infatuation (and that of her classmates) with the racers: "I surprised myself admiring the build of 'Charlot' [Charles Pélissier, the youngest of three racing brothers and France's best sprinter], the physique of Jean Aerts, the elegance of Di Paco." She almost fainted when Georges Speicher thanked her with a smile for a beer she had handed him. Racers wandered through host communities in their tight-fitting racing outfits, inciting "matrons to ogle their muscular forms." Ladies "hid their emotion behind light and malicious fans! They stared at Charlot as if discovering the bogeyman." Some female fans were more aggressive, ambushing racers at checkpoints and stage finishes with passionate kisses. One young hotel employee entered the racers' dining hall in Metz and announced that she was going to kiss one racer from each team, only to exceed her self-imposed limit. A team manager had to convince her boss, who fired her in the wake of this scandalous display, to take her back.[51] The Tour's daily ceremonies reinforced the racers' image as desirable men: the press published photographs and descriptions of local beauties offering smiles, bouquets, and kisses to each stage winner. And, as before the war, racers were reported playfully flirting with their female fans.[52]

The organizers' thesis was once again clear: Tour racers appealed to

French women irrespective of social class, from "salesgirls, blonde typists, little seamstresses, . . . café waitresses, ragwomen, and maids" to "duchesses" and bourgeois "sportswomen."[53] If such a comprehensive claim about the redemptive virility of Tour racers offered hope to a nation suffering from a vast demographic deficit, it also blurred class boundaries in ways that cycling novels addressed explicitly. As in press coverage of the Tour, women played a prominent role in cycling novels of the belle époque and interwar period. Romantic intrigues increased dramatic tension and provided writers with opportunities for character development and incidents likely to titillate the adolescent males and young men who no doubt made up the majority of their readers. Unlike L'Auto's Tour coverage, however, many cycling novels featured capricious, scheming, and possessive women—often actresses, stereotypically of doubtful morality—who corrupted the young protagonist and undermined his prospects for success.

In Le Tour de Souffrance (1925) by André Reuze, Blanc-Mesnil criticizes his former companion (an actress) for not having understood that a top racer "must deprive himself of all life's pleasures." "Because of you," he complains, "I was leading the life of a gigolo. Restaurants, the movies, night clubs, dance halls. I went to bed at impossible times." He blames her for his poor performances and refuses to let her accompany him during the Tour for fear that he will succumb to her charms and be unable to keep pace with the main pack.[54] In Microbe (1929) by Jacques Chabannes, the seventeen-year-old racer Gaston Dubois (nicknamed Microbe), although in love with Madeleine, has an affair with the older Germaine. "Through his contact with this unstable and empty woman, Microbe feels those qualities diminish that are profoundly his: he loses his optimism, his energy, and that vast need for ideals that at times filled his heart."[55] In the end, after an injury has ended his athletic career, Microbe and Madeleine become lovers.

Fictional women like Germaine were dangerous sexual predators who exploited naive working-class athletes, stripping them of their moral and physical qualities—qualities that Microbe recognizes he owes to sport: "His courage, his energy, was it not in athletic battles that he had cultivated them? He still needs that physical fatigue, that expenditure of force that strengthen one's character."[56] Blanc-Mesnil and Microbe represent more than physical role models for French youth, who in the wake of World War I were encouraged more than ever to revitalize the nation through sport. By rejecting his lover's pernicious influence and opting instead for a life of rigor and abstinence, Blanc-Mesnil reaffirms sober commitment to hard work as the foundation of success. Microbe also offers an important moral lesson: putting the romantic errors of his youth behind him, he chooses true love over the temporarily seductive but ultimately destructive relationship with the older, presumably more sexually experienced Germaine.[57]

One of the first writers to alert young racers to the dangers of succumbing to their female fans was Henri Desgrange himself. In his turn-of-the-century training manual, he warned racers to avoid the corrupting influence of "pretty little lecherous souls who would be charmed to experiment with you . . . to determine whether your qualities as a man are as remarkable in bed as are your qualities as a racer on the track." In his novel, also written at that time, Desgrange described racers "besieged" by "the unbalanced women who wished to experience the muscular vigor that all these men were showing them": among the upper-class spectators arriving fashionably late at a velodrome for a seventy-two-hour endurance event were "women, in flashy outfits, [who] leaned against the handrail and examined the racers, checking the traces of fatigue upon their faces, their feline pupils lit with the secret desire to know what lads capable of such a *tour de force* would do in their beds."[58]

Like other French sports novelists of the day, Desgrange depicted racers as easy victims of seductive temptresses who sought to satisfy their sexual appetite with athletes of remarkable endurance—sinister versions of the innocent female fans who would soon populate *L'Auto*'s Tour coverage. Of course, not all women were dangerous predators, nor was competitive cycling inevitably a threat to a young man's moral development. Adopting the religious language favored by cycling's proponents, Desgrange argued that because energetic, disciplined training developed a racer's strength, courage, and self-control, he would be a better husband: "Your bicycle . . . is your salvation. It will lead you to marriage, healthy, strong, vigorous, and honest. Only then will you leave it."[59]

By associating promiscuous (upper-class) women with chaos and failure, and faithful (lower-class) women with social stability and individual happiness, these novels (and Desgrange's training manual) sought to defuse widespread concerns in early-twentieth-century France about the social and "racial" impact of women's emancipation, concerns that were often framed in terms of dangerous female sexuality.[60] There remained, however, an unresolved tension. It was the very vigor that sports enthusiasts like Desgrange were seeking to develop in French youth through physical exercise that was appealing to women. As these athletes came almost exclusively from the lower classes, the upper-class women in sports novels who fantasized about or initiated relationships with them violated class boundaries and the fundamental bourgeois principle that an individual's social ascent be achieved by "respectable" means—certainly not by bedding promiscuous women of higher social standing. The latter's attraction to bicycle racers both fed and reflected a bourgeois obsession with the presumed physical and sexual superiority of individuals who were their social, cultural, and intellectual inferiors. Widely celebrated as the embodiment of a heroic physicality, the "giants of the road" reinforced those fears far more than did other workers who would never enjoy the fame and fortune promised to cycling's stars.

For all the motivations converging to transform the Tour racer into a hypermasculine hero during the belle époque and thereafter, it is worth remembering that athletes, particularly professional athletes, did not fulfill the traditional requirements of heroism: resilience, courage, and leadership in a crisis and, above all, the willingness to sacrifice one's self-interest, health, and life for others. Tour racers clearly put their health and lives at risk, but they did so for glory and money, as the organizers and racers themselves readily acknowledged (see chapter 4). Attempts to justify the racers' heroic status by the classic criterion of self-sacrifice were also undermined by team strategies. When a less capable racer supported his team's star, he was simply fulfilling his contract; as he had no chance of winning the Tour himself, this could hardly be presented as a self-sacrificial act. On the other hand, when a gifted young racer capable of winning the Tour was required by team strategy and against his will to sacrifice his chance and assist the established team leader, this did not qualify as a heroic sacrifice either. For one thing, it was involuntary. For another, it violated the fundamental premise of athletic competition: that all contestants with the talent to win be given the opportunity to do so.[61] Not surprisingly, those wishing to construct a heroic mythology about the giants of the road would eschew self-sacrifice and look elsewhere for its foundation.

SUFFERING AND SURVIVAL: THE *RESCAPÉ* AS HERO

From the race's inception, the media, organizers, and racers have consistently agreed that it is the latter's capacity to suffer in an event continually described as a "calvary" that makes them exceptional.[62] In 1919 *Le Matin* evaluated "with a kind of vertigo the amount of physical courage and moral force, of dogged determination, of suffering vanquished, that [the racers'] prowess represents." In 1935 *Le Petit Parisien* described "suffering in the dust of the roads and in the snowy climbs. There are masks of pain, the grimace of effort, the bitter smile of victory." In 1938 *L'Auto* imagined the reaction of a nurse treating racers during the Tour: made of stronger stuff than her usual patients, "they accept suffering as if it was a condition of their occupation."[63] After World War II Jacques Goddet observed that what characterized Tour racers was their acceptance of suffering and risk.[64] He exalted the "inexorable cruelty" of the Tour, which derived from "the physical demand reaching its paroxysm," human suffering "in the flesh," the almost total exhaustion of the racers' moral resources, the bad luck of some, the physical breakdowns that "nail[ed] others to the ground," and the weather that "deployed the somber veil of catastrophes."[65]

Press coverage inevitably evoked the visible evidence of the racers' suffering, noting their "ravaged faces," "their hollow cheeks, their yellow eyes, the froth on their lips" at the end of a stage.[66] *L'Auto,* in particular, also reported the racers' weight loss over the course of the Tour, thereby providing an objective measure of their suffering by charting what the event literally took out of them.[67] Photographs and, later, television coverage offered evidence of another kind. Bloodied racers writhed in pain or lay unconscious on slick roads and in ditches and ravines after horrendous falls. Sprinters crashed near the finish line in a chaos of thrusting limbs and mangled metal. Mouths agape, eyes empty, semiconscious contestants in the throes of a *défaillance* wove pathetically up mountain roads; inconsolable, they wept as they were helped into the *camion balai* (literally, "broom van"), which "sweeps up" racers who simply can go no farther.[68]

The centrality of suffering for Tour participants has always been perfectly clear to even the most successful among them.[69] The five-time winner Bernard Hinault, who raced professionally from the mid-1970s through the mid-1980s, defined cycling as "perhaps the hardest [sport] of all, the one that leads man beyond suffering . . . one of the only ones to combine so intensely suffering and danger and to make them the daily lot of all those who pursue it at a high level."[70] More recently, the seven-time winner Lance Armstrong described the Tour as "unlike any other sporting event. Along the way, there are crashes, sickness, snow, rain and heat—for three weeks."[71] Participating in his first Tour in 1908, Petit-Breton exclaimed: "This is murder! Those bastards [the organizers] want our skin."[72] Seven decades later,

Gérard Moneyron unwittingly resuscitated Petit-Breton's accusations: "Assassins. It's not possible. They're crazy. What purpose does it serve to [have us] do things like that? They're going to make us ride at night as well. They're crazy. We've been in the mountains for ten days."[73]

Reported by the media, such recriminations reinforced the Tour's image as the world's toughest sporting event. On the whole, however, racers have understood that their stoic acceptance of suffering is the foundation of both their immense popularity and their success.[74] Raphael Géminiani, a Tour veteran of the 1940s and 1950s, noted that "the Tour is made of legendary moments, of exploits . . . the legend is made of falls, of blood," and "the champion is the one who knows how to suffer the best."[75] Jacques Anquetil, the first racer to win five Tours (1957, 1961–64), agreed: beyond his physical gifts, he knew "how to push myself beyond my limits and suffer more than the others."[76] Bicycle racers who "suffered the best" rose to the pinnacle of their sport. Those unable to tolerate the agony required by the Tour reinforced the other pillar of the race's century-old heroic ethos: the cult of survival.

The contestants' goal was obviously to finish ahead of the other competitors (or help their team's star do so). Yet, from the earliest Tours, the press and the organizers set a premium not on victory but on survival: just completing the race required "uncommon energy," "extraordinary capabilities and supernatural qualities."[77] "The ideal Tour for me," Desgrange claimed, "would be one in which there were only one finisher at the Parc des Princes."[78] He therefore forbade the use of derailleurs until the late 1930s, imploring racers to "leave gear changes to women and the old, you are the kings, the giants of the road, you must vanquish the obstacles with which it confronts you by your means alone, without recourse to subterfuges unworthy of you."[79] Apparently lost on Desgrange was a curious paradox: the Tour, promoted by *L'Auto* as a modernizing crusade, had been created to publicize the merits of a new technology; yet the paper denied Tour racers the use of technological improvements ordinary bicyclists had enjoyed for a generation. The tension between advances that made cycling easier and the need to preserve the Tour's unmatched difficulty would repeatedly confront the organizers, sponsors, racers, and media, as illustrated by the debate about performance-enhancing drugs (see chapter 6).

The Tour's annual attrition rates reflected its unique harshness. Only 31.1 percent of the riders completed the Tour between 1903 and 1914, and 31.0 percent between 1919 and 1929. In the 1930s 55.0 percent finished, as a result of dramatic reductions in daily and overall distances, the sport's increasing professionalization, the move to national and regional teams, and the organizers' more rigorous selection of *touristes-routiers* and *individuels*. Moreover, the escalation in prize money and economic downturn during that decade provided additional motivation to stay in the race. Attrition increased during the first four Tours after World War II (1947–50), when only 44.6 percent of the racers finished, largely as a result of poor nutrition and of difficult training and racing conditions in the previous years. Over the next half century the percentage of racers completing the Tour steadily increased: 59.8 percent from 1951 to 1960; 63.3 percent from 1961 to 1970; 66.4 percent from 1971 to 1980; and 72.2 percent from 1981 to 1990. The rate dropped to 67.8 percent in the years 1991 to 2000, a decline attributable in large measure to the expulsions and withdrawals resulting from the doping scandal in 1998, when only 96 of 189 racers reached the Champs-Élysées.[80] Between 1947 and 2000, two thirds (65.3 percent) of all Tour participants made it to Paris, almost double the prewar rate (36.8 percent). This trend is attributable to further reductions in the Tour's length, the sport's continuing professionalization, improved equipment, medical care, and nutrition for the racers, and the increasingly scientific use of ever more effective performance-enhancing drugs.

Like weight loss, attrition rates provided statistical confirmation of the Tour's difficulty and thus of the courage and endurance of racers who managed to complete it. Reporters covering the Tour, whether for the print media or, later, for radio and television, referred to the racers as *rescapés* (survivors) and provided frequent updates about the number of contestants remaining in the event. In 1913, for example, the press—from the Catholic *La Croix* to the socialist *L'Humanité*—continually evoked the small numbers of survivors.[81] Describing the final stage for *Le Matin*, the writer Colette (hardly a typical sports journalist) noted that "the selection, admirably achieved by the race's difficulties, leaves, after 115 withdrawals, 25 contestants."[82] Most of the press presented the severe attrition rate of this "veritable race by elimination" in a positive light:[83] "Some, injured, withdrew before having seriously battled. Let us not accuse them. But many others were struck morally and did not have the courage and the energy required to overcome passing *défaillances* and the fatigue inherent to the great road races. . . . It would have been better to fight until the end so as to be part of the glorious phalanx that will be able to say later that it completed the memorable 1913 Tour."[84]

Noting that "never had there been such waste," that year *L'Humanité* provided its readers with a "Table of Withdrawals" indicating how many racers had dropped out during each of the fifteen stages.[85] Also struck by the number of withdrawals, *L'Ouest-Éclair* published a table of the attrition rates for previous Tours.[86] The organizers were at least partially responsible for the inordinately high attrition rate in 1913: to prevent group finishes, which smacked of unseemly collaboration between opponents, Desgrange scheduled the racers' last food checkpoint 140 kilometers from the finish line.[87] He apparently hoped to weaken certain racers and break up the *peloton*. *L'Auto's* obsession with attrition was more than self-serving promotional rhetoric; it was a project to be implemented.

The cult of survival was immediately revived in the wake of World War I and flourished in interwar coverage of the race, with headlines such as "The Tour de France of Eleven Cyclists" and daily articles announcing *abandons* (withdrawals) and lauding the *rescapés* or *survivants*.[88] The press continued to celebrate the "tough" men who completed the Tour.[89] So did many fans. In 1919 the popular French veteran racer Eugène Christophe was leading the Tour in its final days when, as in 1913 (see chapter 4), he suffered a mechanical breakdown. Although he had lost any chance at the overall victory, Christophe repaired his bicycle at a smithy and became one of only eleven racers to finish the Tour.[90] At the race's conclusion, the Paris suburb of Malakoff celebrated its hometown hero, greeting him with cries of "Vive Christophe!" as he entered the town square accompanied by his wife and friends. A twenty-man band struck up a triumphal march when the couple arrived at a local café for a reception in the racer's honor. The mayor gave a speech celebrating "the courage, the tenacity of the valiant hero." This was followed by remarks by a local sports-club president, who presented Christophe with a bronze statuette of a blacksmith, commissioned by the sports and music clubs of Malakoff and the racer's local fans to commemorate his perseverance.[91] Meanwhile, moved by his resilience in the face of such misfortune, *L'Auto* opened a fund for Christophe to which hundreds of fans across France donated sums. The final tally at the end of August exceeded 13,300 francs and was almost entirely the result of donations ranging from a few centimes to a few francs.[92] At a time when most French had little capital to devote to nonessential expenses, many nonetheless insisted on celebrating Christophe's determination to complete the race, perhaps because it echoed their own survival of four years of unprecedented material and human devastation.[93] World War I had been a war of attrition; so too was the Tour.

After World War II, even though attrition rates gradually decreased, *L'Équipe* and *Le Parisien Libéré* revived the Tour's Darwinian ethos to promote the event. "Such a race proposes the eternal theme: man against nature and against his own nature. . . . The weak will step aside on their own." The Tour was "this enormous machine . . . that crushes men and destroys hope."[94] During the first postwar Tour, *L'Équipe* ran a daily column, "The State of Their Health," that confirmed the race's effect on contestants.[95] The rest of the French press also resuscitated the *rescapé* image, wondering how many racers would make it back to Paris. *Le Monde* worried that the youth and inexperience of most of the participants, eighty-four of whom were new to the race, would take its toll. At the end of the Tour, *Le Populaire* noted that "fifty-three men finished. Not *'rescapés.'* The word is not appropriate, but champions in complete control of their faculties."[96] Even in rejecting the term, the socialist paper reinforced the Tour's cult of survival by suggesting that finishing rather than winning made a Tour racer a champion.

The enduring appeal of the Tour's cult of attrition was confirmed, in the years that followed, by the disappointment of commentators when the race did not effect a sufficiently rigorous selection.[97] For the organizers and much of the media, if too many racers reached Paris, the Tour was no longer a test of the very qualities that had always made the "giants of the road" heroic. Such concerns may have motivated article 41 in the regulations of the 1948 Tour, according to which the last-placed racer in the overall classification at the end of each stage would automatically be eliminated.[98] Although it was not maintained, this rule epitomized the Tour's Darwinian character, which was perhaps best summarized by Antoine Blondin, a novelist and journalist at *L'Équipe*. "The Tour de France," he observed, "is made great as much by what it eliminates as by what nourishes it. Its refuse is sublime."[99]

Postwar television coverage and film summaries of the race in movie theaters also adopted the language of attrition, as they showed the racers winding their way through the bombed ruins of cities like Caen.[100] By evoking national suffering and survival, such images reinforced the connection between heroic narratives of the Tour and the experiences of the average citizen. Many a Frenchman in 1947 likely identified with the veteran racer René Vietto when he complained that racers had received red meat only once since the start of the Tour, despite the fact that their "work" required a rich diet; he also requested fresh milk, as canned milk gave him colic.[101]

Although Vietto was the sentimental favorite in 1947, the press devoted considerable attention to Jean Robic, a young Breton newlywed competing in his first Tour. In addition to noting his small stature, press coverage emphasized his courage, determination, and stereotypically Breton stubbornness, pride, and energy.[102] Unlike Vietto, Robic had not been selected for the French national team and was instead a member of the lesser western regional team. Despite this disadvantage, the man *L'Équipe* dubbed *Jean le hargneux* ("the Fierce")[103] won three stages and remained near the top of the overall classification throughout the race. As the racers approached the capital on the Tour's final day, Robic attacked relentlessly, finally dropping his main rivals, including the race leader. By the time he reached the Parc des Princes his lead assured him of the overall victory. Following so closely on the heels of his wedding and the intense press coverage the young couple had received, Robic's victory resonated as a powerful symbol of renewal to a nation confronting the great challenge of postwar reconstruction.

In an initiative reminiscent of *L'Auto's* fund for Christophe in 1919, the organizers opened a *souscription* for a wedding present for the newlyweds. Despite their grim circumstances and the fact that Robic had earned more than six hundred thousand francs from his Tour victory,[104] over the next three months donations poured in from cafés, sports clubs, workers, employees, French occupation troops in Germany, Breton vicars, gendarmes, and other ordinary Frenchmen determined to reward the man *L'Équipe* described as a "remarkable example of audacity and tenacity, courage and reflection." "A Breton," the sports daily observed, "does not go down without using his final cartridges."[105] Three years after the liberation of France and the end of Vichy's shameful collaboration, Robic personified qualities with which many French wished to identify. The powerful appeal of the stubborn and resilient Breton underdog as a symbol of successful national resistance was later confirmed by the enduring success of the *Astérix* comic-book series, whose title character, like Robic a diminutive specimen, repeatedly triumphs over the Roman oppressors of ancient Gaul.

To this day, the cult of suffering and survival informs Tour coverage and the heroism associated with the race since 1903.[106] In a curious irony, that heroic ethos has in recent years been threatened by the Tour's very success: by the exponential increase in global media coverage of the past two decades and the consequently much higher financial and commercial stakes for team sponsors. It has become common for promising young racers who need to adapt gradually to the toughest event in their sport to plan to withdraw before the end of the Tour—before total exhaustion sets in. They do so with the full support of their sponsors, who seek to protect their long-term investment in their young stars.

Such an approach does not sit well with the organizers. In 1994, when the young American Lance Armstrong, the reigning world champion, withdrew after two-thirds of the race, the Tour's director Jean-Marie Leblanc was not pleased. He argued that racers who behaved in such a way "penalized themselves. They also wrong the race, the public, their employers." Leblanc dismissed such attempts "to avoid 'burning out.' . . . I see rather a loss of one's sense of duty, and I even find that humiliating for the individual involved."[107] Although Leblanc did not explicitly make the point, it was clear that a racer who decided to withdraw as part of a long-term career strategy—before physical or psychological breakdown had occurred—rejected survival as his primary objective. In so doing he undermined the Tour's cult of attrition and suffering and the heroic masculinity with which it had long been associated.

A former racer, described by *L'Équipe* as a "fierce defender of values," understood what was at stake: "In the old days, to finish the Tour meant something to a racer." Now, he complained, some racers entered the Tour simply to attempt a one-day exploit, which so exhausted them that they could not continue.[108] Although such an approach gave their sponsors considerable media exposure on the day of the attempted exploit, it clearly violated the Tour's century-old heroic ethos. Yet perhaps all was not lost: by withdrawing, these racers increased the Tour's attrition rate and thereby reinforced the heroic stature of the remaining *rescapés*.

STABLE FAMILIES AND TRADITIONAL GENDER ROLES: THE WOMEN OF THE "GIANTS OF THE ROAD"

Even as they emphasized the hypermasculinity of men who accepted such extreme suffering, heroic narratives about the Tour did not exclude women. In addition to the *spectatrices* whose attraction to these rugged men was continually evoked, from the very first Tour the organizers and other commentators inserted the racers' female kin into their coverage. As conveyed by the media, the experiences of the racers' mothers, wives, fiancées, girlfriends, and even young daughters reinforced gendered representations of the Tour founded on a narrative of separation inspired by objective reality: unlike other athletes (and, indeed, male workers in general), Tour participants left home for a month to make their living, traveling across France and often venturing into neighboring countries. By emphasizing their womenfolk as steadfast, if emotional nurturers of heroic breadwinners, such coverage presented traditional, complementary gender roles, repeatedly under assault throughout the twentieth century, as both positive and natural.

This narrative of separation followed a predictable progression, beginning with the racers' painful departure, continuing with brief, poignant meetings between racers and their female relatives along the itinerary, and concluding with joyful family reunions in Paris at the end of the race.[109] In 1903 Alexandre Foureaux found his wife at the Nevers checkpoint, where "the newlyweds embraced tenderly" before he set off again. The following year in the town of Saintes, *L'Auto* described Philippe Jousselin's wife encouraging him and giving him soup. In 1909 one particularly persistent mother, whose son would win that year's Tour, became a recurring character in *L'Auto*'s coverage. The organizers described the "touching scene" of the "good mother Faber" rushing to embrace her son François at the end of one stage and her presence the following day at the Metz finish line, against his express wishes. At the Tour's conclusion she reappeared, flanked by François and her other son (who had finished sixth), both of whom "were devouring her with caresses. It brought tears to the happy mother's eyes."[110]

The racers' wives, fiancées, and girlfriends often corresponded with them during the race, offering further evidence of the support and commitment they could expect from the devoted women they had left at home.[111] In 1908 *L'Auto* published the letter of one young woman to her fiancé. "I know your courage and your energy well enough to place you in good position," she wrote. "To reward you I am sending you two big kisses, and if my thought[s] can sustain you, I am sending [them] all." Describing her letter as "adorable," *L'Auto* imagined the mixed emotions of this "good little Marie-Louise" at the Carcassonne checkpoint, where her fiancé would barely take the time to sign in and give her "a big kiss" before heading off again: "You will then have to spend fifteen long days without seeing him."[112]

As the above account and the 1909 coverage of François Faber's mother illustrate, the separation was typically described as especially painful for the racer's female relatives.[113] Such anecdotes reaffirmed the enduring stability of traditional gender roles in the belle époque, when fears about the "new woman" abounded: for *L'Auto,* in particular, men remained stoic heroes, women (including those who helped racers in concrete ways) the emotional and ultimately helpless witnesses to their heroism.

Between the wars, Tour coverage paid even more attention to racers' female relatives than before the war, emphasizing the toll the racers' heroism took on their loved ones. In 1937 an article in L'Auto on "the mood of the wives of our champions on the eve of the start" informed readers of the various emotions, ranging from confidence in their husbands to nervousness and worry, with which five women awaited the Tour.[114] At times the moment of separation was explicitly presented in gendered terms: when faced with his wife's emotional reaction to his impending departure for the Tour, one *touriste-routier* admitted that he was "glad to be a man, because it's always the men who leave and the women who stay behind."[115] At the end of a stage or of the Tour itself, mothers, wives, and young daughters were photographed and described tearfully embracing the exhausted, "sweaty and disfigured" athletes, "tough men and good lads" all, with predictably salutary results: "The suffering goes away, happiness blooms."[116] After a final shower and massage at the Parc des Princes, the racers "rejoined their families and enjoyed in their homes the best reward for the formidable effort produced."[117]

Meanwhile, throughout the race, L'Auto, especially, offered anecdotes, real and fictitious, about how wives and girlfriends coped and the emotional support they provided racers in the form of good-luck charms, letters, and telephone calls. Wives kept abreast of their husbands' progress on the radio, showed up along the itinerary or at the end of a stage to comfort and encourage them, and persuaded them to continue when they were injured or demoralized.[118] Some telephoned the paper the evening after a stage for the latest news about their husbands, leading L'Auto to conclude that "they certainly experience emotions, the little wives of our racers . . . with their glorious husbands!!!"[119] On the other hand, the organizers penalized racers whose wives and girlfriends followed them in cars, for such support violated rules regulating the kind of assistance Tour participants could receive.[120] The practice also blurred the line between heroic racers, courageously confronting the Tour's challenges, and their female kin, whom L'Auto preferred to depict at home or in contact with the racers only during a pause in the race.

L'Auto's portrayals of united, hard-working young couples after World War I may have been particularly comforting to readers confronting the era's grim demographic reality: between two and a half and three million

French men had been either killed or wounded in the war. Hundreds of thousands of women had been widowed, hundreds of thousands more would never marry, and millions became, for a time at least, the principal providers for their families. Fictitious, embellished, or real, *L'Auto*'s accounts of the separation and sacrifices racers and their wives endured during the Tour, and the mutual support they extended to each other in the hope of building a better future together, offered a welcome counterpoint to widespread anxiety about disturbing new female stereotypes such as *la garçonne* and *la femme seule*.[121] Readers could hope that a nation endowed with such resilient young couples would in time recover from the catastrophe that had befallen it.[122] Similarly, when *L'Auto* and other newspapers presented the racers' joyful return home as the best reward for a month of dangerous, exhausting labor, they reasserted the value of a domestic ideal that the war's devastating human toll had, at least temporarily, rendered moot for millions of French families.

As we saw earlier, in 1947 the French press devoted considerable attention to Jean Robic's recent wedding. Its coverage emphasized the life of the newlyweds during the race: his fidelity, their correspondence, and her encouragement, which, he happily acknowledged, inspired his exploits.[123] The focus on the role Robic's wife played in his victory signaled an important continuity in Tour coverage after World War II: the racers' female relatives, especially their spouses, were once again given a prominent place.[124] The media revived the familiar narrative of separation, providing an annual inventory of the various ways wives supported their husbands, including visits along the itinerary.[125] Daily photographs showed racers being greeted at the end of a stage or of the Tour itself by their girlfriends, daughters, mothers, and spouses (who were sometimes pregnant), or receiving a visit during a rest day as they relaxed in their hotel rooms. The *Actualités françaises* in movie theaters also included such scenes in its Tour coverage.[126] The press made much of the joy of reunited couples at the Tour's conclusion, which signaled the end of the racers' suffering.[127]

As before the war, Tour coverage emphasized the many emotions—hope, sadness, disappointment, relief, joy, and pride—that the racers' female relatives, particularly their wives, experienced during the race.[128] Perhaps the dominant emotions for racers' spouses were worry and fear, as they listened to radio coverage and telephoned to find out the day's results.[129] Some wives asserted that it was as difficult to follow the Tour on the radio as to compete in it. Evoking the classic statistical measure of Tour heroism, one woman revealed that she had lost more weight than her husband during a recent race.[130] In 1951 Louison Bobet's wife explained:

> During the Tour de France . . . I listen to the radio and switch from one station to the next. . . . I think that all racers' wives are like me: especially during mountain stages we go through all sorts of anguish. I have freed myself from the oppression that grips me only when I learn that Louison has arrived at the finish line.
>
> In the evening, however, when I phone him I try not to let any of my worry show. On the contrary, if he has had problems, I try to improve his morale. I speak to him of Maryse and Philippe [their children]. For him, that's the best drug.[131]

As Mme Bobet's testimony illustrates, Tour coverage continued to emphasize that a stable, happy family life got racers through difficult times during the race.[132] In 1949 *L'Équipe* opined that the only thing preventing Lucien Teisseire from fulfilling his athletic potential and becoming a champion was "a haven, a home . . . which only marriage can offer him." Four years later, in an article titled "The Wives of Tour Racers Play Their Part," the paper happily reported that his wife's support and advice, and the "serenity" and "familial climate" he found with her and their infant daughter, had been instrumental in helping Teisseire resurrect his racing career.[133] Racers' wives were fully aware of their obligations: a wife had to be able to adapt and understand the requirements of her husband's profession, and a racer with an unhappy wife often did not succeed in the sport.[134] Meanwhile, not only was the public encouraged to celebrate the racers' families, but at times it was actually rewarded for doing so: one of the winning entries in a 1954 photo competition for Tour fans was of the 1950 winner Ferdi Kubler and his wife; another was of "the little Maryse Bobet kiss[ing] her champion father [who won his second consecutive Tour that year] under the melting look of Mme Bobet."[135]

As before the war, the Tour's rigid gender order was reinforced by the restricted visitation rights that prevailed for couples during the race. Tour regulations allowed a racer to receive visitors, but only with the authorization of his team manager, "the principle being that the communal life of the team is obligatory, under the control of the Team Manager and the organizers, during the entire event."[136] The latter did not like the racers' wives visiting, even on rest days, a reluctance that one wife (Helen Hoban, formerly Helen Simpson) attributed to old myths about the nefarious impact of women on racers who must "not be led astray." Her contact with her husband during the Tour was limited to phone conversations and, during the one or two scheduled rest days, frustratingly brief visits in between his professional obligations (media interviews, meals, massage, and rest). Although she had driven hundreds of miles to see him, she was not permitted to eat with her husband or stay in the same hotel: the race organizers made racers' wives feel "very small."[137]

So, too, did the team managers. When two women arrived in Jambes during the 1967 Tour to see their husbands, the latter's *directeur sportif* "asked these ladies . . . to go sleep elsewhere." They obeyed, and *L'Équipe* applauded their self-discipline as evidence of their love for their husbands.[138] In recent years, well-paid racers have been able to fly themselves and their spouses to and from the Tour.[139] Still, the marginalization of racers' spouses, and the strict rules regarding their contact with their husbands during the Tour, continue to this day.[140] In 1999 French television ran a story on the wife of a Tour neophyte. She visited him at the end of every stage, but was required to respect team rules and eat at a separate table during the team's meals. A team official said that the visits were allowed because the young couple was very much in love and his wife's presence helped the racer, but that this unusual arrangement would be tolerated only as long as it did not prove disruptive to the team.[141]

If the racers' relatives were the most prominent female "extras" featured in race coverage, other women continued to be integrated into Tour narratives after World War II in ways that reinforced conventional female roles and identities. Nurses followed the race in ambulances, ministering to injured racers.[142] *Spectatrices,* ranging from "beautiful girls in shorts" to "nuns in cornets," awaited the racers along the itinerary. If their numbers, beauty, encouragement of, and attraction to the racers continued to be noted, the "racial" implications of the racers' desirability were not: after World War II, not only was France experiencing a remarkable baby boom, but there was also perhaps a newfound reluctance to convey any message that might smack of eugenics, given the horrific legacy of the Nazis.[143] The gendered reading of the public endured nonetheless. When a racer set off after a terrible fall, "on each side of the road, women crossed themselves upon seeing him pass by like a ghost covered in blood."[144] In the mountains, "the women, the first to be moved to pity, incapable of tolerating the sight of these masks of pain covered in dust, dripping with sweat, grimacing on their machines, cried out with tears in their voices: 'Help them! . . . Push them! . . . But what are you waiting for?'"[145]

Seeking to exploit the assumed sensitivity of women, after World War II some newspapers sent female journalists to cover the race and offer a woman's perspective on the Tour. *L'Humanité* did so regularly, explaining that because women, unlike men, expressed their feelings, their reactions made for more interesting coverage.[146] Proud that the communist paper had made her the only woman covering the 1950 Tour, the communist intellectual Hélène Parmelin acknowledged her outsider status as a woman who knew nothing about cycling; she reported on the three nurses who followed the racers.[147] For the great Italian racer Gino Bartali, a conservative Catholic and two-time Tour champion, Parmelin's race coverage confirmed that women "were everywhere." He wondered who took care of her domestic chores during the race; in an answer he was unlikely to find comforting, she explained that her husband did so.[148] In 1966 Huguette Debaisieux covered the race for *Le Figaro,* also from an explicitly female perspective. She, too, was aware of her exceptional status as one of ten women accompanying the Tour (the others were five majorettes, three nurses, and the singer Annie Cordy). In a twist on Bartali's remarks, Debaisieux placed her participation in the context of the rapidly evolving postwar gender order: "The Tour is, with the Stock Exchange, the National Assembly and the Council of State, one of the last bastions that women have not really succeeded in infiltrating. . . . The Tour is the triumph of the male freemasonry."[149]

Images of women fulfilling traditional roles before World War II had countered the appearance of disturbing new female types who undermined the established gender order. After World War II, not only did French women obtain the right to vote, but the 1960s and 1970s saw the emergence of a new wave of French feminism, new fashions—the miniskirt, in particular—that challenged conventional notions of proper female dress, and new rights for women.[150] Contraceptives were legalized in the late 1960s; in 1972 they were being sold in pharmacies nationwide, and their use increased rapidly. In 1974 abortion was legalized and the purchase of contraceptives, even by minors and without parental consent, began to be reimbursed by the state. The following year, the 1884 divorce law was significantly liberalized. These developments reflected the emergence of a new youth culture that celebrated the individual's right to autonomy and self-fulfillment. This culture in turn sparked new attitudes toward relationships that resulted, in the early 1970s, in a decline in both the marriage rate and the total number of marriages, as well as an increase in premarital cohabitation. The percentage of children born out of wedlock began to climb even as France's thirty-year baby boom came to an end and its birthrate began to decline.[151] Clearly, the institution of marriage and the family unit were undergoing significant change.

It was true, as Debaisieux suggested, that French women had generally made only marginal gains in the workplace, economic parity, and professional politics; in all three areas, significant gender inequalities persisted.[152] Nevertheless, even before many of the advances described above, Bartali's comment suggests that women after World War II were widely seen as more liberated, autonomous, and empowered than ever before, and Parmelin's explanation that her husband had replaced her at home while she reported on the Tour was anecdotal evidence of this new reality. For conservatives and others concerned by the rapid and profound changes in postwar French society, the ever-supportive Tour wife who embraced her domestic responsibilities and subordinated her own professional ambitions to the requirements of her husband's racing career must have been a welcome, if largely symbolic, palliative.

HEROIC SOLDIERS AND WOMEN
ON THE HOME FRONT

The cult of suffering and survival, combined with the narrative of separation, reinforced gendered representations of the Tour by facilitating comparisons of the Tour with war. As the public celebrations of the unlucky Christophe and the victorious Robic attest, each in the immediate wake of a World War, the *rescapé* image could be seamlessly merged with that of the heroic soldier: Christophe had evoked a *poilu* in 1919, Robic a Resistance fighter in 1947.[153] The connection between cycling and war predated World War I and even the first Tour in 1903. As we have seen, in the late nineteenth century, cycling clubs were involved in the military training of French youth at a time when sport was widely seen as the principal way for the French army to overcome the humiliations of Sedan, Fashoda, and Dreyfus. Playing on contemporary concerns about the moral and physical condition of the French army, *L'Auto* claimed that the Tour created its own "elite soldiers of the glorious army of modern sport, mounted upon their frail companions, without Bonaparte to lead them, but, like the old soldiers of the Republic, with the idea of victory firmly anchored in their soul of bronze, . . . [who] are going to storm the *massif* of the Grande-Chartreuse."[154] References to the *grande armée* of the First Republic conferred a measure of historical heroism on the racers and suggested that an army drawing on such specimens was unlikely to suffer the humiliating defeats of recent generations.[155]

If comparing sport to war was hardly an original rhetorical device, the Tour lent itself to such portrayals even more than other athletic events. Each stage became a battle in an annual, three-week campaign, as *L'Auto*'s continual references to "attacks," "strategies," "alliances," "armies," "decisive battles," "veterans," and "road captains" (the team leaders) made clear. Some journalists were fully aware of the press's role in transforming the Tour racer into a heroic warrior: in 1914 *L'Est Républicain* noted the "Homeric hyperbole" employed to describe star racers like "François Faber, the 'hero of Colombes,'" and "the famous Cruppelandt," who were "honored with no less pomp than Achilles and Patroclus, the wise Ulysses, or the king of kings, Agamemnon."[156]

Far from inhibiting military representations of the Tour, World War I inspired interwar press coverage of the race. The contestants who completed the 1919 Tour were "eleven *poilus*," while the happiness of racers reaching a mountaintop in 1926 was compared to that of troops being relieved from trench duty.[157] Articles spoke of "seriously injured" racers, conveying the toll taken by the race with headlines like "the massacre of the innocent cyclists," "a veritable massacre," and "injuries and withdrawals." The Tour was a "sort of athletic guerilla warfare, friendly but without mercy."[158] Accustomed to the language of suffering and survival and to military representations of the Tour, many readers may have seen the comparison between soldiers and racers as natural. What they knew about the horrendous conditions of trench warfare reinforced their understanding of the Tour; what they knew about the race's uniquely harsh conditions reinforced their understanding of the war. *Le Matin*'s description of Tour racers, "these heroes," as "magnificently hideous," "skinny, brown, caked in dust, dripping with sweat," endowed with "supreme energy," their eyes "sunken and haggard," their legs thin, muscular, and often bloody, their faces contorted in "a grimace of suffering and pride," and their clothing tattered and faded, likely resonated with a public who had recently welcomed home such beings from the front.[159]

The fact that, as one regional paper noted, almost all the racers in the 1919 Tour had actually fought in the war further legitimized the comparison. Indeed, *L'Éclaireur de l'Est* attributed the high attrition rates of the first postwar Tour to "the poor health of our youth [which has] survived the global cataclysm."[160] *L'Auto* observed that the war had taken a heavy toll on the great prewar racers, "gloriously dead for the Fatherland," including the Tour winners Petit-Breton and François Faber.[161] In May 1915, during an attack at Garency, Faber abandoned his trench to assist a gravely wounded comrade who was calling for help near the German lines. Faber lifted the man to his shoulders and had almost made it back to his trench when the "giant of Colombes" was felled by a German bullet.[162] Another Tour champion, Octave Lapize, served as a *sergent-pilote* in the war and was killed in a dogfight in 1917.[163] Perhaps aware that Tour racers had fought and died by their side, many soldiers, far from objecting to the comparison, felt a connection to their cycling brethren. In 1919 the real *poilus* of Fontainebleau offered 26.25 francs to the top B category racer, while a veteran from Narbonne who was still under the colors donated 5 francs to the last racer passing through his city. "Please accept it," he implored, "from a little *poilu* who would like to do more but truly cannot."[164]

The narrative of separation took on a special resonance in the wake of World War I. The racers' departure for the Tour was associated, sometimes explicitly, with the familiar image of a soldier leaving his spouse for the front. *L'Auto* described one woman's "moist look, heavy with tenderness and inexpressible love," as she contemplated her husband, "a handsome fellow who leaves for the Tour a little as [one leaves] for war."[165] Another racer's wife could not bring herself to read newspapers or listen to the radio for fear of bad news. Referring to a recent accident involving two prominent racers, she explained:

> You think about the shock that Archambaud's wife and Maes's parents must have felt when they learned about the accident like that, without warning, without details. . . . That's not a life! . . . You go to bed at night with the idea that he still has his arms and legs, but the next day your worry begins again. . . . And the reporters who describe all the risks they take, that they go down the slopes *à "tombeau ouvert"* [at breakneck speed, literally, at "open grave" speed], that expression doesn't seem like much when you read it like that: but me, when I go to sleep at night, I see an open grave and him falling into it! (She wipes away a little tear.) . . . Popularity, glory, does that matter to us women? . . . No, I don't think so! . . . But that glory, we pay for it with our heartbeats![166]

The comparison to soldiers' wives anxiously awaiting news of their husbands' fate at the front, evident to any contemporary reader, provided a powerful point of identification for fans of both sexes, particularly when a racer's wife visited her injured husband in a hospital after a crash.[167]

When racers' female relatives left the "home front" to support their menfolk along the itinerary, their appearance at the race's "front lines," far from blurring gender distinctions, reinforced gendered readings of the Tour. In 1924 at the checkpoint in Lamballe (Brittany), a young woman burst through the crowd to fill a racer's food pouch and give him a kiss before he set off again. She explained tearfully that the man was her brother-in-law: "His brother, my husband, was killed in the war, so you understand!"[168] That year a somber reunion silenced the throng at the end of the Tour: "Beeckman had barely crossed the finish line when a lady dressed in black rushed towards him and took him away. The crowd watched the group leave without saying a word, but they understood that Beeckman was a son and the lady dressed in black a mother."[169]

As reported by the press, such reunions and the reactions of Tour crowds, once again transformed into representative microcosms of the nation, were moving evocations in the war's aftermath of both the redemptive power of family and the tragic losses millions of French families had suffered. Because of its popularity, its difficulty, and its identification with a military campaign, the Tour resonated with the French as no other event could—as a "war" from which soldiers returned home haggard and bloodied, but alive. The race served a double purpose, perhaps best captured by the poignant figure of Mme Beeckman: a widow welcoming home her son, she personified both a nation in mourning and one nurturing a generation of heroic survivors who would ensure its future.[170]

France's experience in World War II—a rapid defeat followed by a four-year German occupation and the collaboration of the Vichy regime—was nothing like the nation's legendary Union Sacrée and heroic defense along the Western Front in World War I. This did not, however, prevent the press from immediately resuscitating martial imagery to describe the race. Postwar Tour coverage was peppered with references to declarations of war, battles, battlefields, and battle orders; legions, captains, and soldiers; corpses, trenches, and wars of movement; attacks, cease-fires, truces, and nights before combat (veillées d'armes). Headlines spoke apocalyptically of "massacres" and "Waterloo," and some years a daily column, "the eliminated of each stage," served as a kind of running list of fallen racers who had withdrawn.[171] Racers' occupations outside cycling were described as their "civilian" jobs; so, too, were their jobs racing for commercial sponsors in other races (until 1962, when the Tour itself turned to sponsored teams).[172] Meanwhile, racers' wives saw themselves as military spouses. One woman described her life in the 1960s and 1970s as "very regimented, very strict, very dedicated," and geared to her husband's training and competitions, all of which left little time for a social life: "It is literally like being in the army."[173]

Specific references to World War II, however, were rare, which was hardly surprising given the French experience of defeat, occupation, and collaboration.[174] In 1958 *L'Équipe* ran a story cautiously associating the French team's poor performance with the chaotic evacuation of French and British troops, under intense German pressure, from Dunkerque in the spring of 1940.[175] Most references to the war evoked heroic figures and activities of the French Resistance. In 1959, when divisions between the stars of the French team threatened its cohesion, the paper noted that "For the unity of the French team, Marcel Bidot [its manager] issues his call of . . . June 18," a reference to de Gaulle's famous BBC broadcast from London in 1940 urging all French to resist the Vichy regime and Nazi occupation.[176] In 1966 *Le Figaro* compared Jacques Goddet, who typically followed the racers standing in his car and attired in a safari outfit, to General Leclerc in 1944: "Yesterday," its journalist reported, "I was in the front lines on board the battle tank of Jacques Goddet. . . . For *L'Équipe*'s editor the stages are army maneuvers." The radio messages transmitted to and from Goddet's car reminded her of the clandestine messages of the Resistance.[177]

Fueled by the racers' suffering and separation from their families, conventional representations of their wives, mothers, daughters, and female fans in Tour coverage reinforced the heroic image of the "giants of the road." There was one kind of woman, however, who could utterly undermine that image by collapsing the distinctions on which the race's heroic narratives were founded: the female bicycle racer.

ARE THERE NO *GÉANTES DE LA ROUTE?*

Beyond the restrictive discourses and representations examined earlier, what was the reality of female cycling in the belle époque? The absence of sales figures for women's bicycles makes an accurate assessment of the numbers of female cyclists impossible.[178] On the other hand, French advertising posters prove that cycle manufacturers clearly identified women as potential customers. These posters often played on male insecurities by portraying women cyclists as both strong and feminine, and celebrating the bicycle as an instrument of female pleasure and emancipation.[179] The research of Catherine Bertho-Lavenir on the Touring Club de France confirms that middle-class women did indeed mount their new bicycles to explore the French countryside.[180] Of greater concern to those who feared that France was mired in a crisis of masculinity, female cyclists were among the first women to penetrate, however tenuously, the male domain of athletic competition.

The first recorded women's bicycle races in France were held in 1868 in Bordeaux and in the Bois de Boulogne in Paris, but female competitors soon encountered resistance. In 1869 a woman using the pseudonym "Miss America" completed the first major road race, Paris-Rouen. She finished twenty-ninth out of the thirty-three contestants who completed the event within the twenty-four-hour time limit, some one hundred participants (four or five of them women) having started the race. The occasional use by women of pseudonyms suggests that they were aware of the hostility their participation in serious bicycle races might spark, especially when they competed against men and once cycling had established itself as the most popular sport of the day. Although an 1882 law extended obligatory gymnastics classes to girls' primary schools, the idea of public athletic competitions for women remained controversial. In 1891 the organizers of the 1,200-kilometer Paris-Brest-Paris race forbade the seven women who signed up from starting the race, no doubt believing that its prodigious distance, the longest in road racing at the time, justified their decision. On the other hand, the 1890s did see the organization of track events for women, including endurance events held over six, eight, and twelve days (with, however, only one or two hours of actual racing each day). A variety of women's records were established, some of which came close to recently recorded male performances, and at least two French women were unofficially crowned female world champion. A decade later Marie Marvingt, who would soon become a record-setting female aviator, actually completed her own Tour de France. When permitted to do so, women continued to compete against men, suggesting that at least some organizers and spectators still found their participation a titillating novelty.[181]

Such initiatives notwithstanding, a broad coalition of commentators and "experts," including doctors, moralists, clergymen, and prominent officials in the physical education and sports movement, rejected female competitions as a "public exhibition." They agreed with Baron Pierre de Coubertin, the founder of the modern Olympic Games, that women's primary role at sporting events was to crown the victors.[182] Some advised female cyclists not to compete in races, arguing that they lacked men's energy and strength. In 1909 *L'Auto* dismissed a female reader's proposal for the creation of a women's Tour de France, claiming that this would require razing the mountains on the itinerary.[183] Given this widespread bias, it is not surprising that although female bicycle races experienced some success, due in large part to their novelty, they did not succeed in firmly establishing themselves prior to World War I.[184] On 17 October 1912, the Union Vélocipédique de France decided no longer to sanction races for women.[185] Perhaps the federation was disturbed by female achievements that undermined claims of male superiority; perhaps it was troubled by the gender chaos implicit in contests pitting the two sexes against each other in a sport that allowed for the precise measurement of physical performances; perhaps it simply gave in to persistent criticism of competitive female cycling as "unfeminine." Whatever its motivations, by removing institutional support from female cycling, the federation eroded the credibility of women's races, dealing them a blow from which they have yet to recover.

Although female cyclists were by the interwar years generally accepted figures, the bias against women's races persisted despite anecdotal evidence, often provided by *L'Auto* itself, that some women demonstrated the physical and moral qualities required for long-distance events. In 1921 one woman rose at four in the morning and cycled ninety kilometers to watch the racers pass by.[186] Occasionally, female cyclists, including champions, sought to keep up with Tour racers during a stage. For the most part *L'Auto* mocked their efforts, pointing out how quickly they had been dropped by the *peloton*.[187] In 1926 another sports paper, *Sportives,* reflected the bias against women's races: "That *sportswomen* go on rides for fun, nobody can object to that, but that women speed 'like giants of the road,' no, a hundred times no!"[188] When two young women actually managed to keep up with the racers for more than 155 kilometers, *L'Auto* applauded their achievement, but rather than suggest that it might justify the inclusion of women in the race or the creation of a women's Tour, the paper encouraged the two to compete for the title of French national women's road-racing champion.[189]

A number of female sports and cycling organizations did attempt to give a new impetus to competitive female cycling between the wars, but their efforts failed to establish its credibility. Although excluded from track events, women competed in their own road and cyclo-cross races. In the 1930s French women set semiofficial records for the hour time trial: in 1938 the women's record was 35.670 kilometers, the men's 45.840 kilometers.[190] For much of the public, such a disparity may have confirmed the long-assumed inferiority of female cyclists and the lack of credibility of their sport.

Rigidly gendered Tour narratives no doubt also played an important role in the marginalization of female cyclists: stressing public physical agony as the heroic standard par excellence violated widely held notions of appropriate womanly conduct. As we have seen, when women were encouraged to exercise, they were urged to so in ways least likely to jeopardize their femininity: women grimacing in pain, bleeding from a fall, or exercising to the point of exhaustion—the common lot of bicycle racers—clearly violated social conventions. Inherited from the nineteenth century, the influential "separate spheres" ideology divided social reality into a private, female sphere of domestic responsibilities and a public, male sphere of work, politics, and war. This dichotomy extended to the notion of physical suffering: private suffering, notably in childbirth, was distinctly female; public suffering—whether in war or its civilian analogue, sport—distinctly male. As before the war, the Tour and top-flight cycling were to remain the exclusive domain of heroic "soldiers" and hypervirile "giants of the road," while female racers were limited to women's events that received little, if any, media attention and were not taken seriously by the public.

"Since women smoke and vote," a Parisian woman exclaimed on the eve of the 1947 Tour, "there is no reason they can't race in the Tour."[191] If such a proposition no doubt still struck most observers as absurd, nevertheless in the 1950s female cycling became an officially recognized sport. Not only did the FFC and UCI (the Fédération Française de Cyclisme and the Union Cycliste Internationale, the French and international cycling federations) create official female road-racing championships, but the UCI reversed itself and agreed to recognize female records.[192] In 1955 a "Tour féminin cycliste" was organized for members of the FFC and FSGT (Fédération Sportive et Gymnique du Travail). It lasted five days and covered 372 kilometers, and its leader wore a white jersey. Thirty-seven of the forty-eight participants completed the race; the top finishers spent barely two hours a day racing.[193] The event was not held again, perhaps because of a lack of interest in a Tour so unworthy of the name, perhaps because the sport was growing so slowly: in 1960 there were only thirty-four *licenciées* in the FFC, in 1975 their number topped four hundred. Thereafter, the sport's development accelerated: in 1982 the FFC had 1,500 female members, who nevertheless represented but 2.66 percent of its total membership.[194] The number of official French competitions for women kept pace, increasing from 120 in 1972 to 444 in 1984.[195] Top female racers were now proving themselves legitimate athletes, in some cases by competing directly if unofficially against men: in 1984 Betsy King covered the itinerary of Bordeaux-Paris, a professional men's race of almost six hundred kilometers, finishing only ten minutes behind the last male competitor to complete the event.[196]

Women's cycling in France reached a potentially momentous turning point in 1983 when one of the Tour's organizers, Félix Lévitan of *Le Parisien Libéré*, decided to hold the first official Tour de France *féminin* the following summer. The timing was hardly a coincidence: recent performances by female marathon runners had emphatically demonstrated women's endurance. Reflecting the ongoing reassessment of female capacities, the 1984 Olympic Games in Los Angeles included two new events: a women's marathon and a women's bicycle road race. Meanwhile, that summer, the first women's Tour took place. Covering 1,080 kilometers in eighteen stages (none of which exceeded 80 kilometers), it was held on the same days and itinerary as the men's Tour, with one key distinction: the female contestants started on average about 60 kilometers from each day's finish line, arriving just ahead of the *caravane publicitaire* and about an hour and a half before the male racers. This arrangement meant that the huge crowds awaiting the men would first witness and—it was hoped—applaud the efforts of their female counterparts.[197]

There were, however, significant organizational hurdles to overcome. Although only about a quarter the length of the men's race, the female Tour violated decades-old international regulations mandating rest time for female racers in a multistage event. The UCI agreed to make an exception for the women's Tour and send an official to the race who would make recommendations about new regulations based on his observations. There were also financial obstacles: given the small budget allocated by the FFC for female cycling, the Tour's organizers agreed to cover the cost of the women's race. Finally, although twelve teams had initially been expected, several refused to enter or withdrew before the start. Some did so for financial reasons, others because they had committed to a race in Colorado, others yet because the women's Tour would conclude just five days before the start of the Olympics and thus disrupt the preparation of racers competing in the

Games. In the end, with numerous top racers absent, thirty-six women took the start. They were divided into six national teams: two French teams and one each from the United States, Canada, Great Britain, and the Netherlands. The winner finished in 29 hours 39 minutes and 2 seconds, just 49 minutes and 5 seconds ahead of the last-place finisher. Only one racer dropped out.[198]

Lévitan's motivation in creating the women's Tour extended beyond the world of sport: "For some time now my wife and I have thought that women do not occupy the position they deserve in society. . . . Woman is the equal of man, when she is not superior to him. Biologically that is proven by the Faculté [medical schools] and scientists. Therefore, we thought about organizing something greater than anything that had been done to this point in cycling for athletic women."[199]

Even before the race got under way, it was clear that the Lévitans were not alone in perceiving the broader implications of a women's Tour. In December 1983 a former sports editor in chief at *Méridional,* a paper with a circulation of one hundred thousand, published a letter in *La Provence Cycliste* decrying the proposed race. Although he claimed to admire women who bicycled for fun and acknowledged their "perfect right to have their own Tour," the writer, a M. Vivaldi, expressed "aesthetic" objections to women's races:

A woman who runs, a woman who jumps, a woman who swims, that's good.

A woman who pedals, that's less pretty. . . .

Can you see them arriving completely exhausted at l'Alpe d'Huez or Avoriaz, all grey from the dust or black from the mud?

Will they dare confront, in this disfigured state, the television cameras without first cleaning up?

The feminine ideal *[l'éternel féminin]* could take one hell of a blow.[200]

M. Vivaldi's views elicited a response in a subsequent issue of *La Provence Cycliste* from a M. Brondi, who was in charge of a regional club of women racers, the Féminines Côte d'Azur. Like Lévitan, he placed the upcoming women's Tour in its broader context, arguing that not only did women assume in their daily lives the same responsibilities as men, but they performed as well in sports and were still progressing. Brondi rejected Vivaldi's claim that female cyclists were not pretty: on the contrary, because cycling was such a tough sport, it "refines the human body."[201] Thus, even as he defended women's athletic abilities and equality to men, Brondi implicitly accepted Vivaldi's assumption that women had an obligation to be attractive and should eschew activities that prevented them from fulfilling that obligation: rather than "disfiguring" women, Brondi simply claimed that competitive cycling actually made them more attractive. Both men were resuscitating century-old concerns about beauty, femininity, and female cycling.

This exchange prefigured the coverage sparked by the first women's Tour in the summer of 1984.[202] On the eve of the race, Lévitan described its organizers as "pioneers" and acknowledged that the Tour *féminin* would never have been created had he not bypassed the national federation, as "the ideas of the men in charge of female cycling are backward, and are not in harmony with the evolution of female cycling. I am convinced that this first Tour de France will give a new dimension to top-flight female cycling." Lévitan predicted that female racers would soon demonstrate the ability to negotiate much tougher and longer stage races than this first women's Tour.[203]

Stressing its length and difficulty, many commentators agreed that the race was a historic initiative and its participants "pioneers" in what *L'Équipe* described as the "misogynous world of cycling," at a time when women were already competing in many important sports.[204] *Le Monde* dismissed the aesthetic and athletic objections of skeptics who believed women should focus on tennis and figure skating.[205] Struck by their high average pace,[206] commentators observed that the racers were putting the lie to longstanding prejudices against female bicycle races.[207] "One must acknowledge," *Le Figaro* concluded, "that all these representatives of the so-called weak sex demonstrated exceptional physical and moral capacities to finish the Tour."[208]

L'Humanité drew attention to the broader implications of the women's Tour. The communist daily observed that "since 1903, the condition of women in French society has changed" and linked the race to earlier victories for women, notably the right to vote, their "massive entry into the world of work," and contraceptive methods that had given them "a certain autonomy that has an impact in all areas." The paper singled out sport, especially competition, as an activity in which women's participation had long been restricted by "an ideology, by a culture that still tends to enclose women in very precise roles: those of mother, housewife, or sex object." Like the first women's Olympic marathon, the first women's Tour would break taboos and contribute to advances for women.[209] The racers, too, were aware of the event's symbolic importance: one of them asserted that "each yellow jersey, each turn of the pedal since Saturday has advanced and will advance female cyclists, but also all women."[210]

In describing the women's Tour, the press deployed the language of attrition and suffering that had always characterized its coverage of the men's race. There were frequent references to the courage, endurance, willpower, and recuperative capacity of the female racers. Their race was "agony" and a "calvary," they "suffered horribly"; one contestant actually acknowledged that she had come "to suffer," but hoped to make it to Paris.[211] "We have learned," *Le Monde* reported, "that they know how to suffer, a cardinal virtue in such an event."[212] As it turned out, all but one of the thirty-six participants completed the race, the one who did not having withdrawn after breaking her collarbone. This outcome presented the press with a dilemma: it could either celebrate the incredibly low attrition rate (which some compared to the much higher rate in the men's event) as evidence of the women's courage, fitness, determination, and resistance to pain, or else conclude that the female Tour was a travesty. Most, including physicians who were interviewed, chose to do the former.[213]

Even as it celebrated the participants' physical and moral qualities, the press addressed aesthetic concerns. On the eve of the start, *L'Équipe* observed that the nonspecialized press was discovering that female cyclists "had no reason to envy any other female athlete with regard to beauty and charm."[214] Women racers were described as "adorable"; their beauty was noted and declared equal to that of other female athletes, while their legs were compared favorably to those of models.[215] "In the mountains they are even more beautiful," *Libération* asserted, countering the view that at the moment of their greatest effort and suffering female racers ceased to be feminine.[216] Describing them as "astonishing Amazons," *Le Figaro* observed that "one is forced to note that cycling does not take away the beauty *[charme]* of all these graceful persons, who take great care of their appearance." The paper concluded that "one can be a 'racer' and feminine" at the same time, and published a photograph of two Dutch competitors putting on makeup before the start of a stage.[217]

Le Figaro's play on the word *coureuse* (literally, "racer"; in slang, a woman who chases men) added an ironic twist to its consideration of female racers and gender: just as it was possible to remain conventionally feminine while competing in a sport long associated with a particularly virile masculinity, the paper playfully implied that in the modern era of feminism and women's rights, it was possible for a woman to be both sexually aggressive and feminine.[218] As during the belle époque, female cycling was linked to broader social trends, which in turn were associated with a more assertive and autonomous female sexuality. At the race's end, *Le Figaro* concluded that the female racers "had demonstrated their beauty *[ont fait une démonstration de charme]*, proving that top-flight competition and femininity were not incompatible."[219] Its coverage, like that of other papers, reproduced the exact terms—grace, beauty, femininity, charm—that had dominated the debate over women cyclists' bloomers a century earlier.

The racers themselves were aware of the challenge they posed to conventional images of female domesticity and femininity. Béatrice Labarthe, a twenty-year-old member of the France B team, hoped that the women's Tour would

> incite people to take young women seriously *[prendre en considération les filles]*. For [the people], [the race] is nothing, it's not [women's] place, and they should be in their kitchen or ironing. It's by showing ourselves as much as possible that we shall succeed in getting our sport to be accepted as much as any other women's sport. During races, I hear the comments of the spectators: "But they don't have big thighs, they aren't monsters."[220]

For Labarthe, as for French commentators who supported the women's Tour, convincing skeptics that women deserved and were capable of contesting such an event required arguing that it would not strip them of their femininity by transforming them into excessively muscular, and therefore monstrous, women.

Negotiating the tension between promoting women as viable Tour racers and arguing that the Tour did not jeopardize their femininity was not easy for the race's proponents. *L'Équipe* portrayed female racers as more emotional than their male counterparts; although athletes, they remained women and therefore "fragile." Yet the paper also noted that during the race they would have to forget that they were women, as they would not have time to fix their makeup or think about their children. Both *L'Équipe* and *Libération* remarked that the effect of the racers' menstrual periods on their performance remained unclear. The sports daily reported that 10 percent of the medical treatment received by racers addressed specifically female problems. These included urinary problems reportedly caused by the fact that, unlike male racers, women could not simply stop by the side of the road during the race to urinate; according to *Libération,* this led to dehydration, as female racers were loath to drink during the race.[221]

Despite the press's unanimous assessment, which was confirmed by the impressions of the racers themselves, that the public along the itinerary had enthusiastically supported the first women's Tour, the race has failed to establish itself as a major sporting event.[222] This may result at least in part from the fact that the women's Tour continues to be much shorter than the men's race: for an event defined by the endurance it requires, this discrepancy is a public-relations catastrophe. After all, female marathoners compete at the same distance as men. Furthermore, attrition rates in the women's race are hardly the stuff of Tour heroism: in 1988, for example, only two of the seventy-nine racers dropped out.[223]

In 1977 a poll in *L'Équipe* found that 95 percent of the respondents were in favor of female bicycle races; a few years later another poll revealed that 88 percent of French women believed that cycling would keep them in shape.[224] Such positive sentiments have not, however, translated into widespread public interest in the sport. This is particularly curious given that Jeannie Longo, the greatest female bicycle racer of all time, is French. Since the late 1970s she has accumulated victories in the women's Tour and other important races, winning dozens of national, world, and Olympic championship medals, most of them gold. Her world hour record is close to the records set by two of cycling's greatest champions, the two-time Tour winner Fausto Coppi in 1942 and the five-time Tour winner Jacques Anquetil in 1956. (Longo has actually covered more distance than either man, albeit on equipment that has since been banned for official world-record attempts.) No female athlete has been more decorated or more dominant during this period.[225]

Given Longo's performances and those of other successful female racers, athletic factors alone cannot explain the ongoing prejudice against competitive female cycling in France. There is likely an enduring, widely held (although largely unacknowledged) aesthetic objection. Despite Longo's assertion that "when one is going all out *[dans l'effort],* there are wrinkles that are beautiful," this view is not widely shared. Female racers are expected to conform to the standards of conventional femininity. Even as she applauded the courage of the contestants, the medical inspector for the 1985 women's Tour noted that "they know how to conserve their femininity: I observed an American contestant who was doing embroidery . . . to concentrate better a few minutes before the start of a time-trial stage!" The successful French racer Marc Madiot acknowledged that he did not like to see women suffer on their bicycles and would like them to adopt a feminine outfit "to bring out their qualities better *[pour mieux les mettre en valeur]*." He suggested "white or pink cycling shorts, sleeveless jerseys or gloves and socks with a little lace."[226] The great Tour champion Bernard Hinault, who supported female cycling, opined that the athletically imposing physiques that had long been the norm for women racers had not helped their sport develop, but that things were changing: "There are some very beautiful girls who race, both in France and abroad."[227]

Hinault's assessment notwithstanding, female bicycle racers have yet to match the success and popularity of female tennis players and figure skaters. It may be that these other athletes, by continuing to dress in skirts and other emblematic, if increasingly revealing, female attire, conform to widely held French views of femininity. They are consequently favored over female bicycle racers, whose outfits and appearance in competition are hard to distinguish from those of men and who thus are seen as having sacrificed their femininity in the pursuit of their sport. If this is so, it would suggest that as the Tour moves into its second century, it still has much to teach us about French attitudes toward gender and heroism.

CONCLUSION

One question raised by the invention and enduring popularity of the "giants of the road," but perhaps better left to psychiatrists and philosophers, is why humans require heroic models in the first place: why, as *La Culture Physique* argued in 1909, the Tour satisfies "that thirst for the supernatural, that need to admire and to create demigods."[228] The seven-time Tour champion and cancer survivor Lance Armstrong has recently described the race as "a contest in purpose-less suffering," and, to the extent that Tour racers could have chosen a career involving less suffering, he is right.[229] The persistence of the Tour's heroic ethos, however, challenges the cultural historian to explore why survival and "purpose-less suffering" have been widely and continually presented as meaningful throughout a century of extraordinary change for both France and its Tour. Two world wars, the Great Depression, foreign occupation, reconstruction and economic modernization, the development of a strong welfare state, the loss of a colonial empire (and defeats in two wars in the process), several regime changes, European integration, and the country's declining influence in international affairs have arguably challenged and transformed France as never before over the course of a single century. Meanwhile, the Tour has been shortened and road surfaces, equipment, training techniques, nutrition, and medical care dramatically improved.

The challenges France has confronted over the past century may provide a partial explanation. If the French ended up on the victorious side in both world wars, it is because they were able, through their own efforts and those of more powerful allies, to outlast their German foes. After World War II, despite losing the wars in Indochina and Algeria, France remained a leader in European affairs, maintained a seat on the United Nations Security Council, and at times played an important international role in the Cold War. The contributions to Christophe's fund in 1919 and to Robic's in 1947 suggest that their contemporaries valued survival, persistence, and resurrection in the face of disadvantages and misfortune.[230] Given the repeated challenges to France's survival and to its global standing over the past century, it is plausible that other generations also identified with and wished to celebrate that particular brand of heroism. For example, Raymond Poulidor, who had a remarkably successful racing career from the late 1950s to the late 1970s, became France's beloved *éternel second,* celebrated more for his courage and persistence in the face of bad luck and losses to great rivals than for his many victories.

Meanwhile, by restricting women to conventional roles, the Tour has long inspired the evocation of idealized, timeless gender identities that appear impervious to the destabilizing changes of the past century.[231] These changes include, of course, reforms that have successfully challenged long-standing restrictions on women's rights and opportunities. The continuing marginal status of the women's Tour, its inability to garner mass interest, media coverage, and the levels of corporate sponsorship that pertain in a number of other female sports, suggest that the "real" Tour remains meaningful to the French in part by remaining *une affaire d'hommes,* a refuge from repeated attempts since the belle époque to redefine French gender roles and identities. For all her spectacular performances, "La Longo" is not considered "*un* géant de la route."

Even if the race has become easier over the past century, the contrast between the Tour and the lives of most French people—a contrast at the heart of the racers' heroic standing—is greater today than it was one hundred years ago. Fans of the race lead far more comfortable lives than their predecessors: manual labor has decreased as the service sector has come to dominate the national economy, legislation has regularly shortened the work week, and the French welfare state is one of the most generous and extensive in the world. In such a society, the very notion of attrition becomes an abstraction. In 1957, when the social and literary critic Roland Barthes argued that Tour racers were engaged in a "solitary struggle for life," the same could no longer be said of the vast majority of their compatriots.[232] A few years later, Jacques Goddet identified the contrast between the demands of the Tour and the increasingly secure and comfortable life of most French as the key to the Tour racer's appeal. The race, he argued, "remains, in the sedentary era of the battle against human pain, an act of heroism . . . it exposes the contestants to suffering, . . . reminds [us] that danger still threatens our activities." The Tour would endure because "more than ever we need great stories, the unexpected, incomparable personalities."[233]

Barthes and Goddet may well be right. For all its improvements, the race remains the most grueling sporting event in the world. Attrition rates have declined, but until recently one-third of the contestants who started the race failed to make it to Paris. Many others, weakened by illness and injury, barely avoided elimination. Ever-expanding television coverage, which requires no rhetorical embellishment, provides stark, incontrovertible evidence of the risk and pain racers accept as their daily lot. Meanwhile, as succeeding generations of commentators have sought to shape public perceptions of the Tour, they have drawn on the language of attrition and suffering deployed by their predecessors. As this language describes a reality most fans now watch on television, they can continually evaluate its appropriateness. Should the day come when the public no longer believes that it accurately reflects the race, the cult of survival and suffering will be in serious jeopardy. So, perhaps, will the Tour.

FOUR

L'Auto's Ouvriers de la Pédale

Work, Class, and the Tour de France, 1903–1939

≡

Every sport is defined by technical rules that govern, for example, when a ball is in play and how it may be manipulated, the playing area and equipment specifications, and the duration of a competition. There are other rules, equally important, that define norms of acceptable conduct and punish acts that violate those norms. These "social" or "moral" rules inscribe athletic competition in the complex fabric of a society's value systems. This was particularly true of the Tour, whose participants came into direct contact with thousands of fans. Between stages racers stayed in hotels and sometimes, during the early Tours, in the homes of local residents. Moving among the local population, surrounded by curious and admiring crowds, they ate in restaurants, drank in bars, and washed at public bath houses. Given their visibility and popularity, any behavior or—more to the point—misbehavior on their part was likely to attract comment.

From the earliest Tours to World War II, L'Auto received complaints about the racers' offensive appearance and conduct, which appeared to confirm late-nineteenth-century bourgeois representations of male working-class cyclists as debasing an activity that had until recently been monopolized by the respectable classes of society.[1] Seeking to counter this persistent criticism and defuse potentially harmful publicity, Henri Desgrange and his staff created and publicized rigid guidelines of proper conduct for Tour racers that had little, if anything, to do with safeguarding the race's competitive integrity. L'Auto also sought to deflect complaints about the racers' conduct by formulating a positive representation of Tour racers as ouvriers de la pédale, or "pedal workers." In doing so the paper drew on a contemporary understanding of cycling, and of the Tour in particular, as hard physical labor.

The *ouvrier de la pédale* image was sufficiently flexible to allow the organizers to portray racers both as humble, disciplined factory workers and as proud, self-sufficient artisans belonging to a self-regulating guild. In either case, *L'Auto* argued, these young workers were being civilized by the race, whose rules transformed them into "elegant" and responsible citizens. In addition to being heroic "giants of the road" who inspired French youth to engage in physical exercise, Tour racers, according to *L'Auto,* were model workers who contributed to social stability and deserved to be emulated by their male working-class fans. At its core, then, the organizers' campaign to portray Tour racers as *ouvriers de la pédale* was an attempt to shape working-class identity in ways that would improve the moral and material condition of the laboring masses and in so doing calm middle-class fears about the challenges those masses posed to the social order.

This was no easy task. For one thing, the hundreds of fines and other punishments imposed annually by the organizers on the racers for violations of the Tour's code of respectable conduct suggest that many racers resisted the imposition of behavioral norms they did not acknowledge as their own—that they refused to relinquish their working-class identity. For another, there is no evidence that their working-class fans held these violations against them; more likely, fans appreciated and identified with their heroes' refusal to bow before race officials. Finally, the vast sums made by the Tour's stars, a consequence of the success of the Tour and of professional cycling in general, created a group of unskilled physical laborers whose wealth and celebrity made them difficult to intimidate.

It was thus not just the uncouth behavior of Tour racers that was problematic, but also their potentially destabilizing socioeconomic ascent. A working-class racer who rejected the values of his social betters, with whom his wealth gave him a measure of (at least) financial equality, challenged bourgeois society in a way no common laborer had before. The organizers' promotion of the Tour racer as an *ouvrier de la pédale* is thus intimately linked to the complex relationship between representations of class, work, and cycling under the Third Republic—and to the hopes and fears those representations inspired. That story begins in the late nineteenth century, when increasing numbers of lower-class men took advantage of plummeting prices to purchase a bicycle and experience a new, exciting, and liberating form of leisure.

THE *CAVALIER CYCLISTE* VERSUS
THE *VÉLOCIPÉDARD*

"[The bicycle] is going to revolutionize social relations, that is easy to predict, although the extent to which it will do so is still impossible to calculate."[2] This claim, made in 1894 by Dr. Just Lucas-Championnière, one of cycling's most fervent enthusiasts, was an explosive one for many of his compatriots, who saw their nation as riven by political, social, and religious divisions. Under the impact of industrialization and urbanization, and with the reintroduction of universal male suffrage in the 1870s, the fledgling Third Republic faced the challenge of peacefully integrating the working classes into a society shaped by bourgeois norms and values. This "social question" was particularly sensitive for the new regime, which owed its birth in part to the massacre and exile of working-class *communards* in 1871, itself a discomforting echo of the Second Republic's brutal repression of its working-class constituency a generation earlier.

Many French no doubt hoped that Lucas-Championnière was correct when he claimed that cycling was a democratic sport that would "bring the nation's children together in common aspirations, by making them accomplish common efforts."[3] Others, however, feared that far from being an instrument of national cohesion, the democratizing bicycle raised the frightening specter of social disruption. As lower-class cyclists discovered a world of speed and leisure that had traditionally belonged to their social betters, their appearance and conduct often flouted the cycling etiquette formulated by bourgeois "experts," suggesting that new, unregulated forms of mass leisure posed a threat to the social order. In response, bourgeois commentators elaborated a discourse of social distinction that contrasted the elegant ideal of the bicycling gentleman with his uncouth, working-class counterpart. By the turn of the century, one's behavior, posture, position, and attire on the bicycle had become important social markers.

Prior to the 1890s, the bicycle's cost made it almost exclusively the toy of the well-to-do. Even so, bicycling faced elitists who dismissed the new sport because it was neither noble, like fencing and riding, nor well established, like boating, gymnastics, foot races, and hunting.[4] To counter such prejudices, proponents of the bicycle went to great pains to establish its social legitimacy by associating the new machine with the traditional mount of the aristocracy. They conceptualized the bicycle as a mechanical horse, a "horse of steel" or "horse of iron," that was "moved and steered by the *Véloceman* who is its horseman."[5] Perhaps inspired by early *draisiennes,* which often featured equine heads in wood protruding from their handlebars, late-nineteenth-century French cycling experts spoke of the "body" and "anatomy" of the bicycle, which "quivers like an animal under its thin skin of nickel and enamel; it whinnies at times, . . . the screams and moans of steel being overworked."[6]

Building on this association, defenders of cycling also borrowed from aristocratic equestrian etiquette to formulate an *équitation cycliste.*[7] The pedals were simply the cyclist's stirrups, the handlebars his reins, and the bicycle, according to an early instruction manual, "must appear to be moving on its own like a horse, with the pedals pulling one's feet along. It must be held on a normal ride by a single hand and pushed delicately with one's feet."[8] This advice confirms the extent to which bourgeois observers believed that "the cycling horseman, like the horseman on a horse, has . . . an obligation to the public, the obligation of elegance," irrespective of the physical risk involved. Maintaining an upright position was essential; an overly inclined position was "inelegant, absurd, useless and harmful": "Just as a horseman out for a ride does not ride like a jockey, so too a cyclist must not ride like a bicycle racer."[9] Such admonitions, reinforced by advertising posters depicting elegantly dressed, straight-backed bourgeois and aristocratic cyclists, were particularly apt in an age of Darwin-inspired self-consciousness. It was essential for bourgeois cycling enthusiasts to demonstrate that the highly evolved middle- and upper-class cyclist was a variation of *Homo erectus* and thus eschewed "a position as depraved as it is inelegant."[10]

The distinction drawn between the gentleman cyclist and the bicycle racer was pivotal. By the turn of the century, almost all racers came from the lower classes. Their bent-over position on the bicycle was designed for maximum speed because maximum speed brought victories, which in turn earned them prize money and sponsorship contracts with cycle and tire manufacturers. Erect posture distinguished bourgeois cyclists from racers and the working-class youths who sped around town imitating their heroes, as well as from messenger boys and delivery men who used the bicycle professionally. For the bourgeois, "the art of cycling consist[ed] of skill, elegance and grace," not the pursuit of speed and efficiency.[11] Physical elegance was closely correlated with moral rectitude: the ungraceful was disgraceful. Dr. Lucas-Championnière might claim that the democratic bicycle endowed everyone with elegance, but many bourgeois believed that one's position on the bicycle reflected one's position in society.[12]

As male workers, shop clerks, and artisans acquired the new machine, these criteria of elegance allowed bourgeois commentators to draw a sharp contrast between their ideal of the gentleman cyclist and a disturbing new working-class stereotype, the *vélocipédard* (or *pédalard*). The latter was characterized by "a striped jersey under his jacket; bared calves (outside the bicycle track); cap pushed back; feet in a false position on the pedals; a barking horn, a disorderly appearance, an always-dry tongue, and a definite fondness for wine merchants"—all of which transgressed bourgeois norms of modesty, self-control, and respectability.[13] The *vélocipédard* embodied and reinforced the fears of many members of the French middle and upper classes that universal male suffrage, urbanization, and industrialization were spawning an increasingly autonomous, self-confident, and assertive working class that chose to reject the "natural" authority of its social betters even as it appropriated their activities. No figure represented the autonomous, upwardly mobile worker challenging the social status quo more than the champion bicycle racer, who earned sums that exceeded many middle-class incomes. Bicycle racers were the first unskilled laborers to turn their physical capital (strength and endurance) into socioeconomic success (fame and fortune). Their success challenged a bourgeois social hierarchy founded on intellectual and social capital (education and relations).

Not all middle-class observers took such a dim view of the social implications of the democratizing bicycle. Some claimed that the new machine offered at least a partial solution to the ongoing challenge of improving the lot of working-class families and thereby reducing class tensions. This inexpensive, rapid mode of locomotion would decrease expenditures in the family budget, reinforce family unity, and improve personal hygiene by encouraging showers after a ride. The bicycle would allow working-class families to move from their squalid, inner-city lodgings to less polluted suburbs, far from cabarets and cafés where the head of the household too often forgot his familial obligations and succumbed to alcoholism, tuberculosis, gambling, tobacco, and loose women.[14]

Perhaps to counter the threatening image of the *vélocipédard*, some commentators made a point of celebrating examples of respectable working-class cyclists. On Sunday, 25 May 1902, the Véloce-Club de Tours organized an excursion to honor *le père* Galloux, an eighty-nine-year-old inhabitant of nearby Ouchamps believed to be the oldest cyclist in France. In 1837,

Galloux, then an apprentice artisan and a *compagnon du devoir,* accomplished his journeyman's tour of France, traveling from town to town on a "wooden horse" he had built: it consisted of two wheels connected by a wooden seat plank, without pedals but with a steering mechanism on which was mounted a carved horse's head. At the reception in Galloux's honor organized by the Ouchamps municipal government, the club president praised the old artisan as a "family man" and "the persevering worker, full of endurance and tenacity, whom we saw earlier astride his respectable wooden horse." His speech evoked a mythical national community of traditional workers whose values and qualities buttressed the social order and who provided a countermodel to the disorderly, disrespectful *vélocipédards* undermining bourgeois society.[15] Desgrange, too, was concerned with the issue of male working-class cyclists. Even before the first Tour de France, he had given considerable thought to the social utility of the new sport, and specifically to the challenge posed by young, working-class professional racers to bourgeois society.

DESGRANGE'S SOCIAL PHILOSOPHY OF SPORT: AN AUTHORITARIAN PATERNALISM

Desgrange addressed many of the concerns raised by critics of the *vélocipédard* in the training manual and cycling novel he wrote in the late 1890s.[16] Although he encouraged working-class youth to use their new opportunities in professional cycling to improve themselves, Desgrange also sought to control their social mobility and restrict their growing independence. He insisted in his training manual that his authority over his imaginary pupil be absolute and uncontested, much as he did later in dealing with Tour racers. Even allowing for the excesses of style, Desgrange's program verged on the totalitarian: "Your muscles, like your brain, must be animated only by my thought. You must . . . fear me, you must dread me, you must consider me your master, and you must no longer belong to yourself."[17]

The relationship now clear to both parties, Desgrange advised his protégé to try many sports between the ages of fifteen and eighteen; only then would he mount a bicycle for the first time. Among the recommended sports were horseback riding and fencing. Perhaps he hoped to make cycling more respectable by presenting it as the final phase of an athletic program that included sports of the upper classes. The avowed goal of this diversified approach was harmonious muscular development, an objective that reflected medical fears about the distorting effects of cycling. Such concerns inevitably had a class dimension. Working-class professional racers were allegedly likely to overdevelop their legs, thus violating the classical ideal of the well-proportioned body. In contrast, the bourgeois gentleman athlete or *sportsman* was an amateur who played a variety of sports that developed his body evenly.[18]

Desgrange's manual also addressed the young man's mental and moral state. In cycling, he argued, "the intelligent man always beats the brute. The great racers are all intelligent: I mean that they have their special intelligence, a clear and lucid understanding of the precise means which they must employ to reach their goal." Tactical intelligence coupled with well-conceived training methods would turn a strong, disciplined athlete into a champion. Desgrange argued that both the athlete and society would benefit if the training regimen included "five or six hours a day" of "some kind of intellectual work": "How many of those who do nothing train seriously; how many, because they have nothing to do, pass the time doing bad things?" Haunted, like many of his peers, by the *café-concert*'s nefarious effect on French working-class youth, Desgrange viewed bicycle racers as naturally undisciplined individuals who required hours of daily mental work—it hardly mattered what kind—to keep them away from tobacco, alcohol, and the corrupting influence of women. Energetic, disciplined training was the salvation of such young men, for it would endow them with the physical and moral qualities on which a healthy, stable society was founded.[19]

Cycling, according to Desgrange, provided another social benefit: far from distracting a racer from his full-time profession, the sport would improve his productivity and job performance by imposing self-discipline on the racer as he prepared all week for his weekend competitions: "No preoccupations, no enemies, no passing love affairs, the week spent quietly waiting for Sunday, and Sunday's victory filling the following week. Your boss, whom I saw, is most pleased with you." Beyond the imaginary pupil to whom he was writing, his potential audience was French workers and employers everywhere. The important theme of bicycle racing's producing model workers, a prominent feature of L'Auto's Tour coverage throughout the Third Republic, was thus already present in Desgrange's vision of the sport in the late 1890s. For Desgrange, however, there was one paradoxical exception to the rule: the professional racer himself, whose "wicked career" made him "habitually lazy" and led him to "lose any idea of the value of money"—a double violation of middle-class values. Desgrange resolved to control his racer's "surplus," obliging the latter to save much of his winnings and spend the rest on fencing lessons and theater tickets. This transparent attempt to effect the cultural and moral *embourgeoisement* of the working-class cycling champion was no doubt intended to defuse potential criticism of racers as enriched *vélocipédards*.[20]

Although by the late 1890s Desgrange managed velodromes and was soon to become one of France's leading organizers of professional sporting events, he remained profoundly ambivalent about professionalism in sports.[21] Unlike his contemporary, Pierre de Coubertin, the founder of the modern Olympic Games, Desgrange stopped short of rejecting professionalism outright. For all his authoritarianism, he was a realist who understood that the success of his sporting ventures depended on great performances by great athletes, who in turn required long hours of training. And as sport became a subject of mass interest, the commercial sponsorship of athletes and thus professionalism in some form were unavoidable. Although Desgrange saw sport as the salvation of an anemic France, his novel, set in the world of professional track cycling, makes clear that he also feared that professional athletes, equal parts "jester" and "gladiator," competing in a base, modern, excessively commercialized version of the Roman circus, would undermine the health and morality of French society.[22]

Desgrange's social philosophy of sport was thus a curious mix of progressivism and conservatism. On the one hand, he encouraged working-class youths to better themselves through sport. On the other, he was determined to control that process in order to ensure that working-class racers buttressed rather than threatened the social order. The tensions in his philosophy of sport were particularly acute when he addressed the new popular hero of his era, the professional bicycle racer. The working-class cycling champion could be a positive social force: his courage, self-discipline, humility, and strength were qualities that, if widely emulated by French workers, would guarantee social stability and national regeneration. If not properly supervised, however, he could become a lazy, promiscuous, enriched brute with little respect for his social superiors or the values of bourgeois society and a disruptive example for his working-class fans. Hence Desgrange's determination, both in his writings and through the Tour de France, to control the behavior, appearance, and socioeconomic rise of young lower-class athletes and present them as model workers who reinforced rather than threatened the social status quo.

It is easy to see why great industrialists like Count Albert de Dion and Gustave Adolphe Clément, who employed hundreds of workers, chose Desgrange to run *L'Auto*. For businessmen like the main shareholders of the new sports daily, controlling workers was of paramount importance to the success of their enterprises. They lived in the fear, born of experience, of worker rebellion and protest; slowdowns, sabotage, and violent, unpredictable strikes plagued the factories of late-nineteenth- and early-twentieth-century France. Beyond Desgrange's obvious qualifications and breadth of experience in French cycling, *L'Auto*'s investors may have believed he offered them something less tangible but potentially just as valuable: a persuasive instrument for effecting social control through *L'Auto*'s sports coverage. Whether or not they truly believed such propaganda would be effective in quelling worker protest, these businessmen must have found *L'Auto*'s editorial line congenial. What they could not have known in 1900, when they hired Desgrange, was that the Tour de France would provide an annual opportunity for communicating a conservative image of disciplined, respectable workers that served the interests of the paper's financial backers, and, more generally, of French elites.

FOR FAME AND FORTUNE: THE TOUR'S "WORKERS"

What in fact were the social and occupational backgrounds of the young men who entered the Tour during the four decades when *L'Auto* organized the race? If they were motivated to compete in the world's toughest race by the prospect of financial gains unequaled in other jobs for which they were qualified, how much could they actually make in the Tour? In other words, was Desgrange's preoccupation with professional cyclists the product of some delusional obsession with working-class emancipation, or was it grounded in an accurate reading of the social origins, motivations, and financial gains of the Tour's participants?

An examination of the occupational histories of 107 Tour racers who competed in at least one Tour between 1903 and 1939 confirms that almost all came from the lower classes (see the appendix). About half of them worked, or had worked, at manual labor—as mechanics, construction workers, industrial workers, traditional craftsmen, and agricultural laborers. The other half were humble clerks and service-sector employees or owners of small businesses (notably cafés, restaurants, and cycle shops); in most cases, racers opened these businesses with prize money they had won in races.

The participation of so many mechanics is not surprising. These young men knew their way around machines, had access to tools, parts, and materials to build and repair their bicycles, and had employers who might be sympathetic to their training needs. A cycle manufacturer could expect a good racer from his establishment to bring valuable publicity. Four of the service-sector employees—three bicycle salesmen and a garage employee—and the three delivery men in my sample, who almost certainly did their work by bicycle, also had jobs useful to aspiring racers. The significant representation of artisans and apprentices in the building trades likely reflects the seasonal nature of their work, which left many with time for a racing career. On the other hand, the relative underrepresentation of unskilled or semiskilled factory workers was probably due to the fact that they lacked the time, energy, and disposable income for training and equipment.[23]

The agricultural sector was also underrepresented. Many farmers were small producers with no time or energy to train and who preferred to invest their profits in their farms than in racing bicycles.[24] Their participation levels in the Tour increased during the 1920s and 1930s as the bicycle gained popularity in rural France and other European countries. Of the twenty-five racers beginning their Tour careers in the 1930s whose parents' occupations have been identified, eleven were in agriculture. By that decade, many young men raised on farms saw cycling as a viable alternative to working the land. Still, agricultural workers represented only 7.2 percent of Tour racers' occupational backgrounds under the Third Republic, whereas agriculture in France, for example, employed 37.4 percent of the active population in 1913 and 31.4 percent in 1938.[25]

The service sector, on the other hand, was well represented. Shop owners developed personal relationships with their staff that made it easier to negotiate leave to race in the Tour. A butcher could leave his shop in his wife's hands or temporarily replace his apprentice with a family member or acquaintance for the duration of the race. Such arrangements no doubt also occurred in manufacturing: in 1906, 32.2 percent of French industrial workers still worked for businesses with no more than ten employees (by 1931, that number had declined to 19.7 percent).[26] Racers working in such establishments would have had an easier time negotiating time off for training and racing than their peers toiling in the anonymity of large factories.

While there is some overlap between the backgrounds of cycling-club members and early Tour racers, the latter generally came from lower social strata. Teachers and students, categories absent from the Tour's *peloton,* were present in many clubs. So too were local notables, industrialists, business-men, and municipal officials, who often occupied positions of authority in a club but did not consider racing appropriate for persons of their social rank.[27] On the other hand, although chimney sweeps, dockers, miners, fac-tory workers, roadmenders, bellboys, and a bargeman entered the Tour, their poorly remunerated jobs generally left them little money for mem-bership dues. Some jobs required considerable travel, making it impossible to participate in club functions. Generally speaking, jobs held by Tour rac-ers were ones a young man would be willing to jeopardize in the hope of reaping the financial rewards and prestige of a strong performance. As one 1925 contestant and former miner observed, "The Tour de France is not as hard as being a miner."[28]

Both the Tour's organizers and its participants happily acknowledged that what motivated racers was glory and money.[29] The two terms were closely linked, as contestants could convert a successful Tour into lucrative appearances in other races, contracts with corporate sponsors, and invest-ment capital and favorable publicity for businesses they planned to open or already owned. Twenty-nine racers, including some who did not complete the race, earned official prize money in the 1903 Tour. The amounts ranged from a small fortune to a pittance. The top five racers in the final standings took home 6,125 francs, 2,450 francs, 1,975 francs, 1,800 francs, and 1,250 francs, respectively. The next seven averaged 721 francs in official prize money, the last eleven only 96 francs.[30]

Of course, racers had to use some of their winnings to cover their ex-penses: in addition to providing for their own food and equipment (when they were not sponsored), and a registration fee of ten francs, they had to pay for lodging between stages. The cost of the latter was reduced to a "strict minimum," according to Géo Lefèvre, thanks to the "business acumen of the main hoteliers of the host cities, who have understood the advantages of being chosen to receive the Tour de France contestants, who will attract considerable crowds to their establishments."[31]

To help defray the racers' costs, the organizers promised those who won less than 250 francs in prize money a five-franc daily *prime de route.*[32] That racers were even paid on rest days indicates that this was a subsistence wage designed to attract those with little hope of earning prize money. This allowance in turn guaranteed the Tour a sufficient number of participants, without which, Desgrange feared, the race would not be taken seriously by the public. In 1904 he decided to offer a prorated daily allowance for contestants who dropped out before Paris in the event that fewer than fifty racers completed the Tour (only fifteen did). He recognized that completing even part of the Tour was an achievement that deserved to be rewarded, and he thereby hoped to attract racers who would otherwise not enter, again ensuring enough competitors to maintain its credibility.[33] In 1910 the five top prizes were 7,525 francs, 4,085 francs, 2,375 francs, 1,570 francs, and 1,310 francs. The sixth through tenth place prizes averaged 839 francs, the eleventh through fifteenth 426 francs, and the sixteenth through twentieth 247 francs. Thanks to the daily "road money," all racers who completed the Tour received at least 145 francs.[34]

The Tour earnings of many racers dwarfed contemporary working-class wages: for example, in Paris, between 1905 and 1910, daily wages for young male workers ranged from 5.10 francs for fitters at the Dion-Bouton Automobile Company to 7.25 francs for joiners.[35] (Desgrange may well have based the 5-franc daily minimum wage on the former figure, given that the company was *L'Auto*'s largest investor.) Meanwhile, the precarious situation of shopkeepers in early-twentieth-century France no doubt helps explain why so many found their way into the Tour's *peloton,* if only to supplement their incomes and generate favorable publicity while they left their stores in the hands of relatives or associates.[36] A racer who planned to enter the Tour in 1904 even decided to give up his store in Paris and become a traveling salesman so that he could train for the race.[37] Even the average *annual* incomes of many white-collar workers—shop assistants, low-level employees of the PTT, teachers, bookkeepers, clerks, accountants, purchasing agents, commercial representatives, and insurance agents—paled in comparison with the fortunes made by the Tour's top finishers in just three weeks of racing.[38]

The example of Gustave Garrigou, the son of a grocer who eschewed the family business and became one of the most successful racers of his day, confirms this point. In 1911 Garrigou was paid 12,000 francs by his sponsor, earned another 7,825 francs in prize money for winning the Tour, and presumably won several thousand more in other races. That year, his income was twelve to fifteen times the annual salary of a skilled worker like a boilermaker (about 2,000 francs) and three times that of a deputy in the National Assembly (9,000 francs).[39] Champions clearly made enough to establish a small business; so did less successful racers, if they competed for several years.[40]

Feeling the financial pinch of the early 1920s, the organizers charged first-category racers 1,000 francs for food and drink and second-category racers 125 francs for lodgings and the transportation of their luggage, and another 500 francs for food and drink if they were sponsored by cycle manufacturers.[41] These costs and postwar inflation notwithstanding, good racers continued to make an excellent living in professional cycling. In 1921 Honoré Barthélémy enjoyed a successful season, including a victory in Paris–Saint Étienne and third place in the Tour de France. After covering his expenses for racing outfits and food, he cleared 14,076 francs.[42] Marcel Bidot, who participated in six Tours in the late 1920s and early 1930s, was a former employee of the Crédit Lyonnais bank. In 1923 he earned 23,000 francs from racing, almost ten times his annual salary at the bank.[43] That year Henri Pélissier earned 17,638 francs in Tour prize money for winning the month-long race (almost ninety times Bidot's 200-franc monthly paycheck at the Crédit Lyonnais), and that figure does not take into account prizes donated by the public or the salary he received from his sponsors.[44]

These success stories notwithstanding, most Tour participants prudently combined their racing careers with another occupation, as even those who had been signed by a cycle or tire company often received no more than two or three hundred francs a month from their sponsors.[45] Auguste Meyer, who raced professionally for the J. B. Louvet team in 1921, kept his job in a food and wine storeroom at the Strasbourg arsenal: "It is true that I owned three racing bikes and all my travel expenses were paid for, but one could not live from racing alone. Later I became a coffee salesman. I would cycle to villages and go door to door. I must have seen twelve customers a day. As I was pretty good at it, I was able to complete my work in an hour. Once it was over, I had a lot of time left for training."[46]

Given the sport's risks and the cost of equipment, even gifted racers like the future Tour winners Henri Pélissier, an apprentice electrician, and André Leducq, who worked in a dairy, maintained other employment, at least early in their racing careers. Racers whose economic circumstances improved often left the sport.[47] Still, former Tour contestants liked to remind the public of their hard-earned economic ascent: in 1920 Gargat, who now headed a large store in Lyon, proudly donated one hundred francs in prize money to the race. Meanwhile, the escalation in prize money in the 1930s as a result of the creation of the *caravane publicitaire* and vastly increased commercial sponsorship meant that even racers with modest results could translate racing careers into a secure middle-class existence.[48]

Desgrange was right. The Tour's "workers" were indeed workers. They were, not surprisingly, motivated by financial gain. And many did use the race to emerge from humble, even precarious economic situations and enter the middle class; the most successful did even better. The racers' social origins, socioeconomic ascent, and celebrity made them useful targets for critics, who indulged their class prejudice as they bemoaned the destabilizing impact on society of uncouth louts earning large sums from such unskilled labor. Rather than deny the racers' working-class identity, the Tour's defenders, most obviously its organizers, embraced that identity and celebrated the racers as model workers. To do so they first had to establish that cycling—the Tour in particular—was work.

THE TOUR DE FRANCE AS WORK

From the very start *L'Auto* peppered its Tour coverage with references to work and workers: a 1904 participant was "that tough pedal worker," prominent racers killed in World War I were honored as "workers of the first hour," and in 1920 Christophe, Steux, and Heusghem were "tough pedal workers who are the honor of their profession." In 1927 *L'Auto* commended a top racer for being a "good pedal worker" who "worked magnificently the whole day." A headline two days later proclaimed: "Our racers begin today their last week of work."[49]

The structure of the Tour, consisting of lengthy daily (or almost daily) stages over several weeks, provided an objective foundation for comparisons to the work days of other laborers. From 1903 through 1926, Tour winners averaged between 12 hours, 10 minutes, and 16 hours, 1 minute, per stage; from 1927 through 1939, between 6 hours, 24 minutes, and 8 hours, 46 minutes.[50] Of course, most other racers spent considerably more time on the route. During the Tour's early decades, racers even worked at night, starting stages in the pitch dark to ensure that the winners arrived in the afternoon to provide results in time for *L'Auto*'s deadline. When average times for stages gradually decreased in the 1930s, they mirrored reductions for French workers in general. In 1936, for example, barely a month after the Popular Front won the legislative elections advocating the eight-hour day, the Tour de France winner averaged just under seven hours per stage.

The linking of the Tour to work was reinforced by the French language, which has two different expressions for the pursuit of a sport. *Jouer au football* (to "play" soccer) emphasizes the ludic dimension of sport: spontaneous, pleasurable play, free of the constraints imposed by organizational structures and imperatives. *Faire du football* (to "do" soccer) implies productive play within an organized framework, involving training sessions and official competitions; taken to its logical conclusion, it leads to professionalism. Above all, *faire* ("to do" or "to make") connotes work. There are two kinds of sport for which French uses only *faire: sports de combat* like boxing or the martial arts—in French as in English, one does not "play" judo or kickboxing—and mechanized sports, such as sailing *(faire de la voile)* and automobile racing *(faire de la course automobile)*. In such sports, the ludic dimension is subordinated to other considerations, such as avoiding a beating or controlling a machine in competition.

This dichotomy is borne out in the particular case of cycling. In French one cannot "play" cycling, one "does" it: *faire du cyclisme.* Pedaling requires no creativity, finesse, or spontaneity, and very little coordination beyond maintaining one's balance. Not only is play absent, but cycling actually resembles unskilled industrial work: pedaling is the repetitive, unthinking application of human muscle power to a machine. And, like industrial production, cycling yields easily quantifiable results. Output is measured in kilometers; the greater the distance traveled in a set amount of time, the greater the cyclist-worker's productivity.

The industrial nature of cycling was not lost on contemporary French commentators. Robert Dieudonné, an interwar sports novelist who contributed frequently to *L'Auto,* addressed this point in his novel *Le marchand de kilomètres.* Its protagonist, a track cyclist, sees himself as an industrial worker who sells kilometers and demands to be paid "according to a piece rate" by his commercial sponsor for his victories and records.[51] Another interwar novelist, who was critical of the Tour, named one of his protagonists Laboureur ("laborer" or "worker" in French), no doubt to convey the association of the Tour with hard physical labor.[52] Even the French expression for assembly-line work, *le travail à la chaîne,* is applicable to cycling, both literally and figuratively. Racers work a chain-driven machine, and when they ride in a paceline, each taking a turn at the front of the pack, the coordination of their efforts evokes assembly-line work, as one racer noted in 1929. For his part, Desgrange described Tour racers as "a magnificent muscular factory in full activity" and praised their "perfect work organization."[53]

French elites also sought to exploit the image of the *ouvrier de la pédale*. In 1910, at a reception in honor of the Tour's visit to Roubaix, the city's mayor, Eugène Motte, drew a parallel between the race and work: "In our industrial city, where everyone works, we are admirers of endurance and energy. You cannot choose a more prosperous city in which to replenish your courage in order to continue the fight. You will always be welcome in Roubaix, and we shall always receive you as friends."[54] Like Desgrange, Motte portrayed the Tour as an exemplary event for industrial—and industrious—workers impervious to the siren call of class conflict because they were prosperous and shared the work ethic of the community. A textile magnate, Motte held office from 1903 to 1912, during which time Roubaix was in fact the scene of considerable conflict pitting the conservative, Catholic *patronat* against militant workers who espoused the Parti Ouvrier's revolutionary syndicalism.[55]

For Motte and like-minded elites, the Tour provided more than entertainment. If properly exploited, the image of popular Tour racers as hardworking, disciplined workers might pacify their employees, much as cycling clubs were often supported by local authorities because they were believed to contribute to the moral edification of working-class youth and thus to social stability.[56] Factory owners frequently gave their employees time off to watch Tour racers pass through their town or by their workplace.[57] When the Peugeot factories did so in 1932, *L'Auto* noted that "the road is lined on both sides with a hedge of men in blue overalls [the traditional garb of French workers], who provide us with a change from our [usual] crowds in their Sunday best."[58] This was a powerful image that reinforced Desgrange's contention that the Tour had a positive role to play in the lives of French workers.[59] Unfortunately for *L'Auto*, that role was continually undermined by the conduct of the Tour racers themselves.

UNE TENUE CORRECTE, S'IL VOUS PLAÎT!
CIVILIZING THE UNCIVILIZED

From the very first Tour and for the balance of the Third Republic, outraged spectators regularly contacted *L'Auto* to condemn the racers' scandalous appearance and conduct. In 1907 the paper acknowledged having received "numerous complaints . . . last year from the different communities through which . . . the Tour de France passed, . . . [by] *sportsmen* . . . about the *tenue* and the uncouthness of certain racers." The organizers promised to be "merciless this time with respect to those whose behavior should happen to provoke the slightest protest."[60] That class played a crucial role in these complaints was confirmed by *L'Auto*'s use of *sportsmen,* a term almost always designating the middle- and upper classes. What the latter found objectionable had little, if anything, to do with cheating. Instead, they criticized the racers' shabby attire, poor hygiene, public urination, coarse language, violent outbursts, and lack of respect for the property of others. The organizers could ill afford to ignore such criticism. Beyond the prospect of losing the support of local communities on which the race depended loomed the question of the racers' public image. Was it not plausible, as a Lyon newspaper wondered, that the public would be less likely to welcome and praise Tour racers if it were aware of their questionable morality?[61]

In response, Desgrange and his staff elaborated an ever-expanding punitive regime that featured annually in *L'Auto*'s pre-Tour coverage: warnings and fines for first-time offenses, larger fines for each additional offense, expulsion from the race and even exclusion from the following year's Tour for an egregious transgression or an accumulation of violations.[62] *L'Auto* justified these rules in moralizing editorials calling on the racers to adopt *une tenue correcte,*[63] a catch-all phrase that referred both to the racers' attire and their conduct. The organizers warned racers that violations would be rigorously punished, implored them to behave better, and congratulated them when they did so. In addition, whenever possible *L'Auto* offered an alternate reading of the racers' allegedly offensive *tenue,* arguing that it should be tolerated—at times even praised—as evidence of their hard-earned status as authentic working-class heroes. This delicate rhetorical balancing act illustrates the challenges confronting the organizers as notions of work, class, and heroism intersected, and at times collided, in narratives about the Tour.

During the Tour's early years the racers' tattered, filthy clothing and exposed flesh offended many middle-class spectators. *L'Auto,* however, rejected such criticism as unreasonable, ridiculing a mayor who apparently shared the concern of his middle-class constituents and reportedly urged the organizers "to add an article to the rules obliging . . . racers to bring along their tuxedos." Given their budgetary limitations, *L'Auto* noted that Tour racers were "not able to have clothes tailored in London . . . or . . . wear the latest fashion."[64] On the contrary, the paper celebrated the racers' "glorious old castoffs" ("rumpled pants, dirty jackets, faded caps"), as apparently did their working-class fans: "The crowd likes to see our heroes stroll about the streets of their town in their rumpled clothes, their jackets made from yellow cloth, their flattened caps and their inelegant shoes; they love these figures of *grognards* [soldiers of the Old Guard of Napoleon I], whereas they would not like fashion plates."[65]

The organizers also defended the racers' tattered racing outfits, even their partial nudity: "Perrucca arrived without his racing shorts *[sans culotte]*. Torrents of rain, mud, sand, [and] his seat had nibbled away at them. Heusghem did not have much more yesterday at La Rochelle. Some tatters, a few rare tatters, had lasted until the finish line."[66] Just as the racers' modest clothing after a stage reinforced their working-class authenticity and popularity, the deplorable condition of their racing outfits became a badge of honor, evidence of their work ethic in the face of horrific conditions. Meanwhile, historically charged references to *grognards* and *sans-culotte* (the latter pun evoking the working-class revolutionaries of 1789), further reinforced the racers' identity as heroic workers.

Suspecting that not all critics would be placated by this favorable reading of the racers' appearance, *L'Auto* also provided examples of properly attired racers. Wattelier returned home from the first Tour "dressed in a superb pair of blue worker's trousers [the classic French worker's *bleu de travail*] that he had bought at Montargis."[67] To members of the middle classes who feared that Tour participants were uncouth workers out to make a quick fortune, Wattelier's wise use of his hard-earned Tour winnings was intended to demonstrate that humble racers sought to improve their lot without violating class boundaries their social superiors were determined to maintain. *L'Auto*'s rhetorical strategies notwithstanding, the competitors' postrace attire continued to be a thorn in the organizers' sides until 1920, when they required each contestant to deposit with Tour officials a suit, which would be returned to him at the finish line, for use in the event his luggage was delayed or lost.[68]

L'Auto was less forgiving of the racers' colorful language, another source of irritation to middle-class observers of the Tour, in part because "their filthy words are so frequent that several sports associations have refused us their assistance." As the race depended on the goodwill of thousands of volunteers and local officials, many of them middle-class, the organizers asked the racers to use "decent language during the stage and in the host towns."[69] *L'Auto* was particularly determined to penalize the racers' vulgarity when it targeted Tour officials (as it frequently did), because such abuse undermined the officials' authority.[70] At times the paper suggested that coarse language was perhaps acceptable when uttered "in the heat of the battle," but, in contrast to its interpretation of their heroic clothing, *L'Auto* rejected the racers' foul language as a source of their popularity: "Some [racers] imagine that the freer their language, the more crude their words, the more they will be noticed and admired. What a mistake! The crowd turns away from them and takes them for louts."[71] The organizers' claim is unconvincing. It is far more likely that the racers' vocabulary constituted a further point of identification for their working-class admirers. Still, by insisting that the crowd rejected such language, *L'Auto* sought to provide a behavioral model for the racers' fans by invoking a "respectable" working-class identity that they allegedly already embraced. No doubt the organizers also hoped that this would calm fears among the Tour's middle-class public that racers provided deviant models for the lower classes.

Abuse of race officials by contestants, at least in the race's first three decades, frequently turned physical as exhausted racers took out their frustrations on the men they held responsible for the regulations and race conditions that caused them so much suffering. On expelling Émile Engel for attacking an official in 1914, Desgrange noted that such violence was "the worst offense a racer can commit, because it relates to the principle of authority."[72] No doubt because he understood the alarm such acts were likely to provoke in the Tour's middle-class public, Desgrange made a point of rehabilitating the racer in the days that followed his expulsion. He noted that Engel's conduct had been perfect on leaving the race: "He asked Baugé [his team manager] to express his regrets for what he had done [and] promised him to be calmer in the future. Baugé and Engel then embraced with tears in their eyes. Engel! Now that's very good."[73] Given that Engel's ejection reflected poorly on his team's sponsor and manager, it is plausible that Desgrange embellished or even fabricated this scene to demonstrate to potential critics that contestants who flouted the authority of race officials meekly accepted punishment and expressed appropriate contrition for their sins. To underscore the point, several days later Desgrange quoted from a letter written by Engel to his manager in which the racer said how depressed he was about no longer being in the race.[74]

Although he preferred to emphasize the expulsion's moral dimension, Desgrange also recognized the economic consequences for both Engel and his sponsor.[75] Engel's attempts to make amends, and his sponsor's determination to publicize those attempts, were in fact more likely motivated by the economic interests of both than the guilt, embarrassment, or shame suggested by Desgrange. Once the violence had occurred, the interest of all three parties converged, and the violent, uncontrolled worker was quickly transformed into a submissive, repentant employee. Engel's offense was hardly exceptional; when the race resumed after World War I, racers continued to be penalized for assaulting officials.[76] As late as 1935, an article was included in the Tour's regulations that addressed "inappropriate" behavior toward officials and established penalties: fifty francs for a first offense, one hundred for a second, and expulsion for a third.[77] Not all violence targeted figures of authority: racers were also fined for fighting among themselves and abusing spectators.[78] Such behavior, although not a direct attack on the race's authority figures, could not be tolerated, for it alienated spectators and made it difficult for Desgrange to argue that the Tour had a moralizing effect on the working classes.

An important part of the Tour's social canon involved personal cleanliness, a mark of middle-class respectability. Desgrange and his staff encouraged the racers to bathe regularly between stages. Occasionally, during the early years of the race, private citizens provided shower facilities at the finish of a stage: in 1911 the racers were "led to the showers" (suggesting either passivity or reluctance) that Count F. de Saintignon, an ironmaster in the northern industrial town of Longwy-Bas, had set up especially for them.[79] The racers' attempts at personal hygiene were not always well received: in the early 1920s, a number of hotels complained that the contestants were using curtains and sheets to wipe off Vaseline after their massages and generally leaving their rooms dirty. L'Auto promised to punish such behavior severely, for, it pointed out, if such conduct were not corrected, the day would come when the racers would be forced to sleep "under the stars."[80] The organizers understandably feared alienating local business owners who lodged and fed the race participants and organizing staff. The offending contestants, modest touristes-routiers and isolés all, had probably never stayed in a hotel before and were apparently intent on making the most of the experience. Bath houses were also sites of unruly behavior by contestants: in 1930 six touristes-routiers were fined fifty francs each for "improper behavior liable to cast discredit on the race" after having caused "a veritable scandal" in a bath house in Perpignan.[81] Perhaps wisely, L'Auto provided no further details.

No offense was more embarrassing to the organizers, given their notions of propriety and determination to win over their critics, than the racers' urinating in full view of the public, particularly in front of women. Racers drank a great deal during the long, hot stages and had to relieve themselves several times a stage. By 1909 the issue had become so explosive that the organizers had installed "obligatory" bathrooms at the checkpoints to counter the "deplorable *laisser-aller*" of recent years. In 1910 they promised to "repress as mercilessly as last year the few offenses that might still occur with respect to this issue."[82] *L'Auto*'s target audience for this campaign was presumably less the contestants, who were informed of the rules directly by the organizers, than dismayed middle-class spectators. To placate them, *L'Auto* adopted an authoritarian tone despite the fact that—or perhaps, precisely because—the offense in question defied regulation. Desgrange's annual reminders to the racers about using the facilities specifically set up for them indicate that his initiative was largely unsuccessful, as do the numerous fines incurred each year by contestants.[83] After World War I, Desgrange and his staff sought to defuse the issue with humorous cartoons and "boys will be boys" anecdotes suggesting that the public should be amused rather than scandalized by the persistence of behavior the organizers were manifestly unable to prevent.[84]

In response to complaints from individuals taken advantage of by racers, *L'Auto* also formulated strict rules against borrowing, begging, and theft. In 1904 a Parisian man wrote the paper that he was owed fifteen francs, which he had lent to a contestant so that he could return home (the racer had also been the man's guest overnight). Géo Lefèvre regretted the incident but noted that "nine times out of ten our road racers are good, honest lads who know how to feel gratitude toward those who have helped them." As a result of such incidents, as late as 1935 the race's regulations included *L'Auto*'s refusal "to accept any responsibility for the debts that the racers might incur during the race."[85] Not surprisingly, *L'Auto* was only too happy to highlight responsible financial conduct by racers. In 1909, the paper reported that a racer who mistakenly believed his friend had paid his restaurant tab in Metz reimbursed La Lorraine Sportive, which had covered the bill as the club "did not want it said that a Frenchman had behaved in such a manner in the annexed provinces." In 1912, *L'Auto* published the letter of a *sportsman* who was grateful that the wheel he had lent to a racer in need (as was permitted by the Tour's rules that year) had been mailed back to him at the end of the race.[86]

Not all spectators were so trusting. In 1922 Jules Matton struck a spectator who refused to lend him a wheel, prompting an outraged reaction from

L'Auto, which suggested that he carry a one-hundred-franc bill on him at all times to avoid future confrontations.[87] In this case the violence seems to have been less offensive to the organizers than was the racer's disregard for private property and financial accountability. Theft also plagued the Tour throughout the Third Republic, most often in the case of "racers finding it both funny and very convenient to steal food or drink from café and restaurant terraces as they pass by."[88] So did begging. In 1921 Desgrange complained that two individuals had passed a plate among the crowd at a finish line on behalf of the racers who, he insisted, had not asked them to do so. In 1926 a racer was fined two hundred francs for "causing a scandal" at the Dijon finish line when he begged among the crowd after having been eliminated from the race.[89]

Desgrange addressed financial offenses because they constituted clear violations of two fundamental bourgeois values: private property and respect for money as the reward for hard work. Moreover, of course, theft was illegal. Such acts also suggested that the Tour did not pay racers enough, leaving Desgrange open to criticism that he exploited his proletarian contestants for personal gain, a criticism we shall explore in the next chapter. Finally, these acts alienated spectators and café and restaurant owners along the race itinerary. That *L'Auto* chose to address the racers' financial and other transgressions publicly indicates that criticism was too widespread to be ignored. With the exception of the issue of inadequate clothing, which seems to have been resolved by the early 1920s, the violations of Tour regulations continued to be a serious problem through the 1939 Tour.[90] After the war, evolving public sensibilities and the continuing professionalization of the Tour's contestants, as amateur and semiamateur categories were eliminated, reduced the number and gravity of many of these violations, and the need for annual calls for *une tenue correcte* faded.

THE TOUR RACER AS RESPECTABLE ARTISAN

Desgrange's rhetoric when addressing the racers' lack of *tenue* drew on the paradigm of the Tour as work. He saw the crisis in terms of a breakdown in work discipline, which he expressed as "his workers" not showing "respect" for the profession that allowed them to earn a living.[91] Desgrange saw himself as the racers' employer during the Tour: the fines he levied on poorly behaved racers resembled those imposed by factory owners since the nineteenth century on disrespectful, unproductive workers. The racers, of course, often had real employers. Full-time professionals answered to sponsors and team managers; the others, when not independent artisans or entrepreneurs, were accountable to foremen, shopkeepers, and office supervisors.

The explicit employer-employee dynamic resulting from *L'Auto*'s portrayal and treatment of the Tour's contestants as workers did not sit well with racers who were used to a significant degree of workplace autonomy or already had an employer in the noncycling world. Moreover, they entered the race hoping to reap prize money that they could translate into increased independence from workplace authority by setting up their own businesses: the supervision and regulation of their "work" during the race was therefore especially irritating. The diverging expectations and interests of the racers and the organizers meant that the imposition of rigorous racing or working conditions was inevitably fraught with tension and conflict. For Desgrange, this crisis in work discipline was particularly galling, as his oft-stated goal was to improve the moral and, within carefully prescribed limits, the socioeconomic condition of Tour participants. As a result, Desgrange and his staff at times sought refuge in a comforting vision of class relations and worker conduct in which the *ouvrier de la pédale* was no longer a disobedient, poorly behaved industrial worker but the idealized artisan of a traditional guild.

As he implored racers to behave respectably and threatened them with punishment if they did not, Desgrange noted that it was "in everyone's interest that the racers be considered serious and well-behaved lads" and avoid becoming "the accomplices of those who . . . dishonor the guild."[92] References to guilds evoked work of a traditional, preindustrial sort: a hierarchical, self-regulating community of hard-working, disciplined artisans who punished occasional offenses, subordinated their self-interest to that of the guild, and embraced middle-class respectability. References to artisans who unflaggingly produced quality goods, defined here in terms of high average pace and athletic exploits, were implicitly reinforced by the mental association between the cycling Tour de France and the journeyman's traditional rite of passage.

Portrayal of the racers as artisans served an additional purpose. From the first Tour, Desgrange was determined to oblige each racer to compete as an independent, self-sufficient contestant even when participating as part of a sponsored team. During a stage, therefore, each racer was required to effect repairs entirely on his own, without help from team officials, teammates, spectators, or local artisans. This was not simply an attempt to counter the growing influence of sponsors who were prepared to help their star racers win in any way they could. It resulted also from Desgrange's conception of a sporting equality of opportunity *(le fair play)* and from his view that cycling was fundamentally an individual exercise pitting each contestant not only against all the others, but also against the weather, the mountains, and mechanical breakdowns. As a result of this mandatory self-sufficiency, a cracked crank, punctured tire, or broken pedal frequently became the stuff of high drama. *L'Auto* was quick to praise the resourcefulness, perseverance, courage, and pride of racers who continued to compete despite time-consuming repairs that cost them any chance at victory. In these accounts the paper transformed the Tour racer into an independent, self-sufficient artisan and the artisan into a national hero. In this way, too, the race mirrored its namesake, the journeyman's Tour de France. Both emphasized work well done, independence, and travel, and both represented a rite of passage that improved the individual both professionally and morally, suggesting that professional and moral progress were intimately related.[93]

The most celebrated case of a racer's repairing his bicycle involved Eugène Christophe, a former locksmith whose impressive mustache had earned him the nickname "the Gaul" (later "the old Gaul"). Christophe's long and successful racing career (1904–26) and his courage in the face of misfortune—mechanical breakdowns cost him at least one Tour victory—earned him the love and admiration of his countrymen and a special place in the race's popular lore.[94] In 1919, as we have seen, his compatriots were so moved by his determination in the face of misfortune that many donated to a fund established in his name by the organizers. Six years earlier, Christophe had reached the top of the Tourmalet in the Pyrenees ahead of the race leader and appeared to be on his way to winning the Tour when he was upended by a car that then ran over his bicycle. Forbidden by the Tour's rules from changing bicycles, Christophe walked fourteen kilometers down the mountain to the nearest smithy in Sainte-Marie-de-Campan, where, under the watchful eyes of Desgrange and several race officials, he borrowed tools and equipment to make the necessary repairs. When one of the officials asked Desgrange whether he could fetch a sandwich from a nearby restaurant, Christophe allegedly exclaimed: "If you are hungry, eat some coal! I am your prisoner and you shall remain my guards to the very end!" The repairs cost Christophe four hours and an additional ten-minute penalty for unauthorized help from a spectator, and thus any chance of winning the Tour that year.[95]

Desgrange and *L'Auto* made much of the incident, presenting Christophe as the embodiment of hard work, uncomplaining obedience, self-sufficiency, perseverance, and respect for hierarchy—the very qualities Desgrange sought to promote through the Tour. Thirty-eight years later, *L'Équipe* held a historical reconstruction to celebrate the famous incident.[96] The reconstruction brought together the incident's surviving actors, including Christophe, now sixty-eight, who inaugurated a commemorative plaque that reads: "Here, in 1913, Eugène Christophe, French bicycle racer, leading the Tour de France, repaired in the smithy his bicycle's fork [which had] broken in the Tourmalet, and did not drop out of the event which he should have won."[97] The fluidity of the *ouvrier de la pédale* image allowed the organizers to emphasize different aspects of the race, depending on which representation—industrial worker or traditional craftsman—best served their interests in a particular instance.

FROM WORKERS TO GENTLEMEN: THE TRANSMISSION OF ELEGANCE

While *L'Auto* promoted Tour racers such as Christophe as authentic working-class heroes, the organizers' stated purpose behind the Tour's social canon was to endow humble "workers" with "an aristocratic urbanity," transforming them into "gentlemen," "well-behaved . . . men of the world," and "messieurs les travailleurs de la route." *L'Auto* frequently sought confirmation of this transformation in the racers' physiognomy and deportment: "Tiberghien . . . has a delicate head, clever eyes and . . . looks like the son of a very noble family disguised as a messenger."[98] The successful Belgian racer Jean Aerts, who had "elegance" and "distinction," was compared to a gentleman and the son of an English lord; "nobility" and "elegance" described the future two-time winner Antonin Magne, who had both the brains and legs to succeed—an obvious reference to Desgrange's classic training manual, *La tête et les jambes,* which argued that success in cycling went to the intelligent racer over the brute.[99] In 1938 a photograph of the young Italian Gino Bartali, who was winning his first Tour, bore a caption praising the "aristocratic ease" of this "master of the mountains."[100]

The target audience for such descriptions was *L'Auto*'s middle-class readers. Late-nineteenth-century bourgeois "experts" had taken great pains to define criteria that distinguished middle-class cyclotourists from *vélocipédards*. Although the racers' outfits, aerodynamic position, and conduct violated this code, *L'Auto* sought to effect their social redemption through repeated references to elegance, distinction, intelligence, and nobility. The coupling of *bicycle* and *elegance* was also reinforced by society affairs regularly held in Paris under the Third Republic.

In June 1939, for example, the Journée de l'Enfance à Bicyclette at the Jardin d'Acclimatation opened with a performance by the Théâtre du Petit-Monde for the hundreds of children assembled, many of whom were accompanied by their "papas sportifs" and "mamans élégantes." Afterwards, competitions, including *concours d'élégance* events for the "charming" children, were held.[101] The following day the Chambre Syndicale Nationale du Cycle organized the Journée Mondaine de la Bicyclette, hailed by *L'Auto* as "a classic Parisian event," which attracted a distinguished audience of prominent cyclophiles, as well as journalists, team managers, racers, and cycle manufacturers.[102] They witnessed a variety of competitions, including *élégance* events for ladies, gentlemen, tandems, and artists; a Lady Mendl Cup, also known as the "Grand Prix for Feminine Elegance"; and an "Elegance Grand Prix for Artists." The jury, presided over by Lady Mendl herself, included two countesses, a marquise, and a prince. The audience also enjoyed "creations of High Fashion and Haute Couture presented by beautifully dressed models."[103]

The event of course also had a commercial dimension. *L'Auto* noted that the many bicycles on display "unquestionably contributed to the elegant tone desired and obtained by the organizing committee" and made the Journée Mondaine "a propaganda event of the first order."[104] At such affairs political, social, and cultural elites joined with commercial and industrial interests to celebrate the upper classes' exclusionary notion of elegance. When *L'Auto* used terms associated with these *journées* and bourgeois *sportsmen* to describe Tour racers, it may have hoped that the latter's critics would, perhaps subconsciously, come to see the race as just another classic, bicycle-inspired festival that celebrated the values of respectable society, elegance foremost among them.

In certain, apparently infrequent instances, other commentators supported *L'Auto*'s presentation of the racers as preoccupied with "elegance" and of the Tour as a sort of finishing school for its lower-class contestants. In 1935 *L'Intransigeant* noted that Tour racers exhibited "a general concern for elegance" as they dressed after a stage finish in Nice. They did not wish to appear out of place while strolling on the city's famous Promenade des Anglais, but instead wanted to blend in with "the elegant men and women in white dresses" (presumably upper-class tourists) they would encounter. The paper concluded that the anonymity conferred by their sartorial elegance would allow racers to "forget for a moment their suffering, their worries." *L'Intransigeant* also reported that all the Belgian racers appreciated and obeyed Jean Aerts's advice about how to dress after a stage, including the race leader Romain Maes, whom Aerts had advised to wear light gray trousers and comb his hair.[105] Such reporting was consistent with *L'Auto*'s representation of Tour racers as a self-regulating "guild" in which those who had already achieved aristocratic elegance helped the others to do so.

L'Auto's obsession with elegance was also reflected in the attention it paid to the racers' handwriting. The paper made a point of assessing the beauty and elegance of their signatures on the checkpoint sign-in sheets. A regular feature in *L'Auto* from the very first Tour, racers' signatures often received prominent coverage.[106] Racers' photographs were often accompanied by their autographs, suggesting that a racer's handwriting was as representative of him as his face. Postcards bearing the signatures of fan favorites or entire teams became popular items with the race's followers, many of whom were avid collectors.[107]

L'Auto's interest in the racers' handwriting continued through the last Tour it organized. In 1939, a contest sponsored by the Edacoto pen company awarded prizes ranging from 250 to 2,000 francs to the six racers with the best signatures at checkpoints "based on the care that each brings to writing properly, legibly and with as neat a penmanship as possible." *L'Auto* indicated that interest in this "happy initiative" was high among the racers; this was probably an overstatement, given the relatively small sums involved in a year when prize money exceeded 900,000 francs. The paper even described a number of racers practicing their handwriting, "in a schoolboy's notebook," no less. When questioned, one allegedly responded: "We are doing what kids do . . . to perfect our handwriting." A few days later, *L'Auto* published an article titled "The racers apply themselves. . . . And the Edacoto pen is the reason for this revival." In addition to giving a sponsor free advertising, *L'Auto* took advantage of the contest to portray the Tour as a classroom where racers applied themselves to the elementary task of improving their handwriting. This improvement had a moral as well as an intellectual dimension. As *L'Auto* noted, "The care with which one signs is proof of great self-confidence, of a tranquility we would always have liked to be able to note in our champions."[108]

L'Auto's obsession with elegance bore witness to an enduring concern inherited from the previous century. Although the term was no longer in use, the *vélocipédard* stereotype continued to obsess Desgrange and his staff. Some critics, impervious to *L'Auto*'s rhetoric of racer self-improvement, dismissed Tour contestants as undeserving of mass adulation precisely because of their class; without the Tour "they would be joiners, carpenters, locksmiths, canal workers, dockers, or *pimpernel merchants*."[109] Despite the annual flood of contradictory evidence (to which *L'Auto* contributed by exhaustively reporting racer misconduct), the organizers invoked the *vélocipédard*'s fin-de-siècle countermodel, the cycling gentleman, to argue that the Tour transformed its racers into aristocratic workers. Rehabilitating Tour racers in the eyes of their middle-class critics was a challenge, as *L'Auto*'s conflation of two mutually exclusive social categories—aristocrat and worker—demonstrates. *L'Auto* sought to resolve this contradiction by simultaneously celebrating the authenticity of the Tour's "workers" and justifying the race as an annually staged working man's bildungsroman. In the meantime, Desgrange had identified another threat to his vision of the Tour as honorable work.

GOOD WORKERS, BAD WORKERS, AND THE "PROBLEM" OF PROFESSIONALISM

On the one hand, the Tour's prestige and credibility required the participation of the best racers, professionals all. On the other, it was the star racers who were most likely to fuel fears about the excessive autonomy and social mobility the Tour afforded working-class men. Their secure financial position gave them the ability to resist the organizers' attempts to enforce "respectable" standards of behavior. As a result, *L'Auto* continually celebrated racers who held a regular job while training for and participating in the Tour: "A blacksmith like Dargassies, a little apprentice butcher like Pothier, . . . an innkeeper like Brange [who] keep up with kings of the road like Garin, Aucouturier, and Muller."[110]

Part-time racers and their supporters often took pride in their dual identity. The Association Sportive de la Boucherie awarded a medal to Lucien Pothier for his performance in 1903, while Jean Dargassies boasted a few days before the 1904 Tour that "people will see what a blacksmith from Grisolles is worth."[111] When the 1913 Tour came through Longwy-Bas, a local racer, Celidonio Morini, was awarded 10.10 francs by his former coworkers in Homécourt.[112] Competing in 1929, Léon Joudelat, a butcher and treasurer of the Étoile Sportive de la Boucherie, received a daily bonus from his bosses and colleagues at the Boucherie Sabatier.[113]

Identification with and support for the race's less successful contestants did not require actually knowing them. Wishing to acknowledge the persistence of a modest racer who, like them, knew the meaning of a hard day's work, iron workers in Rehon donated fifteen francs to the last unsponsored racer to reach Longwy in 1913.[114] Such acts of solidarity suggest that the race's working-class public, like *L'Auto,* saw the Tour as hard physical labor every bit as much as sport.

Several decades after the publication of *La tête et les jambes,* Desgrange's paper continued to hammer home its central message: professional cycling was fraught with the temptations of free time and good pay. Racers needed a full-time outside occupation to "save" them from their natural lack of discipline, guarantee them a regular source of income, and turn them into responsible citizens and models for their fellow workers. In 1929 *L'Auto* argued that Victor Fontan, "simultaneously a bicycle racer, cycle manufacturer, mechanic, industrialist, [and] merchant," was successful precisely because he worked hard at both his athletic career and his other profession, thus avoiding "the danger of long hours of leisure, the temptations of idleness, etc. . . . Look at the result. At forty, or close to it, Fontan is one of our best road-racing stars, and he is the most serious and best-trained racer we have."[115] *L'Auto* praised Louis Péglion after his stage win at Nice in the 1930 Tour for his "healthy conception of social life": in addition to being a professional racer, Péglion ran a tractor and towing company with his brother.[116] In 1936 the paper described a racer's apprenticeship in a butcher shop: "Edgard de Caluwé is being initiated to the subtleties of cutting up prime rib steak and is learning his future profession. . . . [H]e knows . . . that the career of a bicycle racer is but one period in a man's life, and already he is preparing his future."[117] Such examples were intended both to persuade racers and their lower-class fans that sensibly investing the fruits of painful physical labor would improve their lot and to calm middle-class fears that professional racers would use their winnings to flout bourgeois norms as they climbed the social ladder.

Fears and hopes about the permeability of class boundaries informed the plots of cycling novels, particularly during the interwar years. As the fictional hero's victories mount, his income, ambition, and social horizons expand.[118] Fortuné Richard, the protagonist of *Le roi de la pédale* (1925), which was later made into a movie, is a humble hotel bellhop obsessed with cycling, "that school of energy, of willpower, of tenacity, of endurance, . . . of courage." Hired as a mechanic by the Automoto team, he competes as an amateur. Over the objections of his mother, who "prefers poverty to all that glory about which her *petit* is obsessed," and who fears that the race will ruin her son's health, Fortuné enters the Tour de France. He hopes to win a small fortune and move up the social ladder in an era when "the champion is welcomed like the painter, the writer, the musician or the actor." Success in the Tour indeed allows him "to elevate himself in the most beautiful and glorious of aristocracies: that of sport." The narrator emphasizes that such stupefying social promotions are possible only in sport. Fortuné's willpower, tenacity, energy, and superb muscles have made him the most popular man in France, a member of a new aristocracy based on merit and achievement.[119]

Such plots fueled the dreams of lower-class readers by presenting sport as a meritocratic arena of human endeavor in which social and professional success was not restricted by one's origins.[120] Other novels, however, were cautionary tales about the pitfalls of social ascent through sport. *Frangins* (1931) by Robert Dieudonné tells the story of two working-class friends.[121] Marcel, a packer for a soap manufacturer, is ascetic in his approach to cycling, forgoing parties and women for fear that they will "weaken his legs." He becomes the amateur world champion before turning professional. Roger, who works for a bicycle repair shop, is influenced and exploited by a young actress of suspect morals who convinces him to leave his cycling coach. The novel concludes with his fatal crash in a track race. Its moral is clear: the disciplined working-class youth with a respectable, sensible long-term goal—athletic success as a means to socioeconomic improvement—reinforces bourgeois values and thrives. His undisciplined, dissipated friend poses a temporary challenge to those values before perishing.

Dieudonné provided another example of a fictional working-class racer's remarkable socioeconomic ascent, and its limits, in *Bébert ou la vie ratée* (1929).[122] In this novel the ultimate impermeability of class barriers is illustrated by the unbreachable divide separating the title character from the woman with whom he falls in love: Bébert is an orphaned apprentice butcher, Hélène the daughter of a wealthy count who owns a large oil company. In his teens Bébert moves to Paris, where he becomes a delivery boy and begins to race. After several years as a top cyclist, he takes a job in an automobile factory owned by the man who sponsored his racing career. Hélène, meanwhile, makes it clear that she does not love him enough to confront the social prejudices, authority, and sensibilities of her family and social milieu by marrying him.

Although still in love with Hélène, Bébert moves in with his mistress, Emmeline, seven years his senior but from the same social class. He rises up through the ranks in the company, marries Emmeline, and is soon racing cars for his employer. Having won many races, Bébert is admitted to the Automobile Club, a mark of his social as well as professional advancement. On his employer's death, he is named to lead the company. Bébert resigns to become a pilot and found his own aviation business, which is so successful that he is decorated. During World War I, Hélène's husband, a penniless viscount, is killed in Flanders. Bébert becomes a fighter pilot, Emmeline a nurse. Aware that Bébert still loves the widowed Hélène, Emmeline selflessly chooses to care for contagious cases so that she will die and leave Bébert free to pursue his true love. After Emmeline's death, however, Hélène still refuses to marry Bébert. Thus, despite his remarkable professional success and social ascent, Bébert's life is *ratée*—a failure—because he is unable to accept the "insurmountable chasm" that separates him from Hélène and find happiness with a good, loving woman from his own lower-class background.[123]

By the 1930s the debate over sports professionalism, amateurism, and dishonest amateurism ("shamateurism" or, in French, *amateurisme marron*) was raging in France in many sports, including soccer, rugby, and track and field.[124] Purists like the prominent former track star Franck Reichel harked back to the nineteenth-century ideal of the middle-class amateur, who played for fun, camaraderie, and the moral and physical benefits of vigorous, manly exercise. Proficient at a number of sports and imbued with the notion of "fair play," true amateurs never subordinated their love of sport to financial considerations, the requirements of professional competition, and a "win-at-any-cost" mentality. Desgrange, however, recognizing that professionalism in cycling was irreversible and indispensable, had to walk a fine rhetorical line between the corrupting professionalism he had decried since the late nineteenth century and the hypocrisy of part-time jobs offered to officially amateur athletes in return for their services on local teams.

Desgrange's solution was to craft a defense of the "honest professionalism" that prevailed in cycling. Praising the integrity of Tour racers whose open professionalism was morally superior to hypocritical shamateurism, Desgrange noted that professional cyclists came from the working and lower middle classes; that professional sport brought them comforts they were otherwise unable to afford; and that it did so without—and this was Desgrange's key point—turning them into delinquents once their cycling days were over. "Their professionalism," he exclaimed, "will not be a bad example, but a good lesson!" Still, professional cyclists remained problematic role models. Desgrange argued that although racers exemplified willpower, endurance, perseverance, energy, and even "magnificent stubbornness," young Frenchmen must stop short of seeking to become professional cyclists themselves: the Tour was simply too "horrific" a task for them.[125] Taken at face value, Desgrange's entreaty to French youth appears professionally suicidal: if nobody followed in the footsteps of the current professionals, the Tour and cycling in general would be dead within a decade or two.

Desgrange's plea made sense only if its target audience was the French middle and upper classes. Even as he sought to persuade them of the moral rectitude of professional cyclists, he advised their children against pursuing a career in professional cycling in favor of moderate—in other words, amateur—and therefore healthy sport. Desgrange understood that the Tour's continuing success might well require convincing the "respectable classes" that professional cyclists did not threaten the social status quo, either as dishonest, dissipated athletes or as inappropriate role models for their sons. The latter were destined for the liberal professions or a *bonne situation* in commerce, banking, or industry; they should not follow the example of one fictional *lycée* graduate who became a racer and whose bourgeois family despaired at his scandalous career choice and rejection of further studies.[126] Desgrange concluded his defense of cycling's honest professionalism with an idyllic picture of a retired *touriste-routier* diligently working in the bicycle shop he has purchased with his winnings and raising a family with his wife, his *bourgeoise:* "Professionals and professionalism like that? You can't get enough. And we are going to display them with pride for a month before innumerable crowds whose applause and respect they will incite."[127]

Such portrayals of retired Tour racers allowed Desgrange once again to stress notions of hard work, property, discipline, family, and humility that would resonate favorably with his target audience. His reference to the lowly *touriste-routier* category also reinforced his message that Tour racers were nothing more than workers, artisans, and low-level employees working hard in a temporary profession to buy their slice of the middle-class pie and integrate themselves into bourgeois, or at least petit-bourgeois, society. Desgrange's reference to the racer's *bourgeoise* confirms *L'Auto*'s vision of the role of women in the Tour (discussed in chapter 3). As partners in work and family life, they provided a moderating influence on their husbands, who might otherwise have indulged in irresponsible, socially destabilizing behavior. Together, husband and wife sought to realize their eminently respectable dream of financial independence by running a modest but profitable family business. If Desgrange's intent was to defuse fears about working-class professional cyclists breaching carefully guarded class boundaries, his choice of the *touriste-routier* was disingenuous. It was the highly paid stars who were most dramatically bursting through traditional class barriers by earning sums that moved them in a few short years from their modest origins to the economic level of the upper middle classes and beyond.

Whenever possible, *L'Auto* sought to reinforce with concrete examples its conservative ideal of professional racers as safe for bourgeois society. A couple of weeks before the Belgian Maurice de Waele launched his successful bid for victory in the 1929 Tour, *L'Auto* lauded his "solid intelligence, above the Flemish average, which has made him a big merchant, the general representative for Flanders of the brand he rides, the ever sky-blue Alcyon." The paper preferred the "taciturn and victorious de Waele" to any racer "whose good pleasure and joking about have robbed him of energy and legs well before the dance starts."[128] A 1934 article rhapsodized about the imminent retirement of the two-time Tour winner Nicolas Frantz, who planned to devote himself to his bicycle shop and a possible candidacy in the next legislative elections: "Nicolas Frantz, former great champion, merchant, bourgeois, happy father and—who knows?—perhaps a future politician."[129] Frantz's personal trajectory struck every major note in the bourgeois register: family man, businessman, active and responsible citizen of the Republic, he was an exemplary professional racer who had integrated himself into the bourgeoisie and epitomized its values. His upward mobility was worthy of emulation by other racers and, by implication, by working-class fans. *L'Auto*'s readers were presumably intended to infer that Frantz and other racers who made a successful transition from their athletic careers owed their later success to the lessons learned and character forged by grueling athletic challenges, none more humbling than the Tour de France.

The extraordinary sums earned by the most successful Tour racers impelled *L'Auto* to address the nagging issue of whether the race corrupted working-class men who were utterly unprepared to manage such a financial windfall. When the Belgian Sylvère Maes won the 1939 Tour and a prize of at least two hundred thousand francs, *L'Auto* was quick to point out that "Sylvère will not let his new success go to his head. We can remain calm, he is not one to be tempted by the artificial joys of a life that is too easy." Four decades earlier Desgrange had warned his fictitious protégé in *La tête et les jambes* about the moral risks of rapidly acquired wealth; throughout its existence his paper would obsess about successful racers erasing class distinctions by the conspicuous consumption of material goods and immoral pleasures. *L'Auto*'s only recourse was to implore them to demonstrate financial responsibility and moral rectitude in their transition from professional sport to "civilian" life:

> He [Maes] will not go to a deluxe tailor. He will remain faithful to his humble way of life. We shan't see him in society dressed in black tie on the arms of pretty, pearl-covered girls. He will remain the owner of the Café du Tourmalet and will take care of his business with his usual serious approach. He will do his accounting. He will man his till. He will supervise the weekly sales of beer kegs. He will continue to manage his fortune with the same certainty that he managed his Tour de France.
>
> Sylvère! What a magnificent example for featherbrained youth![130]

Unfortunately for *L'Auto,* not all champions were such outstanding models, as the "defections" in 1923 of two former winners, Léon Scieur and Firmin Lambot, confirmed. Colic and a broken crank, respectively, had cost the two stars so much time that they could no longer hope for a top finish, let alone victory. Rather than finish hours behind the winner in Paris, they had dropped out. Their withdrawals may well have been supported, even mandated, by their sponsors, who had nothing to gain from their forging on; indeed, Scieur's health represented a valuable investment that might have been damaged by the effort. Desgrange, however, blamed their withdrawals on their "star complex": "Having won the Tour, Lambot twice and Scieur once, they consider it unworthy of them to be part of the procession of racers such as Bottecchia, Alavoine or Bellenger. . . . They have thus passed from the category of good pedal workers, to which they unquestionably belonged, to the category of bad ones."[131]

The former champions' poor work ethic was a disturbing reminder of what happened to a good worker when he earned too much money. To drive home this point, Desgrange contrasted them with a number of the lesser racers—"those good pedal workers, those indefatigable artisans of our success"—whose morality, conscientiousness, cleanliness, modesty, perseverance, humility, courage, honesty, and indefatigability he praised. He pointed to the quality of their work, equating their products—their respective "Tours de France"—with carefully crafted, unblemished goods manufactured with loving care in an artisan's workshop.[132] Once again, the Tour was a traditional, self-regulating guild with self-imposed quality and behavioral controls, an ideal site for the production of quality work and quality workers. Desgrange did not acknowledge the possibility that lesser racers were motivated by self-interested economic calculation, not a moral commitment to completing a job. Without the twenty-thousand-franc guarantees enjoyed by Scieur and Lambot, other racers persevered in the hope of winning prize money and attracting the attention of sponsors who would sign them to lucrative contracts. L'Auto argued that "to work fiercely and unrelentingly at a task when it has no other usefulness than to serve honor or sport, which is one of the forms of modern honor, is a beautiful act."[133] How many racers agreed?

Desgrange had long been convinced of the dangers of excessive salaries for working-class racers. In the days that followed Engel's expulsion from the 1914 Tour, he identified the real culprit in the deplorable breakdown in work discipline that had occurred: "Almost all of [the racers are] from humble origins, their existence is completely turned upside down one day solely because of their muscular power; they are offered small fortunes, they are showered with attention, their whims are obeyed, and they gradually get to the point where they forget even the essential principle that sport, on which they depend for a living, itself depends solely on discipline. When that happens everything goes wrong, and if you left them to themselves and to their whims, they would lose their jobs."[134]

Thus, the argument went, the Tour's rules benefited racers financially as well as morally. Left to their own devices, like Desgrange's fictitious protégé in La tête et les jambes, they lacked the self-discipline to translate their muscle power into economic gain. Desgrange's solution was to control the racers' finances and shape their behavior through L'Auto's editorials and fines, imposing a sort of moral economy of the Tour from above. But, as the next chapter shows, what Desgrange self-servingly presented as enlightened paternalism intended to improve his workers, others saw as crass exploitation. And where Desgrange saw moral weakness, the Tour's critics saw physical exhaustion.

CONCLUSION

L'Auto's attempt to promote a vision of working-class identity, embodied by honorable, well-behaved *ouvriers de la pédale,* that would bolster rather than threaten the social order was rife with tensions. For one thing, this image encompassed two distinct working-class identities, one modern (the obedient, disciplined industrial worker), the other anachronistic (the traditional independent artisan belonging to a self-regulating guild). Not surprisingly, it was the modern image of the Tour racer as industrial worker that inspired critics of the race during this period, as chapter 5 illustrates. For another, there was an implicit contradiction in celebrating the working-class identity of Tour racers as tough "pedal workers" while arguing that the race instilled in them bourgeois values and that its prize money would usher them into the respectable middle classes. As *L'Auto* itself acknowledged, the Tour was not an event for middle-class youth. Finally, the financial independence that racers gained from successful Tour careers gave them the freedom to flout the bourgeois norms on which the Tour's code of conduct was founded; much to the organizers' chagrin, some openly did so.

As is shown by the hundreds of fines they incurred each year, the racers resisted the Tour's code of conduct and were willing to pay a price, quite literally, for doing so. They publicly rejected the idealized working-class identity *L'Auto* sought to promote through its many rules. Instead, they continued to curse, urinate in public, swipe drinks from cafés, punch each other, race officials, and the occasional spectator, and parade around host communities in the racing outfits that identified them as heroic Tour racers to their legions of (mostly lower-class) fans. In the process, Tour racers more or less consciously asserted an authentic working-class identity, their own sense of themselves. This image was far more likely to resonate with Tour crowds than that of *L'Auto's* sanitized *ouvriers de la pédale*—and far more likely to result in free drinks, invitations to dinner, and attention from female fans.

Clearly, we must evaluate the public reception of *L'Auto*'s celebration of the Tour racer as an *ouvrier de la pédale* with great care. The many gifts racers received from fans of modest means suggest that the latter consciously wished to reward the racers' hard work.[135] Their generosity does not, however, imply widespread endorsement of the ideal of the "good pedal worker," nor the rejection of racers who did not conform to Desgrange's standards, as *L'Auto*'s own reporting confirms. An initiative by *L'Auto* in 1923 also suggests limits to the persuasiveness of the *ouvrier de la pédale* image. That year the paper organized a competition for fans, who were asked to submit drawings depicting how they saw the Tour winner.[136] As promised, *L'Auto* published the winning drawings, many of which predictably portrayed racers holding bouquets and being carried by fans or greeted by cheering crowds.[137] One, however, depicted the winner dreaming of his prize money, two others a sweating or unshaven racer sitting on or grasping the huge sums he had won.[138] Fans who focused on the fortunes made by such champions were unlikely to see them as model artisans or factory workers.

It seems plausible, then, that *L'Auto*'s *ouvrier de la pédale* campaign was aimed primarily at the middle-class readers and bourgeois spectators who expressed outrage at the racers' *tenue*. Even here, the organizers confronted a tension. On the one hand, they established rigid guidelines of appropriate conduct founded on notions of middle-class respectability. On the other, as the withdrawals of Scieur and Lambot in 1923 suggest, at times the interests of the sport's corporate sponsors were at odds with the values the organizers sought to promote through their rhetoric and regulations. *L'Auto* could decry all it wanted the poor work ethic of champions who dropped out; the sponsors of those champions had nothing to gain and much to lose by demanding that they stay in the race only to reach Paris hours behind the winner.

References to Tour racers as *ouvriers de la pédale* did not survive the war.[139] Perhaps this was because of Desgrange's death in 1940 and the retirement and gradual replacement of an older generation of journalists by Jacques Goddet and a new editorial staff at *L'Équipe*.[140] The new journalists and the men for whom they wrote may simply not have shared the sensibilities and concerns of the founding fathers of the race at *L'Auto*. On the other hand, this generational shift has not prevented the enduring, century-old celebration of racers as *géants de la route*. The reasons for the disappearance of the *ouvrier de la pédale* must be sought elsewhere, in the broader transformation of the nation after World War II.

Postwar France experienced extraordinary change as it shifted to an economy shaped by a rapidly expanding welfare state and increasingly dominated by service-sector jobs. Many modest families now had alternatives to the factory or mine and sought to place their sons in large government bureaucracies. Celebrating the physical and moral courage of the "respectable worker" was unlikely to resonate with individuals now aspiring to less strenuous and less dangerous white-collar jobs. Meanwhile, as both the relative and absolute numbers of blue-collar workers declined, so too did fears of violent working-class insurrection and the incentive to present safe models for potentially rebellious workers. Furthermore, shorter work weeks, safer workplaces, earlier retirements, automation, and, later, computerization, have gradually transformed industrial work and with it the very notion of the *ouvrier*.

In such a context, references to "guilds" and "artisans" would be ludicrously anachronistic to most fans, who, unlike those of the first decades of the race, rarely come into contact with craftsmen. Postwar Tour racers themselves came increasingly from nonmanufacturing backgrounds.[141] Two of the most popular, Raymond Poulidor and Bernard Hinault, are from farming families and have been widely celebrated as sons of the soil. Their image transcends industrial class conflict, evoking instead that most traditional, if increasingly rare, of French identities, the simple, hard-working peasant. Finally, gradual professionalization and improved pay (or, more to the point, the public perception of improved pay) make racers less convincing representatives of the laboring poor.

Occasionally, the opportunity to resuscitate Desgrange's old ideal of the Tour racer holding down a job in the real world presented itself after World War II. In 1966 Lucien Aimar took advantage of the rivalry between Jacques Anquetil and Raymond Poulidor to win the Tour, much to everyone's surprise. *Le Monde* noted that, having never truly believed racing success would let him forgo other employment, Aimar worked as a "humble municipal employee," a carpenter at the town hall in Hyères. His mayor described him as a "punctual, serious, extremely skillful and meticulous employee" and noted that because Aimar managed to do a year's work in six months—the off-season—he was paid all year round by the municipal government.[142] *Le Monde,* however, did not editorialize about the value of such an example; nor did *L'Auto*'s heir, *L'Équipe,* evoke artisans and guilds in covering Aimar's victory.

The notion of the Tour racer as an *ouvrier de la pédale* was well and truly dead. Its disappearance does not mean, however, that all references to the Tour as work evaporated after World War II. On the contrary, debates about the working conditions of Tour racers have surfaced periodically since the war, often in relation to the issue of performance-enhancing drug use by contestants. We shall address these debates in chapter 6. But first we must examine a prewar image of Tour racers that turned positive representations of "giants" and "workers" on their heads: the racer as "convict laborer of the road."

FIVE

The *Forçats de la Route*

Exploits, Exploitation, and the Politics of Athletic Excess, 1903–1939

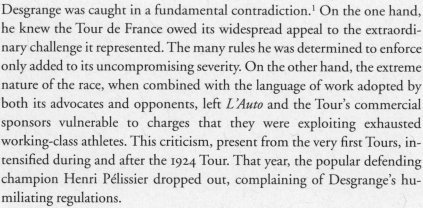

Desgrange was caught in a fundamental contradiction.[1] On the one hand, he knew the Tour de France owed its widespread appeal to the extraordinary challenge it represented. The many rules he was determined to enforce only added to its uncompromising severity. On the other hand, the extreme nature of the race, when combined with the language of work adopted by both its advocates and opponents, left *L'Auto* and the Tour's commercial sponsors vulnerable to charges that they were exploiting exhausted working-class athletes. This criticism, present from the very first Tours, intensified during and after the 1924 Tour. That year, the popular defending champion Henri Pélissier dropped out, complaining of Desgrange's humiliating regulations.

Couched in the language of human and workers' rights and magnified by the communist press in particular, Pélissier's remarks sparked a national debate about the race that lasted through the 1930s. A new representation of the Tour racer was born: the *forçat de la route,* or "convict laborer of the road." A sinister synthesis of "pedal worker" and "survivor," this image of slave labor politicized the race as never before. Critics of the Tour compared the organizers' treatment of racers to modern capitalism's abuse of factory workers, French society's true *forçats. L'Auto,* of course, but also others, rejected this comparison, arguing that professional cycling, and the Tour in particular, represented an opportunity for young men of humble origins to make a good living and that, in any event, these men were not forced to enter the race. The Tour's defenders blamed the affair on Pélissier's poor work ethic: inadequately prepared for the 1924 Tour, he had withdrawn to avoid an embarrassing performance. Furthermore, they argued, a wealthy racer grown soft was hardly an apt symbol of proletarian exploitation.

Whichever side they took, participants in the *forçat de la route* controversy addressed issues that extended well beyond the world of sport. By associating the Tour with broader developments in interwar France, they inserted the nation's most popular sporting event into contemporary French debates about class relations, economic and social justice, and the nature of modern industrial work.

LEGISLATING AGAINST ATHLETIC EXCESS?
THE CASE AGAINST THE TOUR

The magnitude of the Tour as an athletic challenge did not meet with universal approval. Physicians were concerned about excessive physical exercise and, specifically, the harmful effects of endurance events in the new sport of cycling. Politicians and other commentators feared the deleterious impact of long-distance bicycle races on contestants and public alike and called for restrictive legislation that would make such events safe for all involved. Three weeks before the first Tour, the *député-maire* of Sens regretted "that the necessities of existence reduce men to such excesses; . . . laws that regulate work prevent human beings from going beyond the limits of their normal strength except in the event of an urgent obligation; . . . it is up to the public authorities to bring an end to such a state of affairs."[2]

The mayor's criticisms were echoed by the Tour's opponents for the balance of the Third Republic: the race's primary raison d'être was to promote the French cycle industry; its excessive demands on contestants led to exhaustion, injury, sickness, and even death; and it endangered the lives of roadside spectators, to whom it offered a deplorable spectacle. True to his word, the mayor issued a municipal directive relating to long-distance bicycle races that restricted the racers' speeds in his town to a maximum of ten kilometers per hour and required them to proceed on foot when they encountered busy roads or other crowded public spaces. The departmental prefect, representing the French state, authorized its immediate implementation.[3]

The mayor's reference to labor legislation, which confirms that even before the inaugural Tour the association between work and long-distance cycling was firmly established, needs to be contextualized. The decades preceding World War I saw a number of legislative initiatives and reforms under the Third Republic designed to address workers' grievances and improve their work experience and quality of life. Such reforms, many Republicans believed, would guarantee social peace and the political allegiance of increasingly militant, organized industrial workers during a period marked by frequent, disruptive, and often violent strikes. The influence of ideas such as entropy, derived from the new discipline of thermodynamics, also contributed to initiatives to shorten the work day, reduce the risk of accidents, and improve the health of the working classes. Meanwhile, the contemporary scientific focus on fatigue and its elimination resulted in studies on work performance, mental fatigue, and nutrition; their objective was to calculate and conserve the nation's productive capital.[4] L'Auto was thus obliged to defend the rigors of the Tour at a time when considerable attention was being focused on the quality of the French worker's experience.

For much of the nineteenth century, French governments and employers under a variety of authoritarian regimes had resisted attempts by workers to improve working conditions and decrease working hours. Worker organizations had been outlawed during the first French Revolution in 1791, and strikes, illegal until 1864, were vigorously repressed. Early attempts in the 1840s to regulate child labor and limit the working day of adult male workers met with limited success.[5] After the foundation of the Third Republic in 1870, French governments and legislatures proved more sensitive to labor issues. Faced with an expanding working class influenced by socialist and syndicalist ideas, politicians were keenly aware that urban industrialization and universal male suffrage formed a potentially explosive cocktail that labor reforms might defuse. They addressed a number of worker grievances, particularly from the 1890s, as more progressive republicans, the Radicals, became a leading political force.[6] Health and safety regulations and obligatory accident insurance were implemented, although they were weakened by numerous exemptions and procedures favoring employers. Laws relating to old-age pensions were also passed, leading to incremental improvements for workers. Work-related issues became so central to French political life that one of Georges Clemenceau's first acts as the head of a new government in 1906 was to create a Ministry of Labor under the independent socialist René Viviani.[7]

A significant issue that related directly to long-distance bicycle races and may have motivated the Sens mayor's directive was the length of the work-day. As Gary Cross has noted, "France had perhaps the least regulated labor market and the longest worktime of any industrial nation in the late nineteenth century": twelve-hour workdays and seven-day work weeks were the norm for many industrial workers, artisans, and low-level service sector employees. By the late nineteenth century, the reduction of working hours had become the leading demand of organized workers, an important objective of syndicalists and socialists, and a demand frequently expressed during strikes.[8]

Governments of the Third Republic responded by focusing initially on protecting child, adolescent, and female workers. Regulating the hours of adult men—who, unlike women and children, enjoyed full citizenship rights—met with considerable hostility. Liberals believed such measures violated the freedom to work: employers and workers should negotiate terms of employment unhampered by state intervention. Many employers feared that a shorter workday would impair productivity and the international competitiveness of French industry. Nevertheless, laws passed in the early twentieth century reduced working hours and created a weekly day of rest for workers, although inadequate enforcement, employer opposition, and significant exemptions diluted their effect. Working conditions also aroused workers and motivated strikers, leading some reformers to propose compulsory mediation and arbitration. Although a systematic, universal, and compulsory bill was not passed, collective bargaining did become more common in French industry immediately before the war.[9]

Notwithstanding the opposition they faced and their partial scope, imperfect implementation, and inadequate enforcement, labor reforms during this period represented a fundamental shift in how French governments, legislators, employers, and workers addressed the workers' experience and the productive process, especially in industry.[10] The issues involved—the length of the workday, the organization of work, authority in the workplace, and the ability of workers to influence working conditions—were also relevant to the experiences of Tour racers. In this context, the charges made by the mayor of Sens, bolstered by his conviction that public officials should prevent long-distance bicycle races, were criticisms L'Auto could not afford to take lightly, particularly as this mayor sat in parliament, whence he could launch a national campaign against such competitions.

In his spirited response, "A Mayor Who Is Ten Years behind the Times," Desgrange argued that the spectators, merchants, and hotel owners of Sens would suffer the most from their mayor's edict, as the Tour and other races would bypass their town, eliminating a source of revenue and entertainment for the community. He mocked the mayor's contention that road races had caused racer fatalities. On the contrary, long-distance cycling was part of a sports movement that was improving the moral, physical, and intellectual state of French students and soldiers, as the condition of its stars after competitions emphatically confirmed. Races like Marseille-Paris and Bordeaux-Paris required far less energy and were less tiring than a 100-meter foot race or a 200-meter bicycle sprint.[11] That Desgrange made such an argument in one article while extolling the extraordinary physical demands of the Tour in countless others underscores the contradiction in which he was trapped. Criticism of the race as abusive repeatedly forced *L'Auto* to adopt irreconcilable—even ludicrous—positions in its defense.

Unfortunately for Desgrange, the mayor of Sens was not alone in his concerns or determination to intervene. Belgian critics dismissed the Tour as "idiotic," a "mental depravity," and "a base speculation on the frailties of human nature" that covered heroism in ridicule and transformed its injured, bloodied participants into "madmen," "degenerates," and "abnormal" individuals. They decried the poor example such "stupid and immoral" races set for the general population: "For a handful of gold, free men play the role of ancient gladiators and, through the sterile labor of the *forçat*, sprinkle 300-kilometer ribbons of road with their sweat and blood. They arrive panting, broken, exhausted, unrecognizable under the mud, dust and bruises." The Tour's spectators were "gawking onlookers" filled with "base passions," while those who lived off the racers' efforts were "parasites of human stupidity." A legislative solution was required, founded on an understanding that bicycle racing was work: "Parliaments pass laws to limit the work day; they rigorously supervise unhealthy or dangerous industrial establishments. . . . Could they not regulate the maximum effort which the whim of *sportsmen* would have the right to demand of the human machine?"[12]

French commentators agreed. They described the Tour as a "ridiculous event" dominated by the thirst, hunger, and exhaustion of its participants, as a "deviation of sport," and as a "degeneration of our time" that "consisted of making the individual play the role of a motor in which his legs will become pistons."[13] The Tour, according to such views, debased the public and the athletes; the latter were no longer heroes worthy of celebration and emulation but brutalized creatures symbolizing a more general degeneration.

While they echoed some of the misgivings Desgrange had expressed in his novel, these accusations emphatically contradicted *L'Auto*'s claim that the race civilized its participants and made them models of strength, endurance, and courage for a nation insecure about its physical and moral condition. As critics challenged the Tour's cult of suffering and survival, many argued that long-distance races dehumanized racers by transforming them into machines. In so doing they both reflected and challenged an influential contemporary understanding of the human body that had inspired press coverage of the racers since the very first Tour.

THE HERO DEHUMANIZED:
THE BICYCLE RACER AS MACHINE

Comparisons of cycling to industrial work led *L'Auto* and other observers to depict racers not only as workers but as machines, echoing earlier portrayals of cyclists as agents of technological modernity. *L'Auto* described the 1903 Tour champion Maurice Garin as "a fearsome and irresistibly strong resistance machine." Racers struggling through a torrential downpour were "unconscious automata, no longer moved by their will or intelligence but only by a kind of instinct that came from their profession." Covering the Tour for *Le Matin* in 1913, the writer Colette evoked "automata without faces."[14] The image of the locomotive dominated mechanical representations of racers, whose legs became, according to Colette, "two minuscule and indefatigable connecting rods which suffice to move this mechanical tempest."[15] For *L'Auto* they were "formidable connecting rods" falling "straight and hard like pneumatic drills."[16]

Mechanized racers were often seen as tireless, as if the mechanical nature of pedaling implied that they were impervious to pain, suffering, and, above all, fatigue.[17] Such representations, at least when employed by *L'Auto,* were perhaps intended to deflect criticism of the Tour as excessively demanding: if racers were machines, they did not need rest, only regular refueling at the checkpoints where they received food and drink. Although of course fully aware of their own suffering, racers themselves sometimes described themselves in mechanical terms. Apparently explaining a leg injury, in 1907 one contestant noted: "I've got a cylinder that isn't firing, but I'll be all right anyway."[18]

Mechanical representations of racers were buttressed by statistics published in *L'Auto,* such as each racer's *développement,* the distance he covered with one pedal rotation. This indicated which racers had chosen to push a "hard" or big gear and which ones preferred an easier one.[19] (After 1937, when Desgrange allowed all racers to use derailleurs and multiple gears, this statistic was no longer relevant.) *L'Auto* also featured technical articles that explicitly treated the human body as a machine. In 1911 a Dr. Ruffier conducted an "anthropometric examination" of the great François Faber, analyzing the racer's various measurements.[20] In 1939 he studied the chest and waist sizes, weight, and height of seven racers, concluding from ratios involving those measurements that they were well above the norm.[21] A regular contributor to *L'Auto* and *L'Équipe* through the immediate post–World War II years, Charles Faroux explored the "acceptable productivity" and caloric output of the "human machine" or "human motor." During the 1936 Tour, he wrote a series of articles analyzing the pedaling cadences of various racers with respect to their height, weight, nutrition, gear choice, pedal crank length, and wheel size, the power they generated, and the fluidity of their pedaling action under stress.[22]

A few weeks later, in an article titled "The Human Machine," Jean Gilly argued that the frequent comparison of the human body with a machine was quite accurate with respect to its "feeding and structure." Noting the popular practice of describing champions as "handsome machines" and "locomotives," he proceeded to examine the "chassis," "motor," and "body" *(carrosserie)* of the human "machine."[23] By reducing athletic performance to mathematical relationships between quantifiable variables, such articles suggested that the efforts of Tour racers were best understood in terms of output and productivity rather than courage, endurance, and suffering.

Comparisons between man and machine in Tour coverage had their roots in nineteenth-century ideals of efficient work and increased production, and in the resulting scientific interest in precisely measuring the physiological and psychological limits of human performance. As they became interested in quantifying muscular energy, doctors and scientists came to understand the human body as a machine. Some studied the performances and recuperation of top-flight bicycle racers, particularly in endurance events, because the bicycle provided a unique intersection of high-performance sport and experimental science: it could be ridden both to demonstrate and, when employed as an ergometer, to measure performance.

Measurement provided the basis for continual comparisons and, by extension, the promise of virtually limitless human progress. New devices were invented, capable of measuring human physical performance and potential in a variety of areas, including manual labor, military service, and sport. For example, Jules-Étienne Marey's chronophotographs, which broke down a movement into its component parts, could be employed to teach manual laborers a more efficient way of producing goods, just as they could suggest more energy-efficient techniques to athletes.[24] Marey, who began to investigate motion in the 1860s, was convinced that mechanical laws applied to living beings. He viewed the "animal machine" as a motor, which, if properly analyzed, could lead to what one historian has called "a new kind of productivism—the optimum deployment of all forces available to the nation."[25] In the late-nineteenth-century context of European industrial and military competition, and given specific French concerns about demographic stagnation and the debacle of 1870, maximizing human energies had clear implications for the international balance of power and French national security.

The metaphor of the human body as a motor, popularized by scientists in the late nineteenth century, resulted from a new conceptualization of energy and labor inspired by recent scientific discoveries. Chief among them were Hermann von Helmholtz's formulation of the universal law of the conservation of energy in 1847 and, a few years later, Rudolf Clausius's discovery of the second law of thermodynamics, which explained the irreversible decline of energy in entropy. The working body was now seen as a productive machine with measurable energy and output that exemplified the universal process by which energy was converted into mechanical work. As a result, the image of labor was dramatically transformed: the expenditure and deployment of energy came to replace older notions of work founded on human will, technical skill, and moral purpose. Only fatigue distinguished human effort from the operation of an industrial machine capable in principle of perpetual work. But if the human body was governed by the same dynamic laws as industrial machines, would it not be possible to eliminate fatigue and unleash society's latent energies and the triumph of productivism? A variety of scientists and social reformers committed themselves to seeking a cure, and a new science of work was born, inspired by the utopian ideal of a body without fatigue.[26]

Given this conceptual shift, it is hardly surprising that cyclists received particular attention from the scientific community. Desgrange himself defined the Tour as "the greatest scientific experiment [*épreuve de documenta-*

tion] that the sport of cycling has ever given us."[27] While *L'Auto* often described Tour racers as proud guild artisans, the race actually reproduced the work conditions of modern factories, where precisely measured pace and output paralleled a racer's gear choice, pedaling cadence, technique, and aerodynamic position. Efficiency in those areas led to a higher "yield" that, with the inevitability of a mathematical calculation, would presumably lead to victory.[28] Hence the mathematical analysis of Faroux and others, which provided a scientific foundation for evocations of the racers as locomotives, motors, and machines.

An important disjuncture existed, however, between the scientific or social reformist agenda of engineers and fatigue experts and the press's representations of racers as machines. The former sought to eradicate fatigue through the application of scientific knowledge about the way the human body works and thus fully unleash society's productive potential. For the Tour organizers and most of the media covering the race, it was permissible, perhaps even laudable, for a racer to approach his diet, gear choice, or racing position in a scientific manner, but there could be no question of the elimination of fatigue: fatigue and its consequences—suffering and attrition as injured and exhausted racers dropped out—created the drama of the Tour, confirmed that it was the toughest competition in the world, and transformed its contestants into exceptional beings worthy of mass interest. The racers might look like locomotives, even move like locomotives, but theirs was the exquisite suffering of mortal man pushed to his limits, for whom survival *was* victory.

This tension notwithstanding, the Tour's defenders invoked the fantasy of the body without fatigue, which they often fused with the voluntarist discourse of late-nineteenth-century sports enthusiasts. Desgrange noted that "the human body is inexhaustible, when driven by willpower."[29] Alphonse Baugé, a team manager, blended references to "mechanical ghosts" and "human motors" with evocations of "prodigious feats of energy," "beautiful and splendid work," an "atrocious and moving calvary," and "inexhaustible resources, violent courage, stubborn willfulness, and indomitable tenacity."[30] Such rhetoric synthesized the contradictory elements of conventional Tour coverage: the racers were simultaneously tireless, efficient, unfeeling machines and heroic workers whose boundless vitality, courage, and will allowed them to overcome terrible suffering.

Some observers refused to be swayed by such lyricism. *L'Auto* could neither ignore their criticism of the race's inhumane demands nor assert its economic interests in maintaining the Tour's extreme nature, which would simply confirm that it exploited racers for financial gain. Instead, Desgrange shifted his defense of the Tour to a higher plane. In the mid 1920s, in editorials titled "Father Whiphand" and "The Terms of the Contract," he declared that "this is about moral virtues" and expressed indignation at "inelegant withdrawals" by well-paid racers who dropped out without courage or reason and thus violated "unavoidable duties" towards their sponsors and the public.

Desgrange's critique was grounded in two discursive registers he was forever seeking to conflate: on the one hand, the language of work (contractual obligations, good salaries, employers, work ethic); on the other, the language of personal morality (virtue, integrity, elegance, duty, courage, mission, indignation).[31] At the heart of his frustration was the fact that contestants refused to race hard in every stage. In 1926 the unprecedented length of the Tour certainly played a part in this passivity, as did Lucien Buysse's impressive lead over his competitors. Beginning in 1927, Desgrange gradually reduced the length of the race. His willingness to do so proved that he could adapt the Tour to protect its image but also that, much to his frustration, racers could exert influence over their working conditions. Those conditions were already at the center of a great debate launched in the summer of 1924.

RACER REVOLT IN INTERWAR FRANCE

In his attempt to impose autonomy and self-reliance on the Tour's racers, Desgrange required that they finish each stage with all the equipment and clothing with which they had started. In 1924 this rule sparked a controversy involving the defending Tour champion Henri Pélissier, a national celebrity and fan favorite.[32] As stages often began at night in chilly temperatures, Pélissier had taken to wearing several jerseys, gradually peeling them off and tossing them away as the day warmed up. A team manager pointed out to Desgrange that this was a violation of article 48 of the Tour's regulations. Added in 1920, this article was intended to prevent the wasting of sponsor-provided equipment. It was thus part of Desgrange's campaign to instill bourgeois values in the racers, in this instance respect for property, particularly that of others. Desgrange discussed the matter with Pélissier, who informed him that the jerseys were his own and had not been provided by his sponsor. The issue was apparently still unresolved when, at the start of the third stage in Cherbourg, a race official ran his hand down Pélissier's back to check the number of jerseys he was wearing. Enraged, Pélissier declared that he was dropping out of the race. He reconsidered and started the stage, only to withdraw later in the day at Coutances. His brother Francis, an excellent racer in his own right, and the Pélissiers' protégé, Maurice Ville, also dropped out to express their solidarity with the aggrieved champion.

The brothers' withdrawal was big news, as they were two of the most gifted and successful French racers of their day. Henri had begun his racing career in 1911, rapidly accumulating prestigious victories in one-day *classiques* such as the Tour of Lombardy (which he won three times), Paris-Roubaix (twice), Milan-San Remo, Bordeaux-Paris, and Paris-Tours. He also placed in the top three in the French road-racing championship five times between 1919 (when he won) and 1924. Before dominating the 1923 Tour at the advanced age of thirty-four, he had finished a close second to the Belgian Philippe Thys in 1914. The younger brother, Francis, although a professional only since 1919, had already won Bordeaux-Paris twice and the French road-racing championship three times.[33]

The incident assumed unexpected proportions when the prominent journalist Albert Londres, covering the race for *Le Petit Parisien,* interviewed the three racers while they sat at a café sipping hot chocolate. They showed him the drugs they took simply to survive the race, including cocaine for their eyes, chloroform for their gums, cream for their knees, and three boxes of pills that Francis Pélissier mysteriously referred to as "dynamite." Describing the race as a calvary, Henri Pélissier evoked the diarrhea and weight loss experienced by Tour racers and used the English term "hard labour" to characterize the Pyrenees. He expressed outrage at having to check with Desgrange before throwing away his own clothing: "It is not enough that we are obliged to cycle like brutes, [we must also] freeze and suffocate. Apparently that, too, is part of sport." Pélissier also mocked the rules requiring self-sufficiency of Tour racers:

> We do things you would not force mules to do. We aren't lazy, but in the name of God, don't bother us. We do not want to be humiliated! . . . When we are dying of thirst, before we place our water bottles under the running water, we must make certain that someone fifty yards away isn't pumping it. Otherwise: penalization. To drink, you have to pump [the water] yourself! The day will come when they will put lead in our pockets because they will

have decided that God made man too light. . . . Sport is becoming completely mad.[34]

No doubt inspired by his recent trip to French Guyana, where he had reported on the penal colony, and moved by the racers' accounts of the Tour, Londres referred to them in his article as *les forçats de la route,* the convict laborers of the road.[35] Having already reported on the stomach and eye ailments and frequent punctures experienced by Tour participants, he now expanded his critique of the race in a series of scathing articles. Londres described rainy, cold, and windy conditions; badly paved roads and dangerous crowds at finish lines; the pain and injuries experienced by racers, one of whom had lost an eye; and their fear as they negotiated perilous mountain roads. He discussed with a doctor the bacteria in the dust of the roads and exposed regulations requiring racers to continue on foot when they were no longer capable of cycling in order to avoid a five-hundred-franc fine. His headlines trumpeted "Tour de France, Tour of Suffering!" and stressed the race's terrible attrition rate. The racers were empty cadavers; passive, accepting lambs; cows being led to slaughter.[36] For the first time, the various charges that had been made against the Tour since 1903 were brought together for a large audience.

In a letter published in the communist daily *L'Humanité* a few days after his interview with Londres, Henri Pélissier accepted "excessive fatigue, suffering, pain" as part of his profession. He asserted, however, that racers wished "to be treated as men and not as dogs" by "well-behaved, competent and impartial officials," and demanded "the right to control our person as we think fit, without having [Desgrange's] permission." Contradicting *L'Auto's* argument that a racer who withdrew violated contractual obligations, Pélissier noted that "our Directors were very satisfied with the results we have obtained for them and . . . have understood perfectly the kind of harassment against which we have had to revolt. It is not us they blame." He invoked workers' and human rights to support his claim to dignity, liberty, and respect, and rejected Tour regulations requiring self-sufficiency as well as Desgrange's moral authority over the racers, whose behavior was beyond reproach.

Pélissier's dismissal of Desgrange's authority was particularly damaging because it was not part of a broader challenge to authority per se. He acknowledged the legitimacy of a social hierarchy based on "great moral worth, knowledge, talent, [and] genius," but refused to submit to "enriched autocrats" like Desgrange.[37] The racer's views, like Desgrange's, were founded on the image of the Tour as work, but instead of a civilizing process that transformed racers into respectable members of society, he portrayed the race as a dehumanizing factory where workers toiled long hours in the harshest conditions, their every move controlled by the mean-spirited agents of their capitalist boss.

THE HERO DEHUMANIZED:
THE BICYCLE RACER AS BEAST

In making their case against the Tour, both Pélissier and Londres compared racers to a variety of animals exploited by humans. Such representations refuted *L'Auto*'s depictions of conscientious "pedal workers," superhuman "giants of the road," and efficient man-machines emblematic of the advanced industrial age. Ironically, *L'Auto*'s Tour coverage had from the race's earliest years been peppered with allusions to racers as beasts. "Admirable human beasts" and "handsome beasts of combat" when the race was going well, in less favorable circumstances they were "pathetic, bewildered, injured beasts," as when Gustave Garrigou collapsed on the road "with the great, weary gesture of an animal fatally struck." When hiding from their fans, contestants were "poor, hunted beasts . . . holed up in all the hotels of the city."[38]

In addition to using the generic *bête, L'Auto* compared contestants to specific animals, including gazelles, alligators, zebras, and buffalo. These comparisons allowed the sports daily to evoke the racers' physical, moral, and mental qualities. They were as courageous as lions, as aggressive and powerful as boars and bulls, as clever and adroit as monkeys, as sly and patient as tomcats, as small as mice, as strong as oxen, as slow as crabs, and, in the case of good climbers, as light as birds and fleas.[39] Before television coverage, fans were thus able to create mental images of the contestants whose exploits they followed in the press and on radio. Gaston Rebry, for example, was nicknamed the "Bulldog" for his flat nose, courage, aggressiveness, persistence, and racing position.[40] On the eve of his retirement from racing, the organizers praised the "great conscientiousness" of the two-time Tour champion Antonin Magne by comparing his legacy to that of "great race-horses who give their name to the year they were born."[41]

Such portrayals allowed *L'Auto* to draw distinctions between racers, particularly when they were described as different members of a single species: "[Ezquerra] was the eagle of the Galibier [a major peak in the Alps]. Trueba is now only its falcon, while Canardo was only its swallow, and Montero its sparrow."[42] The Tour champions Maurice Garin and François Faber were "pure-breeds"; well-prepared stars were "horses ready for the Derby"; promising young racers were "foals"; and teams were "stables" of racers.[43] Racers themselves occasionally indulged in such comparisons: describing himself as "a pure-breed," in 1919 Henri Pélissier dismissed his adversaries as "cart-pulling horses."[44] *L'Auto* also saw the *peloton* as a "pack" of bulldogs, greyhounds, sheepdogs, Saint Bernards, skinny dogs, and nasty little dogs *(roquets)*.[45] Paul Le Drogo was a Saint Bernard "because of his general robustness, his equanimity, his humility and above all his unwavering attachment to the greyhound." The "feline greyhound" in question was his brother Ferdinand, "often the victim of a sensitivity and a nervousness that result in both the best and the worst things."[46]

Although aware of its predilection for canine comparisons,[47] *L'Auto* did not consider the implications of repeatedly describing Tour contestants as subhuman, nor the fact that it privileged comparisons to dogs and horses, animals domesticated and raced by humans. References to racers as horses might appear to echo late-nineteenth-century representations of the bicycle as a mechanical steed, but there was a crucial distinction: the bourgeois *cavalier cycliste* had been the rider; the lower-class Tour racer was the horse. Meanwhile, the sports daily was not alone in employing bestial images in Tour coverage, as the socialist *Le Populaire*'s analysis of Pélissier's 1923 Tour victory illustrates:

> The eldest Pélissier won thanks to his physical qualities, thanks to his exceptional athletic ability, but also thanks to his remarkable intelligence. He is not a racing machine, [nor] a plough horse who pushes his machine everywhere in all weather, he is a greyhound, with a lucid and clear-sighted mind. An unparalleled tactician, he has a feel for racing, and he knows his profession. Better than all others, he knows where he should switch his back tire, change gears, and take advantage of his small gear to make the decisive effort at the right moment.[48]

Emphasizing Pélissier's intellect and professional expertise did not inspire *Le Populaire* to portray him as a skilled artisan, as an engineer maximizing his machine's productivity, or even as a general marshaling his resources in the successful prosecution of a military campaign. Instead, much as *L'Auto* had lauded Magne by comparing him to a racehorse, the Socialist paper evoked a dog, equally servile, to praise Pélissier.[49] That a paper devoted to the cause of French workers would embrace the image of the bestial racer suggests that by the early 1920s that image was firmly established.

Bestial representations of racers during the Tour's early decades may have been rooted in a nineteenth-century understanding of the relationship between suffering, race, and class. European observers almost always described non-European "savages" as less sensitive to pain than Europeans, and this belief in turn contributed to the subhuman image of "primitive" peoples at that time. Similar conclusions were also drawn about lower-class Europeans, whose assumed insensitivity to pain suggested that they were especially suited to sports like boxing. Some "experts" also observed that a dynamic muscular physique generally excluded a cultivated sensibility.[50] Hence the very capacity to suffer that motivated descriptions of Tour contestants as heroic and superhuman may also have inspired their depiction as primitive and subhuman. Just as it had done in describing the racers as machines, by continually crossing the rhetorical line between the respectable pedal worker and the lower-class beast in its race coverage, *L'Auto* provided its critics with a vocabulary they employed to decry the brutal, dehumanizing treatment of Tour contestants.

INVENTING THE *FORÇAT DE LA ROUTE*

Henri Pélissier had actually used the term *forçat* as early as 1919 to complain about the inhumane conditions of the first postwar Tour. Recognizing that such language reinforced its celebration of the event as the most grueling in all of sport, *L'Auto* had responded by confirming Pélissier's "martyrdom."[51] Five years later Desgrange acknowledged that *Le Petit Parisien*'s coverage would not be as easy to deflect: "The word creates an image. It helps to paint a picture. It evokes a contrast and, as the public is not required to think, it immediately enjoys considerable success."[52]

Forçat in fact painted two pictures, neither of which reflected well on the Tour. The most obvious reference was to penal colonies, particularly Guyana, the destination of convicted criminals who had escaped the death penalty in the great judicial "affairs" of late-nineteenth- and early-twentieth-century France. By the interwar years Guyana had, in the words of one historian, become a "myth." Exasperated parents threatened their offspring with the prospect of "ending up at Cayenne," and the press titillated millions of readers with real and imagined accounts of convict revolts and escape attempts. Londres's investigative series in *Le Petit Parisien,* which ran from August to October 1923, was published as a book, inspired a play and a song, and fueled a media storm that contributed to a series of reforms and attempts by the new governor of the penal colony to end its most egregious abuses.[53] Although obviously unaware of the longer-term impact of his reporting, in the summer of 1924 Londres would certainly have been conscious of the massive public interest in *forçats* as he searched for a compelling image to convey the plight of Tour racers and increase *Le Petit Parisien*'s sales.

The term had a second, derivative meaning that explicitly challenged *L'Auto*'s portrayal of the racers as pedal workers and cast a critical light on its depiction of the race as productive, modern industrial labor. The increasingly mechanized, rationalized factories of nineteenth-century France, with their numerous rules and fines, had inspired references to industrial penal colonies, workers as convicts, and foremen as guards, which came into general usage between 1860 and 1880. Labor newspapers often included an "abuse column" or columns about factory conditions titled "The Review of Penal Colonies." In the Nord *département* (and presumably elsewhere), workers' and socialist papers—*Le Forçat, Le Cri du Forçat* (The Convict's Cry), *La Revanche du Forçat* (The Convict's Revenge), *Le Réveil du Forçat* (The Convict's Awakening)—self-consciously embraced the term, which was also prominently featured in the "Internationale." Written to commemorate the Paris Commune shortly after its defeat in 1871, this anthem of the international working-class movement (and later of international communism) begins, "Arise, the cursed of the earth!/Arise, slave laborers of hunger!"[54] Clearly, by 1924 *forçat* was a familiar term that evoked horrific, exploitative labor.

The impact of the Londres-Pélissier interview on public opinion was considerable because of the popularity of the Tour, the celebrity of both men, and the language they used. At least one sports club, the Amicale de la Jeunesse Parisienne, organized a debate, to which it invited Tour racers and organizers alike, on the following topic: "Indictment of the Tour de France: Is the Tour de France a penal colony? Are the racers convict laborers?"[55] Meanwhile, the Parisian and provincial press of all political hues addressed Pélissier's complaints. Some, like the conservative *Le Figaro* and *Le*

Temps and the Catholic *La Croix,* reported the incident in neutral terms, without editorializing.[56] Others, however, chose sides.

EXPLOITING THE *FORÇAT DE LA ROUTE*

Not surprisingly, the most aggressive criticism of the race sparked by the *forçat* controversy came from those who saw the defense of workers as their fundamental mission. The communist daily *L'Humanité* immediately seized on the affair with dramatic headlines about the "rebellion" of the Pélissier brothers, who were brandishing "the banner of revolt." Like Henri Pélissier, *L'Humanité* accepted Desgrange's vision of the Tour as work, only to turn it on its head. The racers who had dropped out were "strikers," the Tour a vast commercial operation with "absurd regulations" organized by sports profiteers who exploited the "cycling proletariat." *L'Humanité* contrasted "the commercial calculations" of morally bankrupt bourgeois spectator sport with the "severe . . . and disinterested joy" of the pure communist sporting ideal. It was "the duty of sporting communists to exploit the Pélissier incident to denounce forcefully the maneuvers of the sports profiteers" and "begin to unveil the hidden side of the Tour de France."[57]

This position represented a shift for *L'Humanité.* During the three previous Tours, its coverage had generally been limited to brief updates and stage results. Although aware of the terrible attrition rate and rigors of the race, *L'Humanité* had echoed *L'Auto*'s most cherished themes, emphasizing the difficulty of the racers' task and their exceptional will, courage, energy, popularity, and recuperative powers. Its criticism was muted at best and accompanied by the recognition that the Tour was an extraordinary and impressive event, if not the most sporting.[58] *L'Humanité* may have begun to adopt a more critical stance toward the race's commercialism in the early days of the 1924 Tour, before the Pélissiers dropped out, but the shift to outright opposition and to an explicitly political reading of the race was a direct result of the Pélissier incident.[59]

L'Humanité sustained its critique of the Tour for the balance of the interwar period, hoping its readers would recognize that the race was part of the capitalist class's cynical "bread and circuses" manipulation of the laboring masses.[60] Satirizing *L'Auto*'s coverage, the communist paper denounced the organizers' "ferocious and at times criminal exploitation" of "the 'giant' pedal workers" and evoked "the pain and suffering of all the exploited [racers] of M. Desgrange."[61] Tour contestants endured cold, rain, hunger, thirst, fatigue, climbs, lack of rest, sleep deprivation, and lengthy stages in order to generate an ever-increasing profit for Desgrange. They were obliged to race at the hottest time of the day to prevent the evening papers from scooping *L'Auto* by reporting the day's results: "Like an exploiter in the factory, he [Desgrange] requires ever-greater productivity with less security and more fatigue. The result: punctures, accidents, falls, death, men in hospital."[62] The communist paper assailed the practice of subdividing a day's racing into half-stages (introduced in the 1930s), particularly when time trials were involved, as these were especially demanding.[63]

L'Humanité also noted the injustice implicit in the existence of different categories of racers, arguing that *domestiques* should not have to forfeit their own chances in supporting their team leader. The paper complained that the privileged "aces," backed by entire teams, received the best equipment. Meanwhile, the *individuels* or *touristes-routiers,* whom *L'Humanité* compared to factory and construction workers, were paid less, penalized more harshly by the organizers, and placed at a competitive disadvantage by the race's regulations (for example, they did not receive new inner tubes when theirs punctured).[64] This double standard, the paper asserted, was a conscious attempt to divide and conquer Desgrange's "workers."[65] In fact, as we have seen, it was the commercial sponsors, not Desgrange, who insisted on fielding teams to maximize their top racers' chances of winning. Wishing to use the Tour as a case study in exploitation and class conflict, the communist paper was not interested in such fine distinctions. Instead, undermining *L'Auto*'s claims that the Tour transformed racers into "aristocratic" workers, *L'Humanité* argued that the organizers' unfair practices were creating "an aristocracy" that was not founded on merit; the paper concluded, "That is not sport."[66]

L'Humanité contrasted the profit-driven immorality of bourgeois sporting events like the Tour with the disinterested purity of races organized by the communist Fédération Sportive du Travail.[67] The paper hoped to convince working-class members of corporate sports clubs established by the French *patronat* in the interwar years to join communist clubs created in the early 1920s under the unifying banner of the FST.[68] As Richard Holt has noted, there was "a good deal of understandable anxiety on the Left about the very existence of such [corporate] clubs. The Communist *Sport Ouvrier* warned its readers that 'the ruling class seeks to infiltrate the habits, styles of life and thought of its adversaries without their knowing it' and that corporate sports 'will undermine the critical spirit and foster a climate of discipline and respect toward bourgeois chaos and its institutions.'"[69]

To further arouse the class consciousness of French workers, *L'Humanité* promoted its own model Tour "worker." In the 1930s the paper praised the unsponsored racer René Bernard for being a "class-conscious worker" who belonged to a "revolutionary cooperative" and a trade union. It claimed that Desgrange had refused to name Bernard to the French national team because he had been a delivery man for *L'Humanité,* and had penalized him more heavily than the stars of the national team to prevent him from placing well in the overall classification.[70] *L'Humanité* hoped to rally the Tour's working-class fans behind a racer who symbolized class-conscious rebellion and thereby encourage "the exploited [workers] of commercial cycling to organize themselves for the struggle against their bosses, whose rapaciousness is no longer in need of being demonstrated."[71] This was unrealistic: stars did not wish to jeopardize the fortunes they could make by antagonizing Desgrange, and lesser racers lacked the clout to confront him successfully. Nevertheless, *L'Humanité* asserted that the "exploited" racers were favorably disposed to the paper, "because they know that every day we defend their justified demands."[72]

As its frequent references to factories, productivity, exploitation, proletarians, workers, bosses, and strikers make clear, the implications of *L'Humanité*'s critique of the Tour transcended sport. The paper hoped to capitalize on Henri Pélissier's immense popularity, his act of revolt, and public interest in the race to launch a communist campaign against modern industrial capitalism. Workers who shunned bourgeois sport might also by extension reject bourgeois society in its totality.[73] When the 1924 Tour concluded with the victory of Bottecchia, an Italian mason, *L'Humanité* grudgingly acknowledged the small fortune he had won but reminded its readers that "for every Bottecchia who moves thus from proletarian poverty to the petty comforts of the *petit bourgeois,* how many other racers will remain convict laborers of the road?"[74]

Both Desgrange and his communist critics saw the Tour as fitting into a larger debate about class relations and social justice in France. For the former, the Tour symbolized economic opportunity and the peaceful integration of the working class into bourgeois society. For the latter, the race was "the exact copy of the rationalized work supervised by the warder of galley slaves in the great factories": "He [Desgrange] . . . threatened . . . his employees who are not doing the work at the rationalized pace he was demanding. . . . He swore . . . that the articles of the regulations, created by him, the boss, allow him to inflict sanctions that will force the workers to work more. . . . Most of the men hired by the company are exhausted. . . . The 'father' of the Tour is perplexed. How can you make racers who can't go any further race?"[75]

L'Humanité's linking of Desgrange's obsession with maximum productivity to the degrading exploitation of workers under modern industrial capitalism reflected the growing influence in France of recent theories of industrial management, particularly Taylorism. Frederick Winslow Taylor's ideology of scientific management, developed in the United States at the end of the nineteenth century, sought to increase worker productivity and implement an optimum work pace. Functional foremen, time and motion studies, new work-routing systems, and bonus payment plans and other incentives were designed to increase efficiency and managerial control, motivate workers, and subdivide production in ways that reduced reliance on skill. In fulfilling their various tasks, workers were to adhere strictly to instruction sheets drawn up by factory planning departments. Taylor argued that although this approach appeared to transform the worker into "a mere automaton," factory workers under scientific management were more efficient and productive than the self-employed, autonomous artisan, precisely because the workers forfeited their monopoly of technical knowledge to management's planners.[76]

The obedience demanded of workers found an obvious counterpart in the discipline Desgrange sought to impose on Tour racers. Desgrange, too, justified his approach by claiming it would allow racers to develop their potential to the fullest, but, whereas L'Auto sought to present a double image of the Tour racer as both artisan and modern factory worker, Taylor unequivocally celebrated the latter. Despite Taylor's disclaimer, scientific management, like competitive long-distance cycling, seemed to transform workers into automata: workers were seen as machines potentially capable of infinite productivity and resistant to fatigue once their bodies had been subjected to "scientifically designed systems of organization."[77] Such a view was entirely consonant with many late-nineteenth-century theories about athletic training and with Desgrange's claim regarding the potentially "inexhaustible bodies" of properly trained racers. The parallel between Tour racers—specifically Pélissier's anger at the interference of Tour officials with his ability to decide how best to do his job—and the plight of "Taylorized" workers was not lost on communist critics of the modern factory.

According to Taylor, the greatest obstacle to attaining maximum pace and productivity was loafing. This was one of the reasons work processes and paces were to be devised by management's planning departments, rather than by the workers themselves. The benefits of scientific management were then measured mathematically in the form of increased output.[78] Desgrange, too, was obsessed with the racers' pace. Before the first Tour he decided that racers averaging under twenty kilometers per hour for a stage would forfeit their daily minimum wage.[79] Designed to maintain the race's image as heroic work rather than subsidized cyclotourism, the minimum-pace requirement amounted to imposing productivity standards below which racers would no longer be paid for work deemed unsatisfactory. Desgrange was behaving like a Taylorite industrialist. He relented at the Tour's conclusion, awarding *primes de route* to racers who had completed stages at under twenty kilometers per hour.[80] By then it was no doubt clear to him that they had given their best effort and that the Tour's integrity, both as a sporting event and as an example to the masses, had not been compromised by those unable to complete stages within the prescribed time limit. Thereafter, however, whenever Desgrange believed that racers had failed to meet the minimum required pace through lack of effort, he threatened to, and occasionally did, punish their poor work ethic, at times canceling prizes and bonuses.[81] In this way, too, the Tour replicated the factory, where worker protest often took the form of a slowdown and the boss responded with fines.

Both Desgrange and Taylor believed that they were contributing to a solution of the "social question." The "Taylorized" factory worker, laboring in a maximally efficient system, would share in its benefits as increasing productivity raised wages for workers and profits for employers, erasing class conflict over these issues.[82] This promise of increased wages notwithstanding, the two men also shared the paternalistic view that too much money in the hands of workers was dangerous: additional income would simply be spent on alcohol and other immoral expenditures, which in turn would reduce workers' productivity.[83]

Building on a keen interest in industrial rationalization among late-nineteenth-century French engineers, Taylor's ideas found an audience in France in the early 1900s, when a number of his works were translated. His *Principles of Scientific Management* sold twenty thousand copies between 1912 and 1924 in France, one-third of them before the war. Beginning in 1908, initial attempts to implement Taylorism in France were generally not very successful. French industrialists were more likely to invest in the tangible, immediate benefits of new machinery than in a system like Taylor's, which required considerable time and expense to implement. Between 1910 and 1914, the diffusion of scientific management in France received a new impetus as the French economy experienced an upturn and French industrialists, notably automobile and tire manufacturers, faced increased American competition.[84]

If French industrialists were increasingly open to Taylor's ideas, labor hostility and the persistence of skilled personnel in the French automobile industry nevertheless remained obstacles. The trade union press argued that Taylorism was simply a way of organizing "overwork" or "exhaustion" *(le surmenage),* which deskilled workers and robbed them of their dignity. *La Guerre Sociale* saw Taylorism as "the insane intensification of work to the point of slavery." Alphonse Merrheim, the syndicalist leader of the metalworkers' union, described it as "the most ferocious, the most barbaric system of work devised by capitalists." Both *L'Humanité,* until 1920 the official organ of French socialism, and Merrheim predicted that the new system would transform men into "thoughtless machines" and "automat[a] ruled by the automatic movements of the machine." Automobile workers struck against attempts to impose a work pace determined by time and motion studies in which they had had no say. Inspired by the continuing influence of the artisanal tradition in France, workers and their representatives opposed efforts to subdivide production and erode worker autonomy. They saw Taylorism as a final and fatal blow to their professional status as skilled craftsmen.[85]

The language of this critique was identical to that of opponents of long-distance bicycle races, who decried the dehumanization involved in the repetitive, unskilled application of human muscle power. Socialists argued that sport was valuable precisely because capitalism disabled, warped, and destroyed workers' bodies in the factory, but they repudiated professional cycling in part because they associated it with Taylorism: "Our sport does not accept Taylor's method[,] . . . nor does it adjust to velodrome dividends."[86] Criticism of Taylorism extended beyond the trade-union and socialist press, particularly from 1913, when *L'Auto's* own Charles Faroux launched a vigorous attack against Taylor's ideas. His articles sparked a widespread debate in the French press about scientific management and contributed, according to one account, to the 1913 strike at Renault, where many workers read the sports daily and became alarmed at Faroux's depiction of scientific management.[87]

Such criticism notwithstanding, many French trade unionists and socialists before, during, and especially after World War I reacted more positively to Taylorism. They saw in its promise of increased labor productivity and efficiency an argument for shorter work hours and higher wages. The modernization of French industry would improve its international competitiveness and, in turn, the living standards and work experiences of French factory workers. The war's devastating impact on the labor supply increased interest in management theories that promised improved worker productivity. Faced with employers who often increased work hours to increase production, the largest French labor organization, the CGT (General Confederation of Labor), supported such theories, arguing for "maximum production in a minimum time for maximum wages with a minimum of fatigue." Despite these trends, between the end of the war and 1927 Taylorite innovations and scientific management remained the exception in French industry, even if some leading automobile manufacturers integrated American assembly-line production, systems of organization, factory layouts, and machines.[88]

By the late 1920s, Taylor's techniques were being received more enthusiastically in France, which emerged as one of Europe's leaders in applying scientific management. The idea of rationalization came to dominate both the debate between labor and employers and the thinking of the French labor movement.[89] French factory workers, however, seem to have resisted the trend toward greater rationalization, for it rendered even harsher their already difficult working conditions. Their resistance took many forms, including absenteeism, following the pace of the slowest worker (particularly when they were being timed), high turnover rates, and resistance to shop-floor discipline.[90] This behavior paralleled the withdrawals, slowdowns, and rules violations of Tour racers seeking to control their working conditions and maintain a degree of autonomy. In 1929 and 1930, *L'Humanité* published communist trade-union reports that condemned the new factories for reducing workers into a "vast army . . . making the same mechanical movements under the watchful eyes of the company's . . . stooges."[91] The language of such reports clearly informed its critique of the Tour. *L'Humanité* rejoiced each time racers thwarted "the boss's regulations" and rebelled against the pace requirements—described as rates of production (of kilometers)—by initiating a "productivity strike" (slowdown).[92]

Criticism of the Tour as abusive work in the wake of the Pélissier incident was not confined to the communist Left. The satirical Parisian paper

Le Canard Enchaîné took the Tour to task in a series of humorous cartoons that highlighted the dangerous conditions faced by racers and the callousness with which they were treated by race officials.[93] In 1925 André Reuze, undoubtedly inspired by the Pélissier incident and possibly even by one of Londres's headlines, dedicated his novel *Le Tour de Souffrance* to the Tour racers, "sandwich men of the cycle manufacturers, useless heroes, heroes nevertheless . . . as a testimony of sympathy, admiration and pity."[94] Noting that "the incidents that bring *Le Tour de Souffrance* to life are but . . . the adaptation of real events," Reuze described all manner of dirty tricks by teams to ensure that their racers won, and he parodied Desgrange's editorials praising the Tour, which he criticized as the inhumane commercial exploitation of racers who risked their lives for little financial gain.[95] No friend of the Pélissiers in 1924, *L'Intransigeant* nevertheless criticized the organizers in 1937 for subdividing a day's racing into two or three segments to increase profits. Racers facing three mini-stages in a day would naturally choose not to race hard all the time.[96] That year, noting that the racers were not "pieceworkers" and their work not "piece work," *Paris-Soir* criticized the organizers for imposing a minimum pace: fatigue and strategy would occasionally result in uninteresting stages and slower speeds because racers entered the Tour to win, not to entertain the organizers and the press.[97]

In part motivated by the grievances addressed in chapter 2, Breton journalists and their readers in the 1930s assailed the Tour's commercialism, symbolized by the recently created *caravane publicitaire,* as well as Desgrange's cynical exploitation of "the weaknesses of men" who "cycle six thousand kilometers in a row for just a few one-hundred-franc bills." The Tour's rules, including fines for not racing fast enough, reflected Desgrange's "ingenuity in forcing them to work." Like *L'Humanité,* Breton critics were appalled that he required racers to cycle during the hottest time of the day and placed the *domestiques* at such a financial and competitive disadvantage. In 1939 some Bretons were still invoking the slave labor of penal colonies to criticize the organizers: *La Province* claimed that if prisoners were punished by being forced to complete the Tour, the League of the Rights of Man would intervene. Illustrating a familiarity with the mechanical and bestial images of racers analyzed above, the paper noted that racers were men, not machines, and that the League for the Protection of Animals was too distracted by its campaigns against cock- and bullfights to address what was being done to Tour racers.[98]

Not all commentators took the Pélissiers' side. Although critical of the Tour's regulations, *L'Écho de Paris* suggested that Henri Pélissier's "ill humor" and poor conditioning had led to his withdrawal. Other critics, particularly right-wing papers like *L'Action Française* and *L'Intransigeant,* rejected characterizations of the Tour as a penal colony and its racers as convict laborers. They claimed that Pélissier's jerseys did in fact belong to his sponsors, who had opposed the racers' withdrawal; accused the brothers of attempting to destroy the very event that had brought them fame and fortune; and argued that they were losing the respect of their fans. To support this last point, common folk were interviewed: a gendarmerie lieutenant asserted that the racers were being "severely criticized"; a peasant assailed their poor work ethic and hypersensitivity. Meanwhile, a Tour racer noted that no one was forced to enter the race, downplayed its difficulties, and suggested that journalists were overly sensitive about race conditions. He referred to his "little sporting goods store," a reminder of the economic benefits that motivated Tour racers. The implied question was obvious: could a self-employed shop owner be an exploited proletarian? By emphasizing the economic gains and free will of Tour racers and discrediting Henri Pélissier as a wealthy racer grown soft, his critics (particularly on the right) hoped perhaps to defuse the potentially explosive example of his rebellion, which the communists were so determined to exploit.[99]

If *L'Humanité*'s critique of the Tour was shared by some Parisian and provincial (including right-wing) papers, the communists did not initially succeed in uniting the French Left against the race. *Le Peuple,* the organ of the CGT, limited itself to a brief discussion of the Pélissier incident, in which it seemed to blame the racers' irritability more than Desgrange's rules.[100] More striking was the position of the socialist daily, *Le Populaire,* which emphatically rejected the image of Tour racers as *forçats*. The paper argued that, unlike real workers, racers were free to choose their career, that the Tour was not the "murderous" event described by "certain experts in brainwashing" (a reference to *L'Humanité*), and that the racers' "demands" were "in no way comparable with those of true workers." Stars made large sums, thanks to the Tour and sponsorship contracts; professional cycling allowed these "former farmhands or former workers" to escape a more humble fate. Even *domestiques* did far better in professional cycling than "if they had stayed on the farm . . . or in the mine." When *Le Populaire* drew attention to the success of a socialist racer, it did so without turning him into a symbol of working-class resistance to capitalist exploitation. The paper did, however, deplore the commercial dimension of events like the Tour and invited "true *sportsmen*" to join the Socialist Fédération Sportive et Gymnique du Travail, which was the "only way of achieving pure sport, freed of all commercial and advertising contingencies."[101]

Explaining the divergence between communist and socialist views of the Pélissier incident requires reviewing the state of French left-wing politics after World War I. Participants in the French Socialist Congress of December 1920 were discouraged by the inability of international socialism to prevent the butchery of World War I, by their poor performance in the 1919 legislative elections, and by the failure of the general strike of May 1920. Impressed by the successful Russian Revolution, a majority voted to form the French Communist Party (PCF) and join Lenin's Communist International. *L'Humanité* became the organ of the new party. The polarization of the French Left was exacerbated in 1922, when the General Confederation of Labor also split in two: most members remained in the CGT, which adopted a reformist line, while the old revolutionary syndicalists and new communists formed the CGTU, close to the communist line. Two years later, the socialists, but not the communists, participated in the center-Left coalition that won the 1924 legislative elections, with the socialists receiving slightly more than twice as many votes as the PCF. Especially after 1924, the PCF subordinated its autonomy to Moscow's directives. From 1928 to 1934, consistent with the class warfare strategy imposed by the Comintern, the French communists targeted the socialists, whom they dubbed "social-fascists," as their principal political enemies and accused them of leading the working class in a strategy of class collaboration.[102]

The communist assault on the socialists exacerbated tensions between the two camps, whose rivalry was played out in the controversy over the *forçats de la route*. The terms of that debate, the language of work, virtually obligated self-identified representatives of the working class to react, whether to embrace the racers as emblematic proletarians or reject that comparison as illegitimate. *Le Populaire* saw the debate about the Tour as an opportunity to attack the French communists' credibility, dismissing the reporters covering the Tour for "the paper inspired by Moscow" as hopelessly prejudiced puppets contaminated by the Soviet doctrinal line. Determined to distinguish itself from its rival, *Le Populaire* rejected *L'Hu-*

manité's depiction of the Tour as harsh industrial labor, noting that old racers had completed similar events without suffering exhaustion and portraying the race as a month of (paid) vacation for the *touristes-routiers:* "Don't talk to us anymore of convicts!"[103] As a result, for a decade or so the socialist paper's stance was difficult to distinguish from that of many conservative and far-right-wing papers.

The Nazis' rise to power in Germany in January 1933 and the ominous, though unsuccessful, attempt by the French far Right to overthrow the Third Republic in February 1934 led to a dramatic shift by the PCF. Following Stalin's new Popular Front strategy, the French communists now united with the socialists and other progressive forces to block the momentum of antidemocratic, far-right-wing movements. Both parties contributed to the victory of their electoral coalition in 1936, with the Socialists winning about 20 percent of the vote and the Communists exceeding 15 percent for the first time. The resulting Popular Front government was led by the socialist Léon Blum.[104]

The new coalition strategy of the mid-1930s apparently influenced *Le Populaire*'s Tour coverage, which became indistinguishable from the communist critique. Echoing Pélissier's language of 1924, the paper described the Tour as the deadliest "hard labour" and criticized the "at times superhuman labor" demanded by Desgrange of the racers, who, like manual laborers confronted with harsh daily work, expended their energy with great care: "Threats [and] exhortations will change nothing for this is a manifestation of the revolt of muscles of which too much is asked." Celebrating the "rebellions of the 'giants of the road,'" *Le Populaire* now embraced the worker-racer comparison. As *L'Humanité* had since 1924, it accused Desgrange of exploiting the *individuels,* who barely managed to break even during the Tour, and criticized the team system for favoring arbitrarily selected leaders, who were not always the best racers, and depriving *individuels* of any chance to win the race.[105]

L'AUTO DEFENDS THE TOUR

Given the high profiles of Henri Pélissier and Albert Londres and the attacks launched by *L'Humanité* in particular, *L'Auto* had to respond immediately and forcefully to charges that the racers were brutalized, exploited *forçats.* For the balance of the interwar period, Desgrange and his staff continually sought to restore the Tour's image and defuse the controversy, which the race's critics were forever reigniting.

Desgrange's first step was to punish Henri Pélissier by fining him one hundred francs for verbal insults and threats towards Tour officials and five hundred francs for dropping out and convincing his brother to do the same.[106] In the years that followed, Desgrange added articles to the race's regulations to discourage racers emboldened by Pélissier's example. The 1925 regulations warned that any racer harming the Tour's image by dropping out and encouraging others to do likewise would be banned from the following year's Tour, and that "any understanding among the racers in view of protests of any kind, or against the officials' decisions, any understanding to delay the finish, etc. . . . will be rigorously punished."[107] The Tour's regulations in the 1930s continued to prohibit racers from constituting "a little soviet"—a highly charged phrase given the political polarization of the period—in order to protest or rebel collectively, and promised to penalize any racer who created offensive, harmful, or untrue publicity about the organizers.[108]

In forbidding collective action by racers, Desgrange denied them a right enjoyed by French workers since 1884, when the Third Republic formally recognized the right to form unions, which had been tolerated since 1868.[109] The anomalous position of Tour racers did not escape André Reuze. In *Le Tour de Souffrance,* a top racer complains: "Workers, employees, servants, artists, all corporations have the right to unionize, to defend themselves. . . . Not us. It's the barracks. You make a move, I throw you into it. You complain, I beat you. All the while the manufacturers, the race organizers beat their drums on our backs, and the gullible public applauds without understanding. Just wait, maybe things will change when the lads organize themselves."[110]

The organizers were especially fearful that racer solidarity and unionization would lead to slowdowns. Such actions suggested that racers were rebelling against excessive requirements, eroded Desgrange's authority over the contestants, and undermined *L'Auto*'s depiction of the Tour as a site for the production of hard-working, uncomplaining "pedal workers" to be emulated by workers nationwide. Slowdowns also made for a less spectacular event and increased the public's wait along the itinerary. While collective initiatives by racers were forbidden, Desgrange permitted individual racers to lodge complaints with the race director within forty-eight hours of the end of the stage in which the incident had occurred, but they had to pay fifty francs for each complaint lodged (*touristes-routiers* paid five francs). Desgrange may thus have hoped to discourage frivolous complaints and bad publicity, but the fee involved meant that racers had to pay simply to seek justice. Racers could also appeal to the Commission Sportive of the French cycling federation, but if they had been expelled from the Tour for a flagrant violation, they could not continue to compete while awaiting its ruling.[111] Desgrange thus maintained considerable leverage over the Tour participants.

Beyond these practical measures, *L'Auto* sought to discredit the very notion of Tour racers as slave labor. Noting that Henri Pélissier had dropped out of the 1919 and 1920 Tours, complaining that the race was a "*forçat's* job," the paper acknowledged that it "may seem the job of a convict for those whose muscles are insufficient or who lack courage." Success in cycling, as in other professions, was determined by willpower and disciplined training: any task, however simple, would seem like hard labor if one did not apply oneself fully.[112] Although on the defensive, Desgrange hoped perhaps to exploit the Pélissier incident as yet another lesson for French workers.

L'Auto also parodied Tour coverage à la Albert Londres, characterized by what it claimed were the emotional allusions of "literary journalists" to convicts of the road, human livestock, martyrs, and victims of capitalism and the organizers' sadism.[113] Desgrange dismissed these "literary exaggerations" and urged his critics to study cycling before they unjustly accused him of exploiting these *forçats*.[114] Before a stage over the sharp-edged paving stones of northern France, he mockingly described the Tour as an "infernal cycle," explaining that he was employing the term "for effect, and to convince you, if my excellent colleague Albert Londres has not already succeeded in doing so, that 'Tour de France' signifies convict!"[115] These treacherous roads were a stretch of the Paris-Roubaix race known as "the hell of the north"—a nickname that contributed to the epic portrayal of road racing that Desgrange generally endorsed.

Criticism of the Tour's abusive nature obliged its organizers to adopt a tone and arguments in direct contradiction with those they normally used to sell the sport. For example, cartoons in *L'Auto* ridiculed the notion of the Tour as exploitative "hard labour" and of the racers as convicts, instead presenting the race as a month of vacation for the contestants. Racers were quoted thanking the organizers for the opportunity "to go on a beautiful trip for a month in the most diverse regions of our superb France." *L'Auto* concluded that they did "not appear to take the Tour de France for a penal colony." The paper's portrayal of the Tour as working-class cyclotourism contradicted its classic depiction of the Tour as so harsh that racers considered returning to unloading coal or factory work, and indicates the extent to which the organizers had been stung by criticism following the Pélissier incident.[116]

Desgrange was particularly sensitive to accusations that the Tour exploited poor workers: "Who are these convicts? Two racers who suffer from ophthalmia, who prepared themselves poorly and who sense that they are beaten. He [Albert Londres] listens obligingly to their social demands because, according to [these] rebels, [who are] millionaires, moreover—and they brag about it in front of their friends—it is capitalist society that exploits them."[117]

Desgrange drew a sharp distinction between professional cyclists who had chosen "this honorary profession" and "workers in mines, coal-bunkers, [and] polders, who struggle their entire lives, and for what profit?" He listed the Tour's prize money to prove that racers were not *forçats,* describing them at the end of the race as fresh and looking forward to translating their Tour celebrity into lucrative racing opportunities in France, Belgium, and Italy. Noting disingenuously that the Tour had existed for twenty years without references to the racers as *forçats,* Desgrange pointed out that no racer had ever died during the race, and suggested that there was nothing wrong with "cocaine and dynamite when what's involved is simply calming one's eyes, irritated by the tar of recently resurfaced roads, or taking a little stimulant for the effort of the final kilometers."[118]

Desgrange no doubt feared that if representations of the Tour as exploitative labor and racers as rebellious workers prevailed, sponsors and communities along the itinerary would no longer support the race. Municipal officials like the conservative prewar mayor of Roubaix, who sought to identify their working populations with the "pedal workers" of the Tour de France, would cease to view the analogy as conducive to social peace—quite the contrary. Desgrange perhaps also worried that widespread criticism of the Tour would inspire obstructionists. He quoted a letter from "a poor crank" who, having read Londres's articles, considered Desgrange "a dirty sports profiteer and a sinister swindler" and promised "to prevent your next Tour de France and to prevent you at the same time from debasing the French *race.*"[119]

At least one contemporary cycling novel echoed Desgrange's concerns about the political exploitation of cycling by the Left. In *Microbe* (1929), the father of the title character is a socialist dreamer killed in a May Day demonstration. His father's fate and his own victories in the Tour and other races transform Microbe into a popular hero.[120] After a fall cuts short his career, he decides to realize his father's dream of a fraternal society. Tragically, demonstrators inspired by Microbe are involved in a shootout with police and soldiers that leaves five dead. Microbe turns himself in to the authorities. While continuing to call for fraternity from his jail cell, he rejects politics and refuses to be used by anarchists, communists, and socialists eager to exploit his case. Ultimately, he is released from jail and settles down with the woman he loves. The moral of the story was clear: however laudable his objective, a working-class sports champion is doomed to failure whenever he seeks to employ his fame in ways that destabilize the social order. Lower-class readers were presumably to reject public disorder and violence as a means of effecting social change. For their part, middle-class readers could be comforted by the fact that in the end Microbe comes to his senses, refuses to be exploited by radical politicians, and accepts his humble station in society.

A DEATH ON THE TOUR

Shortly after the Pélissier incident, Desgrange had defended the Tour by noting that no contestant had ever died during the race. After 1935 he was no longer able to make that claim. That year, as the Spaniard Francesco Cepeda descended the Galibier mountain, one of his tires peeled off its rim, causing him to crash at high speed. He was taken in a coma to a hospital in nearby Grenoble, where he died a few hours later.[121] Press coverage of the first racer fatality on the Tour was uneven. Many of the mass-circulation dailies and other papers barely mentioned it, limiting themselves to noting "the terribly unfortunate crash," the minute of silence observed in honor of the "unlucky racer" before the start of the Nice-Cannes stage, and his funeral.[122] Others acknowledged the "serious question of the accidents"; some blamed these on the Tour's commercialism, which had resulted in increasing numbers of vehicles on the itinerary.[123] *L'Auto* covered the news of Cepeda's death in three brief paragraphs at the bottom of page 3 in its July 15 issue.[124] For the next three days it briefly addressed the tragedy, usually on page 3, concluding with Cepeda's funeral. Most papers thus gave

Cepeda's death relatively little attention, and *L'Auto* seemed only too ready to bury both the racer and the story. The organizers no doubt understood that, a decade after the Pélissier affair, a fatality would only reinvigorate the Tour's critics, perhaps even enhance their credibility.

In the days that followed Cepeda's death, two issues came to the fore that were indeed relevant to the debate about the exploitative nature of the Tour: Cepeda's social class and *L'Auto*'s responsibility for his death. *L'Auto*'s biographical article on Cepeda described him as a merchant and municipal judge, a social position Robert Dieudonné confirmed in his column: "Poor little Cepeda! He was not, like Trueba, a little peasant who hoped to make his fortune on the roads of France. He was the son of a bourgeois family: his father is at the head of a business where his son was employed. I can see the father shrugging his shoulders when the son left to compete yet again in the Tour de France: 'As if you needed it!'"[125]

Dieudonné implied that although it was natural for a peasant or worker to risk death during the Tour in the hope of improving his economic situation, the Tour was not an event for bourgeois sons with secure jobs. Writing in *Paris-Soir,* the journalist Gaston Bénac, a former associate of Desgrange's, also drew a class distinction between Cepeda and Vicente Trueba. The former was a "pure amateur" who was "so sporting, so loyal, so disinterested," and so happy to be included in the Tour that he had accepted his contract without even reading it. His teammate Trueba, however, had negotiated his contract line by line. At the same time, Bénac deployed the language of dutiful work so typical of *L'Auto*'s coverage of the Tour, describing Cepeda as "an athlete fallen in the middle of his career, in the middle of his duty—I could say—while he courageously accomplished his task."[126]

L'Auto's critics on the French Left, now united, disagreed. *Le Populaire* described Cepeda as "a humble worker of sport."[127] *L'Humanité* identified him as a "simple little mechanic," the son of humble workers. His father had never been a bank manager, as one provincial paper had reported (or indeed a businessman, as *L'Auto* had indicated). For the communists, in particular, it was imperative that Cepeda, whom "death eliminates . . . from the Tour de France of M. Desgrange," be a proletarian, "one of those who make the fortune of the great profiteers of capitalist sport."[128] A middle-class racer assured of a comfortable life would not illustrate the organizers' exploitation of racers as effectively. Addressing the story of how Cepeda had signed his Tour contract, *L'Humanité* noted that M. Desgrange preferred docile racers who did not make demands, as those who negotiated lacked a "sporting spirit."[129] Far from proving his comfortable economic circumstances, Cepeda's passivity confirmed that he was an intimidated, humble worker.

Both left-wing papers accused *L'Auto* of a callous disregard for the dead racer. *Le Populaire* criticized *L'Auto* for not having rendered an appropriately "solemn and supreme homage to someone who, alas, died to some extent for [the organizer]," and for having relegated its eulogy to Cepeda to a few lines at the bottom of a page, "long after the 'exploits' of the pseudo-giants of the pseudo-road."[130] *L'Humanité* expressed disgust at *L'Auto's* inadequate coverage of Cepeda's accident, deploring the fact that not a single high-ranking official from *L'Auto* had bothered to attend his funeral and noting that only a few lines in the paper had been devoted to the funeral oration.[131]

Le Populaire and *L'Humanité* held the organizers responsible for Cepeda's death. *Le Populaire* faulted them for not obliging racers to wear helmets, which were required in races organized by the socialist sports federation. Concluding that "the 1935 Tour was indeed the race of death," it attributed Cepeda's fatal fall and the falls of other racers to wheel rims of poor quality.[132] Meanwhile, *L'Humanité* launched a sustained front-page attack on the Tour's organizers and sponsors for exploiting racers, in this case to the death. Noting that "the accident of a racer in the Tour is a work accident and that a withdrawal constitutes for him an important loss of income," it chastised bourgeois papers for whom such accidents were simply "pretexts for sensational clichés and photographic close-ups."[133] *L'Humanité* implicated the poor quality of the roads in accidents and equipment breakdown, as well as "the ever more brutal regulations" by which Desgrange was seeking to increase "productivity—in other words, speed." A future Tour winner, the Belgian Sylvère Maes, claimed that he wanted to withdraw: "I have a family, I don't want to kill myself."[134]

More ominously, *L'Humanité* agreed with *Le Populaire* that the many falls in the 1935 Tour were due to defective tires provided by *L'Auto:* Desgrange had been paid by a maker of wheel rims to use its products for the bicycles provided to Tour racers. In the mountains, the friction caused by frequent braking caused these rims to heat up. The heat loosened the adhesive tape that held tires in place, and they peeled off, with disastrous consequences for the racers. Once they had realized they might be risking their lives, the paper reported, many racers paid for their own wooden rims.[135] *L'Humanité's* case against the Tour was clear: seeking to maximize sponsorship income, the capitalist organizers had provided racers with defective equipment that had led to "work accidents," including a fatality. Never had the Tour's participants been so self-evidently *forçats*.

CONCLUSION

From the sport's earliest years in the late nineteenth century, French physicians, politicians, and other commentators had expressed concern about the toll long-distance bicycle races took on contestants. Many of these critics argued that the sport was both a symptom and a source of a broader degeneration afflicting French society at a time of acute anxiety about France's position in an increasingly tense and polarized Europe. Emphasizing its repetitive, unskilled nature, observers also frequently associated endurance cycling with modern industrial labor. Influenced by these concerns and the industrial image of the race, opponents of the Tour through the interwar years accused *L'Auto* of exploiting racers to increase its profits and those of the race's commercial sponsors.

In making their case, the Tour's critics, including racers, employed the language of work favored by Desgrange himself, but to opposite effect. Pointing to pace requirements, fines, and the Tour's many regulations, they undermined *L'Auto*'s presentation of the race as the work of traditional artisans or as the honorable, efficient labor of disciplined factory workers. Instead they offered an apocalyptic vision of the Tour as a grossly unjust and repressive event that both reflected and reproduced capitalist exploitation of workers in modern, rationalized factories nationwide. In so doing, critics charged the Tour with dehumanizing racers by transforming them into machines and beasts. These accusations were facilitated by widespread depictions of racers as automata and animals, views that were themselves grounded in recent influential theories about the human body, its capacity for work, and its resistance to suffering.

Ironically, *L'Auto* failed to recognize the extent to which it had, as the leading purveyor of such images, contributed to the rhetorical arsenal of the Tour's opponents, even as it dismissed their "literary exaggerations." In seeking rhetorical flourishes to sell the Tour and help fans conjure up images of their heroes, the sports daily had developed representations of racers as respectable workers, indomitable machines, and primitive beasts. The problem for *L'Auto* was that, as evocative as they were, these portrayals were contradictory: human beings—even bicycle racers and factory workers—were neither machines nor animals. Seizing on this tension, critics cast the Tour and industrial modernity in an unfavorable light: dehumanized by exhausting, dangerous, and repetitive work, the Tour racer, like the factory worker, became a convict laborer.

The 1939 Tour was completed barely a month before World War II broke out, and Desgrange died the following year. The race would not be run again until eight long and painful years had passed. Military defeat, foreign occupation, and the collaborationist Vichy regime were to leave a bitter legacy, which the nation confronted gradually in the postwar period. In the summer of 1947, amid the rubble of bombed ruins and the beginnings of reconstruction, the French once again lined roads and town squares to hail their heroes, whose reappearance many took as a symbol of national rebirth and a first step on the return to normalcy. The Tour racers clearly remained *géants de la route*. And, like the crowds that greeted them along the itinerary, they were survivors. Whether they were still *forçats de la route* was a more complicated question, addressed in the chapter that follows.

SIX

What Price Heroism?

Work, Sport, and Drugs in Postwar France

≡

As the Tour de France prepared to celebrate its seventy-fifth anniversary in the summer of 1978, European professional cycling was at a generational crossroads. The Belgian Eddy Merckx had retired that spring after an unparalleled career: in addition to winning five Tours de France, the "Cannibal" had won five Tours of Italy, one Tour of Spain, numerous shorter stage races, three professional road-racing world championships, and some thirty prestigious one-day *classiques*. In 1972 he had established a new hour record that still stood. Although Merckx had not won the Tour since 1974 and had been declining in recent years, his retirement and those of his longtime rivals—the Frenchman Raymond Poulidor, the Italian Felice Gimondi, and the Spaniard Luis Ocaña—marked the end of an era.

Younger rivals could now look forward to finishing their careers freed of Merckx's intimidating presence in the *peloton*. They included the Belgians Lucien Van Impe (the 1976 Tour winner) and Michel Pollentier, the Dutchman Joop Zoetemelk, the Frenchman Bernard Thévenet (victorious in 1975 and 1977), and the Italian Francesco Moser. Meanwhile, a new generation of racers, led by the recently crowned French road-racing champion Bernard Hinault, hoped that their time had come to dominate the sport and its most famous event.

What was shaping up as a festive, suspenseful competition turned ugly, however, in the southwestern town of Valence-d'Agen when the racers crossed the finish line on foot to protest against what they deemed unacceptable work conditions. A few days later, Pollentier won the mountainous Alpe d'Huez stage and donned the yellow jersey. What should have been a great moment for the Tour—one that might have erased the troubling image of racers refusing to compete a few days earlier—rapidly degenerated into scandal: Pollentier was discovered cheating at the urine test required of stage winners and immediately expelled from the race.

Both the racers' "strike" and the doping scandal were intimately related to the issue that had dogged the organizers since 1903: the Tour's extreme nature. Although the organizers did not revive the *ouvrier de la pédale* image and the media only occasionally referred to *forçats de la route* in postwar debates about race conditions, notions of work and workers' rights were once again at the heart of the matter. The issue of doping, however, added a disturbing new twist to the debate. The practice was as old as the sport itself; what changed after the war was the growing perception that French society had a drug-abuse problem. Responding to mounting concern over the previous decade about France's new public-health crisis, in 1965 the French parliament passed its first antidoping law. This legislation targeted athletes, particularly bicycle racers, who were not only the most visible drug users but, because of their popularity, also those most likely to be emulated by young people, who were seen to be particularly at risk in the emerging drug culture.

Once again, the Tour was at the center of a larger societal debate as a result of its identification with work. And, once again, that debate threatened the celebration of a distinctive Tour heroism based on suffering and survival. For if what made the "superhuman" exploits of the "giants of the road" possible was not their exceptional moral and physical qualities, but their pervasive and increasingly sophisticated doping (including dangerous and illegal drugs), how could one defend the race's existence, let alone promote its participants as individuals worthy of mass adulation? Over the past half century the Tour's stakeholders—the organizers, racers, sponsors, media, and public—have offered a variety of responses to that question. To date, and despite being rocked in 1998 by the greatest doping scandal in its history, the Tour and the contradictions inherent in its century-old heroic ethos have survived largely intact, though not unblemished.

SUFFERING, SURVIVAL, AND WORK: CELEBRATING THE TOUR IN POSTWAR FRANCE

As the French lined the roads of the first postwar Tours, the press once again celebrated the race as a particularly arduous form of labor and revived the cult of survival, emphasizing the event's attrition rates and the natural, physical, and psychological challenges faced by racers.[1] Although no longer "pedal workers," Tour racers were still portrayed as humble, hard-working men who chose their profession freely and were idolized by the working class. As before the war, the racers' exceptional moral and physical qualities transformed them into quasi-divine laborers who exceeded human limits.[2]

The racers themselves continued to see the Tour as particularly dangerous (and, for many, poorly paid) work, characterized by suffering and sacrifice.[3] Their occasional refusal to "work" after the war went neither unnoticed nor unpunished. When they paused to bathe in the Mediterranean during a particularly hot stage in 1950, the press humorously reported their escapade; not amused, the organizers fined them.[4] Two years later, the racers slowed their pace for more than half of the sun-drenched, two-hundredkilometer sixteenth stage between Perpignan and Toulouse; this time the organizers responded by canceling the day's prize money. To do so they invoked a prewar rule requiring stage winners to average at least thirty kilometers per hour to qualify for prize money (the Belgian André Rosseel, who won the stage, had averaged twenty-nine kilometers per hour). Although Desgrange had died twelve years earlier, his determination to oblige the racers to maintain a high level of "productivity" had clearly survived.

The organizers' decision sparked a debate in which the press generally sided with the racers, who wondered why, if prizes could be eliminated when the pace was too slow, they were not doubled for stages during which the racers competed hard all day.[5] Commentators pointed out that the 1952 itinerary was especially difficult, the weather that year particularly hot, and the early stages unusually fast, and that after the slowdown the racers had covered the last eighty kilometers of the stage at a very fast pace. Even Desgrange, they noted, had avoided canceling prize money. Instead, he had reduced prizes by 10 or 25 percent, or paid a few contestants to race hard, thus guaranteeing a sufficiently high average pace for the stage winner even as the rest of the pack meandered along.[6]

Unmoved by these arguments, Jacques Goddet justified the cancellation of prize money in a lengthy editorial titled "Why the Racers Must Be Harshly Treated." Describing the slowdown as a "115-kilometer-long strike," he claimed that he had to be "the merciless and rigid moralist who assumes that the human carcass is made in such a way that it is possible for our guys to fight to the hilt every day for almost four weeks." The "inadmissible" slowdown rendered the Tour ridiculous in the public's eyes and left the racers vulnerable to claims that they were "lazy" or "comedians." As the "modern" Tour provided racers with "a whole array of substantial [financial] rewards," the organizers could only interpret the racers' "passivity" as a conscious decision to forfeit those rewards. Yet Goddet contradicted himself by acknowledging that neither their physical limits nor race tactics would allow racers to go all out from start to finish.[7] Meanwhile, his coorganizer, Félix Lévitan, responding to a radio journalist's criticism of the racers' uncompetitive conduct, defended them as having simply taken a day off during a very eventful, exciting Tour.[8]

The organizers' contradictory positions were echoed by some in the media. *Le Figaro* acknowledged that the racers were simply adhering to the time-honored practice of granting themselves an easy day to recover from earlier efforts. Nevertheless, it described as "laudable" Goddet's attempts to circumvent this tradition through the carefully positioned difficulties of the race and "severe additions" to the regulations, since the "absolute principle" of cycling, like all sports, was *la lutte* (struggle, fight, competition). At the same time, the paper found the rule invoked to deny the racers their prize money "abusive": "One must be reasonable in establishing the work regime *[tableau de travail]* one wishes to impose on them."[9] *Le Figaro*'s ambivalence resulted from its dual understanding of the Tour: as an athletic event, the race had to uphold the competitive principle without which sport is meaningless; as a form of employment, however, it appeared to violate contemporary French labor standards.

Prominent racers, such as the retired two-time Tour winner André Leducq and the young Breton star Louison Bobet, rallied to the racers' defense.[10] Bobet, who was not competing in 1952 but soon became the first racer to win three consecutive Tours, argued that "one has to know what it is to suffer on a bike to understand that one cannot do battle continuously at the pace at which today's races are run, and that the racers, who are never but men like any others, cannot always feel aggressive passions." He noted the paradox that the very reporters who had taken the organizers to task for organizing a ferociously difficult Tour now complained of the calm in the *peloton*.[11] Yet Bobet's position itself was ambiguous. His claim that Tour racers were normal men contradicted his evocation of their exceptional suffering, which set them apart from common mortals in two ways: it transformed them into heroes, and it qualified them—and only them—to decide when a day's racing had to be less than heroic to allow them to recover and contest future stages in a way that would meet the expectations of the fans, sponsors, organizers, and media. The Belgian racers, meanwhile, threatened to withdraw from the Tour to register their outrage at the organizers' refusal to pay their compatriot.[12] No doubt to avoid further criticism, the race commissioners agreed to grant Rosseel his prize money "if the rules are respected from here to Paris."[13]

This incident and the reactions it provoked demonstrate that the tensions and contradictions that had characterized debates about the Tour during its first half century were very much alive as it embarked on its second. The racers continued to describe their sport as dangerous, painful physical labor. The paradox they could never entirely resolve was that it was precisely the risks and suffering they confronted, and the public's appreciation of their endurance and courage in doing so, that both guaranteed and jeopardized their ability to earn a living. The organizers, while admitting that the racers were incapable of racing hard all the time, sought to force them to do just that, lest the race's image suffer when contestants slacked off. As Le Figaro's coverage shows, media commentary was also fraught with contradictions as journalists attempted to reconcile the enduring identification of the Tour with work with the competitive ethos of sport. As for the Tour's spectators, they apparently accepted the delay—some even defended the slow pace under such hot conditions—and were twenty thousand strong at the finish line in Toulouse.[14] A quarter century later, the strike at Valence-d'Agen sparked yet another debate about the Tour's working conditions. This time the public along the itinerary was not so understanding.

THE STRIKE OF VALENCE-D'AGEN

On 11 July 1978, after a particularly difficult, hotly contested Pyrenean stage from Pau to Saint-Lary-Soulan, the racers were driven to Tarbes, the start of the next day's stage. Because of heavy traffic, some arrived at their hotels very late; by the time they had been massaged and fed, it was midnight. Tour racers had long been frustrated by itineraries requiring transfers that robbed them of precious recovery time. To make matters worse, the racers had to rise at five o'clock for a 7:30 start, as the following day's racing was to be run in two half-stages: Tarbes to Valence-d'Agen, and Valence-d'Agen to Toulouse. Because of the detour through Valence-d'Agen, the racers would cover 254 kilometers instead of the 180 that actually separated Toulouse from Tarbes.

Exhausted by a short night's sleep after a difficult mountain stage and angry at being made to ride this additional distance, the racers decided, as one of them put it, that "too much thought was being given to the Tour's profitability and not enough to the racers." They resolved to cycle the entire first leg slowly before walking to the finish line in Valence-d'Agen. Apprised of this disastrous turn of events during the stage, Goddet offered to maintain the prize money if the racers raced the final kilometers. The latter, however, persisted in their slowdown, arriving two hours late in Valence-d'Agen, where, led by the Tour's stars, they walked the final hundred meters to the finish line. The crowd, which had been waiting for hours under the baking sun and anticipating the arrival of the Tour in the town for months, was furious: the racers had to be protected by the local squadron of the Garde Républicaine, deployed to provide the usual security at Tour finish lines, from enraged fans yelling "Lazy bums!" and "Reimburse us!" Citing the racers' "utter failure to compete," the organizers suspended the half-stage's prize money.[15]

The racers' revolt generated considerable commentary, most of which was couched in terms of labor relations and working conditions. Observers agreed that the racers' act was a "strike," including Jacques Goddet, who acknowledged that the contestants were protesting against working conditions they found "mediocre."[16] The anchor on that evening's television news reported in amused tones that the Tour, a "little company in which only 10 percent of the budget goes to the racers," had fallen prey to the same kinds of "social conflicts" one finds in all businesses. The competing interests involved were those of "the bosses" (the organizers), management (the team managers), and "the people who produce—and here it is effort that produces the spectacle—in other words, the racers."[17] *Le Monde* suggested that racers were experiencing their own delayed May 1968, when massive strikes by students and workers had paralyzed the country. *L'Humanité* praised them for refusing to be treated like "sheep" or intimidated by the organizers, who were guilty of a "harsh reaction, the reaction of an employer." Even the conservative *Le Figaro* evoked the racers' collective "revolt" against their "working conditions" as "the discontent of the base against an authoritarian and paternalistic business."[18] In the days that followed, the organizers, team managers, media, fans, current and retired racers, and the mayor of Valence-d'Agen, speaking for his community, engaged in a contentious debate in which several familiar issues emerged.

A variety of prominent commentators criticized the strike. Goddet revived Desgrange's arguments based on the racers' contractual obligations to the organizers and team sponsors and their moral obligation to the public. Like his predecessor, he distinguished between "responsible professionals" and racers who behaved like "rascals" and presented a "deplorable image" of the sport. He noted that the organizers consulted with team managers on average three times before determining each Tour's rules, expectations, and itinerary, which were then made public. Any racer entering the Tour did so of his own free will, implicitly accepted the race conditions, and therefore "must obey what had become his contract."[19] The regional press magnate and *député-maire* of Valence-d'Agen, Jean-Michel Baylet, also criticized as a "moral fraud" the unprofessional conduct of "scandalous" racers who "simply refused to honor their contract." They had thereby negated a considerable financial investment and six months of preparation by his town, which had hoped to turn the Tour's first visit into a great celebration.[20]

Former racers also took the *peloton* to task. Raphael Géminiani, the manager of the Fiat team and a top French racer in the 1940s and 1950s, advocated punishing the stars who had organized the strike for denying "modest racers . . . the opportunity to be noticed and earn a living." He believed that the schedule was a "false pretext" and held the "mafia" of top racers—first and foremost Hinault's Renault team—responsible for "blocking the race" in order to prevent any changes in the overall classification while they recovered from earlier efforts.[21] The retired five-time Tour winner Jacques Anquetil agreed that the top racers had intimidated lesser racers into accepting the slowdown but criticized the latter for not having attacked. He argued that by disrespecting the spectators, the racers had discredited themselves and possibly jeopardized their chances to cash in on their Tour performances in subsequent races, should the public's resentment last.[22] The Jobo team manager, Guy Faubert, argued that "the racers are here to do their work. It is not because it is sunny that the miner does not go down into the mine." Like the Pélissiers' critics, who had dismissed comparisons of Tour racers with "real" workers, Faubert contrasted lazy, irresponsible racers with uncomplaining, hard-working industrial laborers.[23]

In response to this barrage of criticism, racers argued that they were simply protecting their health from an ill-conceived schedule and itinerary that deprived them of time for rest, relaxation, and meals. They complained about noisy hotels, which made their short nights even less restful, and an overly busy racing season.[24] Addressing the Tour's excessive demands, racers argued, like their predecessors, that they were neither animals, nor robots, nor machines.[25] Some prominent team managers and former racers took their side. Describing as "inhuman" the conditions that led to the protest, they feared for the safety of exhausted racers and agreed that the detour via Valence-d'Agen was financially motivated and the racing season far too busy.[26] Most press commentators concurred, blaming the incident on the Tour's hypercommercialism and the organizers' greed.[27] Sympathetic to the racers' plight, *La Croix* wondered how professional sport was to be reconciled with the demand for panache and the spectacular, and *Le Matin de Paris* concluded that the Tour was "excessive" and "too difficult." *Le Monde* compared the incident to the Pélissier affair, "which had alerted [public] opinion a half century ago to the 'extravagances' of despotic regulations."[28]

Goddet responded that the early start had been designed to ensure that racers cycled during the cool morning hours and enjoyed almost three hours to eat and rest in Valence-d'Agen before the second leg. Noting that he had long favored limiting a day's racing to 160 or 180 kilometers, he argued that transfers and half-stages reduced the time spent on flat terrain, where the racing was boring, allowed stages to conclude more often in regions whose topography generated exciting racing, and thus gave more racers a chance to distinguish themselves.[29] He did not, however, explain why the two legs on the day of the strike had covered 254 kilometers, nor did he acknowledge that the itinerary maximized the Tour's profitability by increasing the number of host communities.

The racers clearly identified themselves as workers. Echoing earlier opponents of long-distance cycling, they argued that the lack of sleep they were afforded was "contrary . . . to labor legislation," claimed that like any employees they had the right to strike, and compared their protest to strikes by factory workers. When a journalist noted that bicycle racing was not like other professions, a veteran racer responded that "it wasn't, but little by little it is becoming so." Racers, including André Chalmel (the president of the French racers' union) and Hinault (its vice president), identified a "lack of dialogue" between the organizers and the racers as a major factor in their decision to strike and demanded *la concertation*—consultation with the organizers through union or team representatives on future itineraries.[30] Chalmel noted that a slowdown in the 1977 Paris-Nice stage race by racers protesting against the same conditions had resulted in an "impeccable" edition of the race in 1978. Racers, he argued, were not seeking better pay or easier stages; rather, they sought to guarantee their rest and recovery time and their right to influence their working conditions by a more frequent and systematic consultation with race organizers.[31]

Papers rallying to the racers' cause generally agreed that they were professional workers endowed with the rights afforded all workers. This view allowed commentators to exploit the racers' act of rebellion, "an affair of our era," in order to deplore the confrontational nature of French labor relations and the working conditions of manual laborers in general.[32] Referring to the racers as the *ouvriers spécialisés,* or unskilled workers, of the Tour, *Libération* compared them to other manual workers, like assembly-line workers at Citroën, whose work pace had been increased over the years and who, like the racers, responded with slowdowns.[33] *L'Humanité* mocked critics who could not accept that professional athletes might "demonstrate like workers at Renault," thereby depriving the organizers, journalists, and mayor of Valence-d'Agen of their *forçat de la route* spectacle.[34]

Like other papers, the communist daily revived the image of racers as convict laborers, which had generally lain dormant since World War II.[35] As it had a half century earlier, *L'Humanité* sought to exploit the Tour to make a broader point about economic and social injustice in France. The *prolétariat du cycle* of 1924 were now "miserable little *smicards du vélo*" (minimum-wagers of the bike), whom *L'Humanité,* like *Libération,* compared to automobile workers, the epitome of unskilled, overworked, industrial labor.[36] The target of the communist critique of the Tour, once the rationalized factories of interwar France, was now the unfair labor practices and hostility to worker protests for better pay and working conditions in a country that, the paper did not need to remind its readers, had been governed by the Right since the founding of the Fifth Republic twenty years earlier.

The public seemed less willing to acknowledge the racers' rights as professional workers, perhaps because many fans mistakenly believed they all made a very good living from racing.[37] "If athletes start [striking] as well," a disillusioned spectator wondered, "where are we headed?"[38] One of the race's nicknames had long been "the truce of July." For many fans the Tour represented a separate sphere in which the conflict that characterized French labor relations was replaced by heroic, uncomplaining athletes volunteering for the most grueling of competitions. The racers' strike now undermined this idealized vision of the race.

No doubt shocked by the crowd's hostility, racers addressed the role of the public's expectations in determining their working conditions. "Today's public always wants its money's worth," Charly Rouxel noted. "It wants the spectacular, blood, speed, emotions. . . . We will have to explain to them that, while we are not and do not wish to be average Joes, nor are we supermen."[39] Jacques Anquetil, however, countered that "bicycling is not like other sports. One must learn to accept its demands which have created its legend." The organizers also evoked the Tour's legend to justify the detour to Valence-d'Agen: its mayor and his mother ran an important regional daily, *La Dépêche du Midi,* which had from the Tour's earliest days celebrated the racers' exploits, thereby contributing to the glorious reputations that allowed them to earn a living. Baylet noted that by finishing the stage on foot "the giants were killing their legend" and jeopardizing their professional futures by alienating the public and perhaps even sponsors who might decide that cycling was too risky an investment.[40]

The tension between Tour racers' image as "giants" enduring unparalleled suffering and their very real, human limits was once again front and center. Racers understood that rejecting their superhuman image and mobilizing against the imposition of long hours of grueling work potentially undermined their unique appeal. They consequently sought a middle ground, accepting tough stages but demanding the elimination of lengthy transfers and multiple daily legs, as well as conditions more conducive to recuperation.

In the meantime, damage control was the order of the day. Rouxel announced that Tour racers were offering to race for free later in the season at Valence-d'Agen to compensate for the local population's loss of a competitive Tour stage.[41] Hinault apologized publicly to Baylet for the impact of the strike on his community and assured the public that no future protest was planned, as "from now on they [the organizers] will ask for our opinion." Perhaps to demonstrate his goodwill, he attacked at the start of the second leg but was quickly reeled in by a *peloton* moving at a rapid pace.[42] For his part, the mayor noted that Valence-d'Agen would welcome future Tours, while the organizers promised to donate the half-stage's prize money to the city's social services.[43] Absent a consensus on the racers' rights as professional workers, an uneasy truce had emerged. A few days later, the Pollentier doping scandal broke, forcing all parties once again to address the Tour's cult of survival and the racers' working conditions.

Human beings have been using natural substances to enhance their ability to work, travel, fight, and compete in sport for millennia. These substances, primarily plants, were believed to and often did increase strength and endurance, eliminate or delay feelings of fatigue and hunger, generate a sensation of euphoria, and otherwise stimulate physical and mental capacities.[44] Toward the end of the eighteenth century, chemists succeeded in extracting compounds such as morphine, ephedrine, and strychnine from plants, allowing them to create purer forms of the effective substances and calculate more accurate doses. In the nineteenth century, scientists first synthesized drugs from simple organic elements; they could now create artificial substances more potent than those found in nature. As a result, athletes had access to a range of virtually pure extracts and synthesized molecules from which the performance-enhancing "magic potions" of modern sport's early decades were derived. Practitioners of the new discipline of sports medicine encouraged doping as part of the scientific campaign against fatigue, whose objective was to explore and measure human potential: the emerging science of performance included testing drugs on bicycle racers, boxers, and jockeys. Facing long and difficult competitions, suffering from a variety of ailments, and hoping to gain economic security, racers turned to a variety of more or less effective (and more or less dangerous) substances.[45]

From cycling's early years, doping was characterized by an unscientific, hit-or-miss approach. Racers and their entourages experimented with caffeine, nitroglycerine, maté, opiates, cocaine, arsenic, strychnine, digitalis, strophanthus, nux vomica, kola, camphor oil, ether, and alcoholic beverages, often in combination. Some products acted as stimulants; others suppressed pain.[46] It was no wonder that the mysterious *soigneurs* responsible for preparing racers for competition came to be known as *chargeurs* (loaders) and *dynamiteurs*.[47] The practice met with little opposition in competitive cycling. Henri Desgrange forbade his fictitious protégé in *La tête et les jambes* to use stimulants such as kola or coca, however much the medical establishment might support their "extraordinary" benefits. Yet even as he derided these "poisons" and committed to preparing his racer for a successful career by "natural means," he acknowledged that in endurance events it might be advisable "in a case of absolute necessity to give you for a period an artificial vigor."[48]

The public attitude toward sports doping was one of acceptance, at times even encouragement: roadside spectators often handed racers champagne, widely believed to be an effective stimulant. This was hardly surprising. The substances used by athletes were on sale in their local pharmacy, often at moderate prices; it seemed reasonable that endurance athletes should have access to drugs their fans could purchase freely. Furthermore, the production of medicine was not yet regulated, and the press was full of advertisements vaunting the latest miraculous remedies. One of the most popular tonics during this heyday of "medicinal wines" was *le vin Mariani*, which combined wine with coca leaves and was recommended by the medical establishment, including the Academy of Medicine. In such a climate, the fact that racers were using cocaine was hardly a matter of concern, particularly as its addictive nature was not yet known. Ignorance as to the possible risks of certain drugs clearly contributed to this pharmacological free-for-all. The true cause of drug-related injuries, illnesses, or deaths among athletes was either concealed from the public or impossible to establish reliably, given the embryonic state of medical diagnosis and sports medicine. Even when a drug was known to be dangerous, the public assumed that it was safe in moderate doses and blamed the athlete for taking it in excessive amounts.[49] For example, small doses of strychnine, a drug popular among racers for decades, stimulate breathing; in large doses, it can lead to death by respiratory arrest.[50]

Racers in the interwar years continued to avail themselves of a wide variety of drugs, including cocaine, chloroform, caffeine, and "biodynamine," which contained magnesium, calcium, and "a little strychnine," and was intended for people suffering from fatigue. The normal dose was a spoonful each morning, but racers drank an entire bottle at once. Some used it only when in contention toward the end of a race. Many racers doped only for important races, as they typically had a week or two to recover and train between events. As doping remained the province of shadowy *soigneurs* with no medical training, some racers were leery about ingesting what was handed them. Pierre Choque, who won Bordeaux-Paris in 1936, eschewed the kola and eggs with port his *soigneur* had prepared for him, perhaps remembering the numerous racers who had dropped out of the race three years earlier suffering from suspicious stomach ailments. Although Jacques Goddet described the kola as "innocent," he lauded Choque for showing the attentiveness of a pharmacist preparing medicine in his drugstore.[51] Goddet's attitude and the lack of public outcry in the wake of the Pélissiers' admissions in 1924 that racers resorted to drugs to survive the Tour confirm that during this period there was still little, if any, public concern about the dangers of doping.

French physicians, however, had begun to take a more critical look at the practice in the late 1920s, expressing doubts in their professional publications as to its actual benefits. Most doctors were by now convinced of the dangers of cocaine, digitalin, and strychnine, if more divided on arsenic, phosphorus, and alcohol. Around 1930 the medical community, increasingly concerned about the threat performance-enhancing drugs posed to the health of athletes, began to oppose their use. Despite these warnings most French, European, and international sports federations did not take action against performance-enhancing drugs until after World War II.[52]

After 1945 racers increasingly turned to amphetamines.[53] First developed in the early 1930s and massively used by soldiers during the war, the new drugs spread throughout the world and were used in a broad range of activities by individuals attracted to their stimulant properties. Amphetamines decreased feelings of hunger and fatigue, motivated one to action, perhaps even increased willpower and self-confidence. In France they were sold over the counter until June 1955.[54] In the 1950s and 1960s, consuming the drug before a race, rather than during the event at the onset of fatigue or when a great effort was required, became part of the bicycle racer's preparatory ritual. It stimulated breathing and increased endurance, at least temporarily.[55]

There was, however, a darker side to the new drug, as Dr. Pierre Dumas, the Tour's official physician at the time, noted: "Amphetamine[s] conceal the warning signs of fatigue, stifle the body's cries of distress. [They] thus allow an individual of iron will to go beyond his own capacities, with catastrophic consequences." The drug increased anxiety and stress, caused trembling and serious palpitations, and led to sudden collapses as a result of the lack of sleep made possible by its stimulant effect. It could also provoke hyperthermia, making it difficult for athletes, especially in endurance events under a hot sun, to stay properly hydrated.[56] These risks rarely discouraged racers from turning to this latest miracle drug. For every concerned racer, who, like the Frenchman Apo Lazaridès, saw "ghosts pedaling in the *peloton*," there were others willing to run the risk of serious illness, injury, or death to continue earning a living from the sport.[57]

Anecdotal evidence confirms that doping by racers in the early postwar era was widespread, particularly the use of amphetamines. The Italian *campionissimo* Fausto Coppi, a two-time Tour winner, relied on a doctor for the pharmacological support that helped him dominate the sport in the late 1940s and early 1950s. Bernard Gauthier, who won Bordeaux-Paris four times in the 1950s, acknowledged taking performance-enhancing drugs. Roger Rivière unapologetically admitted to doping for his hour world record in 1958: "It's not a secret, racers who want to have a long career follow the advice of a doctor who knows them and only gives them that which suits their temperament. It has been said of me that I was a 'laboratory' racer whose performances [were] 'brought along' by a very precise preparation. I would happily take that as a compliment, since it proves that I know what I want and what to do to achieve it."[58]

Amphetamine-induced racer deaths, notably that of a Danish cyclist at the 1960 Olympic Games, contradicted such faith. Other racers sometimes barely survived drug-induced crises: the Frenchman Jean Mallejac was revived in extremis from an amphetamine-induced collapse by the Tour's doctor on the Mont Ventoux in 1955. Seven years later, fourteen racers dropped out of the Tour, claiming to be suffering from food poisoning. Nonracers who had consumed the same fish dish were, curiously, unaffected, and it is more likely that the racers were experiencing the ill effects of morphine doping.[59] Despite this disturbing record, many racers during this period, including the sport's stars, argued that, unlike other drugs, the stimulants prescribed by their doctors were both safe and, given the nature of their sport, necessary.[60] Any attempt to launch an antidoping campaign would have to come from outside the world of competitive cycling.

A NEW CRUSADE?

On 1 June 1965, the French parliament passed legislation targeting the use of stimulants in athletic competitions.[61] The law provided for fines for athletes who "knowingly used one of the substances, determined by regulation of the public authorities, that are intended artificially and temporarily to increase [the athlete's] physical potential and are liable to harm [the athlete's] health" (article 1). Individuals convicted of knowingly facilitating such use would be punished by a prison term of one month to one year or a fine of five hundred to five thousand francs, or both (article 2). These punishments could be doubled if the use of banned substances caused injury or death (pursuant to articles 319 and 320 of the Penal Code, which addressed involuntary injury and homicide).[62] Article 3 laid out the testing procedure: on the request of a physician representing the State Secretariat for Youth and Sports, the police could require a competitor suspected of a doping violation to submit samples and undergo "medical, clinical, and biological tests designed to establish proof of the use of a substance targeted" by the law. Any individual refusing to comply with these procedures would be punished according to article 2. Finally, article 4 allowed for those convicted under the first three articles to be prohibited for a period ranging from three months to five years from competing in, organizing, or assuming any responsibilities in an athletic competition. A couple of weeks before the 1966 Tour, the Ministry of Youth and Sports issued a decree identifying the substances banned by the 1965 law.[63]

No law is passed in a vacuum. Although the public's attention was rarely drawn to the issue of doping in cycling in the years immediately after the war, from the mid-1950s momentum had been building in France and elsewhere in Europe to engage medical, sports, and public officials in a vigorous antidoping campaign.[64] The Tour de France was a particular target of those determined to control a practice they saw not only as a threat to the integrity of sport but as a public-health crisis. For one thing, it was the most difficult event in a popular endurance sport known for widespread doping. For another, the Tour's official physician, Dr. Pierre Dumas, was one of the earliest and most committed proponents of a proactive regulatory approach to the problem. In 1955 he had revived Mallejac on the Mont Ventoux, ironically just a few weeks after the French government had published a decree requiring a prescription to obtain amphetamines, until then available over the counter.[65] The Avignon hospital where Mallejac was treated attributed his collapse to sunstroke and a *crise de foie* (bilious or liverish attack) without mentioning the racer's use of stimulants. After an investigation, the Tour organizers dismissed a *soigneur* without acknowledging his role in the racer's near-fatal doping. Mallejac's close call, nevertheless, received considerable coverage.[66]

Incensed by the health risks racers were taking (and perhaps by the unwillingness of the Avignon hospital and Tour organizers to confront the problem head on when they had the chance), and having witnessed during his nightly tour of their hotel rooms the panoply of substances racers took, Dr. Dumas committed himself to a campaign against doping. He understood that although doping was a problem in virtually all sports, the visibility of racers who collapsed during road races placed them front and center in the debate.[67] Three months after the 1955 Tour, he urged the doctors and physical therapists of the Société Médicale Française d'Éducation Physique et de Sport to wage a war against doping through educational workshops for *soigneurs* and racers and a public-information campaign. The organization agreed to condemn doping as unsporting and dangerous; to invite sports federations to do the same and to insist that each of their member clubs engage a practicing physician; to provide *soigneurs* with medical, pharmacological, and dietary information; and to educate athletes about the dangers of doping.[68]

These good intentions bore little if any fruit.[69] Dumas continued to see evidence of widespread doping during his visits to racers' rooms during the Tour.[70] Racers' physicians faced pressure from both the athletes and their commercial sponsors, who sought to increase their racers' *rendement* ("productivity" or "output"—that is, performance) through doping and thereby maximize their investment in the form of favorable publicity.[71] The complex ethical questions this practice posed for physicians were underscored by a conversation during the 1960 Tour among Dumas, his two assistants, a Belgian surgeon, and the Italian doctor responsible for "the biological preparation" of Gastone Nencini, the Tour winner that year.[72] Did a doctor have the right to administer drugs to a healthy individual to increase his *rendement?* Was there a distinction between helping a racer recover from the extraordinary demands of his sport and treating him in ways that increased his *rendement?* Was it ethical to prevent the "normal manifestation" of fatigue and pain, the body's natural "alarm signals"? Did doctors have the right to modify "the natural physiology" of athletes through the administration of drugs and transform them into supermen? Might not insufficiently researched new medicines have dangerous long-term effects? Although the notion of increasing the racers' *rendement* had been present from the early years of the sport, physicians like Dumas posed a new challenge to the Tour's cult of suffering and survival: if racers could complete the Tour only with the help of drugs that made their "superhuman" exploits possible, and if it was unethical to transform athletes chemically into supermen, should not the Tour be abolished or at the very least altered so as no longer to require performance-enhancing drugs?

Momentum for antidoping measures in sport continued to build in the early 1960s, as public opinion became increasingly concerned about drug use by young people. A succession of professional conferences about doping in sport, although not extensively covered by the press, may have contributed to a growing public awareness of the problem.[73] French television began to cover the issue. A popular investigative news program interviewed racers during the 1961 Tour about the picturesque expressions they used to refer to doping. Clearly uncomfortable, racers refused to answer or claimed it was "a professional secret" and difficult to talk about on television. An uneasy Jacques Anquetil, in the process of winning his second Tour, claimed not to have heard such expressions much during the race. The program filmed a young West German racer being given a shot of what he claimed were vitamins and reported that he had withdrawn from the Tour shortly thereafter.[74]

The 1962 Tour was a turning point for the antidoping campaign. In the wake of the fourteen withdrawals for "food poisoning," the Tour's medical service issued a communiqué. Noting that some racers sought to accomplish things that were "incompatible with their physiological possibilities," and that their pursuit of such performances took place without the slightest "medical and psychological control," the medical service proposed to return to its old practice of daily post-stage tours of the racers' hotel rooms. The racers were sufficiently angered by the communiqué to flirt with the idea of a fifteen-minute strike during the Aix-en-Provence–Antibes stage. A few days later, Dumas and the medical inspector of the Isère *département* for the youth and sports ministry agreed to organize the first European Conference on Doping and the Biological Preparation of the Competitive Athlete. Sponsored by the French high commissioner for youth and sports, Maurice Herzog, a celebrated mountain climber who, ironically, had admitted to using stimulants to conquer the world's great peaks, the conference took place at Uriage-les-Bains (Isère) on 26 and 27 January 1963.[75]

The assembled European experts—athletes, former champions, doctors, lawyers, sports officials, coaches, and sports journalists—formulated a motion condemning doping. They defined the practice as "the use of substances and of all means designed artificially to increase [an athlete's] *rendement,* in preparation for or during competition, and which might harm the sports ethic and the physical integrity of the athlete." The conference suggested ways to combat the practice and emphasized the need to continue working on administrative and technical measures to eliminate doping. These included information campaigns targeting athletes, educators, doctors, and the public; antidoping legislation; the harmonization of national sports regulations; studies of the behavior of athletes in competitive conditions and of the effects of drugs on athletes; a regularly updated list of both doping and drug-testing methods; the training of sports-medicine professionals capable of providing appropriate advice to athletes about their diet, training, and hygiene; and the inclusion of a clause in the statutes of every sports federation requiring its members to agree not to dope and to submit to drug testing.[76]

In the months that followed, other conferences with similar objectives were held in Italy and Spain. In June 1964, an International Symposium on Doping was organized by the Research Committee of the International Council of Sport and Physical Education of UNESCO in Brussels.[77] Antidoping laws were passed in Belgium and France in 1965 and in Italy in 1971. In 1967 the UCI drafted its first list of banned substances; a year later, drug tests were conducted for the first time at the Olympic Games.[78]

RIGHTS AND REBELLION: THE FIRST ANTIDOPING TESTS

On 28 June 1966, the first drug tests of Tour racers took place in Bordeaux. Two physicians, delegated by the Ministry of Youth and Sports and accompanied by a ministry officer, descended unannounced on the racers' hotels after the stage and chose several racers to undergo drug tests, including the French star Raymond Poulidor. Each racer was required to provide information about his diet and any medical treatment he was undergoing, allow the doctors to check his entire body for needle marks, and provide a urine sample, which was sent in two sealed flasks to a laboratory in Paris and police headquarters in Bordeaux. Two of the younger racers were asked to open their suitcases, although these were apparently not searched.[79]

Reactions to the tests were mixed. Félix Lévitan affirmed that the organizers had been in favor of testing for several years before the 1965 law was passed and described the tests as "an honor" for the race, a contribution in the "crusade" to prevent athletes from drugging themselves and young fans from emulating them.[80] *Le Figaro* also supported the law's intent, which was "to protect the individual from himself and forbid him, in particular, from going beyond his limits by recourse to toxic products," and thereby preserve equality of opportunity and the natural athletic hierarchy. The paper suggested testing athletes whose exploits were at the limits of human possibilities (without explaining how these limits were to be identified), presumably because such performances were inherently suspect and thus fell within the purview of the new law.[81]

Other commentators, however, noted the difficulties inherent in applying the law, the problematic focus on athletes, and potential violations of human dignity and of an individual's right to control his or her body.[82] The law's application was a delicate matter, as the authorities had to prove that the doped athlete had "knowingly" taken prohibited products. The absence of any international antidoping legislation further complicated the situation, as racers competed throughout western Europe under a variety of national legal codes. Furthermore, test results would not be known for several days, raising the disturbing possibility that a victor might be celebrated by the organizers, media, and fans only to be sanctioned once his positive test results came back from the laboratory.[83] If on the evening of 28 June the racers were divided as to whether to comply with the tests, the following morning they seemed united in opposition.[84] Shouting "No to pissing in test tubes!" they walked their bicycles for the first fifty meters of that day's stage.[85] Their protest sparked considerable commentary among the press, team managers, and the racers themselves, and raised issues that have been central to the debate about doping ever since.

The first question was whether the racers' protest had truly been unanimous. Jacques Anquetil, the five-time Tour champion and apparent leader of the protest, maintained that it had been; other prominent racers disagreed. They claimed that they considered it normal to be subject to French law while in France, that they opposed the protest, and that it had not been supported by the whole *peloton*.[86] Arguing that the apparently unanimous act was actually the result of threats by one or more influential instigators "without a mandate" and that the majority of racers had not been consulted, the organizers opened an investigation that they hoped would lead to an "exemplary punishment" that would "prevent any further such incident."[87] The investigating officials soon acknowledged the impossibility of identifying those responsible for the protest and issued a communiqué criticizing the racers' initiative, which had discredited their sport, and warning them that any future such incident would have "serious consequences."[88]

The issue of the *peloton*'s unanimity was important to both the racers opposed to the testing procedures and the organizers. For the former, it was critical to present a unified front if there was to be any chance of reforming the procedures. For the organizers, however, the racers' protest, especially if it was unanimous, undermined Lévitan's claim that the drug tests were an "honor" for the Tour. For decades *L'Auto* had claimed that the Tour inspired the fragile young men of France to develop their strength, endurance, and character through sport, while its critics had argued that the race contributed to French degeneration. Desgrange's heirs now sought to associate the Tour with the public-health crusade of their times, but the racers' public protest suggested instead that the Tour was symptomatic of the broader drug problem. A disillusioned Lévitan acknowledged that the protest demonstrated that the racers, "a band of drug addicts who are discrediting the sport of cycling," were troubled by the determination of the authorities to fulfill their "moralizing objective" and incapable of reforming their unhealthy habits.[89]

The second issue was whether antidoping legislation restricted the racers' right to work and unfairly discriminated against athletes. The two questions were linked: how could the drug tests be a fair restriction of the racers' work when athletes—specifically professional bicycle racers—were singled out for testing while other occupations were left unaffected? Many racers were upset at this double standard.[90] They understood that their own professional survival depended on producing and rapidly recovering from feats of prodigious endurance; doing so required stimulants. Anquetil argued that the racers were not systematically opposed to educating their younger peers about the pitfalls of doping, but that experienced professionals had proved that they could be trusted to medicate themselves responsibly in order to compete. As a result, they found this new interference in their work by the Tour organizers and the state difficult to accept, particularly since, although justified by a public-health imperative, it did not target other professions affected by drug abuse.[91]

Other commentators, such as the team manager Raphael Géminiani, *Le Monde,* and *L'Humanité,* agreed that the law was discriminatory: the fivefold increase in the sale of stimulants over the previous decade could hardly be attributed to sixty French professional bicycle racers.[92] *L'Équipe*'s Antoine Blondin criticized the selective application of the law and argued that racers were professionals, that the very nature of sport was to seek victory, and that "we should not show ourselves too punctilious about the means deployed to achieve this end."[93] His boss, Jacques Goddet, however, argued that racers should respect the law, and most team managers agreed. Some noted that the 1965 law was not discriminatory, as it did not exclusively target cyclists.[94] This was technically true, as any athlete could be tested, but the vast majority of those tested during the law's initial implementation were in fact bicycle racers.

A related question was whether the testing procedures violated the racers' human dignity and civil rights.[95] Racers claimed they were willing to accept testing if it was done with utter discretion to preserve their dignity; Anquetil remarked that their motivation was "the defense of the moral person of the professional bicycle racer." Some commentators argued that police searches of the racers' suitcases and clothing were abusive and deprived the racers of their civil rights.[96] Goddet, however, countered that professional bicycle racers represented a very small group who made a living from sport, some of whom earned considerable amounts of money, and that their exceptional visibility required them to submit to "exceptional restrictions."[97] In fact, at that time most racers—including Lucien Aimar, the surprise winner of the 1966 Tour—barely eked out a living in the sport.[98] This reality was largely irrelevant to Goddet: he believed that, as public heroes, racers had special responsibilities.

Therein lay a fundamental contradiction that Goddet did not acknowledge. Heroes are by definition worthy of emulation. The heroic status of Tour racers was conditioned by their exploits, which were made possible, according to Anquetil and others, only by the use of stimulants. Now that the use of stimulants (and other drugs) was deemed an important social problem requiring legislative and regulatory attention, the prospect of young people emulating the heroic behavior of Tour racers was, to say the least, problematic. The drug tests thus had a polarizing effect: one camp favored an all-out campaign against stimulants, whereas the other was concerned that human dignity, individual autonomy, and the right to work would be sacrificed in the process.[99]

Even those who acknowledged that the racers' rights had been violated argued that those rights were trumped by public-health considerations. At stake was the health of the racers and, by extension, that of the public, particularly young people. Goddet asked that instead of opposing the drug tests, racers, who were well aware of the "ravages" caused by doping to their health, collaborate with the necessary "purification" of sport.[100] According to *Le Figaro,* most racers understood that the battle against drug use was a public-health issue; it was not right to consider all professional cyclists "vulgar drug addicts." Still, the Bordeaux tests were a good warning: "The fear of the gendarme is excellent medicine against doping."[101] For *L'Humanité,* the solution was an educational campaign in high schools, universities, clubs, and amateur teams in all sports.[102]

At least one young racer admitted that the testing had made him rethink his approach. Rather than risk a positive test and a suspension that might jeopardize his career, he would forgo the exploit he had been planning for the mountains.[103] His was a healthy choice, praised by *L'Humanité*, but one—ironically enough—founded on the assumption that exploits, the key to Tour celebrity and professional success, were impossible without recourse to banned stimulants. As for the *peloton*'s brief "strike" in 1966 against the drug tests, it came to an abrupt end when a racer who opposed the protest attacked, obliging the others to go after him. "To take the start of the Tour," his team manager explained, "is to sign a moral contract. You accept the rules and all their implications, or you don't enter the race."[104] In a terrible irony that would only become clear a year later, the racer whose manager uttered those words was Tom Simpson.

A DEATH ON THE TOUR

On 13 July 1967, one of the hottest days in Tour history, the temperature soared to 45 degrees Celsius (113 degrees Fahrenheit) in the shade as the thirteenth stage took the racers 211.5 kilometers from Marseille to Carpentras. Lying 8 minutes 20 seconds behind the race leader Roger Pingeon after the Alps, the Englishman Tom Simpson was determined to take his best shot at overall victory and the economic windfall it represented. Simpson was one of the stars of the *peloton*, with impressive victories in *classiques* like the Tour of Flanders (1961), Bordeaux-Paris (1963), Milan–San Remo (1964), and the Tour of Lombardy (1965), as well as the 1965 road-racing world championship. Earlier in the 1967 season he had shown excellent form, winning the one-week Paris-Nice stage race and two stages of the Tour of Spain. Doubts lingered, however, about his ability to sustain the effort required to win the Tour de France. Although he had led the race for a while before finishing sixth in 1962, Simpson had shown a tendency to weaken in the Tour's second half, dropping out in 1965 and again in 1966.[105]

One hundred and fifty kilometers into the stage, the *peloton* confronted the 21.5 kilometers and 7.5-degree average incline of the formidable Mont Ventoux, whose summit, at 1,909 meters, dominates the surrounding countryside. The "bald mountain" holds a special place in Tour lore. A solitary peak in southeastern France, its top half is a rocky, plantless moonscape mercilessly exposed to the midsummer sun.[106] Although not as high as some of the climbs in the Pyrenees and Alps and often the only major obstacle in the stage that includes it, the Mont Ventoux's forbidding profile has long tempted racers to take drugs, as Mallejac's close call in 1955 reminds us. Pursuing Raymond Poulidor and Julio Jimenez, who had attacked earlier, Simpson began to zigzag a few kilometers from the summit and fell; he was put back on his bicycle by two spectators. A few hundred meters farther up the climb, he collapsed on the side of the road in convulsions. A spectator gave the now-unconscious racer mouth-to-mouth resuscitation until Dr. Dumas reached him and, assisted by a Tour nurse, administered first aid. A helicopter then transported Simpson to the hospital in Avignon. Despite every effort to revive him, he never regained consciousness and was pronounced dead at 5:40 P.M. An autopsy revealed the presence in his body of amphetamine and methamphetamine, whose toxicity had been increased by the heat and Simpson's fatigue. The same drugs were found in his jersey pocket. The physicians who conducted the autopsy concluded that the amphetamine had not directly caused Simpson's death but had allowed him to go beyond his limits in difficult climatic conditions, which might also have contributed to his physical distress and exhaustion. Heat prostration had led to a fatal heart attack.[107]

The following day—France's national holiday, no less—every major French daily carried news of Simpson's death in prominent front-page stories, with extended coverage in the national and sports sections. Three decades earlier Francesco Cepeda's fatal accident had certainly not been ignored by the press, despite *L'Auto*'s desire to muffle bad publicity, but Simpson's death took place in a dramatically changed media environment. The public had seen grim images of what had transpired on the Mont Ventoux, including photographs of Dumas attempting to revive the fallen racer. Simpson's collapse had been captured by French television and was later covered on the program *Panorama* in a segment titled "Farewell to Tom Simpson."[108] Media attention and public interest were heightened when many commentators, including Dumas, immediately raised the possibility that doping was involved, even though the official autopsy results were not made public until early August, after the race.[109] For their part, the racers observed a minute of silence in Carpentras at the start of the next stage, which they allowed Simpson's friend and compatriot, Barry Hoban, to win uncontested as a tribute to his fallen teammate.[110]

The question of who was responsible for Simpson's death reignited the debate about the Tour's excessive nature.[111] The journalist Jean Bobet, a former racer and the brother of the three-time Tour champion Louison Bobet, emphasized the accumulation of fatigue over a busy season, especially in stage races like the Tour, when "high averages over excessively long distances are demanded of exhausted racers." Simpson's peers pointed to his ability to go "beyond his limits." "Tom," a teammate noted, "was capable of pedaling to the death."[112] While the 1966 Tour winner, Lucien Aimar, attributed Simpson's death to a combination of the sun and his efforts, other racers were less coy: "If all the racers who doped to get over a mountain had died on the road," some racers claimed, "European mountains would be strewn with monuments to their memory."[113]

Like Bobet, Jacques Anquetil accused the organizers of asking too much of the racers. The solution, he argued, lay in reducing certain difficulties and, especially, the number of races.[114] A doctor had told him that to avoid doping, a racer should limit himself to fifty days of racing a year. Anquetil himself raced between 230 and 235 days a year and had bicycled half a million kilometers over his career, an average of about thirty-five thousand kilometers a year. Yet even as he argued for reducing the sport's difficulty, Anquetil, apparently undeterred by rumors implicating prohibited drugs in Simpson's death, renewed his advocacy of educated doping by experienced professional racers. He pointed out that racers had been taking stimulants for fifty years; without them they would average twenty-five kilometers an hour.[115] The often horrendous race conditions, like those of the Mont Ventoux, required pharmacological support. When a reader of *L'Humanité* asked him why the top racers did not simply refuse to enter excessively difficult events and thus force the organizers to reform the Tour de France, Anquetil responded that "if anyone could do it, it would no longer be the Tour."[116]

Anquetil's contradictions are instructive. The appeal of most sports depends on the skills of their best practitioners, which set them apart from other human beings. The Tour's appeal, as we have seen, lies less in its participants' skill than in the exceptional endurance and courage they demonstrate in completing the race. Compromising the Tour's uniquely grueling nature would empty the race of meaning. On the other hand, maintaining its unequaled difficulty led racers to resort to illicit and risky chemical means to reduce their suffering and allow them to earn a living.

Other observers agreed with Anquetil that extreme demands led to doping, but, rather than seek to resolve the tensions inherent in the Tour's cult of suffering and survival, they criticized the race and its organizers. A Parisian doctor claimed that "without doping, the Tour de France is an impossible enterprise" for all but one or two rigorously prepared "phenomenal athletes."[117] Citing Simpson's public admission of doping two years earlier, *L'Aurore* noted that he had evoked "the professional racers' obligation to obtain the maximum *rendement* . . . by all means," which inevitably led to doping.[118] *Le Monde* blamed his death on "a certain mystical conception of sport" and on a hubris that led athletes to push themselves beyond "the limits that nature assigns to the human machine" and become "ritual victims" sacrificed to the crowd.[119] One of its readers accused the organizers of torture, sadism, and an "unacceptable conception of sport" that led them to impose race conditions that "obliged racers to use or abuse" drugs. Demonstrating an evident familiarity with the organizers' most cherished themes, he noted that they wished to provide crowds with "the spectacle of suffering" and wanted people to speak "of hell, of calvary, etc." He argued that the organizers should have canceled the stage, reduced it by half, or rescheduled it so that the racers negotiated the Mont Ventoux in the evening.[120]

Seeking to deflect this criticism, the Tour organizers held Simpson responsible while stressing the noble financial motivation—his family responsibilities—that had led him "to go beyond his limits" and perhaps seek "artificially to raise himself to the level of his rivals."[121] *L'Équipe*'s Blondin argued, against the evidence, that the Mont Ventoux climb was particularly "benign" that year and that the racers had climbed it with a smile. He claimed that *le surmenage cycliste* (overwork in cycling) was a useless notion: everything possible had been done to preserve the racers from their own abusive ambitions and pursuit of glory. Ultimately, the question of how far to push their limits could only be answered by the racers themselves. The Tour was not too hard, Lévitan asserted; Goddet, citing the recent deaths of nine mountain climbers and automobile racers, implied that Simpson's death, however tragic, hardly made the Tour the world's most dangerous sporting event.[122] Lévitan charged some critics with taking advantage "of the slightest incidents to blow them up disproportionately"—a grotesque statement given that the "slightest incident" in question was nothing less than a racer's death. He argued that the Tour did not kill, that it was neither inhuman nor excessive, and that the organizers did not have "an unacceptable conception of sport." Had not a hundred racers negotiated the

Mont Ventoux without health problems? Did not other sports hold competitions in terrible weather?[123]

Goddet sought to place the "plague" of doping in its broadest context. He argued that it was not just cycling or sport in general, but "modern life" itself that was affected and that "all legal, moral, spiritual, [and] scientific forces must work together to bring back the good moral order."[124] Although in favor of "the administration of certain nontoxic products" and of improving "the *rendement* of the human machine," he balked at the greater freedom advocated by Jacques Anquetil.[125] Goddet believed that Simpson's death did not require a fundamental modification of the sport, but he admitted that "important corrections" in the Tour's itinerary and schedule could be implemented to protect the racers from "their own errors" (a phrase that absolved the organizers of any responsibility for the racers' doping) and to ensure that the Tour continued to evolve as it always had, consistent with "the march of modern times, which tend toward acceleration." The solution to the doping problem, which was ravaging all of modern society, was a campaign uniting the public authorities, doctors, educators, and the media.[126]

The tension between this campaign and the modern celebration of "acceleration" with which Goddet wished to associate the Tour apparently escaped him. Indeed, he argued against an "emasculated event" that would irreparably harm the exhilarating, exemplary nature of "the beautiful, free spectacle of the Tour." The racers were "voluntary martyrs" who were "unanimous in accepting the demands of road racing as it exists, with its difficulties and imperatives." They owed their prestige to the race's *légende*, to its rigor, and to their own will and resistance to suffering. Goddet took his "ignorant" critics to task for attacking the Tour's excesses, which, he argued, protected racers by requiring them to prepare flawlessly, adopt an ascetic self-discipline, refuse to cheat, and know their bodies and limits perfectly.[127] This counterintuitive argument—never more paradoxical than in the wake of Simpson's drug-related death—reflected the challenge facing the organizers: how could they reconcile their professed commitment to discourage doping, by reforming the Tour, with the race's much-celebrated extreme image, which they, like Anquetil and other racers, understood was the foundation of its popularity and economic viability?

Now as before the war, the debate over the Tour's nature was shaped by terms associated with industrial modernity, specifically the *rendement* and *surmenage* of human "machines." The Tour's critics saw the modern obsession with ever-more-efficient, ever-faster racers as a profoundly unhealthy, immoral conception of sport, founded on excess, exhaustion, and suffering. The Tour's defenders, on the other hand, blamed overly ambitious racers for doping, castigated "ignorant" commentators for their unjustified criticisms, and continued to celebrate the race's contribution to improved, "accelerated" human performance. For them, references to machines and productivity were not indictments of the Tour's industrial exploitation of the racers; as Goddet's endorsement of "the administration of certain nontoxic products" makes clear, these were positive terms associated with scientific—specifically, pharmacological—modernity. In the wake of Simpson's death, the Tour was once again inserted into debates about the modern world, its dangers, and its possibilities.

THE MORE THINGS CHANGE . . .

If Simpson's death just one year after the first drug tests raises the question of their effectiveness in the battle against doping, at least testing would presumably generate reliable data as to the extent of the practice in professional cycling.[128] In 1966, of the thirty-seven athletes (most of them cyclists) tested in France, twelve tested positive. All were bicycle racers, including six Tour competitors whose tests revealed the use of amphetamines and methamphetamine.[129] The percentage of positive tests in France dropped rapidly after 1966, to 1 or 2 percent by the mid-1970s, even as the total number of tested athletes increased dramatically.[130] Bicycle racers remained the prime targets of testing, representing 87.4 percent of the 7,535 athletes tested during the first ten years of the law's application.[131] Although this trend would seem to confirm the resounding success of the French antidoping campaign, it was in fact largely attributable to several factors that allowed athletes to avoid detection while continuing to dope.

For one thing, the French government soon turned over the responsibility for drug tests to the sports federations, which were plagued by an obvious conflict of interest.[132] What federation would wish to attract negative publicity, perhaps even jeopardize the future of its sport, by exposing widespread doping? In the 1968 Tour, for example, the testing procedures were so lax that doped racers were systematically able to provide containers of urine that was not their own. Furthermore, random, unannounced testing, critical to the success of any antidoping campaign, often gave way to announced tests, allowing racers to interrupt their doping regime or take other measures to ensure a negative result. Some racers in the 1968 Tour of Italy injected water into their bladders before being tested after a stage in order to dilute traces of illicit drugs. When they arrived at the Tour de France, they insisted that tests take place after each stage, presumably to give them time to implement the same procedure and thereby avoid detection. Racers also ingested masking agents like diuretics and vitamin C to cover their continued amphetamine use, and some turned to drugs like corticosteroids, testosterone, and anabolic steroids, which were not detected by the tests of that period.[133]

The dynamic that has characterized the recent history of high-performance sport was thus launched in professional cycling in the late 1960s. Many racers and their support staff sought to stay one step ahead of the ability of laboratories to detect prohibited drugs; and the laboratories, once apprised of the new drugs being taken, attempted to devise new tests that would detect their use. When the laboratories were successful, or when athletes and their entourages were careless, racers tested positive. In the late 1960s and 1970s, most of the top racers, in addition to numerous racers of mediocre ability, were caught at least once.[134] Occasionally racers admitted their use of prohibited performance-enhancing products. Having tested positive, Bernard Thévenet acknowledged using cortisone for a three-year period, during which he won the 1975 and 1977 Tours de France. His observation that the practice was widespread among racers led to his ostracism by his peers.[135] Some, like Freddy Maertens, remained defiant and, echoing Anquetil, justified their drug use as a professional right.[136]

While most cases were clear-cut, some incidents, often involving high-profile racers, raised important questions about the fairness of the tests, the consistency with which sanctions were applied, and the legality of a process that denied racers fundamental rights enjoyed by all other citizens.[137] Opponents of testing were thus regularly offered opportunities to discredit the whole system. In 1971 the 1967 Tour winner Roger Pingeon tested positive for amphetamines and was suspended for four months by the FFC. Denying that he had used the drugs, Pingeon took his case to court. In response, the federation, applying rules in effect since the early 1900s, canceled his professional license, in effect making it impossible for him to continue earning a living at the sport. The Paris administrative tribunal in turn voided the FFC's decision on procedural grounds, a decision supported by the Council of State, which noted that no such punishment could be taken before Pingeon's case was heard by the FFC.[138]

In addition to violating the procedural guarantees afforded all citizens under French law, the antidoping campaign suffered from at least two other major flaws. In 1969 French courts dismissed the cases of two racers who had tested positive in the 1966 Tour because it was impossible to prove, as the 1965 law required, that the racers had knowingly taken prohibited drugs. Furthermore, the Bordeaux Chambre Correctionnelle judged that racers could not be convicted of doping if they had taken a product prescribed to them by their doctor to treat an ailment. This was a fundamental right, and it was unreasonable to deny racers appropriate treatment for genuine afflictions simply because the medicine in question contained prohibited ingredients.[139]

The most notorious case occurred during the 1969 Tour of Italy. On the verge of winning the race for the second consecutive year, Eddy Merckx tested positive after an easy stage for which no racer, especially the world's best, would have normally required an illicit boost. Expelled from the race and suspended for a month, Merckx tearfully proclaimed his innocence. Rumors of dirty tricks, surreptitious doping by agents of his competitors, and laboratory error abounded, fueled by the fact that the beneficiary of Merckx's expulsion was none other than the Italian favorite Felice Gimondi, who himself had tested positive in the 1968 Tour of Italy. Observers raised legitimate doubts about the conditions in which the testing had been done and noted differences between the French and Italian regulations defining prohibited substances. Merckx's sponsor hired a private detective to uncover any malfeasance targeting its champion.

As public outrage at this perceived injustice mounted, especially in Merckx's native Belgium, the Belgian minister of sport asked the foreign minister to request that his Italian counterpart ensure that an exhaustive investigation was conducted. During a parliamentary session, two Italian senators asked the Italian minister of tourism and spectacles whether Merckx's expulsion for "involuntary" ingestion of doping products was consistent with "the law of sport, the rules of hospitality and even with the requirements of reciprocity in our compatriots' sports competitions abroad." The Belgian and Italian cycling federations also became involved, the former defending Merckx, the latter the legitimacy of its testing procedures. For their part, the Tour de France's organizers were dismayed that the Belgian's suspension would prevent him from entering their race: without Merckx, public interest would flag, with potentially dire financial and commercial consequences for the Tour. Taking into consideration the strange conditions surrounding Merckx's positive test, the International Federation of Professional Cycling decided to give him the benefit of the doubt, and the UCI lifted his suspension.[140] Merckx then went on to one of the most decisive Tour de France victories in history.

These cases illustrate the significant procedural issues—both scientific and legal—that plagued the issue of drug testing from the start, as well as the existence of powerful interest groups and institutions likely to oppose the punishments that ensued from a positive result. These included the public and politicians responding to public pressure; courts determined to uphold the legal and procedural rights of professional racers, including the right to work and the right to medical care, which sports federations sometimes violated; commercial sponsors defending racers who, if penalized for doping, would bring the sponsors bad publicity and be unable to represent them during the suspensions; organizations representing professional racers; and race organizers, who had much to lose if a top racer was denied the right to enter their event. Of course, organizers had potentially even more to lose when a star was caught doping *during* an event.

THE YELLOW JERSEY DISGRACED

In 1978 Michel Pollentier entered the Tour de France following an impressive series of victories that included the Tours of Italy and Switzerland, the Dauphiné Libéré stage race, and the Belgian professional road-racing championship.[141] After winning the Alpe d'Huez stage, he was the Tour's new leader. Before providing a urine sample for the drug test to which all stage winners had to submit within an hour of finishing, Pollentier retired to his hotel, where he changed clothes.[142] Knowing he would test positive for a banned substance, he wedged a rubber bulb filled with another person's urine under his armpit. A tube leading from the bulb was taped to his back; it ran between his buttocks and ended under his penis. Pollentier planned to provide "clean" urine at the medical caravan by pressing his arm against his flank and forcing the urine down the tube. Unfortunately for the Belgian, the medical inspector in charge of the test that day discovered the tube and promptly drafted a report accusing Pollentier of fraud. As required by the regulations of the UCI and consistent with French law, the racer was immediately expelled from the Tour, fined five thousand Swiss francs, and suspended from competition for two months.[143]

The incident generated considerable commentary because it was the first time in Tour history that the race leader had been caught doping and expelled. A number of the issues raised since the 1965 law's passage resurfaced: the relationship between doping and sportsmanship; inconsistencies in the administration of the drug tests; the challenge of protecting human dignity and workers' rights on the one hand and public health on the other; and the link between doping in sports and broader trends. Behind these issues lurked the discomforting question raised in the wake of Simpson's death: was it possible to reconcile doping by racers, which was designed to make the Tour easier, with the celebration of heroic survival that had always been at the core of the race's *légende* and popular appeal?

Édouard Seidler and Pierre Chany argued in *L'Équipe* that Pollentier had "committed a crime" against the Tour, top-level cycling in general, and his peers. His attempt to cheat at the drug test would inevitably raise doubts about the exploits of other racers. This was unfair, as the behavior of the majority of professional racers was "reasonable and often enlightened" and their performances therefore presumably untainted by the use of illicit drugs. That two respected, knowledgeable sports journalists could express such views, despite the fact that the sport's recent history was peppered with positive tests by most of the world's best racers, including several Tour winners, bears testimony to the enduring appeal of the Tour's heroic ideal and *L'Équipe*'s interest in maintaining it. That ideal could only be preserved if fraudulent acts like Pollentier's were understood to be exceptions to the rule. Chany did, however, acknowledge the moral laxity and corrupt sports ethic of some racers (another racer had in fact been caught cheating at the urine test a few minutes before Pollentier).[144]

Chany's reference to a sports ethic raised the issue of the moral role of sport in society: was sport, as its defenders so often claimed, a special area of human endeavor distinguished by an uncompromising commitment to honorable competition, fair play, and respect for rules? Jacques Goddet argued that sport in contemporary society was indeed a symbol of integrity *(loyauté)* that should remain impervious to the "turpitudes" that characterized everyday life and all human beings. The spectacle of athletes going beyond their limits was a moving one; the role of journalists was to sing the praises of "these transcendent beings who, before our eyes, transform themselves into supermen." Confronted with Pollentier's dishonesty, Goddet wondered whether the exploits that brought joy to millions of fans were only made possible by "prohibited means" and "chemical concoctions": "if the desire to win or to perform brilliantly engenders such errors, the sports ethic, whose foundation is morality, is thereby seriously undermined."[145] Yet again the problem of the "excessive" Tour was posed.

As in 1967, many commentators argued that racers could not negotiate the Tour's extreme demands without dangerous performance-enhancing drugs. They condemned the excess, immorality, and obsession with profitability, exploits, and spectacle that characterized professional sports, accused the Tour's organizers of hypocrisy, and urged major reforms in the event and cycling in general.[146] In response, Goddet argued that doping was not specific to the Tour, nor to cycling, nor even to sports, but a consequence of human nature: humans were motivated by personal satisfaction, financial rewards, and the desire to please, perform brilliantly, elevate themselves, and dominate. As a result, the species was constantly seeking "ways to improve its simple human capacities. The era of progress pushes us to explore secret domains."[147]

In light of this human drive for self-improvement, Goddet singled out Tour racers as having a special role to play in modern society. He asked whether doping should in fact be forbidden to top-flight athletes, "those who have the responsibility of seeking always to carry higher and farther the threshold of human physical power." "Are they not," he wondered, "experimental individuals, apt to serve technical knowledge as well as science itself?"[148] Once an opponent—at least in his rhetoric—of performance-enhancing doping by racers, Goddet now embraced the West's century-old obsession with the athlete as a glorified human laboratory rat and justified the pharmacological initiatives and competitive ambitions of Tour racers as serving a higher scientific purpose from which all humanity might one day benefit.[149] This position was utterly at odds with the antidoping campaign led by Dumas and others since the late 1950s. Although still apparently concerned about drug use in society, Goddet now asserted that athletes were a select category of individuals whose drug-taking furthered the human pursuit of "progress."

Numerous commentators, team managers, and racers criticized the inconsistencies, arbitrariness, and generalized laxity of the tests, which had subverted the antidoping campaign and misled racers into believing that cheating would be tolerated.[150] Pollentier noted that the medicine he had taken, alupin, simply helped him to breathe better; although this was the first time he had taken it in France, he had used it in Belgium (where it was sold over the counter), Italy, and Switzerland.[151] Both Pollentier and his teammate Maertens claimed that the organizers wanted a Frenchman to win and resented the fact that a team of Belgians had monopolized the important jerseys.[152] *Libération* agreed that tests seemed to target certain racers while allowing others, often local favorites, to evade detection. Tour officials, according to an unnamed source, had gone after Pollentier to punish the Flandria team for their prominent role in leading the general strike at Valence-d'Agen. His expulsion also greatly improved the chances for overall victory of the young French favorite Bernard Hinault (although, given Hinault's role in the strike at Valence-d'Agen, this example of the organizers' alleged chauvinism was not entirely convincing).[153] The Belgian paper *La Nouvelle Gazette* suggested that the Tour was "unhealthy" for foreigners, given the recent history of positive tests that had penalized foreigners to the benefit of French racers.[154]

As in 1966, two main positions on the doping issue emerged. One, emphasizing the health dimension of the problem and the obligation of governments to protect their citizens, held that uncontrolled doping would lead to catastrophe. The other, based on workers' rights, argued that professional racers, like all manual and intellectual workers, had the right to choose their doctor and medicine.[155] The medical community was polarized: some physicians believed racers required "care" (the racers' euphemism for drugs) to maintain the "infernal cadences" imposed by the race schedule; others opposed doping on medical and moral grounds and urged a reduction in the number of races.[156] Racers continued to resent their sport being singled out and to find the strict application of the doping test, which required them to strip from waist to knees and to pull up their sleeves to their elbows, an embarrassing violation of their human dignity.[157]

Prominent figures in the world of French cycling suggested reforming the antidoping regime in ways that returned considerable control to the racers over their bodies and labor. Anquetil advocated drastically reducing the list of illicit doping products, arguing that only two or three were actually dangerous. Making the others illegal led racers to take products that were undetectable but much more dangerous than the prohibited drugs.[158] Richard Marillier, the national technical director of the French Cycling Federation, argued that racers were "physical laborers" *(travailleurs de force)* who could not get by simply with the nutrition and medical care of the "common man." Paradoxically, despite their particularly difficult work, racers could not take a day off when they felt ill or weak during the Tour; nor could they take medicine or stimulants available to an ordinary person, because such products contained banned ingredients that resulted in positive drug tests. Marillier's solution was that each team's physician be required to inform the doctor of his national cycling federation about any treatment provided an ailing racer that involved a banned substance.[159]

In an editorial titled "Does Your Body Belong to You?" Goddet, too, wondered whether restrictions on what racers could put into their bodies undermined their rights, which were quite particular given the nature of their work. While he agreed that the government was responsible for the collective health of its citizens, and that this duty entailed combating drugs and alcoholism, he wondered whether public officials might not draw useful distinctions according to social or professional categories: the current prohibition on performance-enhancing substances in cycling had unintended, corrupting consequences, including "the uncontrolled consumption of mysterious products with still-unknown effects." Goddet suggested that the medical profession establish "reasonable prescriptions" and that racers participating in difficult races like the Tour be monitored by a physician. Such a system would establish the "habeas corpus" of the professional bicycle racer.[160]

These proposals represented a significant departure from the traditional view, long upheld by Goddet and his predecessors, that what separated Tour racers from the common man was their exceptional courage and endurance. Rather than enforce existing laws and regulations against doping and thus "clean up" the sport, Anquetil, Marillier, and Goddet advocated decriminalizing many substances: the problem was not doping per se, but the fact that so many drugs were illegal or prohibited. If their destiny was indeed to be "transcendent supermen," Tour racers had to be allowed access to products that helped make them so. As Roger Bastide has noted, drugs had become an *instrument de travail* (a work tool) for racers confronted by the great demands of their sport and the pressure of living up to their heroic status.[161] Since 1903, Tour critics had argued that professional racers, as workers, were endowed with the same rights as other workers under French law, including the right to limit the danger and duration of their work. What was different now was that, in addition to arguing for shorter stages and more time for rest and recuperation, as they had at Valence-d'Agen, some racers (as well as the Tour organizer and a prominent FFC official) were advocating the racers' right to use stimulants and other banned drugs to help them surmount the Tour's many obstacles.

Surely these were contradictory demands. If the race were made easier, there would be no need to allow the use of prohibited drugs. If, however, the racers were allowed free access to stimulants, painkillers, and other performance-enhancing substances (as had been the case before the mid-1960s), it would be harder to justify reducing the Tour's length and difficulty. For decades the modus vivendi within the sport had been to make the Tour extremely difficult while tacitly allowing the use of a variety of drugs. The recent emergence of drugs as a widely recognized societal problem had spawned the legislation of the mid-1960s, effectively outlawing this arrangement. The sport and its various interest groups now confronted an awkward choice: they could jeopardize the heroic status of Tour contestants by reducing the event's difficulty or else jeopardize that status by allowing racers to use drugs and risk being seen as addicts in a society increasingly concerned about widespread drug abuse.

Some commentators did indeed present the doping scandal as a reflection of a more general decadence. *Libération* feared that the glorious days when the Tour, "that jewel of our cultural patrimony," was a truly epic event and France had a future were over now that the nation had become so "soft." Drugs had first seduced young people; they now contaminated healthy racers.[162] (In fact, as we have seen, racers were taking drugs long before public attention focused on substance abuse in other professions and among French youth.) According to *La Croix*, cycling had created an atmosphere that justified doping at a time when many intellectual workers, including doctors, also took drugs.[163] *L'Humanité* linked what it perceived as the increasing demands and danger of the Tour to the "race for profits" in contemporary society. The hectic racing schedule was a result of uncontrolled capitalism. "Behind the beautiful legend of the Tour," the paper's headline trumpeted, lay "commercial profits and (sometimes) the miserable lives of racers," most of whom barely eked out a living from professional racing.[164] Marillier of the French Cycling Federation acknowledged that the expectations of commercial sponsors were higher than ever before. If that was indeed the pressure that had motivated Pollentier, Marillier was willing to concede that the Belgian racer was at least partially a victim.[165] As had been the case since 1903, the Tour's immense popularity and the kind of work it required made it a compelling metaphor for commentators disturbed by broader trends.

Notwithstanding these attempts to link racers' doping to a more general crisis of modern society, public opinion on doping during this period seems to have been characterized by indifference, ambivalence, and, at best, temporary concern. A few weeks before the Pollentier scandal, a poll in *Le Pé-lerin* revealed that 34 percent of the respondents opposed doping because it subverted fair competition, and 57 percent because it put the athlete's life at risk; yet only 53 percent would cease to respect and admire a great champion convicted of doping. (One wonders how many condemned doping because they knew this was the "right" answer to give.)[166] The public might support drug testing for athletes, as 75 percent of *L'Équipe*'s readers did in another poll in 1978, but its lack of concern (or rapid forgiveness) was continually confirmed by the ever-increasing numbers of fans who lined the itinerary, bought newspapers in July, or followed the race on television.[167]

Further evidence of the public's indifference is the fact that commercial sponsors generally took no action to penalize racers caught doping.[168] Had sponsors had any indication that the public was more than temporarily and superficially troubled by such violations, they would surely have sought to contain the damage to their image, perhaps even withdrawn from the sport.[169] Instead, they tended to defend their racers and exercise pressure to have doping punishments reduced or rescinded. Meanwhile, the press generally failed to pursue doping stories beyond the initial splash of publicity their revelation sparked, which increased newspaper sales, and eagerly resumed positive coverage of the racers' exploits rather than linger on the illegal or banned substances that made them possible in the first place. The position of the sports press, in particular, was ambiguous: delving responsibly and uncompromisingly into doping would tarnish the image of the competitions and champions from whose coverage it made a living. It would also antagonize athletes, whom sports journalists often revered and on whose cooperation they relied.[170]

Ultimately, the Pollentier scandal of 1978 had no discernible long-term effect on the public's attitude or the racers' behavior. The very next year, Joop Zoetemelk became the first Tour racer to test positive for anabolic steroids, which he acknowledged having used in 1978 without provoking a positive test.[171] The curious doping affairs involving the German star Dietrich Thurau in 1980 suggest that interested parties in professional cycling continued to exercise behind-the-scenes pressure to help racers escape punishment.[172] In 1988 the Tour was again rocked by a possible doping scandal involving the race leader when French television leaked rumors of a positive test by Pedro Delgado. Although used to mask the presence of steroids and banned by the International Olympic Committee, the drug involved, probenecid, was not on the UCI's list of prohibited drugs in 1988 (the UCI banned it the following year). As he had not in fact violated cycling's anti-doping rules, Delgado remained in the race. A few days later, before a largely enthusiastic crowd on the Champs-Élysées, he became only the third Spaniard in history to win the Tour. As in the Merckx incident in 1969, this brief affair reached the highest levels of government. Facing mounting public concern that the French were seeking to rob the popular Delgado of his victory, the Spanish government contacted the French minister of education, youth and sports, Lionel Jospin, and sent a representative to witness the laboratory test on Delgado's second sample. If the Spanish were presumably satisfied by the ultimate resolution of the affair, for his part Jospin refused to attend the Tour's closing ceremony honoring Delgado.[173]

The French public continued to react to doping revelations with a curious mix of ambivalence, naïveté, and denial. In the wake of the much-publicized 1988 doping affairs of Delgado and the Canadian Olympic sprinter Ben Johnson, a 1989 study revealed that 44 percent of the French public believed that doping contaminated all sports, 79 percent wished that it be stopped, and 47 percent feared that if a child of theirs was a gifted athlete, he or she would be confronted by the issue. However, 70 percent of the respondents rarely or never believed that the athletes they watched were taking performance-enhancing drugs. As Patrick Laure notes, what such data illustrate is the public's frustration: on the one hand, fans wish to admire, even idolize, athletes who perform exceptionally; on the other, they confront the "potentially artificial character of these records" and fear being played for fools.[174]

A new, presumably more rigorous French law on doping in sports was passed in 1989.[175] Confirming the need for a more aggressive campaign against doping, in 1990 the recently retired racer Paul Kimmage published a memoir in which he described in grim detail the nature and extent of doping among his peers in the 1980s; in the process, he implicated Stephen Roche, who in 1987 had won the Tours of Italy and France and the road-racing world championship.[176] In the 1990s, testing of athletes in France increased, but the percentage of positive tests remained so far below the level of doping suggested by anecdotal evidence as to be meaningless, except to demonstrate that athletes and their support staff continued to find ways to circumvent the testing procedures and the capacity of laboratories to detect the use of prohibited drugs.[177] In 1995, for example, the FFC conducted 1,235 drug tests, only 20 (1.61 percent) of which were positive.[178] Such results suggest that the governing bodies of the sport, as well as the public authorities, were unwilling to commit the resources required for an effective, sustained campaign against doping. In 1998 that would change.

On the eve of that year's Tour de France, French customs officials intercepted a vehicle of the prominent Festina team at the Franco-Belgian border and found a large supply of banned performance-enhancing drugs. The doping scandal that ensued disrupted the Tour as never before: police investigators descended on the race, searched the racers' rooms and belongings, and carted some of them off to prison cells, where they were often harshly treated and forced to submit samples for drug testing. Implicated in the expanding investigation, some teams were expelled; others, fearful that they soon would be, withdrew. With the crisis escalating, the remaining contestants stopped racing: television viewers the world over were treated to the startling spectacle of ad hoc negotiations during a stage between the organizers and the racers, who agreed to resume competing only after being promised that they would be treated with dignity and respect for the balance of the race.[179]

As shocking as it was to millions of casual spectators and the fans of implicated racers, the scandal confirmed what critical observers familiar with developments in the sport over the previous decade had known or suspected: professional racers were continuing to use a whole range of performance-enhancing drugs. In addition to the traditional amphetamines and corticosteroids, these now included anabolic steroids, human growth hormones, and erythropoietin (EPO). EPO was at the center of the 1998 scandal. A synthetic hormone that increases the number of oxygen-carrying red cells in the blood, it is of particular benefit to athletes in endurance sports like cycling. The drug, however, has a dangerous side effect: it thickens the blood, increasing the risk of strokes and heart attacks, especially when the user is resting or sleeping. Informed observers, including physicians, hold EPO responsible for the mysterious deaths since the late 1980s of a number of racers, including a fairly prominent Dutch professional.[180]

In the wake of the 1998 doping scandal, the French National Assembly passed antidoping legislation of unprecedented scope and ambition. The new law required French professional bicycle racers to submit regularly to a battery of tests so that officials would be able to establish a physiological baseline for each and chart their condition over the course of their careers, and thus presumably be able to identify suspicious anomalies that suggested doping.[181] The issue has been kept in the public eye by media coverage of other, more recent doping "affairs" and by the publication of memoirs by racers and other individuals with inside knowledge of professional cycling, including many of the principal actors in the drama of July 1998. Some of these works were implausible, self-serving accounts designed to exculpate their authors. Others, however, provided an unprecedented, credible, and horrifying window into a sport contaminated by widespread, illicit, and potentially life-threatening doping.[182]

CONCLUSION

There are striking continuities between the interwar *forçats de la route* debate and postwar controversies over the Tour's excessive demands on its contestants. In both cases, the language of labor, of workers' rights and contractual responsibilities, helped to shape the rhetoric of all sides. In neither case did a consensus emerge as to whether racers were endowed with the same rights as other workers and employees. And in both cases it was the very core of the Tour's mass appeal, the image of heroic survivors confronting exceptional suffering, that proved problematic for the organizers, racers, and media. If all three parties clearly profited from the Tour's reputation as the world's most grueling sporting event, only the racers actually suffered. Yet even they sought to couch their demands for better working conditions in language that did not undermine the Tour's *légende,* which they understood was the foundation of their popularity and allowed them to earn a living. Finding such language proved a difficult, perhaps even an impossible, task. On the other hand, when the organizers were attacked for the merciless conditions they imposed on the racers, they too found it hard simultaneously to deflect criticism and celebrate the Tour's extreme nature.

Until the mid-1960s it was widespread (and for the most part legal) doping that allowed many racers to negotiate the tension between the Tour's "superhuman" demands and their own human limits, often at considerable risk to their health. And it was the organizers' tacit acceptance of the practice that allowed them to maintain the Tour's difficulty. *Le dopage* was the dirty little secret behind the race's heroic mythology. Although it did not prevent racers from suffering terribly, it gave them a timely boost and eased their aches and pains long enough for many to complete the race and for some to produce exploits that were, in a certain sense, superhuman. However flawed, intermittent, and hypocritical it has often been, the antidoping campaign of the past four decades has exposed the extent and danger of the racers' reliance on illegal performance-enhancing drugs. In the process it has challenged the organizers, media, public, and athletes themselves to confront the contradictions on which the Tour's appeal is founded.

Those contradictions have taken the form of questions that remain relevant, never more so than in the wake of the 1998 scandal. Is doping the only way to reconcile the pursuit of *rendement* with the reality of *surmenage?* If so, is it a professional right, as Anquetil, Maertens, and finally even Goddet argued? Goddet's ambivalent reaction to the Pollentier scandal is instructive. At first he deplored the racer's attempt to cheat the public of genuine exploits; such fraudulent conduct by a *géant de la route* undermined the moral significance Goddet wished to attach to the Tour and to sport in general. Yet he soon contradicted this initial impulse, as well as the anti-doping position he had taken in the 1960s, by arguing that Tour racers were "supermen," "transcendent beings," and "experimental individuals." Given the role top-flight athletes were called on to play in a modern society obsessed with improving human capacities, should they not be exempt from the government's otherwise laudable crusade against drug abuse?

In a curious twist, Goddet had resuscitated the late-nineteenth-century ideal of the body without fatigue. What he did not see, or refused to acknowledge, was that, given the essence of the Tour's appeal, more liberal doping rules for racers were a risky proposition. Most high-performance sports are characterized by the demonstration of exceptional skill. The Tour de France, however, is defined by the expenditure of exceptional energy, the deployment of exceptional courage, and the acceptance of exceptional suffering. Would crowds still be drawn to the race if they perceived the racers' energy to be pharmacologically enhanced, to the point that neither extreme suffering nor its corollary, great courage, were part of the equation?

That question was posed in the 1990s, at least for some informed observers, when racers ascended the Tour's toughest climbs and completed its stages day after day at unprecedented speeds and with little apparent fatigue. In the wake of the 1998 scandal and with the "purification" of the sport purportedly under way, recent Tours have actually been even faster. Equally troubling, credible revelations by racers themselves, although dismissed by their peers and downplayed by some of the sport's officials, confirm that doping remains widespread. So do positive drug tests and court cases involving racers and their doctors. These developments have done little to harm the racers' popularity: the crowds that have lined the Tour's itinerary in recent years have been as large and, in most cases, as enthusiastic as before the 1998 scandal. During that time France's most popular racer has been Richard Virenque, who, as a member of the Festina team in 1998, initially denied having doped, despite the overwhelming evidence against him, only to recant after charges were brought against him. For the time being, the Tour's century-old cult of suffering and survival has proved remarkably resilient in the face of unprecedented revelations of doping by racers. It is difficult to see this as a good thing.

Epilogue

≡

One of the distinctive features of the modern era has been the emergence of mass commercialized spectator sport and its emblematic figure, the professional athlete. In France, the earliest and most celebrated manifestation of this new social type was the bicycle racer, while the Tour de France rapidly developed into the often ground-breaking epitome of modern sport. As a result, from its creation the Tour and its participants were caught up in French debates about the nature of progress and the complex relationship between progress and modernity.

As the Tour de France enters its second century, it is worth reflecting on the major narratives that the French generated about the race during its first hundred years as they confronted the forces that were changing their lives. Some of these narratives have clearly receded into history. It seems implausible, for example, that the bicycle will ever again be celebrated as a preeminent symbol of technological modernity, even if over the past quarter century the machine has undergone major improvements—a point to which we shall return. Nor is it likely that Tour racers will be promoted as a proud community of guild artisans or highly efficient factory workers, or that the *peloton* will be decried as industrial slave labor. Reductions in the race's length, improvements in racing conditions, and increases in the racers' incomes, as well as the evolution of industrial production techniques, major gains in workers' rights, and the dominance of the service sector in the French economy, give such images little traction.

Other Tour narratives have survived as the race enters its second century. Yet even these appear to have been undergoing important, if often subtle, changes over the past two decades. During this period of transition, as earlier in the race's history, Tour narratives have been challenged, even under-mined, by their internal tensions. The race's future may depend on whether its stakeholders—the organizers, racers, sponsors, public, media, UCI, and, most recently, the French government—are able to resolve these contradic-tions.

One tension centers on the symbolic charge of the race's itinerary. To what degree can the Tour's route be exploited to make broader geopolitical statements and still remain distinctively French? Although the organizers have to date refused to extend the itinerary across the Atlantic, future routes may reflect the ongoing process of European integration. One can imagine an opening to the east to mark the recent admission to the EU of former Soviet-bloc countries. On the other hand, widespread French concerns about the potential negative impact of the EU's eastward expansion, not to mention the rejection in 2005 by French voters of the European constitu-tion, could just as well dampen enthusiasm for such plans. Recalling the hostility sparked by their Maastricht Treaty–inspired itinerary in 1992, the organizers may prefer to select itineraries bereft of political symbolism, or whose symbolism is uncontroversial.

If the race is unlikely to include North America in its itinerary anytime soon, Americans have nevertheless personified the globalization of the event over the past quarter century. In 1986 Greg LeMond became the first non-European to win the race. Although LeMond did so as a member of a team sponsored by a French company, Lance Armstrong, the second Amer-ican to win the race, won his Tours riding for American teams (US Postal and Discovery Channel), and it was possible to watch his victories live on American television. Today the race is profoundly international. Although East Asian, South Asian, and African racers have yet to participate (with the exception of a North African team in the early 1950s and the occasional white South African racer in recent years), racers now come from North and Latin America, Australia, New Zealand, and, since the end of the Cold War, Eastern European countries and former Soviet republics. Meanwhile, North and South American, as well as European, companies have become major sponsors of the Tour and of professional cycling in general. The forces of globalization currently shaping world affairs have clearly not spared the world's greatest bicycle race.

The two American Tour winners, LeMond and Armstrong, also epito-mize the enduring appeal of the Tour's classic heroic narrative. In 1989 LeMond returned from an almost fatal hunting accident that kept him out of cycling for two years to win the race in the last stage, a time trial finishing on the Champs-Élysées during which he made up a fifty-second deficit to win the Tour by eight seconds, the smallest margin of victory in the event's history. His resurrection was confirmed the following year, when he won the Tour for a third and final time. A decade later, having survived a life-threatening bout with cancer, Armstrong entered the 1999 Tour, which, to almost everyone's surprise, he went on to win. He has since set the record of seven Tour victories before retiring after his final victory in 2005. LeMond and Armstrong suffered, they survived, and ultimately they triumphed.

Yet both men have also contributed to recent and ongoing challenges to classic Tour heroism. The sums that began to pour into the rapidly globalizing sport of cycling in the 1980s increased the financial stakes for team sponsors. As a result, racers and their support staff came under unprecedented pressure to find a competitive advantage over their opponents. To do so, teams sought to exploit the latest scientific and technological knowledge: they maximized their racers' muscular effort by improving their racing position and adopting lighter and more aerodynamic clothing and equipment. In his famous time trial victory in 1989, LeMond used triathlon handlebars and a streamlined helmet to minimize wind resistance. Following the example of downhill skiers and applying methods used in the design of automobiles, Armstrong conducted wind-tunnel experiments to identify the most efficient racing position. Like his rivals, he was attentive to technological innovations such as new designs and lighter materials for his bicycle and racing apparel.[1] As LeMond's victory in 1989 demonstrated, every second counts: advantages once believed to be inconsequential might actually yield the winning margin, even in a race of over three thousand kilometers.

A new, scientific culture of high performance has been emerging in recent decades. This new approach to the sport undermines the classic Tour themes of suffering and survival and the race's *légende*, its history of remarkable feats of courage and endurance by exceptional champions. The purpose of all these innovations, after all, is to allow the racers to be ever more efficient physiologically: to cycle faster by eliminating or reducing the obstacles to greater speed, notably their weight and wind resistance. From the early 1980s to the early 1990s, for example, the hour record was raised a stunning seven kilometers: none of the record holders was on a par with the sport's legendary figures, but they all experimented successfully with new lightweight materials and aerodynamic designs. Aware that such performances by lesser racers risked trivializing the exploits of past champions, the UCI responded: not only did it ban a range of innovations, but it also erased from the sport's official record book accomplishments achieved with the banned equipment. For the good of the sport and its premier event, the pursuit of maximal efficiency *(rendement)* had to be reined in and suffering restored to its rightful place in cycling lore.

The current tension between suffering and *rendement,* conventional Tour heroism and scientific innovation, has of course been a familiar theme in the race's history. Desgrange, after all, banned the use of derailleurs until the late 1930s to ensure that the race did not become so easy as to deny its participants ample opportunity to demonstrate their heroic qualities. At its core, this tension centers on diverging and ultimately irreconcilable images of human achievement: is Tour prowess the result of human courage and persistence in the face of great and unavoidable pain, or is it the mathematically ordained outcome of carefully prepared, tireless man-machines, an image that has its roots in the reconceptualization of the human body that occurred in the nineteenth century?

The renewed obsession with improving *rendement* that characterizes the new cult of scientifically enhanced performance has a darker side. In addition to technological innovation, attempts have been made to augment by pharmacological means the physiological capacities of racers. Steroids, testosterone, and human growth hormone serve this purpose, as do drugs like EPO that increase oxygen-carrying red blood cells and thus improve endurance. Resorting to these substances has allowed racers to train more intensely, race faster, and reduce their recovery time; the last, in particular, is critical to completing a three-week race during which rest is at a premium.

Tour statistics over the past quarter century illustrate the extent to which racers have improved their performances. From 1981 through 1990, Tour winners averaged 37.369 kilometers per hour. Beginning in 1991, in the first fifteen Tours of what one might dub "the EPO era" (even if EPO is not the only drug implicated in the sport's many recent doping scandals), the winners have averaged 39.661 kilometers per hour, a significant increase.[2] Moreover, they have not been winning by greater margins than earlier Tour champions: to the contrary, the time gaps separating the top racers from each other, as well as the gaps between those racers and the rest are, if anything, decreasing. It is thus not just the stars but the whole *peloton* that is going faster than ever before.

Although some commentators and racers explain this remarkable collective improvement by emphasizing changes in technology and training, many also attribute it to a far more systematic and sophisticated approach to doping. Notwithstanding the promises of the sport's stakeholders to address the doping crisis aggressively in the wake of the 1998 Tour, anecdotal, circumstantial, and scientific evidence of widespread doping has tended to increase over the past seven years: positive drug tests, admissions by racers and former racers (and members of their support staff), evidence presented in legal proceedings, and even—sadly—mysterious racer deaths all suggest the alarming scope of the phenomenon, which has implicated many top racers as well as their less accomplished, lesser-known peers.[3]

Numerous racers, including stars, have tested positive since the 1998 Tour. Among the most prominent are the American Tyler Hamilton and the Spaniard Roberto Heras. The former tested positive for blood doping (involving the transfusion of another person's blood) in August 2004 on winning the Olympic time trial in Athens, and again in September during the Tour of Spain. Because Hamilton's positive test in the Olympics was not confirmed by his second sample (known as a B sample), which had been mistakenly frozen and thus compromised, he kept his gold medal.[4] His positive test during the Tour of Spain, however, was confirmed by his B sample; he was then fired by his team and given a two-year suspension by the UCI.[5] In 2005, Heras won his record-setting fourth Tour of Spain, only to test positive for EPO after the penultimate stage; he was then stripped of his victory.[6]

Most tragic is the tale of Marco Pantani, arguably the most popular Italian athlete of the past two decades and the winner of the scandal-plagued 1998 Tour de France. Implicated in a number of doping scandals both before and after his Tour de France victory, Pantani was expelled from the 1999 Tour of Italy when, on the verge of winning the race for the second year in a row, he was found to have a hematocrit level above the allowable maximum of 50 percent, suggesting the use of a substance (like EPO) that increased the number of red cells in his blood. (He was acquitted in October 2003 of this doping charge.)[7] In the years that followed, despite suffering from bouts of depression, Pantani occasionally showed flashes of his earlier form but was never able to sustain the performance level that had been his until 1999. In February 2004, he was found dead in his hotel room from a cocaine overdose. Many fans, especially in his native Italy, saw Pantani as the victim of persecution by overly aggressive authorities. Pantani was honored by the organizers of the 2004 Tour of Italy, who dedicated one of its great mountain stages to his memory; they also planned to place a black marble bust of Pantani at the top of the mountain where he first demonstrated his climbing prowess in the 1994 Tour of Italy.[8]

Many racers who did not test positive for illicit performance-enhancing substances have been compromised by overwhelming circumstantial evidence and, in some cases, by their own admissions.[9] In 2002, the Lithuanian Raimondas Rumsas, a virtual unknown riding in his first Tour de France at the age of thirty, unexpectedly placed third in the race. On the day the Tour ended, his wife, Edita, was arrested by customs officials at the French-Italian border; a search of her vehicle revealed that she was transporting EPO, anabolic steroids, corticosteroids, testosterone, and human growth hormone, which, despite the couple's denials, could only plausibly have been intended for her husband.[10] In early 2004, the French Cofidis team was rocked by a doping scandal that led to a legal investigation. The affair, which implicated several racers and a staff member, involved amphetamines, EPO, human growth hormones, testosterone, and anabolic steroids. One of the racers, Philippe Gaumont, noted how easily drug tests could be circumvented and claimed that the vast majority of professional racers were doping.[11] After initially and categorically denying that he was involved, the Scot David Millar, Cofidis's top racer and the reigning professional time-trial world champion, admitted to using EPO after a search of his home uncovered empty syringes that had once contained the drug. He claimed that, as the team's leader, he had felt pressure to achieve results and admitted to doping at the time of his victory in the world championship time trial the previous year (for which he had not tested positive). Fired by Cofidis and suspended for two years by the British cycling federation, Millar planned to return to professional cycling after his suspension.[12] These and other such cases illustrate how easy it is for racers who dope to avoid positive tests.

In the wake of so many doping scandals, official investigations, court cases, and unexpected performances, it has become increasingly difficult to deny—although racers and officials in the sport continue to do so—either that doping pervades top-flight cycling or that it is fundamentally different from the practice that characterized the sport into the 1970s.[13]

The Tour's cult of suffering and survival is once again under assault. As it has for decades, the Tour continues to eliminate racers who finish a stage *hors délai* by exceeding the maximum time allowed for each stage (this limit is based on the stage winner's time and varies depending on whether the stage is mountainous or flat). Although this rule guarantees a certain amount of attrition each year, that rate of attrition has been steadily declining since the 1950s, a trend at least partly attributable to ever more effective doping. In 2002, the year of the Rumsas affair, 153 of the 189 racers—a stunning 81 percent—who started the race completed it, suggesting that illicit doping extended well beyond the hapless couple. Even before the Rumsas affair broke, the doctor responsible for the race's drug testing during the previous three years estimated that 40 percent of Tour racers were still using banned substances.[14] In 2005, 155 of the 189 starters (82 percent) completed the Tour.

It is sobering to juxtapose the recent antidoping campaign and rhetoric of the French government and the sport's officials with these attrition rates and also with another trend: the Tours since the 1998 doping scandal have included the fastest in history. They have been won at an average speed of 40.277 kilometers per hour—almost three kilometers per hour faster than the average speed of Tour winners between 1981 and 1990, a period dominated by two of the most gifted Tour champions in history, Bernard Hinault (1981, 1982, 1985) and Greg LeMond (1986, 1989, 1990). Despite initiatives to improve drug testing, racers and their support staff maintain a comfortable advantage over the authorities: not a single positive was recorded among the 143 urine tests and 21 blood tests conducted on racers during the 2005 Tour de France, which turned out to be the fastest ever.

The public's reaction to date makes it difficult to argue that the Tour's image has been tarnished by these developments: every July millions of spectators flock to the itinerary, and hundreds of millions more watch daily television coverage.[15] Not surprisingly, given the public's response—or lack thereof—to so many doping scandals, commercial sponsors have almost all stayed the course; they recognize that they still have much to gain from their association with professional cycling. In recent years, only one major team sponsor, Mapei, has withdrawn from the sport because of concerns about its racers' doping. For its part, after much public soul-searching, the Cofidis team suspended operations for a brief period in the spring of 2004. Having fired the offending racers and publicly recommitted to racing "clean," the team returned to competition in time to enter that year's Tour de France.

The Tour's continuing popularity raises important questions. Can the classic cult of suffering and survival that has shaped its appeal since 1903 accommodate growing public awareness of generalized doping by racers? Is the race's heroic ethos now merging with, or even giving way to, a new cult of scientifically generated performance founded on both technological and pharmacological advances?

Once again, the complex figure of Lance Armstrong illustrates the ambiguities that plague the Tour's image. American commentators have tended to favor a heroic narrative that attributes Armstrong's remarkable performances to his natural physical ability, mental toughness, exceptional work ethic, and scientific—but above-board—preparation.[16] As a result, in the United States Armstrong's reputation has until very recently remained pristine: his well-publicized battle with cancer and subsequent fund-raising efforts for his cancer charity, combined with the American public's general ignorance about cycling, have to date sheltered him from the kind of critical scrutiny recently directed at high-profile American athletes suspected of doping in other sports.[17]

In France (and elsewhere in Europe), however, Armstrong's Tour victories have been met with considerable skepticism by fans and commentators, including newspapers such as *Le Monde* and *Libération*. Well-informed observers of the sport remember a young racer in the early 1990s who performed well in one-day and short stage races but never demonstrated the ability to race time trials or climb well enough to prevail in the Tour, let alone win it seven times.[18] They question whether such improvement can be explained solely by weight loss, a more intense and scientific approach to training, and a newfound sense of mission that has given him increased focus and motivation. They are alarmed by Armstrong's relationship with Dr. Michele Ferrari, an Italian physician who has publicly endorsed the use of EPO by athletes and was convicted in the fall of 2004 in Italy of "sports fraud" and "abusive exercise of the profession of pharmacist" for facilitating illegal doping by athletes. They are all the more skeptical because the duration of that relationship coincided with Armstrong's development into a racer capable of winning major Tours.[19] Finally, they wonder how a racer who has always claimed to be "clean" consistently defeated top racers who have been found guilty of doping. No less a figure than Greg LeMond, who finished his career just as Armstrong began his (and just as this new wave of more sophisticated and effective doping got under way), has publicly questioned the authenticity of Armstrong's exploits and expressed concern about his relationship with Ferrari.[20] So too have others with an intimate, first-hand knowledge of the sport.[21]

Undeterred by questions about the legitimacy of his victories, and having announced that he would retire after the race, Armstrong entered and convincingly won the 2005 Tour de France at a record speed of 41.654 kilometers per hour. For the first time in the event's history, the winner was handed a microphone at the final ceremony in Paris to make a few remarks to the huge crowd assembled near the finish line on the Champs-Élysées. In a veiled attack on those who continued to charge that he and other racers owed their extraordinary performances to illicit doping, Armstrong pitied the "cynics" and "skeptics" who refused to appreciate the sport of cycling. A month later, however, his critics were unexpectedly provided with new ammunition against the now-retired champion.

In late August 2005, *L'Équipe* revealed that urine samples taken from Armstrong after six different stages during his first Tour victory in 1999 had been tested in 2004 by France's leading drug-testing laboratory and had come back positive for EPO. The samples had been provided to the laboratory in 1999, at a time when no reliable urine tests for EPO existed, with the understanding that they would remain anonymous and would be used simply to verify whether tests subsequently developed by the laboratory were effective in identifying the presence of EPO in urine. Investigative journalists at the sports daily had, however, obtained documents that included the code number given to Armstrong's samples; armed with that information, they were able to identify racers, including Armstrong, whose code numbers appeared on other documents containing the test results.

Armstrong vigorously denied the validity of the test results, impugned the integrity of the newspaper, and evoked an anti-American conspiracy to explain the affair. As there were no B samples available to confirm or invalidate the test results, he could not be stripped of his 1999 Tour victory. In the media firestorm that followed, doping experts and officials, racers and former racers, politicians, the sport's officials, race organizers, and journalists reacted in a variety of ways. Some found the timing of *L'Équipe*'s revelations suspect; the newspaper, which is owned by the same company that owns the Société du Tour de France, which organizes the race, had made the test results public only after Armstrong had completed his final Tour, rather than during the race, when such revelations would have been far more damaging to the event. Some questioned whether the results of six-year-old drug tests were relevant for assessing the current state of the sport. Others, however, interpreted the results as confirmation of what they had long suspected about the American champion's extraordinary performances since 1999, about the truthfulness of his repeated claims to be racing without using illicit substances, and, more generally, about the sport's unresolved doping crisis. Still others, including the Tour's organizer Jean-Marie Leblanc, a former racer, expressed disappointment and shock at the revelations but did not think they should tarnish Armstrong's entire career. Leblanc soon took a more aggressive stance, however, charging Armstrong with having deceived fans and race officials by doping, an accusation Armstrong angrily dismissed.[22]

It is too soon to know what consequences the Armstrong affair and future allegations of racer doping, whether or not they are confirmed, will have on the Tour, professional cycling, and the campaign against doping in sport. A few weeks after the story broke, opinion polls in France, Germany, Italy, and Spain revealed that 79 percent of the individuals polled associated cycling with doping (in France alone the figure was a staggering 97 percent).[23] But will this association have a strong enough impact to endanger the Tour? Or will the public once again deny, rationalize, or ignore the racers' doping and throng the route of future Tours to celebrate the remarkable performances of their heroes?

As it did so often during its first century, the Tour de France is providing a public forum for a debate about the nature of progress. Once again, that debate is shaped by considerations that are difficult to reconcile with each other: the dream of virtually limitless human improvement, the ethos of suffering and survival, the rights of individuals to control their own bodies and of workers to control their working conditions, and the desire to shield public health and public morality from the broader implications of top-flight athletic competition.[24] The tensions between these ideals have never been more relevant, for beyond the age-old, if increasingly sophisticated, practice of performance-enhancing doping looms an even more radical and troubling prospect: genetic manipulation designed to maximize athletic potential.

It is unclear how this debate will evolve. Given the ongoing doping crisis in cycling and other sports, the Tour will most likely continue to feature prominently in discussions about progress and the possibilities, as well as the dangers, of modernity. During its first century the race served as a public platform for often heated discussions among the French about what it meant to be a worker or an employer, a man or a woman, a communist or a conservative, French or Breton. As medical and pharmacological advances accelerate, and as racers avail themselves, legally or otherwise, of new drugs and therapies, the Tour is likely to be part of a global conversation about an even more fundamental question: what does it mean to be human?

Appendix
Racers' Occupations

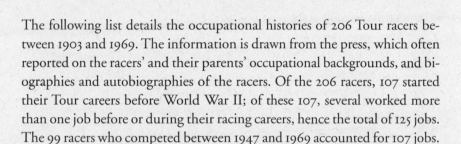

The following list details the occupational histories of 206 Tour racers between 1903 and 1969. The information is drawn from the press, which often reported on the racers' and their parents' occupational backgrounds, and biographies and autobiographies of the racers. Of the 206 racers, 107 started their Tour careers before World War II; of these 107, several worked more than one job before or during their racing careers, hence the total of 125 jobs. The 99 racers who competed between 1947 and 1969 accounted for 107 jobs.

I. *Racers' jobs before and during their racing careers, 1903–39:* 125 (100%)
    A. *Manual labor:* 66 (52.8%)
        a. *Mechanics:* 16 (12.8%)
        b. *Building trades:* 16 (12.8%): 6 masons, 3 carpenters, 2 apprentice carpenters, 2 electricians, 1 apprentice electrician, 1 brickyard apprentice, 1 construction worker
        c. *Industrial workers:* 9 (7.2%): 3 miners, 2 metal workers, 1 rubber-factory worker, 1 broom-factory worker, 1 steel-factory worker, 1 cigar-box-factory worker
        d. *Traditional crafts:* 9 (7.2%): 2 locksmiths, 1 blacksmith, 1 typographer, 1 saddler, 1 cabinetmaker, 1 mirror cutter, 1 apprentice boilermaker, 1 cobbler
        e. *Agricultural laborers:* 9 (7.2%): 3 peasants, 2 farmers, 2 herdsmen, 1 vineyard worker, 1 farm worker
        f. *General labor:* 7 (5.6%): 3 delivery men, 1 bargeman, 1 chimney sweep, 1 roadmender, 1 docker

B. *Nonmanual labor:* 59 (47.2%)
  a. *Small businessmen:* 31 (24.8%): 14 cycle merchants,
     manufacturers, or workshop owners, 7 inn, café, or restaurant
     owners, 3 butchers, 1 grocer, 1 apple merchant, 1 fish merchant,
     1 baker, 1 linen merchant, 1 tractor-towing company owner,
     1 merchant
  b. *Clerical/service sector:* 24 (19.2%): 10 store or office employees,
     4 salesmen, 4 apprentice butchers, 2 bellboys, 1 illustrator-
     reporter, 1 taxi-driver, 1 submarine quartermaster, 1 draftsman
  c. *Entertainers:* 4 (3.2%): 1 clown-acrobat, 1 actor, 1 opera
     baritone, 1 banjo player
II. *Racers' jobs before and during their racing careers, 1947–69:* 107 (100%)
  A. *Manual labor:* 72 (67.3%)
    a. *Industrial workers:* 20 (18.7%): 17 workers (including
       10 metalworkers), 3 miners
    b. *Agricultural laborers:* 17 (15.9%): 12 agricultural workers,
       peasants, or farmers, 2 shepherds, 1 gardener, 1 wine grower,
       1 lumberjack
    c. *Building trades:* 16 (15.0%): 6 electricians, 4 carpenters,
       2 construction painters, 1 mason, 1 plasterer, 1 plumber,
       1 construction worker
    d. *Traditional crafts:* 10 (9.3%): 2 printers, 2 cobblers, 1 cooper,
       1 typographer, 1 watchmaker, 1 turner, 1 cabinetmaker, 1 tailor
    e. *Mechanics:* 9 (8.4%)
  B. *Nonmanual labor:* 35 (32.7%)
    a. *Small businessmen:* 20 (18.7%): 7 café owners, 4 cycle
       merchants, 3 bakers, 1 butcher, 1 oyster seller, 1 greengrocer,
       1 florist, 1 milkman, 1 shirt-shop owner
    b. *Clerical/service sector:* 15 (14.0%): 12 employees, 1 accountant,
       1 teacher, 1 mailman

NOTES

ABBREVIATIONS

APPP   Archives de la Préfecture de Police de Paris

CIEREC   Centre Interdisciplinaire d'Études et de Recherches sur l'Expression Contemporaine

INTRODUCTION

1. There have been some notable exceptions to this neglect. Some thirty-five years ago, Eugen Weber's articles on sport in fin-de-siècle France suggested a number of important themes that could profitably be explored through the serious study of sport. A decade later, Richard Holt published the first rigorous, book-length historical analysis of sport in modern France (including a chapter on cycling); it remains the foundational work in the field.

The Tour itself has inspired a wealth of often beautifully illustrated, generally hagiographic histories—heavy on anecdote and light on analysis—written by journalists who covered the race. There has, however, been remarkably little critical, scholarly study of the race. Jacques Calvet's monograph, written a quarter century ago, on the at times conflicting interests of the race's stakeholders (the organizers, racers, media, and commercial sponsors) is an excellent study of the relationship between the Tour's economics and its heroic mythology. Georges Vigarello's chapter on the race in the *Lieux de mémoire* collection edited by Pierre Nora was the first, based on primary sources, to connect the Tour to important questions of history, memory, and identity. (Roland Barthes suggested some of these connections in his piece on the Tour in *Mythologies* a half century ago; although at times insightful, his reflections on the race's meanings remain largely speculative, as they are not grounded in primary sources.) *La République du Tour de France, 1903–2003,* by Jean-Luc Boeuf and Yves Léonard, is a welcome addition to this fledgling field. Although its authors' use of primary sources is at times limited (they cite only three newspapers in their bibliography), they do an excellent job of relating the race to the broader narrative and several major themes of twentieth-century French history. Finally, Eric Reed's dissertation on the Tour's cultural and commercial history is a thought-provoking contribution, notably in its examination of sponsorship and the motivations, interests, and experiences of host communities. See the bibliography for these and other works on French sport and the Tour.

2. See, in particular, Lynn Hunt, ed., *The New Cultural History* (Berkeley: University of California Press, 1989).

ONE. *LA GRANDE BOUCLE*

1. On the unifying impact of universal conscription, public schooling, and the railroads under the early Third Republic, see Eugen Weber, *Peasants into Frenchmen: The Modernization of Rural France* (Stanford, CA: Stanford University Press, 1976).

2. See Stephen Kern, *The Culture of Time and Space, 1880–1918* (Cambridge, MA: Harvard University Press, 1983); Christophe Studény, *L'invention de la vitesse: France, XVIIIe–XXe siècle* (Paris: Éditions Gallimard, 1995).

3. For the Bon Marché's role in this transformation, see Michael B. Miller, *The Bon Marché: Bourgeois Culture and the Department Store, 1869–1920* (Princeton, NJ: Princeton University Press, 1981).

4. See Charles Rearick, *Pleasures of the Belle Epoque: Entertainment and Festivity in Turn-of-the-Century France* (New Haven, CT: Yale University Press, 1985); Eugen Weber, *France, Fin de Siècle* (Cambridge, MA: Belknap Press, 1986); Vanessa R. Schwartz, *Spectacular Realities: Early Mass Culture in Fin-de-Siècle Paris* (Berkeley: University of California Press, 1998); Jean-Pierre Rioux and Jean-François Sirinelli, eds., *La culture de masse en France de la Belle Époque à aujourd'hui* (Paris: Librairie Arthème Fayard, 2002).

5. On the invention and early years of Drais's new machine, see Jacques Seray, *Deux roues: La véritable histoire du vélo* (Rodez: Éditions du Rouergue, 1988), 13–14, 19–47; Jean Durry, *Le vélo* (Paris: Éditions Denoël, 1976), 16–17.

6. Seray, *Deux roues,* 71–72, 97, 99, 102–3. Prior to Michaux's invention of the pedal, significant technological improvements had been devised on both sides of the Atlantic, but they received little attention and were not incorporated into the basic design of the *draisienne.* Durry, *Le vélo,* 17; Seray, *Deux roues,* 145, 148.

7. French provides more precise terms than English, distinguishing between *bicycle* (a machine whose pedals are directly attached to one of the wheels by cranks, and of which the *grand bi[cycle]* is the most imposing model) and *bicyclette* (a ma-

chine that transfers power to the rear wheel by means of a chain and sprockets). All of these were types of *vélocipèdes* or *véloces*, as were tricycles and quadricycles.

8. Seray, *Deux roues*, 113, 114, 124, 125, 128, 136, 146, 147, 185; Durry, *Le vélo*, 19. Until the late nineteenth century, cyclists were limited to one speed on the *bicycle*, because the pedal cranks were directly attached to the wheel itself. In the case of the *bicyclette* (the bicycle with chain), two gears were available, one on either side of the rear wheel. The rider dismounted and turned the rear wheel around to change gears before climbing a hill, for instance.

9. Eugen Weber, "Gymnastics and Sports in Fin-de-Siècle France: Opium of the Classes?" *American Historical Review* 76 (February 1971): 80–82.

10. Ronald Hubscher, ed., *L'histoire en mouvements: Le sport dans la société française (XIXe–XXe siècle)* (Paris: Armand Colin, 1992), 83.

11. *L'Écho de Longwy*, 17 January 1909; *Le Longovicien*, 21 January 1909.

12. Michel Bouet, *Signification du sport* (Paris: Éditions Universitaires, 1968), 357–58; Pierre Chany, *La fabuleuse histoire du cyclisme*, vol. 1, *Des origines à 1955* (Paris: Nathan, 1988), 30; Georges Cadiou, *Les grandes heures du cyclisme breton* (Rennes: Ouest-France, 1981), 12; René Kuhn, Alfred North, and Jean-Claude Philipp, *Le cyclisme en Alsace de 1869 à nos jours* (Strasbourg: Éditions Publitotal, 1980), 7.

13. Chany, *La fabuleuse histoire du cyclisme*, vol. 1, 30–31, 99; Jean-Marie Durand, *Les as du vélo: Le Tour de France cycliste, 1869–1939* (Marseille: Delta-Repro, 1983), 19–20, 22–23, 25–27, 30, 32, 35–36; Jack Rennert, *100 ans d'affiches du cycle* (Paris: Henri Veyrier, 1974), 3.

14. Chany, *La fabuleuse histoire du cyclisme*, vol. 1, 119, 133–36. See also Richard Holt, *Sport and Society in Modern France* (Hamden, CT: Archon Books, 1981), 86–91, 94–95.

15. Bruno Dumons, Gilles Pollet, and Muriel Berjat, *Naissance du sport moderne* (Lyon: La Manufacture, 1987), 80; Hubscher, *L'histoire en mouvements*, 81; Georges Renoy, *Le vélo au temps des belles moustaches* (Brussels: Rossel Édition, 1975), 85–87.

16. Holt, *Sport and Society in Modern France*, 90–91.

17. Hubscher, *L'histoire en mouvements*, 107; Pierre Sorlin, *La société française*, vol. 1, *1840–1914* (Paris: B. Arthaud, 1969), 239; Rearick, *Pleasures of the Belle Epoque*, 11.

18. Georges Pagnoud, *Ces Bretons qui passionnent le cyclisme français* (Paris: Solar Éditeur, 1974), 42; Marie-José Drogou and Raymond Humbert, *La Bretagne: Mémoire de la vie quotidienne* (Paris: Temps Actuels, 1981), 249; Cadiou, *Les grandes heures du cyclisme breton,* 40; Jean-Paul Ollivier, *L'histoire du cyclisme breton* (Paris: Éditions Jean Picollec, 1981), 236.

19. For more on French cycling clubs during this period, see Christopher Thompson, "Bicycling, Class, and the Politics of Leisure in Belle Epoque France," in *Histories of Leisure*, ed. Rudy Koshar (Oxford: Berg Publishers, 2002), 131–46.

20. Hubscher, *L'histoire en mouvements*, 81, 141–42; Archives Municipales de

Montbéliard-Service Éducatif, *Sport et société dans la région de Montbéliard à la fin du 19e siècle* (Montbéliard: Archives Municipales de Montbéliard, 1980), 8.

21. Departmental Archives of Meuse, series 251M1 (Associations: Sociétés sportives: Autorisations: Dissolutions).

22. Statutes of the Cyclistes Lunévillois and the Pédale de Baccarat, Departmental Archives of Meurthe-et-Moselle, series 4M85 (Associations Vélocipédiques). For a detailed description of one club's excursion at the turn of the century, see Paul Sainmont, *Le Véloce-Club de Tours et le doyen des cyclistes de France* (Tours: Librairie Péricat, 1902).

23. Holt, *Sport and Society in Modern France*, 86.

24. Eric S. Reed, "The Tour de France: A Cultural and Commercial History" (PhD diss., Syracuse University, 2001), 35, 39.

25. Hubscher, *L'histoire en mouvements*, 81, 83.

26. Jacques Marchand and Pierre Debray, *Pour le Tour de France, contre le Tour de France* (Paris: Berger-Levrault, 1967), 22; Durry, *Le vélo*, 17, 22; Seray, *Deux roues*, 164; Rennert, *100 ans d'affiches du cycle*, 6; Reed, "The Tour de France," 40.

27. *Rennes-Vélo*, 1 March 1899; advertisements in *Le Longovicien* and *L'Écho de Longwy* during this period.

28. Seray, *Deux roues*, 155; Dumons, Pollet, and Berjat, *Naissance du sport moderne*, 31; *L'Écho Sportif* (Nancy), 1 January 1905; *L'Auto-Revue de l'Est*, 20 September 1903; *Rennes-Vélo*, 1 December 1898; Hubscher, *L'histoire en mouvements*, 80.

29. Chany, *La fabuleuse histoire du cyclisme*, vol. 1, 100; Hubscher, *L'histoire en mouvements*, 84, 86.

30. Marchand and Debray, *Pour le Tour de France*, 20–21.

31. The first sports newspaper was *Le Sport* ("journal des gens du monde"), founded by Eugène Chapus on 17 September 1854. Hubscher, *L'histoire en mouvements*, 502. On the early history of the cycling press, see Renoy, *Le vélo au temps des belles moustaches*, 65–67; Louis Baudry de Saunier, *L'art de bien monter la bicyclette*, 3rd ed. (Paris, 1894), 157; Louis Baudry de Saunier, *Recettes utiles et procédés vélocipédiques* (Paris, 1893), 139–40; Hubscher, *L'histoire en mouvements*, 86, 502–3, 506; Dumons, Pollet, and Berjat, *Naissance du sport moderne*, 132–33.

32. Chany, *La fabuleuse histoire du cyclisme*, vol. 1, 63–83, 91, 103.

33. Jacques Calvet, *Le mythe des géants de la route* (Grenoble: Presses Universitaires de Grenoble, 1981), 10; Édouard Seidler, *Le sport et la presse* (Paris: Armand Colin, 1964), 28.

34. Seidler, *Le sport et la presse*, 28.

35. Claude Bellanger, Jacques Godechot, Pierre Guival, and Fernand Terrou, eds., *Histoire générale de la presse française* (Paris: Presses Universitaires de France, 1972), vol. 3, 279, 299, 584. On the development of a mass press in France at this time, and its strategies for generating sales (particularly the *fait divers*), see Edward Berenson, *The Trial of Madame Caillaux* (Berkeley: University of California Press, 1992), 208–39, and Schwartz, *Spectacular Realities*, 26–43.

36. Géo Lefèvre, *Ceux que j'ai rencontrés (en 60 ans de vie sportive): Souvenirs et anecdotes* (Paris: Éditions SOSP, 1962), 17–19; Pierre Chany, *La fabuleuse histoire du Tour de France* (Paris: Éditions Nathan, 1991), 20. All translations are mine unless otherwise indicated.

37. Chany, *La fabuleuse histoire du Tour de France,* 19.

38. Nicolas Spinga, "L'introduction de l'automobile dans la société française entre 1900 et 1914: Étude de presse" (maîtrise d'histoire contemporaine, Université de Paris X—Nanterre, 1972–73), 12.

39. Jacques Goddet, *L'équipée belle* (Paris: Éditions Robert Laffont, SA, et Stock, 1991), 15; Spinga, "L'introduction de l'automobile," 19; Chany, *La fabuleuse histoire du Tour de France,* 18.

40. The French automobile industry was the leading producer of automobiles in the world at the time. It was overtaken by the American auto industry in 1904 but remained the dominant car industry in Europe until the First World War. See James M. Laux, *The European Automobile Industry* (New York: Twayne Publishers, 1992), 8; James M. Laux, *In First Gear: The French Automobile Industry to 1914* (Montreal: McGill-Queen's University Press, 1976), 210–12, 215–16; James M. Laux, *The Automobile Revolution: The Impact of an Industry* (Chapel Hill: University of North Carolina Press, 1982), 74.

41. In addition to being one of France's earliest and leading automobile manufacturers, Dion helped found the Automobile Club de France (1895) and the Aéro Club de France (1898). He was also among those arrested in June 1899 at the Auteuil races for attacking President Émile Loubet. For this incident he was criticized in the pages of Giffard's paper, in which Dion had been an early investor. According to Eugen Weber, this was what prompted him and his nationalist friends, like Michelin, to found *L'Auto-Vélo.* Dion won election as a Nationalist in the monarchist and Catholic Loire-Inférieure, first as a departmental councilor, then as a deputy, and finally as a senator. Weber, *France, Fin de Siècle,* 207, 209.

42. Eugen Weber, "Pierre de Coubertin and the Introduction of Organized Sport in France," *Journal of Contemporary History* 5, no. 2 (1970): 21; Chany, *La fabuleuse histoire du Tour de France,* 19; APPP, BA/1697, "Henri Desgrange [Directeur Sportif]," Rapport de la Direction Générale des Recherches, 1ère Brigade, 1 October 1901.

43. In his book *Images du Passé* (Paris, 1937), C. Baudin argues that this political rivalry incited Dion to launch his own paper, but Spinga believes that this is an insufficient explanation for the creation of the paper, especially as several other leaders in the automobile industry were among the original investors. Spinga, "L'introduction de l'automobile," 21–22.

44. See the speech by Baron de Zuylen de Nyevelt, 25 May 1901, to the annual Assembly General of the Automobile Club de France, in Spinga, "L'introduction de l'automobile," 21.

45. Ibid., 19–20, 175–76. The other initial investors from these industries were Clément Cycles and Automobiles (50 shares), Michelin Tires (20), the Aster Auto-

mobile Company (12), Charron, Girardot, & Voigt Automobiles (10), Panhard L.-F. Automobiles (10), La Française Cycles (5), Renault Automobiles (2), and Hurtu Cycles and Automobiles (1). The automobile industry was further represented by the aforementioned president of the Auto-Club de France (20 shares), and one of its founding members, Gustave Rives (5 shares).

46. Ibid., 22. The initial directors were Zuylen de Nyevelt, Dion, Chasseloup-Laubat, Michelin, and an administrator delegate of the Aster Automobile Company. The majorities of succeeding councils of administration in 1904, 1905, and 1908 continued to comprise businessmen from the automobile and related industries, including Darracq himself in 1904, the year *Le Vélo* closed its doors. Other members were either from the aristocracy or personalities from the automobile world, such as G. Rives (from 1901) who was the organizer of the Salons de l'Auto de Paris. Ibid., 21, 23–24.

47. *L'Auto-Vélo,* 16 October 1900, quoted in Reed, "The Tour de France," 49. The translation is his.

48. Some of the material in this section appeared in Christopher Thompson, "Controlling the Working-Class Hero in Order to Control the Masses? The Social Philosophy of Sport of Henri Desgrange," *Stadion* 23 (2001): 139–51.

49. This biographical sketch is drawn from the following sources: APPP, BA/1697; Goddet, *L'équipée belle;* Nicolas Spinga, "L'introduction de l'automobile." Another account has Desgrange starting out as a notary's clerk, but this may simply be a reformulation of his job with the Parisian solicitor.

50. That record was 35.325 kilometers, established on 11 May 1893 at the Buffalo Velodrome in Neuilly. At the time a racer could set records alone "without a trainer" or "with trainers" (other racers or motorcyclists who allowed the rider to achieve much higher speeds by shielding him from the wind). Desgrange would go on to set a number of other records (*L'Auto,* 10 May 1923).

51. Desgrange's involvement in the press extended beyond sport. In 1903 he was the editor in chief of *Le Petit Bleu,* a paper specializing in the arts. Four years later he decided to launch his own literary and artistic paper, *Comoedia.* Unable to generate sufficient readership and new information on a daily basis, and confronted with advertisers who insisted on favorable reviews of their shows (an unacceptable compromise for Desgrange), *Comoedia* soon foundered.

52. They were, respectively, *La tête et les jambes* (Paris: L. Pochy, 1898) and *Alphonse Marcaux,* 2nd ed. (Paris: L. Pochy, 1899).

53. APPP, BA/1697, Rapport de la Direction Générale des Recherches, 1ère Brigade, 1 October 1901.

54. APPP, BA/1697, Rapport, 16 February 1895; APPP, BA/1697, Rapport de la Direction Générale des Recherches, 1ère Brigade, 1 October 1901; APPP, BA/1697, Rapport de la Direction Générale des Recherches, 1ère Brigade, 20 November 1903; APPP, BA/1697, Préfet de Police au Ministre du Commerce, de l'Industrie, des Postes et des Télégraphes, 25 November 1903.

55. Calvet, *Le mythe des géants de la route,* 134, 135; Bellanger et al., *Histoire générale de la presse française,* vol. 3, 383–84.

56. Calvet, *Le mythe des géants de la route,* 36; Marchand and Debray, *Pour le Tour de France,* 30.

57. Hubscher, *L'histoire en mouvements,* 506.

58. Bellanger et al., *Histoire générale de la presse française,* vol. 3, 383–84. Both Calvet, *Le mythe des géants de la route,* 36, and Dumons, Pollet, and Berjat, *Naissance du sport moderne,* 134, set the figure for *L'Auto*'s daily circulation in July 1913 at 284,000.

59. Berenson, *The Trial of Madame Caillaux,* 209, 228. In 1909 *L'Auto*'s average daily circulation of 100,000 trumped those of *Le Figaro* (29,000) and the socialist *L'Humanité* (75,000). Hubscher, *L'histoire en mouvements,* 58.

60. The total daily press circulation in France, including the burgeoning provincial press, increased from 1.5 million in 1875 to 12.5 million in 1914. Roger Price, *A Social History of Nineteenth-Century France* (New York: Holmes & Meier, 1987), 354.

61. Seidler, *Le sport et la presse,* 55; Hubscher, *L'histoire en mouvements,* 506.

62. Holt, *Sport and Society in Modern France,* 101–2.

63. *L'Auto,* 31, 19 May, 23 June 1903.

64. Ibid., 27 June 1903.

65. Ibid., 7, 9, 5 July 1903, 25 May, 21 June 1904, 8, 30 July, 23 May 1905.

66. Ibid., 6 August 1905,

67. *Le Toulouse Cycliste* (n.d.), quoted in *L'Auto,* 30 July 1903.

68. See "Ode au véloce" by M. Deckert, quoted by Maurice Martin in his preface to Baudry de Saunier, *L'art de bien monter la bicyclette,* 11; Berenson, *The Trial of Madame Caillaux,* 46–47; Seray, *Deux roues,* 156; Dr. Just Lucas-Championnière, *La bicyclette* (Paris: Léon Chailly, 1894), 7.

69. Garsonnin, *Conférence sur la vélocipédie faite à Tours le 31 mars 1888* (Rouen: Imprimerie Julien Lecerf, 1888), 4, 7.

70. Baudry de Saunier, *Recettes utiles et procédés vélocipédiques,* 13.

71. Departmental Archives of Ille-et-Vilaine, series 4M221 (Manifestations Sportives-Courses Cyclistes 1899–1914, 1925, 1934, 1940), speech of Vice-Président M. Perdriel at the banquet of the Vélo-Cycle Rennais, 22 February 1903.

72. Garsonnin, *Conférence sur la vélocipédie,* 4, 7, 9.

73. Baudry de Saunier, *L'art de bien monter la bicyclette,* 26. The emphasis is his.

74. Baudry de Saunier, *Recettes utiles et procédés vélocipédiques,* 33, 135.

75. Seray, *Deux roues,* 164.

76. Garsonnin, *Conférence sur la vélocipédie,* 13; Lucas-Championnière, *La bicyclette,* 6.

77. See, for example, *Journal de Rennes,* 9 October 1905; *L'Est Républicain* (Nancy edition), 15 August 1911; *Le Longovicien,* 19, 22 September, 17 October 1907, 28 May, 20 August 1908.

78. A. Berruyer, *Manuel du véloceman ou notice, système, nomenclature, pratique,*

art et avenir des vélocipèdes (Grenoble: Typographie de F. Allier Père et Fils, 1869), 15; Baudry de Saunier, *Recettes utiles et procédés vélocipédiques,* 51–52; Municipal Archives of Sens, *arrêté municipal,* 28 October 1893, regulating the traffic of velocipedes.

79. Garsonnin, *Conférence sur la vélocipédie,* 21. The earliest attempt to use the *vélocipède* professionally may go back to 1832, when mail carriers reportedly tried, without success, to use the new machine on their rounds. Berruyer, *Manuel du véloceman,* 12.

80. Garsonnin, *Conférence sur la vélocipédie,* 22–24. The telegraphist was quoted in *La Revue du Sport Vélocipédique* 178 (February 1887).

81. Renoy, *Le vélo au temps des belles moustaches,* 75.

82. Roger Bastide, *Petit-Breton: La Belle Époque du cyclisme* (Paris: Éditions Denoël, 1985), 199–200; Garsonnin, *Conférence sur la vélocipédie,* 36; André Glarner, ed., *Le sport en France* (La Haye: International Bridge of Trade, 1929), 101.

83. Seray, *Deux roues,* 168. For a list of works on the military application of the bicycle published at this time, see Keizo Kobayashi, *Pour une bibliographie du cyclisme: Répertoire des livres en langue française édités entre 1818 et 1983; La bicyclette sous tous ses aspects* (Paris: Fédération Française de Cyclotourisme, Fédération Française de Cyclisme, 1984), 31–34.

84. Labor, one of the major manufacturers at the time, took note of the outcome of the Russo-Japanese War and issued a poster depicting Russian cossacks vainly attempting to catch a Japanese soldier mounted on one of its bicycles. Jean Durry, *Le sport à l'affiche* (Paris: Éditions Hoëbeke, 1988), 14–15.

85. M. Clémentel (a former French minister of war), quoted in Paramé, "Cyclisme militaire: Un rapport," *Nancy-Sportif,* 4 December 1913; René-Félix Le Hérissé, *Le cyclisme militaire* (Paris: Henri Charles-Lavauzelle, Éditeur Militaire, 1897), 46. An official of the French cycling federation claimed that the battles of Forbach and Rezonville in August 1870 would have been resounding French victories if only cyclists had been employed to convey critical information quickly. Garsonnin, *Conférence sur la vélocipédie,* 44.

86. Seray, *Deux roues,* 177; Lieutenant H. Gérard, *Le problème de l'infanterie montée résolu par l'emploi de la bicyclette* (Paris: Librairie Militaire L. Baudoin, 1894), 14. In the early 1900s, General Langlois called for the creation of at least one battalion of cyclists for each cavalry division, two or three being preferable. P. Nudant, *Deux journées de manoeuvres: Infanterie et cyclistes en liaison avec la division de cavalerie* (Paris and Nancy: Berger-Levrault et Cie., Éditeurs, 1907), 33. See also Charles Humbert (deputy from the Meuse and president of the Union Vélocipédique de France), "Que devient la Question Cycliste?" *L'Union Verdunoise,* 23 June 1907.

87. Gérard, *Le problème de l'infanterie,* 91; idem, *L'infanterie cycliste en campagne* (Paris, Nancy: Berger-Levrault et Cie., Libraires-Éditeurs, 1898), 82. See also *Rennes-Vélo,* 1 August 1899; Humbert, "Que devient la Question Cycliste?"

88. Seray, *Deux roues,* 170–72; Renoy, *Le vélo au temps des belles moustaches,* 70;

Hubscher, *L'histoire en mouvements*, 80; Gérard, *Le problème de l'infanterie*, 22–23. For a detailed examination of military cycling in belle époque France, including these debates, see Christopher S. Thompson, "The Third Republic on Wheels: A Social, Cultural, and Political History of Bicycling in France from the Nineteenth Century to World War II" (PhD diss., New York University, 1997), 86–106.

89. Renoy, *Le vélo au temps des belles moustaches*, 70; Le Hérissé, *Le cyclisme militaire*, 12–13. In 1895 Charles Morel became the first cycle manufacturer to commercialize this model. The weight of the Gérard folding bicycle was ultimately reduced from 16.5 to 13.5 kilograms before World War I. Seray, *Deux roues*, 172, 174–75.

90. Seray, *Deux roues*, 174, 175.

91. M. D. Bellencontre, *Hygiène du vélocipède* (Paris: L. Richard, Libraire-Éditeur, 1869), 38.

92. Garsonnin, *Conférence sur la vélocipédie*, 35; Berruyer, *Manuel du véloceman*, 9.

93. The evolving nomenclature for the bicycle and its technological cousins also testifies to the machine's hold on the French public imagination. The original terms for the new machine—*vélocifère, célérifère, vélocipède,* and *véloce*—all referred explicitly to its potential for speed, one of the bicycle's most striking features at a time when most people had not ridden in a train and the car had yet to be invented. Gradually, however, these machines became known by terms that described their mechanical structure: *bicycle, grand bi(cycle), bicyclette, tricycle,* and *quadricycle,* for example. The novelty of the bicycle was beginning to wear off, and, in an era of motorized machines that traveled faster, had been replaced by an increasingly sophisticated appreciation of the structure of each variant. Whether celebrating speed or describing a complicated machine, however, this new vocabulary emphasized the bicycle's modernity.

94. Bellencontre, *Hygiène du vélocipède*, 34–35; Garsonnin, *Conférence sur la vélocipédie*, 39.

95. Berruyer, *Manuel du véloceman*, 72–73.

96. Baudry de Saunier, *L'art de bien monter la bicyclette*, 23, 25. The emphasis is his.

97. Maurice Martin preface to Baudry de Saunier, *L'art de bien monter la bicyclette*, 14; Berruyer, *Manuel du véloceman*, 73. At this time, at least in the provinces, stores often did not specialize in bicycles but sold them along with other recently invented machines—cars, motorcycles, and sewing machines—all of which mechanics were expected to be able to repair. Commercial differentiation occurred later, as consumers became more sophisticated.

98. The Bon Marché department store in Paris issued a series of cards depicting heroic French colonial officers on bicycles confronting crocodiles and hostile natives. Fox bicycles sought to convey the value of its machines with a postcard that showed a French colonial official refusing to exchange his bicycle for a pile of elephant tusks; these were offered by an African eager to acquire the technological

marvel that epitomized the superiority of French civilization over his own. Another postcard was a photograph of a French colonial official showing off "the first bicycle in Haute-Sanga (Cougourta)" to a crowd of curious Africans.

99. Some of the material in this section appeared in Christopher Thompson, "Regeneration, *Dégénérescence,* and Medical Debates about the Bicycle in Fin-de-Siècle France," in Thierry Terret, ed., *Sport and Health in History* (Sankt Augustin, Germany: Academia Verlag, 1999), 339–45.

100. Dumons, Pollet, and Berjat, *Naissance du sport moderne,* 105; Anson Rabinbach, *The Human Motor: Energy, Fatigue and the Origins of Modernity* (New York: Basic Books, 1990), 224.

101. Quoted in Pierre Charreton, *Les fêtes du corps: Histoire et tendances de la littérature à thème sportif en France 1870–1970* (Saint-Étienne: CIEREC—Université de Saint-Étienne, 1985), 39–40.

102. Dr. Philippe Tissié, *L'éducation physique* (Paris: Librairie Larousse, 1901), 19. For an account of Tissié's career, see Hubscher, *L'histoire en mouvements,* 32, 185; Pierre Arnaud, ed., *Le corps en mouvement: Précurseurs et pionniers de l'éducation physique* (Toulouse: Éditions Privat, 1981), part 1, chapter 6.

103. Tissié, *L'éducation physique,* 20.

104. Robert A. Nye, *Crime, Madness, and Politics in Modern France: The Medical Concept of National Decline* (Princeton, NJ: Princeton University Press, 1984), 226, 320–22. See, for example, Émile Zola, "Lettres parisiennes," *La Cloche,* 6 October 1872; Jules Vallès, "Le sport," in *La Rue à Londres* (chapter 21); Jean Richepin, "La statue vivante," *L'Auto-Vélo,* 16 November 1902. They are quoted in Nicole Priollaud, ed., *Le sport à la une* (Paris: Liana Levi, 1984), 23–26, 27, 36.

105. Garsonnin, *Conférence sur la vélocipédie,* 49. Nye, *Crime, Madness, and Politics,* 328–29.

106. To ensure the fitness of its cycling infantrymen, the French army established a selection process that included a ninety-kilometer course to be completed in under six hours (for general staff cyclists) and a forty-eight-kilometer test in under four hours for regimental cyclists. Baudry de Saunier, *Recettes utiles et procédés vélocipédiques,* 143–44.

107. On mobilization drills, see *Rennes-Vélo,* 1 May 1897. A *brevet militaire d'estafette cycliste* advertised in *L'Est Républicain* (Nancy edition), 15–16 August 1912, indicated maximum times of two and a half, five, and nine hours respectively for these three distances, suggesting that for the longest race a slower pace was acceptable. A competition for soldiers and civilians organized by the prominent tire manufacturer Wolber in partnership with *L'Est Républicain* just a few weeks before the outbreak of the war included marksmanship and reconnaissance events as well as cycling and foot races. *L'Est Républicain* (Nancy edition), 12 July 1914. In the years prior to World War I these competitions were extended to include departmental, regional, and national championships. In 1914 the departmental championship events in Ille-et-Vilaine were organized by Wolber, with additional spon-

sorship from the French cycling federation, *Le Petit Parisien, L'Auto,* and several large regional dailies. Departmental Archives of Ille-et-Vilaine, series 4M221 (Manifestations Sportives-Courses Cyclistes 1899–1914, 1925, 1934, 1940).

108. When the Union Cycliste Nancéene did so for the Army's 20th Corps in 1913, the race was followed by a marksmanship event. *L'Est Républicain* (Nancy edition), 4 June 1913.

109. At the end of 1912, 6,100 such clubs received subsidies from the Ministry of War (up from 3,600 in 1909). Although the main curriculum of these associations was composed of gymnastics, marksmanship with rifle or canon, elementary topography, hiking, hygiene, and riding and caring for horses, other skills such as canoeing, swimming, and cycling could be added. *Annuaire 1913: Union des Sociétés de Préparation Militaire de France* (Paris, 1913), 24, 26–28. Some cycling clubs, like the Union Cycliste de Longwy in 1909, wished to be recognized as a *société de préparation militaire* and promised to create a military preparation section. *Le Longovicien,* 28 January 1909. Although patriotism was certainly a motivating factor, the promise of a government subsidy probably also played a part in such decisions.

110. See, for example, Georges Paramé, "À Monsieur Raymond Poincaré, Haut Protecteur du Sport Cycliste," *Nancy-Sportif,* 9 July 1914. The pretext for Paramé's article was the attendance of Poincaré and his minister of war, Adolphe Messimy, at the Grand Prix Cycliste held at the Vincennes track, which Paramé saw as an official recognition of the importance of the sport for French society.

111. Lucas-Championnière, *La bicyclette,* 23–24. French doctors devoted countless articles, lectures, pamphlets, theses, books, and conferences to the subject. Journals addressing the topic included *Revue Scientifique, France Médicale, Lancet, Normandie Médicale, Gazette Médicale, Bulletin Médical,* and *Bulletin de l'Académie de Médecine.* Dr. Eugène Guillemet, *La bicyclette: Ses effets psycho-physiologiques* (Paris: J.-B. Baillière et Fils, Éditeurs, 1897), 111–13. At the 1894 congress of the Association pour l'Avancement des Sciences in Caen, there was an important debate on the medical advantages and disadvantages of the bicycle. Médecin-Major de 1ère classe Salle, *La reine de la route: Éléments de physiologie et notions d'hygiène pratique à l'usage des officiers-cyclistes* (Paris: Henri Charles-Lavauzelle, Éditeur Militaire, 1899), 98. For an exhaustive list of French medical writings on the bicycle and cycling during this period, see Kobayashi, *Pour une bibliographie du cyclisme,* 61–69.

112. Lucas-Championnière, *La bicyclette,* 17–18, 30–31, 34–35; Dr. Charles Lavielle, *Sur une arthrite spéciale du pied avec déformation observée chez les vélocipédistes* (Paris: Gustave Doin, 1891); Salle, *La reine de la route,* 96–97; Bellencontre, *Hygiène du vélocipède,* 24; Guillemet, *La bicyclette,* 55–56, 59, 61; Dr. Élie Mirovitch, *De l'influence de la vélocipédie sur la vision et conseils d'hygiène pour les yeux des vélocipédistes* (Paris: A. Malone, Éditeur, 1897), 3–12; Dr. Ludovic O'Followell, *Bicyclette et organes génitaux* (Paris: Librairies J.-B. Baillière et Fils, 1900), 37–38, 56, 58–59.

113. Salle, *La reine de la route,* 88–91; Lucas-Championnière, *La bicyclette,* 11, 30–32,

34–35, 38; Tissié, *L'éducation physique*, 56; Bellencontre, *Hygiène du vélocipède*, 25, 30; Guillemet, *La bicyclette*, 30, 32, 37, 56, 175; Garsonnin, *Conférence sur la vélocipédie*, 38; Dr. Monin, quoted in Renoy, *Le vélo au temps des belles moustaches*, 57.

114. Salle, *La reine de la route*, 85; Guillemet, *La bicyclette*, 77, 99, 102–4; Dr. Philippe Tissié, *Études sur l'entraînement physique* (Bordeaux: Imprimerie G. Gounouilhou, 1897), 15.

115. Rabinbach, *The Human Motor*, 19, 40, 42–44, 146; John Hoberman, *Mortal Engines: The Science of Performance and the Dehumanization of Sport* (New York: Free Press, 1992), 92–93.

116. Tissié, *Études sur l'entraînement physique*, 1–2, 19; Tissié, *L'éducation physique*, 17; William Schneider, *Quality and Quantity: The Quest for Biological Regeneration in Twentieth-Century France* (Cambridge: Cambridge University Press, 1990), chapter 3; Anne Carol, *L'histoire de l'eugénisme en France: Les médecins et la procréation XIXe–XXe siècle* (Paris: Seuil, 1995).

117. Rabinbach, *The Human Motor*, 7, 146; Tissié, *L'éducation physique*, 18, 107; Tissié, *Études sur l'entraînement physique*, 19; Bouet, *Signification du sport*, 452; Hoberman, *Mortal Engines*, 159, 324.

118. Hoberman, *Mortal Engines*, 5, 9, 13–14.

119. Lucas-Championnière, *La bicyclette*, 9.

120. *L'Auto*, 28 June 1913. Like Lefèvre, Desgrange also noted the Tour's beneficial impact on the cycle industry as French youths, inspired by Tour racers, invested in their own bicycles. The devastation unleashed by four years of trench warfare only reinforced his arguments. In 1934 Desgrange continued to describe sport as a "magnificent school of courage, of willpower, of energy . . . of integrity" and "the foundation of all virtues," for exercise maintained not only one's physical condition, but also one's "moral energies." *L'Auto*, 24 July 1934.

121. Chany, *La fabuleuse histoire du Tour de France*, has greatly facilitated my examination of the race's development.

122. Until 1928 the distances announced by the organizers were rarely those actually covered by the racers, but they were sufficiently accurate to establish the scale of the challenge. For distance and time figures, as well as the statistics relating to the number of racers who started and finished each Tour, see ibid., 793–899; Pierre Chany, *La fabuleuse histoire du cyclisme*, vol. 2, *De 1956 à nos jours* (Paris: Nathan, 1988), 397–410.

123. On the Tour's mountains, see Paul Boury, *La France du Tour: Le Tour de France, un espace sportif à géométrie variable* (Paris: L'Harmattan, 1997), chapter 7.

124. See *L'Équipe, 50 ans de sport, 1946–1995* (Issy-les-Moulineaux: L'Équipe; Paris: diff. Calmann-Lévy, 1995), 15–21; Seidler, *Le sport et la presse*, 123; Bellanger et al., eds., *Histoire générale de la presse française*, vol. 4, 201; Goddet, *L'équipée belle*, 106–7, 120, 146–52; Christophe Penot, *Jean-Marie Leblanc, gardien du Tour de France: Entretiens avec Christophe Penot* (Saint Malo: Éditions Cristel, 1999), 227; Chany, *La fabuleuse histoire du Tour de France*, 785; Reed, "The Tour de France,"

193–97. After 1965, the Groupe Amaury became a "multimedia publicity empire built around a large number of periodicals, several televised sporting events, and the French capital's premier sports and entertainment venues." Reed, "The Tour de France," 271–73. For the reasons behind Lévitan's dismissal, see Chany, *La fabuleuse histoire du Tour de France,* 736–37; Reed, "The Tour de France," 412–13.

125. Reed, "The Tour de France," 66.

126. Ibid., 234–44.

127. *L'Auto,* 1, 4, 20, 21 July 1903. See chapter 4 for more on the financial incentive the Tour represented for racers, almost all of whom came from the lower classes.

128. Ibid., 26 July 1908.

129. Ibid., 8 July 1907, 1 August 1910, 5 May 1920.

130. For a long list of such donations, see ibid., 23 July 1924.

131. Ibid., 1 July 1903.

132. Ibid., 13 July 1908. *La Vie au Grand Air's* fairy statuette had been awarded in 1903 to the cycle manufacturer whose bicycle was ridden by the victor. Starting in 1908, the new prizes were offered to the racers themselves.

133. Ibid., 16 June 1924.

134. Ibid., 16 June 1929. This was not as great an increase over prewar prize money as it might initially seem because of postwar inflation.

135. By the late 1920s, the French bicycle industry no longer enjoyed the dynamic growth of earlier decades, as demand for bicycles was tapering off. Faced with the cost of fielding a team in the Tour—two hundred thousand francs for Alcyon in 1929—cycle manufacturers asked their racers to take pay cuts or withdrew their sponsorship entirely. Reed, "The Tour de France," 140–41, 145, 156–57.

136. Ibid., 144.

137. *L'Auto* also profited from advertisements purchased by sponsors in its pages. In return, the paper regularly publicized and praised their services and products in its race coverage. Ibid., 148–49.

138. *L'Auto, supplément gratuit,* 26 June 1931.

139. The *caravane publicitaire* was of particular value to producers of alcoholic beverages, as it allowed them to gain national exposure while bypassing the legal obstacles the government had created to alcohol-related advertisements in the media. Reed, "The Tour de France," 151.

140. *L'Auto,* 4 July 1935, 22, 10 June 1937.

141. Ibid., 11 July 1936. See chapter 4 for a discussion of the costs incurred by racers participating in the Tour.

142. Ibid., 6 August 1935.

143. On how the city of Pau sought to exploit the Tour to attract new tourists, see Reed, "The Tour de France," 126–36.

144. Ibid., 146–47, 152. Reed calculates that the contributions demanded of host communities in the 1930s typically increased by a factor of between five and twenty-five over those in the 1920s.

145. Seidler, *Le sport et la presse,* 66, 69–70; Bellanger et al., *Histoire générale de la presse française,* vol. 3, 479–80, 584–85; Hubscher, *L'histoire en mouvements,* 506; Calvet, *Le mythe des géants de la route,* 36; Dumons, Pollet, and Berjat, *Naissance du sport moderne,* 134.

146. As a result of this competition, *L'Auto*'s circulation began to slip, even during the Tour. The paper's competitiveness was also damaged by the increased salaries mandated by the June 1936 Matignon agreements under the recently elected Popular Front government. By 1939 its daily circulation had dropped to 164,000 issues, with only 20 percent of that total in the Paris region, and Desgrange and Goddet sold the paper to Patenôtre. Seidler, *Le sport et la presse,* 78, 80–81; Raymond Barrillon, *Le cas Paris-Soir* (Paris: Armand Colin, 1959), 6, 54, 61, 65–67, 74, 268; Raymond Manévy, *Histoire de la presse, 1919–1939* (Paris: Correa, 1945), 250; Bellanger et al., *Histoire générale de la presse française,* vol. 3, 479–80, 524–25; Reed, "The Tour de France," 79, 179, 190, 431. On the other hand, the organizers benefited from increased coverage of the Tour, which made it a more attractive option for sponsors.

147. Jean-François Remont and Simone Depoux, *Les années radio* (Paris: Éditions Gallimard, 1989), 7–9; René Duval, *Histoire de la radio en France* (Paris: Éditions Alain Moreau, 1979), 57, 87–89, 123–26, 158, 169, 268–74, 282–87; Pierre Miquel, *Histoire de la radio et de la télévision* (Paris: Librairie Académique Perrin, 1984), 34–35, 48–49; Roland Dhordain, *Le roman de la radio de la TSF aux radios libres* (Paris: La Table Ronde, 1983), 36; Hubscher, *L'histoire en mouvements,* 518.

148. *L'Auto,* 18 July 1937. For the technological adjustments and innovations implemented by radio stations in their Tour coverage, see Reed, "The Tour de France," 169–73.

149. Duval, *Histoire de la radio en France,* 90; Jean-Paul Ollivier, *Gino Bartali: Gino le pieux* (Paris: Éditions PAC, 1983), 75; Bellanger et al., *Histoire générale de la presse française,* vol. 3, 472–73.

150. Hubscher, *L'histoire en mouvements,* 518.

151. Reed, "The Tour de France," 166–68, 173–75.

152. Marcel Huret, *Ciné Actualités: Histoire de la presse filmée, 1895–1980* (Paris: Henri Veyrier, 1984), 28–30, 33, 36, 50, 54, 56, 63–64, 68, 85–87.

153. On Tour-related films both before and after World War II, see Hubscher, *L'histoire en mouvements,* 500–501; Jean Durry, *L'en-cycle-opédie* (Lausanne: Édition-Denoël, 1982), 313, 323–24, 326–27, 329; Dumons, Pollet, and Berjat, *Naissance du sport moderne,* 96.

154. After the war, the French state became much more involved in ensuring the smooth running of the race. It provided the expertise of the civil engineering corps, gendarmes for security along the itinerary, and an elite military motorcycle squad to accompany the Tour. The Groupe Amaury continued to seek to improve the planning, publicity, and organization of the race by the Société du Tour de France. Reed, "The Tour de France," 204, 247–58, 260–62, 413, 415–19.

155. Yvette Horner, *Du Tour de France à l'opéra musette* (Paris: Éditions Filipacchi, 1987), 100–101; *L'Équipe,* 28–29 June, 15 July 1952; Goddet, *L'équipée belle,* 290–92.

156. Line Renaud (with Danièle de Caumon and Louis Valentin), *Les brumes d'où je viens . . .* (Paris: France Loisirs, 1989), 149–53; Horner, *Du Tour de France à l'opéra musette,* 9–16, 102–7, 109, 112–13, 120.

157. Raymond Marcillac and Christian Quidet, *Sport et télévision* (Paris: Albin Michel, 1963), 150–52; Jacques Mousseau and Christian Brochand, *L'aventure de la télévision des pionniers à aujourd'hui* (Paris: Éditions Fernand Nathan, 1987), 10–11, 15, 27, 29; Miquel, *Histoire de la radio et de la télévision,* 191–93, 195, 197; Raymond Marcillac, *20 ans de télé et d'athlétisme* (Paris: Raoul Solar, 1967), 208.

158. *L'Équipe,* 30 June 1950; Marcillac and Quidet, *Sport et télévision,* 26. In 1958, for example, viewers were treated for the first time to live television coverage of racers climbing the Pyrenees, their descent towards Luchon, and the Mont Ventoux time trial. From 1962 the final thirty kilometers—instead of the final three hundred meters—of each stage were filmed, thanks to smaller cameras and wireless technology that allowed the use of handheld cameras on motorcycles. Mousseau and Brochand, *L'aventure de la télévision,* 75; Hubscher, *L'histoire en mouvements,* 521; Wladimir Andreff and J.-F. Nys, *Le sport et la télévision* (Paris: Dalloz, 1988), 145. See also Reed, "The Tour de France," 218–22.

159. Miquel, *Histoire de la radio et de la télévision,* 194, 197, 271; Mousseau and Brochand, *L'aventure de la télévision,* 33, 37, 39, 41, 54; Huret, *Ciné actualités,* 141–42; Joffre Dumazedier, *Télévision et éducation populaire: Les télé-clubs en France* (Paris: UNESCO, 1955), 17, 43, 48–49, 78, 80–81; Joffre Dumazedier, *Vers une civilisation du loisir?* (Paris: Éditions du Seuil, 1962), 62, 155. In 1957 the expanding possibilities and profits of television coverage resulted in a conflict between the Tour organizers and French television. The latter argued that the public had a right to be kept informed by television about the Tour—a public event granted special access to the national road network—as quickly and completely as it was by radio and the press. The organizers, while recognizing the public's right to be informed, wanted a distinction to be drawn between news coverage and spectacles (such as the Tour), from which the television stations could turn a profit. No agreement was reached; as a result, that year viewers were denied live coverage and instead saw the previous day's racing accompanied by commentary. The dispute was resolved before the 1958 Tour. Mousseau and Brochand, *L'aventure de la télévision,* 66.

160. Reed, "The Tour de France," 222–23. In part boosted by interest in the race, the number of television sets in France increased to four million in 1962 and thirteen million in 1973. By 1986, 93 percent of French homes had at least one television. Miquel, *Histoire de la radio et de la télévision,* 271, 290; Jean Cazeneuve, *Sociologie de la radio-télévision,* 6th ed. (Paris: Presses Universitaires de France, 1986), 50–51, 84. Meanwhile, as Eric Reed notes, radio experienced its "golden age" in the

1950s in France, while television lagged far behind. By 1964 virtually the entire population owned or had access to a radio. Reed, "The Tour de France," 210.

161. Reed, "The Tour de France," 212, 226–30, 268–70.

162. Marchand and Debray, *Pour le Tour de France,* 50.

163. The yellow jersey was sponsored for the first time in 1948 by Les Laines Sofil, which paid the race leader a daily sum (in 1950 the total prize money provided by Sofil was 1,850,000 francs). In 1979 Miko (an ice-cream manufacturer) paid the organizers 650,000 francs for the right to sponsor the yellow jersey. Recently the yellow jersey has been sponsored by the Crédit Lyonnais bank. The green jersey, which is awarded based on a points system for stage finishes and is thus usually worn by a top sprinter, is sponsored by PMU (the off-track betting concern). The "king of the mountains" championship, now sponsored by the Champion supermarket chain, was first sponsored in 1949 by Vittelloise. That year Martini sponsored the overall team competition. Calvet, *Le mythe des géants de la route,* 80, 85n.29; *L'Équipe,* 14 June 1950. On the promotional strategies of Miko and the Crédit Lyonnais, see Reed, "The Tour de France," 274–83.

164. These included the yellow jersey of the overall leader, the green points jersey, the white jersey worn by the racer with the best aggregate position in the other main classifications, team classifications by time and by points, the best mountain climber, the best young racer, the "hot spots" classification based on special sprints during stages, the most combative, most pleasant, most unlucky, and most elegant racers (the last rewarding the "moral as much as the physical elegance" of the individual), the best teammate, and the best breakaway. Calvet, *Le mythe des géants de la route,* 82–83.

165. Chany, *La fabuleuse histoire du Tour de France,* 721; Penot, *Jean-Marie Leblanc,* 238.

166. Reed, "The Tour de France," 392–401.

167. Calvet, *Le mythe des géants de la route,* 80.

168. Boury, *La France du Tour,* 380–81; Robin Magowan, *Tour de France: The Historic 1978 Event,* 2nd ed. (Boulder, CO: Velopress, 1996), 180–81. In recent years, the organizers have limited the number of sponsors and created three categories of sponsorship. Reed, "The Tour de France," 421–24.

169. Chany, *La fabuleuse histoire du Tour de France,* 785; *En attendant le Tour,* France 2, 20 July 1995; Boury, *La France du Tour,* 198–99, 210–11; Andreff and Nys, *Le sport et la télévision,* 39, 145, 147; Jacques Marchand, *La presse sportive* (Paris: Presse et Formation, 1989), 22. The 1998 Tour's revenues have been estimated at 250 million francs, 14 percent of which were derived from the fees paid by host communities, 30 percent from television rights, and 56 percent from commercial sponsorship. Penot, *Jean-Marie Leblanc,* 231–32. This figure, however, must be advanced with caution, as the Groupe Amaury has consistently refused to make public its profits. Like *L'Auto* before the war, *L'Équipe* has benefited from public interest in the race. While its average circulation rapidly stabilized at 200,000 to 240,000, and

although the Parisian and provincial press further developed their sports sections, during the Tour *L'Équipe's* circulation exceeded half and sometimes even three-quarters of a million. Emmanuel Derieux and Jean Texier, *La presse quotidienne française* (Paris: Armand Colin, 1974), 51; Calvet, *Le mythe des géants de la route,* 178; Seidler, *Le sport et la presse,* 101, 119; Dumazedier, *Vers une civilisation de loisir?,* 33, 60; *L'Équipe,* 5 July 1949, 15 July 1953; Marchand, *La presse sportive,* 28–29; Hubscher, *L'histoire en mouvements,* 263.

170. Reed, "The Tour de France," 247; Goddet, *L'équipée belle,* 174, 199.

171. Quoted in Marchand and Debray, *Pour le Tour de France,* 51, 71–72.

172. Goddet, *L'équipée belle,* 290, 291.

173. Penot, *Jean-Marie Leblanc,* 236.

TWO. ITINERARIES, NARRATIVES, AND IDENTITIES

1. Of course, people from various social strata experienced travel in different ways; yet those very differences evolved in large part as elites reacted to encroachment from below of a form of leisure they had until recently monopolized.

2. *L'Auto,* 24 April 1919.

3. *Le Petit Journal,* 11 February, 4 January 1919.

4. *L'Intransigeant,* 28 April 1919.

5. *L'Auto,* 26, 27 April 1919.

6. *Le Petit Journal,* 5 January, 20, 27 March 1919.

7. Philippe Bernard, *La fin d'un monde 1914–1929* (Paris: Éditions du Seuil, 1975), 108–10; François Caron, *Histoire économique de la France XIXe–XXe siècle* (Paris: Armand Colin, 1995), 186–87; Jeremy D. Popkin, *A History of Modern France,* 2nd ed. (Upper Saddle River, NJ: Prentice Hall, 2001), 203.

8. *Le Matin,* 21 April 1919; *L'Intransigeant,* 19 April 1919; Pierre Chany, *La fabuleuse histoire du cyclisme,* vol. 1, *Des origines à 1955* (Paris: Nathan, 1988), 245.

9. *L'Auto,* 19 April 1919.

10. Roger Bastide, *Petit-Breton: La Belle Époque du cyclisme* (Paris: Éditions Denoël, 1985), 266–67; *Le Petit Parisien,* 4 May 1919; *Le Petit Journal,* 3 May 1919; *L'Auto,* 29, 30 April, 3, 4, 5 May 1919; *L'Éclaireur de l'Est,* 17 April, 11 May 1919; *L'Ouest-Éclair,* 3, 5 May 1919.

11. *Le Petit Journal,* 30 April, 2, 5, 12 May 1919.

12. *L'Auto,* 29 April, 2, 3 , 4, 5, 7 May 1919; *Le Petit Journal,* 29 April, 5 May 1919; *L'Éclaireur de l'Est,* 6, 13 May 1919.

13. Bastide, *Petit-Breton,* 266–67.

14. *Le Petit Journal,* 12 May 1919; *L'Auto,* 12 May 1919.

15. The French Revolution abolished guilds, but *compagnonnages* were tolerated well into the nineteenth century.

16. Georges Vigarello, "Le Tour de France," in Pierre Nora, ed., *Les lieux de mémoire,* vol. 3 (Paris: Éditions Gallimard, 1997), 3802, 3807; Bernard Guenée, "Des limites féodales aux frontières politiques," in ibid., vol. 1, 1118; Daniel Nordman, "Des limites d'État aux frontières nationales," in ibid., vol. 1, 1129–31.

17. *L'Auto,* 13 July 1939.

18. *Le tour de la France par deux enfants* had sold three million copies by 1887; six million copies had been printed by 1901. Jacques Ozouf and Mona Ozouf, "*Le tour de la France par deux enfants:* Le petit livre rouge de la République," in Nora, ed., *Les lieux de mémoire,* vol. 1, 277–301; Anne-Marie Thiesse, *Ils apprenaient la France: L'exaltation des régions dans le discours patriotique* (Paris: Éditions de la Maison des Sciences de l'Homme, 1997), 8.

19. Thiesse, *Ils apprenaient la France,* especially 1, 3–9, 16–34, 36–53, 55–63, 85, 87–88, 90–91; Mona Ozouf, *L'école de la France: Essais sur la Révolution, l'utopie et l'enseignement* (Paris: Gallimard, 1984), 187–95. France's "unique" natural and geographical diversity was celebrated by the most prominent contemporary French geographer, Paul Vidal de La Blache. Geographers like Vidal de La Blache emphasized the causal relationship between the natural environment and the behavior, character, and material culture of the people who lived there, thus minimizing the significance of other factors such as history and social arrangements. Vidal de La Blache devoted relatively little attention to urban and industrial France, deploring French industrialization's destructive, "artificial" character. Both Vidal de la Blache and the influential nineteenth-century French historian Jules Michelet argued that France's remarkable diversity led to relationships of reciprocity and solidarity among French people. Traditional images of the French peasant were reinforced by contemporary artists, notably the painter Jean-François Millet. Jean-Yves Guiomar, "Le *Tableau de la géographie de la France* de Vidal de La Blache," in Nora, ed., *Les lieux de mémoire,* vol. 1, 1073, 1075–77, 1081, 1083–85, 1090–92; Eugen Weber, "L'hexagone," in ibid., 1173; Marcel Roncayolo, "Le paysage du savant," in ibid., 1007–8, 1010, 1012–14.

20. Thiesse, *Ils apprenaient la France,* 96–102.

21. Daniel Nordman, "Les Guides-Joanne, Ancêtre des Guides Bleus," in Nora, ed., *Les lieux de mémoire,* vol. 1, 1037, 1040–42, 1046–50, 1056, 1062–63. See also André Rauch, *Vacances en France de 1830 à nos jours* (Paris: Hachette, 1996), 54–59; Catherine Bertho-Lavenir, *La roue et le stylo: Comment nous sommes devenus touristes* (Paris: Éditions Odile Jacob, 1999), 60–62. In 1900 Michelin published its first *Guide Michelin* to France. Designed to facilitate and promote automobile tourism, these guides, like the *Guides-Joanne,* included detailed itineraries and maps. Stephen L. Harp, *Marketing Michelin: Advertising and Cultural Identity in Twentieth-Century France* (Baltimore, MD: Johns Hopkins University Press, 2001), chapter 2.

22. *L'Auto,* 5 June 1907, 1 June 1908, 2 July 1905.

23. Ibid., 1 June 1908, 10 June 1904, 5, 6, 15, 16, 17, 19, 29 June 1920.

24. *L'Auto* was perhaps sensitive about this perception because it was occasionally accused of favoring Parisian racers and neglecting provincial racers in its race coverage. See *Le Petit Calaisien*'s accusations about the unfair treatment of the northern racer Félix Goethals by *L'Auto*'s journalists in *L'Auto*, 16 July 1921. The concept of a France divided between Paris and the provinces goes back to the ancien régime and was reinforced by the centralizing, "Jacobin" tendencies of French republicanism. See Alain Corbin, "Paris-Province," in Nora, ed., *Les lieux de mémoire*, vol. 2, 2851–88; Maurice Agulhon, "Le centre et la périphérie," in ibid., 2889–2906.

25. *L'Auto*, 16 May 1903, 23 May 1904.

26. Ibid., 12 July 1921, 2 July 1904; see also ibid., 29 June 1920.

27. *L'Est Républicain* (Nancy), 12 July 1911.

28. *L'Auto*, 30 June 1912.

29. Ibid., 5 June 1920.

30. See the initiatives of *L'Éclaireur de Nice*, *Le Petit Niçois*, *L'Éclaireur de l'Est*, *La Dépêche Dauphinoise*, and *La République du Var*. *L'Auto*, 1, 18 June 1920, 14 June 1921, 13, 30 June, 7 July 1922, 15 June 1926.

31. See, for example, *L'Auto*, 18 June 1928. The regions were Alsace-Lorraine, Champagne, Normandy, Upper Brittany, the Southeast, Île-de-France, the North, the Midi, and the Côte d'Azur. Ibid., 12 July 1921, 12 July 1926, 8, 13, 21 May 1928.

32. The regional teams in 1930 were the North, Normandy, the Midi, Provence, the Riviera, the Southeast, Alsace-Lorraine, Champagne, and Île-de-France; in 1939, North/East/Île-de-France, the West, the Southwest, and the Southeast. Pierre Chany, *La fabuleuse histoire du Tour de France* (Paris: Nathan, 1991), 812, 824.

33. *L'Auto*, 3 July 1938, 6 April 1935, 30 March 1936, 10, 11, 12 May 1937. Qualifying competitions were sponsored by a radio station and by La Suze, Dubonnet, and Pernod.

34. For the role of reading—particularly novels and newspapers—in the creation of a sense of shared nationhood, see Benedict Anderson, *Imagined Communities* (London: Verso, 1991), 24–46.

35. See, for example, *L'Auto*, 29 July 1907, 30 July 1908, 26 July 1909, 16 July 1910, 30 June 1912, 7 July 1914, 10 July 1926, 29 June 1927.

36. Ibid., 1 July 1927.

37. Ibid., 7 July 1927.

38. See, for example, its descriptions of crowds in La Rochelle and Paris in ibid., 26 June 1904 and 6 July 1909, respectively.

39. Ibid., 25 July 1930. For the example of Châteaubriant in 1932, see ibid., 8 July 1932.

40. Ibid., 13 July 1932.

41. Jean Durry, *L'en-cycle-opédie* (Lausanne: Édition-Denoël, 1982), 317. Tour-related songs, including the official selections, were often composed and performed by well-known singers, bands, and music-hall stars of the day. See the brochure ac-

companying the compact disc *Le vélo en chansons, 1927–1950* (Compacts Radio France).

42. "Les Champions de la Route" (1934). Among the other songs were "Ah! Les Voilà!" (1936), "A Qui le Tour?" (1937), and "On Tourne autour du Tour" (1938).

43. "Ah! Les Voilà!" (1936).

44. "Les Tours de France" (1927).

45. Workers were often given several hours off, if not the entire day, to watch the Tour racers go through their town. *L'Auto,* 1 July 1914, 24 July 1929, 25 July 1930, 26 July 1932, 24 June 1933; *Le Nouvelliste de Bretagne, Maine, Normandie, Anjou,* 9 July 1939.

46. *L'Auto,* 7 July 1906. The Dreyfus affair had since the late 1890s divided France between those, primarily on the Left, who believed the army had framed the Jewish officer Alfred Dreyfus, and those, primarily on the Right (conservatives, nationalists, Catholics, and anti-Semites), who defended the army.

47. *L'Auto,* 17 July 1927.

48. Ibid., 26 July 1908, 8 July 1932, 27 June 1933. The organizers often noted the support the race and cycling in general received from priests. Ibid., 24, 28 July 1908.

49. Ibid., 5 August 1908.

50. Ibid., 27 June 1933, 8 July 1907. Others also reported the diversity of the Tour's crowds and the unifying function of the race. *L'Est Républicain* (Nancy), 24 July 1913.

51. *L'Auto,* 27 June 1933.

52. Ibid., 4 July 1903, 8 July 1907, 5 July 1909, 17 May 1910, 20 May 1913, 19 May 1914, 14, 16 July 1920, 26 June 1922, 21 June 1925 *(supplément gratuit),* 18 May 1926. Other papers provided such information: see *L'Humanité,* 9 July 1914.

53. Nordman, "Les Guides-Joanne," 1051, 1054, 1055; Rauch, *Vacances en France,* 59.

54. For examples of such initiatives, see *L'Auto,* 2 July 1910, 26 June 1913, 21 June 1922, 4, 10 July 1933, 12 January, 3, 13 June 1934, 22, 30 June 1937, 20 June 1938. Although geography was a required course in French primary schools from 1867, students were initially more likely to be exposed to maps of specific regions than to maps of the entire country: *Le tour de la France par deux enfants,* for example, did not include a map of the nation until the 1905 edition. Weber, "L'hexagone," 1179–80.

55. *L'Auto,* 24 June 1923, 2 July 1927, 5 July 1932.

56. Ibid., 4, 8 July 1924, 20 June 1928, 5, 26, 30 July 1934.

57. Ibid., 22 June 1928.

58. Ibid., 5 August 1923.

59. Ibid., 11 July 1922, 4 June 1928.

60. Ibid., 21 July 1934.

61. For information about this initiative and the published essays, see ibid., 15 April 1935; 25 May 1935; 1, 3, 4, 5, 6, 7, 13, 16, 19, 20, 21, 22, 23, 24, 25, 27 July, 1 August 1935. See also ibid., 4 May 1938.

62. Ibid., 8 March 1938.

63. Ibid., 15 July 1903. For similar descriptions of Arles, Toulouse, and Quimperle (Brittany), see, respectively, ibid., 9 July 1903 (2nd ed.), 18 July 1904, 25 July 1906. On the writing style adopted by tourist and travel literature under the Third Republic, see Bertho-Lavenir, *La roue et le stylo,* especially 51–58, 114–21.

64. See, for example, *L'Auto*'s photographs from June through early August 1907. In the weeks preceding the race, *L'Auto* also published photographs of the French countryside and towns on the itinerary. See, for example, *L'Auto,* 22 May 1909, 18, 25 May, 5, 18 June 1910, 22 May 1919. For the explosion of photographic illustrations in tourism publications of the period, which intentionally emphasized an "eternal" rural France, see Bertho-Lavenir, *La roue et le stylo,* 263–86.

65. *L'Auto,* 12 June 1920, 5 July 1903. See also ibid., 24 June 1903, 28 June 1924, 21 June 1927.

66. The racers did in fact occasionally indulge in local tourism, as when they toured Toulouse during a rest day in 1908. Ibid., 29 July 1908.

67. For details of such initiatives, see ibid., 10 July 1922, 6 July 1924, 13 July 1926, 4 June 1931, 15 June 1933, 19 July 1935, 28 June 1936. Meanwhile, also determined to celebrate France's cultural and gastronomic diversity and promote tourism, Michelin launched its first regional guidebooks in the mid-1920s (Harp, *Marketing Michelin,* 256–64).

68. *L'Auto,* 10 July 1935.

69. Ibid., 24 July 1929, 8 July 1928, 29 July 1932.

70. A. J. P. Taylor, *The Struggle for Mastery in Europe, 1848–1918* (Oxford: Oxford University Press, 1954), 217; Popkin, *A History of Modern France,* 136.

71. Jean-Marie Mayeur, "Une mémoire-frontière: L'Alsace," in Nora, ed., *Les lieux de mémoire,* vol. 1, 1163. The duchy of Lorraine, located within the Holy Roman Empire, fell partially under French control beginning in the late thirteenth century. It was returned to its dukes in 1697 before being turned over to the dispossessed king of Poland in 1737 and, on his death in 1766, to France. In 1815, as part of the second Peace of Paris, Prussia annexed portions of the province. Alsace was a territory of the Holy Roman Empire for eight centuries; during this period it was divided into numerous smaller political units, which were gradually incorporated into the French kingdom under Louis XIV in the seventeenth century. Dan P. Silverman, *Reluctant Union: Alsace-Lorraine and Imperial Germany, 1871–1918* (University Park: Pennsylvania State University Press, 1972), 2, 7–10; Stephen L. Harp, *Learning to Be Loyal: Primary Schooling as Nation Building in Alsace and Lorraine, 1850–1940* (DeKalb: Northern Illinois University Press, 1998), 10–12.

72. Robert Gildea, *The Past in French History* (New Haven, CT: Yale University Press, 1994), 194; Christian Félix, *Alsace-Lorraine et Union sacrée* (Lyon: Horvath, 1991), 66–67, 80, 86–91, 154–56; Mayeur, "Une mémoire-frontière: L'Alsace," 1151, 1163–64; Popkin, *A History of Modern France,* 156, 157, 163; Mona Siegel, " 'History Is the Opposite of Forgetting': The Limits of Memory and the Lessons of History

in Interwar France," *Journal of Modern History* 74 (December 2002): 777–78; Ozouf, *L'école de la France*, 195, 207–10, 214–30; Nordman, "Les Guides-Joanne," 1059, 1061, 1064, 1066–67; Ariane Chebel d'Appollonia, *L'extrême-droite en France de Maurras à Le Pen* (Brussels: Éditions Complexe, 1988), 45–46, 49, 53–54; Nordman, "Des limites d'État aux frontières nationales," 1127–29, 1138, 1139, 1141, 1142; Guiomar, "Le *Tableau de la géographie de la France* de Vidal de La Blache," 1075; Weber, "L'hexagone," 1175.

73. *L'Auto*, 7 July 1906, 14 July 1908, 8 July 1910; Vigarello, "The Tour de France," 3810. The Tour's passage through Alsace-Lorraine coincided with what Eugen Weber has described as a "nationalist revival" in France in the decade preceding the outbreak of war. Eugen Weber, *The Nationalist Revival in France, 1905–1914* (Berkeley: University of California Press, 1959). *L'Auto* also commemorated rare instances of successful French resistance in 1870, notably that of Belfort. *L'Auto*, 14 July 1907, 19 July 1914.

74. *L'Auto*, 17 July 1910, 29 July 1932, 10 July 1907, 8 July 1910. On the German policies designed to integrate Alsace-Lorraine into the Reich, see Silverman, *Reluctant Union*, especially chapters 3–5, 7–8; Harp, *Learning to Be Loyal*, especially chapters 2–7.

75. *L'Auto*, 21 May, 16 July 1908, 2 July 1911, 1 July 1912.

76. Ibid., 5 August 1914, 30 June 1919.

77. Ibid., 28 June, 21 July 1919. Other commentators agreed. *L'Ouest-Éclair*, 28 June 1919; *Le Matin*, 28 July 1919. Meanwhile, *L'Auto* and *L'Éclaireur de l'Est* paid their respects to French champion racers killed in the war. *L'Auto*, 23 June 1919; *L'Éclaireur de l'Est*, 29 June 1919.

78. *L'Auto*, 28 June 1919. *L'Éclaireur de l'Est* embraced the symbolic reconquest effected by the Tour with equal enthusiasm, referring to "the stage of the invaded regions." *L'Éclaireur de l'Est*, 25 July 1919.

79. *L'Auto*, 23, 26, 20 July 1919.

80. Ibid., 24 July 1919; Eric S. Reed, "The Tour de France: A Cultural and Commercial History" (PhD diss., Syracuse University, 2001), 115. Complementing and in fact predating *L'Auto*'s patriotic use of the Tour's itinerary to commemorate the heroism of French soldiers on the Western Front, Michelin produced its own guides to World War I battlefields even before the end of the war. See Harp, *Marketing Michelin*, chapter 3.

81. *L'Auto*, 22 July 1919, 19 July 1921, 18 July 1923, 23 June 1926, 12, 13, 14 July 1928. The race offered additional evidence of the reintegration of Alsace-Lorraine into the national community, such as French-speaking Alsatian spectators and Tour participants from the two provinces (ibid., 18 July 1924, 19 June 1921).

82. Antoine Prost, "Les monuments aux morts: Culte républicain? Culte civique? Culte patriotique?" in Nora, ed., *Les lieux de mémoire*, vol. 1, 199–223; Daniel J. Sherman, "Art, Commerce, and the Production of Memory in France after World War I," in *Commemoration: The Politics of National Identity*, ed. John R. Gillis

(Princeton, NJ: Princeton University Press, 1994), especially 186–92, 199–207; Siegel, " 'History Is the Opposite of Forgetting,'" 785, 787, 788; Annette Becker, *Les monuments aux morts: Patrimoine et mémoire de la Grande Guerre* (Paris: Éditions Errance, 1988), 9, 12, 21. On the debate in the French educational establishment about sustaining and shaping the collective memory of the war in future generations, see Siegel, " 'History Is the Opposite of Forgetting,'" especially 780–82, 789–98.

83. *L'Auto,* 14 June, 14 July 1928.

84. Reed, "The Tour de France," 111–22.

85. Jack E. Reece, *The Bretons against France: Ethnic Minority Nationalism in Twentieth-Century Brittany* (Chapel Hill: University of North Carolina Press, 1977), 14–18; Commission "Histoire" de Skol Vreizh, *Toute l'histoire de Bretagne des origines à la fin du XXe siècle* (Morlaix: Skol Vreizh, 1997), 402–7, 411–23; Commission "Histoire" de Skol Vreizh, *Histoire de la Bretagne et des pays celtiques de 1789 à 1914* (Morlaix: Skol Vreizh, 1980), 216; Michel Raspaud, "Stade Rennais: Standard-Bearer of Breton Identity," in *Sport in the Making of Celtic Cultures,* ed. Grant Jarvie (London: Leicester University Press, 1999), 73.

86. Jean Delumeau, ed., *Histoire de la Bretagne* (Toulouse: Privat Éditeur, 1969), 465, 468–70, 479; Commission "Histoire" de Skol Vreizh, *Histoire de la Bretagne et des pays celtiques de 1789 à 1914,* 110–11, 114; Michel Nicolas, *Le séparatisme en Bretagne* (Brasparts: Éditions Beltan, 1986), 11, 315; Reece, *The Bretons against France,* 44–49; Alain Déniel, *Le mouvement breton, 1919–1945* (Paris: François Maspéro, 1976), 35, 39, 41–43, 46–47, 123, 131, 133; Yannick Guin, *Histoire de la Bretagne: Contribution à la critique de l'idéologie nationaliste* (Paris: François Maspéro, 1982), 204–6; Michel Lagrée, "Brittany, between Ireland, Scotland and France," in Jarvie, *Sport in the Making of Celtic Cultures,* 47; Marie-José Drogou and Raymond Humbert, *La Bretagne: Mémoire de la vie quotidienne* (Paris: Temps Actuels, 1981), 39–40. On the battle over Breton since the French Revolution, see also Maryon McDonald, *We Are Not French: Language, Culture, and Identity in Brittany* (London: Routledge, 1989), chapters 1–3; Reece, *The Bretons against France,* 31–34.

87. Gildea, *The Past in French History,* 200–202; Commission "Histoire" de Skol Vreizh, *Histoire de la Bretagne et des pays celtiques de 1789 à 1914,* 266–69; Nicolas, *Le séparatisme en Bretagne,* 19–21, 315; Déniel, *Le mouvement breton,* 9, 21, 23, 29; Reece, *The Bretons against France,* 5–22, and chapter 3.

88. Delumeau, *Histoire de la Bretagne,* 490; Gildea, *The Past in French History,* 202–3; Louis Doucet, *Pays et gens de Bretagne* (Paris: Librairie Larousse, 1982), 10; Nicolas, *Le séparatisme en Bretagne,* 22–23, 313–14; Déniel, *Le mouvement breton,* 134, 153, 216; Commission "Histoire" de Skol Vreizh, *Histoire de la Bretagne et des pays celtiques de 1914 à nos jours* (Morlaix: Skol Vreizh, 1983), 117–18; Lagrée, "Brittany, between Ireland, Scotland and France," 43, 45–49; Philip Dine, "Sporting Assimilation and Cultural Confusion in Brittany," in Jarvie, *Sport in the Making of Celtic Cultures,* 117–19, 121–23; Commission "Histoire" de Skol Vreizh, *Histoire de*

la Bretagne et des pays celtiques de 1789 à 1914, 160–62. On interwar Breton autonomism and nationalism, see Reece, *The Bretons against France,* chapters 4–6.

89. Georges Cadiou, *Les grandes heures du cyclisme breton* (Rennes: Ouest-France, 1981), 12, 22, 26–28, 38, 40–45, 48, 204, 207, 212; Georges Pagnoud, *Ces Bretons qui passionnent le cyclisme français* (Paris: Solar Éditeur, 1974), 26, 40–42, 45; Jean-Paul Ollivier, *L'histoire du cyclisme breton* (Paris: Éditions Jean Picollec, 1981), 7, 23, 236; Lagrée, "Brittany, between Ireland, Scotland and France," 41, 51–52; Dine, "Sporting Assimilation and Cultural Confusion in Brittany," 126–27; Jean Boully, *Les stars du Tour de France* (Paris: Bordas, 1990), 185, 193.

90. Dine, "Sporting Assimilation and Cultural Confusion in Brittany," 127; *L'Ouest-Éclair,* 5, 8, 9, 10, 13 July 1935; *La Bretagne Sportive,* 13 August 1936; Reed, "The Tour de France," 107–9. Reed notes that Breton racers like Le Grévès, who moved to Paris and signed with national brands, were sometimes rejected by the local press as no longer true Bretons.

91. For Brest's experience as a host community during this period, see Reed, "The Tour de France," 104–11.

92. *La Province,* 26 July 1933, 7 July 1937.

93. *La Bretagne Sportive,* 11 October 1935.

94. Ibid., 29 April, 16 July 1936. See also ibid., 9 July 1936.

95. Ibid., 25 June, 9 July, 29 April, 6 August 1936, 22 July 1937. Local papers emphasized the large, excited crowds at the Rennes finish line and the support of local elites in organizing the Tour's visit to the city. *Le Nouvelliste* (Rennes), 22 July 1933; *L'Ouest-Éclair,* 21, 22 July 1933, 12 July 1939; *La Bretagne Sportive,* 22 July 1937; *Le Nouvelliste de Bretagne,* 23 July 1937; *Le Nouvelliste de Bretagne, Maine, Normandie, Anjou,* 23 July 1937, 12, 13 July 1939. In fact, Rennes made a mediocre impression on the organizers: in 1933 the security and crowd control provided by the municipal government were apparently less than satisfactory, and in 1937 the uncooperative attitude of local hotel owners almost cost the city its stage. *La Bretagne Sportive,* 10, 17 June, 15, 29 July 1937; *Le Nouvelliste de Bretagne, Maine, Normandie, Anjou,* 24 July 1937; *Les Nouvelles de l'Ouest,* 23 July 1937. On the other hand, when the Tour passed through Rennes without stopping, the press reported the "icy welcome" it received. *L'Ouest-Éclair,* 29 July 1934, 28 July 1935.

96. *La Bretagne Sportive,* 11 October 1935, 9 July 1936. In 1934 Breton autonomists reportedly made a threat against the Tour. *L'Ouest-Éclair,* 29 July 1934.

97. *La Bretagne Sportive,* 9, 23 July 1936.

98. *Les Nouvelles Rennaises et de l'Ouest,* 27 July 1933; *L'Ouest-Éclair,* 29 July 1934; *La Province,* 5, 26 July 1933, 7, 28 July 1937, 22 July 1939; *Les Nouvelles de L'Ouest,* 11 January, 26 June, 9, 23, 30 July 1937; *La Bretagne Sportive,* 10, 19 October 1935, 29 April, 25 June, 2, 9, 16 July 1936.

99. The sensitivity of the Breton press may have been stoked by a recent conflict between the Stade Rennais, the top soccer team in Brittany, and the French soccer federation, which, like *L'Auto,* was a powerful, Paris-based sports institution seem-

ingly intent on controlling Breton participation in the nation's sporting life. Raspaud, "Stade Rennais," 74.

100. See, for example, *L'Humanité*, 21, 29 July 1935.

101. Ibid., 15, 17, 27, 29 July 1935.

102. Ibid., 20 July 1935.

103. Jean Touchard, *La gauche en France depuis 1900* (Paris: Éditions du Seuil, 1977), 197, 200–203; Stéphane Courtois and Marc Lazar, *Histoire du Parti Communiste Français* (Paris: Presses Universitaires de France, 1995), 99–111, 117–27; Serge Berstein, *La France des années 30* (Paris: Armand Colin, 1988), 48–49.

104. See, in particular, Robert O. Paxton, *Vichy France: Old Guard and New Order, 1940–1944* (New York: Columbia University Press, 1972).

105. Reed, "The Tour de France," 182–87. On the sports policy of the Vichy regime, see Ronald Hubscher, ed., *L'histoire en mouvements: Le sport dans la société française (XIXe–XXe siècle)* (Paris: Armand Colin, 1992), 188–98; Jean-Louis Gay-Lescot, "La politique sportive de Vichy," in Jean-Pierre Rioux, ed., *La vie culturelle sous Vichy* (Brussels: Éditions Complexe, 1990), 83–115.

106. Reed, "The Tour de France," 187–88; Jacques Goddet, *L'équipée belle* (Paris: Éditions Robert Laffont, SA, et Stock, 1991), 119–23. The efforts of *L'Auto* and Goddet to protect French sport from exploitation and manipulation by the Germans and Vichy are detailed in "Rapport sur *L'Auto:* Sa constitution, son activité, son rôle durant les cinq dernières années (1939–1944)," which *L'Auto* produced at the liberation in an unsuccessful attempt to avoid being banned for publishing during the occupation. I am grateful to Serge Laget for providing me with a copy of this unpublished document.

107. Reed, "The Tour de France," 188–90; Goddet, *L'équipée belle*, 129–30; "Rapport sur *L'Auto*," 23–25.

108. The organizers made a point of thanking the German authorities for doing all they could to facilitate the organization of the race. *La France Socialiste*, 6 October 1942.

109. Ibid., 3–4, 5, 6 October, 28 September 1942.

110. Ibid., 12–13, 28 September 1942.

111. Ibid., 21, 25 September 1942. The racers were lodged in a school in Poitiers and a seminary in Le Mans. Ibid., 30 September, 1 October 1942.

112. Ibid., 28 September, 6 October 1942.

113. Ibid., 30 September 1942; Goddet, *L'équipée belle*, 131; Reed, "The Tour de France," 190–92; "Rapport sur *L'Auto*," 26–27. For Laval's enthusiastic support for expanding the race in the future, see *La France Socialiste*, 3–4, 5, 6 October 1942.

114. Reed, "The Tour de France," 192–93; Goddet, *L'équipée belle*, 131.

115. Reed, "The Tour de France," 195–99; Goddet, *L'équipée belle*, 143–51; *L'Équipe*, 17 June, 10, 22, 25 July 1946. For the struggle over the rights to the Tour, see *L'Équipe*, 16 December 1946, 6, 23, 27, 28 January, 6, 7 February, 24, 25 April, 2 May, 5 June 1947.

116. Popkin, *A History of Modern France,* 251.

117. *L'Équipe,* 6–7 April, 17 June 1946.

118. *Le Figaro,* 25 June, 22, 23 July 1947; *Le Populaire,* 25 June 1947; Chany, *La fabuleuse histoire du Tour de France,* 347. The press reported that the race's popularity in 1947 matched and even exceeded that of prewar Tours. *Le Parisien Libéré,* 26 June 1947; *La Croix,* 20–21 July 1947; *Le Figaro,* 26 June, 20–21, 22 July 1947; *Le Populaire,* 25, 26 June, 2, 22 July 1947.

119. Quoted in Noël Couëdel, *Tour de France: La fête de juillet* (Paris: Calmann-Lévy, 1983), 22.

120. *L'Équipe,* 25 June 1947.

121. Ibid., 21 July 1947.

122. France 3, "Le Tour de France: Son histoire, notre histoire," *Témoins sports,* 20 July 1986.

123. *Le Populaire,* 9 July 1947.

124. Quoted in Chany, *La fabuleuse histoire du Tour de France,* 347.

125. *Le Monde,* 24 June 1947; *Le Populaire,* 25 June 1947.

126. *Le Parisien Libéré,* 25, 19 June 1947.

127. *Le Figaro,* 20–21 July 1947; *Le Populaire,* 25 June, 22 July 1947; *La Croix,* 20–21 July 1947; *Liberté de Normandie,* 25 June 1947.

128. *Le Parisien Libéré,* 19, 21 June 1947; *L'Équipe,* 26 June 1947.

129. Popkin, *A History of Modern France,* 250; Jean-Pierre Rioux, *La France sous la Quatrième République,* vol. 1, *L'ardeur et la nécessité, 1944–1952* (Paris: Éditions du Seuil, 1980), 33–36; Caron, *Histoire économique de la France,* 204.

130. Rioux, *La France de la Quatrième République,* 33n.1; Gabriel Désert, ed., *La Normandie de 1900 à nos jours* (Toulouse: Privat, 1978), 309–17.

131. Rioux, *La France de la Quatrième République,* 33n.1; Désert, *La Normandie de 1900 à nos jours,* 312–13, 315.

132. Caen Municipal Council minutes, 4 January 1946, 10–11. The mayor's outrage was perhaps exacerbated by the city council's acrimonious negotiations with the provisional government to obtain the necessary funds to address the crisis. The tone of the Parisian press in turn was perhaps informed by leaks from the office of the minister of reconstruction, who was clearly frustrated by his dealings with the city council. See the correspondence between the two parties in the minutes, 15–28. On postwar recovery and reconstruction efforts in Normandy, see Désert, *La Normandie de 1900 à nos jours,* 318–48.

133. Caen Municipal Council minutes, 28 February 1946, 124.

134. Ibid., 24 March 1947, 148–53.

135. *Journal National,* 24 July 1947.

136. *L'Équipe,* 9 June, 20 July 1947.

137. *Liberté de Normandie,* 19, 10, 11 July 1947; *Ouest-France,* 21 July 1947.

138. See, for example, *France-Soir* and *Combat,* 20–21, 22 July 1947.

139. *Le Centre Républicain,* 5, 20 December 1951, 16 January 1952; *Le Patriote*

(Valmy), 22 December 1951. For the negotiations between the Tour organizers and the various interested parties in Vichy, see *La Tribune,* 23 November 1951.

140. Chany, *La fabuleuse histoire du Tour de France,* 831.

141. Rauch, *Vacances en France,* 15–16. Medicinal bathing at the seaside developed in France during the last third of the eighteenth century. André Rauch, *Vacances et pratiques corporelles* (Paris: Presses Universitaires de France, 1988), 13–62. On baths and curing under the ancien régime in France, see Douglas Peter MacKaman, *Leisure Settings: Bourgeois Culture, Medicine, and the Spa in Modern France* (Chicago: University of Chicago Press, 1998), chapter 1.

142. MacKaman, *Leisure Settings,* 4–5, 44, 48, 53–55, 121, 122, 138–39; Michèle Cointet, *Vichy Capitale, 1940–1944* (Paris: Librairie Académique Perrin, 1993), 22, 24–25.

143. Rauch, *Vacances en France,* 29–32, 34–38; MacKaman, *Leisure Settings,* 129–31; Adam Nossiter, *The Algeria Hotel: France, Memory, and the Second World War* (Boston: Houghton Mifflin Company, 2001), 122.

144. Nossiter, *The Algeria Hotel,* 121; MacKaman, *Leisure Settings,* 65. For the employment and profits generated by the thermal-spa industry at the turn of the century nationwide, see MacKaman, *Leisure Settings,* 66.

145. Rauch, *Vacances en France,* 18–19. According to MacKaman, during the nineteenth century, "spas helped France's emerging bourgeoisie create and refine an acceptable practice of leisure and pleasure on vacation" largely inspired by aristocratic practices, such as "visiting, promenading, dancing, reading, and the annual pleasures of the social season." *Leisure Settings,* 2, 5.

146. MacKaman, *Leisure Settings,* 6, 51–52; Nossiter, *The Algeria Hotel,* 102, 121.

147. *L'Industrie Hôtelière du Bourbonnais* 26 (December 1949), 35 (September 1950), 44 (June 1951). On the difficulties of the region's tourism industry and its response, see *Auvergne, Bourbonnais, Velay (Organe de Liaison de la Fédération des Syndicats d'Initiatives et Offices du Tourisme),* 1er trimestre 1951, and 3 (April 1952).

148. As part of the budget for the city's 1951 summer season—its *Fêtes de saison*—the council awarded a three-hundred-thousand-franc subvention to the organizers of a "Tour" for cyclotourists that paused overnight in Vichy in early June. It involved a variety of spectacles, included French radio stars, and was expected to attract more than seven hundred participants who would need hotel rooms. Vichy Municipal Council minutes, 24 November 1950; Vichy Commission des sports, minutes, 9 October 1951; *La Montagne,* 20 October 1951. For criticism of Vichy's inclusion in this event, see *Le Patriote* (Valmy), 24 October 1951.

149. *L'Industrie Hôtelière du Bourbonnais* 48 (October 1951).

150. Ibid. 47 (September 1951); *L'Aurore du Bourbonnais,* 14 October 1951, 20 January 1952.

151. Vichy Municipal Council minutes, 26 November 1951, 29 February, 31 March 1952.

152. *Vichy-Cannes: Plages et Villes d'Eaux* 28 (December 1951); *Tourisme: Plages et Villes d'Eaux* 32 (April 1952).

153. The city spent the spring and early summer making the necessary arrangements. *Tourisme: Plages et Villes d'Eaux* 29 (January 1952), 30 (February 1952); Vichy Municipal Archives, Commission Municipale des Travaux, minutes, 11 June 1952. Preparations for the Tour's visit were widely covered by local newspapers, including *La Montagne, La Liberté du Massif Central, La Tribune, Espoir,* and *Le Patriote* (Valmy).

154. *L'Industrie Hôtelière du Massif Central* 52 (February 1952); *Tourisme: Plages et Villes d'Eaux* 29 (January 1952), 30 (February 1952); *L'Aurore du Bourbonnais,* 2 December 1951; *La Tribune,* 23 November 1951; *La Liberté du Massif Central,* 10 November 1951; *La Liberté du Massif Central,* 26 January 1952. According to *Vichy-Cannes: Plages et Villes d'Eaux* 27 (October–November 1951), the Tour's passage in Clermont-Ferrand, another hydropathic center, had attracted large crowds and been "the great event of the 1951 season."

155. *Tourisme: Plages et Villes d'Eaux* 29 (January 1952), 30 (February 1952). Another local paper noted that some had initially mocked the "fanciful" itinerary of the 1952 Tour, but the article did not explain why. *Le Patriote* (Valmy), 18 July 1952.

156. *La Liberté du Massif Central,* 19 July 1952; *La Montagne,* 19–20 July 1952; *Tourisme: Plages et Villes d'Eaux* 36 (August 1952).

157. *La Liberté du Massif Central,* 18, 21 July 1952; *La Montagne,* 19–20 July 1952; *Le Patriote* (Valmy), 20 July 1952.

158. *Le Patriote* (Valmy), 18 July 1952; *La Montagne,* 19–20 July 1952; *Tourisme: Plages et Villes d'Eaux* 36 (August 1952).

159. *Tourisme: Plages et Villes d'Eaux* 29 (January 1952).

160. *Le Patriote* (Valmy), 15 March, 22 July 1952. See also *Le Bourbonnais républicain* (Moulins), 20 July 1952.

161. *Journal de Vichy: Journal des Baigneurs,* 20–21 July 1952.

162. *La Croix,* 20–21 July 1952.

163. *Le Monde,* 20 July 1952; *Le Populaire,* 15 January, 19–20, 21 July 1952; *La Croix,* 19, 20–21, 22 July 1952; *L'Humanité,* 19, 21, 22 July 1952; *Le Parisien Libéré,* 18, 19–20, 21 July 1952.

164. See, in particular, Henry Rousso, *The Vichy Syndrome: History and Memory in France since 1944,* trans. Arthur Goldhammer (Cambridge, MA: Harvard University Press, 1991). See also Eric Conan and Henry Rousso, *Vichy: An Ever-Present Past,* translated and annotated by Nathan Bracher (Hanover, NH: University Press of New England, 1998); Henry Rousso, *Vichy: L'évènement, la mémoire, l'histoire* (Paris: Gallimard, 2001).

165. Rousso, *The Vichy Syndrome,* 7, 18–20.

166. Nossiter, *The Algeria Hotel,* 109–11.

167. Cointet, *Vichy capitale,* 19, 26, 167–69; Nossiter, *The Algeria Hotel,* 103, 105, 114, 129–30, 135, 209.

168. Cointet, *Vichy capitale,* 100–109; Nossiter, *The Algeria Hotel,* 113, 114.

169. Cointet, *Vichy capitale,* 94–96, 98, 100.

170. Nossiter, *The Algeria Hotel,* 139–40; Cointet, *Vichy capitale,* 256, 259, 263, 264.

171. Cointet, *Vichy capitale,* 110–12, 140–54.

172. Nossiter, *The Algeria Hotel,* 106, 112, 114, 117, 182, 184, 194, 195–96.

173. Rousso, *The Vichy Syndrome,* 28–59. For the case of Oradour-sur-Glane, see also Sarah Farmer, *Martyred Village: Commemorating the 1944 Massacre at Oradour-sur-Glane* (Berkeley: University of California Press, 1999).

174. Nossiter, *The Algeria Hotel,* 101, 98.

175. In 1984 *Le Monde* noted: "The Tour de France presents this peculiarity of reminding us of history along its itineraries, and even of being able to make us forget for a moment *[le temps d'un regard]* the battles that its contestants fight in favor of those, far more serious, that throughout the ages have been fought by men in search of liberty and pride." *Le Monde,* 14 July 1984.

176. Jacques Goddet, interview with the author, 21 July 1999.

THREE. THE *GÉANTS DE LA ROUTE*

1. Jeremy D. Popkin, *A History of Modern France,* 2nd ed. (Upper Saddle River, NJ: Prentice Hall, 2001), 158, quoted in Jean Bouvier, *Les deux scandales de Panama* (Paris: Julliard, 1964), 158.

2. Popkin, *A History of Modern France,* 164, quoted in Raoul Girardet, *L'Idée coloniale en France de 1871 à 1962* (Paris: La Table Ronde, 1972), 149.

3. See, in particular, Charles Rearick, *Pleasures of the Belle Epoque: Entertainment and Festivity in Turn-of-the-Century France* (New Haven, CT: Yale University Press, 1985); Vanessa R. Schwartz, *Spectacular Realities: Early Mass Culture in Fin-de-Siècle Paris* (Berkeley: University of California Press, 1998).

4. Pierre Charreton, *Les fêtes du corps: Histoire et tendances de la littérature à thème sportif en France, 1870–1970* (Saint-Étienne: CIEREC—Université de Saint-Étienne, 1985), 8, 23–24, 86, 104–6, 110–11.

5. See, for example, La Française's advertisements in *L'Auto,* 3, 16, 19 July 1903, 9 July 1904. Even when advertisements did not include pictures of the racers, they reinforced the racers' name recognition.

6. *L'Auto,* 19 June, 2 July, 31 May 1903.

7. Preface by Georges Speicher in Jean Buzançais, *La patrouille du Tour de France* (Paris: Éditions de l'Arc, 1948), 5–6.

8. *L'Auto,* 24 June 1903. See also ibid., 1 July 1903. The organizers expressed gratitude toward *Le Toulouse cycliste* (*L'Auto,* 24 June 1903) and papers in the Avignon region (*L'Auto,* 6 July 1903) and Lyon (*L'Auto,* 10 July 1904).

9. Ibid., 19 July 1903.

10. Ibid., 15 July 1907.

11. The book in question is Victor Breyer and Robert Coquelle, *Les géants de la route: Bordeaux-Paris* (E. Brocherioux, 1899). Cited in Roger Lajoie-Mazenc,

L'homme-horloge: Gustave Garrigou; Itinéraire d'un enfant de l'Aveyron devenu Géant de la route (La Primaube: Graphi Imprimeur, 1996), 34.

12. *L'Auto,* 20 July 1910.

13. See, for example, *L'Est Républicain* (Nancy), 29 June 1906; *La Bretagne Sportive,* 29 April 1936.

14. *L'Ouest-Éclair* (Rennes), 28 July 1905.

15. *Le Toulouse cycliste* (n.d.), quoted in *L'Auto,* 30 July 1903.

16. J.-C. Lyleire and H. Le Targat, *Anthologie de la littérature du sport* (Lyon: Presses Universitaires de Lyon, 1989), 24–25.

17. Jean Durry, *L'en-cycle-opédie* (Lausanne: Édition-Denoël, 1982), 352.

18. The lithographic poster in color was developed in the nascent mass-consumer culture of the late Second Empire in response to the growing need of manufacturers to advertise their wares. The first sports posters appeared between 1870 and 1885; prominent among them were those vaunting the merits of the bicycle, which, as we have seen, was emerging as a symbol of modern, industrial, consumer society. Jean Durry, *Le sport à l'affiche* (Paris: Éditions Hoebeke, 1988), 11, 14.

19. Ibid., 92–93.

20. Ibid., 14; Jacques Augendre, *Le Tour de France: Les exploits et les hommes, les sommets du Tour de France* (Paris: Éditions Solar, 1991), 25. A year earlier, Peugeot had produced a similar poster comparing Napoleon's record to the achievements of another great French racer, Émile Frioul.

21. *L'Auto,* 16 July 1903.

22. Three important developments converged at this time to spark the mass demand for postcards: virtually universal literacy, the perfecting of photography, and a reliable national postal service.

23. Félix Potin, France's earliest grocery chain, produced a collector's album of photographic portraits of the great figures of the belle époque. In addition to statesmen, scientists, artists, and writers, the series included prominent athletes, including bicycle racers. My thanks to Professor Scott Blair for bringing the existence of such albums to my attention and showing me his.

24. *Journal de Rennes,* 29 July 1905. The fictional Croïmans, a Belgian *touriste-routier* competing in the Tour, noted that "I display my bike, covered in mud and dust, in the window of my store when I get home, and I sell anything I want to." André Reuze, *Le Tour de Souffrance* (Paris: Arthème Fayard, 1925), 115–16.

25. Alphonse Baugé, *Messieurs les coureurs: Vérités, anecdotes et réflexions sur les courses cyclistes et les coureurs* (Paris: Librairie Garnier Frères, 1925), 80; Roger Bastide, *Petit-Breton: La Belle Époque du cyclisme* (Paris: Éditions Denoël, 1985), 123.

26. For a more detailed examination of female cycling and the debates it spawned with respect to women's emancipation, see Christopher Thompson, "Un troisième sexe? Les bourgeoises et la bicyclette dans la France fin de siècle," *Le Mouvement Social* 192 (July–September 2000): 9–39.

27. Reversing some of the sex-based inequalities of the Napoleonic Code of 1804,

the Third Republic increased the financial autonomy of women, entitled them to partial participation in public life (though not to the vote), and eroded the husband's formal authority within the family, not least by granting wives the right to initiate divorce proceedings. See Eugen Weber, *France, Fin de Siècle* (Cambridge, MA: Belknap Press, 1986), 87, 92–94; Edward Berenson, *The Trial of Madame Caillaux* (Berkeley: University of California Press, 1992), 106–9, 160; Theodore Zeldin, *France 1848–1945: Ambition and Love* (Oxford: Oxford University Press, 1979), 356, 358; Angus McLaren, *Sexuality and the Social Order: The Debate over the Fertility of Women and Workers in France, 1770–1920* (New York: Holmes & Meier, 1983), 179; Francis Ronsin, *Les divorciaires: Affrontements politiques et conceptions du mariage dans la France du XIXe siècle* (Paris: Éditions Aubier, 1992), 181–284; Roger Price, *A Social History of Nineteenth-Century France* (New York: Holmes & Meier, 1987), 78; Deborah L. Silverman, *Art Nouveau in Fin-de-Siècle France: Politics, Psychology, and Style* (Berkeley: University of California Press, 1989), 65–66.

Female enrollment in secondary schools and universities increased dramatically during this period. Access to higher education translated into access to the professions: by 1906, France had 573 female doctors, 3 percent of the total. In 1911, 7.5 percent of working women had careers in the liberal professions. In 1906, almost one in eight (12.2 percent) working women was an employer. By the end of the twentieth century, 45 percent of French working women were employed outside the home. See Françoise Mayeur, *L'enseignement secondaire des jeunes filles sous la Troisième République* (Paris: Presses de la Fondation Nationale des Sciences Politiques, 1977), 162; Susanna Barrows, *Distorting Mirrors: Visions of the Crowd in Late Nineteenth-Century France* (New Haven, CT: Yale University Press, 1981), 54–55; Price, *A Social History of Nineteenth-Century France*, 213, 344; Weber, *France, Fin de Siècle*, 94–96; Zeldin, *France 1848–1945*, 344–45, 351, 359; Annelise Maugue, *L'identité masculine en crise au tournant du siècle 1871–1914* (Paris: Éditions Rivages, 1987), 176; Berenson, *The Trial of Madame Caillaux*, 112–13.

Between 1870 and 1914, the French birthrate fell 27.4 percent. Deaths outnumbered births for 1890–95, 1900, 1907, and 1911. Between 1872 and 1911, the French population increased by 10 percent, while Germany's population grew by 58 percent. Between 1885 and 1895 alone, while France increased its population by a scant quarter of a million, Germany's grew by eight million. See Weber, *France, Fin de Siècle*, 89; Berenson, *The Trial of Madame Caillaux*, 161; McLaren, *Sexuality and the Social Order*, 179; Robert Nye, *Masculinity and Male Codes of Honor in Modern France* (New York: Oxford University Press, 1993), 77–78; Karen Offen, "Depopulation, Nationalism and Feminism in Fin de Siècle France," *American Historical Review* 89 (June 1984): 658.

28. McLaren, *Sexuality and the Social Order*, 11, 154. For the history of antifeminism (including its relationship to natalist concerns) under the early Third Republic, see Christine Bard, ed., *Un siècle d'antiféminisme* (Paris: Fayard, 1999), especially chapters 1, 3, and 6.

29. On the contemporary debate about appropriate cycling attire for women, see Thompson, "Un troisième sexe?" 18–22. During the belle époque, French feminists launched newspapers, held congresses that received considerable press coverage, and established a number of French women's organizations that were often affiliated with international bodies. By the late nineteenth century, the "woman question" had become a central and polarizing theme of French cultural production and political discourse, widely treated in the press, literature, and theatrical works. See Offen, "Depopulation, Nationalism and Feminism in Fin de Siècle France," 649, 655–56. For a history of French feminism under the early Third Republic, see Laurence Klejman and Florence Rochefort, *L'égalité en marche: Le féminisme sous la Troisième République* (Paris: Presses de la Fondation Nationale des Sciences Politiques, 1989); Claire Moses, *French Feminism in the 19th Century* (Albany: State University of New York Press, 1984), chapters 8 and 9. For coverage of the issue of divorce in contemporary plays, books, and the press, see Ronsin, *Les divorciaires,* 187–92, 200–207, 211–19.

30. Weber, *France, Fin de Siècle,* 203.

31. For the debate on the implications of cycling for female sexuality, see Thompson, "Un troisième sexe?" 22–25.

32. Ruth Harris, *Murders and Madness: Medicine, Law, and Society in the Fin de Siècle* (Oxford: Oxford University Press, 1989), 186. On "uncontrollable" women's passions, see also Joëlle Guillais, *La chair de l'autre: Le crime passionnel au XIXe siècle* (Paris: Éditions Olivier Orban, 1986), especially chapters 5 and 6; Berenson, *The Trial of Madame Caillaux;* Ann-Louise Shapiro, *Breaking the Codes: Female Criminality in Fin-de-Siècle Paris* (Stanford, CA: Stanford University Press, 1996), especially chapters 3–5. This anxiety seems to have been a response to evidence that middle-class women were in fact increasingly taking control of their sex lives, claiming an equal right to sexual pleasure, and thus challenging the late-nineteenth-century male obsession with having a woman entirely shaped by and for oneself. See Annelise Maugue, "The New Eve and the Old Adam," in *Emerging Feminism from Revolution to World War,* ed. Geneviève Fraisse and Michelle Perrot (Cambridge, MA: Belknap Press, 1993), 524; Weber, *France, Fin de Siècle,* 90.

33. On the bicycle as "the technological partner of the New Woman," see Silverman, *Art Nouveau,* 67.

34. See, for example, Dr. Philippe Tissié, *L'éducation physique* (Paris: Librairie Larousse, 1901), 54; Dr. Just Lucas-Championnière, *La bicyclette* (Paris: Léon Chailly, 1894), 44; Garsonnin, *Conférence sur la vélocipédie faite à Tours le 31 mars 1888* (Rouen: Imprimerie J. Lecerf, 1888), 12; Dr. Raymond Martin, "Les avantages du sport vélocipédique," *L'Écho Sportif* (Nancy), 7 January 1905. On contemporary views of marriage, divorce, and the family, see Berenson, *The Trial of Madame Caillaux,* especially chapter 4. At least one contemporary novel rejected the view that the bicycle reinforced marriage and stabilized society: the two young married couples of Maurice Leblanc's 1898 novel *Voici des ailes!* (Paris: Paul Ollendorff Éditeur)

become so intoxicated by the sartorial, sensual, and sexual liberation they experience during their bicycle trip that not only do both women ride bare-breasted, but by the end of the trip the couples have swapped spouses! Stephen Kern, *The Culture of Time and Space* (Cambridge, MA: Harvard University Press, 1983), 111.

35. Berenson, *The Trial of Madame Caillaux,* 189–90; Nye, *Masculinity and Male Codes of Honor,* 219–20; Michel Bouet, *Signification du sport* (Paris: Éditions Universitaires, 1968), 394. See also Pierre Arnaud, *Le militaire, l'écolier, le gymnaste: Naissance de l'éducation physique en France (1869–1889)* (Lyon: Presses Universitaires de Lyon, 1991).

36. Berenson, *The Trial of Madame Caillaux,* 113; Maugue, *L'identité masculine en crise,* 53–54. On the construction of masculinity in nineteenth- and early-twentieth-century France, see Nye, *Masculinity and Male Codes of Honor;* André Rauch, *Crise de l'identité masculine 1789–1914* (Paris: Hachette Littératures, 2000); Angus McLaren, *The Trials of Masculinity: Policing Sexual Boundaries, 1870–1930* (Chicago: University of Chicago Press, 1997).

37. Robert A. Nye, *Crime, Madness and Politics in Modern France: The Medical Concept of National Decline* (Princeton, NJ: Princeton University Press, 1984), 325; Bouet, *Signification du sport,* 402–3.

38. Berenson, *The Trial of Madame Caillaux,* 114–15; Maugue, "The New Eve," 526, 529.

39. For a discussion of the *vraie femme,* the conservative countermodel to the "new woman," see Berenson, *The Trial of Madame Caillaux,* especially 92, 98, 100–102, 114, 116.

40. Harris, *Murders and Madness,* 21–22, 207; Berenson, *The Trial of Madame Caillaux,* 11, 103. For the often-contradictory positions taken by French physicians on the issue of female cycling, see Thompson, "Un troisième sexe?" 14–17.

41. C. de Loris, *La femme à bicyclette: Ce qu'elles en pensent* (Paris: Ancienne Maison Quantin Librairies—Imprimeries Réunies, 1896), 40.

42. Louis Baudry de Saunier, *L'art de bien monter la bicyclette,* 3rd ed. (Paris, 1894), 86–87.

43. *La Revue Sportive du Nord Est* (Nancy), 1 December 1910.

44. Ronald Hubscher, ed., *L'histoire en mouvements: Le sport dans la société française (XIXe–XXe siècle)* (Paris: Armand Colin, 1992), 102.

45. *L'Auto,* 3 July 1903, 10 July 1910, 21 July 1912, 22 July 1909, 15, 8 July 1911.

46. Ibid., 9 July 1903, 9 July 1909, 25 July 1913, 25 July 1905, 4 August 1904.

47. For examples of such incidents involving the top racers Émile Georget, Louis Trousselier, and François Faber, see ibid., 23 July 1903, 25 July 1906, 12 July 1909. Occasionally, racers took advantage of gullible *admiratrices:* in 1914 an anonymous *isolé* apparently passed himself off as Philippe Thys, that year's winner, to impress one of Thys's female fans. This successful impersonation was uncovered when Thys received a letter from the woman in question thanking him for the hours they had spent together after the stage finish in Bayonne. Ibid., 18 July 1914.

48. For an illuminating examination of how such fears mobilized postwar French society, see Mary Louise Roberts, *Civilization without Sexes: Reconstructing Gender in Postwar France, 1917–1927* (Chicago: University of Chicago Press, 1994).

49. *L'Auto,* 23 July 1920, 10 August 1921, 5 July 1923, 4 July 1924, 27 June, 5 July 1925, 27 June 1926, 23 July 1932, 11 June, 11 July 1937, 25 July 1938.

50. Ibid., 25 June 1925, 26 July 1935.

51. Ibid., 22 June 1926, 22 July 1935, 19 June 1928, 3, 24 July 1930, 18 June 1929, 25 July 1930, 28, 29 July 1932.

52. See, for example, ibid., 27 June 1928, 24 July 1931, 8 July 1932, 19 July 1936, 25 June 1926, 29 June 1927, 25 July 1932.

53. Ibid., 17 July 1925, 10 August 1921, 5 July 1926.

54. Reuze, *Le Tour de Souffrance,* 62–63.

55. Jacques Chabannes, *Microbe* (Paris: La Nouvelle Société d'Édition, 1929), 76–77.

56. Ibid., 113–14. For another example of the role played by dangerous women in this genre, see Robert Dieudonné, *Frangins* (Paris: Éditions des Portiques, 1931).

57. Even in the rare cycling novel whose main character is not from the lower classes but rather a bourgeois, chaotic female relationships prove distracting, disastrous, and even fatal. See Théodore Chèze, *Claude Lenoir* (Paris: Librairie Moderne, 1907). For another example featuring a racer who comes from a "good" (middle-class) family, see Robert Dieudonné, *Le Vainqueur* (Paris: Albin Michel, 1922).

58. Henri Desgrange, *La tête et les jambes* (Paris: L. Pochy, 1898), 103; idem, *Alphonse Marcaux,* 2nd ed. (Paris: L. Pochy, 1899), 58–59, 209.

59. Desgrange, *La tête et les jambes,* 24, 166.

60. For interwar debates about popular, contemporary fiction that addressed gender roles and identities, see Roberts, *Civilization without Sexes.*

61. In 1934, when the gifted young René Vietto was required by the French national team's strategy to help the 1931 champion Antonin Magne win his second Tour, Vietto's "sacrifice" sparked widespread debate in the French press, questioning the legitimacy of Magne's victory and the team's strategy. See Christopher Thompson, "René Vietto et le Tour de France de 1934: Un sacrifice héroïque ou un héros sacrifié?" *Histoire et Sociétés: Revue européenne d'histoire sociale* 7 (July 2003): 35–46. In 1985 a similar conflict occurred between the established French star Bernard Hinault and his young American teammate Greg LeMond.

62. See, for example, *L'Auto,* 29 July 1906; *Les Vosges Sportives,* 3 July 1913.

63. *Le Matin,* 28 July 1919; *Le Petit Parisien,* 4 July 1935; *L'Auto,* 14 July 1938.

64. *Actuel 2,* ORTF 2, 16 July 1973.

65. *L'Équipe,* 8–9 July 1967.

66. See, for example, *L'Auto,* 18 July 1907, 22 July 1908; *Le Matin,* 28 July 1919; *L'Humanité,* 6 July 1967.

67. See, for example, *L'Auto,* 2 August 1911, 29 June 1914; *Le Populaire,* 4 July

1929. See *L'Auto*, 29 July 1912, for a photograph of the winner Odile Defraye being weighed at the end of the Tour. In 1923, forty-two racers lost an average of 3.05 kilograms. *L'Auto*, 24 July 1923. Ottavio Bottecchia lost almost three kilograms during his victorious 1925 Tour, Antonin Magne four when he won in 1931. *L'Auto*, 21 July 1925, 1 August 1931.

68. Like television coverage, documentaries about the Tour tend to emphasize such images, often set to dramatic music. See, for example, "Le Tour de France: Son histoire, notre histoire," *Témoins sports*, France 3, 20, 27 July 1986.

69. Paul Robert Cazala, a member of the French national team in the 1959 Tour, noted that he had learned to suffer a great deal while working in his father's cornfields as a teenager but that professional cycling had brought him suffering of a different order ("bien d'autres souffrances"). *L'Équipe*, 19, 15 June 1959.

70. Bernard Hinault (with Bernard Pascuito), *Moi, Bernard Hinault, champion des champions* (Paris: Calmann-Lévy, 1981), 105–6.

71. *USA Today*, 17 February 2004.

72. Quoted in Georges Pagnoud, *Ces Bretons qui passionnent le cyclisme français* (Paris: Solar Éditeur, 1974), 20.

73. "Autour du Tour," TF1, 2 January 1976. Moneyron apparently did not know that a few decades earlier racers had indeed ridden at night.

74. When a young racer in André Reuze's instructively titled novel *Le Tour de Souffrance* wants to drop out of the Tour because he is in too much pain, his manager responds, "To suffer, that is noble, that is beautiful, that moves the crowds," and attributes the great popularity of another racer of "average ability" to the fact that "he knows how to suffer" (98–99).

75. *Actuel 2*, ORTF 2, 16 July 1973.

76. Roger Bastide, *Doping: Les surhommes du vélo* (Paris: Raoul Solar, 1970), 140. On retiring, the thirty-eight-year-old Johan Museeuw, one of the top racers of the past fifteen years, acknowledged in an interview with *L'Équipe*: "I still want to ride, to train, to suffer." *New York Times*, 18 April 2004.

77. *L'Humanité*, 27 June 1914; *L'Auto*, 15 July 1907.

78. Quoted in Roger Bastide, *Petit-Breton: La Belle Époque du cyclisme*, 94. See also *L'Équipe*, 23 July 1946.

79. Jacques Seray, *Deux roues: La véritable histoire du vélo* (Rodez: Éditions du Rouergue, 1988), 185. See also Desgrange's explanation for why the derailleur would not be allowed in the 1933 Tour (*L'Auto*, 21 May 1933) and the positive reactions of derailleur manufacturers to the announcement that derailleurs would be allowed in the 1937 Tour (*L'Auto*, 29 June 1937).

80. The aggregate numbers of racers who completed the Tour in these periods are: 1903–1914, 387 of 1,246; 1919–1929, 447 of 1,441; 1930–1939, 469 of 852; 1947–1950, 203 of 455; 1951–1960, 726 of 1,214; 1961–1970, 838 of 1,324; 1971–1980, 853 of 1,284; 1981–1990, 1,314 of 1,820; 1991–2000, 1,288 of 1,899.

81. See, for example, *L'Ouest-Éclair*, 22 July 1913; *L'Intransigeant*, 27, 28 July 1913;

Le Temps, 11, 15–16, 20, 27 July 1913; *Le Matin*, 27 July 1913; *La Croix*, 22 July 1913; *L'Humanité*, 20 July 1913; *Le Petit Parisien*, 28 July 1913.

82. *Le Matin*, 28 July 1913.

83. *L'Intransigeant*, 28 July 1913. For other examples, see *La Croix*, 18 July 1913; *Le Temps*, 27 July 1913.

84. *L'Intransigeant*, 27 July 1913. *L'Humanité* also referred to "the savage elimination of the road" and the "phalanx of glorious athletes" who made it back to Paris. *L'Humanité*, 27, 23 July 1913.

85. *L'Humanité*, 28 July 1913.

86. *L'Ouest-Éclair*, 19 July 1913.

87. *L'Intransigeant*, 9 July 1913. Desgrange continued to rail against group finishes after the war. *L'Auto*, 25 July 1932.

88. See, for example, *Le Matin*, 28 July 1919; *Le Petit Journal*, 27 July 1919; *L'Intransigeant*, 25 July 1919; *Le Petit Parisien*, 28 July 1919, 26 July 1937; *La Croix*, 18 July 1919; *Le Temps*, 17 July 1919, 17 July 1934; *L'Ouest-Éclair*, 29 July 1919, 18 July 1935; *L'Éclaireur de l'Est*, 10 July 1919; *L'Humanité*, 11 July 1923; *Le Populaire*, 22 July 1923; *Paris-Soir*, 12, 13 July 1935.

89. *L'Action Française*, 10 July 1919. See also *L'Ouest-Éclair*, 28 June, 2, 6 July 1919.

90. Pierre Chany, *La fabuleuse histoire du Tour de France* (Paris: Éditions Nathan, 1991), 159.

91. *L'Auto*, 2 August 1919.

92. For lists of donors, see ibid., 29, 30, 31 July, 1, 2, 3, 5, 6, 7, 8, 11, 12, 13, 14, 15, 18, 19, 20, 21, 31 August 1919. For Christophe's thank-you letter, see ibid., 24 August 1919.

93. Confirming this parallel, many French at this time also contributed modest private donations for the erection of war memorials. Jay Winter, *Sites of Memory, Sites of Mourning: The Great War in European Cultural History* (Cambridge: Cambridge University Press, 1995), 89.

94. *L'Équipe*, 23 July 1946; *Le Parisien Libéré*, 25 June 1947.

95. *L'Équipe*, 13 July 1947.

96. *Le Monde*, 24, 29–30 June 1947; *Le Populaire*, 22 July 1947. See also *La Croix*, 3 July 1947.

97. See, for example, *Le Monde*, 16–17, 23–24 July 1950, 5 July 1966.

98. Lajoie-Mazenc, *L'homme-horloge*, part 2, *Les Aveyronnais dans le Tour de France cycliste*, 81.

99. *L'Équipe*, 6–7 July 1957. Jacques Goddet noted in a headline that "they [Tour racers] don't all die, but all are struck." Ibid., 23 July 1954. In 1973 Raphael Géminiani called for the rule's resurrection as a way of toughening the Tour. A racer who disagreed no doubt spoke for many of his peers, whose job security and earning potential would have been jeopardized by the rule. *Actuel 2*, ORTF 2, 16 July 1973.

100. The narrator of the film summary of the 1950 Tour referred frequently to

the number of survivors at various moments of the race. *En attendant le Tour,* France 2, 7 July 1995. A year earlier, coverage of the fifth stage included footage of a still badly damaged Caen being rebuilt. Ibid., 6 July 1995.

101. *L'Humanité,* 1 July 1947.

102. See, for example, *Le Monde,* 4, 15, 20–21 July 1947; *Le Populaire,* 22 July 1947.

103. *L'Équipe,* 3 July 1947.

104. Ibid., 24 July 1947.

105. Ibid., 24, 21 July 1947 For a running list of donations to Robic's fund, see ibid., 24, 25, 30 July, 5, 7, 12, 21, 26 August, 3, 5, 16, 17 September, 22, 24 October 1947. The final total was 20,820 francs.

106. See, for example, the documentary "Le Tour de France: Son histoire, notre histoire," *Témoins sports,* France 3, 20, 27 July 1986. See also *L'Équipe,* 19 July 1994.

107. *L'Équipe,* 19 July 1994.

108. Ibid., 19 July 1994. Racers did indeed celebrate completing the event and in so doing endorsed the cult of survival. Describing his arrival on the Champs-Élysées at the end of the 1986 Tour, Paul Kimmage noted: "Two hundred and ten riders had started. One hundred and thirty-two had finished. I was 131st, I had survived. I was a 'Giant of the Road.'" Paul Kimmage, *Rough Ride: Behind the Wheel with a Pro Cyclist* (London: Yellow Jersey Press, 1998), 92.

109. At the end of the 1906 Tour, the winner, René Pottier, was described as falling "into the arms of his young wife." *L'Auto,* 30 July 1906.

110. Ibid., 3 July 1903, 22 July 1904, 8, 9 July, 2 August 1909.

111. See, for example, ibid., 15 July 1907. Mail for racers was generally sent to the hotels where they were to be lodged.

112. Ibid., 22 July 1908.

113. At the end of the first Tour, for example, Jean Dargassies was summoned home to Grisolles by "a tearful telegram from his wife." Ibid., 21 July 1903.

114. *L'Auto,* 30 June, 13 July 1937. *Paris-Soir*'s 1937 coverage included an article devoted to the "sorrows and joys of a racer's mom" by Roger Lapébie's mother. *Paris-Soir,* 25 July 1937. She admitted to *L'Auto* that when her son was racing, she was consumed with fear: "I am not curious to see him suffer, and I can't wait for the Tour to be over."

115. Ibid., 22 June 1925. In 1932 "Mme Stoepel . . . cried so hard at her husband's departure." Ibid., 19 July 1932.

116. *Le Matin,* 28 July 1919. As Mme Faber had before the war, occasionally a winner's mother emerged as a central figure in interwar press coverage. Such was the case of the mother of Romain Maes in 1935. See *L'Auto,* 28, 29 July 1935; *Paris-Soir,* 21, 26, 29 July 1935; *Le Petit Parisien,* 29 July 1935; *L'Intransigeant,* 30 July 1935. In 1921, when Henri Collé was greeted at the end of a stage in Geneva by his young daughter, the crowd roared its approval. *L'Auto,* 18 July 1921. For other examples of interwar press coverage of racers being greeted by their female kin, see *L'Auto,* 29

July 1919, 16 July 1924, 23 June 1927, 29 July 1930, 9 July 1932, 30 July 1936, 12, 21, 28 July 1938, 31 July 1939.

117. *L'Humanité,* 25 July 1921.

118. See, for example, *L'Auto,* 29 June 1925, 3 July 1930, 17 July 1934, 15 January 1935, 29 July 1936, 30 June 1937, 21 July 1938, 24, 26 July, 3 August 1939. See, in particular, "How Mme Jaminet conceives of her role of racer's spouse," ibid., 2 July 1938. *L'Auto* imagined letters from wives to their racer husbands, in which one fictitious wife admitted that "I have never found a month so long." Ibid., 27 July 1934.

119. Ibid., 3 July 1933. One of the emotions evoked by *L'Auto* was the wives' fear that their husbands would be unfaithful during the race. Ibid., 30, 31 July 1932, 9 July 1933, 20 July 1935.

120. For *L'Auto*'s rules about women following their husbands or boyfriends during a stage, see ibid., 23, 24 July 1921. Victor Cosson was penalized fifty francs for the repeated presence along the route of his fiancée (ibid., 28 July 1939), a fact he still remembered sixty years later (interview with the author, 15 July 1999).

121. See Roberts, *Civilization without Sexes,* on the cultural impact in postwar France of this major demographic imbalance.

122. *L'Auto* even reported on the assistance some journalists covering the race received from wives who accompanied them. *L'Auto,* 15 July 1931.

123. For example, *L'Équipe* covered Mme Robic's presence at the time trial in Vannes: *L'Équipe,* 18 July 1947. See also *Le Parisien Libéré,* 1 July 1947; *Sports-Ouest,* 10 July 1947; *L'Équipe,* 1, 14 July, 2 August 1947.

124. See, for example, coverage of Louison Bobet's mother and wife visiting him in 1948. *L'Équipe,* 18 July 1948.

125. One racer's wife, who was expecting a child during the Tour, helped her husband pack on the eve of the start. Ibid., 6 July 1955. Once the race had started, wives mobilized to provide racers with clean laundry (*Sports-Ouest,* 10 July 1947), encouraged them to do well (*L'Équipe,* 11 July 1952), consoled them when they did poorly or lost the yellow jersey (*L'Équipe,* 17 July 1948, 18 July 1952), and at times even chided their husbands' teammates for not having done more to protect their leads (*Sports-Ouest,* 8 July 1948).

During a lull in a stage, the *peloton* often slowed down to allow racers to spend a moment with their families—usually their wives, young children, and mothers—at the side of the road. See, for example, the cases of Raymond Poulidor in 1967 (*Le Parisien Libéré,* 22–23 July 1967) and the Irish racer Stephen Roche in 1984 (*L'Équipe,* 5 July 1984).

126. For photographs of racers embracing wives, mothers, and daughters, see *L'Équipe,* 18, 26 July 1948, 23 July 1953, 2 August 1954, 31 July 1956, 4, 21 July 1958, 24 July 1967; *L'Humanité,* 1, 5 August 1950, 21 July 1952; *Le Parisien Libéré,* 10, 22–23 July 1967, 18 July 1984. For newsreels, see, for example, scenes from the coverage of the 1950, 1952, 1953, and 1955 Tours in INA NEWS 12, Ref. 2109, "Le dossier: Les grandes figures du Tour de France, 1947–1992."

127. The caption of a photograph in a Breton sports paper of Jean Robic's wife kissing him through the fence at the Parc des Princes read: "The joy of the return. After a month apart, Mme Robic is reunited with her husband at the Parc. A big kiss rewards the headstrong 'Biquet' for all his suffering." In the same issue, another photograph with the caption "It ends with a kiss" showed the French racer Jacques Marinelli embracing his "delicious fiancée." *Sports-Ouest,* 28 July 1949.

128. In 1949 Mme Robic was quoted as hoping her husband would come home with the yellow jersey. *Sports-Ouest,* 23 June 1949. One young newlywed tearfully said goodbye to her husband, who had interrupted their honeymoon to take part in the race. *L'Équipe,* 13 July 1956. In 1958 *L'Équipe* devoted a paragraph to describing Charly Gaul's wife fighting back tears as her husband donned the yellow jersey after a time-trial victory. Flaring nostrils, reddening eyelids, tightening throat: nothing escaped the journalist's keen eye. *L'Équipe,* 19–20 July 1958. After Jacques Anquetil's withdrawal due to illness in 1966, *Le Figaro* noted that "the spouses of men who live dangerously are the only ones to rejoice at their capitulation." *Le Figaro,* 12 July 1966.

See also *L'Équipe, numéro spécial* of 8 July, 21–22 July 1951; *Le Figaro,* 10 July 1947.

129. *L'Équipe,* 6 July 1949, 27 July 1950.

130. Ibid., 26 June 1953.

131. Ibid., 3 July 1951. Perhaps inspired by Mme Bobet's words, a few weeks later the caption of a photograph of Louison Bobet and his wife described the latter as "Louison's drug." Ibid., 21–22 July 1951.

132. In 1953, shortly before the first of Bobet's three consecutive Tour wins, *L'Équipe* devoted an article to the "kissing scene" between the Bobets, describing Christiane Bobet as the "goddess of Victory, all dressed in white." Ibid., 23 July 1953. In 1984 *Le Parisien Libéré* published a photograph of a stage winner, Pascal Jules, in bed with his wife and infant son, implicitly linking his victory to a happy, stable family life. *Le Parisien Libéré,* 7–8 July 1984. That year Stephen Roche kept a picture of his wife and newborn son in his jersey pocket throughout the Tour. *L'Équipe,* 5 July 1984.

133. *L'Équipe,* 20 May 1949, 26 June 1953. In 1967 the press was unanimous in attributing Roger Pingeon's Tour victory to his wife's support: she had convinced him to stick with racing when he became discouraged and thought about returning to his career as a plumber. Ibid., 10 July 1967; *Le Parisien Libéré,* 10 July 1967; *La Croix,* 25 July 1967; *Le Monde,* 20 July 1967. At the end of the Tour, Pingeon publicly dedicated his victory to his wife. *L'Équipe,* 24 July 1967.

134. Helen Hoban, interview with the author, 25 July 1999. Helen Hoban was married to the English racer Tom Simpson, and, after his death during the 1967 Tour (see chapter 6), to another English racer, Barry Hoban.

135. *L'Équipe,* 3 August, 20 July 1954.

136. Ibid., 4 July 1956.

137. Helen Hoban, interview with the author, 25 July 1999. Having experienced

similar ostracism at the hands of the Tour organizers, the wife of the 1973 Tour winner Luis Ocaña described the racers' wives as "persona non grata" on the Tour. Michel Milenkovitch, ed., *50 Histoires du Tour de France* (Paris: Éditions du Sport, 1997), 60. *Le Figaro* observed that Janine Anquetil saw her husband, the five-time Tour champion Jacques Anquetil, only ten minutes a day during the Tour: "Segregation is de rigueur for the warrior's rest." *Le Figaro,* 24 June 1966.

138. *L'Équipe,* 6 July 1967.

139. Helen Hoban, interview with the author, 25 July 1999.

140. For a racer's account (and resentment) of the segregation of racers and their wives and girlfriends during the 1987 Tour, see Kimmage, *Rough Ride,* 128.

141. France 2, "Autour du Tour," 24 July 1999.

142. *L'Équipe,* 19 July 1948.

143. Ibid., 27 July 1953, 17 July 1950, 6 July 1948. During the first postwar Tour, an American observer compared the Tour racers' female fans to those of Clark Gable and Frank Sinatra in the United States. Ibid., 13 July 1947. The role of *admiratrices* as extras confirming the racers' heroic status was reinforced by beauty contests designed to select the Tour's most attractive female spectators. In 1947 the Judex watch company sponsored a "Miss Tour de France" competition, whose top three finishers (selected from among the daily "Miss Stages") received a variety of prizes and were invited to participate in the "Miss France" competition. Ibid., 21–22 June, 25 July 1947; *Le Parisien Libéré,* 10 July 1947. In 1953 there was a "One Woman a Day" contest (*L'Équipe,* 11–12 July 1953); in 1955, another "Miss Tour de France" contest (*L'Équipe,* 29 July 1955). In 1984 the reigning Miss France visited the Tour and awarded a bouquet to one of the stage winners. *Le Parisien Libéré,* 11 July 1984.

144. *L'Équipe,* 3 July 1958.

145. Ibid., 13 July 1949.

146. *L'Humanité,* 3 August 1950. In 1966 Janine Anquetil was hired by Radio Luxembourg to offer her insights (and insider's perspective) each evening about that day's stage. *Le Parisien Libéré,* 22 June 1966.

147. *L'Humanité,* 14 July, 9 August, 25 July 1950. In a similar move, *Le Petit Parisien* had sent a female journalist to cover the 1937 Tour. She wrote a daily column clearly intended to come "from a woman's perspective," which served to reinforce the sense that the race was a naturally gendered experience.

148. *L'Humanité,* 19 July 1950. Gino Bartali won the Tour in 1938 and 1948. One of his nicknames was "Gino le pieux" ("Gino the devout"). In the immediate postwar era, the Italian public was divided between partisans of Bartali, seen as the embodiment of a traditional Italy, and fans of his great rival, the younger Fausto Coppi (the winner of the 1949 and 1952 Tours), who was widely seen to personify the more progressive, secular values of a modernizing, democratic Italy. See Jean-Paul Ollivier, *Gino Bartali: Gino le pieux* (Paris: PAC Éditions, 1983); Daniele Marchesini, *Coppi e Bartali* (Bologna: Società editrice il Mulino, 1998).

149. *Le Figaro,* 21 June 1966.

150. On new rights for women and French feminism during this period, see Claire Duchen, *Women's Rights and Women's Lives in France, 1944–1968* (London: Routledge, 1994), chapters 6 and 7; idem, *Feminism in France from May '68 to Mitterrand* (London: Routledge & Kegan Paul, 1986).

151. Serge Berstein and Jean-Pierre Rioux, *La France de l'expansion,* vol. 2, *L'apogée Pompidou, 1969–1974* (Paris: Éditions du Seuil, 1995), 218–21; Jean-Jacques Becker (with Pascal Ory), *Crises et alternances, 1974–1995* (Paris: Éditions du Seuil, 1998), 38–43.

152. On French women and politics during this period, see Duchen, *Women's Rights and Women's Lives,* especially chapter 2; Gill Allwood and Khursheed Wadia, *Women and Politics in France, 1958–2000* (London: Routledge, 2000). On gender inequalities in employment, especially as reflected in the underrepresentation of women in the liberal professions and upper management positions, see Duchen, *Women's Rights and Women's Lives,* chapter 5. On the issue of equal pay in the 1960s and 1970s, see Amy G. Mazur, *Gender Bias and the State: Symbolic Reform at Work in Fifth Republic France* (Pittsburgh, PA: University of Pittsburgh Press, 1995), especially chapters 1–4.

153. French infantrymen in World War I were known as *poilus* (hairy ones), a nickname that emphasized their virility and evoked the mustaches so many of them sported.

154. *L'Auto,* 15 July 1907.

155. At other times the racers' miserable state after a particularly difficult mountain stage evoked painful memories of Napoleon's retreat from Russia. Ibid., 21 July 1935. For other references to Tour racers as French soldiers, see ibid., 8 August 1905, 4 July 1923, 14 July 1925, 31 July 1932.

156. *L'Est Républicain* (Nancy), 4 July 1914.

157. *Le Matin,* 28 July 1919; *L'Auto,* 8 July 1926.

158. *L'Ouest-Éclair,* 12, 6, 18 July 1935; *Le Temps,* 17 July 1934.

159. *Le Matin,* 28 July 1919.

160. *L'Éclaireur de l'Est,* 17 July 1919.

161. *L'Auto,* 23 June 1919.

162. Chany, *La fabuleuse histoire du Tour de France,* 155.

163. *L'Équipe,* 16 July 1957.

164. *L'Auto,* 16 June, 11 July 1919.

165. Ibid., 20 June 1927. When Maurice Archambaud signed on as member of the French national team for the 1935 Tour, his wife, speaking "with tears in her voice," explained her sadness: "It's that . . . again you are going to take him away from me for a month." Ibid., 11 June 1935.

166. Ibid., 17 July 1934. In an interview, the wife of Georges Speicher evoked the difficulty of the month-long separation from her husband and the patience required of a racer's wife. She explained that although she listened to race coverage

on the radio, she had turned it off when her husband had crashed the previous year, waiting instead for someone to call to explain his condition. Ibid., 4 July 1938.

167. Ibid., 7 July 1935.

168. Ibid., 28 June 1924.

169. Ibid., 20 July 1924.

170. Women's "natural" maternal and protective role inspired a 1938 competition: Tour spectators were invited to enter photographs of female spectators, one of whom would be selected at the race's conclusion as the "Godmother of the 1939 Tour de France." Ibid., 4 July 1938.

171. *L'Équipe,* 11, 14 July 1949, 14, 23, 24–25 July 1954, 2 August 1955, 28 June, 12, 30 July 1956, 4, 5, 21 July 1967; *Le Parisien Libéré,* 22 June 1966, 5, 8 July 1967; *Le Populaire,* 15–16 July 1950. Describing Tour racers as "itinerant cadavers" in 1975, the racer Régis Delépine wondered whether "people are going to take us for survivors of Buchenwald." His comparison of racers to the ultimate postwar image of the devastated survivor, admittedly in questionable taste, would have been inconceivable for athletes in other, less demanding sports. "Autour du Tour," TF1, 2 January 1976.

172. See, for example, *L'Équipe,* 14 July 1948, 13 July 1956.

173. Helen Hoban, interview with the author, 25 July 1999.

174. American journalists were understandably less inhibited. For one covering the first postwar Tour, the vehicles carrying equipment and food for the racers evoked "a liberating army." *L'Équipe,* 13 July 1947.

175. Ibid., 28–29 June 1958.

176. Ibid., 18 June 1959.

177. *Le Figaro,* 27 June 1966.

178. One survey of cyclists leaving Paris on a Sunday morning in the summer of 1893 found that women comprised only 192 of the total of 5,653; meanwhile, of the 1,138 members of the Touring Club de France in 1891, only 14 were women. Richard Holt, "The Bicycle, the Bourgeoisie and the Discovery of Rural France, 1880–1914," *British Journal of Sports History* 2 (May 1985): 130.

179. For an analysis of the evolving depiction of women in cycling posters during this period, see Thompson, "Un troisième sexe?" 34–37.

180. Catherine Bertho-Lavenir, *La roue et le stylo: Comment nous sommes devenus touristes* (Paris: Éditions Odile Jacob, 1999), chapters 4–6; idem, "Le voyage: Une expérience d'écriture; La revue du Touring Club de France," in *Par Écrit: Éthnologie des écritures quotidiennes,* ed. Daniel Fabre and Martin de la Soudière (Paris: Éditions de la Maison des Sciences de l'Homme, 1997), 273–97.

181. In 1894 a Mme Beylot was one of the seventy-two contestants in the inaugural Paris-Évreux race. Occasional "handicap" track races pitted top female racers against male stars: a Breton woman took advantage of a four-kilometer head start to defeat her male opponent in a twenty-five-kilometer event at the Vél d'Hiv in Paris in 1897. On competitive female cycling during this period, see Françoise

Laget, Serge Laget, and Jean-Paul Mazot, *Le grand livre du sport féminin* (Belleville-sur-Saône: FMT Éditions, 1982), 269, 275, 286–96; Hubscher, *L'histoire en mouvements,* 298–99; Georges Renoy, *Le vélo au temps des belles moustaches* (Brussels: Rossel Éditions, 1975), 92; Jean-Marie Durand, *Les as du vélo: Le Tour de France cycliste, 1869–1939* (Marseille: Delta-Repro, 1983), 35; Georges Cadiou, *Les grandes heures du cyclisme breton* (Rennes: Ouest-France, 1981), 28; Allen Guttmann, *Women's Sports: A History* (New York: Columbia University Press, 1991), 102; Rémy Pigois, *Les petites reines du Tour de France* (Limoges: Imprimerie A. Bontemps, 1986), 13, 15, 21.

182. Bouet, *Signification du sport,* 395–96; Hubscher, *L'histoire en mouvements,* 102. See also Jacques Gleyse, "L'image de la femme dans les discours sur l'EP et le sport de 1870 à 1930. Un 'fait social total'?" in *Histoire du sport féminin,* vol. 2, *Sport masculin—sport féminin: éducation et société,* ed. Pierre Arnaud and Thierry Terret (Paris: L'Harmattan, 1996), 41–57.

183. *La Revue Sportive du Nord Est* (Nancy), 1 December 1910; *L'Auto,* 7 August 1909.

184. Hubscher, *L'histoire en mouvements,* 300.

185. Laget, Laget, and Mazot, *Le grand livre du sport féminin,* 296.

186. *L'Auto,* 10 July 1921.

187. See, for example, ibid., 8 July 1929, 12, 15 July 1932.

188. Quoted in *L'Humanité,* 30 June 1984.

189. *L'Auto,* 3 July 1928.

190. Laget, Laget, and Mazot, *Le grand livre du sport féminin,* 296, 298–300; Pigois, *Les petites reines,* 21. On French attempts to organize women's sports in the interwar period, see Hubscher, *L'histoire en mouvements,* 303–5.

191. *L'Équipe,* 25 June 1947.

192. Pigois, *Les petites reines,* 24, 29; Laget, Laget, and Mazot, *Le grand livre du sport féminin,* 300–301, 303.

193. Pigois, *Les petites reines,* 69, 341; Laget, Laget, and Mazot, *Le grand livre du sport féminin,* 303.

194. Pigois, *Les petites reines,* 37. In 1972, when he was introduced to the French female world champion, the president of France, Georges Pompidou, exclaimed: "It exists, female cycling?" *L'Équipe,* 30 June–1 July 1984.

195. Pigois, *Les petites reines,* 38; Laget, Laget, and Mazot, *Le grand livre du sport féminin,* 305.

196. Pigois, *Les petites reines,* 37.

197. Augendre, *Le Tour de France,* 143; Pigois, *Les petites reines,* 68; *Le Parisien Libéré,* 30 June–1 July 1984.

198. On the creation of the women's Tour, the obstacles faced by its organizers, and the 1984 race itself, see Pigois, *Les petites reines,* 68–75, 276–94.

199. Ibid., 71.

200. Ibid., 70.

201. Ibid. Meanwhile, on the 12 November 1983 Forum Sport–RMC radio program *L'Équipe*, the defending Tour champion Laurent Fignon observed that he had never liked women's cycling: "I like women, but I prefer to see them doing something else." *L'Humanité*, 30 June 1984.

202. A sampling of major Parisian dailies indicates that although many did cover the women's Tour, they often did so sporadically or minimally, providing stage results and the updated overall standings with little or no commentary. See, for example, *Le Figaro*, *Le Monde*, *Libération*, *La Croix*, and even *Le Parisien Libéré*, which organized the race. *L'Humanité* did not provide daily commentary but did have a fairly regular "Tour Féminin" report.

203. *Le Parisien Libéré*, 30 June–1 July 1984. Lévitan believed that they should be able to cover between one hundred and two hundred kilometers daily and climb two or three mountains in a row.

204. Ibid.; *Le Figaro*, 30 June–1 July, 2 July 1984; *L'Équipe*, 25 June, 30 June–1 July 1984. One participant acknowledged that three-quarters of the racers had never climbed the kinds of mountains included in the women's Tour. *L'Équipe*, 29 June 1984. *Libération* was less impressed with an event whose creation had been met with "the greatest indifference," and whose participants were lost amidst the "immense" attention focused on the male racers. *Libération*, 30 June–1 July 1984.

205. *Le Monde*, 5 July 1984.

206. Ibid.; *La Croix*, 7 July 1984.

207. *Libération*, 7–8 July 1984; *L'Équipe*, 23 July 1984.

208. *Le Figaro*, 23 July 1984. Noting their remarkably fresh state at the end of the Tour, some of the racers recommended lengthening the stages.

209. *L'Humanité*, 30 June 1984.

210. Betsy King, quoted in ibid., 2 July 1984.

211. *L'Équipe*, 5, 12 July 1984; *Le Parisien Libéré*, 9 July 1984; *Le Monde*, 20 July 1984 (the paper noted that the women's endurance and recuperative powers were equal to and perhaps even greater than those of the male racers). *Le Figaro* noted that the experts hoped that "some of these young ladies would reach the Champs-Élysées." *Le Figaro*, 30 June–1 July 1984.

212. *Le Monde*, 5 July 1984.

213. Ibid., 2 July 1984; *L'Équipe*, 2, 16, 21–22 July 1984; *La Croix*, 24 July 1984; *Le Parisien Libéré*, 9 July 1984; *Libération*, 7–8 July 1984.

214. *L'Équipe*, 30 June–1 July 1984.

215. *Libération*, 7–8 July 1984; *L'Équipe*, 13, 16 July 1984.

216. *Libération*, 7–8 July 1984.

217. *Le Figaro*, 7–8 July 1984.

218. No doubt to avoid this connotation, the regulations of the women's Tour referred to the participants as *concurrentes* ("contestants" or "competitors").

219. *Le Figaro*, 23 July 1984.

220. *L'Équipe*, 25 June 1984. One of the physicians on the women's Tour noted

of the racer Judith Painter: "It is difficult to explain how her legs can be so slender; let's say that quality is not proportional to volume." Ibid., 16 July 1984.

221. Ibid., 16 July 1984; *Libération,* 7–8 July 1984. Fifteen years after the first women's Tour, Jacques Goddet confirmed that the stages of subsequent women's Tours had not been lengthened because of the problem raised by women urinating. Interview with the author, 21 July 1999.

222. For positive assessments see *L'Équipe,* 3 July 1984; *La Croix,* 7, 24 July 1984; *Le Figaro,* 2, 7–8, 23 July 1984; *Le Monde,* 5 July 1984. In 2004 the women's Tour was canceled. Its organizers hoped that this would be only a temporary setback, but it was not held in 2005 either.

223. Phil Ligett, *Tour de France* (London: Harrap Books, 1989), 136–38.

224. Pigois, *Les petites reines,* 58; Laget, Laget, and Mazot, *Le grand livre du sport féminin,* 306.

225. For Longo's athletic achievements and records, see Jean Boully, *Les stars du Tour de France* (Paris: Bordas, 1990), 83–85; Hubscher, *L'histoire en mouvements,* 311–12; Longo's official website (http://jeannielongo.free.fr).

226. Pigois, *Les petites reines,* inside cover flap, 245–46, 253.

227. Ibid., 256–57.

228. Quoted in *L'Auto,* 30 July 1909. *L'Auto,* too, referred to the racers as "demigods." See, for example, ibid., 4 August 1909.

229. Lance Armstrong (with Sally Jenkins), *It's Not about the Bike: My Journey Back to Life* (New York: Berkley Books, 2001), 215.

230. As noted in chapter 2, Aragon saw the Tour racers' effort, sweat, and "voluntary pain" in 1947 as a "lesson of national energy" and believed the race proved "that France is alive."

231. Perhaps no single feature of the Tour illustrates this point more than the daily ceremonies at the end of a stage, during which, to this day, the stage winner and the racers wearing the prestigious jerseys receive bouquets and kisses from local beauties.

232. Roland Barthes, *Mythologies* (Paris: Éditions du Seuil, 1957), 109.

233. Jacques Goddet, *Les noces du Tour* (1963), quoted in Jacques Marchand and Pierre Debray, *Pour le Tour de France, contre le Tour de France* (Paris: Berger-Levrault, 1967), 71–72.

FOUR. *L'AUTO'S OUVRIERS DE LA PÉDALE*

1. See, for example, *L'Auto,* 21 June 1904.

2. Dr. Just Lucas-Championnière, *La bicyclette* (Paris: Léon Chailly, 1894), 46. Some of the material that follows first appeared in Christopher Thompson, "Bicycling, Class, and the Politics of Leisure in Belle Epoque France," in *Histories of Leisure,* ed. Rudy Koshar (Oxford: Berg, 2002), 131–46.

3. Lucas-Championnière, *La bicyclette,* 46–47.

4. Garsonnin, *Conférence sur la vélocipédie faite à Tours le 31 mars 1888* (Rouen: Imprimerie Julien Lecerf, 1888), 12. For other examples of such prejudice, see Maurice Martin, preface to Louis Baudry de Saunier, *L'art de bien monter la bicyclette,* 3rd ed. (Paris: n.p., 1894), 10–11; *Rennes-Vélo,* 1 November 1897.

5. Garsonnin, *Conférence sur la vélocipédie,* 24; A. Berruyer, *Manuel du véloceman ou notice, système, nomenclature, pratique, art et avenir des vélocipèdes* (Grenoble: Typographie de F. Allier Père et Fils, 1869), 21.

6. Baudry de Saunier, *L'art de bien monter la bicyclette,* 45–46; idem, *Le cyclisme théorique et pratique* (Paris: Librairie Illustrée, 1892), 161–219; Martin, preface to Baudry de Saunier, *L'art de bien monter la bicyclette,* 10–11.

7. Baudry de Saunier, *L'art de bien monter la bicyclette,* 18.

8. M.D. Bellencontre, *Hygiène du vélocipède* (Paris: L. Richard, Libraire-Éditeur, 1869), 8; Médecin-Major de 1ère classe Salle, *La reine de la route: Eléments de physiologie et notions d'hygiène pratique à l'usage des officiers-cyclistes* (Paris: Henri Charles-Lavauzelle, Éditeur Militaire, 1899), 51; Berruyer, *Manuel du véloceman,* 64–65. To this day, the French term for the bicycle seat is the word for saddle, *la selle.*

9. Baudry de Saunier, *L'art de bien monter la bicyclette,* 79, 80–81; Dr. Philippe Tissié, *L'éducation physique* (Paris: Librairie Larousse, 1901), 55–56; Salle, *La reine de la route,* 51–52.

10. Salle, *La reine de la route,* 50.

11. Berruyer, *Manuel du véloceman,* 54.

12. Lucas-Championnière, *La bicyclette,* 40.

13. Louis Baudry de Saunier, *Recettes utiles et procédés vélocipédiques* (Paris, 1893), 25. Many moralizing middle-class commentators, even some who viewed the bicycle favorably, linked such cyclists to the toxic cocktail of idleness and alcohol. See Salle, *La reine de la route,* 16; *Le Parisien de Paris,* 28 November 1897, quoted in Jacques Seray, *Deux roues: La véritable histoire du vélo* (Rodez: Éditions du Rouergue, 1988), 163; Garsonnin, *Conférence sur la vélocipédie,* 16.

14. Bellencontre, *Hygiène du vélocipède,* 35–38; Garsonnin, *Conférence sur la vélocipédie,* 41; Baudry de Saunier, *Recettes utiles et procédés vélocipédiques,* 97; Dr. J. Basset, *De l'influence de la bicyclette sur la diminution de la tuberculose à Toulouse* (Toulouse, 1905), 7–8.

15. For a complete account of the excursion and festivities surrounding the celebration of *père* Galloux, see Paul Sainmont, *Le Véloce-Club de Tours et le doyen des cyclistes de France* (Tours: Librairie Péricat, 1902).

16. Some of the material that follows first appeared in Christopher Thompson, "Controlling the Working-Class Sports Hero in Order to Control the Masses? The Social Philosophy of Sport of Henri Desgrange," *Stadion* 27 (2001): 139–51.

17. Henri Desgrange, *La tête et les jambes* (Paris: L. Pochy, 1898), 15–16.

18. See Christopher Thompson, "Regeneration, *Dégénérescence,* and the Medical

Debates about the Bicycle in Fin-de-Siècle France," in *Sport and Health in History,* ed. Thierry Terret (Sankt Augustin, Germany: Academia Verlag, 1999), 341.

19. Desgrange, *La tête et les jambes,* 14, 18, 19, 21–24, 31, 34, 103, 166.

20. Ibid., 10, 96–97, 152. Desgrange's emphasis on the racer's laziness was contradicted by the fact, obvious even to a casual observer, that bicycle racing was extraordinarily time- and energy-consuming, an aspect of the sport Desgrange and his journalists endlessly glorified in their coverage of the Tour.

21. I disagree with Jacques Goddet's characterization of Desgrange as a "determined supporter of professionalism in his writings." See Jacques Goddet, *L'équipée belle* (Paris: Robert Laffont SA et Stock, 1991), 20.

22. Henri Desgrange, *Alphonse Marcaux,* 2nd ed. (Paris: L. Pochy, 1899), 88–90.

23. In 1905, only 3 percent of a French worker's expenses covered nonessential items; in 1930 that figure was still a paltry 4.7 percent. Parisian workers had an advantage over their provincial counterparts: in 1907 9.2 percent of their income was available for nonessential items; in 1937 that figure had increased to 19.2 percent. Alain Beltran, *Un siècle d'histoire industrielle en France: Industrialisation et sociétés 1880–1970* (Éditions SEDES, 1998), 141, 151. This may explain why young men from the Paris area were disproportionately represented in the early Tours.

24. On pre–World War II French agriculture, see Antoine Olivesi and André Nouschi, *La France de 1848 à 1914* (Paris: Éditions Nathan, 1981), 241–43, 252–56; Maurice Agulhon, André Nouschi, and Ralph Schor, *La France de 1914 à 1940* (Paris: Éditions Nathan, 1993), 165–67.

25. Jean-Charles Asselain, *Histoire économique de la France du XVIIIe siècle à nos jours,* vol. 2, *De 1919 à la fin des années 1970* (Paris: Éditions du Seuil, 1984), 76.

26. Beltran, *Un siècle d'histoire industrielle en France,* 72.

27. For more on the composition of French cycling clubs before World War I, see Christopher Thompson, "Bicycling, Class, and the Politics of Leisure," 137–39.

28. *L'Auto,* 17 July 1925.

29. For statements by the organizers, see ibid., 2 July 1903, 1 June 1907, 23 June 1938. For statements by racers, see ibid., 17, 19 June 1920.

30. Ibid., 24 July 1903.

31. Ibid., 4 June, 29 May 1903. In 1904 the registration fee was refunded to racers finishing below twenty-second place. Ibid., 24 May 1904.

32. Ibid., 21 July 1903.

33. In 1907 the five-franc per diem arrangement resulted in a distribution of more than six thousand francs to the less successful racers. Ibid., 11 June 1908.

34. Ibid., 1 August 1910.

35. Lenard Berlanstein, *The Working People of Paris, 1871–1914* (Baltimore, MD: Johns Hopkins University Press, 1984), 44.

36. Christophe Charle, *Histoire sociale de la France au XIXe siècle* (Paris: Éditions du Seuil, 1991), 183, 185.

37. *L'Auto,* 18 May 1904.

38. Roger Price, *A Social History of Nineteenth-Century France* (New York: Holmes & Meier, 1987), 209; Berlanstein, *The Working People of Paris,* 65–66; Charle, *Histoire sociale de la France au XIXe siècle,* 205; Jacques Ozouf and Mona Ozouf, *La République des instituteurs* (Paris: Éditions du Seuil, 1992), 299, 303.

39. Roger Lajoie-Mazenc, *L'homme-horloge: Gustave Garrigou; Itinéraire d'un enfant de l'Aveyron devenu Géant de la route* (La Primaube: Graphi Imprimeur, 1996), 25, 26, 37–38.

40. For store rental and purchase figures in Paris at the time, see Jean-Pierre Daviet, *La société industrielle en France 1814–1914* (Paris: Éditions du Seuil, 1997), 246.

41. *L'Auto,* 16, 17 May, 1 June 1922.

42. Alphonse Baugé, *Messieurs les coureurs: Vérités, anecdotes et réflexions sur les courses cyclistes et les coureurs* (Paris: Librairie Garnier Frères, 1925), 50–52.

43. Jacques Augendre, *Marcel Bidot: Souvenirs, ou l'épopée du Tour de France* (Troyes: Éditions de la Maison du Boulanger, 1996), 8, 10, 11, 17, 19, 21, 23, 36.

44. *L'Auto,* 24 July 1923.

45. Eric S. Reed, "The Tour de France: A Cultural and Commercial History" (PhD diss., Syracuse University, 2001), 92.

46. René Kuhn, Alfred North, and Jean-Claude Philipp, *Le cyclisme en Alsace de 1869 à nos jours* (Strasbourg: Editions Publitotal, 1980), 21.

47. André Leducq and Roger Bastide, *La légende des Pélissier* (Paris: Presses de la Cité, 1981), 10–17, 26, 31. Two 1903 Tour contestants did not return the following year: Rodolfo Muller, the manager of the J. Conte stores in Paris, could not afford to leave his job for three weeks, and Arthur Pasquier had opened his own shop. *L'Auto,* 15 June 1904. A potential 1933 participant, Paul Amet, decided not to take part when, after the death of his mother, his relatives offered him "une bonne situation dans le commerce" that no longer allowed him to cycle competitively. *L'Auto,* 20 June 1933.

48. *L'Auto,* 13 June 1920. See ibid., 6 July 1937, 12 July 1938, for the examples of Léo Amberg and Jules Lowie, respectively.

49. Ibid., 28 June 1904, 23 June 1919, 5 July 1920, 9, 11 July 1927.

50. These averages were calculated by dividing each winner's overall time by the number of stages, excluding the Tours of 1905 through 1912, when the classification was calculated on a points system and times were not officially recorded.

51. Robert Dieudonné, *Le marchand de kilomètres* (Paris: Éditions Berger-Levrault, 1932), 41, 47.

52. André Reuze, *Le Tour de Souffrance* (Paris: Arthème Fayard, 1925).

53. *L'Auto,* 4 July 1929, 12 July 1924.

54. Ibid., 5 July 1910.

55. Patricia Hilden, *Working Women and Socialist Politics in France, 1880–1914: A Regional Study* (Oxford: Clarendon Press, 1986), 13, 225. Revolutionary syndicalism eschewed peaceful participation in parliamentary politics as a way to improve the

lives and working conditions of the exploited masses and looked instead to a presumably violent general strike of all workers to destroy capitalism and reorganize productive relations and society along equitable lines.

56. On attempts by elites during the belle époque to use cycling clubs to supervise, control, and "improve" lower-class men, see Christopher Thompson, "Bicycling, Class, and the Politics of Leisure," 138–39.

57. See, for example, *L'Auto,* 24 July 1929.

58. Ibid., 26 July 1932.

59. What is not clear is whether supervisors believed the race exerted a positive influence on their employees or whether workers seeking to disrupt the monotony of their workday negotiated the time off with their foremen. The latter, recognizing that many of their employees would desert their work stations to watch the race in any case, may have preferred to be seen as benevolently granting them permission to do so than be confronted with an unnegotiated *fait accompli.*

60. *L'Auto,* 25 June 1907.

61. *Lyon Républicain,* 1912 (n.d.), quoted in *L'Auto,* 13 July 1922.

62. In 1939 Desgrange continued to insist that "the racer is under our control and subject to the requirements of the rules during the entire race." *L'Auto,* 8 June 1939.

63. See ibid., 25 June 1907, 21 May 1910, 27 April, 5 June 1920, 21 June 1921, 19 June 1923, 3 June 1925, 10 June 1931.

64. Ibid., 29 July 1911, 21 May 1910. Although *L'Auto* claimed that this particularly "backward" mayor was the exception, Desgrange indulged in some unsubtle economic blackmail, reminding mayors of host communities that "their simple duty is to receive with a smile people who, without asking for anything, entertain a part of their city for thirty-six hours."

65. Ibid., 22 July 1908, 21 May 1910. The organizers insisted that racers who sauntered around town after a stage in their racing outfits did so because the suitcases containing their regular clothes had not yet arrived, but it is plausible that they enjoyed their celebrity and wore their racing gear to attract attention, female admirers, gifts, and free drinks and meals.

66. Ibid., 23 July 1912.

67. Ibid., 2 July 1903.

68. Ibid., 20 June 1920.

69. Ibid., 6 July 1914, 21 May 1910.

70. See, for example, ibid., 13 July 1912, 3 July 1920, 3 July 1922, 6 July 1926, 4 July 1928, 8 July 1931, 9 July 1933.

71. Ibid., 25 June 1907, 21 June 1904, 21 May 1910.

72. Ibid., 16 July 1914. See also ibid., 13 July 1914.

73. Ibid., 18 July 1914.

74. Ibid., 26 July 1914, *édition spéciale.*

75. Ibid., 16 July 1914.

76. See, for example, ibid., 14 July 1923, 26 June 1924, 3 July 1931.

77. Ibid., 6 June 1935.

78. See, for example, ibid., 29 June 1922, 19 July 1935.

79. Ibid., 3 July 1911.

80. Ibid., 7 June 1923.

81. Ibid., 18 July 1930.

82. Ibid., 21 May 1910.

83. See, for example, ibid., 2 July 1911, 30 June 1912.

84. For examples of cartoons, see ibid., 10, 12 July 1927. For examples of anecdotes, see ibid., 22 June, 1 July 1922, 15 July 1925, 31 July 1932, 24 June 1937. Television coverage after World War II and changing sensibilities defused this issue entirely: viewers are now used to camera shots, sometimes taken discreetly from hovering helicopters, of dozens of racers relieving themselves on the side of the road, to the light-hearted commentary of reporters. Only a racer who makes no attempt to find a spot where the public is absent or sparse is sanctioned today.

85. Ibid., 9 August 1904, 19 June 1935.

86. Ibid., 13, 27 July 1909, 3 August 1912.

87. Ibid., 5 July 1922.

88. Ibid., 18 June 1920. See similar reminders to the racers in ibid., 1 June 1935, 30 June 1938.

89. Ibid., 20 July 1921, 21 July 1926.

90. In the 1930s *L'Auto* occasionally suggested that there was less need to impose a behavioral code on the contestants, as they were "better selected" and therefore better behaved. Ibid., 10 June 1931, 29 May 1934. This assertion is contradicted by the published lists of offending racers fined during that decade and by the organizers' admission in 1932 of the need "to continue perfecting the rules because the racers will continue to perfect ways to circumvent them." Ibid., 18 July 1932.

91. Ibid., 6 July 1914.

92. Ibid., 25 June 1907. The organizers also portrayed the racers' trainers, once condemned as poorly behaved (ibid., 28 July 1908), as having subsequently eliminated "the bad elements," leaving "only respectable subjects who do not behave scandalously in train stations [nor] swear at the public at the checkpoints." Ibid., 24 July 1914. They, too, were a moral, self-regulating working community, whose improvement confirmed the Tour's civilizing influence.

93. Ronald Hubscher, ed., *L'histoire en mouvements: Le sport dans la société française (XIXe–XXe siècle)* (Paris: Armand Colin, 1992), 469.

94. Jacques Augendre, Roger Bastide, Gianni Marchesini, and Jean-Paul Ollivier, *Le dictionnaire des coureurs* (La Maison du Sport, 1988), 923.

95. See Pierre Chany, *La fabuleuse histoire du Tour de France* (Paris: Éditions Nathan, 1991), 144.

96. See *L'Équipe* for the week of 31 May–6 June 1951.

97. Ibid., 31 May 1951.

98. *L'Auto,* 26 June 1924, 5 June 1920, 3 June 1925, 27 June 1923.

99. Ibid., 8 June, 31 May 1929.

100. Ibid., 23 July 1938.

101. Ibid., 2 June 1939.

102. Ibid., 3 June 1939. The audience in the grandstand included the president of the Chambre Syndicale Nationale du Cycle; Louis Renault and his wife; a deputy from the Meuse known for defending the cause of the bicycle; Henri Desgrange and his companion, Jane Deley; Jacques Goddet; and a member of one of France's oldest families, Gontaut-Biron (presumably the one who, under the pseudonym Pépin, had participated in the 1905 and 1907 Tours).

103. *L'Auto*, 3 June 1939.

104. Ibid.

105. *L'Intransigeant*, 16 July 1935.

106. See, for example, *L'Auto*, 20 July 1903, 1 August 1905, 24 June 1910, 18, 26 July 1912. To this day, Tour contestants are required to sign in at the beginning of each stage in a ritual celebration of the "surviving" racers.

107. See, for example, ibid., 19 July 1907, 25 June 1913.

108. Ibid. 8, 13 July 1939.

109. *Lyon Républicain* (n.d.), quoted in *L'Auto*, 25 July 1911. Emphasis in original.

110. *L'Auto*, 1 July 1904.

111. Ibid., 25 July 1903, 21 June 1904.

112. *L'Écho de Longwy*, 7 July 1913.

113. *L'Auto*, 18 June 1929.

114. *L'Écho de Longwy*, 24 July 1913.

115. *L'Auto*, 30 May 1929.

116. Ibid., 19 July 1930.

117. Ibid., 29 January 1936. *L'Auto* did not always keep its facts straight. In 1939 the paper lauded the Belgian Albertin Disseaux for having the will to participate in the Tour despite being from a financially comfortable family. This praise came only two years after an article describing him as a "kid who climbs the rungs of the social ladder one by one and who finds himself—thanks to his valor and courage—at the head of a small fortune that allows him to blossom with each breath of life." Ibid., 17 July 1937, 14 July 1939. Occasionally Desgrange came out in favor of "specialization" and full professionalism in cycling. When he did so in 1925, he compared professional racers who specialized in racing the Tour (as opposed to other events) to workers *(ouvriers)* who specialized in one specific task in their workplace. Ibid., 13 July 1925. In this instance Desgrange evoked the modern industrial worker, rather than the skilled guild artisan, to make his case.

118. See, for example, the racer Blanc-Mesnil's experience in Reuze, *Le Tour de Souffrance*.

119. Henri Decoin and Pierre Cartoux, *Le roi de la pédale* (Paris: Ferenczi et Fils, 1925), 11, 83, 80, 102, 105.

120. Pierre Charreton, *Les fêtes du corps: Histoire et tendances de la littérature à thème sportif en France 1870–1970* (Saint-Étienne: CIEREC—Université de Saint-Étienne, 1985), 143–44, 146–47. As Charles Rearick has noted, interwar French popular culture celebrated heroic "little people" from the urban lower classes, including Tour winners like André Leducq and Georges Speicher, as resilient, humorous, good-natured, and unpretentious *mômes* (kids), *faubouriens* (residents of working-class suburbs), *gens du peuple* (common people), and *titis parisiens* (streetwise brats). Charles Rearick, *The French in Love and War: Popular Culture in the Era of the World Wars* (New Haven, CT: Yale University Press, 1997), especially chapters 4 and 5.

121. Robert Dieudonné, *Frangins* (Paris: Éditions des Portiques, 1931).

122. Robert Dieudonné, *Bébert ou la vie ratée* (Paris: La Nouvelle Société-d'Édition, 1929).

123. Ibid., 90.

124. In 1929, for instance, *L'Auto* ran a series of articles titled "Should Bicycle Racers Have a Job outside Sports?" (see no. 2 in this series in *L'Auto,* 2 May 1929). For the interwar debate about professional soccer in France, see Alfred Wahl, *Les archives du football: Sport et société en France (1880–1980)* (Paris: Éditions Gallimard/Julliard, 1989), 244–60; Geoff Hare, *Football in France: A Cultural History* (Oxford: Berg, 2003), 19–22. On shamateurism and professionalism in interwar French rugby, see Philip Dine, *French Rugby Football: A Cultural History* (Oxford: Berg Publishers, 2001), 69–70, 81, 84–91.

125. *L'Auto,* 26 June 1931, *supplément gratuit.*

126. Dieudonné, *Frangins,* 157.

127. *L'Auto,* 26 June 1931, *supplément gratuit.*

128. Ibid., 12 June 1929.

129. Ibid., 25 April 1934.

130. Ibid., 28 July 1939.

131. Ibid., 8 July 1923.

132. Ibid.

133. Ibid., 18 July 1933.

134. Ibid., 16 July 1914.

135. In 1923, when *L'Auto* opened a fund for Jean Alavoine, who had crashed and withdrawn from that year's Tour while well placed in the overall standings, it had received 8,197 francs by mid-August. Ibid., 14 August 1923.

136. Ibid., 8 June 1923.

137. See, for example, ibid., 23 June, 10, 13, 14, 16 July 1923.

138. Ibid., 17, 28, 29 July 1923.

139. Prizes for the "most elegant" racer continued to be awarded after World War II by sponsors (such as sportswear manufacturers) who wished to associate their products with elegance and sport, and race coverage often noted the physical elegance of certain champions, notably Hugo Koblet and Jacques Anquetil, but these

references to elegance were no longer correlated with representations of racers as exemplary physical laborers.

140. Interviewed by the author on 21 July 1999, an alert Jacques Goddet, then well into his nineties, did not appear to recall the image of the *ouvrier de la pédale*, although he did recall other details of Tour history before World War II.

141. See the appendix. A 1976 study of the occupations of the parents of French professional racers discovered that 50 percent were in agriculture; only 17 percent were workers and 13 percent shopkeepers. Jacques Calvet, *Le mythe des géants de la route* (Grenoble: Presses Universitaires de Grenoble, 1981), 98.

142. *Le Monde,* 16 July 1966.

FIVE. THE *FORÇATS DE LA ROUTE*

1. For an earlier version of this chapter, see Christopher Thompson, "The Tour in the Inter-War Years: Political Ideology, Athletic Excess and Industrial Modernity," *International Journal of the History of Sport* 20 (June 2003): 79–102.

2. *L'Auto,* 9 June 1903.

3. Municipal Archives of Sens, Arrêté relatif aux courses vélocipédiques à grande distance, 28 May 1903.

4. Anson Rabinbach, *The Human Motor: Energy, Fatigue, and the Origins of Modernity* (New York: Basic Books, 1990), 23, 72.

5. Roger Price, *A Social History of Nineteenth-Century France* (New York: Holmes & Meier, 1987), 212, 245; Judith F. Stone, *The Search for Social Peace: Reform Legislation in France, 1890–1914* (Albany: State University of New York Press, 1985), 124–25; Gary Cross, *A Quest for Time: The Reduction of Work in Britain and France, 1840–1940* (Berkeley: University of California Press, 1989), 37, 39, 42–43; Roger Price, ed., *Documents on the French Revolution of 1848* (London: Macmillan, 1996), 50.

6. The Radicals came to power at the height of the Dreyfus affair in 1899, when much of the Left coalesced in defense of the Jewish officer.

7. Stone, *The Search for Social Peace,* 62–65, 90, 96, 103–22.

8. Ibid., 101, 124; Cross, *A Quest for Time,* 56–57, 71–72, 82–83, 235; Price, *A Social History of Nineteenth-Century France,* 210–11.

9. Cross, *A Quest for Time,* 48, 49, 51, 98; Price, *A Social History of Nineteenth-Century France,* 214; Stone, *The Search for Social Peace,* 62, 101, 124–27, 129, 132–39, 147–59; Christophe Charle, *Histoire sociale de la France au XIXe siècle* (Paris: Éditions du Seuil, 1991), 303.

10. Stone, *The Search for Social Peace,* 134.

11. *L'Auto,* 9 June 1903. See also ibid., 8 August 1911.

12. See ibid., 27 July, 19 August 1909, 8 August 1912. The Belgian critics quoted

were a newspaper in Tournai, a socialist on the Brabant Provincial Council, and *La Jeunesse Progressiste.*

13. Quoted in *L'Auto,* 13 July 1923.

14. Ibid., 3 July 1903, 20 July 1912; *Le Matin,* 28 July 1913. For other such descriptions by the organizers, see *L'Auto,* 3 June 1929, 28 June 1931, 7, 11 July 1932. See also *Le Petit Parisien,* 4 July 1935.

15. *Le Matin,* 28 July 1913.

16. *L'Auto,* 28 May, 21 July 1929. See also *L'Auto,* 20 July 1931, 26 July 1938, 30 June 1934.

17. Desgrange noted that the legs of André Leducq (a future two-time Tour champion) "rotate harmoniously like a perfectly round spinning wheel indefatigably unwinding its wool." Ibid., 23 June 1928.

18. Ibid., 10 July 1907.

19. See ibid., 4 July 1914, 29 June 1919, 27 June 1920, 26, 25 June 1921, 24 June 1923, 22 June 1924, 21 June 1925, 19 June 1927, 17 June 1928, 30 June 1929, 27 June 1933. In 1921, for example, the racers' *développements* were almost all between five and six meters. Ibid., 26 June 1921.

20. Ibid., 18 July 1911.

21. Ibid., 8 August 1939.

22. See Faroux's articles in ibid., 15, 16, 21, 26, 29, 30 July 1936. For a similar postwar piece by Faroux, see *L'Équipe,* 17 July 1946.

23. *L'Auto,* 28 August 1936.

24. John Hoberman, *Mortal Engines: The Science of Performance and the Dehumanization of Sport* (New York: Free Press, 1992), 5–6, 9, 13–14, 19, 25, 68, 189.

25. Rabinbach, *The Human Motor,* 90, 119. For more on Marey's career, see ibid., chapter 4.

26. Ibid., 1–4, 10, 44, 59, 60, 133, 137, 183.

27. *L'Auto,* 27 July 1906.

28. Jules Amar, a French industrial ergonomist and fatigue expert and the author of *Le Moteur Humain* (1913), was convinced that "a scientifically predetermined optimum speed and position achieve a maximum amount of work with a minimum amount of fatigue" and tested his theory in sports. Rabinbach, *The Human Motor,* 48, 188.

29. *L'Auto,* 15 July 1922.

30. Alphonse Baugé, *Messieurs les coureurs: Vérités, anecdotes, et réflexions sur les courses cyclistes et les coureurs* (Paris: Librairie Garnier Frères, 1925), 41.

31. *L'Auto,* 17 July 1925, 14 July 1926.

32. The following account is drawn from Pierre Chany, *La fabuleuse histoire du Tour de France* (Paris: Éditions Nathan, 1991), 196–200.

33. For a summary of the Pélissiers' racing careers, see Jacques Augendre, Roger Bastide, Gianni Marchesini, and Jean-Paul Ollivier, *Le dictionnaire des coureurs* (La Maison du Sport, 1988), 987–88.

34. *Le Petit Parisien,* 27 June 1924.

35. Guyana became a French penal colony in the mid-nineteenth century. See Jacques-Guy Petit et al., *Histoire des galères, bagnes et prisons, XIIIe–XXe siècles: Introduction à l'histoire pénale de la France* (Toulouse: Éditions Privat, 1991), 227–59.

36. For Londres's series of articles on the Tour, see *Le Petit Parisien,* 23, 27, 29 June, 2, 3, 5, 7, 9, 13, 19, 20 July 1924.

37. *L'Humanité,* 1 July 1924.

38. See *L'Auto,* 18, 24, 9 July 1906, 17 July 1907, 9 July 1912, 18 July 1931, 5 July 1936.

39. See ibid., 6 June 1906, 23, 31 July 1907, 4 June, 6 July 1910, 14, 19, 21 July 1929, 30 June, 15 July 1930, 5, 13, 15, 22 July 1931, 20 May 1932, 10, 25 July 1933, 8 May, 18 July 1936. Racers were at times collectively a beast: *L'Auto* referred to "our great snake of almost 80 racers." Ibid., 8 July 1935.

40. Ibid., 30 July 1932, 28 June 1934; *L'Équipe,* 4–5 July 1953.

41. *L'Auto,* 31 July 1938.

42. Ibid., 11 July 1934.

43. See ibid., 3 July 1903, 7 July 1911, 9 July 1919, 21 June 1928, 29 May 1929, 23 May 1934, 6 July 1928.

44. Ibid., 9 July 1919.

45. See ibid., 28 June 1907, 7 July 1911, 20 June 1914, 6, 23 June, 18 July 1929, 20 May, 30 July 1932, 28 June 1934, 23 June 1938. See also *L'Équipe,* 19 June 1950, 4–5 July 1953.

46. *L'Auto,* 6 June 1929.

47. Ibid., 15 June 1929. The greyhound, known for its speed, was perhaps the most frequently invoked dog. See *Le Populaire,* 22 July 1923; *L'Auto,* 10 June 1929, 14 July 1933, 23 May, 23 June 1934, 6 June 1935.

48. *Le Populaire,* 23 July 1923.

49. Occasionally, commentators invoked the racers' almost bestial strength as their defining trait and as evidence that they were primitive "individuals without a profession and without work," who lacked the skill and work ethic associated with meritorious human labor. *La Jeunesse Progressiste* (n.d.), quoted in *L'Auto,* 8 August 1912.

50. Hoberman, *Mortal Engines,* 49, 51, 52, 56, 58, 59, 61.

51. *L'Auto,* 6 July 1919.

52. Ibid., 30 June 1924.

53. Michel Pierre, "La transportation (1848–1938)," in Jacques-Guy Petit et al., *Histoire des galères, bagnes et prisons,* 253–54. Londres's investigative work on the penal colony in Guyana was sufficiently well known for him to be invited to author the preface of an interwar study by Eugène Dieudonné, *La vie des forçats* (Paris: Librairie Gallimard, 1930). This work went through at least twenty-two editions, offering further evidence of the contemporary appeal of the topic.

54. Michelle Perrot, "On the Formation of the French Working Class," in *Work-*

ing-Class Formation: Nineteenth-Century Patterns in Western Europe and the United States, ed. Ira Katznelson and Aristide R. Zolberg (Princeton, NJ: Princeton University Press, 1986), 90, 100; idem, "Le regard de l'Autre: Les patrons français vus par les ouvriers (1880–1914)," in Le patronat de la seconde industrialisation, ed. Maurice Levy-Leboyer (Paris: Les Éditions Ouvrières, 1979), 295; idem, "The Three Ages of Industrial Discipline," in Consciousness and Class Experience in Nineteenth-Century Europe, ed. John M. Merriman (New York: Holmes & Meier, 1979), 16; idem, Les ouvriers en grève, France 1871–1890 (Paris: Mouton & Co., 1974), 295; Stewart Edwards, The Paris Commune, 1871 (Chicago: Quadrangle Books, 1971), 40; R. Palme Dutt, The Internationale (London: Lawrence & Wishart Ltd., 1964), 11. For the text of the "Internationale" and the English translation I have quoted, see Robert Tombs, The Paris Commune, 1871 (London: Longman, 1999), 220–23.

55. L'Auto, 26 July 1924.

56. See Le Figaro, 27 June 1924; Le Temps, 28 June 1924; La Croix, 27 June, 1 July 1924. Le Petit Journal Illustré does not seem to have mentioned the incident in its race coverage. See, for example, Le Petit Journal Illustré, 29 June 1924.

57. L'Humanité, 27, 28, 29 June, 21 July 1924.

58. Ibid., 25 July 1921, 24 June, 11 July 1923.

59. Ibid. 21 June 1924.

60. Ibid., 1 August 1932.

61. Ibid., 7 July 1932, 22 July 1935.

62. Ibid., 19, 17, 21 July 1935.

63. Ibid., 26 July 1935.

64. Ibid., 13 July 1932, 10, 15, 16, 19, 23, 29 July 1935. Paris-Soir agreed that the touristes-routiers were treated unfairly by Desgrange. Paris-Soir, 15 July 1935.

65. L'Humanité, 1, 2 August 1932, 10, 15, 16, 29 July 1935.

66. Ibid., 15 July 1935.

67. Ibid., 2 July 1924, 6 July 1932.

68. Ibid., 1 July 1924; Richard Holt, Sport and Society in Modern France (Hamden, CT: Archon Books, 1981), 204.

69. Holt, Sport and Society, 204. The issues of Sport Ouvrier cited by Holt are those of 5 October 1923 and 6 December 1924. The translations are his.

70. L'Humanité, 31, 15, 17 July 1932, 11, 12 July 1935.

71. Ibid., 31 July 1932.

72. Ibid., 28 July 1935.

73. Richard Holt notes that although it is difficult to document the rank and file's response to communist sports-related propaganda, anecdotal evidence suggests that readers of Sport Ouvrier resisted or were ignorant of the communist ideology of sport. Holt, Sport and Society, 211. While it spent considerable portions of its race coverage denouncing Desgrange, L'Humanité also provided its readers with a narrative summary of each stage. No doubt recognizing that many of its readers

remained fans of the sport, *L'Humanité* thus hoped to discourage workers from buying "bourgeois" papers with their "bourgeois" coverage of the Tour.

74. *L'Humanité,* 21 July 1924.

75. Ibid., 6, 26 July 1932.

76. Harry Braverman, *Labor and Monopoly Capital: The Degradation of Work in the Twentieth Century* (New York: Monthly Review Press, 1974), 90–91, 118, 131, 133–34; Cross, *A Quest for Time,* 106; David S. Landes, *The Unbound Prometheus: Technological Change and Industrial Development in Western Europe from 1750 to the Present* (Cambridge: Cambridge University Press, 1969), 321–22; Charles S. Maier, "Between Taylorism and Technocracy: European Ideologies and the Vision of Industrial Productivity in the 1920s," *Journal of Contemporary History* 5, no. 2 (1970): 29; Georges Friedmann, *The Anatomy of Work: Labor, Leisure and the Implications of Automation,* trans. Wyatt Rawson (New York: Heinemann Educational Books, 1961), 86–87.

77. Rabinbach, *The Human Motor,* 2.

78. Braverman, *Labor and Monopoly Capital,* 88, 97, 100.

79. *L'Auto,* 1 July 1903.

80. Ibid., 19 July 1903.

81. Ibid., 1 June, 25 July 1929, 7 June 1930, 12 July 1931, 22 July 1933.

82. Maier, "Between Taylorism and Technocracy," 31; George G. Humphreys, *Taylorism in France, 1904–1920: The Impact of Scientific Management on Factory Relations and Society* (New York: Garland Publishing, 1986), 83–84, 91–92.

83. Humphreys, *Taylorism in France,* 65.

84. Aimée Moutet, "Les origines du système de Taylor en France: Le point de vue patronal (1907–1914)," *Le Mouvement Social* 93 (October–December 1975): 15, 18–21, 23–33; Humphreys, *Taylorism in France,* 49, 76–81, 93–102, 116–23; Cross, *A Quest for Time,* 106; Maurice Levy-Leboyer, "Innovation and Business Strategies in Nineteenth- and Twentieth-Century France," in *Enterprise and Entrepreneurs in Nineteenth- and Twentieth-Century France,* ed. Edward C. Carter II, Robert Foster, and Joseph N. Moody (Baltimore, MD: Johns Hopkins University Press, 1976), 116; Richard F. Kuisel, *Capitalism and the State in Modern France: Renovation and Economic Management in the Twentieth Century* (Cambridge: Cambridge University Press, 1981), 28. For the specific French conditions and background that shaped efforts to promote and implement Taylorism in France—particularly attempts by French employers to assert greater discipline and restrict worker autonomy—see Humphreys, *Taylorism in France,* chapter 2.

85. Moutet, "Les origines du système de Taylor," 38–41, 43, 48; Humphreys, *Taylorism in France,* 4, 10, 13–14, 105–9, 113, 127–30; Levy-Leboyer, "Innovation and Business Strategies," 116; Cross, *A Quest for Time,* 106; Rabinbach, *The Human Motor,* 241. For an overview of workers' reactions to industrial rationalization in early-twentieth-century France, see also Gary Cross, "Redefining Workers' Control: Rationalization, Labor Time, and Union Politics in France, 1900–1928," in

Work, Community, and Power: The Experience of Labor in Europe and America, 1900–1925, ed. James E. Cronin and Carmen Sirianni (Philadelphia: Temple University Press, 1983), 143–72.

86. *L'Humanité,* 7 July 1913.

87. Humphreys, *Taylorism in France,* 109–11. The business press tended to favor Taylor's ideas, the press of the Left was predictably hostile, and specialized papers devoted to the concerns of industry were divided. Moutet, "Les origines du système de Taylor," 42–43.

88. Moutet, "Les origines du système de Taylor," 44, 46; Humphreys, *Taylorism in France,* 3–4, 13, 130–34, 172–74, 221–24, 230, and chapter 5; Sylvie Van de Casteele-Schweitzer, "Management and Labour in France, 1914–39," in *The Automobile Industry and its Workers: Between Fordism and Flexibility,* ed. Steven Tolliday and Jonathan Zeitlin (New York: St. Martin's Press, 1987), 58–60; Rabinbach, *The Human Motor,* 260–61, 271; Cross, *A Quest for Time,* 105–11, 151–52, 157–59, 195, 200–204, 209; Maier, "Between Taylorism and Technocracy," 38. For a detailed examination of wartime scientific management in France, see Humphreys, *Taylorism in France,* chapter 4.

89. Kuisel, *Capitalism and the State,* 77, 83, 86; Moutet, "Les origines du système de Taylor," 33–34; Van de Casteele-Schweitzer, "Management and Labour in France," 63; Cross, *A Quest for Time,* 204, 209, 211–12; Maier, "Between Taylorism and Technocracy," 50–51. For an overview of the impact of Taylorism in Europe in the 1920s, see Maier, "Between Taylorism and Technology," 27–61; for the French case, see 37, 57–58 in particular. For communist attitudes towards rationalization during the interwar period, see also Van de Casteele-Schweitzer, "Management and Labour in France," 71.

90. Patrick Fridenson, "Automobile Workers in France and Their Work, 1914–1983," in *Work in France: Representations, Meaning, Organization, and Practice,* ed. Steven Laurence Kaplan and Cynthia J. Koepp (Ithaca, NY: Cornell University Press, 1986), 523–27. For a different view, which argues for less worker resistance to rationalization while acknowledging high turnover rates and voluntary departures, see Van de Casteele-Schweitzer, "Management and Labour in France," 64–65. Van de Casteele-Schweitzer argues that by the late 1920s "Taylorism had become part of people's mentalities" in the French automobile industry (68).

91. Quoted in Cross, *A Quest for Time,* 212.

92. *L'Humanité,* 9, 22 July 1932, 28 July 1935.

93. *Le Canard Enchaîné,* 2, 9 July 1924.

94. André Reuze, *Le Tour de Souffrance* (Paris: Arthème Fayard, 1925).

95. Ibid., 153, 172–77, 230–32.

96. *L'Intransigeant,* 19 July 1937.

97. *Paris-Soir,* 21 July 1937.

98. *La Bretagne Sportive,* 19 October 1935, 16 July 1936, 15 July 1937; *Voici,* 4 July 1936, quoted in *La Bretagne Sportive,* 9 July 1936; *La Province* (Rennes), 7, 28 July

1937, 22 July 1939; *Les Nouvelles de l'Ouest* (Rennes), 30 July 1937; *Les Nouvelles Rennaises et de l'Ouest,* 20 July 1933.

99. *L'Action Française,* 30 June 1924, 31 July 1935; *L'Intransigeant,* 29, 30 June, 20 July 1924; *L'Écho de Paris,* 27, 30 June 1924.

100. *Le Peuple,* 27 June 1924.

101. See *Le Populaire,* 8, 17 July 1928, 6, 25 July 1929, 1 July 1937.

102. Michel Winock, *Le socialisme en France et en Europe, XIXe–XXe siècle* (Paris: Éditions du Seuil, 1992), 82–85. This mutual hostility also led to competing socialist and communist sports federations and clubs and was played out in their sports papers. Holt, *Sport and Society,* 204–5.

103. *Le Populaire,* 25 July 1929, 17 July 1928.

104. Winock, *Le socialisme,* 85–86. The reconciliation between French socialists and communists led to the unification of their rival sports federations in 1934. Holt, *Sport and Society,* 205.

105. *Le Populaire,* 29 July 1935, 19, 27 July 1937.

106. *L'Auto,* 29 June 1924.

107. Ibid., 1 June, 22 May 1925. See also the 1926 regulations in ibid., 1 June 1926.

108. Ibid., 6 June 1932, 10 June 1931, 10 June 1930, 14 June 1932.

109. Price, *A Social History of Nineteenth-Century France,* 245–46.

110. Reuze, *Le Tour de Souffrance,* 212–13.

111. *L'Auto,* 3 June 1925.

112. Ibid., 30 June 1924.

113. Ibid., 8 July 1929. For two examples of such parodies, see ibid., 8, 15 July 1924.

114. Ibid., 20 July 1924, 20 June 1925, 8 July 1929. Jacques Goddet, Desgrange's young assistant, was more conflicted as to the legitimacy of "literary" critiques of the Tour, acknowledging that they had some basis in reality. Ibid., 25 July 1931.

115. Ibid., 17 July 1924.

116. Ibid., 18 July 1924, 21 June 1927, 28 July, 30 June 1924, 26 July 1909, 28 July 1939.

117. Ibid., 20 July 1924.

118. Ibid., 22 July 1931, 12, 20 July 1924.

119. Ibid., 20 July 1924.

120. Jacques Chabannes, *Microbe* (Paris: La Nouvelle Société d'Édition, 1929).

121. Chany, *La fabuleuse histoire du Tour de France,* 295.

122. *Le Petit Parisien,* 15, 16 July 1935; *L'Ouest-Éclair,* 15, 17 July 1935; *Le Temps,* 13, 17 July 1935; *L'Intransigeant,* 17, 29 July 1935; *La Croix,* 16 July 1935; *L'Action Française,* 12, 13, 17, 24 July 1935.

123. *L'Action Française,* 31 July, 14 August 1935; *La Croix,* 21–22 July 1935.

124. *L'Auto,* 15 July 1935.

125. Ibid., 16, 17 July 1935.

126. *Paris-Soir,* 16 July 1935.

127. *Le Populaire,* 22 July 1935.

128. *L'Humanité,* 16 July 1935.

129. Ibid., 17 July 1935.

130. *Le Populaire,* 22 July 1935.

131. *L'Humanité,* 15, 17, 29 July 1935.

132. *Le Populaire,* 30, 29 July 1935.

133. *L'Humanité,* 12 July 1935.

134. Ibid., 13 July 1935.

135. Ibid., 14, 15 July 1935.

SIX. WHAT PRICE HEROISM?

1. *Le Monde,* 16 July 1952, 27 July 1950; *Le Figaro,* 20–21 July 1947; *Le Populaire,* 8 July 1947.

2. *Le Figaro,* 20–21 July 1947; *L'Équipe,* 6 July 1949; *Le Populaire,* 8 July 1947.

3. See the comments of René Vietto in *L'Humanité,* 16 July 1947; of Jean Robic in *L'Équipe,* 18 July 1955; of Robert Cazala in *L'Équipe,* 19 June 1959; and of Roger Hassenforder in René Kuhn, Alfred North, and Jean-Claude Philipp, *Le cyclisme en Alsace de 1869 à nos jours* (Strasbourg: Éditions Publitotal, 1980), 181.

4. Pierre Chany, *La fabuleuse histoire du Tour de France* (Paris: Nathan, 1991), 382; *Le Monde,* 1 August 1950; *La Croix,* 1 August 1950; *Le Populaire,* 31 July 1950.

5. *Le Monde,* 12 July 1952; *L'Humanité,* 15 July 1952.

6. *La Croix,* 13–14 July 1952; *Le Monde,* 13–14 July 1952.

7. *L'Équipe,* 12–13 July 1952.

8. *Le Parisien Libéré,* 12 July 1952.

9. *Le Figaro,* 12–13 July 1952.

10. *Le Parisien Libéré,* 12 July 1952.

11. *L'Équipe,* 12–13 July 1952.

12. *Le Monde,* 13–14 July 1952.

13. *Le Parisien Libéré,* 14 July 1952.

14. *L'Équipe,* 12–13 July 1952.

15. This account of the racers' "strike" at Valence-d'Agen is drawn from Chany, *La fabuleuse histoire du Tour de France,* 675–76; Noël Couëdel, *Tour de France: La fête de juillet* (Paris: Calmann-Lévy, 1983), 19–20, 22; Robin Magowan, *Tour de France: The Historic 1978 Event,* 2nd ed. (Boulder, CO: Velopress, 1996), 102–3; "A Strike on the Tour," 8 P.M. news, IT1, 12 July 1978; *L'Équipe,* 13 July 1978; *La Croix,* 13 July 1978; *Le Figaro,* 13 July 1978; *Le Matin de Paris,* 13 July 1978; *Libération,* 13 July 1978. Only *L'Humanité* downplayed the public's displeasure, noting that it had not been informed of the reasons behind the racers' anger. *L'Humanité,* 13 July 1978.

16. *L'Équipe,* 13 July 1978.

17. "A Strike on the Tour."

18. *Le Matin de Paris,* 13 July 1978; *Le Monde,* 14 July 1978; *Libération,* 13 July 1978; *L'Humanité,* 13 July 1978; *Le Figaro,* 13 July 1978.

19. *L'Équipe,* 13 July 1978. Lévitan, meanwhile, threatened to open the race to "amateur" racers from communist Eastern Europe, who he believed would not strike. *Le Matin de Paris,* 14 July 1978. The irony of a highly commercialized Western European sporting event turning to racers from the communist dictatorships of Eastern Europe, in the belief they would be more docile than their rebellious peers in the West, was lost on most commentators.

20. For Baylet's widely reported statements, see *L'Humanité,* 13 July 1978; *Le Matin de Paris,* 13 July 1978; *Le Figaro,* 13 July 1978; *L'Équipe,* 13 July 1978; *Libération,* 13 July 1978; *La Croix,* 13, 14–15 July 1978; *La Dépêche du Midi,* 13 July 1978.

21. *L'Équipe,* 13 July 1978; *Le Matin de Paris,* 13 July 1978; *La Dépêche du Midi,* 13 July 1978.

22. *L'Équipe,* 13 July 1978. See also comments by Raymond Poulidor and Jean-Pierre Genet in *Le Matin de Paris,* 13 July 1978.

23. *Libération,* 13 July 1978; *La Croix,* 13 July 1978. See also criticism of the strike by Henri Anglade in *Le Figaro,* 13 July 1978, and Maurice de Muer in *La Dépêche du Midi,* 13 July 1978.

24. *L'Équipe,* 13 July 1978; "A Strike on the Tour"; *Libération,* 13 July 1978; *La Dépêche du Midi,* 13 July 1978. The 1978 Tour was particularly difficult. See Magowan, *Tour de France,* 17; Chany, *La fabuleuse histoire du Tour de France,* 871.

25. *L'Équipe,* 13 July 1978; *L'Humanité,* 13 July 1978; *La Dépêche du Midi,* 13 July 1978.

26. See comments by team managers Louis Caput (Mercier), Peter Post (Raleigh), Fred de Bruyne (Flandria), and Cyrille Guimard (Renault), and by the 1937 winner Guy Lapébie and the five-time champion Eddy Merckx in *L'Équipe,* 13 July 1978; *La Croix,* 13 July 1978; *La Dépêche du Midi,* 13 July 1978; *Le Matin de Paris,* 13 July 1978.

27. *Libération,* 13 July 1978; *Le Matin de Paris,* 13 July 1978; *L'Humanité,* 14 July 1978; *La Croix,* 14–15 July 1978.

28. *Le Matin de Paris,* 13 July 1978; *La Croix,* 14–15 July 1978; *Le Monde,* 14 July 1978.

29. *L'Équipe,* 13 July 1978.

30. Cyrille Guimard, the manager of Hinault's Renault team, claimed that the strike was "necessary" and "healthy" and would modify "the balance of power between the racers, whose opinion has never been asked, and the organizers." *Le Matin de Paris,* 13 July 1978; *Libération,* 13 July 1978; *La Croix,* 13 July 1978.

31. *Le Monde,* 14 July 1978; *L'Équipe,* 13, 18 July 1978; *La Croix,* 13 July 1978; *Le Matin de Paris,* 13 July 1978; *L'Humanité,* 13 July 1978; *La Dépêche du Midi,* 13 July 1978; "A Strike on the Tour."

32. *Libération,* 13 July 1978; *Le Matin de Paris,* 14 July 1978; *Le Figaro,* 13 July 1978; *La Croix,* 14–15 July 1978.

33. *Libération,* 13 July 1978.

34. *L'Humanité,* 13, 14 July 1978.

35. Many papers noted the historical precedent of the Pélissiers' withdrawal in 1924 and the resulting furor over the *forçats de la route* image introduced by Albert Londres. See, for example, *La Croix,* 14–15 July 1978; *Libération,* 13 July 1978.

36. *L'Humanité,* 14 July 1978.

37. See the exchange between Hinault and a spectator reported in *L'Équipe,* 13 July 1978.

38. *Libération,* 13 July 1978.

39. *L'Équipe,* 13 July 1978.

40. Ibid.; *La Dépêche du Midi,* 13 July 1978.

41. *L'Équipe,* 13 July 1978.

42. *La Croix,* 14–15 July 1978; "A Strike on the Tour"; Magowan, *Tour de France,* 104.

43. *La Dépêche du Midi,* 13 July 1978; *L'Équipe,* 13 July 1978.

44. Patrick Laure, *Le dopage* (Paris: Presses Universitaires de France, 1995), 15–39, 41, 47; Jean-Pierre de Mondenard, *Dopage: L'imposture des performances; Mensonges et vérités sur l'école de la triche* (Paris: Éditions Chiron, 2000), 8–10. The etymology of the word *doping* itself is rooted in hard manual labor: the Dutch settlers of seventeenth-century New Amsterdam fed their construction workers a mysterious porridge, *doop* ("mixture") in their slang, which they believed had a stimulating effect. The porridge was apparently so toxic that it caused a number of deaths and was outlawed in 1666. René Guillet, *Le doping de l'homme et du cheval* (Paris: Masson et Cie., 1965), 9; Roger Bastide, *Doping: Les surhommes du vélo* (Paris: Raoul Solar, 1970), 17; Laure, *Le dopage,* 8. Laure notes another explanation which attributes the word to the Boers of late-eighteenth-century South Africa, who used *doop* to designate a strong alcohol used by the Bantus in ceremonial rituals.

45. Laure, *Le dopage,* 46–47, 61–62; Bastide, *Doping,* 13–14, 21–22; John Hoberman, *Mortal Engines: The Science of Performance and the Dehumanization of Sport* (New York: Free Press, 1992), 6, 63, 92–93, 97, 124, 133.

46. Bastide, *Doping,* 37, 39, 63–64, 99; Laure, *Le dopage,* 26, 49, 59–60, 63–65, 69, 71–74, 75; Mondenard, *Dopage,* 10–14. The alcoholic beverages used as stimulants by racers included rum, champagne, port (sometimes mixed with egg yolks), cherry brandy, red wine, beer, and cognac.

47. André Noret, *Le dopage,* 2nd ed. (Paris: Éditions Vigot, 1990), 201.

48. Henri Desgrange, *La tête et les jambes,* 7th ed. (Paris: Imprimerie Henri Richard, 1930), 155.

49. Laure, *Le dopage,* 49, 56–58, 66–67, 201–5; Michel Bourgat, *Tout savoir sur le dopage* (Lausanne: Éditions Favre, 1999), 78.

50. Jean-Paul Rapp, *Le doping des sportifs (ou la science détournée),* 2nd ed. (Paris: Éditions Médicales et Universitaires, 1978), 36.

51. Mondenard, *Dopage,* 14; Pierre Chany, *La fabuleuse histoire du cyclisme* (Paris:

ODIL, 1975), 451; idem, *La fabuleuse histoire du cyclisme,* vol. 1, *Des origines à 1955* (Paris: Nathan, 1988), 286; Bastide, *Doping,* 63–64, 83–84; Laure, *Le dopage,* 58–59; Victor Cosson, interview with the author, 15 July 1999. Cosson finished third in the 1938 Tour de France.

52. Laure, *Le dopage,* 176–78, 207.

53. Bastide, *Doping,* 86–87; Russell Mockridge, completed by John Burrowes, *My World on Wheels: The Posthumous Autobiography of Russell Mockridge* (London: Stanley Paul, 1960), 96, 131; Mondenard, *Dopage,* 23, 105–7, 169–70; Noret, *Le dopage,* 32–33.

54. Laure, *Le dopage,* 49–53; Noret, *Le dopage,* 200.

55. Laure, *Le dopage,* 194; Bourgat, *Tout savoir sur le dopage,* 74.

56. Bourgat, *Tout savoir sur le dopage,* 73–74; Bastide, *Doping,* 113–14, 193.

57. Bastide, *Doping,* 114. For the comments of Alfred de Bruyne, another cautious racer, see Mockridge, *My World on Wheels,* 133. One estimate is that 70 percent of Tour racers during the 1950s were doping. Rapp, *Le doping des sportifs,* 141.

58. Bastide, *Doping,* 201–2.

59. Admissions by racers continued into the mid-1960s, after which antidoping legislation in France and other European countries discouraged such openness. For these and other examples of doping by racers during this period, see J.-P. de Mondenard and Bernard Chevalier, *Le dossier noir du dopage: Les produits, les dangers, les responsables* (Paris: Hachette, 1981), 181–85; Bastide, *Dopage,* 42–44, 87–90, 96–98, 104–9, 117, 122–24, 186, 188–90, 192–93, 199–203, 206–7; Laure, *Le dopage,* 53–54, 91–93, 96–97, 99, 107–8; Guillet, *Le doping de l'homme et du cheval,* 24–26; Rapp, *Le doping des sportifs,* 25, 34–35, 145; Bourgat, *Tout savoir sur le dopage,* 63; Noret, *Le dopage,* 147; Mondenard, *Dopage,* 38, 178–80.

60. Laure, *Le dopage,* 206. See comments by Louison Bobet (Mockridge, *My World on Wheels,* 130); Raphael Géminiani (Roger Bastide et al., "Le Tour devant les stimulants," *But et club, le miroir des sports* 919 [12 July 1962], quoted in Mondenard, *Dopage,* 117); and Jacques Anquetil (*Miroir Sprint,* 9 May 1966, quoted in Mondenard, *Dopage,* 116).

61. Loi # 65–412 du 1er juin 1965, tendant à la répression de l'usage des stimulants à l'occasion des compétitions sportives. *Journal Officiel de la République Française,* 2 June 1965; *Le Parisien Libéré,* 29 June 1966. Other laws established punishments (one month to five years in prison and a fine of 60 to 1,800 francs) in cases in which the administration of doping substances led to illness or prevented an individual from working. *Le Parisien Libéré,* 29 June 1966.

62. Rapp, *Le doping des sportifs,* 174.

63. For the specific drugs listed, see Décret # 66–373 du 10 juin 1966, portant réglement d'administration publique pour l'application de la loi # 65–412 du 1er juin 1965, tendant à la répression de l'usage des stimulants à l'occasion des compétitions sportives. *Journal Officiel de la République Française,* 14 June 1966.

64. There were some exceptions to this rule. *Le Monde* occasionally addressed the

issue, sometimes as part of a broader critique of the Tour. *Le Monde,* 10 August 1950, 16 July 1952. Jean Leulliot, an organizer of bicycle races, noted in *Route et piste* the "too many strange deaths" of racers in the wake of the 1952 amateur championships. Bastide, *Doping,* 188–89.

65. Laure, *Le dopage,* 179; Bastide, *Doping,* 29. See *Journal Officiel de la République Française,* 24 June 1955.

66. Laure, *Le dopage,* 179, 206; Bastide, *Doping,* 106–9. Laure argues that the Mallejac incident was the only one of many doping incidents to receive considerable coverage between 1950 and 1965, evidence of the "apparent passivity of the public" during this period.

67. Bastide, *Doping,* 102–4, 107, 109, 188; Rapp, *Le doping des sportifs,* 20.

68. Mondenard, *Dopage,* 267. See also *L'Équipe,* 27 October 1955. Mondenard, during his tenure as the federal physician of the FFC, assisted Dumas in the campaign against doping. Rapp, *Le doping des sportifs,* 142.

69. From the mid-1950s the police conducted occasional drug raids on racers at competitions in Italy, Switzerland, and Belgium to discourage doping. Bastide, *Doping,* 129–31.

70. Ibid., 117.

71. Ibid., 119.

72. Ibid., 117–120.

73. Ibid., 253; Laure, *Le dopage,* 207.

74. *Cinq colonnes à la une,* 7 July 1961.

75. Bastide, *Doping,* 122–26. Bastide gives 26 and 27 February 1963 as the dates for the conference, but all other sources indicate that it actually occurred a month earlier. A few days before the Uriage conference, a meeting of medical experts from ten countries had led the Comité de l'Éducation Extra-scolaire (of the Council of Europe), meeting in Strasbourg on 22 January 1963, to call for an end to doping. Guillet, *Le doping de l'homme et du cheval,* 3. See the "Practical Recommendations" of the Council of Europe's Section of Physical Education and Sports for an example of European initiatives envisaged at the time. Guillet, *Le doping de l'homme et du cheval,* 87–89.

76. Guillet, *Le doping de l'homme et du cheval,* 3–4, 83–85; Rapp, *Le doping des sportifs,* 105, 167.

77. Guillet, *Le doping de l'homme et du cheval,* 4.

78. Rapp, *Le doping des sportifs,* 167–68; Noret, *Le dopage,* 161–62. For national and European-wide antidoping laws and initiatives, see Patrick Laure, ed., *Dopage et société* (Paris: Ellipses, 2000), 363–92. For one of the UCI's first lists of banned products, see Bastide, *Doping,* 253–55.

79. *L'Équipe,* 29 June 1966.

80. *Le Parisien Libéré,* 29 June 1966.

81. *Le Figaro,* 29, 30 June 1966.

82. *L'Équipe* noted that the doctors had not followed the letter of the law, which required officials to test only those racers suspected of doping; furthermore, nee-

dle marks were problematic evidence, as they could result from the use of an authorized substance. *L'Équipe,* 29 June 1966.

83. *Le Monde,* 30 June 1966.

84. *L'Équipe,* 29 June 1966; *Le Parisien Libéré,* 29 June 1966; *Le Monde,* 30 June 1966.

85. *L'Humanité,* 30 June 1966. The racers also targeted Dr. Dumas with derisive chants: "A test tube for Dumas!" and "Dumas, pipi! Dumas, pipi!" Bastide, *Doping,* 156.

86. *Le Parisien Libéré,* 30 June 1966. Rik Van Looy and Jan Janssens, in particular, disputed Anquetil's claims.

87. *Le Monde,* 1 July 1966; *L'Équipe,* 30 June 1966; *L'Humanité,* 30 June 1966; *Le Parisien Libéré,* 30 June 1966. *Le Figaro* also believed that certain "leaders" were responsible for the protest. *Le Figaro,* 30 June 1966. Although some racers claimed their protest was a "strike" (*Le Figaro,* 30 June 1966), the organizers initially attributed the "antidoping rebellion" to the racers' "bad mood." *L'Équipe,* 30 June 1966; *Le Monde,* 1 July 1966; *Le Parisien Libéré,* 30 June 1966. This explanation infantilized the protesting racers, emptying their act of social significance: they were not adult workers, rebelling against the arbitrary authority of their employers and the state, but children who had thrown a tantrum when confronted with parental discipline intended to protect their health. Nevertheless, the term *strike* seeped into the organizers' coverage of the incident as well as that of other papers. See, for example, *Le Figaro,* 30 June 1966; *L'Humanité,* 30 June 1966.

88. See the text of the *communiqué des commissaires* in *Le Monde,* 1 July 1966.

89. *L'Humanité,* 30 June 1966; *Le Monde,* 1 July 1966. Some team managers also criticized the racers' protest, which seemed to constitute an admission that they could not race without stimulants. *Le Parisien Libéré,* 30 June 1966.

90. *Le Monde,* 1 July 1966; *Le Parisien Libéré,* 30 June 1966; *L'Humanité,* 30 June 1966.

91. Anquetil implied that the very high pace of the previous stage (over forty-six kilometers per hour) would have been impossible without banned stimulants. *Le Parisien Libéré,* 30 June 1966. The pace had in fact attracted attention. *Le Parisien Libéré* described it as "alarming," while *Le Monde* noted the fortuitous timing of the tests, given the record-setting pace of the stage. *Le Parisien Libéré,* 29 June 1966; *Le Monde,* 30 June 1966.

92. *Le Parisien Libéré,* 30 June 1966; *Le Monde,* 1 July 1966; *L'Humanité,* 30 June 1966.

93. *L'Équipe,* 30 June 1966. Antoine Blondin was a serious novelist, a member of the Hussards literary movement, and a former right-wing activist. He believed that sports writing was underestimated as a literary genre and became France's leading sports journalist, renowned for the quality of his prose: see Philip Dine, *French Rugby Football: A Cultural History* (Oxford: Berg Publishers, 2001), 51, 137–38. Several collections of his sports articles have been published, some posthumously.

94. *L'Humanité,* 30 June 1966; *Le Parisien Libéré,* 30 June 1966.

95. *Le Figaro* noted that many racers felt that tests were "a threat to their human and professional dignity." *Le Figaro,* 30 June 1966.

96. *L'Équipe,* 30 June 1966; *Le Monde,* 1 July 1966; *L'Humanité,* 30 June 1966. Blondin defended the racers for simply expressing the "desire of the individual to control his own body *[disposer de soi-même]*." *L'Équipe,* 30 June 1966.

97. *L'Équipe,* 30 June 1966.

98. *Le Monde,* 16 July 1966.

99. *Le Monde,* 1 July 1966.

100. *L'Équipe,* 30 June 1966.

101. *Le Figaro,* 30 June 1966. The racers' protest did not disrupt the drug testing of racers on the 1966 Tour. For coverage of other tests, see *L'Équipe,* 4 July 1966; *Le Parisien Libéré,* 4 July 1966.

102. *L'Humanité,* 30 June 1966.

103. Ibid.

104. *Le Parisien Libéré,* 30 June 1966.

105. Ibid., 12 July 1967; Bastide, *Doping,* 178–79; Jacques Augendre, Roger Bastide, Gianni Marchesini, and Jean-Paul Ollivier, *Le dictionnaire des coureurs* (La Maison du Sport, 1988), 1013; Magowan, *Tour de France,* 139.

106. For Simpson's own description of climbing the Mont Ventoux, see Magowan, *Tour de France,* 139.

107. Rapp, *Le doping des sportifs,* 19; Bastide, *Doping,* 180–83; Mondenard, *Dopage,* 173, 175–76; Laure, *Le dopage,* 110–11; Magowan, *Tour de France,* 140.

108. Laure, *Le dopage,* 111, 114; *Panorama,* ORTF 1, 14 July 1967. For photographic coverage of Simpson's death see, in particular, *Le Parisien Libéré,* 14 July 1967; *L'Équipe,* 14 July 1967.

109. For the official autopsy report, made public on 3 August 1967, see *L'Équipe,* 4 August 1967, quoted in Mondenard, *Dopage,* 175–76.

110. *Panorama,* ORTF 1, 14 July 1967; *Le Monde,* 16–17 July 1967.

111. See, for example, *La Croix,* 19, 26 July 1967.

112. *Le Monde,* 15, 28, 16, 17 July 1967; Bastide, *Doping,* 187.

113. *Panorama,* ORTF 1, 14 July 1967; Laure, *Le dopage,* 112.

114. *L'Humanité,* 14, 15 July 1967. In 1967 Anquetil acknowledged widespread doping by racers in a series of articles published in the weekly *France-Dimanche,* for which revelations the French Cycling Federation excluded him from the national and world championships. Anquetil then backtracked, blaming the journalist with whom he had worked for taking advantage of him. Bastide, *Doping,* 146–48. In 1969, however, Anquetil claimed in a *Sports Illustrated* article that all racers doped and that anyone who said otherwise was lying: "Since we are constantly asked to go faster to make ever-greater efforts, we are obliged to take stimulants." *Sports Illustrated,* 30 June 1969.

115. *L'Humanité,* 25 July 1967; ibid., 15 July 1967, quoted in *Le Monde,* 16–17 July 1967.

116. *L'Humanité,* 14, 25 July 1967.

117. *Le Parisien Libéré,* 17 July 1967; *L'Est Républicain,* 17 July 1967, quoted in Laure, *Le dopage,* 113.

118. Quoted in *Le Monde,* 15 July 1967. Simpson had admitted doping to *The People* a few months after the passage of the 1965 antidoping law in France. *Le Monde,* 15 July 1967. See *Le Monde,* 25 and 28 September 1965, for the paper's initial coverage of Simpson's revelations to *The People.*

119. *Le Monde,* 18 July 1967. *L'Est Républicain* wondered how many other racers had the same drugs as Simpson in their jersey pockets as they climbed the Mont Ventoux. *L'Est Républicain,* 15 July 1967, quoted in Laure, *Le dopage,* 113.

120. *Le Monde,* 19 July 1967.

121. Simpson already had two young children; his wife was pregnant with their third child, whom she lost four months into her pregnancy, less than two weeks after her husband's death. *L'Équipe,* 27 July 1967. When Goddet met Helen Simpson in Avignon to attend the departure of her husband's coffin, she says she had the distinct impression that the organizers believed her husband had brought shame on the Tour and that they wished to avoid making his death a big issue: beyond Goddet's attendance at the funeral, the organizers did nothing to help her and her two young daughters. *L'Équipe,* 17 July 1967; Helen Hoban, formerly Helen Simpson, interview with the author, 25 July 1999. For the way the Tour organizers planned to honor Simpson's memory on the last day of the 1967 Tour, see *Le Parisien Libéré,* 18 July 1967.

122. *Le Parisien Libéré,* 14 July 1967; *Panorama,* ORTF 1, 14 July 1967; *L'Équipe,* 14 July 1967.

123. *Le Parisien Libéré,* 20 July 1967.

124. *L'Équipe,* 14 July 1967. Goddet also put doping in its broader context in *L'Équipe,* 15–16 July 1967.

125. Ibid., 15–16 July 1967.

126. Ibid., 25 July 1967.

127. Ibid.

128. For the results of testing in Belgium and Italy in 1965, see Bastide, *Doping,* 128–29; Mondenard, *Dopage,* 250.

129. Mondenard and Chevalier, *Le dossier noir du dopage,* 238; Laure, *Le dopage,* 109; Bastide, *Doping,* 158.

130. For percentages of positive tests during this period, see Noret, *Le dopage,* 159; Bastide, *Doping,* 251; Rapp, *Le doping des sportifs,* 183.

131. Mondenard, *Dopage,* 82.

132. For the relevant text from the French minister of youth and sports, François Misoffe, to the French sports federations, see Rapp, *Le doping des sportifs,* 171–73.

133. Magowan, *Tour de France,* 143; Mondenard and Chevalier, *Le dossier noir du dopage,* 200; Laure, *Le dopage,* 116; Mondenard, *Dopage,* 40, 91–92. Like amphetamines, cortisone and corticosteroids have a stimulant effect that help racers fight fatigue in endurance events and can produce a euphoric effect, but the abuse of such drugs is held responsible for the wave of tendinitis and bronchitis suffered by racers during this period. Testosterone and anabolic steroids dramatically increase the assimilation of protein; the resulting muscular development increases athletes' power and allows them to train harder. Rapp, *Le doping des sportifs,* 62; Laure, *Le dopage,* 126–28, 180; Mondenard, *Dopage,* 39.

134. These racers included Eddy Merckx, Freddy Maertens, Hermann Van Springel, Walter Godefroot, Michel Pollentier, Felice Gimondi, Roger Pingeon, Lucien Aimar, Bernard Thévenet, Luis Ocaña, Joop Zoetemelk, and Joaquin Agostinho. For details about the cases of racers who tested positive and various doping affairs during this period, see Mondenard, *Dopage,* 19, 271–72; Rapp, *Le doping des sportifs,* 40, 142–43, 174; Mondenard and Chevalier, *Le dossier noir du dopage,* 185–88, 212–15, 222–23, 235, 237–38, 240–41.

135. Mondenard, *Dopage,* 25, 167; Laure, *Le dopage,* 128.

136. Mondenard and Chevalier, *Le dossier noir du dopage,* 233, 241.

137. When none of the top finishers of the 1966 professional World Championship road race submitted to drug tests in a timely fashion, as required, the UCI suspended them for several weeks. The racers appealed their suspensions and continued to compete. Facing criticism from the French and Italian organizations of professional cycling and a lawsuit by the sponsor of the newly crowned world champion, the UCI soon backed down and voided the suspensions. Bastide, *Doping,* 141–44.

138. Noret, *Le dopage,* 164–65. This issue had surfaced a few years earlier, when defenders of Désiré Letort, who tested positive after winning the 1967 French professional road-racing championship, argued that in voiding his victory the FFC had violated his civil rights and the procedural guarantees afforded him by French law. Bastide, *Doping,* 158–63.

139. Mondenard and Chevalier, *Le dossier noir du dopage,* 239; Noret, *Le dopage,* 139–40.

140. For the affair involving Merckx's positive drug test during the 1969 Tour of Italy, see Laure, *Le dopage,* 115; Bastide, *Doping,* 212–24; Noret, *Le dopage,* 229–33.

141. Magowan, *Tour de France,* 18.

142. In addition to the stage winner, four other racers were tested after each stage: the overall race leader, the stage runner-up, and two racers drawn at random. Ibid., 128.

143. Ibid., 129; Chany, *La fabuleuse histoire du Tour de France,* 679–80; *L'Équipe,* 18 July 1978.

144. *L'Équipe,* 18 July 1978.

145. Ibid.

146. *Le Matin de Paris*, 18 July 1978; *Libération*, 18 July 1978; *L'Humanité*, 18 July 1978; *La Croix*, 18, 19 July 1978. In 1977 some racers spent 280 days on their bicycles. In 1978 Freddy Maertens was entered by his team manager in 220 races, of which he remarkably won fifty-six. Mondenard and Chevalier, *Le dossier noir du dopage*, 206.

147. *L'Équipe*, 18 July 1978.

148. Ibid.

149. See Hoberman, *Mortal Engines.*

150. *Le Matin de Paris*, 18 July 1978; *Le Figaro*, 18 July 1978; Magowan, *Tour de France*, 129, 135–36.

151. Magowan, *Tour de France*, 128; *L'Équipe*, 18 July 1978. In one of his statements, however, Pollentier asserted that the drug was a new product that helped him to breathe at high altitude. This statement contradicted his claim that he had already used the product in Belgium, a country hardly known for its mountainous terrain. *Le Figaro*, 18 July 1978.

152. *Le Figaro*, 18 July 1978; Magowan, *Tour de France*, 133.

153. *Libération*, 18 July 1978.

154. *Le Monde*, 19 July 1978.

155. *L'Humanité*, 18 July 1978.

156. *La Croix*, 18 July 1978.

157. *Le Figaro*, 18 July 1978; *L'Humanité*, 18 July 1978.

158. *L'Équipe*, 18 July 1978. See also the racer Charly Rouxel's comments about amphetamines. *L'Équipe*, 13 July 1978.

159. Ibid., 18 July 1978.

160. Ibid. See also Goddet's comments in *Le Figaro*, 18 July 1978.

161. Bastide, *Doping*, 242.

162. *Libération*, 18 July 1978.

163. *La Croix*, 19 July 1978.

164. *L'Humanité*, 18 July 1978.

165. *L'Équipe*, 18 July 1978.

166. Mondenard and Chevalier, *Le dossier noir du dopage*, 226–27.

167. Ibid., 227.

168. An exception to this rule in 1978 were the contracts of racers with the Fiat–La France, Renault-Gitane, and T. I. Raleigh teams, which allowed for dismissal of a racer caught taking illicit substances. These three teams were unusual in that they were sponsored by bicycle manufacturers who wanted their racers' victories to be attributed to their superior equipment rather than to drugs. Magowan, *Tour de France*, 53.

169. Mondenard and Chevalier, *Le dossier noir du dopage*, 227.

170. Mondenard, *Dopage*, 202–9.

171. Laure, *Le dopage*, 150–51.

172. On the Thurau affairs, see Noret, *Le dopage*, 239–42.

173. Ibid., 245–51; Laure, *Le dopage,* 133–34; Bourgat, *Tout savoir sur le dopage,* 98.

174. Laure, *Le dopage,* 211. Laure also cites a 1993 study which found that the French public ranked cycling second (72 percent) behind track and field (85 percent) as the sport most affected by doping. Another study in the 1990s found that a vast majority of the French (92 percent) believed doping and money to be the two most serious threats to sport. Bourgat, *Tout savoir sur le dopage,* 27.

175. For the details of the so-called *loi Bambuck* and the antidoping measures that ensued from it in the 1990s, see Laure, *Dopage et société,* 368–70; Bourgat, *Tout savoir sur le dopage,* 115–24.

176. Paul Kimmage, *Rough Ride: Behind the Wheel with a Pro Cyclist* (London: Yellow Jersey Press, 1998), especially 30, 51, 55, 57–58, 80–81, 88, 91, 92, 96–98, 102–3, 125, 143–44, 146, 147, 148, 149, 169, 170, 176–78, 200, 230–35, 237–38, 244. The doping described by Kimmage involved vitamins B6 and B12, iron, amphetamines, cortisone, testosterone, caffeine, and hormones. A number of the drugs were taken both in pill form and by injection (including self-administered shots during races).

177. Bourgat, *Tout savoir sur le dopage,* 22; Mondenard, *Dopage,* 234–36.

178. Kimmage, *Rough Ride,* 248.

179. For additional accounts of the 1998 Tour doping scandal, see Fabrice Lhomme, *Le procès du Tour: Dopage; Les secrets de l'enquête* (Paris: Éditions Denoël, 2000); Nicolas Guillon and Jean-François Quénet, *Un cyclone nommé dopage: Les secrets du "Dossier Festina"* (Paris: Éditions Solar, 1999); Jeremy Whittle, *Yellow Fever: The Dark Heart of the Tour de France* (London: Headline, 1999); Samuel Abt and James Startt, *In Pursuit of the Yellow Jersey: Bicycle Racing in the Year of the Tortured Tour* (San Francisco: Van der Plas Publications, 1999).

180. Bourgat, *Tout savoir sur le dopage,* 12, 28–30, 65, 82, 89, 92–97; Mondenard, *Dopage,* 20–22, 25, 32, 42–44, 181–83; Laure, *Le dopage,* 135–36; Kimmage, *Rough Ride,* 245–58.

181. For the text and an explanation of the 1999 law, see *Le dopage hors jeu, Rapport d'information no. 1499, déposé en application de l'article 145 du Règlement par la Commission des Affaires Culturelles, Familiales et Sociales sur la loi relative à la protection de la santé des sportifs et à la lutte contre le dopage,* presented by Alain Néri, *député* (Paris: Assemblée Nationale, 1999).

182. For continued reporting on doping in cycling after the 1998 scandal, see Nicolas Guillon and Jean François Quénet, *Le dopage: Oui ça continue* (Paris: Éditions Solar, 2000); Jean-François Quénet, *Le procès du dopage: La vérité du jugement* (Paris: Éditions Solar, 2001). The most credible memoirs include those of Willy Voet, the Festina employee driving the vehicle stopped by customs officials in 1998; Bruno Roussel, the Festina team manager; Daniel Baal, the president of the FFC and vice president of the UCI at the time of the 1998 scandal; and the racers Jérôme Chiotti, Erwann Menthéour, Christophe Bassons, Pascal Richard, and Thierry Bourguignon. See Willy Voet, *Massacre à la chaîne: Révélations sur 30 ans de tricherie*

(Paris: Calmann-Lévy, 1999); Bruno Roussel, *Tour de vices* (Paris: Hachette Littératures, 2001); Daniel Baal, *Droit dans le mur: Le cyclisme mis en examen* (Grenoble: Éditions Glénat, 1999); Jérome Chiotti, *De mon plein gré* (Paris: Calmann-Lévy, 2001); Erwann Menthéour, *Secret défonce: Ma vérité sur le dopage* (Paris: Éditions Jean-Claude Lattès, 1999); Christophe Bassons, *Positif* (Paris: Éditions Stock, 2000); Pascal Richard, *Géant de la route, forçat de la vie: Le vrai visage d'un cycliste* (Geneva: Éditions Factuel, 2001); Thierry Bourguignon, *Tours et détours* (Paris: Botega Éditions, 2000). The self-serving accounts include those of Bernard Sainz, who was for decades a shadowy figure in the world of professional cycling and was implicated in the doping of the 1990s; and two books by Richard Virenque. See Bernard Sainz, *Les stupéfiantes révélations du Dr. Mabuse* (Paris: Éditions Jean-Claude Lattès, 2000); Richard Virenque (with Guy Caput and Christian Éclimont), *Ma vérité* (Monaco: Éditions du Rocher, 1999); Richard Virenque (with Jean-Paul Vespini), *Plus fort qu'avant* (Paris: Éditions Robert Laffont, 2002).

EPILOGUE

1. See, for example, Lance Armstrong's innovations in preparation for the 2004 Tour de France. *New York Times,* 19 April 2004.

2. My thanks to John Hoberman for providing me with the data from which I generated these figures.

3. In June 2003 the twenty-three-year-old French racer Fabrice Salanson died in his sleep; the autopsy did not reveal the presence of illicit drugs but attributed his death to cardiac and coronary anomalies. In February 2004 the twenty-one-year-old Belgian racer Johan Sermon also mysteriously died in his sleep. Although it is impossible to be certain as to the cause of either death, it is also difficult to rule out EPO. The drug thickens the blood and thus increases the chances of a stroke (particularly when the body is at rest for any length of time and the blood flow slows as a result), but it does not remain long in the user's body.

4. Both the blood and urine of racers are separated into A and B samples at the time they are drawn. In the event a racer's A sample comes back positive, his B sample is tested; it, too, must be positive for the racer to be found guilty of doping.

5. Hamilton has consistently and vigorously proclaimed his innocence. Two other prominent racers from Hamilton's Phonak team, including the racer who finished second in the 2004 Tour of Spain, were also found guilty of blood doping that year. As a result, the recently created Pro Tour in professional cycling, which organizes many of the sport's major races, denied Phonak a permit to compete in its events. Faced with no longer being commercially viable, the team fired its top staff to demonstrate its commitment to clean racing in the hope that the UCI would grant it the required permit.

6. A gifted climber, Heras had raised eyebrows by almost winning the penulti-

mate stage, which was a time trial, an event in which he had never performed well. Although his case had not fully run its course as this book was being completed, barring a successful appeal, Heras will almost certainly be fired by his team and banned from competition for two years by the Spanish cycling federation. Three years earlier, another Spaniard, Aitor Gonzalez, had been stripped of his Tour of Spain victory for doping. Meanwhile, two of Heras's teammates were expelled from stage races earlier in 2005 for registering hematocrit levels that exceeded the allowable maximum of 50 percent (an indication of their use of a boosting agent such as EPO), leading some in the Spanish press to charge that the team manager, Manolo Saiz, was behind his racers' doping violations.

7. Pantani's hematocrit level (54 percent) during the 1994 Tour of Italy was so high that it could plausibly be explained only by the use of EPO. In 1995, Pantani exhibited an even higher hematocrit level (60 percent) during the Milan-Turin race. *The Sunday Times,* 22 February 2004. At the time of his death Pantani still faced a trial for doping and sports fraud during the 2001 Tour of Italy, when insulin was found in his hotel room. It is worth noting that the 50 percent maximum permissible hematocrit level established by the UCI in 1997 is a threshold that implicitly tolerates doping: as David Walsh has noted, "Cyclists at the peak of their fitness will normally register a hematocrit of 40–43. A few have naturally high hematocrit levels, about 47 or 48, but this is rare, and Pantani was not among this small minority" (ibid.).

8. *Libération,* 19 February 2004. On Pantani's fall from grace and drug problems, see also *The Observer,* 22 February 2004.

9. The most sensational voluntary admission of recent years was that of the Spaniard Jesús Manzano. In a series of articles published by the Spanish sports daily *As* in late March 2004, Manzano described in great detail how he and other professional racers doped. As a result of his revelations, his former team, Kelme, was excluded from that summer's Tour de France by the race organizers.

10. Edita Rumsas, who spent the next two and a half months in jail, claimed, fantastically, that the drugs were for her mother. Her husband, who had left France immediately after the Tour, denied having used illicit drugs but refused to return for questioning by French authorities. One of his four blood tests, toward the end of the Tour, had, in fact, suggested the use of EPO, but the follow-up urine test required in such instances had been negative. (As the urine test signals only the presence of EPO consumed during the previous seventy-two hours, this result was hardly exculpatory, but it did prevent the organizers from taking any action against the racer.) Rumsas's team kept him on in the wake of the scandal, and he was named Lithuanian athlete of the year. The following spring, he finished sixth in the 2003 Tour of Italy, only to be found to have tested positive for EPO during an unannounced test conducted by the UCI before the race's sixth stage. That summer, the Lithuanian cycling federation suspended him for one year. In 2004, the French judge in charge of the 2002 case issued international arrest warrants for the

racer and the Polish doctor who had prescribed the substances discovered in Edita Rumsas's vehicle, charging both men with smuggling "prohibited merchandise."

11. In an interview with *Le Monde,* Gaumont explained how racers scheduled their consumption of illicit substances to avoid testing positive—a strategy that worked because the "unannounced" tests actually only occurred during team training camps and races. Moreover, he claimed that only the top racers could afford the cost of transfusions during a stage race like the Tour. Such transfusions, Gaumont argued, are critical because they allow a racer to increase his hematocrit, which is otherwise naturally depleted over the course of such a grueling event—and to do so without leaving any traces of EPO use. *Le Monde,* 15 March 2004. A few days later, the Spaniard Jesús Manzano went public with his revelations about doping in the sport (see note 9). He, too, explained how easily racers avoided testing positive by injecting EPO in the off-season and then drawing and storing their artificially boosted, highly oxygenated blood for use later in the season. Manzano noted that if drug tests during races were truly unannounced, racers would not have the time to inject diluting agents into their bloodstream that reduce their hematocrit level to under the legal 50 percent limit and thus allow them to test negative. *Libération,* 26 March 2004.

12. Another top racer, the recently retired Johan Museeuw, was implicated in 2005 in the biggest doping scandal in recent years in his native Belgium. He was formally charged with having in his possession in August 2003 illicit doping substances, including EPO, that had been banned by the World Anti-Doping Agency.

13. For a most insightful exploration of the "law of silence" that governs the topic of doping among professional cyclists, as well the often disingenuous rhetoric deployed by racers, their support staff, the sport's officials, and race organizers to avoid addressing the issue, see John Hoberman, " 'A Pharmacy on Wheels': Doping and Community Cohesion among Professional Cyclists Following the Tour de France Scandal of 1998," in *The Essence of Sport,* ed. Verner Møller and John Nauright (Odense: University Press of Southern Denmark, 2003), 107–27.

14. *The Guardian,* 30 July 2002.

15. On the public's reaction of indifference, often tinged with sympathy for the athletes, in this and other doping scandals, see Hoberman, " 'A Pharmacy on Wheels,' " 108–10; John M. Hoberman, *Testosterone Dreams: Rejuvenation, Aphrodisia, Doping* (Berkeley: University of California Press, 2005), chapter 6.

16. See, for example, Edward F. Coyle, "Improved Muscular Efficiency Displayed as 'Tour de France' Champion Matures," *Journal of Applied Physiology* 98 (June 2005): 2191–96. Coyle calculates that Armstrong increased his muscular efficiency when cycling by 8 percent between 1992 and 1999. Taking into account Armstrong's reduction in body fat and weight loss of about seven kilograms during that period, Coyle calculates that the racer's power-to-body-weight ratio improved by 18 percent. Coyle acknowledges, however, that the reasons for Armstrong's "extremely low maximal blood lactate concentration" are unclear, as are "the physio-

logical mechanisms responsible for" the 8 percent improvement in Armstrong's muscular efficiency and "the stimuli that provoked this adaptation."

17. Armstrong has often affirmed that when he returned to the sport after his bout with cancer, he was motivated to win by a sense of responsibility to the cancer community (see, for example, *Charlie Rose,* PBS, 1 August 2005). There is no reason to question the authenticity of such a noble and understandable sentiment. At the same time, such statements make Armstrong a difficult target for skeptics who wonder whether his remarkable performances are due in part to illicit doping. One may also wonder whether an individual motivated by so worthwhile a cause might be willing to use illicit means to win races: winning would allow him to offer an inspirational example of recovery and triumph to cancer patients as well as to raise public awareness and funds for cancer research.

18. This record represents a departure from the typical trajectory of successful Tour racers. From the first Tour in 1903 to the early 1990s, in virtually every case winners and top contenders in the race demonstrated their potential from the very beginning of their professional careers. Only in the past decade and a half has the Tour been won by racers who did not demonstrate that kind of potential early in their careers and whose first Tour performances were mediocre. Miguel Indurain, Lance Armstrong, and Bjarne Riis, winners between them of thirteen of the fifteen Tours between 1991 and 2005, fit this profile. Of the two remaining Tours during this period, one (in 1998) was won by the late Marco Pantani, who was found to have doped during much of his career; the other (in 1997) was won by Jan Ullrich, at that time a teammate of Bjarne Riis and a former East German, whose early years in the sport coincided with the final years of the German Democratic Republic, a Communist regime known for the systematic, state-sponsored doping of its elite athletes.

19. Ferrari worked for professional cycling teams before setting up his own practice. In addition to Armstrong, other top racers who consulted with him include some of the most successful Italian cyclists of the past decade and a half, as well as the Russian Pavel Tonkov, the Swiss Tony Rominger, and the Spaniard Abraham Olano. A less successful racer, the Belgian Axel Merckx (the son of the greatest racer of all time, Eddy Merckx), has also consulted with Ferrari. Eddy Merckx, a friend of Armstrong's, has repeatedly defended the latter against accusations of doping. For his part, Armstrong expressed disappointment at the verdict against Ferrari, a man he described as his "old friend" and "adviser." For a detailed explanation by Armstrong of his relationship with Ferrari, see *USA Today,* 14 July 2004.

20. See, for example, LeMond's interview in *Le Monde,* 15 July 2004. Another racer who questioned Armstrong's performances was Christophe Bassons. Bassons noted that although Armstrong had physiological capacities virtually identical to his own (as measured by standard tests), the American was capable of pushing a much harder gear and thus of deploying far more energy than Bassons during a 1999 Tour time trial. Christophe Bassons, *Positif* (Paris: Éditions Stock, 2000), 193.

A young racer ostracized by his peers for the public position he took against doping during the 1999 Tour de France, Bassons was reportedly warned by Armstrong, who suggested that he leave the sport, to be quiet on the subject. Hoberman, " 'A Pharmacy on Wheels,' " 110–11; *Libération,* 24 August 2005.

21. For the most comprehensive case that Armstrong has been doping, see Pierre Ballester and David Walsh, *L.A. Confidentiel: Les secrets de Lance Armstrong* (Paris: Éditions de la Martinière, 2004). Walsh, an award-winning English journalist for the *Sunday Times,* has been the most assiduous reporter to investigate the possibility that Armstrong has been doping. Armstrong lost his legal bid in France to force the book's publisher to insert a sheet in each copy of the book in which he denied its allegations of doping. Armstrong has also sued the book's publisher and the French news magazine *L'Express,* which published excerpts from the book, for libel.

22. For coverage of the affair, see in particular *L'Équipe, Libération,* and *Le Monde* beginning in late August 2005, when the positive tests were made public by the sports daily. Leblanc's surprise appears disingenuous: he enjoyed a front-row seat from which to witness the ever-faster speeds of Tour racers after the 1998 doping scandal, when one might reasonably have expected slower Tours had the drug-testing campaign truly been effective.

23. *L'Équipe,* 5 October 2005. In the United States, an unscientific poll conducted immediately after the revelations by the sports cable television network ESPN indicated that 72 percent of respondents did not believe that Armstrong was guilty of doping. *Libération,* 25 August 2005. Of course, these results also mean that almost three in ten respondents did not believe he was innocent, a large number given that the American public is far less knowledgeable about the sport than are most Europeans and Armstrong is extremely popular in the United States.

24. The difficulty of negotiating the contradictions that plague his sport was perhaps best captured by the late Marco Pantani: "In cycling," he affirmed, "there is not a culture of doping, but rather a culture of champions, meaning: self-improvement. That means doing things that are forbidden, but that are only forbidden if they catch you." Hoberman, " 'A Pharmacy on Wheels,' " 114; the translation is Hoberman's.

BIBLIOGRAPHY

ARCHIVAL SOURCES

Archives of the Paris Préfecture de Police. BA/1697. "Henri Desgrange [Directeur Sportif]."

Caen Municipal Archives. Municipal Council minutes.

Departmental Archives of Ille-et-Vilaine. Series 4M221 (Manifestations sportives—courses cyclistes 1899–1914, 1925, 1934, 1940).

Departmental Archives of Meurthe-et-Moselle. Series 4M85 (Associations vélocipédiques).

Departmental Archives of Meuse. Series 251M1 (Associations: Sociétés sportives: Autorisations; Dissolutions).

Rennes Municipal Archives. Series Rx103 (Sociétés sportives: Cyclisme, motocyclisme, sports athlétiques) and Municipal Council minutes.

Sens Municipal Archives.

Vichy Municipal Archives. Minutes of the Municipal Council and Commission des Sports.

INTERVIEWS

Cosson, Victor. Interview with the author. 15 July 1999.

Goddet, Jacques. Interview with the author. 21 July 1999.

Hoban, Helen (formerly Simpson, Helen). Interview with the author. 25 July 1999.

PERIODICALS

L'Action Française

L'Aurore du Bourbonnais

L'Auto

L'Auto-Revue de l'Est

L'Auto-Vélo

Auvergne: Bourbonnais: Velay (Organe de Liaison de la Fédération des Syndicats d'Initiatives et Offices du Tourisme)

Le Bourbonnais Républicain (Moulins)

La Bretagne Sportive

Le Canard Enchaîné

Le Centre Républicain

Combat

La Croix

La Dépêche du Midi

L'Écho de Longwy

L'Écho de Paris

L'Écho Sportif (Nancy)

L'Éclaireur de l'Est

L'Équipe

Espoir

L'Est Républicain (Nancy)

Le Figaro

La France Socialiste

France-Soir

The Guardian

L'Humanité

L'Industrie Hôtelière du Bourbonnais

L'Industrie Hôtelière du Massif Central

L'Intransigeant

Journal de Rennes

Journal de Vichy: Journal des Baigneurs

Journal Officiel de la République Française

Libération

Liberté de Normandie

La Liberté du Massif Central

Le Longovicien

Le Matin

Le Matin de Paris

Le Monde

La Montagne

Nancy-Sportif

The New York Times

Les Nouvelles de l'Ouest

Les Nouvelles Rennaises et de l'Ouest

Le Nouvelliste (Rennes)

Le Nouvelliste de Bretagne

Le Nouvelliste de Bretagne, Maine, Normandie, Anjou

The Observer

L'Ouest-Éclair

Ouest-France

Le Parisien Libéré

Paris-Soir

Le Patriote (Valmy)

Le Petit Journal

Le Petit Journal Illustré

Le Petit Parisien

Le Peuple

Le Populaire

La Province

Rennes-Vélo

La Revue Sportive du Nord Est (Nancy)

Sports Illustrated

Sports-Ouest

The Sunday Times

Le Temps

Tourisme: Plages et Villes d'Eaux

La Tribune

L'Union Verdunoise

USA Today

Vichy-Cannes: Plages et Villes d'Eaux

Les Vosges Sportives

PRIMARY SOURCES

Armstrong, Lance. *It's Not about the Bike: My Journey Back to Life.* With Sally Jenkins. New York: Berkley Books, 2001.

Baal, Daniel. *Droit dans le mur: Le cyclisme mis en examen.* Grenoble: Éditions Glénat, 1999.

Basset, Dr. J. *De l'influence de la bicyclette sur la diminution de la tuberculose à Toulouse.* Toulouse, 1905.

Bassons, Christophe. *Positif.* Paris: Éditions Stock, 2000.

Baudry de Saunier, Louis. *L'art de bien monter la bicyclette.* 3rd ed. Paris, 1894.

———. *Le cyclisme théorique et pratique.* Paris: Librairie Illustrée, 1892.

———. *Recettes utiles et procédés vélocipédiques.* Paris, 1893.

Baugé, Alphonse. *Messieurs les coureurs: Vérités, anecdotes et réflexions sur les courses cyclistes et les coureurs.* Paris: Librairie Garnier Frères, 1925.

Bellencontre, M. D. *Hygiène du vélocipède.* Paris: L. Richard, Libraire-Éditeur, 1869.

Berruyer, A. *Manuel du véloceman ou notice, système, nomenclature, pratique, art et avenir des vélocipèdes.* Grenoble: Typographie de F. Allier Père et Fils, 1869.

Bourguignon, Thierry. *Tours et détours.* Paris: Botega Éditions, 2000.

Buzançais, Jean. *La patrouille du Tour de France.* Paris: Éditions de l'Arc, 1948.

Chabannes, Jacques. *Microbe.* Paris: La Nouvelle Société d'Édition, 1929.

Chèze, Théodore. *Claude Lenoir.* Paris: Librairie Moderne, 1907.

Chiotti, Jérome. *De mon plein gré.* Paris: Calmann-Lévy, 2001.

Decoin, Henri, and Pierre Cartoux. *Le roi de la pédale.* Paris: Ferenczi et Fils, 1925.

Desgrange, Henri. *Alphonse Marcaux.* 2nd ed. Paris: L. Pochy, 1899.

———. *La tête et les jambes.* Paris: L. Pochy, 1898.

———. *La tête et les jambes.* 7th ed. Paris: Imprimerie Henri Richard, 1930.

Dieudonné, Robert. *Bébert ou la vie ratée.* Paris: La Nouvelle Société d'Édition, 1929.

———. *Frangins.* Paris: Éditions des Portiques, 1931.

———. *Le marchand de kilomètres.* Paris: Éditions Berger-Levrault, 1932.

———. *Le vainqueur.* Paris: Albin Michel, 1922.

Le dopage hors jeu: Rapport d'information no. 1499, déposé en application de l'article 145 du Règlement par la Commission des Affaires Culturelles, Familiales et Sociales sur la loi relative à la protection de la santé des sportifs et à la lutte contre le dopage. Presented by Alain Néri, *député.* Paris: Assemblée Nationale, 1999.

Garsonnin. *Conférence sur la vélocipédie faite à Tours le 31 mars 1888.* Rouen: Imprimerie Julien Lecerf, 1888.

Gérard, H. *Conséquences tactiques de la création de l'infanterie cycliste.* Paris: Henri Charles-Lavauzelle, Éditeur Militaire, 1903.

———. *L'infanterie cycliste en campagne.* Paris, Nancy: Berger-Levrault et Cie., Libraires-Éditeurs, 1898.

———. *Le problème de l'infanterie montée résolu par l'emploi de la bicyclette.* Paris: Librairie Militaire L. Baudoin, 1894.

Goddet, Jacques. *L'équipée belle.* Paris: Éditions Robert Laffont, SA, et Stock, 1991.

Guillemet, Dr. Eugène. *La bicyclette: Ses effets psycho-physiologiques.* Paris: J.-B. Baillière et Fils, Éditeurs, 1897.

Hinault, Bernard. *Moi, Bernard Hinault, champion des champions* With Bernard Pascuito. Paris: Calmann-Lévy, 1981.

Horner, Yvette. *Du Tour de France à l'opéra musette.* Paris: Éditions Filipacchi, 1987.

Kimmage, Paul. *Rough Ride: Behind the Wheel with a Pro Cyclist.* London: Yellow Jersey Press, 1998.

Lavielle, Dr. Charles. *Sur une arthrite spéciale du pied avec déformation observée chez les vélocipédistes.* Paris: Gustave Doin, 1891.

Lefèvre, Léo. *Ceux que j'ai rencontrés (en 60 ans de vie sportive): Souvenirs et anecdotes.* Paris: Éditions SOSP, 1962.

Le Hérissé, René-Félix. *Le cyclisme militaire.* Paris: Henri Charles-Lavauzelle, Éditeur Militaire, 1897.

Loris, C. de. *La femme à bicyclette: Ce qu'elles en pensent.* Paris: Ancienne Maison Quantin Librairies—Imprimeries Réunies, 1896.

Lucas-Championnière, Dr. Just. *La bicyclette.* Paris: Léon Chailly, 1894.

Menthéour, Erwann. *Secret défonce: Ma vérité sur le dopage.* Paris: Éditions Jean-Claude Lattès, 1999.

Milenkovitch, Michel, ed. *50 Histoires du Tour de France.* Paris: Éditions du Sport, 1997.

Mirovitch, Dr. Élie. *De l'influence de la vélocipédie sur la vision et conseils d'hygiène pour les yeux des vélocipédistes.* Paris: A. Malone, Éditeur, 1897.

Mockridge, Russell. *My World on Wheels: The Posthumous Autobiography of Russell Mockridge.* Completed by John Burrowes. London: Stanley Paul, 1960.

Nudant, P. *Deux journées de manoeuvres: Infanterie et cyclistes en liaison avec la division de cavalerie.* Paris: Berger-Levrault et Cie., Éditeurs, 1907.

O'Followell, Dr. Ludovic. *Bicyclette et organes génitaux.* Paris: Librairies J.-B. Baillière et Fils, 1900.

Penot, Christophe. *Jean-Marie Leblanc, gardien du Tour de France: Entretiens avec Christophe Penot.* Saint Malo: Éditions Cristel, 1999.

"Rapport sur *L'Auto:* Sa constitution, son activité, son rôle durant les cinq dernières années (1939–1944)." Unpublished manuscript.

Renaud, Line. *Les brumes d'où je viens. . . .* With Danièle de Caumon and Louis Valentin. Paris: France Loisirs, 1989.

Reuze, André. *Le Tour de Souffrance.* Paris: Arthème Fayard, 1925.

Richard, Pascal. *Géant de la route, forçat de la vie: Le vrai visage d'un cycliste.* Geneva: Éditions Factuel, 2001.

Roussel, Bruno. *Tour de vices.* Paris: Hachette Littératures, 2001.

Sainmont, Pierre. *Le Véloce-Club de Tours et le Doyen des Cyclistes de France.* Tours: Librairie Péricat, 1902.

Sainz, Bernard. *Les stupéfiantes révélations du Dr. Mabuse.* Paris: Editions Jean-Claude Lattès, 2000.

Salle, Médecin-Major de 1ère classe. *La reine de la route: Eléments de physiologie et notions d'hygiène pratique à l'usage des officiers-cyclistes.* Paris: Henri Charles-Lavauzelle, Éditeur Militaire, 1899.

Tissié, Dr. Philippe. *L'éducation physique.* Paris: Librairie Larousse, 1901.

———. *Études sur l'entraînement physique.* Bordeaux: Imprimerie G. Gounouilhou, 1897.

Virenque, Richard. *Ma Vérité.* With Guy Caput and Christian Éclimont. Monaco:
Éditions du Rocher, 1999.

———. *Plus fort qu'avant.* With Jean-Paul Vespini. Paris: Éditions Robert Laffont,
2002.

Voet, Willy. *Massacre à la chaîne: Révélations sur 30 ans de tricherie.* Paris: Calmann-
Lévy, 1999.

SECONDARY SOURCES

Abt, Samuel, and James Startt. *In Pursuit of the Yellow Jersey: Bicycle Racing in the
Year of the Tortured Tour.* San Francisco: Van der Plas Publications, 1999.

Agulhon, Maurice. "Le centre et la périphérie." In *Les lieux de mémoire,* edited by
Pierre Nora. Vol. 2. Paris: Éditions Gallimard, 1997.

Agulhon, Maurice, André Nouschi, and Ralph Schor. *La France de 1914 à 1940.*
Paris: Éditions Nathan, 1993.

———. *La France de 1940 à nos jours.* Paris: Éditions Nathan, 1995.

Allwood, Gill, and Khursheed Wadia. *Women and Politics in France, 1958–2000.*
London: Routledge, 2000.

Anderson, Benedict. *Imagined Communities.* London: Verso, 1991.

Andreff, Wladimir, and J.-F. Nys. *Le sport et la télévision.* Paris: Dalloz, 1988.

Annuaire 1913: Union des Sociétés de Préparation Militaire de France. Paris, 1913.

Archives Municipales de Montbéliard-Service Éducatif. *Sport et société dans la région de Montbéliard à la fin du 19e siècle.* Montbéliard: Archives Municipales de
Montbéliard, 1980.

Arnaud, Pierre. *Le militaire, l'écolier, le gymnaste: Naissance de l'éducation physique
en France: Sociabilités et formes de pratiques sportives.* Lyon: Presses Universitaires
de Lyon, 1986.

———, ed. *Les athlètes de la République: Gymnastique, sport et idéologie républicaine, 1870–1914.* Toulouse: Bibliothèque Privat, 1981.

———, ed. *Le corps en mouvement: Précurseurs et pionniers de l'éducation physique.*
Toulouse: Éditions Privat, 1981.

Arnaud, Pierre, and J. Camy, eds. *La naissance du mouvement sportif associatif en
France (1869–1889).* Lyon: Presses Universitaires de Lyon, 1991.

Asselain, Jean-Charles. *Histoire économique de la France du XVIIIe siècle à nos jours.*
Vol. 2. *De 1919 à la fin des années 1970.* Paris: Éditions du Seuil, 1984.

Augendre, Jacques. *Marcel Bidot: Souvenirs, ou l'épopée du Tour de France.* Troyes:
Les Éditions de la Maison du Boulanger, 1996.

———. *Le Tour de France: Les exploits et les hommes, les sommets du Tour de France.*
Paris: Éditions Solar, 1991.

Augendre, Jacques, Roger Bastide, Gianni Marchesini, and Jean-Paul Ollivier. *Le dictionnaire des coureurs.* La Maison du Sport, 1988.

Ballester, Pierre, and David Walsh. *L.A. Confidentiel: Les secrets de Lance Armstrong.* Paris: Éditions de la Martinière, 2004.

Bard, Christine, ed. *Un siècle d'antiféminisme.* Paris: Fayard, 1999.

Barrillon, Raymond. *Le cas Paris-Soir.* Paris: Armand Colin, 1959.

Barrows, Susanna. *Distorting Mirrors: Visions of the Crowd in Late Nineteenth-Century France.* New Haven, CT: Yale University Press, 1981.

Barthes, Roland. *Mythologies.* Paris: Éditions du Seuil, 1957.

Bastide, Roger. *Doping: Les surhommes du vélo.* Paris: Raoul Solar, 1970.

———. *Petit-Breton: La Belle Époque du cyclisme.* Paris: Éditions Denoël, 1985.

Becker, Annette. *Les monuments aux morts: Patrimoine et mémoire de la Grande Guerre.* Paris: Éditions Errance, 1988.

Becker, Jean-Jacques. *Crises et alternances, 1974–1995.* With the collaboration of Pascal Ory. Paris: Éditions du Seuil, 1998.

Bellanger, Claude, Jacques Godechot, Pierre Guival, and Fernand Terrou, eds. *Histoire générale de la presse française.* Vols. 3 and 4. Paris: Presses Universitaires de France, 1972.

Beltran, Alain. *Un siècle d'histoire industrielle en France—industrialisation et sociétés 1880–1970.* Paris: Éditions SEDES, 1998.

Berenson, Edward. *The Trial of Madame Caillaux.* Berkeley: University of California Press, 1992.

Berlanstein, Lenard. *The Working People of Paris, 1871–1914.* Baltimore, MD: Johns Hopkins University Press, 1984.

Bernard, Philippe. *La fin d'un monde 1914–1929.* Paris: Éditions du Seuil, 1975.

Berstein, Serge. *La France des années 30.* Paris: Armand Colin, 1988.

Berstein, Serge, and Jean-Pierre Rioux. *La France de l'expansion.* Vol. 2. *L'apogée Pompidou, 1969–1974.* Paris: Éditions du Seuil, 1995.

Bertho-Lavenir, Catherine. *La roue et le stylo: Comment nous sommes devenus touristes.* Paris: Éditions Odile Jacob, 1999.

———. "Le voyage: Une expérience d'écriture; La revue du Touring Club de France." In *Par écrit: Éthnologie des écritures quotidiennes,* edited by Daniel Fabre and Martin de la Soudière. Paris: Éditions de la Maison des Sciences de l'Homme, 1997.

Boeuf, Jean-Luc, and Yves Léonard. *La République du Tour de France, 1903–2003.* Paris: Éditions du Seuil, 2003.

Bouet, Michel. *Signification du sport.* Paris: Éditions Universitaires, 1968.

Boully, Jean. *Les Stars du Tour de France.* Paris: Bordas, 1990.

Bourgat, Michel. *Tout savoir sur le dopage.* Lausanne: Éditions Favre, 1999.

Boury, Paul. *La France du Tour: Le Tour de France, un espace sportif à géométrie variable.* Paris: L'Harmattan, 1997.

Braverman, Harry. *Labor and Monopoly Capital: The Degradation of Work in the Twentieth Century.* New York: Monthly Review Press, 1974.

Cadiou, Georges. *Les grandes heures du cyclisme breton.* Rennes: Ouest-France, 1981.

Calvet, Jacques. *Le mythe des géants de la route.* Grenoble: Presses Universitaires de Grenoble, 1981.

Carol, Anne. *L'histoire de l'eugénisme en France: Les médecins et la procréation XIXe–XXe siècle.* Paris: Éditions du Seuil, 1995.

Caron, François. *Histoire économique de la France XIXe–XXe siècle.* Paris: Armand Colin, 1995.

Cazeneuve, Jean. *Sociologie de la radio-télévision.* 6th ed. Paris: Presses Universitaires de France, 1986.

Chany, Pierre. *La fabuleuse histoire du cyclisme.* Paris: ODIL, 1975.

———. *La fabuleuse histoire du cyclisme.* Vol. 1. *Des origines à 1955.* Paris: Éditions Nathan, 1988.

———. *La fabuleuse histoire du cyclisme.* Vol. 2. *De 1956 à nos jours.* Paris: Éditions Nathan, 1988.

———. *La fabuleuse histoire du Tour de France.* Paris: Éditions Nathan, 1991.

Charle, Christophe. *Histoire sociale de la France au XIXe siècle.* Paris: Éditions du Seuil, 1991.

Charreton, Pierre. *Les fêtes du corps: Histoire et tendances de la littérature à thème sportif en France 1870–1970.* Saint-Étienne: Centre Interdisciplinaire d'Études et de Recherches sur l'Expression Contemporaine—Université de Saint-Étienne, 1985.

Chebel d'Appollonia, Ariane. *L'extrême-droite en France de Maurras à Le Pen.* Brussels: Éditions Complexe, 1988.

Cointet, Michèle. *Vichy Capitale, 1940–1944.* Paris: Librairie Académique Perrin, 1993.

Commission "Histoire" de Skol Vreizh. *Histoire de la Bretagne et des pays celtiques de 1789 à 1914.* Morlaix: Skol Vreizh, 1980.

———. *Histoire de la Bretagne et des pays celtiques de 1914 à nos jours.* Morlaix: Skol Vreizh, 1983.

———. *Toute l'histoire de Bretagne des origines à la fin du XXe siècle.* Morlaix: Skol Vreizh, 1997.

Conan, Eric, and Henry Rousso. *Vichy: An Ever-Present Past.* Translated and annotated by Nathan Bracher. Hanover, NH: University Press of New England, 1998.

Corbin, Alain. "Paris-Province." In *Les lieux de mémoire,* edited by Pierre Nora. Vol. 2. Paris: Éditions Gallimard, 1997.

Couëdel, Noël. *Tour de France: La fête de juillet.* Paris: Calmann-Lévy, 1983.

Courtois, Stéphane, and Marc Lazar. *Histoire du Parti Communiste Français.* Paris: Presses Universitaires de France, 1995.

Coyle, Edward F. "Improved Muscular Efficiency Displayed as 'Tour de France' Champion Matures." *Journal of Applied Physiology* 98 (June 2005): 2191–96.

Cross, Gary. *A Quest for Time: The Reduction of Work in Britain and France, 1840–1940.* Berkeley: University of California Press, 1989.

————. "Redefining Workers' Control: Rationalization, Labor Time, and Union Politics in France, 1900–1928." In *Work, Community, and Power: The Experience of Labor in Europe and America, 1900–1925,* edited by James E. Cronin and Carmen Sirianni. Philadelphia: Temple University Press, 1983.

Daviet, Jean-Pierre. *La Société Industrielle en France 1814–1914.* Paris: Éditions du Seuil, 1997.

Delumeau, Jean, ed. *Histoire de la Bretagne.* Toulouse: Privat Éditeur, 1969.

Déniel, Alain. *Le mouvement breton, 1919–1945.* Paris: François Maspéro, 1976.

Derieux, Emmanuel, and Jean Texier. *La presse quotidienne française.* Paris: Armand Colin, 1974.

Désert, Gabriel, ed. *La Normandie de 1900 à nos jours.* Toulouse: Privat, 1978.

Dhordain, Roland. *Le roman de la radio de la TSF aux radios libres.* Paris: La Table Ronde, 1983.

Dine, Philip. *French Rugby Football: A Cultural History.* Oxford: Berg Publishers, 2001.

————. "Sporting Assimilation and Cultural Confusion in Brittany." In *Sport in the Making of Celtic Cultures,* edited by Grant Jarvie. London: Leicester University Press, 1999.

Doucet, Louis. *Pays et gens de Bretagne.* Paris: Librairie Larousse, 1982.

Drogou, Marie-José, and Raymond Humbert. *La Bretagne: Mémoire de la vie quotidienne.* Paris: Temps Actuels, 1981.

Duchen, Claire. *Feminism in France from May '68 to Mitterrand.* London: Routledge & Kegan Paul, 1986.

————. *Women's Rights and Women's Lives in France, 1944–1968.* London: Routledge, 1994.

Dumazedier, Joffre. *Télévision et éducation populaire: Les télé-clubs en France.* Paris: UNESCO, 1955.

————. *Vers une civilisation du loisir?* Paris: Éditions du Seuil, 1962.

Dumons, Bruno, Gilles Pollet, and Muriel Berjat. *Naissance du sport moderne.* Lyon: La Manufacture, 1987.

Durand, Jean-Marie. *Les as du vélo: Le Tour de France cycliste, 1869–1939.* Marseille: Delta-Repro, 1983.

Durry, Jean. *L'en-cycle-opédie.* Lausanne: Édition-Denoël, 1982.

————. *Le sport à l'affiche.* Paris: Éditions Hoëbeke, 1988.

————. *Le vélo.* Paris: Éditions Denoël, 1976.

Dutt, R. Palme. *The Internationale.* London: Lawrence & Wishart, 1964.

Duval, René. *Histoire de la radio en France.* Paris: Éditions Alain Moreau, 1979.

Edwards, Stewart. *The Paris Commune, 1871.* Chicago: Quadrangle Books, 1971.

L'Équipe. 50 ans de sport, 1946–1995. Issy-les-Moulineaux: L'Equipe; Paris: diff. Calmann-Lévy, 1995.

Farmer, Sarah. *Martyred Village: Commemorating the 1944 Massacre at Oradour-sur-Glane.* Berkeley: University of California Press, 1999.

Félix, Christian. *Alsace-Lorraine et Union sacrée.* Lyon: Horvath, 1991.

Fourastié, Jean. *Les trente glorieuses.* Paris: Fayard, 1979.

Fridenson, Patrick. "Automobile Workers in France and Their Work, 1914–1983." In *Work in France: Representations, Meaning, Organization, and Practice,* edited by Steven Lawrence Kaplan and Cynthia J. Koepp. Ithaca, NY: Cornell University Press, 1986.

Friedmann, Georges. *The Anatomy of Work: Labor, Leisure and the Implications of Automation.* Translated by Wyatt Rawson. New York: Heinemann Educational Books, 1961.

Gay-Lescot, Jean-Louis. "La politique sportive de Vichy." In *La vie culturelle sous Vichy,* edited by Jean-Pierre Rioux. Brussels: Éditions Complexe, 1990.

Gildea, Robert. *The Past in French History.* New Haven, CT: Yale University Press, 1994.

Glarner, André, ed. *Le sport en France.* La Haye: International Bridge of Trade, 1929.

Gleyse, Jacques. "L'image de la femme dans les discours sur l'EP et le sport de 1870 à 1930: Un 'fait social total'?" In *Histoire du sport féminin.* Vol. 2. *Sport masculin—sport féminin: Éducation et société,* edited by Pierre Arnaud and Thierry Terret. Paris: L'Harmattan, 1996.

Guenée, Bernard. "Des limites féodales aux frontières politiques." In *Les lieux de mémoire,* edited by Pierre Nora. Vol. 1. Paris: Éditions Gallimard, 1997.

Guillais, Joëlle. *La chair de l'autre: Le crime passionnel au XIXe siècle.* Paris: Éditions Olivier Orban, 1986.

Guillet, René. *Le doping de l'homme et du cheval.* Paris: Masson et Cie., Éditeurs, 1965.

Guillon, Nicolas, and Jean-François Quénet. *Un cyclone nommé dopage: Les secrets du "Dossier Festina."* Paris: Éditions Solar, 1999.

———. *Le dopage: Oui ça continue.* Paris: Éditions Solar, 2000.

Guin, Yannick. *Histoire de la Bretagne: Contribution à la critique de l'idéologie nationaliste.* Paris: François Maspéro, 1982.

Guiomar, Jean-Yves. "Le *Tableau de la géographie de la France* de Vidal de La Blache." In *Les lieux de mémoire,* edited by Pierre Nora. Vol. 1. Paris: Éditions Gallimard, 1997.

Guttmann, Allen. *Women's Sports: A History.* New York: Columbia University Press, 1991.

Hare, Geoff. *Football in France: A Cultural History.* Oxford: Berg, 2003.

Harp, Stephen L. *Learning to Be Loyal: Primary Schooling as Nation Building in Alsace and Lorraine, 1850–1940.* DeKalb: Northern Illinois University Press, 1998.

———. *Marketing Michelin: Advertising and Cultural Identity in Twentieth-Century France.* Baltimore, MD: Johns Hopkins University Press, 2001.

Harris, Ruth. *Murders and Madness: Medicine, Law, and Society in the Fin de Siècle.* Oxford: Oxford University Press, 1989.

Hilden, Patricia. *Working Women and Socialist Politics in France, 1880–1914: A Regional Study.* Oxford: Clarendon Press, 1986.

Hoberman, John. *Mortal Engines: The Science of Performance and the Dehumanization of Sport.* New York: Free Press, 1992.

———. " 'A Pharmacy on Wheels': Doping and Community Cohesion among Professional Cyclists Following the Tour de France Scandal of 1998." In *The Essence of Sport,* edited by Verner Møller and John Nauright. Odense: University Press of Southern Denmark, 2003.

———. *Testosterone Dreams: Rejuvenation, Aphrodisia, Doping.* Berkeley: University of California Press, 2005.

Holt, Richard. "The Bicycle, the Bourgeoisie, and the Discovery of Rural France, 1880–1914." *British Journal of Sports History* 2, no. 1 (May 1985): 127–39.

———. *Sport and Society in Modern France.* Hamden, CT: Archon Books, 1981.

Hubscher, Ronald, ed. *L'histoire en mouvements: Le sport dans la société française (XIXe–XXe siècle).* Paris: Armand Colin, 1992.

Humphreys, George G. *Taylorism in France, 1904–1920: The Impact of Scientific Management on Factory Relations and Society.* New York: Garland Publishing, 1986.

Hunt, Lynn, ed. *The New Cultural History.* Berkeley: University of California Press, 1989.

Huret, Marcel. *Ciné actualités: Histoire de la presse filmée, 1895–1980.* Paris: Henri Veyrier, 1984.

Jarvie, Grant, ed. *Sport in the Making of Celtic Cultures.* London: Leicester University Press, 1999.

Kern, Stephen. *The Culture of Time and Space, 1880–1918.* Cambridge, MA: Harvard University Press, 1983.

Klejman, Laurence, and Florence Rochefort. *L'égalité en marche: Le féminisme sous la Troisième République.* Paris: Presses de la Fondation Nationale des Sciences Politiques, 1989.

Kobayashi, Keizo. *Pour une bibliographie du cyclisme: Répertoire des livres en langue française édités entre 1818 et 1983; La bicyclette sous tous ses aspects.* Paris: Fédération Française de Cyclotourisme, Fédération Française de Cyclisme, 1984.

Kuhn, René, Alfred North, and Jean-Claude Philipp. *Le cyclisme en Alsace de 1869 à nos jours.* Strasbourg: Éditions Publitotal, 1980.

Kuisel, Richard F. *Capitalism and the State in Modern France: Renovation and Economic Management in the Twentieth Century.* Cambridge: Cambridge University Press, 1981.

Laget, Françoise, Serge Laget, and Jean-Paul Mazot. *Le grand livre du sport féminin.* Belleville-sur-Saône: FMT Éditions, 1982.

Lagrée, Michel. "Brittany, between Ireland, Scotland and France." In *Sport in the Making of Celtic Cultures,* edited by Grant Jarvie. London: Leicester University Press, 1999.

Lajoie-Mazenc, Roger. *L'homme-horloge: Gustave Garrigou; itinéraire d'un enfant de l'Aveyron devenu géant de la route.* Including part 2, *Les Aveyronnais dans le Tour de France cycliste.* La Primaube: Graphi Imprimeur, 1996.

Landes, David S. *The Unbound Prometheus: Technological Change and Industrial Development in Western Europe from 1750 to the Present.* Cambridge: Cambridge University Press, 1969.

Laure, Patrick. *Le dopage.* Paris: Presses Universitaires de France, 1995.

———, ed. *Dopage et société.* Paris: Ellipses, 2000.

Laux, James M. *The Automobile Revolution: The Impact of an Industry.* Chapel Hill: University of North Carolina Press, 1982.

———. *The European Automobile Industry.* New York: Twayne Publishers, 1992.

———. *In First Gear: The French Automobile Industry to 1914.* Montreal: McGill-Queen's University Press, 1976.

Leducq, André, and Roger Bastide. *La Légende des Pélissier.* Paris: Presses de la Cité, 1981.

Levy-Leboyer, Maurice. "Innovation and Business Strategies in Nineteenth- and Twentieth-Century France." In *Enterprise and Entrepreneurs in Nineteenth- and Twentieth-Century France,* edited by Edward C. Carter II, Robert Foster, and Joseph N. Moody. Baltimore, MD: Johns Hopkins University Press, 1976.

Lhomme, Fabrice. *Le procès du Tour: Dopage; Les secrets de l'enquête.* Paris: Éditions Denoël, 2000.

Ligett, Phil. *Tour de France.* London: Harrap Books, 1989.

Lyleire, J.-C., and H. Le Targat. *Anthologie de la littérature du sport.* Lyon: Presses Universitaires de Lyon, 1989.

MacKaman, Douglas Peter. *Leisure Settings: Bourgeois Culture, Medicine, and the Spa in Modern France.* Chicago: University of Chicago Press, 1998.

Magowan, Robin. *Tour de France: The Historic 1978 Event.* 2nd edition. Boulder, CO: Velopress, 1996.

Maier, Charles S. "Between Taylorism and Technocracy: European Ideologies and the Vision of Industrial Productivity in the 1920s." *Journal of Contemporary History* 5, no. 2 (1970): 27–61.

Manévy, Raymond. *Histoire de la presse, 1919–1939.* Paris: Correa, 1945.

Marchand, Jacques. *La presse sportive.* Paris: Presse et Formation, 1989.

Marchand, Jacques, and Pierre Debray. *Pour le Tour de France, contre le Tour de France.* Paris: Berger-Levrault, 1967.

Marchesini, Daniele. *Coppi e Bartali.* Bologna: Società Editrice il Mulino, 1998.

Marcillac, Raymond. *20 ans de télé et d'athlétisme.* Paris: Raoul Solar, 1967.

Marcillac, Raymond, and Christian Quidet. *Sport et télévision.* Paris: Albin Michel, 1963.

Maugue, Annelise. *L'identité masculine en crise au tournant du siècle 1871–1914.* Paris: Éditions Rivages, 1987.

———. "The New Eve and the Old Adam." In *Emerging Feminism from Revolu-*

tion to World War, edited by Geneviève Fraisse and Michelle Perrot. Cambridge, MA: Belknap Press, 1993.

Mayeur, Françoise. *L'enseignement secondaire des jeunes filles sous la Troisième République.* Paris: Presses de la Fondation Nationale des Sciences Politiques, 1977.

Mayeur, Jean-Marie. "Une mémoire-frontière: L'Alsace." In *Les lieux de mémoire,* edited by Pierre Nora. Vol. 1. Paris: Éditions Gallimard, 1997.

Mazur, Amy G. *Gender Bias and the State: Symbolic Reform at Work in Fifth Republic France.* Pittsburgh, PA: University of Pittsburgh Press, 1995.

McDonald, Maryon. *We Are Not French: Language, Culture, and Identity in Brittany.* London: Routledge, 1989.

McLaren, Angus. *Sexuality and the Social Order: The Debate over the Fertility of Women and Workers in France, 1770–1920.* New York: Holmes & Meier, 1983.

———. *The Trials of Masculinity: Policing Sexual Boundaries, 1870–1930.* Chicago: University of Chicago Press, 1997.

Miller, Michael B. *The Bon Marché: Bourgeois Culture and the Department Store, 1869–1920.* Princeton, NJ: Princeton University Press, 1981.

Miquel, Pierre. *Histoire de la radio et de la télévision.* Paris: Librairie Académique Perrin, 1984.

Mondenard, Jean-Pierre de. *Dopage: L'imposture des performances—Mensonges et vérités sur l'école de la triche.* Paris: Éditions Chiron, 2000.

Mondenard, Jean-Pierre de, and Bernard Chevalier. *Le dossier noir du dopage: Les produits, les dangers, les responsables.* Paris: Hachette, 1981.

Moses, Claire. *French Feminism in the 19th Century.* Albany: State University of New York Press, 1984.

Mousseau, Jacques, and Christian Brochand. *L'aventure de la télévision des pionniers à aujourd'hui.* Paris: Éditions Fernand Nathan, 1987.

Moutet, Aimée. "Les origines du système de Taylor en France: Le point de vue patronal (1907–1914)." *Le Mouvement Social* 93 (October–December 1975): 15–49.

Nicolas, Michel. *Le séparatisme en Bretagne.* Brasparts: Éditions Beltan, 1986.

Nora, Pierre, ed. *Les lieux de mémoire.* Paris: Éditions Gallimard, 1997.

Nordman, Daniel. "Des limites d'état aux frontières nationales." In *Les lieux de mémoire,* edited by Pierre Nora. Vol. 1. Paris: Éditions Gallimard, 1997.

———. "Les Guides-Joanne, Ancêtre des Guides Bleus." In *Les lieux de mémoire,* edited by Pierre Nora. Vol. 1. Paris: Éditions Gallimard, 1997.

Noret, André. *Le dopage.* 2nd ed. Paris: Éditions Vigot, 1990.

Nossiter, Adam. *The Algeria Hotel: France, Memory, and the Second World War.* Boston: Houghton Mifflin Company, 2001.

Nye, Robert A. *Crime, Madness, and Politics in Modern France: The Medical Concept of National Decline.* Princeton, NJ: Princeton University Press, 1984.

———. *Masculinity and Male Codes of Honor in Modern France.* New York: Oxford University Press, 1993.

Offen, Karen. "Depopulation, Nationalism and Feminism in Fin de Siècle France." *American Historical Review* 89 (June 1984): 648–76.

Olivesi, Antoine, and André Nouschi. *La France de 1848 à 1914.* Paris: Éditions Nathan, 1981.

Ollivier, Jean-Paul. *Gino Bartali: Gino le pieux.* Paris: Editions PAC, 1983.

———. *L'histoire du cyclisme breton.* Paris: Éditions Jean Picollec, 1981.

Ozouf, Jacques, and Mona Ozouf. *La République des instituteurs.* Paris: Éditions du Seuil, 1992.

———. "*Le tour de la France par deux enfants:* Le petit livre rouge de la République." In *Les lieux de mémoire,* edited by Pierre Nora. Vol. 1. Paris: Éditions Gallimard, 1997.

Ozouf, Mona. *L'École de la France: Essais sur la Révolution, l'utopie et l'enseignement.* Paris: Éditions Gallimard, 1984.

Pagnoud, Georges. *Ces Bretons qui passionnent le cyclisme français.* Paris: Solar Éditeur, 1974.

Paxton, Robert O. *Vichy France: Old Guard and New Order, 1940–1944.* New York: Columbia University Press, 1972.

Perrot, Michelle. "On the Formation of the French Working Class." In *Working-Class Formation: Nineteenth-Century Patterns in Western Europe and the United States,* edited by Ira Katznelson and Aristide R. Zolberg. Princeton, NJ: Princeton University Press, 1986.

———. *Les ouvriers en grève, France 1871–1890.* Paris: Mouton & Co., 1974.

———. "Le regard de l'Autre: Les patrons français vus par les ouvriers (1880–1914)." In *Le Patronat de la seconde industrialisation,* edited by Maurice Levy-Leboyer. Paris: Les Éditions Ouvrières, 1979.

———. "The Three Ages of Industrial Discipline." In *Consciousness and Class Experience in Nineteenth-Century Europe,* edited by John Merriman. New York: Holmes & Meier, 1979.

Petit, Jacques-Guy, et al. *Histoire des galères, bagnes et prisons, XIIIe–XXe siècles: Introduction à l'histoire pénale de la France.* Toulouse: Éditions Privat, 1991.

Pigois, Rémy. *Les petites reines du Tour de France.* Limoges: Imp. A. Bontemps, 1986.

Popkin, Jeremy D. *A History of Modern France,* 2nd ed. Upper Saddle River, NJ: Prentice Hall, 2001.

Price, Roger. *A Social History of Nineteenth-Century France.* New York: Holmes & Meier, 1987.

———, ed. *Documents on the French Revolution of 1848.* London: Macmillan, 1996.

Priollaud, Nicole, ed. *Le sport à la une.* Paris: Liana Levi, 1984.

Prost, Antoine. "Les monuments aux morts: Culte républicain? Culte civique? Culte patriotique?" In *Les lieux de mémoire,* edited by Pierre Nora. Vol. 1. Paris: Éditions Gallimard, 1997.

Quénet, Jean-François. *Le procès du dopage: La vérité du jugement.* Paris: Éditions Solar, 2001.

Rabinbach, Anson. *The Human Motor: Energy, Fatigue and the Origins of Modernity.* New York: Basic Books, 1990.

Rapp, Jean-Paul. *Le doping des sportifs (ou la science détournée).* 2nd edition. Paris: Éditions Médicales et Universitaires, 1978.

Raspaud, Michel. "Stade Rennais: Standard-Bearer of Breton Identity." Translated by David Bailey. In *Sport in the Making of Celtic Cultures,* edited by Grant Jarvie. London: Leicester University Press, 1999.

Rauch, André. *Crise de l'identité masculine 1789–1914.* Paris: Hachette Littératures, 2000.

———. *Vacances en France de 1830 à nos jours.* Paris: Hachette, 1996.

———. *Vacances et pratiques corporelles.* Paris: Presses Universitaires de France, 1988.

Rearick, Charles. *The French in Love and War: Popular Culture in the Era of the World Wars.* New Haven, CT: Yale University Press, 1997.

———. *Pleasures of the Belle Epoque: Entertainment and Festivity in Turn-of-the-Century France.* New Haven, CT: Yale University Press, 1985.

Reece, Jack E. *The Bretons against France: Ethnic Minority Nationalism in Twentieth-Century Brittany.* Chapel Hill: University of North Carolina Press, 1977.

Reed, Eric S. "The Tour de France: A Cultural and Commercial History." PhD diss., Syracuse University, 2001.

Remont, Jean-François, and Simone Depoux. *Les années radio.* Paris: Éditions Gallimard, 1989.

Rennert, Jack. *100 ans d'affiches du cycle.* Paris: Henri Veyrier, 1974.

Renoy, Georges. *Le vélo au temps des belles moustaches.* Brussels: Rossel Édition, 1975.

Rioux, Jean-Pierre. *La France sous la Quatrième République.* Vol. 1. *L'ardeur et la nécessité, 1944–1952.* Paris: Éditions du Seuil, 1980.

Rioux, Jean-Pierre, and Jean-François Sirinelli, eds. *La culture de masse en France de la Belle Époque à aujourd'hui.* Paris: Librairie Arthème Fayard, 2002.

Roberts, Mary Louise. *Civilization without Sexes: Reconstructing Gender in Postwar France, 1917–1927.* Chicago: University of Chicago Press, 1994.

Roncayolo, Marcel. "Le paysage du savant." In *Les lieux de mémoire,* edited by Pierre Nora. Vol. 1. Paris: Éditions Gallimard, 1997.

Ronsin, Francis. *Les divorciaires: Affrontements politiques et conceptions du mariage dans la France du XIXe siècle.* Paris: Éditions Aubier, 1992.

Rousso, Henry. *Vichy: L'évènement, la mémoire, l'histoire.* Paris: Éditions Gallimard, 2001.

———. *The Vichy Syndrome: History and Memory in France since 1944.* Translated by Arthur Goldhammer. Cambridge, MA: Harvard University Press, 1991.

Schneider, William. *Quality and Quantity: The Quest for Biological Regeneration in Twentieth-Century France.* Cambridge: Cambridge University Press, 1990.

Schwartz, Vanessa R. *Spectacular Realities: Early Mass Culture in Fin-de-Siècle Paris.* Berkeley: University of California Press, 1998.

Seidler, Édouard. *Le sport et la presse.* Paris: Armand Colin, 1964.

Seray, Jacques. *Deux roues: La véritable histoire du vélo.* Rodez: Éditions du Rouergue, 1988.

———. *1904: The Tour de France Which Was to Be the Last.* Translated by Richard Yates. Denver, CO: Buonpane Publications, 1994.

Shapiro, Ann-Louise. *Breaking the Codes: Female Criminality in Fin-de-Siècle Paris.* Stanford, CA: Stanford University Press, 1996.

Sherman, Daniel J. "Art, Commerce, and the Production of Memory in France after World War I." In *Commemorations: The Politics of National Identity,* edited by John R. Gillis. Princeton, NJ: Princeton University Press, 1994.

Shorter, Edward, and Charles Tilly. *Strikes in France, 1830–1968.* Cambridge: Cambridge University Press, 1974.

Siegel, Mona. " 'History Is the Opposite of Forgetting': The Limits of Memory and the Lessons of History in Interwar France." *Journal of Modern History* 74, no. 4 (December 2002): 770–800.

Silverman, Dan P. *Reluctant Union: Alsace-Lorraine and Imperial Germany, 1871–1918.* University Park: Pennsylvania State University Press, 1972.

Silverman, Deborah L. *Art Nouveau in Fin-de-Siècle France: Politics, Psychology, and Style.* Berkeley: University of California Press, 1989.

Smith, Robert A. *A Social History of the Bicycle: Its Early Life and Times in America.* New York: American Heritage Press, 1972.

Sorlin, Pierre. *La société française.* Vol. 1. *1840–1914.* Paris: B. Arthaud, 1969.

Spinga, Nicolas. "L'Introduction de l'automobile dans la société française entre 1900 et 1914—Étude de Presse." Maîtrise d'histoire contemporaine, Université de Paris X—Nanterre, 1972–1973.

Stone, Judith F. *The Search for Social Peace: Reform Legislation in France, 1890–1914.* Albany: State University of New York Press, 1985.

Studény, Christophe. *L'invention de la vitesse: France, XVIIIe–XXe siècle.* Paris: Éditions Gallimard, 1995.

Taylor, A. J. P. *The Struggle for Mastery in Europe, 1848–1918.* Oxford: Oxford University Press, 1954.

Thiesse, Anne-Marie. *Ils apprenaient la France: L'exaltation des régions dans le discours patriotique.* Paris: Éditions de la Maison des sciences de l'homme, 1997.

Thompson, Christopher. "Bicycling, Class, and the Politics of Leisure in Belle Epoque France." In *Histories of Leisure,* edited by Rudy Koshar. Oxford: Berg Publishers, 2002.

———. "Controlling the Working-Class Hero in Order to Control the Masses? The Social Philosophy of Sport of Henri Desgrange." *Stadion* 27 (2001): 139–51.

———. "Regeneration, *Dégénérescence,* and Medical Debates about the Bicycle in Fin-de-Siècle France." In *Sport and Health in History,* edited by Thierry Terret. Sankt Augustin, Germany: Academia Verlag, 1999.

———. "René Vietto et le Tour de France de 1934: Un sacrifice héroïque ou un héros sacrifié?" *Histoire et Sociétés: Revue européenne d'histoire sociale* 7 (July 2003): 35–46.

———. "The Tour in the Inter-War Years: Political Ideology, Athletic Excess and Industrial Modernity." *International Journal of the History of Sport* 20, no. 2 (June 2003): 79–102.

———. "Un troisième sexe? Les bourgeoises et la bicyclette dans la France fin de siècle." *Le Mouvement Social* 192 (July–September 2000): 9–39.

Tombs, Robert. *The Paris Commune, 1871.* London: Longman, 1999.

Touchard, Jean. *La gauche en France depuis 1900.* Paris: Éditions du Seuil, 1977.

Van de Casteele-Schweitzer, Sylvie. "Management and Labour in France 1914–39." In *The Automobile Industry and Its Workers: Between Fordism and Flexibility,* edited by Steven Tolliday and Jonathan Zeitlin. New York: St. Martin's Press, 1987.

Vigarello, Georges. "Le Tour de France." In *Les lieux de mémoire,* edited by Pierre Nora. Vol. 3. Paris: Éditions Gallimard, 1997.

Wahl, Alfred. *Les archives du football: Sport et société en France (1880–1980).* Paris: Editions Gallimard/Julliard, 1989.

Weber, Eugen. *France, Fin de Siècle.* Cambridge, MA: Belknap Press, 1986.

———. "Gymnastics and Sports in Fin-de-Siècle France: Opium of the Classes?" *American Historical Review* 76, no. 1 (February 1971): 70–98.

———. "L'hexagone." In *Les lieux de mémoire,* edited by Pierre Nora. Vol. 1. Paris: Éditions Gallimard, 1997.

———. *The Nationalist Revival in France, 1905–1914.* Berkeley: University of California Press, 1959.

———. *Peasants into Frenchmen: The Modernization of Rural France.* Stanford, CA: Stanford University Press, 1976.

———. "Pierre de Coubertin and the Introduction of Organized Sport in France." *Journal of Contemporary History* 5, no. 2 (1970): 3–26.

Whittle, Jeremy. *Yellow Fever: The Dark Heart of the Tour de France.* London: Headline, 1999.

Winock, Michel. *Le socialisme en France et en Europe, XIXe–XXe siècle.* Paris: Éditions du Seuil, 1992.

Winter, Jay. *Sites of Memory, Sites of Mourning: The Great War in European Cultural History.* Cambridge: Cambridge University Press, 1995.

Zeldin, Theodore. *France 1848–1945: Ambition and Love.* Oxford: Oxford University Press, 1979.

FILM AND TELEVISION SOURCES

Actuel 2. ORTF 2, 16 July 1973.

"Autour du Tour." TF1, 2 January 1976.

"Autour du Tour." France 2: 24 July 1999.

Charlie Rose. PBS, 1 August 2005.

Cinq colonnes à la une. 7 July 1961.

"Le dossier: Les grandes figures du Tour de France, 1947–1992." INA NEWS, no. 12, Ref. 2109.

En attendant le Tour. France 2: 6, 7 July 1995.

Journal National. 1947.

Panorama. ORTF 1, 14 July 1967.

"A Strike on the Tour." 8 P.M. news, IT1, 12 July 1978.

Témoins sports. "Le Tour de France: Son histoire, notre histoire." France 3: 20, 27 July 1986.

INTERNET SOURCE

http://jeannielongo.free.fr. Official website of Jeannie Longo.

INDEX

ball bearings, 10
Ballester, Pierre, 343n21
Ballon d'Alsace, 34
banning of newspapers, 81, 293n106
Barrès, Maurice, 95, 104
Bartali, Gino, 123–24, 165, 308n148
Barthélémy, Honoré, 153
Barthes, Roland, 140, 269–70n1
Basques, 61–62
Bassons, Christophe, 338n182, 342–43n20
Bastide, Roger, 248
bath houses, 160
bathing in Mediterranean, 217
Baudry de Saunier, Louis, 23–24, 27
Baugé, Alphonse, 159, 188
Bayard-Clément bicycle, 15
Baylet, Jean-Michel, 221, 224
BBC, 128
beasts, Tour racers as, 192–94, 203, 323nn39,47,49
Beaujolais wineries, 48
Bébert ou la vie ratée (Dieudonné), 170–71
Bécaud, Gilbert, 45
begging, 161–62
Belgian critics of Tour, 184, 321–22n12
Belgian teams, 37, 41, 167, 173, 174, 219, 319n117
Belle Jardinière department store, 16, 41
bells on bicycles, 25
Bénac, Gaston, 211
Bernard, René, 198
Bertho-Lavenir, Catherine, 129
bias. *See* prejudices
bicycles: invention of, 10, 270–71nn5–8; shops, 15, 102, 150, 173, 277n97, 298n24
bicyclette, 270–71nn7,8, 277n93
La Bicyclette, 16
Bidot, Marcel, 128, 153
"biodynamine," 226
biographies, 100
birthrate, French, 103–4, 106, 122–24, 298–99nn27,28
Bismarck, 7
Blair, Scott, 298n23
Bleuets, 61
Blondin, Antoine, 115, 234, 239, 333n93, 334n96

blood tests, 262, 339n4, 341n11
bloomers, 103, 106, 136
Blum, Léon, 206
Bobet, Christiane, 121, 306n124, 307nn131,132
Bobet, Jean, 238
Bobet, Louison, 2, 121, 218, 238, 306n124, 307nn131,132
Bobet, Maryse, 121
Bobet, Philippe, 121
Boeuf, Jean-Luc, 269–70n1
Bol d'Or race, 12
Bon Marché department store, 8, 16, 270n3, 277–78n98
Bordeau sisters, 45
Bordeaux Chambre Correctionnelle, 243
Bordeaux-Paris race, 16, 17, 132, 184, 190, 226, 228, 236
Bordeaux race (1868), 11
borrowing by Tour racers, 161–62
Bottecchia, Ottavio, 174, 198, 302–3n67
Boucherie Sabatier, 169
Boulanger (General), 95
boules, 62
bourgeois society: and cycling clubs, 14, 151, 271n19, 272n22; as cycling fans, 62, 110; and deaths of Tour racers, 211–12; and elegance, 144–45, 165–68, 319n102; and female cyclists, 104–5, 300n32; and *forçats de la route*, 196–98, 210, 324–25n73; and *ouvriers de la pédale*, 5, 141–42; and Pélissier incident, 189; and professionalism in sports, 169, 172–73; and *une tenue correcte*, 157–62; and Tour racers as artisans, 163, 177–78; and Tour racers as elegant gentlemen, 165–68; vs. *vélocipédards*, 143–46, 148, 166, 168; at Vichy, 87
Bourguignon, Thierry, 338n182
boxing, 52, 96, 100, 155, 194, 225
"B" racers, 36, 126, 136
breakaways, 1, 284n164
Brest, 74
La Bretagne Sportive, 74–75
Breton Autonomist Party, 73
Breton language, 72–75
Breton Nationalist Party, 73

Napoleon I, 101, 124, 158, 298n20, 309n155

Napoleon III, 7, 63, 86

Napoleonic Code (1804), 298–99n27

National Breton Party, 72–73

national holiday (July 14), 13, 26, 237

national identity, 51, 55–61, 178, 286n19; and Alsace-Lorraine, 67, 289n71, 290n73; and unity in diversity, 59–67, 287n34, 288n50

nationalists, 56, 67, 75, 288n46, 290n73

national lottery, 81

national teams, 37–38, 40–41, 47, 61, 81, 113, 116, 302n61, 303n69, 309n165; of female cyclists, 133

Nazis, 35, 77–81, 91, 122, 128, 206, 293n106

Nencini, Gastone, 230

newlyweds, 116, 118, 120, 307n128

newspapers. *See* press, French

newsreels, 44, 306n126

"new woman," 105, 106, 118, 300n33, 301n39

night cycling, 112, 154, 189, 303n73

nitroglycerine, 225

Nora, Pierre, 269–70n1

Normans, 61–62

Nossiter, Adam, 91

La Nouvelle Gazette, 247

Le Nouvelliste de Bretagne, 73

novels, 99–100, 297–98nn11,24, 300–1n34; and dangerous women, 107–9, 302nn56,57; and *forçats de la route,* 203, 207, 209–10; and *ouvriers de la pédale,* 155, 165, 169–71, 174–75, 320n120; and suffering, 303n74

nurses, 122–23, 237

nux vomica, 225

Nye, Robert, 29

Ocaña, Luis, 2, 215, 307–8n137, 336n134

occupational histories of Tour racers, 149–52, 168–69, 267–68, 315nn23,24, 321n141

Officier de la Légion d'Honneur, 20

Olano, Abraham, 342n19

Olivier brothers, 15

Olympic games, 31, 130, 132–34, 137, 148, 228, 232, 260

"One Woman a Day" contest, 308n143

Oradour-sur-Glane, massacre of, 92

L'Ouest-Éclair, 100, 114

Ouest-France, 85

ouvriers de la pédale (pedal workers; representation of Tour racers), 5, 141–79; as artisans, 142, 150, 162–65, 175, 178, 318n92; and authoritarian paternalism, 146–49; as elegant gentlemen, 165–68, 319n102, 320–21n139; and financial incentives, 149–54, 315nn31,33, 316n47; and professionalism in sports, 148–49, 162, 168–76, 315n21, 318n90, 319n117, 320nn120,124; and *une tenue correcte,* 156–62, 317nn62,64,65, 318nn84,90; and Tour as work, 154–56

ouvriers spécialisés, 223

overexercising, 30–31

overwork, 201, 223, 239–40, 254

Painter, Judith, 312–13n220

Palmes Académiques, 20

Panama Canal, 95

Panhard-Levassor, 18

Panhard L.-F. Automobiles, 273–74n45

Panorama (TV show), 237

Pantani, Marco, 260–61, 340nn7,8, 342n18, 343n24

Paramé, Georges, 279n110

Parc des Princes, 20, 41, 46, 81, 112, 116, 119, 307n127

Pardon (Brittany), 13

Paris-Brest-Paris race, 11–12, 17, 32, 73, 129

Paris-Brussels race, 16, 101

Paris–Clermont-Ferrand race, 16

Paris Commune, 7, 14, 195

Paris-Évreux race, 310–11n181

Paris Grand Prix, 101

Le Parisien Libéré, 35, 81–83, 115, 132, 307n132, 312n202

Paris-London dirigible race (1906), 17

Paris-Milan race, 12

Paris-Nantes race, 73

Paris-PTT/*Intran/Match,* 43

Paris-Rennes race, 73

Paris-Roubaix race, 12, 17, 53–54, 190, 208

Paris-Rouen airplane race (1911), 17

Paris-Rouen auto race (1894), 17

sports press, 16–22, 35, 42, 97, 99, 105, 107, 193–94, 250, 272n31. *See also* press, French; *names of newspapers and magazines*
Sprint, 42
sprinters, 80, 107, 111, 184, 251, 284nn163, 164
Stade Rennais, 292–93n99
stages of Tour, 32, 34, 35, 44, 284n163; and Alsace-Lorraine, 68–69; and antidoping rebellion, 333n91; and Brittany, 74–75, 292n95; and Caen, 84–85; and deaths of Tour racers, 237–39; and *géants de la route,* 107, 118, 301n47, 308n143, 313n231; and *ouvriers de la pédale,* 154, 167, 316n50, 319n106; and regional diversity, 60, 64–65; and Tour de France *féminin,* 134, 313n221; and Valence-d'Agen strike, 219–20, 222, 224; and Vichy, 86, 88
Stalin, Joseph, 206
State Secretariat for Youth and Sports, 229
steroids, 250, 259
stimulants, 225, 227–29, 231, 234–36, 238, 249, 331n61, 333n91, 334n114, 336n133
Strasbourgeois, 70
strikes: by industrial workers, 149, 182–83, 201, 205, 220, 316–17n55; by Tour racers, 219–24, 231, 247–48, 328n15, 329nn19,26,30, 333n87
strophanthus, 225
strychnine, 225–27
suffering, 110–17, 138, 140, 265, 303nn69,74,76; and doping, 216, 230, 238–41, 255, 258–59, 261–62; and female cyclists, 131, 135; and *forçats de la route,* 185–86, 188, 191, 194; and protests by Tour racers, 218
summits, 34, 40, 43, 283n158
Sunday Times, 343n21
sunstroke, 229
surmenage. See overwork
survival, 110–17, 265, 304n84, 305n108; and doping, 216, 230, 255, 258, 261–62; and *forçats de la route,* 185
suspensions, 242, 244, 261, 336n137, 340–41n10
La Suze, 287n33

syndicalists, 156, 182–83, 201, 205, 316–17n55
syndicat d'initiatives (Vichy), 88–89

Taylor, Frederick Winslow, 199–201
Taylorism, 199–202, 325–26nn84,85, 87–90
teams, 33–34, 36–38, 284n164; criticism of, 197, 206; of female cyclists, 133, 136; and *géants de la route,* 110, 112–13, 116, 128, 302n61, 309n165; and *une tenue correcte,* 159–60; and Tour racers as artisans, 163–64; and traditional gender roles, 121–22. *See also* team names
technological innovations, 8, 21, 24, 27, 38, 49, 258–59; and *géants de la route,* 112; in moving pictures/sound, 44; in radio coverage, 43–44, 282n148; in television coverage, 46, 283n158; and Tour racers as machines, 185
Teisseire, Lucien, 121
téléclubs, 46
television coverage, 45–49, 257, 262, 283–85nn158–160,169; of Caen, 85; and commercial sponsors, 34; of deaths of Tour racers, 237; of doping, 231, 250, 252; and *forçats de la route,* 192; and *géants de la route,* 111, 113, 115, 122, 140, 303n68; of Valence-d'Agen strike, 220
Le Temps, 195–96
tendinitis, 336n133
tennis, 96, 134, 138
une tenue correcte, 156–62, 317nn62,64,65, 318nn84,90
la terre et les morts, 67
Terront, Charles, 12
testosterone, 242, 259, 261, 336n133, 338n176
La tête et les jambes (Desgrange), 109, 165, 169, 174–75, 225–26, 274n51
textbooks, 56–59, 61
Thann race (1869), 11
theater, sport as, 98–99
Théâtre du Petit-Monde, 166
theft, 161–62
thermodynamics, 182, 187
Thévenet, Bernard, 215, 242, 336n134

Thiers, Adolphe, 7
"third category" of quasi-amateurs, 37
Third Republic, 3, 7–8, 56, 58–59, 62–63,
    66, 206, 270n1; and Breton coun-
    ternarrative, 72–76; and communist
    counternarrative, 77; and labor re-
    forms, 181–83, 207; and *ouvriers de la
    pédale*, 142–43, 147, 150, 162, 166; and
    scandals, 95; and Vichy regime, 80;
    and women's emancipation, 103,
    298–99nn26–28, 300n29
Thurau, Dietrich, 250
Thys, Philippe, 190, 301n47
Tiberghien, 165
times of Tour, 33, 154–55, 259, 316n50,
    333n91
time trials, 33–34, 44, 88, 197, 258, 261, 263,
    283n158, 339–40n6
Tissié, Philippe, 28–29, 31
Tonkov, Pavel, 342n19
top racers, 36–37, 259–60; as celebrities,
    102; and commercial sponsors, 197; in
    cycling films, 45; and doping, 238,
    242, 244–45, 341n11; and female fans,
    301n47; as *ouvriers de la pédale*, 154;
    on postcards, 101; at Valence-d'Agen,
    221. *See also names of racers*
Le Toulouse Cycliste, 23, 100
Le Tour de France (documentary film), 45
Tour de France auto race (1899), 17
tour de France des compagnons, 56–57, 65
Tour de France *féminin*, 98, 132–39,
    311n194, 312–13nn202–204,208,
    211,218–222,225
Le tour de la France par deux enfants, 57, 61,
    288n54
Le Tour de Souffrance (Reuze), 108, 203,
    207, 303n74
Tour-Expo, 47–48
Tour féminin cycliste, 131
Touring Club de France, 59, 65, 129
tourism, 41, 51, 59–60, 65–66, 281n143,
    286n21, 289nn66,67; and Vichy,
    87–88, 92, 295n148
touristes-routiers, 37; of attrition rates, 113;
    complaints by, 208; and criticism of
    Tour, 197, 206, 324n64; and host
    communities, 41; and professionalism

in sports, 172–73; and *une tenue cor-
    recte*, 160; and traditional gender
    roles, 119
tourist guidebooks, 59, 64–65, 286n21,
    289nn63,67, 290n80
Tourmalet (Pyrenees summit), 34, 44, 62,
    164–65
Tour of Belgium, 101
Tour of Flanders, 236
Tour of Italy, 215, 243–44, 251, 260–61,
    336n140, 340–41nn7,10
Tour of Lombardy, 190, 236
Tour of Spain, 215, 236, 260, 339–40nn5,6
Tour of Switzerland, 244
Tour racers: antidoping rebellion by, 233–36,
    333nn87,89, 334nn95,96,101; as artisans,
    142, 150, 162–65, 175, 178, 318n92;
    bathing in Mediterranean, 217; as
    beasts, 192–94, 203, 323nn39,47,49;
    from Brittany, 73–76, 292n90; cate-
    gories of, 36–37; and commemoration
    of war dead, 54, 68–69, 126, 290n77;
    deaths on Tour, 210–13, 228, 236–41,
    260, 334nn106,108,109,114, 335nn118,
    119,121, 339n3; as elegant gentlemen,
    165–68, 319n102, 320–21n139; and fe-
    male fans, 97, 105–10, 301n47, 308n143;
    as heroic soldiers, 124–28, 309n155,
    310n171; as machines, 185–89, 240,
    322nn17,19,28; occupational histories
    of, 149–52, 169, 267–68, 315nn23,24,
    321n141; and Pélissier incident, 189–92,
    198, 222, 330n35; and professionalism
    in sports, 148–49, 162, 168–76, 315n21,
    318n90, 319n117, 320nn120,124; and re-
    gional diversity, 60–61, 287n24; as
    rescapés, 110–17, 304n84, 305n108; slow-
    downs by, 200, 207, 217–22; and *une
    tenue correcte*, 156–62, 317nn62,64,65,
    318nn84,90; times of, 33, 154–55, 259,
    316n50, 333n91; and tourism, 65–66,
    289n66; and traditional gender roles,
    117–24; Valence-d'Agen strike by,
    215–16, 219–24, 247–48, 328n15,
    329nn19,26,30. *See also* doping; *forçats
    de la route; géants de la route;* heroic
    mythology; *ouvriers de la pédale*
trade unions, 198, 201–2, 204–5, 207

traditional gender roles, 117–24,
    305nn109,113–116, 306nn118–126,
    313n231; and home front, 97, 106,
    124–28
transatlantic Tours, 93–94, 257
transfusions, 341n11
Trénet, Charles, 45
Trousselier, Louis, 301n47
Trueba, Vicente, 193, 211

UCI (Union Cycliste Internationale),
    131–32, 232, 244, 250, 259–60, 332n78,
    336n137, 338n182, 339n5, 340–
    41nn7,10
Ullrich, Jan, 342n18
Union Cycliste de Longwy, 279n109
Union Cycliste Nancéene, 29
Union Sacrée, 78
Union Vélocipédique de France (UVF).
    See French Cycling Federation
United Nations Security Council, 139
unity in diversity, 59–67, 287nn24,34,
    288n50
urbanization, 58, 143, 145, 286n19
urinary problems, 136–37, 313n221
urinating in public, 157, 160–61, 318n84
urine tests, 216, 232–33, 241–42, 244–45,
    260, 262, 264, 336n142, 339n4,
    340–41n10, 343n22
US Postal team, 257

Valence-d'Agen strike, 219–24, 247–48,
    328n15, 329nn19,26,30
Van Impe, Lucien, 215
Van Springel, Hermann, 336n134
Vars (Alps summit), 34
Vél d'Hiv, 310–11n181
Le Vélo, 17–18, 20, 23, 97, 99, 274n46
véloce (cycle), 277n93
Véloce-Club de Tours, 145
Véloceman, 144
Véloce-Sport, 16
vélocifère (cycle), 277n93
vélocipédards (working-class cyclists),
    143–46, 148, 166, 168
vélocipède (cycle), 10, 270–71n7, 277n93
Le Vélocipède Illustré, 16
Vélodrome de la Seine, 19–20

velodromes, 12–13, 21, 45, 73, 85, 88, 148.
    See also names of velodromes
Vercingetorix, 100
Versailles, Treaty of, 68
Le Vésinet suburb of Paris, 62
Vichy (town), 85–92, 295nn141,144,145,148,
    296nn153,155
Vichy-Paris stage, 86, 88–89
Vichy regime, 35, 77–81, 89–91, 128,
    293n106
Vidal de La Blache, Paul, 286n19
La Vie au Grand Air, 101, 281n132
La vie des forçats (Dieudonné), 323n53
La Vie insurance company, 41
Vietto, René, 115–16, 302n61
Vigarello, Georges, 269–70n1
Ville, Maurice, 190
villes-étapes, 54, 74–75, 84, 86, 92
le vin Mariani ("medicinal wine"), 226
Virenque, Richard, 255
Virot, Alex, 43
visitation rights for Tour racers, 121–22,
    307–8nn137,140
vitamin B6, 338n176
vitamin B12, 338n176
vitamin C, 242
Vittelloise, 284n163
Vivaldi, 133–34
Viviani, René, 182
Voet, Willy, 338n182
Voici des ailes! (Leblanc), 300–1n34
vraie femme. See "new woman"
vulgar language, 157–59

wages, working-class, 9, 150, 152, 200, 202,
    315n23
Walsh, David, 340n7, 343n21
war memorials, 69–70, 304n93
warning bells, 25
Waterloo, battle of, 101
Wattelier (racer), 158
wealth. See financial incentives for Tour
    racers; prize money
Weber, Émile, 28
Weber, Eugen, 269–70n1, 273n41, 290n73
weight loss, 111, 113, 190, 302–3n67
welfare state, French, 138, 140, 178
Western Europe, 93

western front (World War I), 52–55
wheel rims, 210, 212
white jersey, 131, 284n164
wind-tunnel experiments, 258
wine, 76, 226
withdrawals, 1, 33; Desgrange on, 174, 189;
    by female cyclists, 135; by *géants de la
    route,* 114, 116–17, 127, 188; and
    Pélissier incident, 180–81, 204, 207–8
wives: and divorce, 123, 298–99n27,
    300–1nn29,34; and home front, 97,
    126–28, 309–10nn165,166; and tradi-
    tional gender roles, 117–24,
    305nn109,113, 306nn118–126,
    307nn127,128,131–134; and visitation
    rights of, 121–22, 307–8nn137,140
Wolber tire company, 16, 39–40,
    278–79n107
"woman question," 300n29
women. *See entries under* female; women's
    emancipation
women's emancipation: and dangerous
    women, 109, 302n48; and female cy-
    clists, 97–98, 103–5, 134, 298–99nn26–
    28, 300nn29,31,32; and World War I,
    106; and World War II, 123–24,
    309nn150,152
"wooden horse," 146
workers' rights, 180, 182–83, 191, 202, 207,
    216, 223; of racers, 224, 234, 242–43,
    245, 247–48, 265, 336n137
working class: and alcoholism, 28–29, 145,
    147, 314n13; *cavalier cycliste* vs.
    vélocipédard, 143–46; as *communards,*
    7, 14, 143; as cycling fans, 12, 63, 142,
    156, 158–60, 169, 173, 217, 288n45;
    317n59; and doping scandals, 216; in
    England, 21–22; and *forçats de la*

route, 205; housing for, 66; identity
    of, 5, 142, 154, 158–59; and industrial-
    ization, 56, 58, 143, 145, 197–98; and
    labor reforms, 182; models of bicycles
    for, 11; and paid vacations, 41; Tour
    racers as, 109–10, 149–50, 155, 222;
    wages of, 9, 150, 152, 200, 202,
    315n23; and World War II, 89. See
    also *forçats de la route; ouvriers de la
    pédale*
working hours, 9, 154, 182–83, 202
working women. *See* female workers
World Anti-Doping Agency, 341n12
World War I, 15, 20, 25, 35, 37, 44,
    278–79n107, 280n120; and Alsace-
    Lorraine, 68–69, 290–91nn73,74,
    77,78,80–82; and Brittany, 73; and
    Circuit des Champs de Bataille,
    52–55; and *géants de la route,* 102, 106,
    114, 119–20, 124–27, 304n93, 309n153;
    and *ouvriers de la pédale,* 154; and so-
    cialism, 205
World War II, 34–35, 37, 77–83,
    293nn106,108, 294n118; and amphet-
    amines, 227; and Caen, 83–85, 115; and
    géants de la route, 115–16, 127–28,
    310nn171,174; and *ouvriers de la pé-
    dale,* 177–79; and Vichy, 85–92 (*see
    also* Vichy regime)

yellow jersey, 47, 49, 81, 135, 215,
    284nn163,164, 306n125, 307n128
youth culture, 123

Zay, Jean, 65
Zoetemelk, Joop, 2, 215, 250, 336n134
Zola, Émile, 96
Zuylen de Nyevelt, Baron de, 18, 274n46

Text: 11/14 AGaramond
Display: Franklin Gothic, Adobe Garamond
Compositor: Binghamton Valley Composition, LLC
Printer and Binder: Maple-Vail Manufacturing Group